The Unknown Callas

OPERA BIOGRAPHY SERIES, NO. 14

Series Editors
Andrew Farkas
William R. Moran

Frontispiece: Mary as Leonore, *Fidelio,* Odeon of Herodes Atticus, Athens, August 1944.

Published in 2001 by
Amadeus Press (an imprint of Timber Press, Inc.)
The Haseltine Building
133 S.W. Second Avenue, Suite 450
Portland, Oregon 97204, U.S.A.

Printed in Hong Kong

ISBN 1-57467-059-X

Library of Congress Cataloging-in-Publication Data

Petsalis-Diomidis, N., 1943–
       The unknown Callas : the Greek years / Nicholas Petsalis-
Diomidis; with a foreword by the Earl of Harewood.
            p.   cm.—(Opera biography series; no. 14)
       Includes bibliographical references and indexes.
       ISBN 1-57467-059-X
       1. Callas, Maria, 1923–1977. 2. Sopranos (Singers)—
Biography. I. Harewood, George Henry Hubert Lascelles, Earl
of, 1923–   II. Title. III. Series.

       ML420.C18 P43   2000
       782.1′092—dc21
       [BB]
                                                                00-040155

The Unknown Callas

THE GREEK YEARS

—⚏—

Nicholas Petsalis-Diomidis

with a foreword by the Earl of Harewood

AMADEUS PRESS
Portland, Oregon

Maria Callas lived in Greece from 1937 to 1945 [aged thirteen through twenty-one]. . . . That is the fundamental formative period for an opera singer and the most important period in the development of a human being.

Renzo Allegri
(*La vera storia di Maria Callas*, Milan 1991)

—⚡—

In all the vast Callas literature there is one big gap, at least eight years of total darkness: the Athens years, from 1937 to 1945.

Leonardo Bragaglia
(*L'arte dello stupore*, Rome 1977)

—⚡—

May I remind you that I had an eight-year career in Greece during World War II? That's when I really got most of my experience.

To John Gruen
(*The New York Times*, 31 October 1971)

Contents

Foreword

T he art of biography is complex. Facts are important; so is their interpretation. Research can throw light onto periods hitherto obscure, but a plethora of detail can turn the obscure, which is undesirable, into the opaque, which is disastrous. One of the odd things about the relatively short but incomparably brilliant career of Maria Callas is that it is usually thought of as lasting from her Italian début in 1947 to her last operatic appearance in London in 1965, or maybe the last concerts in 1974. But nobody who thinks about it with any care could ever possibly imagine that that was the whole story.

I myself was lucky enough to hear her in Ponchielli's *La Gioconda* in the open-air at Verona on 2 August 1947—lucky too that by a series of wholly fortuitous circumstances I sat next to her at dinner after the performance and so began an acquaintance that ripened over the years into friendship. She was an absolutely new and important entrant on the Italian scene, a young soprano with a splendid voice and a powerful sense of how to communicate drama to a huge audience. The voice itself was not only very large but highly individual, not at all the smooth, creamy sound of the conventional leading soprano most people enjoy on records, but something more resinous, earthier, certain to make you sit up and take special notice—equally certain to make you remember what you had heard. That, I suppose, is the impression most people took away with them in 1947 after a performance of some splendour, notable for a very strong cast combining the new—Richard Tucker on his European début as well as Callas—with the experienced—Carlo Tagliabue and Elena Nicolai as well as the great conductor, Tullio Serafin.

What none of us seems to have asked at the time is how this phenomenon came to burst on the scene without any apparent pedigree or performance background. We heard vaguely that she had been a member of a basically Italian troupe engaged to tour America but foundering when insufficient money had been raised to meet union requirements in advance of the first night. She had then sung for Giovanni Zenatello and been engaged by him for the Arena di Verona, and her success had been immediate. But of what came before Verona we heard nothing. That she had in Greece been a pupil of Elvira de Hidalgo came out in interviews with the diva, but of experience in Greek performance virtually nothing emerged until much later. Yet there were singers she had performed with in Greece, witnesses to her peregrinations between New York and Athens, members of her family, friends. Only slowly did rumours of performances of *Tosca* and *Fidelio* percolate from Greece, and only now after the painstaking researches of Mr. Petsalis-Diomidis is the full story told.

And very fascinating it is! It is of course one of struggle, but mainly of struggle against war-time conditions in Athens rather than against lack of opportunity. Plainly, Athens was not at the centre of the operatic world, equally plainly Callas was cast where need directed rather than where careful planning might have suggested. But this book indicates a career evolving rather than a diva arriving in the Arena di Verona on 2 August 1947 as if by parachute from another planet. That might sound romantic, but it is far less interesting than the story Mr. Petsalis-Diomidis has to tell.

Lord Harewood
London

Preface

M aria Callas (1923–1977) is one of the most written-about artists in history and certainly the most written-about singer in the history of opera. However, in all the hundred or so books and various publications about her that have already appeared around the world, her origins and her life up to September 1945 are covered in very few and decidedly sketchy pages.[1] The simple reason for this is that not one of Callas's biographers has researched her early years, and particularly the crucial Greek years, from 1937 to 1945. In 1960 Leo Riemens, in his own earliest Callas biography, wrote that her Greek period was "like a blank patch on the map of her life," awaiting to be uncovered by future biographers. Since then, biographers have had very little to say about the younger Callas, basing their conclusions almost exclusively on her mother's memoirs and on statements Maria made in later life, often in the context of their open feud. They all made a point of mentioning the main psychological traumas she suffered during her childhood and the salient events of her life in Greece during World War II, but in most cases they borrowed from each other, perpetuating errors and inaccuracies, thus, by frequent repetition in print, giving the patina of truth to stories that often have no basis in fact. But when there is to all intents and purposes a gap of eight very important years in the subject's life, it is bound to give rise to dangerous inaccuracies and distortions. This is especially true in the case of Maria Callas, where the gap covers the crucial formative years of her adolescence, her first serious studies, and the start of her career, with all the early experiences, enthusiasms, disappointments, and battles—battles in which she usually gave of her best.

Non-Greek writers on Callas, of course, can always plead in self-justification —or at least in extenuation—their ignorance of Greek, which is a difficult language to learn. The fact remains, however, that few of them took note of the existence and importance of this gap, while not one observed even the elementary rules of serious historiography. Some of the most conspicuous cases in point are the books published in Britain, France, and Italy in 1997, obviously timed to cash in on the twentieth anniversary of Callas's death. But even Greek writers gave only perfunctory attention to Callas's Greek years, the two best known among them,

Stelios Galatopoulos (1976) and Arianna Stassinopoulou (1980), failing to appreciate the importance of her origins and her life until 1945. This is particularly unfortunate because several people who would have been invaluable sources of information—Maria's mother, her teacher Elvira de Hidalgo, her maestro Leonidas Zoras, her rival Zozo Remoundou, and others mentioned in the pages that follow—were still alive. Yet, instead of researching conscientiously, both these writers, like the non-Greek-speakers, contented themselves with retailing unattributed rumors, scurrilous gossip, and questionable facts recorded by Maria's mother in her memoirs. Polyvios Marchand (1983) first stressed the importance of Callas's Greek years, by publishing a chronicle of her musical studies, concerts, and stage performances in Greece. His book, however, has no thread of narrative running through it, nor does it refer to her private life, which was so closely bound up with her professional career. Finally, in his third book on Callas, Galatopoulos (1998) —who asserts to have spoken at length with Maria herself but has produced no evidence to prove that the discussions really took place—again failed to attribute to her origins and to the first twenty-two years of her life their deserved importance, as this book intends to show.

It is most regrettable that not one of the numerous general managers of the Greek National Opera has bothered to organize its archives, thus preserving the records of the history of the G.N.O. and, indeed, of opera in Greece since 1940. Once I had reduced the chaotic jumble of the surviving precious dossiers to some semblance of order, I searched through them only to discover that the personal file for Marianna Kaloyeropoulou (the name she used when signing her first contract in 1940) was nowhere to be found. Its disappearance should be dated to some time since 1982, when Elli Nikolaidi asked the G.N.O. for material about Callas on Marchand's behalf. She was given photocopies of certain documents, but unfortunately only a selected few: the first contract, which has since been published in part by Marchand, and four reports to the disciplinary board, which are published for the first time in the pages that follow. As these are typical of the papers in the files that have survived, it is clear that in 1982 the Kaloyeropoulou file was still in existence.

Fortunately the National Opera in its early years was part of the National Theater, and so until May 1944 its affairs were dealt with by the latter's board of governors. Although many of the archives of the National Theater are kept in a squalid and wet basement, several days of painstaking research yielded a certain amount of useful material. Much more valuable, however, were the personal papers of Theodoros Synadinos, a former governor of the National Theater who was general manager of the G.N.O. from February 1945 to May 1946. The value of these papers is obviously enhanced by the fact that the G.N.O. archives are to all intents and purposes nonexistent and those of the National Theater not much better. Furthermore, whereas it seemed reasonable to expect that other material would be found in the archives of the German and Italian occupation forces, very little has survived. What remains is scattered far and wide and chronologically fragmented, and most of it is general news. During the war the arts were used by the occupation authorities mainly as a propaganda tool. They were therefore of comparatively minor importance, and the few reports and papers on the subject, if not destroyed by chance, were among those earmarked for destruction as soon as circumstances appeared to demand it.

A major part of my research consisted of conversations with well over a hundred people who knew Maria Callas during that period in her life. Some were close to her, others less so, but all were there with her, either at the conservatory, at her first appearances with the Greek National Opera, or in her everyday life. To all those who helped me I offer my sincere thanks. As I see it, they have not only assisted me but have helped to preserve a good deal of historical evidence relating to the period in question which was otherwise in danger of being lost forever. I was touched by the willingness with which most people I approached agreed to talk to me, often in spite of personal problems of their own due to their advanced age. In particular, I should like to single out Elli Nikolaidi, who died suddenly before we had finished our conversations. Sadly, many others will also never see the final product of the work to which they contributed, among them Yannis (Zannis) Kambanis and Mireille Fléri, who died in 1991 and 1996, respectively. The names of all those who offered their testimony are to be found in the text and the Notes; their status, their connection with Maria, and the dates of our first conversations are listed in Sources, Bibliography, and Abbreviations.*

A most important source of material for this book has been Maria Callas herself. When I came to make systematic transcripts of all her radio, television, and press interviews I was astonished to see what a wealth of primary material had so far remained almost untapped. Maria made numerous statements about her youth, both orally and in writing, directly or reported by others. Wherever I have quoted

---

*The only person who flatly refused to help me was Athina Spanoudi (d. 1999), who might have been able to remember some events from the viewpoint of her mother, Sophia Spanoudi, a leading figure in the Greek musical world at that time. A few others were unwilling to cooperate as much as they might have done, namely the bass Nikos Zachariou (Nicola Zaccaria), the soprano Anthi Zacharatou, and Christos Mangliveras. Zachariou, at the time a young chorus member and comprimario with the G.N.O., gave me his cooperation initially but then suddenly refused to help any more, mainly pleading that Maria should be "left in peace." Zacharatou, who could also have been of considerable assistance, especially with regard to the important events of 1945, when Theodoros Synadinos was general manager of the G.N.O., either evaded or declined to answer most of my questions. Lastly, Christos Mangliveras, the brother of the baritone Vangelis Mangliveras, with whom Mary had her most serious love affair before she married, gave me some useful material in conversation but would only let me use two postcards and selected excerpts from two letters from Mary to his brother. He had at least thirteen more, he said (on one occasion he put the figure as high as twenty), material that would illuminate not only her time in Athens but her New York years from 1945 to 1947 as well. Unfortunately, after Christos Mangliveras's death, in December 1999, only one of the two postcards and the two letters were found.

her own words in this book they are *in italics* so that they stand out more clearly. It seems hardly necessary to stress the significance of Maria's personal testimony, but it is worth quoting something she herself said on the subject: "*There are many quotes that I've 'said,' that I've never really said.*"[2] What is more, Maria was prone to sudden mood swings and often contradicted herself, sometimes deliberately and sometimes by mistake or through carelessness, which means we must be cautious when assessing the worth even of her personal testimony. We should attach greater weight to her oral statements, which are definitely authentic, than to the statements attributed to her in published interviews, which may be distortions of her words or even pure invention. The reliability of the published interviews also depends, of course, on the reputation of the interviewer or the publication in which they appeared.

Readers will find that most of the facts about this period of Callas's life have never been published before: they are taken either from my own interviews or from hitherto unused documentary records. Some, always quoted with an acknowledgment of their source, will be recognized from other books and articles, notably the memoirs of Maria's mother and sister. Both of these precious primary sources should be treated with caution, however, as they are flawed by numerous omissions and errors—not always deliberate, of course. Maria herself, in a moment of anger, described her mother's book as "*a humiliating pack of lies,*"[3] but surely her accusation is as suspect as its object. Readers may also recognize a good many of the events of Maria's musical career chronicled by Polyvios Marchand, a book which many other writers have made free with, usually without even mentioning the author's name.

Besides these sources, I have consulted a multitude of books, newspapers, and periodicals published in Greece, America, Britain, France, Italy, Germany, Belgium, and the Netherlands. Special mention should be made of the two daily newspapers published in Athens by the occupation authorities: *Deutsche Nachrichten in Griechenland* (April 1941 to October 1944) and *Il Giornale di Roma* (September 1941 to September 1943). Unfortunately, only 136 and 126 issues, respectively, of these publications are to be found in Greek public libraries, all dating from before Maria had made her breakthrough with *Tosca* in the summer of 1942. I had to do my research in Berlin and Florence, but even in Germany there are no copies of any issue of the *Deutsche Nachrichten in Griechenland* after 30 April 1944, while in Italy only 140 of the 500-odd issues of *Il Giornale di Roma* for 1942 and 1943 could be found in public libraries. If the missing numbers are discovered, some further useful material should become available.

The reader will find references not only to opinions and recollections that Maria disclosed after 1945, but also to events that occurred in her later life. In general, they are events hitherto overlooked or unknown, which are interpreted, confirmed, or disproved in the light of the new biographical material. I have not given a detailed account of the great prima donna's life after September 1945, most of which is well known; but in Postscripts I and III some events up to her death and after are either revealed for the first time or interpreted in a different light, while Postscript II provides a reassessment of her historic contribution to opera. All in all, I have done my best to enable the reader to form a picture of Maria Callas which is as complete and truthful as I could make it, while avoiding the repetition of stories too well known to need repeating.

Throughout her childhood in America Maria Callas was never called anything but Mary. When she came to Greece she remained Mary to her relatives and close friends, though her other friends and acquaintances, fellow students, and fellow musicians also knew her as Maria or even Marianna. She herself liked to be known as Marianna (at school in New York she was often called Mary Anna), and from 1944 she used Marianna Kaloyeropoulou as her stage name. In this book I have tried to use the name which seems most appropriate: "Mary" is the general rule, but wherever I am referring to the post-1947 period—whether in the narrative or in quoting words spoken or written by her in later life—I considered it more accurate to use "Maria," by which name she was then generally known.[4] My intention in adopting this practice has been to give a chronological point of reference in each case. Callas biographers have often been guilty of misinterpretations and fallacious arguments, especially when writing about her early years, as a result of overlooking the circumstances and causes of certain statements made by the post-1947 Maria about the pre-1947 Mary.

This book was first published in Greek in 1998, and I wish to thank Timothy Cullen very warmly for translating it so well. Indeed, I fully agree with those who have already commented that the reader feels as if the book were originally written in English. Although some of the material omitted from the English translation would undoubtedly interest fanatical Callas buffs, most of it refers to the historical background and to events, people, and institutions on the periphery of Callas's life in Greece. The Greek edition also includes photographs and documents in Greek that were omitted, as being of less interest to the English-speaking reader. On the other hand, not only have some minor errors been corrected and the text order moved in some places to improve the readability, but new material has been added in some relatively uncharted areas, both interesting and meaningful to the development of the story. In other words, this book is not a mere translation of the Greek but a revised and amplified, although shorter, new book.

I wish to thank Jackie Callas, Maria's sister, very specially for her most precious twofold assistance. In the course of many long and searching discussions— on subjects distant in time but quite often still painful—long-forgotten events were brought back to life, others were confirmed, rejected, or interpreted, and several people were remembered and appraised. Her memories and her views, always expressed with candid openness—including her refusal to discuss certain points—were always edifying, even when they contained factual errors or ideas with which I did not agree. Jackie's second major help, for which I am grateful to her, was her permission—as holder of her sister's rights—to freely use Maria's spoken or written words, contained in the worldwide Callas literature and interviews. Last but not least, she also allowed me to quote equally freely from her own memoirs as well as from those of her mother.

My thanks to Lord Harewood who wrote the Foreword. Responsible for the most complete and precious spoken interview with Maria Callas—his friend for thirty years, who revealed to him on that occasion more than she ever had or would to anybody else about her early years—he was immediately appreciative of the subject and method of my research and writing. "Although I did not meet Maria until August 1947, everything you say about her makes absolute sense in the light of what I knew later on," he wrote to me; and there could have been no greater encouragement.

My thanks also to John Ardoin, who, after reading a few chapters of this book, spoke about it to Eve Goodman of Amadeus Press with what must have been compellingly persuasive words (at least judging from the speed and enthusiasm with which both Amadeus and myself—who already knew of their excellence in the field—embarked on the project of publishing *The Unknown Callas*). Crucially productive and rewarding in this process was my cooperation with Franni Bertolino Farrell, who edited the manuscript with singular verve, occasional panache, extreme insight and tact—and above all with lots of humor.

Finally, the two other people I wish to thank expressly are Dr. Polyvios Marchand and Renzo Allegri. The first is the good friend who very early on, during the stages of this book's "conception," offered me extremely precious material on Callas collected by him over many years; and after laying this "trap," he never tired of encouraging my research, reading each chapter as it was completed and urging me on to the next with irresistible enthusiasm. As for Renzo Allegri, although a potential "antagonist" (he was writing his own books on Callas at the time), he responded to my approach straightaway, we exchanged enlightening correspondence, and I will always remember my visits to his beautiful home, in the country where Callas spent twelve great years of her life. Renzo not only offered me invaluable photographic and documentary material (including letters of Maria's mother) but also gave me the leads that enabled me to approach Italians whom Maria had known intimately during the war in Greece.

—⚭—

The Maria Callas who appears in these pages is a very different person from the one created by her previous biographers: here we have Maria Callas demythologized and portrayed as true to life as possible. To some extent she was herself responsible for the largely false picture that has prevailed up to now. That is why some biographers have been led astray: in general, they took her own statements at face value and overlooked the significance of certain facts about her early life that she herself distorted or never mentioned.

The two most important facts are these: first, that the key to her psychological problems was that her love for her father had been maimed by a mother suffering from frustration in many areas of her life; and secondly that her mother's attitude and conduct throughout the time they lived together in Greece, and especially during the occupation, built up in Mary a suppressed resentment which gradually transformed into lifelong hatred. When Maria later condemned her mother for the way she had treated her father and for her conduct during the occupation, she would in effect be casting herself as the avenger—and the victim—both of the unfair treatment of her father, and of the wrongs that she believed she herself had suffered *or committed* through her mother's example, and with her mother's encouragement.

Besides these fundamental reappraisals and the first-ever description of the time Callas spent in Greece, from March 1937 to September 1945, the reader will find that many myths are exploded and errors corrected: for example, that in her early years she was always a sullen, downtrodden girl, unattractive and devoid of sex appeal, that she took up singing against her own wishes, that she left Greece to escape the persecution of her professional rivals, or that the Callas phenomenon was a product of Italy and all that she learned there after leaving Greece. The public broadsides exchanged between mother and daughter from 1950 onward provided journalists and biographers with a mass of material which they often deliberately misinterpreted for the sake of sensationalism. By quoting statements out of context and without precise dates they distorted the truth, and their anachronistic arguments created the trashiest parts of the Callas mythology.

It is true of all really great international celebrities that their greatness stands above and unaffected by the course of time and historical events. But it is also their fate that their private lives should be pried into with excessive, and sometimes obsessive, interest. The consequences of this interest, all too often, are that legends are woven around their names and become widely accepted; that their characters and the facts of their life are distorted; and that the most intimate and secret corners of their personalities are prized open, often with ghoulish and offensive curiosity. Maria Callas was an international celebrity par excellence, and I am no exception as regards the arousal and pursuit of my interest. Inevitably, therefore, I shall probe into purely personal matters, whose appeal to the public is enhanced by the fact that they relate to an international celebrity who also happens to be a young woman. Some readers may think that the descriptions of certain intimate aspects of her private and professional life are unnecessary; however, I considered it would be a dereliction of the biographer's duty as historian to keep silent about facts brought to light by the research.

Maria Callas was Greek through and through: both her parents were full-blooded Greeks, and although she spent only eight and a half of the fifty-four years of her life (from the age of thirteen and a half to about twenty-two) actually living in Greece, these were the years that had the greatest formative effect on her character and her sense of national identity, such as it was. Until the late 1950s, whenever she was in the United States or addressing an American audience she had been in the habit of emphasizing that she was born in New York and possessed American citizenship as her birthright.[5] Similarly, when she was speaking to Italians, and in general during the time when she was married to Meneghini, she liked to stress that she lived in Italy and was married to an Italian, whose name she had added to her own. In 1957, however, when she revisited Greece for the first time after an absence of twelve years, she stated flatly, "*The blood in my veins, my character, my thoughts, all are Greek,*" and "*My blood is Greek, and no one can alter that!*" Thereafter she made many more statements in the same vein;[6] she came back to Greece frequently, three times to sing and the others privately; she had a long-standing relationship with a man who was Greek to his fingertips; and she worked with many of her compatriots, both in Greece and elsewhere.

Yet toward the end of her life, when she was permanently settled in Paris, she bared her innermost feelings in an interview with a Greek journalist and friend: "*Somehow I feel as if my roots had been cut—if I ever had any roots! I was born in America, yet I have never thought of myself as American. My parents were both Greek, I spent my youth in Athens and first sang in public there, yet I can't say for sure that I am Greek. Afterward I lived in Italy, got married there, built my career, and yet I never thought of myself as Italian. Now I am living in Paris, my home and my friends are here, but I definitely don't think of myself—nor do others think of me—as French. What the hell am I? I once told a very good friend of mine about this quandary and he said to me, 'But you are Maria Callas, and the whole world is your country and all its people your compatriots. Isn't that enough for you?' What do you think? Should I be satisfied with that?*"[7] Her work, and hence her reputation, had transformed Mary Kaloyeropoulou into Maria Callas and made her a citizen of the world—that, of course, is what her supportive friend implied. All the same, it cannot be denied, nor should the importance of the fact be overlooked, that she was born one hundred percent Greek, the daughter of two obscure Greek immigrants in New York.

David A. Lowe, the editor of a book about Maria published in 1987, came to the pessimistic conclusion that "a persuasive and revelatory intimate biography of Callas . . . is in fact an impossibility." In his view, "the woman herself was ultimately inaccessible," her privacy remained "largely intact—for all time," and "the total picture emerges as a jigsaw puzzle that can never be assembled because too many pieces were missing from the very beginning."[8] It is my hope that this book supplies many of the missing pieces. Maria herself wanted very much to write her autobiography, to "*set the record straight,*" as she told her secretary Nadia Stancioff in 1970. Toward the end of her life, finding that she did not have the strength to do it, she finally resigned herself to remaining silent, justifying herself on the grounds that if she had told the truth too many people would have been hurt. "*If I did [write my autobiography], I would have to tell the truth, and that would hurt too many people. As I am a woman who cannot invent the truth, it has to be [the real truth], and therefore it is better for me to be silent,"* she once said.[9] Today, surely, Maria would no longer be afraid of hurting a lot of people, as most of those she did not want to hurt are no longer alive. This applies particularly to her early life, spent in America and Greece well over fifty years ago. I am therefore taking the liberty of assuming that Maria—who was basically a straightforward and honest person herself—would have given her blessing to my attempt to "set the record straight," especially with regard to her unknown early years, which tell us so much about her character and hence about the whole course of her later life.

—⚊—

Please, Andrea, if you or anyone else you know has any old photographs of me from those years in Athens, or any reviews or other papers, please pack them up and send them to me. I'll need them for my memoirs.

I see you remember it all, Maria.

Of course I remember. Could anyone forget times like those?

To Andreas Paridis, Paris 1969
(Yorgos Pilichos, *Ta Nea,* 29 March 1969)

PART ONE

Origins and Childhood
(1923–1937)

CHAPTER 1

Roots

George Kaloyeropoulos was born in the early 1880s[1] at Neohori in the province of Ithomi, near the plane trees and willows that line the banks of a seasonal tributary of the Pamisos. Only two kilometers away lies Meligalas, a small country town with a station on the railway line to nearby Kalamata, the capital of Messinia. Vassilis Kaloyeropoulos, a well-off farmer of his own land, and his wife, Fotini, had four children: Mitsos, George, Tassos, and Tassia. Tassos died of tuberculosis when he was eighteen; Mitsos inherited the family home at Neohori; George was sent to Athens to study pharmacology; and Tassia was married off with a dowry and went to live at Sandani, the ancient Andania, a neighboring village of some three hundred souls.[2]

Very little is known about George's early life. When he left school at Meligalas in about 1902 he was a tall, slim, good-looking young man, quiet and rather reserved but popular with the girls. He may have spent the next few years doing his military service[3] and then helping the family at Neohori, before going to Athens to study pharmacology at the university. In 1915, when he was about thirty and was still living in Athens, he met Litsa Dimitriadou, an attractive blonde at least ten years his junior. With his good looks and smart appearance, backed up by the air of maturity that went with his age and his prospects as a pharmacist, he swept her off her feet immediately. No doubt George was attracted both by her looks and by the fact that she came from a "good" family, which would help a young man from the provinces like him to climb the social ladder.

On the background of the Dimitriadis family, all writers up to now have unquestioningly accepted the version given by Evangelia (Litsa) Kaloyeropoulou, *née* Dimitriadou, the mother of Maria Callas, in her book: namely, that the family came from Constantinople, but that Litsa's grandfather had moved to Stylis in Phthiotis, a district in east central Greece.[4] However, the facts are rather different. Mary's great-great-grandfather Petros, the earliest Dimitriadis, of whom hardly anything is known, came from the island of Kea (also known as Tzia) in the Cyclades. Born in about 1780, he moved to Constantinople for reasons now unknown and settled there with his wife, a woman from Kythira (Cythera) whose maiden name was Varvarigou. Their son Konstantinos was born on 28 February 1813, probably in Constantinople, but around 1820 mother and son went back to Kea. There they were joined by Petros, who had fled from Constantinople with nothing but the clothes on his back, when the Greek War of Independence broke out in 1821 and the Greeks of Constantinople suffered the repercussions. Thereafter nothing more is heard of him.

Konstantinos Dimitriadis, a boy with literary leanings, had lessons with Ioannis Psaras, a future professor at the Ionian Academy in Corfu, and in 1825, when he was only twelve, he was construing Xenophon faultlessly, as he wrote in his unfinished memoirs. In November 1825 he went to Nafplion to look for work, and from there he was sent to the besieged town of Mesolonghi by his self-appointed guardian Panos Rangos, a member of the National Assembly belonging to a well-known family from the Valtos district of western Greece. He went on to become secretary to Panos's brother, General Ioannis Rangos, described as "relatively well educated in comparison with the other generals of that period." In spite of his tender age he fought in several engagements in central Greece, including the final battle at Petra. When the independent state of Greece was established and a regular army formed, Konstantinos decided on a military career. He distinguished himself in the counterinsurgency actions against rebellious factions opposed to King Otho, and in the drive to clear the country of bandits. In 1874 he retired from the army with the rank of colonel following a quarrel with the war minister, Dimitrios Grivas. He spent the rest of his life at Stylis, a small town on the Malian Gulf which was the port for Lamia, the capital of Phthiotis, about 17 kilometers away.[5]

Litsa, who makes extravagant claims for her illustrious forebears, says in her memoirs that the family of her *great*-grandfather was "immensely wealthy" and that he went as a young man to Stylis, where he bought "vast estates" and raised a family of seven children.[6] The truth is that in the 1840s her grandfather Konstantinos Dimitriadis happened to be posted to the area around Lamia, then close to the northern frontier of Greece, where he met and married Marigo, the daughter of a wealthy local named Doukas Filon. So the "vast estates" near Stylis—about one hundred forty acres—came to him as his wife's dowry. The newlyweds made their home there around 1850 in a fine big house surrounded by orchards and extensive olive groves. The evidence suggests that they lived happily and very comfortably. The estate was just below the house, and on it there was a chapel dedicated to Ayios Kirykos, about 100 meters from the shore. When Konstantinos died in 1888, his children buried him in front of the chapel and put up a memorial surmounted by his bust in marble.[7]

Konstantinos and Marigo, who outlived her husband by many years, had three sons and two daughters.[8] The eldest son, Petros Dimitriadis (1850/53?–1916), inherited his father's intelligence and his love of music. He spoke French and Italian and was generally acknowledged to have a very good tenor voice, with which he sang soulful Greek *kantades* and all the best-known arias from the popular Italian operatic repertoire. But "the nightingale of Stylis," as he was known locally, never had singing lessons and always felt rather bitter about that. Litsa once described him as one who looked for comfort in singing at any hour of the day. "Often during a meal he would stun the family and the servants as he stood up, threw his napkin aside, put his hand on his chest and abandoned himself in an Italian *romanza*, while his eyes shone through the tears of his emotion." The story that a touring Italian tenor named Esposito heard him sing and canceled his own concert on the grounds that Petros sang better than he did, presumably contains at least an element of exaggeration.[9] Evidently, however, Petros did have one serious weakness: he gambled heavily at cards. And so, when he met and fell in love with fifteen-year-old Frosso Lourou, her father Efthymios Louros, a senior fellow officer of his, was unwilling to let him marry her. Petros is said to have threatened to elope, whereupon her father gave way to prevent scandal.

Frosso Lourou (1870/72?–1956) was a strikingly beautiful girl with fair hair and blue eyes, nicknamed "Helen of Troy's sister" or "Faust's Marguerite." Her father was an army officer who rose to be commandant of the palace guard, while her mother Eleni belonged to the Klaras family from Lamia, a name well known from the War of Independence.[10] It was said that Frosso never really loved her husband because she had lost her heart to a cavalry officer she had seen passing in front of her window. But she was made to marry Petros in a big wedding at the Church of Saint George Karytsis in central Athens, in 1887 or early in 1888. A guard of honor was formed of Efthymios Louros's and Petros's own fellow officers, and the guests included some of the cream of Athenian society. After their marriage Petros and Frosso lived for a time in the Makriyanni area behind the Acropolis, where Petros had apparently inherited some property. From then until 1912 or 1913, wherever Petros happened to be posted, they would go with their children to spend long periods at the house at Stylis as often as he could get leave from the army. However, although they had eleven children (two of whom died in infancy) in a period of just over twenty years, it seems that the bond of conjugal love and affection was always missing from their home life.[11]

Of the four sons who survived, the eldest was Konstantinos (Konstas), born in 1888 probably at Stylis. A sensitive and artistic youth with a gift for music and poetry, he went to university, traveled to Constantinople, started writing for literary magazines, and won the respect and support of distinguished playwright Polyvios Dimitrakopoulos, several of whose texts were used for operettas and popular songs. Unfortunately for Konstas, he fell in love with a girl "beneath his station," whom he asked to marry him in 1910. When she refused, thinking that the well-off Dimitriadis was making fun of her, the impulsive Konstas pulled his gun and shot himself in front of her very eyes. His mother ran to Constantinople just in time to hear her twenty-two-year-old son ask her pardon, "for in a moment of madness he had forsaken all his family obligations," referring to his yet unmarried sisters. His faithful dog Mephistopheles accompanied the funeral cortège to the family tomb at Stylis and stayed there, refusing food and drink, until he too died and was buried beside Konstas.[12]

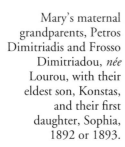

Mary's maternal grandparents, Petros Dimitriadis and Frosso Dimitriadou, *née* Lourou, with their eldest son, Konstas, and their first daughter, Sophia, 1892 or 1893.

The eldest daughter and second child of Petros and Frosso was Sophia (1891–1966), born at Kalambaka, where her father was stationed at the time. Next came Litsa, who happened to be born at Stylis, followed by two more girls, Ekaterini (Kakia) (1897–1989) and Kalliopi (Pipitsa) (1898–1981), born at Almyros and Tyrnavos, respectively. The next son, Doukas (1902–1965), born at Halkis, was named after his maternal grandfather. He was a fair-haired, blue-eyed boy who was the darling of his grandmother Marigo Dimitriadou. Efthymios (1905/06?–1961) also had blue eyes, bright as buttons, but his hair was dark. A very good-looking boy, he was Litsa's favorite among her younger brothers.[13] The next to be born was Altana (1906/08?–1920/22?), like Konstas a very introverted child from an early age, and also devoutly religious. The youngest of the family was Filon, born at

Stylis in 1909, just a year before the suicide of his eldest brother. In general, the male members of this large family had inherited the genes of their good-natured, artistic father, while the daughters had a harder streak to their character more in keeping with their mother's Louros blood. But most of Petros and Frosso's children, boys as well as girls, had the fair hair and light blue eyes of the Louros side of the family.[14]

One of the girls who inherited both the blue eyes and the hardness of character was Litsa. In her book she says that she was born at Stylis on New Year's Day, 1898, because the family was vacationing there at the time. Actually, she was born the third child of Petros and Frosso in 1894 or 1895. She was christened Elmina Evangelia but was called Litsa (the usual abbreviation for Evangelia in Greece). Nothing is known about her early years, from which we may assume that nothing of any consequence occurred to disturb her comfortable childhood at Stylis. One of the traits she appears to have inherited from her forebears was a love of acting and the theater, but even if she ever actually expressed a wish to become an actress, the family's strict code of propriety would certainly not have allowed such a thing to happen. She consoled herself by studying the mandolin and the guitar, but no amount of parental disapproval could have killed off her urge to act up before an audience, to be acclaimed and applauded. These inclinations of hers, which circumstances forced her to suppress, were to remain with her always and to exert a profound influence not only on her own life but also on those of her daughters.

Exactly when Petros and Frosso moved to Athens is not known, nor can we be sure that they continued to visit the estate at Stylis regularly for summer or other holidays, as Litsa wrote. Nor is it by any means certain that the family was as well-off as their second daughter claimed: "We were rich. With my brothers and sisters I spent much of my childhood in Stylis, where my father had estates, orchards, and olive groves." On the contrary, a box of jewelry which Frosso had brought with her as part of her dowry had to be sold off to pay Petros's gambling debts. His mother, old Marigo, aware of the danger, made a will bequeathing the family house and land to her favorite grandson, Doukas.[15] It must have been in 1913 or thereabouts, soon after being wounded in action in the Balkan Wars, that Petros, semi-paralyzed and short of money, decided to settle permanently in Athens with his family. His son Doukas being still under age, and old Marigo having died, he contrived to sell the Stylis property to his nephew Iraklis Kambouris, who offered to "help out" and bought it for a song. The family moved to Athens and rented a house in Kolonaki, near Vassilissis Sofias Avenue; the children continued their schooling at the Omirion Lykion, also in Kolonaki. After a very short time, however, they moved again to a large two-story house on Jean Moréas Street, off Veikou Street behind the Acropolis.[16]

Litsa was an attractive, vivacious young girl when she met George Kaloyeropoulos, in unknown circumstances. Evidently old Petros instinctively disapproved of George as a prospective son-in-law from the outset. "You will never be happy with him," he warned Litsa, and added, "If you marry that man, I will never be able to help you." But Litsa, by nature stubborn and self-willed, took no notice of her father's advice and introduced George to her mother, who was still quite young, liked male company, and proved by no means impervious to the young pharmacist's smooth manner: "My beautiful mother . . . wanted me to marry him, for he could charm all women and he had charmed her as well as myself."[17]

Petros Dimitriadis, the retired colonel crippled by hemiplegia, did not manage to prevent the marriage of his beloved daughter. But, as it turned out, nor was he present to give it his blessing. In August 1916, with the country divided against itself and in political turmoil, Petros—beset by who knows what worries and strains and saddened by the conspiracy between mother and daughter—died suddenly of a stroke. Litsa would remember him telling her shortly before he died that music made him think of the waves hitting the rocks of Cape Sounion. We do not know whether the decision to go ahead with Litsa's marriage to George had already been made, or whether the way was cleared for them by the death of "the nightingale of Stylis." In any event the wedding took place just sixteen days later in an Athenian church, with almost indecent haste. It was probably a small family affair, and Litsa wore only a plain white dress because the family was in mourning.[18]

CHAPTER 2

Meligalas

The newly married couple went to live at Meligalas, then a thriving little town of two thousand inhabitants and the hub of a rural area some 30 kilometers north of the busy port of Kalamata. George decided to open a pharmacy of his own, as there were none in any of the surrounding villages. He found suitable ground-floor premises on the main shopping street, brought basic stock and equipment down from Athens, and started mixing drugs and making up herbal remedies to his own recipes. Soon he was making plenty of money, and was highly regarded locally. The living quarters over the shop were big enough for George and Litsa, a cook, two maids, and a handyman, with room to spare for the children they hoped to have soon. The two upper floors were reached from the pharmacy by a broad wooden spiral staircase.

It did not take long for Litsa to realize that she and George were not suited to each other. George was well known in the neighborhood and had a wide circle of friends outside the family, whom he avoided introducing to his wife. His work in the pharmacy kept him busy all day, and it was not the sort of work Litsa could help him with. She, for her part—a twenty-two-year-old expectant mother, brought up in the Athenian middle class—suddenly found herself plunged into the alien world of a small provincial town, a world with different codes of behavior and a different pace of life. Their obvious incompatibility was revealed in her conversations with George, which more and more often would end in painful arguments and quarrels. Nor was she wrong, for in fact the two of them were ill-matched in many crucial respects.

One of the differences between George and his new bride was the disparity of their social backgrounds, and Litsa's harping on the fact was typical of her middle-class snobbery. "George Kaloyeropoulos was of a less good family than ours," she notes in her memoirs, in a matter-of-fact tone; but later in the book she gets carried away and says that in her mother's family tree there were "generals, diplomats, a bishop, and a sprinkling of counts and countesses"! As time went on, these gibes of hers about her social superiority over the provincial pharmacist with inferior tastes, who lacked her own "artistic" refinement, were brought out with increasing frequency and vulgarity, and later she would even come out with them in front of the children.[1] Unquestionably the social status of Litsa's army family was higher, from the viewpoint of the world at large, than that of George's "peasant" family. On the other hand one should not overlook the differences between the social criteria of rural Greece and those of urban society in the wider Athens area, to which Litsa's people really belonged. Thus the Kaloyeropoulos family, though provincial, had a high standing in their own community, whereas the Dimitriadis family, though middle class and higher up the social ladder, were of no consequence in Athenian society except insofar as they basked in the reflected glory of Konstantinos Louros, Frosso's cousin, who was the royal family's obstetrician.

In character, too, George and Litsa were ill-matched. George was easygoing and undemonstrative, he had no great ambitions, financial or social, and his total lack of feeling for any of the arts was to cause him a lot of friction with his wife. By contrast Litsa, who was full of life, had imagined that at least some of the dreams stifled by parental pressure in Stylis and Athens would come true for her. She began to see that at Meligalas she would still not know where to channel her energy or be able to satisfy the innate but undeveloped proclivity for music and the theater. What is more, though Litsa's pregnancy must have somehow limited the pleasures that marriage had introduced her to, the thirtyish heartthrob of Meligalas had no intention of denying them to himself. Evidently he had already embarked on discreet extramarital liaisons which, in a small country town where everyone knows everyone else's business, could not possibly remain secret. It did not take long for the observant Litsa to guess the reason for his unexplained late homecomings, and we may be sure that her fiery character led to fierce arguments and a withering of their feeling for each other. "Within six months I knew that my father was right and that I would never be happy with my husband. But I was determined to be a good wife to him, and I did my best. I had servants, a cook and maids, and I helped them, for my mother had trained me to be a good housekeeper and to cook, and when I was busy I could forget that I was unhappy."[2] These few words constitute one of the three paragraphs in which Litsa dismisses her life at Meligalas from the autumn of 1916 to July 1923. Yet in those seven years three major events occurred—two births and a death—and George was to make a very serious decision.

The first event was the birth of a daughter on 4 June 1917. This gave Litsa an excuse to go back to Athens and spend some time with her family—and more than an excuse, because both on medical grounds and for reasons of social propriety it was considered right for the baby to be delivered by Litsa's "celebrated" uncle Konstantinos Louros. Soon after the birth Litsa returned to Meligalas with little Yakinthi (Hyacinth), later to be known as Jackie, who started her life in that large house of cool, darkened rooms, surrounded by the chatter of the servants. She still remembers the big wooden staircase leading down to her father's pharmacy, fragrant with strange and intoxicating aromas, full of beautiful jars, tubes, and bottles. And she would watch her father working on his magic potions or serving the customers: "My mother always seemed to be upset by something so that at that time I preferred my father with his smile and his moustache twirling and the way the young ladies giggled when he held on to their hands as he gave them their change. . . . Father, so [my mother] said, could never resist a pretty face and his position in the pharmacy gave him plenty of opportunity to follow his bent."[3]

The other two major events of this period were the birth and death of Vassilis, the son who, in accordance with tradition, was given the name of George's father. He too was born in Athens, probably early in 1920, with Louros again in attendance. He was a beautiful boy with fair hair and blue eyes—a real chip off the old Dimitriadis-Louros block. The arrival of a son and heir lessened the friction between George and Litsa, both of whom doted on the little boy. The future seemed rosier, but in the summer of 1922 Vassilis died of meningitis. Maria recalled in 1959, "*I know I had a brother, Vassilis, but the subject was always carefully avoided at home. All I know about it, I suppose my sister must have told me later.*" A doctor had been called, but he could find no explanation for the high temperature. "*That evening, however, his temperature rose still higher, the next morning he was unconscious and three days later he was taken to the cemetery.*"[4] Jackie, who was five at the time, described the doom-laden atmosphere of those days and recalled how the first thing her mother did, on returning from the funeral in deep mourning, was to scold her for skipping on the stairs. Her father, gentle and conciliatory as usual, tried unsuccessfully to calm her down, but no sooner had the emotional scar begun to heal than the marital rows erupted anew, now fiercer than ever. Usually they were started by Litsa, regardless of whether or not George had given her any cause for complaint or needled her with his maddening impassivity, retiring into his shell and sitting in silence for hours on end. "He stayed in the house less and less and didn't smile as he had before," Yakinthi would later remember.[5]

By the spring of 1923, in spite of the strained relations with George and the shock they had been through, Litsa found that she was pregnant again. Feeling calmer now, she lost no time in telling Yakinthi that she would soon have another brother just like Vassilis.[6] Yet the peace in the household was precarious. George had had enough of Litsa's tantrums, which were damaging his reputation in the small and narrow-minded community of Meligalas. Litsa, for her part, felt growing resentment at the way her philandering husband expected to be allowed to do just as he liked. So it was perhaps inevitable that the example of Leonidas Lanzounis, George's old friend who had recently emigrated to New York, should have given George the idea of packing up and setting off with his pregnant wife and their young daughter to make a fresh start in the New World.

When he wrote and asked Lanzounis what he thought about it, the answer he received was discouraging. America was not the place for George, said Leonidas. How would he support himself to begin with, until he had learned English in order to pass the examination without which it was impossible to get a work permit? Nevertheless, disregarding his friend's advice and keeping the matter entirely to himself, George secretly worked out the details of his bold plan. Probably around June 1923[7] he made the great decision, but even then he told nobody about it until he had sold the business and booked the passage on a liner sailing from Patras in mid July. "One morning I heard Mother shouting hysterically, then my father began slamming doors and the servants hid away," as Jackie recalls. "No one would tell me what was happening. . . . [Until] gradually the word America crept into my consciousness and then suddenly there were boxes and cases everywhere."[8]

Litsa complained incessantly about George's "crazy behavior," hurling at him over and over again that "only the uneducated, the peasants, did such a thing." George did not react, nor did he immediately reveal to his wife the destination of their impending journey. Evidently he was afraid she might object to the plan and have time to arrange for herself to live with her mother in Athens. But the idea never even occurred to Litsa: after all, she was pregnant, she had six-year-old Yakinthi to look after, and she had no private means. And at least it meant that she would be leaving Meligalas, a place where she had been unhappy and had recently lost her son. So, however much she may have shouted and thrown tantrums, she went along with George's decision. But she did go back to Athens for one last visit, to say good-bye to her family. In fact she even suggested taking her favorite brother, eighteen-year-old Efthymios, to America with her, but her mother would not allow her.[9]

There can be no doubt that George's decision to emigrate came as a complete surprise, especially in view of his usual lack of enterprise. He himself never gave a convincing explanation of the reasons that had led him to such a drastic move. In 1959 Maria referred to *several friends who had already emigrated and wrote to tell him about their thriving businesses and comfortable homes.* As for Litsa, although she would never say it publicly, she would one day reveal to Yakinthi that her father "had fled from Meligalas because he had got the mayor's daughter pregnant."[10] It certainly seems strange that George made the decision just when his life appeared to be getting back to normal after the loss of Vassilis. His business was doing well, he was making a fair amount of money, and socially the Kaloyeropoulos family was well established as one of the leading families in Meligalas. Undoubtedly a combination of reasons led him to his decision. The first, and probably the one that clinched the matter for him, was Litsa's overwrought state of mind. Although she was calmer now that she was pregnant again, her continual outbursts had been exhausting and embarrassing. At the same time Litsa was taking him to task over his infidelities with increasing frequency, and George probably thought that in New York he would have more scope, more freedom. And, of course, if he had indeed left the mayor's daughter pregnant, his position in a tiny community must have become untenable. Finally, getting away from the place where little Vassilis had died must have been another factor behind George's decision. He had become obsessed, it seems, by the idea that his son's death had been due to the unhygienic conditions prevailing in Greece in those days. *"In any case, he wanted to get away from Athens [sic] to spare the family another such disaster. You see, my mother was pregnant again,"* as Maria would say in 1959.[11]

Once the decision had been made, the hurried preparations for the departure must have taken up all their time and attention. George wound up his affairs, negotiated the sale of his thriving business, and made arrangements for the voyage. Litsa meanwhile supervised the disposal of the household effects and the packing for the voyage. By the end of it all, exhaustion and an awareness of their shared responsibility for the great adventure ahead must have brought a long-forgotten feeling of family unity and human warmth into the lives of the harassed couple, even if only for a few moments and perhaps not until they were on the train. To six-year-old Yakinthi, no doubt, it was all a great adventure. She was quiet and reserved by nature, but even she could hardly have concealed her immense excitement on that day in 1923, probably sometime between 15 and 20 July, when the train pulled out of Meligalas station to take them to Patras via Kyparissia.[12] When the isles of Kefallinia and Zakynthos had been left behind and the ship was crossing the Ionian Sea toward Sicily, George could hardly have imagined that he would not be seeing Greece again until 1960. Still less, perhaps, could Litsa, then five months pregnant, have had any idea that it would be fourteen long years before she came back to Greece—with two daughters but without her husband.

CHAPTER 3

America! America!

George was sufficiently prosperous at that time to be able to afford a good cabin for the long and tiring voyage. Litsa spent much of her time closeted in there, often prostrated by seasickness aggravated by her pregnancy: "I was not happy about coming to the United States. . . . All the way across the Atlantic I was wretched." From time to time she made the effort to go to the dining salon, that hub of shipboard social life, to keep an eye on Yakinthi's table manners. The sight of the Statue of Liberty and the skyscrapers of Manhattan must have given the untraveled immigrants their first idea of the enormous difference of scale that they would have to adapt to. According to Litsa, the port of New York was strangely subdued when the ship docked there on 2 August 1923.[1] Sirens hooted mournfully and all the flags were at half-mast, since on that very day President Warren G. Harding had died in San Francisco, aged fifty-seven. Litsa burst into tears: she was physically and emotionally exhausted and, being a superstitious woman, she felt that this atmosphere of death was a bad omen.[2]

On George's instructions, Leonidas Lanzounis had found them an apartment, the first of the many places they were to live during the next fourteen years. It was at 87 Sixth Avenue, near Ditmars Boulevard on Long Island, in Astoria in the borough of Queens, just across the East River from Manhattan. Even then Astoria was jokingly known as "Little Athens" because so many Greeks lived and worked there. Litsa immediately set to work furnishing and decorating the apartment. She only had to buy furniture for she had brought carpets, lace, embroidered cushion covers, and icons with her from Meligalas, and these were enough to make the apartment feel quite like home—an ordinary Greek lower-middle-class home. "Some things hardly changed: we spoke Greek and lived among Greek immigrants, so the sensation of being in a foreign place was much lessened," Jackie wrote later.[3]

It has often been said—and many writers have been content to repeat the allegation—that George found work immediately in the pharmacy of a department store. But this must have happened later, because when he arrived he knew no English at all. Not wishing to remain idle, he taught Greek in a school, and he probably worked as an assistant in a Greek drugstore in Astoria. George, how-

ever, failed to match his lifestyle to his income, with the result that the fairly substantial sum he had brought from Meligalas was gradually frittered away. According to his friend Lanzounis, "George, when he came to New York, he came like a
banker, but he ate up his money right away. He came from a small town and acted
like a big shot!"[4] It has to be said that Lanzounis, in voicing his disapproval of
George's extravagance, was making no allowance for Litsa's constant demands for
money, chiefly in order to keep up appearances. In the early days, however, before
they began to feel the pinch financially, most of the couple's attention was taken
up with their new environment, new acquaintances, George's prolonged absences
at work, and, above all, Litsa's pregnancy.

Maria, in a private conversation only three years before she died, said that
Litsa had sent George to ask an astrologer when the best time to conceive a son
would be.[5] It seems a safe assumption that Litsa's third pregnancy, coming as it did
so soon after the loss of Vassilis, was intended to fill the void left by that bereave-
ment. In anticipation of the birth of a boy, Litsa made everything blue: not only
his clothes, which she knitted herself, but even the walls of the room where
Yakinthi slept on her own. In this way the first four months in New York went
quickly. Litsa made some new friends, mostly Greeks living in Astoria, while Yakinthi, who became fluent in English in about a year, soon acquired a new name:
when they arrived in America she had been entered in the immigration register as
"Jakynthi," and from then on she was called Jackie, even by her parents.[6]

On Sunday, 2 December 1923, a fine day, Leonidas took Litsa to the Flower
Hospital at Fifth Avenue and 105th Street, in Manhattan, where he had made
arrangements for her. He stayed in the labor ward, but only in his capacity as a
family friend, as he was an orthopedic surgeon. The birth was straightforward,
and Litsa was delivered of a healthy girl weighing twelve and a half pounds, which
is unusually heavy. When Leonidas took the baby in to Litsa she was shattered to
learn that it was a girl, because she had never allowed such an idea to enter her
head. He did his best to cheer her up, complimenting her on her bonny newborn.
But her reaction was one of strong aversion, and it was not until four days later that
she looked at her daughter, who had black hair and felt heavy in her arms, for the
first time. Naturally, accounts of Litsa's reaction have been adorned with imaginative embellishments, some of the "psychologists" (mostly French) speculating
that the initial rejection by her mother might well have left the newborn with a permanently scarred personality.[7]

Until 1987, when Nadia Stancioff, Callas's secretary in the early 1970s, published the particulars recorded on her birth certificate, opinions were divided with
regard to the exact date of her birth. Her name was actually registered as Sophie
Cecelia Kalos, whereas previous researchers had been looking for Callas or Kallas,
Kaloyeropoulos or Calogeropoulos. Litsa's maiden name was given as Demes,
rather than Dimitriadou or any other phonetic rendering of her Greek name.[8]
And the date of birth was 2 December 1923, as always correctly stated on her

American passport and often confirmed by Leonidas Lanzounis. It was disputed later by Litsa, who maintained that her daughter was born on 4 December, although she herself gave Mary's date of birth as 3 December when she enrolled her at school. Having once got the fact wrong, of course, Litsa stubbornly refused to countenance any other version. Maria herself contributed to her biographers' confusion by writing in her memoirs: *"I prefer the fourth of December, first, because I have to believe what my mother says. Second, it's Saint Barbara's Day, the patroness of the artillery, a proud and combative saint whom I like in a special way."*[9] Yet she always celebrated her birthday on 2 December.

As for the name Kalos, evidently the Americans found "Kaloyeropoulos" such a tongue twister that George decided to simplify it, as did many immigrants with long surnames. We do not know when the name Callas came into general use, but from the time the family arrived in America the name Kaloyeropoulos was presumably shortened first to Kalos (as on the birth certificate) and then to Callas.* George and Litsa also had difficulty in deciding on their daughter's Christian name, as they had both taken it for granted that they were going to have another Vassilis. Litsa wanted to call her Sophia but George suggested Cecilia, a name virtually unknown in the Orthodox Church. Both names, albeit with slightly different spellings, were entered on her birth certificate, and in the end the parents compromised with Maria, but both of them called her Mary from the very beginning. "Among ourselves we called her Mary, both in America and here [in Greece] later," her sister Jackie says.[10]

On 26 February 1926, after an unusually long delay, Mary was christened Sophia Cecilia Anna Maria at the Greek Orthodox Cathedral of the Holy Trinity

---

*LITSA (14) states that the name was changed by court order at about the time of Mary's christening (in 1926), but that they themselves continued to use both names and their Greek friends still called them by their Greek name. The name Sophie Cecelia Kalos remained on Maria Callas's official papers until 18 March 1966, when she renounced her U.S. citizenship at the American embassy in Paris. (See also *The Maria Callas International Club Magazine*, no. 15, June 1995.) As a result, after she got married in Italy, on 21 April 1949, her first Italian identity card, issued at Zevio near Verona on 6 September 1949, bore this name (*Gente*, 2 Nov. 1992). It was under this name that she had all her U.S. passports issued and renewed, starting in New York (16 February 1937), then in Athens (4 August 1945), and subsequently in Washington (10 June 1947), Venice (12 May 1950), and Milan (12 May 1952, 12 May 1954, 4 June 1958, and 19 June 1962). In Greece the problem of the surname did not arise, because she always used the Greek name, Kaloyeropoulou, except on one occasion when, for a concert on 30 March 1945, shortly before she left Greece, she used Callas as her professional name (but as *Mary* Callas, not Maria) for the first time. Before she left the U.S. for Italy, however, on her application to the State Department for the renewal of her passport on 2 June 1947, she would state: *"My professional name is Maria Callas."* (Photocopied documents pertaining to Maria Callas's American citizenship and passports, kindly provided by Jackie Kaloyeropoulou.) The suggestion put forward by some writers, that the name Callas was chosen because it is almost an anagram of La Scala, is an anachronistic piece of imaginative invention. Maria herself made the matter quite clear: *"I kept the name Callas because Kaloyeropoulou is too long for a poster and too difficult to pronounce, except in Greece."* (MARGRIET.)

Mary in her mother's arms, with Jackie and George Kaloyeropoulos, probably at her christening, New York, 26 February 1926.

at 319 East Seventy-fourth Street, in Manhattan. Her godfathers were Lanzounis and another doctor named Karouzos, one of the new family friends. She seemed to love it when Father Methodios Kourkoulis dipped her into the font: "She splashed around and didn't want to get out. She didn't mind the sacred oil smeared on her head, and she didn't complain when they cut her curls as is customary," Lanzounis recollected some sixty years later. But she screamed bloody murder when they dressed her.[11]

—⚶—

As one of Maria's biographers has suggested, if the baby had been a boy the relations between George and Litsa might not have deteriorated as rapidly as they did.[12] In her book Jackie comments ruefully that the compromise over their second daughter's name was "the last time that diplomacy would prevail in the war that was to break out between husband and wife." When the quarreling resumed, Litsa found herself looking back nostalgically at the "paradise" of Meligalas. She reviled her husband for having "brutally transported" the family to a foreign land and "thrown away the opportunity to better himself" in Greece. "Chagrin at her own foolishness drove her into paroxysms of recrimination and regret," notes Jackie, who adds, "We never played with dolls although we had them. How could we when the only example of motherhood we knew was a woman forever bemoaning the fact that she had married our father?" The effects of that warfare were felt by both girls, though the consequences were different. Jackie must surely have been severely traumatized, while Mary, though still far too young to be fully aware of what was happening, retreated behind a barrier of truculence.[13]

Talking about her childhood in late 1956, Maria would say: "*I have no particular recollection, except the vague intuition that my parents were not suited to each other.*" In fact, Litsa never let up on George and often attacked him in front of the girls. "*My husband's indifference to me made me irritable and nervous,*" Litsa claims in self-defense, admitting that although she tried not to let the two girls know this, she didn't "always succeed."[14] Naturally enough, Litsa channeled all her abundant energy into the upbringing of her children. In those early years in New York she was even fussier than she had been at Meligalas about whom they mixed with. She would not let the girls go to any of their friends' houses except for the very few that she considered socially acceptable. Social status soon became an obsession with her. And she was a real martinet when it came to dealing with the children's trivial everyday misdemeanors. Like several other traits of Mary's character, it is most likely that her gluttony and impertinence were caused partly by the unreasonable punishments and pressures imposed on her by her hysterical mother. Jackie, too, remained unforgiving toward Litsa to the end, but she reacted in her own way. She never crossed swords with her mother openly, as Maria did eventually: being a more docile character, she behaved like an obedient daughter and accepted scathing criticism uncomplainingly.[15]

But Jackie was all the while recording instances of Litsa's tyrannical treatment of herself and Mary (who had no doubt begun her own mental record of events) and, more particularly, of their father. Reading her memoirs of this period, one is struck by the deep undercurrent of resentment that comes through in her descriptions of her mother's overbearing and insensitive behavior. It only needed one of the girls to step slightly out of line for Litsa to remind the culprit how stupid and feckless she was: "Sometimes she would go on and on, building up to a crescendo, so that I would run weeping to my room. I was only happy alone with Mary." After school Jackie would play with Mary and, like any girl with a baby sister, teach her to walk. When she had done her homework she would read Mary stories, such as "Goldilocks and the Three Bears" and "Little Red Riding Hood," in the seclusion of their shared bedroom. Then at eight o'clock sharp they had to go to bed, whether they were tired or not.[16]

There is no reason to doubt that Mary did start singing at a very early age, but that does not mean that her singing was any different from that of other toddlers. Litsa admits that she cannot remember when she began to suspect that Mary might have an exceptional voice. "*As for my vocation, there were never any doubts,*" says Maria in her memoirs, with a strong dash of irony. "*My father tells of how I sang while still in the cradle, hurling vocalises and high notes so unusual for an infant that even the neighbors were stupefied.*" She had no precise recollection of the first songs she sang. "*But from what my parents say, I must have begun very early indeed, more or less in the cradle.*"[17] Various little incidents that occurred when Mary was young have been seized upon, with hindsight, as early signs of her genius. For example, one of her favorite nursery rhymes is supposed to have been the cautionary tale of Little Polly Flinders, who sat among the cinders: "Her mother came and caught her, / And whipped her little daughter / For spoiling her nice new clothes." Mary is said to have sung this jingle over and over again, putting a wealth of meaning into it, according to the unverified source of the story. But the most popular story in the Callas literature concerns Mary and the pianola that Litsa persuaded George to buy in 1926. No doubt Litsa saw the new acquisition as a fine status symbol and she bought pianola rolls of perforated paper, nearly all of arias from well-known operas: "We were raised to the sounds of grand opera and my mother's incessant nagging," Jackie remarks neatly.[18]

Most biographers describe how Mary, aged three or four, discovered that she could make music by pumping the pedals with her hands, as she could not reach them with her feet. The story is probably true, but it can hardly be called significant, as a three-year-old girl would in any case have pumped away at the pedals. Others make a point of the fact that, from a very early age, Mary could not stand the Greek popular songs that her father liked to listen to, to remind him of home. This was simply a result of the brainwashing she had received from Litsa, whose musical pretensions had exposed both girls to a constant diet of Bellini, Verdi, and Puccini. Finally there is the story, probably more a matter of legend than of fact, that little Mary loved going to church to hear the chanting. The family's Sunday visits to the nearest Greek Orthodox church from wherever they were living (from 1931 or 1932 it was Saint Spyridon's in Washington Heights) were primarily social events, because in Greek communities the world over churchgoing is also regarded as an ideal opportunity to keep up with one's acquaintances and mix with society at a level that would otherwise be out of one's reach.[19]

When Litsa was asked later who had discovered Maria's "golden voice," she would answer without hesitation, "I did, when she was three, in Astoria." Yet she admits in her book that it was not until Mary was ten years old that she realized she was "gifted with a magnificent voice." Maria herself was in fact quite consistent and never attempted to deny that it was her mother who had discovered her talent. At the same time, however, she accused Litsa of having put such pressure on her that she had deprived her of the pleasures of childhood: "*As soon as she became aware of my vocal gifts [she] decided to make of me a child prodigy as quickly as possible,*" she says in her memoirs. "*And child prodigies never have genuine childhoods. It's not a special toy that I remember—a doll or a favorite game—but, rather, the songs that I had to rehearse again and again, to the point of exhaustion, for the final test at the end of a school year.*"[20] And this was by no means the only time Maria spoke out on the subject.

She reverted to it on many occasions, one of the last being as late as 1973: "*I was made to sing when I was only four, and I hated it. That's why I've always had this love-hate relationship with singing.*" And on being asked whether she would have wanted a child of hers to be a singer, she answered, "*That would be her own decision; I'd never hound her as I was hounded. Oh, I got enough spankings!*" She had actually said much the same back in 1957: "*No! Decidedly no! There must be a law against it. . . . Children should have a wonderful childhood. I have not had it—I wish I had.*" And in 1971 she said, "*When I was young I longed so much to go [to the circus]. . . . I used to dream about it. . . . But I was never taken to see one. There ought to be a law against making children work and depriving them of childish memories—it's disgraceful!*"[21] However, Maria's recollections of the pressure put upon her in her childhood were colored by the way her mind worked in later life and were not entirely accurate. Although it can hardly be denied that Mary was ill-disposed and aggressive to her mother from a very early age, it will become clear that very little of the resentment she felt was due to Litsa's incipient efforts to push her into a musical career. The fundamental cause of most of her childhood traumas was the pain caused to her by the cruelly despising and humiliating way her mother treated her father, almost daily and often in her presence.

CHAPTER 4

First Clouds on the Horizon

While George Kaloyeropoulos was working as a sales assistant he was also struggling to learn English, so that he could pass the examination and open a pharmacy of his own. In 1928, shortly before he took the exam, the family moved across the river to Manhattan.* Litsa sent Jackie to the local grade school and kept four-year-old Mary at home. The humdrum routine of her everyday life must have made her understand that her dreams of climbing the social ladder and "being somebody" were not going to come true in New York either. In the words of Leonidas Lanzounis, "The only thing George had was good looks and beautiful bearing: tall, straight, distinguished. He wasn't ambitious, not even particularly interested in money, and that made Litsa more annoyed and nervous."[1]

Litsa grew more and more depressed and disillusioned, sometimes dangerously so. "She had periods of deep melancholia affected by the phases of the moon," Jackie records. "She was at her worst at regular intervals and it was explained during one of her rows with Father when he suddenly asked if the moon was full." Her moods of black melancholy alternated with hysterical outbursts of aggression, and then George was the obvious target: she would vent her frustration at him, raging over the most trivial issues. On these occasions even the long-suf-

---

*It is very difficult to unravel the correct sequence and chronology of the many places the Kaloyeropoulos family lived between 1928 and 1931. Besides LITSA and JACKIE, there are only two sources that provide any useful information on actual addresses: STANCIOFF (50) says that the family moved from Astoria to West Thirty-fourth Street, off Ninth Avenue, to be near George's pharmacy in Hell's Kitchen, and that before settling in Washington Heights they made nine moves in eight years, going from one drab apartment to another, but she gives no particulars; SCOTT (7) gives a list of seven addresses (240 West Thirty-fourth Street, 465 Columbus Avenue, 64 West 135th, 520 West 139th, 609 West 137th, 569 West 192nd, and 561 West 180th), but he gives no dates. His addresses are taken from the records of the Board of Education of the City of New York, which means that they cover the period from 1929 to 1937, Mary's school years in New York. Her last address, however, before leaving America, as stated on her passport application and the necessary oath of allegiance sworn in New York on 15 February 1937, was 520 West 183rd Street. (Photocopied documents kindly provided by Jackie Kaloyeropoulou.)

fering George found it difficult to restrain himself in the face of her vitriolic abuse. "She had a devilish temper, calling her husband a *zóo* and *vláhos*—an animal and a peasant, in that order—reminding him of her distinguished background . . . and [saying] how she regretted the day she had ever married him and later bore him three lovely children."[2] As for George, although there is no firm evidence, it seems that he liked to get out and enjoy the company of other women as he had done at Meligalas, rather than stay at home and listen to his wife's endless nagging. Sooner or later, of course, Litsa found out about it, and there is no doubt that George's philandering was in a large measure responsible for the breakdown of the marriage. However, his transgressions took place outside the home and were therefore not obvious to the girls; whereas Litsa, with her ebullient character, her outbursts and lamentations, appeared worse than she really was.

Jackie and Mary observed the frequent scenes between their parents in silence, as children usually do in that situation. *"Most of the time there were quarrels raging in the house,"* Maria recollected in 1959.[3] In one corner was their mother, the person closest and most necessary to them in their life. In the other was their peace-loving working father, who was constantly under attack, usually for no obvious good reason. It was only natural that the girls felt they were being torn apart. In the early years the balance was tilted—or appeared to be tilted—in favor of Litsa, who had bewildered the children with her outspoken but convincing tirades against their father, saying that he was a lazy good-for-nothing, that he had no taste and was in one or another way "inferior": after all, how could anyone listen to bouzouki music when they might be listening to opera? Both Jackie and Mary reacted against the way Litsa tried to impose her views. *"I remember he loved Greek dance,"* Mary once said. *"He'd put on one of his favorite records but it never lasted long; my mother would rush over and change it for an aria, and that was sure to start an argument."* According to Jackie, Litsa was always complaining about her husband's "stupidity, laziness, and lack of anything that she told us was correct in life." In the end, whenever George came back after one of his absences, Jackie found herself wondering whether this pleasant, smiling man, by now almost a stranger, really was the monster her mother made him out to be.[4]

The other area in which George and Litsa failed completely as parents was their inability to offer their children parental love. Litsa was simply unable to provide the girls with the warmth and affection they needed, and this caused tension to build up inside her. The one obvious way in which the tension manifested itself was in her constant nagging of the children over their lapses from her perfectionistic standards. It was Jackie who bore the brunt of these attacks: "She was a terrible tyrant," she wrote later, "but not so hard on Mary, who was younger. I was the one who got it in the neck. She took it out on me, because I was the elder." Jackie even claims that when she was ten she seriously thought of drowning herself in the river. This may be an exaggeration, but it does indicate the joylessness of their life, the emptiness of their home environment, the void created by their sad parents.

"Without Mary it would have been totally unbearable. . . . When neither parent was around, Mary would come to me for company. She would cuddle up to me and I would try to give her the love we never seemed to get."[5]

George was always more gentle and did try sometimes to get closer to the children. Without making any real attempt to understand the way his mind worked, Litsa later commented that "indifference rather than affection was the situation between [him and the children]."[6] George was an introvert, not given to showing his feelings; at home he found it difficult to communicate with the girls, nor did he ever dare to interfere in Litsa's dealings with them. His intervention one day, when his wife hit Jackie over the head with an umbrella, was so unusual that it was regarded as quite an event. Sometimes, however, he took the girls out without Litsa, and then he treated them like grown-ups. Maria later described an incident that occurred when they were out for a Sunday walk with their father: *"I remember, as a child, my father used to say that when we walked by an ice cream parlor I would all of a sudden stop and pull [his] jacket, without saying a word. I would look at him, not at the ice cream parlor, and he had caught on after a while; but he would play the comedian and ask, 'What are you asking for, what do you want? Will you tell me?' And I wouldn't say a word, I was just looking at him like mad."* To Giuseppe di Stefano, when she repeated this story, she added several years later, *"I wanted him to work out for himself what I wanted."*[7]

As this story shows, a strong bond existed between George and Mary. Indeed, her deep affection for her weak father, combined with the overbearing competitiveness of her mother, played a crucial role in the formation of her character. She felt very early on that she was more or less on her own in life and realized that she would therefore have to rely more on herself than on anyone else. In reaction against the weakness of her beloved but too easygoing father, she went to the other extreme and always pushed herself hard, with a sometimes ruthless determination to succeed. Furthermore, by competing with her own mother from an early age, sometimes openly but more often secretly, Mary became not only tough but occasionally aggressive. As we shall see, it was this affection for her father, coupled with his desertion by Litsa in 1937 and again in 1951, that eventually sealed the dramatic rift with her mother. And her own frustrated feelings toward her father, as well as the years she spent without him from 1937 till 1945, were what made her nearly always turn to older men in search of support, affection, and love.

—m—

Meanwhile, in spite of the oppressive atmosphere at home, life went on. The summers of 1928 and 1929 stand out, the first for an unpleasant event and the second for a pleasant interlude. The unpleasant event was a near-fatal accident that has been variously described and has become part of the Callas mythology, often grossly exaggerated. According to Litsa, one day in July 1928, as she, George, and Mary came out of the apartment building to meet Jackie from school, Mary slipped from her mother's grasp and darted into the street toward her sister. A car hit her and dragged her several yards, while all the bystanders stood frozen with horror. Maria described the incident in 1956: "*I saw Jackie, who was playing ball on the other side of the street. . . . I ran to her to give her a kiss and then ran away, red and embarrassed, precipitously crossing the street just at the moment when a car was coming along at great speed. I was knocked over and dragged to the end of the street.*" She was taken, probably unconscious, to Saint Elizabeth's Hospital on Fort Washington Avenue.[8]

How long Mary actually remained hospitalized is not known, but as a concussion case she is unlikely to have been kept there for more than a few days, and there is no reason to question the diagnosis of Dr. Polyvios Koryllos, an eminent professor at New York University. Mary was probably fully recovered within two or three weeks at most, but Litsa maintained that for some time afterward she was nervous and irritable. "When she recovered, she had lost her bright coloring and was no longer a happy, loving, laughing little girl but was highly nervous, often bad tempered with her family and sometimes sullen." Maria later recalled, "*As far as I can remember, during the days I spent in the hospital after a road accident when I was five, the long hours of fever and hazy consciousness were full of strange kinds of music, melodious sounds that were confused but attractive and stimulating.*" And in 1956 she said, "*The American newspapers . . . called me 'lucky Maria' on that occasion, because I managed to recover in almost miraculous fashion after being unconscious for twelve days, and everyone . . . at the hospital considered me a hopeless case.*"[9]

In the summer of 1929, just after George had opened his own pharmacy, Litsa took the two girls, then aged twelve and five and a half, to Tarpon Springs in Florida. It was the first time Mary had been on a long journey and the first time they had taken a vacation. They stayed with Litsa's cousin Hariklia Kritikou, *née* Lourou, who was married to a successful businessman. The long train journey south must have been an exciting experience for mother and daughters alike. The Kritikos family lived only half an hour away from Clearwater Beach, where the six young cousins—Jackie, Mary, and the four Kritikos children—spent most of their days. "As Mother did not dare nag us in such company we were in heaven. I think Mary was happier than I have ever known her," Jackie recalls. "But then our only thoughts were to run in the sand and splash in the water. We were not to know that that holiday marked the end of such happiness as we were to know in America. From then on, life was to get very hard indeed."[10]

It need hardly be said that, as the family's expenditure far exceeded its income, when George at last obtained his license in early 1929, he no longer had the capital he needed to start his own business. So he asked his old friend Lanzounis, who by this time had made good, to lend him about ten thousand dollars, no mean sum in those days. With it George opened the Splendid Pharmacy at 483 Ninth Avenue in June 1929.[11] This dockside district, even then known as Hell's Kitchen, had a large population of Greek immigrants and not only would George seem to be assured of customers but he would not have need of his poor English. The family

Jackie and Mary (right) playing with their Kritikos cousins, Tarpon Springs, Florida, summer 1929.

had been living in an apartment only a few minutes away from Ninth Avenue, but after a few months of good business, George gave in to Litsa's pressure to move again, somewhere further uptown. This time they went to a two-bedroom apartment (like all the Kaloyeropoulos homes in New York) probably on 135th or 137th Street, off Riverside Drive, which runs along the Hudson River.[12]

Things did seem to be looking up, and the pharmacy continued to do well. George now worked harder, and he was very skillful at making up his own medicines. Besides these, the pharmacy also sold snacks, sandwiches, soft drinks, stockings, perfumes, and even paperbacks. In the words of Maria, who appears to have been looking at this part of her past through rose-colored glasses: "*My father opened a very lovely pharmacy, and at the beginning everything went well. The business prospered, and we lived in an elegant apartment in the center of town.*"[13] Although the pharmacy was in a disreputable neighborhood—a fact which was later to give rise to a lot of scurrilous remarks, including the malicious story that Mary had been known as "The Queen of Hell's Kitchen"—George's efforts seemed to be bearing fruit at last. But fate was about to play a nasty trick on the Kaloyeropoulos family, as on so many others: just as George started building up his business capital, the world economy collapsed.

CHAPTER 5

Discovering a Voice

On Thursday, 24 October 1929, the New York stock market collapsed, plunging America—and the whole world—into a prolonged economic crisis. In the space of three days more than two hundred people committed suicide in New York City alone. Unemployment almost tripled by year's end, more than six hundred banks failed, hundreds of millionaires and thousands of other wealthy people were ruined overnight. The financial crash and its aftermath, the Great Depression, which hit the poor as well as the rich, inevitably affected George Kaloyeropoulos at the Splendid Pharmacy, though not immediately as severely as those in some other lines of business. People still needed their medicines, but as the pharmacy's main sources of income had been sweets and sundries, sales dwindled steadily and the debts mounted. As usual, George kept the bad news to himself: Litsa was not told how bad the financial situation really was, and for some time the family maintained its lifestyle.

A most unpleasant incident in the running war between Mary's parents led Litsa into a grand theatrical gesture. One day, when she was helping George at the cash register as she sometimes did, a male customer paid her a gracefully turned compliment. He was being no more than polite, but George overreacted. This angry scene, coming as it did from a husband who was a notorious womanizer, was too much for Litsa, who took an overdose of drugs, probably belladonna. The ambulance arrived soon after the girls came home from school, so they were just in time to witness the traumatic events. Litsa had passed out, but she was rushed to the hospital and soon regained consciousness. On being asked why she put up with a situation that inspired such a drastic step, she answered simply, "My children." George used his contacts to hush up Litsa's suicide attempt and subsequent recovery; but the crisis, which dragged on for over a month, finally signaled the end of the marriage: "From then on," Jackie remarks, "they would live under the same roof as irritable strangers." Eventually George had to close the Splendid Pharmacy, and his new job as a salesman of pharmaceutical products kept him away from home, often for days at a time. He dyed his fine moustache black and lived pretty much the life of a bachelor. As he confided later to Jackie, his work offered him an escape from "the incessant nagging over which he had no control." Litsa, for her part, would have had the children believe that George was almost solely responsible for the Wall Street crash. Deprived of the easiest target for her pent-up feelings, she now devoted all her energies to bringing up her family. But the new state of affairs at home, resulting from the complete breakdown of her relationship with George, had grave consequences for the children—not only Jackie, now thirteen, but also Mary, who was not yet seven.[1]

Despite the difficult situation, George remained a conscientious head of the family. He changed his job several times but kept on working as hard as he could, and in about 1931 he successfully launched on the market his own patented ointment for gingivitis, which he sold to dentists and druggists. The profits from this business enabled the family to move to a "small but respectable" apartment in the middle-class residential area of Washington Heights. They lived in this neighborhood until Litsa and the children left for Greece, starting on 180th or 181st Street, soon moving further out to 569 West 192nd Street, where they stayed for about five years, and ending at 520 West 183rd Street. Jackie was enrolled at the George Washington High School and Mary at Public School 189, a few blocks away from home at 189th and Amsterdam. She had started school in September 1929, just a month and a half before the Wall Street crash. Unfortunately for her, the frequent moves to ever cheaper apartments, mostly on the West Side between 130th and 140th Streets, meant that by 1932 she had been to five different schools. Each time, just as she was beginning to settle down and make friends, another move would make it impossible for her to put down firm roots, contributing to the sense of insecurity that dogged her all her life.[2]

Yet despite these recurrent upheavals Mary did well at her studies, receiving grades of A, B+, or B throughout her school career. She was a natural hard worker and was always near the top of her class. The impossibility of making lasting friendships, combined with her father's increasingly frequent absences, probably intensified the emotional void she felt at home and drove her to seek refuge in books. It was during this bleak period that she acquired the facility for learning and the lasting tendency to be overconscientious about her school duties and duty in general. Whenever faced with a negative situation, she instinctively tried to make something positive out of it. Similarly, again and again during her career, she turned the unusual qualities and even the shortcomings of her voice to her own advantage.

In the early days the Kaloyeropoulos family spoke Greek at home. Then, as George and Litsa's English improved and the children attended their English-speaking schools, they conversed in a hodgepodge of both languages which was neither good Greek nor good English. Mary's English was then much better than her Greek, of course, but she never learned to speak either language without throwing in words and phrases from the other. In America she never had any Greek lessons but simply picked up the language by ear, mainly from her parents at home, with the result that when she went to Greece she spoke it rather poorly and could not yet write it. Later in life, when she knew Italian too—the language she probably learned best of all—her peculiar mixture of Greek and English became sprinkled with Italian idioms.

Most of the people they knew were Greeks: George was on good terms with a number of Greek doctors and druggists, and the best friends of the family were the Papajohns (originally Papayannis, from Aigion in the Peloponnese), who lived near them in Washington Heights. The girls used to play with the Papajohn children, who probably spoke a similar mixture of English and Greek. Their aunt, Alexandra Papajohn—who would later become George's second wife—was described by Jackie as "a buxom handsome woman in love with life, a marked contrast to our slim but difficult mother." If Jackie found the contrast a welcome relief, it naturally attracted George even more. Little Mary seems to have sensed this attraction, for she gave vent to unsuspected feelings of strong hostility toward Alexandra. On one occasion, with the unerring instinct of a child, she even begged her mother to send her out of the house. Jackie, who interpreted this merely as an early sign of Mary's "neurotic possessiveness," was generally much easier to get along with and had acquired a close friend in her class at school, Clare Poretz. It was only when she had spent a few weekends at Clare's home that she realized what was wrong with her own home: "The Poretzes loved each other," as she wrote later.[3]

Litsa sometimes took the girls out for special treats, which were of four kinds: visiting the public library at Forty-second Street and Fifth Avenue, going to an occasional movie in winter, attending the Goldman band concerts in Central Park in the summer, and eating out at a Chinese restaurant in Washington Heights on Thursday evenings. All these pleasures—books and records, the cinema, concerts, and good food—remained important to Maria for the rest of her life. And it was on these outings, as well as during Clare's visits to their house, that Litsa showed the girls her best side. She would then forget her domestic and financial problems and her delusions of grandeur and turn into an amusing friendly companion. She would teach the girls the tango and foxtrot in the living room at home, and she enjoyed "play acting" when she was out with Jackie, Mary, and Clare, pretending that the chop suey was really roast pheasant, or that their local Chinese restaurant was a banquet hall in a Renaissance palace. "At such moments," Jackie recalls, "Mother was the most magical person on earth."[4]

It is impossible not to feel some sympathy for Litsa, who was starved of any kind of artistic nourishment in her life with George. She does not appear to have had any real talent, but she would probably have been a different person—and easier to live with—if she had had a chance to move in a different environment from the one imposed on her by her uncultured husband and the circumstances of their life. Only once in all the fourteen years she was in New York did she go to the Metropolitan Opera, and then the tickets were bought by Lanzounis, not George. Leonidas, who was then working at the New York Orthopedic Hospital, was also

Mary (left) and Jackie (right) with their friends George Vasson and Clare Poretz, New Jersey 1933.

an excellent godfather to Mary. Outside the family he was the one fixture in their world, and he brought a touch of color into their generally gray life. From him Mary could be quite sure of getting presents on her name day and her birthday, and at Easter and Christmas. Sometimes he would take her out to Sunday brunch at the Longchamps on Tenth Street or some restaurant in Greenwich Village, after which they would go for a walk in Washington Square. On these occasions Mary was in seventh heaven.

Jackie and Mary shared a bedroom all the time they were in New York—in fact they slept in the same big bed. Once or twice a year Mary would decide on a new color scheme, white or blue or pink or yellow, and repaint the bedstead and all the rest of the furniture in their room. Litsa recalls that both girls were "good cooks and very clean housekeepers." Once they had finished their homework, they might occasionally read a book (Litsa kept urging them in vain to read the "great classics"), but almost all their time was spent listening to music. And, apart from

Mary and Jackie (front row) with their father (back left), Alexandra Papajohn (at his side), Litsa (next to Alexandra), and other members of the Papajohn family, New York, Inwood Park, 1934.

the increasingly rare occasions when George managed to put on one of his old favorite Greek popular songs, music to Jackie and Mary meant opera. For the fact is that Litsa had managed to get a phonograph and from then on all her savings were spent on records, which took the place of the old pianola rolls. Now, every day, the family's two-room apartment resounded to the voices of Caruso, Galli-Curci, and other great operatic stars. The pianola, of course, still gave great pleasure to the two girls: they treated it rather as a plaything, pretending to be famous pianists. Complications set in, however, when Litsa, who had encouraged this game of make-believe, started to share it herself.[5]

It is difficult to know, at this distance in time, whether Litsa's encouragement of her daughters' musical talents was prompted by genuine maternal interest or whether, as so many of her critics have alleged, it was really motivated by egotism.

Mary and Jackie with a
young Papajohn.

Most probably the truth of the matter is that, once Litsa had planted the idea of music (and opera in particular) in their minds and accustomed them to the sound of music in the home, they willingly and apparently spontaneously allowed themselves to be ensnared by its charms. The idea of a musical career for her daughters would surely have passed through Litsa's mind, and it was perfectly legitimate that she would investigate the possibilities. It is true, of course, that by pushing her daughters toward a life in music and the opera she would vicariously satisfy her own musical and theatrical instincts, which had been suppressed by her upbringing. From quite early on, when she saw that her daughters were ready to take the bait, she saw them in her imagination as stars who would one day take the world by storm. What mother has not had dreams of this kind? To accuse her, as nearly all Maria's biographers have done, of being motivated only by the selfish ambition of lifting herself out of the middle-class obscurity to which her marriage had condemned her, seems arbitrary and is surely an exaggeration.

Certainly, as Mary made spectacular progress with her music, that thought did take shape in Litsa's mind, feeding on her innate ambition and her personal and social vanity. What is even more certain is that, as time went on, her initial instinct developed into an article of faith and came to be the be-all and end-all of her existence. What happened from then on has provided fuel for the accusations made by Maria in later life and the criticisms leveled against her. But even though Litsa must bear much of the responsibility for the subsequent disintegration of her relationship with Mary, it would be wrong to deny her the credit for setting her daughter on the path to a musical career, for that is something she really did achieve virtually on her own. She herself admitted that she had "pushed" her daughter when she realized that she was "endowed with a voice beyond dreams"; and there is no reason to dispute the claim Litsa makes for herself that in 1950, when she saw her for the last time in Mexico, Maria thanked her because, "of all those who helped her with her career, I was the first to discover her voice and push her."[6]

Litsa decided to replace the pianola with an upright piano, and in the school year 1931–32 she engaged Signorina Sandrina as a piano teacher, at first only for Jackie. George, faced with serious financial worries, objected to this "unnecessary" extra expense, but Litsa insisted and he was forced to give in. Jackie threw herself into her piano lessons with enthusiasm and soon Mary was having lessons too. Signorina Sandrina, an Italian woman of about thirty, came just once a week for a few months only—"We couldn't afford to have her more often"—but that was long enough for her to teach Mary the rudiments of music.[7] Meanwhile, the eight-year-old had started having elementary music and singing lessons at school. All at once music, which on the radio, the pianola, and the phonograph had been soulless and mechanical, began to come alive and to give her new pleasure. Above all, it now became a part of her life and showed signs of developing into a major preoccupation: "*At the time when I started the piano I also had my first bitter struggles as a self-taught singer. Up to then I had heard a lot of music on the radio, mainly American songs, light pieces which I could learn with the greatest of ease. But when I was confronted with the world of opera I was overcome by terrible feelings of despondency—and at the same time a thrilling sense of intoxication.*"[8]

To say, however, that Mary was acclaimed as a star and behaved like a prima donna from the time she started school, as some have alleged, is of course an overstatement. We may nevertheless be sure that her young head was turned by her precocious vocal prowess and the acclaim that greeted her performances. When she was nine or ten she started singing at school concerts and other functions (she was then at P.S. 164, at 164th and Wadsworth). One of the teachers told her she had "a nightingale in her throat," and thirty years later some of her schoolmates recalled that they had signed her autograph album with best wishes to "the future great singer" or "the girl with the golden voice." This collection of early compliments was later seized upon by the press and magnified, until it became "the nine-year-old prima donna's fan club."[9] The fact remains, though, that singing soon became for Mary an invaluable source of personal satisfaction and self-confidence. One of her most frequently published pronouncements is the famous dictum, *"When I sang, I [felt that I] was really loved."*[10]

Once she had started piano lessons, Mary was soon able to play some of the songs she liked to sing. One of these was "La Paloma" by Sebastián Yradier, then at the height of its popularity, which was for a long time the number-one piece in her very limited repertoire. Litsa told a story which has found its way into all the biographies: "Then came a day I shall never forget. Maria was ten. We were then living in Washington Heights. She had been a very good pianist since she was a little girl, and she was playing the piano and singing 'La Paloma.' When I went into the room I looked out and saw that a great crowd of people—about two hundred of them—were standing under the window, applauding her. Only when she stopped singing did they go away." The "crowd" probably consisted of a dozen or so passers-by who stopped for a moment to listen and clapped as they drifted away. Still, that was enough for the ecstatic Litsa: "At that moment," she recalled, "I knew Maria had a voice that must be trained, and I began to make plans for the golden future before her."[11]

Quite possibly Mary's precocious musical talent developed out of a childish rivalry with her elder sister. There were frequent scenes over who should play the piano first, and for how long. Both girls together would sing along with the arias they heard on the radio or the phonograph. In the early days Jackie had had more practice at singing and inevitably outdid her sister. But Mary already had the competitive spirit that springs naturally from the younger sibling's sense of always coming second, added to which her innate musical ability quickly redressed the balance. Every evening, often until eleven o'clock, the piano resounded with music of all kinds, including piano arrangements of extracts from arias and endless finger exercises, mostly Hanon or Czerny. Litsa, of course, observed the situation with great gratification, while her daughters, as Jackie remarked bitterly, acted as "the passive agents of her schemes."[12]

When the family acquired a phonograph—the records they either bought or borrowed from the library at two for a dime—Mary heard the voices of some of the best singers of the day for the first time.[13] But it was the radio that first gave her an opportunity to hear opera regularly: from the end of 1931 complete performances were broadcast live from the Met, usually on Saturday afternoons. The first of those historic broadcasts was Humperdinck's *Hänsel und Gretel* on Christmas Day, 1931. It was followed the next day by the second and third acts of *Norma*, conducted by Tullio Serafin with Giacomo Lauri-Volpi as Pollione and Rosa Ponselle in the title role. By the end of February 1937, when Mary left New York, the National Broadcasting Company had aired a total of 108 performances of forty-four different operas. In twelve of these (*Aida, Il Barbiere di Siviglia, Fidelio, La Forza del Destino, Lucia di Lammermoor, Norma, Rigoletto, La Sonnambula, La Traviata, Tristan und Isolde, Il Trovatore,* and *Die Walküre*) Maria was one day to star on stage, and she would make complete recordings of three more (*La Bohème*, *Carmen*, and *Pagliacci*).[14]

"When you wish to discuss singers," Geraldine Farrar once remarked, "there are two you must put aside. One is Caruso, the other is Rosa Ponselle. Then you may begin." And when Lotte Lehmann asked her how one could get a voice like Ponselle's, Farrar answered, "By special arrangement with God!" Rosa Ponselle, like Mary a daughter of immigrants, was twenty-seven years older than she and then at the zenith of her brief career, which ended in 1937, the very year Mary entered the National Conservatory in Athens. Maria later spoke about Ponselle with admiration and respect, although interestingly enough she never tried to meet her in person. So much was said about the "likenesses" between them that Maria had an irrational jealousy of Ponselle. When, in 1954, there was a recurrence of the wobble in Maria's voice that Elvira de Hidalgo had managed to eliminate, or at least bring under control, she was advised by Walter Legge, the general manager of EMI, to go to Ponselle for assistance. "*I will not see that woman!*" she snapped, no doubt under considerable strain at the time. "*She started out with better material than I did!*" Yet it is a fact, as she herself admitted later, that she was indirectly and without realizing it influenced by Ponselle in many respects through her lessons with de Hidalgo and Tullio Serafin, both of whom had worked with Ponselle in the "old school" of bel canto.[15]

It is not known whether Mary heard Ponselle's famous *Norma* on 26 December 1931; even if she did, the impression it made on her would not have had anything to do with its musical value, as she was only just eight at the time. But she must have heard a large number of operas between 1932 and early 1937: "*When I think that I stole so much of my homework [time] just to listen to these Saturday broadcasts when I was a child, it just, well, gives me a bit the jitters to have to do it [myself] today,*" she said in 1956 at the Met broadcast of *Lucia*, this time with herself in the title role.[16] The first opera she remembered hearing was probably *Aida*, and that may have been when she was nine or eleven, on 2 April 1932 or 27 January 1934, both times with Elisabeth Rethberg singing one of her best-known roles under the baton of Tullio Serafin. As for Ponselle, Mary could have heard her nine times in this period: as Leonora in *Il Trovatore* (1932), as Donna Anna (1932, 1934, and 1935), as Selika (1934), as Violetta (1935), and as Carmen (February and March 1936 and January 1937).[17]

Although much has been written about how often Mary heard Ponselle in her childhood and how strongly she was influenced by her, we cannot be sure that she did actually hear her sing during this period. On this point, as on so many others, Maria herself is responsible for the confusion and uncertainty. On one occasion, when asked which was the first complete opera that had made an impression on her, she replied, " *'Aida,' on the radio. But 'Carmen' even more, with Rosa Ponselle: an outstanding artist, with a warm and luminous voice, my idol during my adolescence. And at the same time my despair, too. Because the timbre of my voice, unlike hers, was dark . . . and there were problems with the range of my voice at the top of the register.*[18] No doubt Maria was getting her dates muddled and confusing her childhood recollections with memories of the time when Elvira de Hidalgo was working with her in Athens to lighten the tone of her voice. But we cannot ignore her categorical statement that Rosa Ponselle was her idol, and so we may perhaps assume that she did hear her as Carmen at least once, in one of the two historic 1936 performances of *Carmen* (1 February and 28 March), which divided the critics and may have contributed to the premature termination of Ponselle's career, or in that of 9 January 1937, which was also broadcast by NBC.

However, we have to remember that even then Mary was only just thirteen and had not yet had any proper singing lessons; so it would not have been until much later that she was able to hear recordings of Ponselle and form a serious opinion of her singing. This happened after her return to New York in October 1945, and the first time she "knowingly" listened to Ponselle's voice, with critical attention, was in fact in Mexico City in 1950: "*No, no, I never heard her,*" she protested to Carlos Díaz Du-Pond, the assistant of the administrator of the Ópera Nacional Antonio Caraza-Campos, who offered to play Ponselle records for her. "*I heard her on a record—not even in Greece, because during the war we didn't have records like that—so I never heard her until I came here, to America.*" And when Díaz Du-Pond said that her singing reminded him of that of Ponselle, she told him: "*I am very anxious to listen to her records, because Maestro Serafin has told me the same thing.*"[19]

Apart from maestro Tullio Serafin, who until early 1937 conducted no fewer than fourteen Metropolitan performances aired live, the great singers whom Mary may well have heard on the Met broadcasts in those New York days include Giuseppe de Luca, Beniamino Gigli, Giacomo Lauri-Volpi, Emanuel List, Giovanni Martinelli, Lauritz Melchior, Max Lorenz, Ezio Pinza, Tito Schipa, Friedrich Schorr, Lawrence Tibbett and, of the female singers (besides Ponselle and Rethberg, with fourteen broadcasts each), Lucrezia Bori (thirteen), Kirsten Flagstad (seven), Frida Leider (six), Lotte Lehmann, Bidú Sayão, Grace Moore, and Maria Jeritza. And she definitely heard at least one of the four broadcasts of *Lucia di Lammermoor* with the Met's French star Lily Pons (whom she could have heard on twelve occasions in all). The one that we know she did hear, on the evidence of an anecdote related by George, was one of the two performances broadcast in 1934, on 3 March or, more probably, on 29 December. That day the family and a few friends were sitting around the radio listening to Lily Pons in the Mad Scene when Mary, then aged ten or eleven, suddenly exclaimed that Lucia was out of tune. Impossible, someone remarked: Lucia was Lily Pons, and Lily Pons was a great star. Unabashed, Mary screamed furiously, "*I don't care if she is a star, she sings off key! Just wait and see—one day I am going to be a star myself, a bigger star than she!*"[20]

If this story has not been embroidered in the retelling, by about 1934 or 1935 Mary was already thinking seriously about singing as a future career. If so, however, George was quite unaware of the fact. He disapproved of the way Litsa made young Mary practice more than she "ought to" and reacted negatively to her constant demands for more money to spend on "such frivolities." Although Litsa was a determined woman, this time she failed to get money from him for Mary's lessons. According to her own account, she had to sell her own clothes and to scrimp on the housekeeping to be able to pay out two dollars four times a week for lessons. But this figure is clearly an exaggeration, for Jackie now says that neither of the girls ever had a piano teacher in America apart from Signorina Sandrina, who came just once a week for a few months. Whether or not Litsa actually saved up to pay for lessons, the fact remains that even at this early stage she seems already to have been totally devoted to her children's and more so to Mary's musical future. Roland Mancini, who gave a vivid account of Mary's first introduction to opera, could find no convincing explanation for Litsa's fanaticism and suggested humorously that she must have been inspired by the extraordinary picture of little Adelina Patti, aged seven, standing on a table and singing Amina's famous "Ah! non giunge" from the finale of *La Sonnambula*.[21] And perhaps he was not so far wrong.

—⚉—

My program was set not by myself in life. From the very beginning it was set by my family, my mother mainly, who was commanding the family then. So I had to act accordingly. . . . The program was that, of course, I should become a singer; I should become an artist in any case. . . . I was supposed to study and not to sing immediately. But I am afraid it didn't last that long.

To Lord Harewood, Paris, April 1968

CHAPTER 6

Some "Facts" Reconsidered

Much has been written about the pressure Litsa exerted on Mary to make a musician of her from a very early age. This is particularly relevant to the period from late 1931 through early 1937, when Mary was between eight and thirteen years old. According to the generally accepted view, Mary's impressionable character was "straitjacketed" during these tender years, leaving her with irreparable psychological damage. The line of argument taken by most biographers is that Litsa, pursuing her plan for the advancement of her talented daughters, subjected Mary to far too much pressure for her age, thus depriving her of a normal childhood. What is more, all accuse Litsa of being motivated not so much (or at least not only) by her daughter's interests as by her own ambition for reflected glory through the achievements of Mary and to a lesser extent of Jackie, who for a time also seemed to have a promising future ahead of her. How well does this theory stand up? Which of Mary's traumas were real and which were later accretions invented by her biographers or by Maria herself? And if so, what caused her to make those accusations against her mother?

There is no doubt that the "standard version" is based largely on stories told by Maria herself later on, when she was engaged in an implacable feud with her mother. From about 1955 onward she repeatedly blamed her mother, both in public and privately, mainly for what happened in her childhood. A Greek journalist reported that she had once gone so far as to claim that she had helped to support her parents from the age of eight: *"What terrible years! . . . My sister and I used to do odd jobs for our neighbors to earn a few cents, which we gave to our parents to make ends meet."*[1] This story, which cannot be verified and which, if true, was probably reported in different words from those Maria actually used, was immediately and categorically denied by Litsa. Years after her daughter's death, with still undiminished venom, Litsa would say, "Maria was crazy. Only a crazy daughter would hold her mother to blame for things that never happened!" We cannot be sure exactly which incidents Litsa was referring to, but it is quite astonishing—especially to a Greek—to find a mother using such strong language of her own daughter; and there were many other occasions when she said the most extraordinarily cruel things about her.*

Vitriolic statements made by both Litsa and Maria have provided writers on Callas with a great deal of material which is open to misinterpretation. In Litsa's running feud with her daughter, Maria never fired the first shot; she was always on the defensive, but she instinctively regarded attack as the best form of defense. As we shall see, she could never pass up an argument, never allow a personal challenge to go unanswered; and her answer was often extremely trenchant. But the material of this polemic has often been used anachronistically and wrongly applied to Callas's childhood. And the mutual recriminations of their later life have been interpreted in a way generally condemning Litsa for the way she had brought up her daughter. This, however, remains largely unsubstantiated and it would be wrong to underrate the part played by this mother. Capricious though she was, shockingly though she treated her daughter on occasions, and no matter how damnable and uncontrolled her behavior gradually became, the fact is that the hysterical and unhappy Litsa, frustrated as a wife and overbearing as a mother, was largely responsible for the miracle that led to the transformation of little Mary into Maria Callas. Without her perceptiveness—even if her motives were not altogether altruistic—the chances are that the world of music would have been deprived of one of its brightest stars.[2]

When Litsa was forced to defend herself against the charge that she had overstrained her daughter in the process of "creating" that vocal miracle, she would say, "From the time [Mary] was born, she always wanted to be somebody, to be conspicuous, to stand out from the crowd. '*Mother*,' she said to me once, '*I'm going to be the greatest opera singer of all time! The whole world's going to be talking about me!*'"[3] For her part, Maria would say about Litsa, at every opportunity, "*I'll never forgive her for taking my childhood away. During all the years I should have been playing and growing up, I was singing or making money.*"† On the strength of statements like this, which cannot be verified nor can we be sure what period of Callas's life they refer to, nearly all her biographers have rushed to hasty and facile conclusions. This unfair apportionment of the blame for an "unhappy childhood" to

---

*A. Fotinos, "Maria Callas, a Living Legend," *Evropaia*, 3 Feb. 1983. Litsa's animosity reached such a pitch that when, some time in the early 1970s, contralto Popi Tzavara bumped into her in the street and asked after Mary, Litsa replied, "Mary can't see straight. And I hope she goes completely blind!" The reason for her wrath, of course, was that Maria was not sending her as much money as she thought she deserved. (KOURAHANI.) Litsa's equally horrible "wish" that her daughter get "cancer in her throat" is well known and has been quoted repeatedly. See also Postscript I.

†DE CARVALHO. Maria herself, talking about this statement in an interview with Norman Ross (Chicago, 17 Nov. 1957), said, "*Yes, but condensed words sound much harder. . . . I had said that I was terribly sorry and I really could not forgive her for having taken this childhood away.*" The two statements do in fact sound very different, and such differences of nuance have given rise to all sorts of misunderstandings and exaggerated interpretations.

Litsa, in other words, was mainly the combined result of Maria's often exaggerated accusations and her biographers not stopping to consider that they were mostly made in the heat of an all-too-public feud.

No doubt Litsa was excessively zealous, and no doubt there was an element of self-glorification and vanity in her motives; but most of the other charges laid at her door with reference to the period between late 1931 and early 1937 do not stand up. The underlying cause of the friction between mother and daughter should in fact be sought not so much in Litsa's attitude to Mary as in her behavior toward her husband, George. Maria's cumulative reaction to the way her mother treated her father accounts for a lot of traumas which were bound to come to the surface sooner or later, and eventually did so, but not until the trying experiences in Athens from 1938 to 1945, when the mother of the budding prima donna lost control in many points of her private and social behavior. If we concentrate exclusively on her childhood, however, that is to say the years up to early 1937 in New York, things appear in a different light.

The truth of the matter is that Litsa, performing her duty as a mother, gave Mary a push in the right direction. Whether she did so in response to some mysterious subconscious instinct or consciously willed on to her daughter her own repressed longings is beside the point; probably both are true to some extent. However, apart from Maria's own later statements, which cannot be verified, nowhere has it been said or written that she objected in any way to the musical career that was marked out for her, or that she refused to practice or to take part in any public competition that Litsa pressed her to enter. On the contrary, she herself took a girlish pride in her successes in singing competitions at school and on the radio. And we also know that Mary never found it a hardship, either then or later in life, to practice for hours at a time: she herself found solace in it, and her tireless assiduity was always an object of unqualified admiration to others.

In 1961, on being asked when she had first become aware of her extraordinary musical ability and her musicianship, Maria answered, "*My mother made me realize it. It was always put into my head that I had it—and that I'd better have it!*" At this point she belatedly remembered to re-introduce the theme of the "downtrodden little girl," and when her interviewer countered, not unreasonably, "Your mother was right, wasn't she?", Maria was forced to admit openly, "*Yes, but lots of mothers don't guess right, and they ruin the child. . . . As things turned out, of course, I can't complain.*"* A Greek writer, Yorgos Orfanos, sums it all up so well that no more need be said: "Quietly and uncomplainingly Maria did whatever her mother

---

*PROUSE. In self-defense, Maria went on to champion all downtrodden children, elaborating on the theme she so often returned to: "*But to load a child so early with responsibility is something there should be a law against. A child should not be taken away from its youth—it becomes exhausted before its time.*" We should not forget, of course, that by 1961 Maria had already started suffering from exhaustion and considerable vocal problems.

told her, at first to please her mother and later to avoid argument. But in this, as in everything she turned her hand to, she went the whole hog. . . . Little by little she immersed herself in music up to the eyes, and unwittingly she found herself well and truly 'hooked' on singing and opera. When she eventually realized what had happened, she could never forgive Evangelia for the trick she had played on her. For her mother, without actually realizing it herself, had struck the right chord, pressed the right button." So Maria failed to distinguish in her mind "between the person who was merely the cause of the discovery of her genius and the tribulations inherent in genius itself," Orfanos concludes, "which she wanted and yet did not want, and which she possessed in abundance."[4]

—⁂—

Another matter that many Callas biographers have dwelt on at some length is Litsa's supposed preference for Jackie, dating back to those very early days, and the related question of Mary's feelings toward her sister. Jackie was a pretty, well-turned-out young lady, Mary a plain and rather unattractive girl; in fact some have described her (unfairly, to judge by photographs of her at that age) as fat and spotty. The person who started the myth of Litsa's preference for pretty Jackie at the expense of Mary, the "ugly duckling," was none other than Maria herself in various barbed remarks directed against Litsa over the years. The most serious in its consequences was a statement published in *Time* in 1956: *"My sister was slim and beautiful and friendly, and my mother always preferred her. I was the ugly duckling, fat and clumsy and unpopular. It is a cruel thing to make a child feel ugly and unwanted."* On another occasion Maria said of her mother, *"She took no notice of me and never had a good word to say of me. To make her notice me, I began singing. I knew I had a beautiful voice and it did me good to arouse admiration when I sang. So singing gradually came to be the medicine for my inferiority complexes."*[5]

Like most of the bones of contention between the various members of the Kaloyeropoulos family, this did not really become an issue until long after the event, in the context not only of Maria's feud with her mother but also of the rift between George and Litsa. From quite soon after the move to Greece in 1937 until Mary's return to New York in 1945, Litsa did show a definite preference for Jackie. Her partiality—which was motivated by self-interest at least as much as by concern for Jackie's best interests—became much more pronounced after 1951: by then Maria had become famous and cut herself off completely from her mother, and Jackie had sided with Litsa who had, to some extent, become dependent on Jackie. In her teens and early twenties in Athens Mary drifted apart from Jackie too, and much later said some very unkind things about her. But in Mary's childhood in America, up to the age of thirteen, Litsa showed little favoritism for Jackie, and Mary was on perfectly good terms with her elder sister. It was only natural that Litsa got on better with Jackie, who was considerably older and went along with her opinions in "women's affairs" and other everyday matters; whereas with Mary,

inwardly seething and still very young, communication was difficult from the outset and became more and more so as time went on.

It was only in certain everyday activities that Mary tried to compete with
Jackie. At the piano, for example, aside from the petty quarrels over who was to
have the first turn, "it was never thought that one was more especially gifted than
the other." Mary's competitiveness was simply a healthy part of her normal development, for every intelligent young child naturally tries to "stand tall" and to
assert his or her own views. Not only was there no hostility—open or repressed—
between them, but on the contrary we saw Mary turn to Jackie for consolation and
for the affection that her parents seemed unable to give her. "We were very fond
of each other. I was her protector in a way, as I was older," Jackie confirms. "Mary
felt the need for affection. Her mother never offered it, nor could she find it in her
father, because Mother turned us against him."[6] In fact it was this attitude of
Litsa's toward George that traumatized Mary most. The never-ending barrage of
insults and abuse that her beloved father had to endure from his own wife, her
mother, upset Mary and brought her closer to her sister. So there is no truth in the
common allegations that when the girls were young Jackie was Litsa's favorite and
Mary got on badly with her sister.

To judge by what both Maria and Jackie have said and written, Litsa was
clearly not an affectionate, loving mother. Even more so when we consider her bitterness and the outbursts of invective against Maria over the years. Yet this frustrated and angry mother, who at that early stage was still deluding herself and had
great plans occupying her mind, would one day wake up to reality with a start. She
would then find herself faced with all sorts of unresolved problems which would
prevent her from enjoying Maria's astonishing international success. Maria, too,
would suffer from this rift in later life, but her strong character would enable her
to pursue her brilliant career. Luckily for Litsa, Jackie's docile character and future
unhappy experiences would mean that she would at least have the support and
company of one daughter right to the end of her miserable life. As she would say
in 1958, whereas Maria behaved to her like a "devil," she was luckily living well
with Jackie, her "angel."[7]

—⁂—

John Ardoin, probably the most penetrating analyst of Maria Callas's achievements as a singer and a personal friend of hers, has no hesitation in attributing her
lifelong sense of insecurity to her childhood, "when she was overweight and felt
herself in competition with an older sister for their mother's affection."[8] No doubt
her insecurity did have its roots in her childhood, but not in the causes that Ardoin
suggests. As we have seen, there was no real rivalry with Jackie in those days. And
as for the old story of her "fatness"—in those early years in America—some clarification and rethinking is also called for. Simply because she did put on quite a lot
of weight during her first years in Greece, and really was fat for about six years in

Italy after that, nearly all her biographers have tried to make out that she had always been an unattractive, overweight, complex-ridden girl who filled her emotional void with food, which her unloving mother supplied in great quantities to assuage her own feelings of guilt. Just as the theme of young Mary's "persecution" by her mother has been heavily overplayed, so too the eating exploits of the young female Gargantua have been too readily accepted and exaggerated. The more psychoanalytically minded have even explained that overeating is not only a classic reaction to feeling unloved, but also a self-protective reflex of people who "bury themselves in the shell of their fat."[9]

The myth of the pudgy little girl has been sustained not only by the fact that the older Maria actually was fat as a young woman, but also by her mother's published recollections of her appetite and her favorite foods. We are told that Mary loved spaghetti bolognese and fried potatoes—but what child doesn't? Also that she loved fried eggs with cheese, another favorite with most children, and that she drank a lot of milk and loved her mother's homebaked bread. What could be more natural? The less serious and more sensation-seeking writers on Callas have all concluded that the awful Litsa stuffed little Mary with food as part of her "Operation Prima Donna," having got it into her head that the voice had to be kept "well fed" and that only very fat singers rose to stardom in opera. However, although Litsa really did believe in the necessity of "feeding the voice," we have to believe her when she says that as a child Mary was "plump but not excessively fat," that as a teenager she was "no sylph but certainly no barrel," and that it was only later that she turned into "the 'fat girl' of the Callas legend."[10]

Maria shares the responsibility for distorting the truth in this matter. In later years, when she still had a lingering hang-up about the weight problem she had had between the ages of fourteen and seventeen and twenty-four and thirty, she was in the habit of giving extra color to her words by throwing in exaggerated descriptions of her plain looks, or allusions to her past fatness. This she did in order to stress the general wretchedness of her early life, but also her achievement in turning into the sylph she now was. In an interview given in 1959, for example, after reiterating the "ugly duckling" misery of her childhood, she said that Jackie had always had pretty clothes, whereas she herself had been sent to school wearing her sister's hand-me-downs.[11] But if she really was so fat, how could she have fitted into Jackie's slim-waisted skirts? And although she subsequently blamed her mother for doing nothing about the hormone problem that had caused her to put on weight during the early years in Athens, it is significant that she never accused her of overfeeding her as a child. That story cannot possibly be true, as Mary was never fat in America; she herself declared in 1956, "*It is not true that I was fat when I left America. . . . It is not true that I ate a lot of cheese and olive oil. I never liked cheese. I also remember that I hardly ever had breakfast. My mother used to run after me down the front steps because I would go off in the mornings without even having had a cup of tea or a piece of toast.*"[12]

Litsa, Mary, and
Jackie, New York,
early 1936.

The only two incontrovertible sources of evidence on the subject of Mary's weight are the photographs taken at that time and a report by the nurse at the school she attended when she was eleven. The photographs show a girl who might perhaps be described as well-built, but certainly not fat, and the school nurse's report presents a similar picture: at the age of eleven Mary was already 5 feet 3 inches (1.60 meters) tall and weighed 119 pounds (54 kilos). All the other figures published at various times are undocumented. So it is safe to say that during her childhood in America Mary had no reason to feel embarrassed about her weight. She may not have had Jackie's slim figure nor her beautiful features, but by no stretch of the imagination could it be said that her face was homely or covered with acne. "Nor was she ugly . . . [and] her pimples proved to be a temporary affliction," Litsa says in her book, and Jackie confirms this: "In truth, Mary did not start out as an unattractive child; she was very pretty, dark rather than with my paler looks, and at first no one made unfavorable comparisons."[13]

A much more deep-rooted problem concerned the Oedipus complex under-lying Mary's feelings for her father. George, who for all his faults (which Mary was still too young to perceive) was doing his best to support his family, was a quiet, good-natured man who was not always expecting too much of his children or trying to pick quarrels with them. And this beloved father of hers was the per-son on whom Mary heard her mother pouring scorn and abuse every day. Deep down inside, as one might expect, she began to nurse feelings of hatred and revul-sion for her surroundings, even her physical environment, her home and school. But in her condemnation she did not include her father: "*Nobody loved me and I loved nobody, except my father,*" she was once reported saying.[14] So it is there, in the daughter's wounded and beleaguered love for and pride in her father, that we should look for Mary's deepest trauma.

Fundamentally, the strains between Litsa and Mary were nothing more than the usual problems that arise in any mother-daughter relationship. Litsa's auto-cratic and cynically matter-of-fact character doubtless exacerbated certain situa-tions, and Mary's spirited resistance when under attack surely provoked scenes which left their mark. "*My mother kept demanding too much from me, too much responsibility for a young girl,*" Maria said later. "*It should be illegal for mothers to force their children like that.*"[15] But when she grumbled and complained about the way she was treated by her mother—being pressed to practice her music, being deprived of childhood pleasures, being forced to sing in competitions and at social functions—in reality she was complaining on behalf of her father and punishing her mother for her harshness toward him. Indeed, Leonidas Lanzounis once said that when she was young, Mary got on very well with her mother, a statement to which not enough attention has been paid. Jackie corroborates this view today: "Mother didn't persecute Mary. And it's not true that she loved me more than Mary. In fact she loved Mary more than me; Mary was more her sort of person."[16]

In conclusion, in those early days—and presumably all the time until they went to Greece—relations between mother and daughter may have been poor, but certainly not as stormy as they have been presented by most Callas biogra-phers, a misconception due mainly to the use of anachronistic data and inverse rea-soning. Despite a certain plausibility of some descriptions, the clever but glib clichés fail to convince that Mary's childhood experiences were as harrowing and traumatic as they are generally held to have been.[17]

—∽—

My sister was a beautiful girl, but I was very fat and full of pimples. I was also much too mature for my age—and not very happy. I had no young friends, but I had this sister who was so beautiful and I certainly was the ugly duckling.

To Mary Jane Matz (*Opera News*, 3 December 1956)

CHAPTER 7

"Sing! Sing! Sing Again!"

Maria was sometimes asked what she remembered of her school days, and her answers were contradictory. At one extreme: "*Very happy days, I must say. Carefree days.*" At the other: "*I hated school. I hated everybody,*" a statement which she later denied in writing: "*It's a lie that I hated everybody. Why should I have? It's not true that I wasn't liked at school. No, that was dreamed up.*"[1] Apart from her musical memories, to which we shall return later, little is known about her life at school. Her mother mentioned a little boy who fell in love with her and wrote her notes adorned with hearts and arrows, with tempting references to his fat savings account! Her father recalled that several teachers had congratulated him on his daughter's progress and good conduct. And one of her teachers at P.S. 189, Miss Jessie Sugar, said in 1960 that Mary was "a pleasant, well-behaved girl with no sign of temper."[2]

Maria herself remembered an admonition from the principal of P.S. 164: "Now, children, self-control! Remember that all your life!" But her most interesting reference to her school days came in an interview she gave in Amsterdam in 1959. After remarking tartly that she never went to high school ("*Only to grade school, and I hated it*"), she explained that because of her bad eyesight she had always had to sit in the front row, under the eyes of the teacher. Apparently several of her teachers did not much like her, or at any rate that was how Mary felt as a result of the humiliating petty punishments that were always being inflicted on her. Whenever she was caught eating a sweet, for example, the teacher would haul her out in front of the class and make her hand over what was left of the object of her greed, which she had paid for with her precious savings.[3]

In those early days Mary was basically placid and apparently gentle-natured. Beneath the surface, however, the uneasy atmosphere at home and the bad relations between her parents had heightened the sense of insecurity that one would expect in any child of her tender age, giving her a generally pessimistic outlook on life. Besides all this, she must have felt that in the matter of looks she was less blessed than pretty Jackie, who by this time was growing into a young lady. As a result she was very reserved and taciturn, she found it difficult to communicate except on a superficial level, and her friendships never went deep. Many of these traits stayed with her to the end of her life: *"Even now,"* she said in 1956, *"though I am charged with being conceited, I never feel secure about myself and torment myself with doubts and fears."*[4] We have already seen that Mary was subject to frequent mood swings, bouts of depression alternating with sudden outbursts of exuberance, especially at home and in her behavior toward her mother. Her nervous disposition and bad temper in fact became much more marked after she began her informal and strictly amateur juvenile "career" in 1934.

Mary's first contacts with the world of opera have already been described. Her amazing ability to learn fast enabled her to pick up by ear any piece of music she heard and liked. Sometimes, while walking in the streets of New York, she heard a radio blaring out and picked up a new tune that way. At school she had music class and singing lessons, and it was there that she first learned various songs from operettas and musicals. But right from the beginning, and with Litsa's encouragement, it was opera in particular that possessed an irresistible attraction for her. *"I owe a lot to Bizet,"* Maria said in 1957. *"It was his 'Carmen' that first cast the spell on me, in fact it may have decided the course of my life. I remember how I would wander from one room in the house to another, endlessly singing the provocative Habanera over and over again. And when my family couldn't stand it any longer I would start on Philine's aria, 'Je suis Titania,' from 'Mignon.'"* And then, falling into her habit of interpreting past events with hindsight, she went on frivolously, *"It was after all a way of alternating between a light soprano and a contralto voice so as to leave all doors open, wasn't it?"*[5]

Of course, when she was ten or so and had never had any proper singing lessons, Mary could have had very little instinctive awareness and no acquired knowledge of such technical differences. She simply sang what she heard and liked, without discriminating between the different types of voice required, more or less in the way that a coloratura soprano might "sing" a well-known melody from *Carmen*, or an alto the Queen of the Night's aria, while doing the housework. Partly by making the most of her vocal talents and retentive memory, and partly by using unorthodox vocal techniques and perhaps fudging the notes, no doubt she could achieve some kind of result, though of what kind we can only guess. One thing we can be sure of is that the story repeated unquestioningly, to the effect that when she was about ten she sang Thomas's exhausting and complex aria "Je suis Titania" (without ever having seen the music!) is not just an exaggeration but a perversion of the truth.

In about 1932 or 1933 there happened to be a Swedish singing teacher (whose name we shall probably never know) living in the apartment building opposite the Kaloyeropoulos family. Having heard Mary singing a song that she was playing on the pianola—probably through the same open window from which Litsa had seen the "great crowd" applauding her—he offered to give her some lessons. To Litsa, the combination of his praise and his willingness to teach Mary for nothing was irresistible. Within a month or two at the most he had taught her "La Paloma" and a number of other songs including "A Heart That's Free," a light American waltz that was later popularized by Jeanette MacDonald in the film *San Francisco*. For those few "lessons" Mary was accompanied by Jackie, who today acknowledges condescendingly that the Swede "must have done something for her." Although he coached Mary for only about two months, she recalled, her sister made "astonishing" progress: "From being just another sweet voice, there now appeared the first signs of something special." But Jackie insists that it was not the Swede who drew Litsa's attention to Mary's talent: "He didn't need to—she could see it for herself!"[6]

Twenty-five years later, Maria had only a faint memory of her first anonymous singing teacher: "*Now, I think I did take singing lessons from someone. I can't really recall, it is so far away. I think he was a pianist, I can't remember. But it was something that didn't really count.*"[7] It may not have been very significant in retrospect, but in the cultural wilderness of Kaloyeropoulos family life in Washington Heights in 1933, the picture of the middle-aged Swedish teacher explaining something to the nine-year-old Mary, with Jackie accompanying on the pianola, must have caught the imagination of a woman thirsting for public attention and recognition, as Litsa was. People were already talking about some very young musicians such as Yehudi Menuhin, Ruth Slenczynska, and Marion Talley, who at the age of eighteen had made her début at the Metropolitan; and no doubt the later examples of child prodigies like Mickey Rooney, Shirley Temple, Jackie Coogan, and Deanna Durbin (who sang classical music under the baton of Leopold Stokowski at the age of fifteen) continued to fill Litsa's head with hopes and dreams.

—⁂—

It must have been soon after this that the duo of Mary and Jackie made their first joint appearance in a radio talent-spotting competition for children, with Litsa as their impresario. According to Jackie, "We only took part in one. Mother heard about it on the radio and we went to the studio, where I accompanied her in 'A Heart That's Free.'" Although Jackie maintains that she never accompanied Mary again and that Mary would not have been allowed to go anywhere on her own, it seems certain that she did enter at least one other competition. Maria herself said in 1956, "*At eleven years of age I put my books aside and began to get to know the enervating anxiety and the waiting involved in contests for child prodigies: I was regularly entered in them, for radio contests or for scholarship competitions.*" Perhaps the truth is to be found in her first biographical note, written in Athens in 1943: "At the age of eleven she took part in two competitions organized by the biggest radio networks in America."[8]

The competition Jackie refers to must have taken place in New York in late 1934, when Mary was eleven. It was a competition for juvenile talent in any field, not just singing, with children reciting poetry, telling stories, and so on, and it was broadcast nationwide. Jackie accompanied Mary (who wore her hair in bangs at her forehead) in "La Paloma" and "A Heart That's Free." The studio audience applauded enthusiastically and, according to Jackie and Litsa, the judges awarded her first prize, which was a Bulova watch. But here the problems begin. On three different instances Maria herself said that the watch was a consolation prize, the competition having been won by an accordion player. And in all her accounts she added that the emcee of the competition was the well-known comedian Jack Benny, who was "furious" or "disappointed" that she had not won. It seems odd that neither Jackie nor Litsa ever mentioned such a popular celebrity as Jack Benny; so perhaps they were thinking about a different occasion. Be that as it may, the competition or competitions took place in New York. John Ardoin's assertion that one of Mary's radio performances was broadcast from Chicago probably arises from misinterpretation of an interview Maria once gave in Chicago, for we may be sure that a trip to Chicago would not have gone unremarked by either Jackie or Litsa.[9]

Next we come to the case of the *Major Bowes Amateur Hour*, a radio program in which Maria Callas is said to have taken part. John Ardoin sifted the evidence minutely, hoping to find proof that Mary did appear some time between 1935, when the program started, and March 1937, when she left for Greece. After listening to recordings of all the broadcasts made during that period, he decided that there was only one entrant who could possibly have been Mary: she was a soprano who, under the name of Nina Foresti, sang an abridged version of "Un bel dì" from Puccini's *Madama Butterfly* on 7 April 1935. However, neither the recorded nor the documentary evidence, as it exists today, supports the case that Nina Foresti was the pseudonym of the eleven-year-old Mary. Major Bowes had a short conversation with the girl, who told him that she was born in New York and her father was a druggist—so far so good—but then said that she worked in the toy department of a big store. Clearly this was a girl of at least sixteen, and that is what her voice sounds like in the recording of her singing "Un bel dì." The entry form for Nina Foresti—actually made out in the name of Anita Duval!—begins with a statement to the effect that she has studied music for several years; the address she gives (549 West 144th Street) is not where the Kaloyeropoulos family was living at the time (569 West 192nd or 520 West 183rd Street); and the handwriting is neither Mary's nor Litsa's.[10]

The question first attracted notice in 1966, when a record company issued an album which included this piece. Maria, however, denied that she had ever sung under a pseudonym and the matter was closed. Nadia Stancioff reopened it in 1987, writing that Maria herself had revealed to her that, with her mother's connivance, she had entered a competition under the pseudonym of Nina Foresti, giving her age as sixteen instead of eleven, in order to prevent George from finding out about it. Although Stancioff herself, interestingly enough, said that she still had serious reservations on the subject, Ardoin now had no choice but to accept that the voice on the tape was Mary's. Almost certainly, either Maria was joking or else Stancioff misunderstood what Maria said to her in 1970. What is more, there is actually a letter on file from Nina Foresti's mother saying that, in spite of the family's financial ruin in 1930, Nina had continued with her singing lessons, had sung at concerts, and had made her amateur début as Nedda in Leoncavallo's *Pagliacci*. Furthermore, the handwriting of Nina's mother shows absolutely no resemblance to Litsa's hand. "Completely untrue!" says Jackie, flatly dismissing the Foresti affair. "She was very young, we would have gone together and I would have remembered it. Not as Foresti nor under any other pseudonym. No way!"[11]

—⁓—

The ambitious Litsa seems to have gone to great lengths to enter her daughter in competitions, often lining up for hours to do so. Her pride in her daughter's success (or successes) on the radio was unbounded, though Mary herself does not appear to have been particularly excited about it. "In those days she wanted to be a dentist, not a singer!" Litsa admitted. "Moreover, she was used to winning prizes for singing in school and, I seem to remember, in church and Sunday school too." The fact—if it is a fact—that for a time in her childhood Mary wanted to be a dentist, either because the idea happened to take her fancy or in reaction to what may have been an overdose of music, is in no way remarkable. But quite possibly the ambition of dentistry was not Mary's at all; so at least Jackie believes, as she herself evidently went through a stage of being madly in love with her dentist. We do not know if the much younger Mary was obsessed by any childish craze of this kind. Litsa tells us in her book that both girls were "severely moral" as children. Amazing though it seems nowadays, "in winter they didn't like to go out and play in the snow with the neighborhood children, because the little girls talked about their 'sweethearts.'" This is a measure of the conservative upbringing they had had in Litsa's hands.[12]

　　Because of the way she was brought up, Mary was too introverted to make friends with other girls of her own age. So she had nobody, really, to whom she might have been able to open up and share her thoughts and anxieties, her pleasures, hopes, and dreams. "*I was always much too mature for my age, and not very happy,*" she remarked in 1956. "*I had no young friends. . . . If I could only live it all over again, how I would play and enjoy myself like other girls. What a fool I was!*" Her mother counters with the assertion that Mary was by no means friendless at school; it would, however, be safer to rely on the testimony of a fellow pupil at P.S. 189, Georgette Kokkinaki, who was two years older than Mary: "They were well-mannered, obedient children, overly protected like most Greek girls of our age and background. . . . They kept to themselves. They were a bit . . . uppity, would you say? . . . Mary Ann was a loner. She wasn't invited to many kids' houses and I guess she was not encouraged to have us over. . . . Usually she was very quiet. She wasn't outgoing, but when she sang, those dark expressive eyes flashed." Here, in

Mary Ann at the age of twelve, we can see some of the fundamental traits of character that Maria was to carry with her all her life.[13]

Mary's success as a vocalist at school is beyond question. On one occasion, when she was being teased by some of her schoolmates for having "no voice," she is said to have come back with the provocative retort, *"One day I'll sing at the Metropolitan!"* In 1958 she actually recalled, *"I used to sing every year for the graduation. I was the little singer of the school. I sang operettas and I sang a Chinese prince and a sailor and things like that."*[14] We know of three operettas from which she sang excerpts at school: two were by Gilbert and Sullivan, *The Mikado* and *H.M.S. Pinafore*, and the third was the popular *Countess Maritza* by Imre Kálmán. Mary Ann (or Mary Anna, as she liked to be called at school—and later as well) sang these in or after the school year 1933–34, at P.S. 189. About *The Mikado* we know only that her mother made her costume and that she was probably either Pitti-Sing or Peep-Bo, though it is possible that when she referred to "a Chinese prince" in 1958 she meant Nanki-Poo, the son of the Mikado of Japan, which is actually a tenor part. From *Countess Maritza* she sang, probably in January 1935, "Play, gypsies! Dance, gypsies!": "With her hands on her hips, she twisted to and fro," Georgette Kokkinaki reminisced. "You could tell that she enjoyed it! . . . Even when the chorus joined in, her voice stood out. We were spellbound by her voice." From the third operetta, *H.M.S. Pinafore*, she sang some excerpts at her graduation on 28 January 1937, when she was just thirteen. Probably she had the part of Ralph Rackstraw (this may be the "sailor" she remembered later), another tenor role. A photograph shows her among twenty-two other girls and boys, a fairly tall girl with fine, regular features, with a sailor's jacket and the thick glasses which she had started wearing in 1935.[15]

In the autograph book of one of her classmates Mary wrote then a typical piece of schoolgirl doggerel, *"Being no poet, having no fame, Permit me just to sign my name,"* and signed it "Mary Anna Callas." We shall never know at which of the aforementioned performances she first heard "the roar of the crowd," but she did remember in later life that it had happened at school: *"Ah, well, public school, graduation. . . . I was quite good at it, I suppose, and every year since then I was invited for graduation play."*[16] That first applause she heard from audiences at school—and perhaps in the radio studio as well—gave Mary a taste of the satisfaction and the feeling of power that success brings. And the possession of this new weapon not only boosted her self-confidence but also gave her a sense of being worth something in her mother's eyes. Litsa, for her part, could now hardly conceal her secret plans and hopes for her daughter: "When I told her you will be a great star of this world, she called me crazy: *'Mamma, you are crazy!'* She wouldn't believe it, but I did believe it, I saw it from when she was a little girl."[17] So here we have the mother encouraging her daughter, putting "crazy" dreams into her mind. Not only dreams, of course, but now a burden of responsibility as well. This probably explains why Mary was sometimes seized with panic in those early days: *"And*

Mary (wearing glasses) on her graduation day from P.S. 189, New York,
January 1937.

*above all [I felt] the painful sensation of panic that overcame me when, in the middle
of a difficult passage, it seemed to me that I was about to choke, and I thought in terror that no sound would emerge from my throat which had become parched and dry.
No one was aware of my sudden distress because, in appearance, I was extremely calm
and continued to sing."*[18]

It would seem that Mary got over this sensation of fear before an audience
while she was still at school. In her singing, and her awareness of the impact it had
on the audience, she had found a way of putting up with solitude and an outlet for
her teeming emotions. In fact this was one of the first occasions when, out of a difficult situation, Mary managed to extract what was most profitable for her and, by
building on that, to develop her talents and reach success. She began to convince
herself that she could and should become a famous singer, greater even than those
she heard from the Met every Saturday on the radio. Little by little, the satisfaction
she gained from singing bred in her a strong desire to succeed and win recognition.
As Ardoin rightly remarks, it was not long before Litsa's ambition became essential to the new, and newly ambitious, persona of Mary herself: "Not only did sing-

ing provide an outlet for gaining her mother's approval and attention, but it was a means of combating a shy, introverted nature . . . partly brought on by the quarrelsome nature of her parents."[19] Mary had indeed become a willing recipient of Litsa's encouragement and predictions of international stardom, which she herself now had come to believe in. Just as Antonia in *The Tales of Hoffmann* would not have been content to "Sing! Sing! Sing Again!" at the insistence of Dr. Miracle, so Mary, from now on, would sing because she herself wanted to.

But we must not overlook the fact that amid all this "interaction" and "cooperation" between mother and daughter there seems to have been very little time left over for any demonstration of real love and affection. Although Mary's newly acquired sense of worth and self-assurance did satisfy a part of her emotional needs, they were still only a poor substitute for the feelings that she, like any child of that age, so badly needed. This was something Litsa never understood, and the reason she was so indignant when, in later life, Maria blamed her for actions or omissions which she herself saw as demonstrations of motherly interest, and therefore of love. Of course, it never even entered Litsa's head that the main underlying cause of her daughter's later complaints was actually her lack of understanding for and tolerance of her husband, George Kaloyeropoulos.

—⁕—

I consider a marriage break-up one of the greatest admissions of failure.

To Derek Prouse, London (*The Sunday Times*, 26 March 1961)

CHAPTER 8

A Sudden Upheaval

Unfortunately George Kaloyeropoulos, the beloved but ever-absent father who Jackie says was "by now a mere detail in our lives," was no better at supplying the affection and warmth his daughters so badly needed. "Sometimes he tried to ask Mary and me about our lives, tried to join in whatever we were doing, but it was impossible, we had been too much influenced against him and we felt embarrassed by his attentions." To Mary, these pathetic scenes—and still more the rows between her parents, which may perhaps have diminished in frequency but probably made up for it in intensity—were a source of embarrassment and deep, unexpressed pain as well: "For little Mary it was a living nightmare," Jackie recalls. "She clung to me in desperation. '*I want to hug you*,' she would say. '*Let me cuddle up to you*.' She would get beside me on the sofa and I would comfort her. '*How sweet you smell*,' she said, her face pressed into my neck."[1]

There is not much factual evidence concerning the relations between Mary's parents after Litsa's histrionic suicide attempt and the start of George's new job, which kept him away from home for much of the time. However, the situation must have been growing more and more obvious to Mary who, as she grew older, saw with her own eyes and felt in her bones that the marriage was steadily withering away. "*There they go again . . .*" she would say whenever anything occurred to spark another fight. Litsa admitted that she "didn't always succeed" in keeping the situation hidden from the girls, and, in a burst of frankness, went on to say, "My husband and I did not lead a very peaceful home life, and perhaps this also left its mark on Maria. . . . Ours was not a 'broken home' in the accepted sense, but it was not a very happy one."[2]

At other times, however, Litsa defended herself by going on the attack: "My husband was a womanizer, he was unfaithful to me, squandered all his money on his various lovers. He never looked after us at all, we lived as strangers. Much later my daughters came to realize that I was right." That, at least, was how Litsa wanted to see things, presumably relying not only on her recollection of a number of George's marital infidelities but also on the fact that once, probably between 1935 and 1937, she had caught him with her friend Alexandra Papajohn. Possibly the

74

girls were not fully aware of the liaison, although we saw Mary's instinctive hostility toward Alexandra from a very early age, an attitude that would not change to the day she died.* At all events, Jackie's verdict is unfavorable to Litsa in this respect as well: "Except where my mother was concerned, [my father] was the gentlest of men and [it was] his disgust with her [that] led him to ignore us."[3] Clearly Jackie had little or no hesitation in blaming Litsa for driving their father away from them. But whereas later on Jackie would more or less get over this grudge against her mother, it was to stay with the younger and oversensitive Mary throughout her life, as one of the key elements of her complex and tormented personality.

After graduating from high school in 1935, Jackie paid another visit to the Kritikos family in Tarpon Springs, Florida. This time she was accompanied only by her father, while Mary stayed in New York with Litsa, probably practicing singing for school concerts and radio competitions. On her return Jackie got a modeling job with a garment manufacturing company, thus managing to spend a good deal of time away from the oppressive atmosphere of the family home.[4] Meanwhile Litsa had begun to look for a way of giving Mary a real musical training. As proper lessons were too expensive, however, she began casting about for alternative solutions. Jackie's startling revelation that her mother tried to push her into marriage with their apartment's landlord—a prosperous young lawyer of twenty-five— foreshadows Litsa's amoral mentality a few years later in Greece. Eventually, the combination of the situation at home and the inescapable fact of their poverty made her think of an altogether different solution: if she returned to Greece with the children, not only would she be rid of George but she would be back under the wing of her family, which she thought of as being comfortably established and connected. In Athens—so Litsa's reasoning went as the plan matured in the course of 1936—she would be able to help Mary's studies and musical career, and perhaps that of Jackie too with her piano. And as far as money went, the cost of living would be lower there and the amount George gave them in New York would be more than enough.[5]

---

*F. Filippas, "Maria Callas's Mother Reveals . . . ," *Thisavros*, no. 22, 24 Nov. 1977; EFFIE: "George had been unfaithful to her with her best friend and in desperation Litsa took herself off with her children and came back to her mother." Effie Hadzimitakou, a daughter of Litsa's sister Pipitsa and therefore first cousin to Jackie and Mary, thinks that Mary was unfair to her mother because she was blinded by love of her father. "In all those years, what did Kaloyeropoulos do for Maria? Nothing—until she became famous, and then he came over here and threw his arms round her." There can be little doubt that Litsa eventually told her daughters about George's "betrayal" with Alexandra. "They couldn't help hearing about it," Effie says, "because my aunt was a woman who could never keep quiet about anything!" When Mary went back to New York in 1945 and found her father living with Alexandra Papajohn, she reacted strongly and behaved toward her with open animosity. She never accepted her as her father's partner, and when George eventually married her in 1964 Maria broke off all contact with him, not acrimoniously but finally. See also Postscript I.

Whether it was, as she wrote, that she had a dream in which her dead father told her to go back to Greece and take the girls with her, or (as seems more likely) that the ideal pretext was presented to her when she found out about George's affair with Alexandra, when she finally made the decision nothing was going to stop Litsa. The first thing she had to do was to tell George so as to be sure that he would pay their fares and send them a regular allowance in Greece. Her pride must have been severely wounded when her husband, on hearing that she was about to leave him, kneeled down, crossed himself, and exclaimed joyfully, "At last, my God, you have pitied me!"[6] Naturally enough, George willingly agreed to the financial terms. Not only would he pay their fares, but he would send them a hundred dollars a month for as long as they stayed in Athens. Once George had given her the go-ahead, Litsa told the girls what had been decided over their heads. The prospect of serious musical studies was the bait, especially for Mary, besides being the only plausible way of covering up the real reason for their departure, which was the virtual breakdown of the marriage. "When I left my husband I took my two daughters and came to Greece to get over it," Litsa said later.*

The enforced curtailment of her schooling would probably not have bothered Mary very much at that time, though in later years she held this too against her mother: *"I would very much have liked . . . to become a high school student. But I couldn't: my mother had decided that I should not steal even a moment from a day spent in studying singing and piano."* We may be sure that such reproaches were made with the benefit of hindsight, especially as a few lines further on she says, *"My mother wanted me to become a singer and I was quite happy to second her, but only on the condition that I be able to become a great singer. All or nothing."*[7] What must have been the hardest thing for Mary to bear at this juncture was probably her separation from Jackie, the sister with whom she had shared a bedroom for thirteen long years. Jackie left on her own, on or about 15 December 1936, to stay with the Dimitriadis family in Athens and await the arrival of Litsa and Mary. In her book she recalls that she had a pleasant voyage aboard the *Vulcania*, one of the two ships of the Italia Lloyd Triestino line that sailed regularly between New York and Patras. However, the fact that Litsa sent her ahead on her own, to get her "out of her hair," is interpreted by Jackie as yet another example of her mother's blind

---

*F. Filippas, "Maria Callas's Mother Reveals . . . ," *Thisavros*, no. 22, 24 Nov. 1977. It is interesting from a psychological point of view that in later years Maria did not describe her father as a man who had been virtually abandoned by his wife, preferring to say that he had "advised" Litsa to take the family to Greece, where they would be able to live better on the same money, which he would send them. (MARGRIET.) Similarly, she misrepresented facts about her situation in her first "interview" with the German journalist Friedrich Herzog in July 1943 (see Chapter 25). As late as 1958, in an interview with Hy Gardner in New York, George referred to Litsa's return to Greece with the girls as having been "for a visit." However, Mary's first biographical note (see Chapter 26, note 6), in 1943, states explicitly that she came with her family "to settle" in Greece.

Mary with her mother, New York 1936.

devotion to Mary's musical career: "I knew by then that Mother was quite willing to sacrifice me on the altar of Mary's success."[8]

What Mary was thinking and feeling during the two months and more that she spent alone with her parents can only be imagined. All in all, that Christmas of 1936 would have been very special, and no doubt her beloved Leonidas was particularly solicitous toward her. It seems odd, though, that neither her parents nor her well-off godfather ever once took her to the Metropolitan, as she had by this time made it abundantly clear that she was interested in opera, and there were plenty of performances between Christmas and the end of February.[9] Always ready to please, Litsa would one day, twenty years later, blame it on George, accusing him of refusing to go to the Met or any other singing event. Apart from her daughter's graduation ceremony at P.S. 189 in January, the only other thing she informs us about this last period in New York is that Mary helped to pack their suitcases, "singing while she worked."[10] But the really interesting fact, ignored until now, is that Mary worked as a sales assistant in a music shop for a few weeks, probably in January and February 1937. Later she recalled that the proprietor teased her mercilessly about her ambition of becoming a great opera singer. That did not bother her particularly, however, because in between serving customers she spent her time reading libretti.[11] Here again we see how Mary, a naturally studious girl, was able to make the most of a situation which, though not pleasant in itself, did at least give her access to music books, scores, and libretti for the first time in her life. Indeed, in those few weeks she may well have had her first look at some of the operas she was to sing in later.

On 15 February Mary Anna Callas (as she signed) solemnly swore the oath of allegiance and the State Department issued her American passport no. 367557. It was in the name of Sophie Cecelia Kalos (matching the name on her birth certificate) of 520 West 183rd Street, New York, a student, 5 feet 7 inches tall, with brown hair and brown eyes, who was about to leave on a visit to Greece accompanied by her mother, with the declared intention to return within two years. Litsa and Mary sailed from New York on the *Saturnia* on Saturday, 20 February 1937. George, of course, would have taken them to the docks to see them off. For him, now well into his fifties, their departure marked the end of a period which had not been the happiest of his life. Now he could face the future with a measure of optimism and renewed zest. So, with a new vista before him, he would not have found it too hard to bear the prospect of being separated from his daughters. After all it would be for only a few years, he thought, as they were going to Greece on an extended visit, perhaps for as long as to give the girls a chance to pursue their studies. In any case, George was not the sort of person who thought deeply and worried about things: he simply took life as it came. Looking back at the past in about 1960, he would find that in general he was satisfied with his life. In particular, he was pleased that he had managed to support his family with dignity, without ever having had to send his wife out to work. His biggest regret was that his efforts had not been appreciated by her.[12]

Although there was some consolation in the thought that she would be coming back before too long, Mary must have said good-bye to her father with a very heavy heart. Litsa, not surprisingly, maintains that she was in a cheerful frame of mind: "Maria was excited, as only girls of that age can be. . . . If she was sorry to leave America, she did not say so." Here again Litsa may have been taking a superficial view, but she is not far wrong in her summing-up: "As children, Maria and her sister Jackie . . . lived a comfortable, middle-class existence that was neither rich nor poor. I was a good housekeeper and cook, and we always had plenty to eat and wear. My husband supported us in reasonable comfort." And for once Maria agrees: "*We were never rich, of course, not even well off. But we lived very well. We had a lovely home and my father gave me everything he could.*"[13] If thirteen-year-old girls were in the habit of looking back critically at their past lives, Mary would probably have decided that, apart from the deep and lasting trauma caused by the ever-worsening rift between her parents—and her conviction that Litsa was solely to blame for it— her childhood in America may not have been exactly blissful, but at any rate it had not been particularly unhappy or problematic either. Certainly it was not as harrowing as she herself and her biographers were later to make it out to have been.

OATH OF ALLEGIANCE

Further, I do solemnly swear that I will support and defend the Constitution of the United States against all enemies, foreign and domestic; that I will bear true faith and allegiance to the same; and that I take this obligation freely, without any mental reservation or purpose of evasion: So help me God.

Mary Anna Callas
(Signature of applicant)

Subscribed and sworn to before me this FEB 15 1937 day of ____, 193

[SEAL OF COURT]

Agent, Department of State ()
Clerk of the ____ Court ()

DESCRIPTION OF APPLICANT

Height: _5_ feet, _7_ inches, Age: ____

Hair: _Brown_

Eyes: _Brown_

Distinguishing marks or features: ____
(Any facial marks or scars by which applicant may be identified)

Place of birth: _New York City, New York_
(City and State)

Date of birth: _December 2, 1923_
(Month, day, and year)

Occupation: _Student_

I intend to leave the United States from the port of _New York_
(Port of departure)

sailing on board the _Saturnia_ on _no_ , 193_7_
(Name of ship) (Date of departure)

ADDRESS

I request that my passport be mailed to the following address:

Name: _Sophie C. Kalos_   [NOTE.—A passport will not be mailed to an hotel address unless the hotel is the applicant's place of permanent residence.]

No. and Street: _520 West 183 St_

City and State: _New York_

AFFIDAVIT OF IDENTIFYING WITNESS

I, the undersigned, solemnly swear that I am a citizen of the United States; that I reside at the address written below my signature hereto affixed; that I know the applicant who executed the affidavit hereinbefore set forth to be a citizen of the United States; that the statements made herein by the applicant are true to the best of my knowledge and belief; further, I solemnly swear that I have known the applicant personally for _five_ years.

John Kayloue
(Signature of witness)

If witness has been issued a passport, give number and date of issue or approximate date of issue.

701 W. 177 St. N.Y.C.
(Residence address of witness)

No. ____ Date of issue ____

No lawyer or other person will be accepted as witness to a passport application if he has received or expects to receive a fee for his services in connection with the execution of the application or obtaining the passport.

Subscribed and sworn to before me this ____ day

of ____, 193

Clerk of the ____ Court

at ____

[SEAL OF COURT]

The ... plicatio ... fides a ... Seal, ... impres ... left-ha ... manne ... person ... Do ... graph ...

Two photographs (duplicates) are required; one to be affixed to the application in the space designated above, and the other, bearing the signature of the applicant, to accompany the application unattached. A group photograph should be used if more than one person is to be included in the passport. Photographs must be on thin paper, should have a light background, and be not over 3 by 3 inches nor less than 2½ by 2½ inches in size.

Oath of allegiance with attached photograph of Mary taken in New York, early 1937.

As for Litsa, she was glad to be going because she was to see her family again, but she was sorry to be leaving America, which she had learned to love. In describing her feelings she makes no mention of George, whom, by this time, she probably regarded as belonging to her past. Although it is open to question whether even she was sure she would not be returning one day, she was still attractive, fairly young and vivacious (she always looked less than her age), and no doubt she believed she had a good chance of rebuilding her life.[14] Everything would be easier in Greece, which she imagined as an earthly paradise peopled with myriad well-off, well-loved, well-disposed, well-connected relatives of hers. It may be that she made a conscious effort to justify herself on the grounds that the real purpose of their return to Greece was to provide for the musical future of her daughters, especially Mary. But as the *Saturnia* drew steadily away from the Manhattan skyscrapers, which finally disappeared below the distant horizon, the feeling uppermost in Litsa's mind must have been that at last she had done "what she most wanted"—and that, as Jackie unequivocally concludes, was "to get away from our father. That rather than Mary may have been the prime motivation of all this upheaval."[15] And what an upheaval! A wholesale removal, ruthless and entirely voluntary, which was to alter the lives of the whole family quite dramatically.

—∞—

Without wishing to make myself out to have been a child prodigy, I remember that when I was five there was cheerful and promising singing to be heard in the house in New York where I was born. When I was seven, to satisfy my musical inclinations, I started learning the piano. . . . I was ten when my vocal abilities first gained some sort of recognition in the form of various prizes I won at competitions organized from time to time by Radio New York for budding singers. After that I went with my family to our home country.

To R. Ravazzin, upon her arrival in Verona
(*Il Gazzettino*, 22 July 1947)

A Musical Apprenticeship
(1937–1940)

PART TWO

A Musical Apprenticeship

(1937–1970)

CHAPTER 9

Arriving and Settling Down
in Athens

On the evening of Saturday, 6 March 1937, Litsa found herself back at the port
of Patras, almost fourteen years after she had set off from there for America
with her husband and little Yakinthi. When Litsa later recalled her return voyage,
she was filled with a similar sense of contentment to that which she had evidently
felt during the days of that second Atlantic crossing. Then, probably more than at
any other time before or since, her younger daughter was exclusively and unconditionally "hers."[1] For the fact is that Mary was then completely dependent on her
mother, not only in practical terms but emotionally as well. Even if something
deep down inside her told her that the rift between her parents was irreparable,
Mary instinctively turned her thoughts elsewhere, a distraction from the problems of family and everyday life. What is more, the rosy prospects of musical and
social betterment in Greece, so vividly sketched out for her by her mother, left no
room for misgivings in her thirteen-year-old mind: on the contrary, they made
Mary even more dependent on Litsa.

The first and most serious problem that both mother and daughter had to face
was violent nausea. They spent the first two days on board the *Saturnia* confined
to their lowly tourist class cabin, with none but the maddening company of their
three canaries, who seemed determined to assert their superiority over the two
suffering females by singing incessantly at the top of their voice. Litsa and the two
girls adored their canaries, and very early on Mary had started watching them,
trying to figure out how they produced such an extraordinarily loud trilling from
their tiny throats.[2] Once she had got over her initial seasickness Mary began
exploring the ship, finding her way about and getting to know something about
the other passengers. Most important among her discoveries was the piano in the
tourist class salon, where she immediately sat down and started playing and singing pieces from her self-taught repertoire.* One day the captain happened to hear

---

*Ypatia Louvi, one of Mary's classmates at the Athens Conservatory, said Mary sometimes sang
on the *Saturnia* to make a bit of pocket money from the passengers: "She sang on the ship, as
she told me herself, and earned herself a few pennies, poor thing." (LOUVI.) Given Mary's

her and invited her to sing the plainchant, or alternatively the Ave Maria, at Mass the following Sunday. Mary refused, but when the captain asked her to sing for the officers and two titled Italian ladies instead, she agreed. On the night of the party, Litsa recalls, her daughter was "at first just like any other little girl of thirteen in a blue cotton dress with a white collar, her bangs carefully combed and her face powdered to hide the pimples; but once she sat down at the piano to play her own accompaniment, she was a poised, accomplished artist." Mary had taken off her glasses, her black eyes were "snapping with excitement," and she sang "as though she had been singing at concerts for years."[3]

After the Ave Maria, "La Paloma," and perhaps another song or two, Mary astonished her listeners by singing the Habanera from Bizet's *Carmen*, an extremely demanding aria that calls for a mature, well-trained mezzo-soprano voice and a high level of acting ability. At this distance in time it is hard to imagine what the very young teenager must have sounded like in the first-class salon of the *Saturnia*, especially as she was accompanying herself on the piano. At the end of the aria, where Carmen taunts the captivated Don José with the warning "Prends garde à toi!", Mary, who had probably made sure that a vase of flowers stood nearby, reached out and tossed a carnation to the astonished captain. He laughed, picked it up, and kissed it, eyeing the young girl with some embarrassment. The next day he sent her a bunch of flowers with a note of thanks, the first bouquet she had ever received for a public performance, and with it he sent a doll. "For Maria, who never played with dolls!" Litsa remarks wryly, though it never occurred to her to wonder why Mary had never played with dolls, still less whether she herself might not be at least partly responsible. "*I didn't have toys,*" Maria recalled in 1971. "*There were classical records and books—and the piano until eleven o'clock in the evening. My first and only doll was given to me when I was thirteen, on the boat going to Greece.*"[4] The fact remains—if her mother's memory of the occasion is to be relied on—that even then, with no stage experience behind her, Mary already possessed remarkable aplomb when performing in front of an audience. And in that audacious stroke of throwing a flower to the captain we see a first sign of her innate theatrical and histrionic temperament.*

Mary received her first impressions of Greece and its pellucid, balmy atmos-

---

uncommunicative and proud nature, it is pretty certain that if indeed this happened she would never have told anyone about it. In any case, the story does cast an interesting light on the way Mary was regarded by some of her better-off and socially superior classmates at the Athens Conservatory. See Chapter 16.

*At the première of Spontini's *La Vestale* at La Scala, on 7 December 1954, the great diva Maria Callas would enact a different kind of scene with a carnation: selecting one among the multitude of flowers thrown on to the stage at the end of the performance, she would make a deep curtsy to Arturo Toscanini, who was in attendance, and personally take it to him in his box, sending the audience wild with delight. ("At La Scala, the Triumph of U.S.–born Maria Callas," *Newsweek*, 10 Jan. 1955.)

phere in the last few hours of the voyage, as the *Saturnia* ploughed through the Ionian Sea and she caught sight of the islands of Zakynthos and Kefalonia bathed in the glow of the setting sun. On arrival, however, the idyllic atmosphere changed abruptly when she found herself on the quay, suddenly confronted with the milling crowds and hullabaloo of the Greek waterfront. Never had she heard such a din or witnessed anything to compare with the chaotic scramble of disembarkation. It is easy to picture her sitting on a trunk, surrounded by baggage of all shapes, sizes, and colors, with the three terrified canaries, probably silent now, in their cage nearby. Seeing her on the quay, many of the passengers who had heard the "recital" and appraised the talents of the serious and rather quiet young girl wished her luck in her singing career.

By the time they had cleared customs it was too late even to think of going on to Athens that day; so Mary must have spent her first night on Greek soil with her mother in an inexpensive hotel in Patras. Early the next morning they set off by train on the last leg of their journey. It was a sunny day and the scenery along the north coast of the Peloponnese was at its most glorious. Mary feasted her eyes on the endless succession of mountain peaks and valleys, the constantly changing colors of the sea, the picturesque coves and beaches along the coastline. To her, the blossom-laden trees and shrubs, the wildflowers of every hue, the shimmering silvery gray foliage of the olive trees, and the erect silhouettes of the dark cypresses presented a spectacle that was as new as it was lovely. Even the old-fashioned wooden carriages with their hard seats, the mediocre food in the dining car, and their Greek fellow passengers, who regarded the two "Americans" and their canaries with a mixture of curiosity and awe, all seemed to possess a quaint charm which outweighed their annoyance value. Mary wore a simple dark blue dress with her usual white collar, while Litsa had chosen a gray two-piece ensemble and a striking black-feathered hat, with the avowed intention of impressing the relatives who would be meeting them at the station. Slowly the train made its way past Aigion, Corinth and its famous canal, Megara, Eleusis, station after station, until at last, after the final stretch through the shabby western suburbs, it reached Athens as dusk was falling.[5]

—ɯ—

Meanwhile Jackie, who had arrived at the end of December 1936, had been living with her maternal grandmother on Xanthippis Street, in Sepolia. This area, about three kilometers northwest of Omonia Square downtown, was in those days mostly open countryside and orchards. Such houses as there were, each with its garden planted with orange and lemon trees and usually a vegetable patch as well, were never more than two stories high. Xanthippis Street ran almost as far as the picturesque Skouzé Hill, and like most of the roads outside the city center it was unpaved. The exact position of that rented house, now demolished, is not known, but it was probably near the hill and had a view of the Acropolis. An enclosed porch with a wooden front door led in to a large hall, from which a wide marble staircase went up to the bedrooms.[6]

The matriarch of this household was Litsa's mother, Frosso Dimitriadou, then in her mid sixties but still by all accounts a fine-looking and active woman. Since her husband's death some twenty years earlier she had continued to live in the style to which she was accustomed, surrounded by her children. She was a woman of great spirit who had never allowed anything to get her down—not even the death of her youngest daughter, Altana, some time between 1920 and 1922. She was often to be seen sitting at Yannaki's Patisserie at the corner of Panepistimiou and Kriezotou Streets, surveying the passers-by through her lorgnette. Her children frequently took exception to her extravagances, but in vain. From time to time she would hire two horse-drawn victorias to take the whole family to eat at the fashionable Poisson d'Or, a seaside restaurant in Faliron, miles away on the other side of Athens. The result of this open-handedness was that Frosso had eventually had to sell off such properties as she still owned, including the family house on Jean Moréas Street. From then on she lived on her husband's pension, renting accommodations in less expensive areas such as Sepolia.

The family budget was now extremely tight. The only supplements to Petros's meager pension came from the salaries of Sophia and Kakia, both in their forties but hardworking civil servants. Also living on Xanthippis Street were Doukas, recently divorced, and Pipitsa, one of the two "rebels" of the family, the other being youngest brother Filon, then twenty-eight and living on his own. Living with his own family in Plaka was thirty-two-year-old Efthymios, a gentle, good-looking man with a romantic streak and great love for music. With six mouths to feed on a pension and two civil servants' salaries, nothing was left over on Xanthippis Street to support Litsa and her two daughters. Litsa, in her book, says condescendingly, "Even in 1938 my family wasn't poor, but they were living on salaries and pensions, quite enough for their needs but with little to spare for Maria and me." As for Jackie, she evidently sized up the situation very quickly: "Mother in her unthinking way had built up a complete fantasy about her family. Over the years of absence they had been transformed into people of considerable means. . . . Our immediate circle was basically petit-bourgeois. They listened to Mother's endless stream of ambitious plans, looked at each other and wondered. . . . I suspect that they rather wanted her to have a reasonable holiday, then pack up and go home to her husband."[7]

Although the various members of the Dimitriadis family were temperamental individuals who went their own ways and were not averse to speaking their minds about each other, they did stick together as a family, with the house on Xanthippis Street as its focal point. There they would gather on Sundays for a protracted lunch with a lot of talk and an impromptu theatrical or musical performance. Sophia and Pipitsa sang and played the guitar and mandolin, respectively. Pipitsa was a contralto with a rich, deep tone; for her, however, the pleasures of life, love, and smoking were more enjoyable than singing, and she never tried to develop her voice. Efthymios was also a good singer, a baritone: he often sang at tavernas with his friends, and he was a cantor at the Church of Ayios Vassilios in Koukaki. Kakia and Doukas were not musical, but they joined in the lively conversations which, even if usually on mundane subjects, often had so much drama in them that they were as good as theatrical performances.[8]

The whole family except Frosso—who was not well that day—went down to the railway station late on Sunday afternoon, 7 March 1937, to meet Litsa and Mary. Jackie remembered Mary looking "embarrassed and downcast" and attributed this to "her isolation with Mother whose nervous chatter seemed endless." No doubt Mary's predominant feeling was one of relief at the prospect of no longer being cooped up with her mother all the time. Litsa, with a swagger in her walk and a feather in her hat, now devoted all her attention to her brothers and sisters, whom she scarcely recognized after fourteen years. As soon as she could, Jackie took Mary aside and tried to cheer her up, telling her about all the good things awaiting her in Athens, the house in Sepolia, and their loving and lovable grandmother.[9]

The "Americans" stayed on Xanthippis Street for about a month. In a household with seven women it was naturally regarded as a matter of honor to do the housework and cooking as well as possible. Mary's task was to mop the floors, a duty which she performed with prodigious zeal, not allowing anyone to walk on them until they were completely dry. As for the cooking, it made no difference to her who did it: she always enjoyed the result, and she now began eating more than ever before. Often she would go into the kitchen at the end of a meal and top it off with her favorite snack of fried eggs with cheese or a large slice of bread soaked in water and sprinkled with sugar. Furthermore, as soon as the weather warmed up, members of the Dimitriadis family went out to eat at a local taverna almost every evening, and they would often take Jackie and Mary with them. The girls enjoyed the company of such friendly, easygoing people, but on those occasions they ate even more than they would have done at home. It was at this time, too, that Mary discovered the delights of the *tyrópita*, a kind of cheese pie which she found irresistible. "I'll buy you as many as you like, but mind your figure, my girl!" her uncle Doukas would say after Mary had gulped down two or three while walking around Athens. *"Don't worry, I won't eat when I get home,"* she would answer, knowing as well as he did that this was a promise she would not keep.[10]

Needless to say, Mary, who was already tall but not yet fat, started putting on weight and losing her complexion. The first manifestations of this gluttony (for that is what it was) appeared as soon as Mary arrived in Greece. No doubt the skills of the cooks and the rich oil and starch content of their Greek dishes had something to do with it, but the root cause of her overeating must surely have been the severing of her emotional ties with her father. Now that his name was hardly ever mentioned in the house Mary began suffering from feelings of remorse at having gone off and left him in faraway America. For the time being, music seemed to be the only thing that absorbed her attention so completely that she forgot about food. She sang and practiced every day at the piano, on which her grandmother would put a glass of milk for her, and it often happened that four hours later the milk would still be there, untouched.[11]

Litsa, of course, introduced Mary to her family as "a person of consequence embarking on a brilliant career." Mary did not need much pushing to show off her talents to her newfound relatives, but none of them seemed particularly impressed. The only one who felt that it might be worth seeing if anything could be done with Mary's voice was her uncle Efthymios. Not only did he sing himself, but his colleague and friend Stavros Trivellas was the brother-in-law of Maria Trivella, who taught at the National Conservatory. Jackie describes how Mary sang "La Paloma" (what else?) for Efthymios, whereupon "he only nodded and announced that there were hundreds of girls with pleasant voices." However, he would arrange for her to be auditioned by Trivella, although Litsa should not push Mary too hard while she was still feeling her way in an unfamiliar environment and didn't even speak the Greek language well.[12]

Interestingly enough, there was never any question of Mary's continuing with her secondary schooling in Greece. True, she could not write Greek at that stage, but the main reason she was not sent to a Greek school was her mother's utter determination to exploit her vocal talents. Indeed, with a financial crisis looming, Litsa was already planning to launch Mary on her singing career as soon as possible, in order to bring in a bit of money. In later years Maria was rather bitter about having been taken away from school so early: "*In 1937 I went to Athens and started at the conservatory straightaway—singing lessons, and very soon my first appearance on stage. I made my début when I was only fourteen. So I suppose you might say I didn't get an education. That's the way it is, unfortunately!*"[13] The fact remains that she never received a proper education in anything other than music, and on this point—another of the grievances she held against her mother—nothing can be said in Litsa's defense.

As time went on, the atmosphere in the house on Xanthippis Street became steadily more oppressive. There was a certain amount of bickering between Litsa and her siblings, but Mary, so recently released from the bitter quarreling between her parents, was not worried by the occasional outbreaks of discord. She had a habit of saying whatever came into her head, without thinking much before she spoke. In this she resembled Pipitsa, the youngest of her aunts and the one with whom she got along best. She even persuaded Pipitsa to write in her autograph book that she hoped one day to see her perform at La Scala. Within a short time of her arrival she had also formed a fairly strong attachment to her uncle Doukas, who often took her out with him. When this happened Mary made no attempt to hide her excitement, ignoring the disapproving looks she received from the female members of the household, except the "progressive" Pipitsa.[14] But who else, apart from Doukas, was in a position to give her a few moments away from her mother and the other women? To show her around Athens and the famous sights that she only knew about from books and casual talk?

Mary was particularly happy and talkative when they were out walking in the Royal Garden. Full of confidence in herself, she would chatter away to her uncle about her dreams of a great career. *"Uncle, will you come to hear me at La Scala in Milan?"* she asked him one day. To which Doukas replied in a gently teasing tone: "My dear Mary, does it have to be La Scala? Would no other rung on the ladder be good enough for you?" *"No, really, Uncle, I'm going to sing there, and you're going to come and hear me!"* Once, when Doukas was going out to a taverna in the evening, Mary asked him to take her with him. To prevent a scene with his sisters, Doukas took her out before the usual opening time of the late-night tavernas to a place where his friend Angelos Rakinas played the piano. "Who's the young girl?" Rakinas asked. "She's my niece," Doukas answered with a twinkle in his eye, "who has an idea that one day she's going to sing at La Scala"—whereupon Rakinas offered to accompany her. Mary suggested "Don't Cry, Sweet Marió" (none other than the Greek version of "La Paloma") and off she went. Rakinas was dumbfounded, the windowpanes rattled in their frames, and a small crowd gathered outside, as on that famous occasion a few years earlier in New York.[15]

Even at that early stage, Mary must already have started working out her singing future. It was clear that the only hope of achieving the musical ambitions that her mother had stirred in her was to follow the path chosen for her by none other than Litsa. But just how unrealistic Litsa had been in most practical matters would very soon become apparent, and from then on Mary would start distancing herself from her mother. The process would be painful and traumatic, with alternating periods of partial reconciliation and further estrangement, but it would be irreversible and inexorable. For the time being, however, in those early days in Athens, Mary was entirely dependent on her mother and went along with her plans for her artistic future. As for George Kaloyeropoulos, the only thing that brought Litsa and the girls nearer to him after leaving New York was the readoption of their full Greek surname, Kaloyeropoulou in its female form.

—⁂—

Litsa lost no time in finding out all she could about the conservatories and their teaching staff. The Athens Conservatory, founded in 1871, was the older and the more highly regarded, but it did not have a very strong tradition in singing. What made it particularly interesting for Mary in 1937 was that the famous Spanish soprano Elvira de Hidalgo was teaching there. The National Conservatory had been founded as recently as 1926, but the presence of Manolis Kalomiris, its founder and principal, and the high caliber of its singing teachers were factors in its favor. Generally speaking, the Athens Conservatory was stricter in its entrance requirements and in the teaching of all subjects—not only the electives chosen by the students as their special subjects but also the compulsory classes in theory and rudiments of music. The National Conservatory, on the other hand, adopted a more flexible approach and in certain circumstances would allow especially talented students to "skimp" the compulsory theory subjects.

To Mary, who had had no theoretical musical training and attached little importance to it, and even more to Litsa, who knew nothing whatever about music, the requirements of the Athens Conservatory seemed excessive; perhaps at the National Mary might be able to get by without "wasting time" on theory. Her age was another obstacle, as neither conservatory admitted students under the age of sixteen and all applicants had to have a basic secondary education. Thirdly, the fees—not for Mary alone but for Jackie also, as she too now wanted to go on with her piano—would present a serious problem, as Litsa and her daughters were totally dependent on the money that George had promised to send them. So it looked as if the only way either girl would be able to study music was by winning a full scholarship (not an insuperable obstacle, as both conservatories offered such awards). All in all, therefore, there were plenty of practical problems occupying the minds of Litsa and the girls during their first few weeks after arriving and settling down in Athens.

In addition to these preoccupations, they soon had to start worrying about two more pressing problems: one was where they were to live, as they would obviously have to move soon from Xanthippis Street, and the other was what they were to live on. In the beginning George sent them the hundred dollars a month on which, supplemented by some savings brought from America, the three women managed well enough. After about a month in Frosso's house, however, probably as a result of a quarrel, Litsa decided to rent a small apartment. Accustomed as she was to frequent moves in New York, she thought nothing of moving several times in Athens as well. Most biographers mention only the apartment at 61 Patission Street, and some say that Litsa and the girls moved in there as soon as they arrived in Greece. In reality, however, Litsa and her daughters lived at not less than six and possibly seven different addresses in the three years between spring 1937 and early 1940. First they moved, with their few possessions and no furniture of their own as yet, to an apartment in a house on Ithakis Street, much closer to the city's center.[16]

On Ithakis Street they were near neighbors of Frosso's sister Machi and her husband, Major General Achilleas Koukoulis. Litsa and her daughters were frequent visitors to their house at 116 Thiras Street, where they would usually sit out on the cool first-floor terrace at the back, shaded by the tall trees in the garden. The four Koukoulis daughters, who were first cousins of Litsa's but closer in age to Jackie and Mary, often had parties for their young friends, and Jackie and Mary would attend—chaperoned by their mother, of course. The buffet was always lavish, and the music and dancing made a welcome break from the monotony of the girls' existence. "Sometimes Mary sang at these parties," says Titina, the eldest of the Koukoulis sisters, "and then people hung out of their windows to listen. Litsa would give the order, lightly but firmly. 'Come on, Mary, off you go!' she would say, and Mary did as she was told. I remember her singing Ave Maria and 'La Paloma,' but we didn't have a piano and she sang unaccompanied."[17]

Titina Koukouli was impressed by the way her cousin Litsa more or less commanded Mary to "do her turn": "She really imposed her will on the girls. With one look she withered them into submission!" There is, however, no way of knowing how resentful Mary felt at being subjected to such open pressure by her mother. There must have been times, depending on who was in the audience, when she did not need to be cajoled into singing in public, but doubtless on many occasions, especially in front of strangers, she was coerced by her mother to show off her vocal talents. A reliable witness to Mary's discomfiture in such cases was Jackie, who had recently experienced Litsa's fury directed against herself and her grandmother Frosso, for encouraging her to take a secretarial course. "She got Mary to sing for anyone who had even the vaguest connections with the musical life of Athens," Jackie says, "and how poor Mary loathed it. *I don't want to,*' she wailed to me. *'Please tell her to stop!'*"[18]

Titina Koukouli remembers only one outing with Mary. It was on Good Friday of 1937 or 1938, when they went—probably with other members of the family—to see the Epitaphios procession at the Church of Saint George Karytsis. "It was an opportunity for me to show her the church where her grandmother had been married," she recollects. However, Titina still has vivid recollections of the year she and Mary were friends: "She was a good girl, well-behaved, sensible, reasonable," she says. "Mary was tall for her age, but rather fat and plain; and she was quite unsophisticated and didn't bother about what she wore. Although she already spoke Greek fairly well, you could tell she was a foreigner from her pronunciation and the mistakes she sometimes made." This picture of Mary as she was in 1937–38 tallies with the brief description of herself given by Maria exactly twenty years later: "*When I arrived in Athens I had barely turned thirteen, but I looked older because I was as tall as I am now, stout, and altogether too serious, in my face and clothing, for my young age.*"[19]

Sometime during 1937 or early 1938, something caused the prickly and quick-tempered Litsa to break off relations with the Koukoulis family. "I don't even remember what she was so angry about that time," Titina admits. "But Litsa flew off the handle at the slightest provocation." Mary, who was very fond of her great-aunt Machi and her daughters, secretly continued going to see them on Thiras Street, until one day her visits abruptly ceased. "Litsa must have got wind of it and I expect she said, 'If you go and see those people again, I'll chop your feet off!' After that I completely lost touch with Mary." Although Litsa wielded a rod of iron, here we see young Mary, aged only fourteen, making a first spirited attempt to resist her mother's autocratic rule. However, it was only in her dealings with friends and relations that she tried to assert her independence. Where singing and her future were concerned, she still complied with her mother's ideas and aspirations without demur. "I don't remember Mary ever having talked to us about her

musical ambitions," recalls Titina, "but we knew that she had started having lessons with Trivella."[20]

—⁂—

In later life Maria frequently asserted that she had not chosen a singing career for
herself. In 1970 she stressed, "*Destiny brought me into this career. I couldn't get out.
I was forced into it quite frequently, first by my mother, then by my husband. I would
have given it up with pleasure. This will probably amaze people, but I would have!*"[21]
However, we should not forget that even at that tender age Mary had repeatedly
declared her ambition of singing in the world's greatest opera houses. Also that not
only did she practice the piano and singing on her own for hours at a time (which
even Litsa could hardly have forced her to do), but on her own admission she had
agreed to study singing on condition that she should one day be able to become a
great singer. She had in fact asked her mother to let her study singing, on condition that she won scholarships: "*Winning scholarships represented for me a firm guarantee that my parents were not deluded in believing in my voice.*"[22] Therefore her later
protestations that she was forced to become a singer should be taken with a large
grain of salt.

Admittedly Mary never did pay a penny in fees for her musical studies, as she
always won scholarships. As, however, the Greek conservatories were fairly generous with their awards in those days, Mary, who never closed her eyes to reality,
knew very well that scholarships were by no means a guarantee of future success.
Her self-confidence would have come to her gradually as a result of her progress
and the swift recognition of her talent in Athenian musical circles. But the winning
of scholarships (also awarded to pupils with very mediocre voices, frequently
through string-pulling) was to her an absolute necessity for purely financial reasons
and for the comforting feeling of not being a burden on her mother. This meant
that Mary would not be absolutely dependent on Litsa and would eventually be
able to choose her own career instead of having to abide by objectionable notions
and often misguided admonitions. Litsa was later to declare, "Whatever Maria
has achieved she owes to me. I enrolled her at the conservatory, at enormous sacrifice to myself." But Maria would counter, "*That's not true. She enrolled me at the
conservatory because she knew that that way I would be able to make money faster
than in any other career. And she didn't have to make any sacrifices. From the second
[sic] year of my studies I had a scholarship.*"[23]

After only a month or two on Ithakis Street the family moved again, this time
about two kilometers northwest, to a small furnished house at the uptown end of
Patission Street. In this house, which they loved, Litsa and her daughters spent the
summer and autumn of 1937. During those months, Litsa redoubled her efforts
to enroll Mary at one of the music schools, preferably the Athens Conservatory.
"*My mother tried first to enroll me in the Athens Conservatory, the most important one
in all of Greece; but they laughed in her face. What were they to make—they said—out*

of a thirteen-year-old girl?"[24] The exact date of this initial approach to the Athens Conservatory remains unknown, but it is possible that when Litsa went there to enroll Jackie in Tassia Filtsou's piano class, she asked someone—perhaps the principal, Filoktitis Ikonomidis, himself—if they would take Mary in a singing class for the year starting that September. If that was what happened, we may be sure that Ikonomidis, who always insisted that his young students must have a reasonable grounding in theory of music, would not have considered admitting her.

It was around this time that Mary herself approached the Athens Conservatory and had her first brush with Ikonomidis. In her memoirs Maria mentions only her mother's unsuccessful attempt to enroll her, but that is doubtless because her own experience had left her feeling even more humiliated. Ypatia Louvi—who was then in the advanced class under Loula Mafta, a highly regarded teacher with a strong predilection for classical lieder—remembers: "I was standing near the door when suddenly there was a knock, and in came a fat girl with hideous legs and eyes popping out of their sockets. She told me what she wanted in poor Greek with an American accent, and I passed the message on to Mafta: she was called Kaloyeropoulou and wanted to be auditioned. Mafta agreed and heard her then and there, in front of all of us. She sang only some simple exercises because she didn't know anything except 'Astero' and 'La Paloma.' She sang with a very heavy, ugly voice. 'She sings like a man,' a fellow student told me, 'as if she had a sweet stuck in her throat!' And she had absolutely no idea how to extend the upper range of her voice. 'This isn't the place for you,' Mafta told her. 'Go to an elementary teacher first, learn music, and then come back to be taught by a singing teacher.' So out she went."[25]

Soon afterward, Louvi recalls, Ikonomidis came into the classroom and asked sarcastically who it was that Mafta had been auditioning—"that girl who wanted to learn singing without doing the compulsory subjects." He then told the whole class that on her way out Miss Kaloyeropoulou had happened to meet him, accidentally or on purpose, and had told him that she wanted to enroll at the conservatory "because she had a voice." The first thing he had asked her, he reported, was whether she had done the compulsory subjects: theory, rudiments of music, and so on. When she said no, he had told her that since she had no musical knowledge, she would have to take the compulsory subjects first.[26] Knowing something about Mary's character as it was then and was to develop further later, it is not hard to imagine how she must have felt about her rejection and what sort of things she would have said about it to her mother, who had pushed her into it in the first place and would no doubt have been furious herself.

"When they turned her away," Louvi continues, "young Kaloyeropoulou went to the National Conservatory and we lost her. We heard that she had private lessons in theory and rudiments of music with Leonidas Zoras, and made very rapid progress. She had talent, she picked things up quickly, and she was strong-willed: she really wanted to learn, to get ahead. One day not long afterward, when

I bumped into her on a streetcar, she said quite shamelessly, '*Mr. Ikonomidis told me not to come to the conservatory because I haven't done theory and rudiments. Well, Mr. Ikonomidis can take a running jump. I'm going somewhere else.*' And when I remarked that all the rest of us had done five or six years of theory, she retorted, '*But I came here for singing! I'll get through the theory and rudiments in a year with Zoras.*'[27] Louvi's reminiscences have taken us a few months ahead of the story, to the time when Mary was at the National Conservatory. As to her assertion that Mary had private lessons with Zoras—who, seven years later, would conduct her in d'Albert's *Tiefland*, one of her early triumphs—there does not seem to be any supporting evidence at all. But everything else in the account fits in well with what we know of Mary's cocky self-assurance and with the other known facts and circumstances of her life then.

—m—

I couldn't put up a fight, because in those days we did what our parents wanted. It wasn't the way it is now, when if you hit a child he goes straight to the police . . . . But I was only thirteen. What could I do? Protest? To someone with my mother's forceful temperament?

To Philippe Caloni, Paris 1976

CHAPTER 10

Maria Trivella and the
National Conservatory

One evening in the summer of 1937 Doukas took Litsa, Mary, Jackie, Efthymios, and perhaps some friends out to dinner at a seaside taverna near Piraeus. It was a place frequented by opera singers, who went there not only to eat but to sing, in order to supplement their meager incomes. According to Jackie's recollection of the evening, "To Mary's disgust, she was ordered to take the stage and show what she could do." Jackie sat down at the piano, Mary went through her usual repertoire, after which they went back to their table "to ecstatic applause." Afterward, Yannis (Zannis) Kambanis, a good-looking but very short young man who was an up-and-coming tenor in his last year as a student under Maria Trivella at the National Conservatory, came over to congratulate Mary. Litsa immediately "went into top gear as she attempted to win him over to her cause." If Efthymios failed to arrange an audition, she thought, she would succeed with Kambanis on her side. Kambanis, however, had a different recollection of the occasion. Speaking in 1991, shortly before he died, he said: "Yes, the mother, who was with a group of people at another table, came over and asked me to hear her daughter, who had a good voice. The daughter was sitting at the table looking diffident and not wanting to sing in the taverna. So the mother asked me to try and persuade her to come and see Trivella with me. I did, and the next day Mary came, Trivella heard her and kept her on as a pupil."[1]

That Mary actually sang at the taverna that night is uncertain, and so is whether her audition took place as a result of the taverna evening, as Kambanis says it did, or through the intervention of Stavros Trivellas, Maria Trivella's brother-in-law and a close friend of Efthymios Dimitriadis. The latter seems much more likely: it may be that Kambanis merely put in a word of his own to his teacher and perhaps listened in on one of Mary's first lessons. At all events, when the great day of the audition arrived—probably in early September 1937—Mary was bubbling over with excitement so that she could not stop chattering. The most nervous person, however, was Litsa, who was terrified that perhaps her daughter's voice was not the "pure gold" she hoped it was. Amazing though it may seem, no fewer than six people went along with young Mary to Trivella's tiny house at 5 Hoffmann Street:

besides Efthymios, there were Frosso, Litsa, Kakia, Pipitsa, and Jackie, all dressed in their best and bejeweled—a real family party. Mary, in her white organdy dress and with her hair up, was determined that at the very least this crucial moment would put an end to all the uncertainty and her mother's pressure. Either she would pass the test or else the whole business would be over and done with.

According to Litsa, Mary sang for Trivella "like an opera star in embryo," and Jackie confirms that she sang "better than ever before." Both agree that Trivella was entranced: "But this is talent!" she exclaimed, and said at once that she wanted to have Mary as her pupil. General rejoicing and mutual embracing ensued, with Mary in a bit of a daze and Litsa greatly relieved: "I knew then that I was right," she gushes, "and that Maria was destined to be a great artist."[2] Trivella herself recalled twenty years later: "She was first brought to me in 1937 by her uncle, Makis Dimitriadis, and my brother-in-law, Stavros Trivellas. 'We're giving you a marvelous voice to work on,' they told me. . . . The plump girl was looking at me strangely, with a certain amount of nervous expectancy. 'What's your name?' '*Marianna, Marianna Kaloyeropoulou.*' 'What sort of voice have you got?' '*I've been told I'm a contralto.*' 'Do you want to study singing?' '*Yes! It's my one dream.*' 'You realize, my child, that an artist's life is very hard? To reach the level you aspire to, you need not only a good voice but constant study and practice as well.' '*You'll see! I think you will be very pleased with me.*' 'All right, then. Come back tomorrow and we'll have our first lesson.'"[3]

Trivella's later description of the audition, despite some obvious mistakes, is very illuminating: "It was in the summer of 1937 that I was visited by Mrs. Kaloyeropoulou and her two daughters: Mary, a very plump young girl wearing big glasses for her myopia, and Yakinthi, sweet and slim. . . . 'I have come to put my daughter Marianna into your hands,' she said, 'to be taught music and opera. . . . My Marianna won't give you much trouble because she is obedient, tenacious, and hardworking. . . . As regards the fees, please be very lenient and make them as moderate as you can. I'm afraid our family budget can't stand too much of a strain.' . . . 'I'll listen to her and see what I think,' I answered. . . . I had a feeling that that girl with the short socks and the frosty look behind her glasses was gifted with great talent. Mrs. Kaloyeropoulou sat down, with her younger [sic] daughter Yakinthi standing beside her. I struck up a well-known tune on the piano and Mary Kaloyeropoulou started singing. What I had suspected turned out to be true. Her warm, vibrant voice, though somewhat primitive and completely untrained, attested to the great passion welling up in her heart. The tone of that voice was warm, lyrical, intense; it swirled and flared like a flame and filled the air with melodious reverberations like a carillon. It was by any standards an amazing phenomenon, or rather it was a great talent that needed control, technical training, and strict discipline in order to shine with all its brilliance. All the time that Mary Kaloyeropoulou was singing, I was watching her and I thought she looked beautiful and likable. Two or three times during the audition she snatched off her glasses with a nervous gesture and wiped them with a handkerchief. I confess I wasn't sure whether she was wiping off the perspiration induced by nervous stress or the tears springing from her young heart. When she had finished I turned to her mother and said, with great feeling, 'I will teach your daughter music and opera free of charge, because she is extremely talented. She can come every day and I'll give her lessons.' [Young] Callas embraced me as she left."[4]

The very next day Mary went to Trivella's home for a lesson. "The gemlike quality of her voice was apparent from her first lessons," Trivella said in 1957. "However, as soon as she started doing exercises I realized that she was not a contralto, as I had been told, but a dramatic soprano. . . . I had to work very hard with her to establish the *imposto* of a dramatic soprano. Previously, as far as I could see, some irresponsible self-styled singing teachers had almost ruined her voice, thinking she was an alto." It is beyond question that in those days Mary did not know where her voice really lay and sang pieces with a tessitura that was too low for her. She herself said in 1957, "*The timbre was dark, almost black—when I think of it I think of thick molasses—and I also had problems with the limits [of my voice] in the upper register. All my efforts, then and later, starting in 1937 when I moved to Greece with my mother, were directed toward lightening the tone and acquiring the tonal colors I would need for many—a great many—of the roles I dreamed of.*" And in 1968 she reaffirmed, "*They say I was not a true soprano, I was rather toward a mezzo.*"[5] Trivella's efforts to raise the tessitura of Mary's voice and lighten her tone were to be continued, and indeed redoubled by Mary's next teacher, a year or two later. But there had definitely not been any "self-styled singing teachers" who had considered her an alto, as Trivella imagined. Mary herself, in trying to sing pieces that were far too difficult and outside her range during her childhood in America, such as "Je suis Titania," had transposed them automatically to the key that suited her best, lowering her voice and darkening her tone. It is quite likely that these early efforts of hers were the cause—at least a contributory cause—of the excessive vibrato or wobble that was to plague Mary from the time of her first lessons in Athens.

On the question of fees Trivella may well have been willing to teach Mary for nothing, but there was also the matter of enrolling her at the National Conservatory, and all scholarship decisions rested with its principal, Manolis Kalomiris, to whom she doubtless spoke about it. The real problem was Mary's age, as she was not yet fourteen and the minimum age for admission to the conservatory was sixteen. "I had to lie about her age," Litsa admits in her memoirs. "I said she was sixteen! Fortunately for all of us Maria looked and acted older than her years."[6] Many years later, when she was feuding with her mother, Maria cited this deception as yet another example of Litsa's domineering behavior and scheming: "*My mother was very ambitious . . . so she wanted me to be what she would have wanted to be. I don't know what that would have been. . . . She pushed me. At thirteen I had to go to the conservatory in Greece. We had to change my age. . . . We lied about it.*"[7] Yet that first lie could not have really bothered her very much then. Her strict moral principles and her habit of criticizing everything her mother did came later, when she was going through the difficult stage of adolescence.

—ɷ—

Maria Trivella, a small, plumpish woman with light brown hair and dark eyes, was born in Mytilini, on the island of Lesbos, in 1894, the daughter of Aryirios Adalis, a fine architect who had studied under Hansen and Ziller in Vienna and Munich, and his wife, Penelope, *née* Grimani.[8] She therefore grew up in a cultured, well-to-do home. She was educated at a Catholic convent school in Mytilini, was a personal friend of novelist Stratis Myrivilis, and at seventeen she became engaged to Athanasios Trivellas, an engineer officer in the Greek army who was then stationed on the island. After some time in Athens, Trivellas went to France for further training in Montpellier and Paris, where somebody happened to hear his wife sing and encouraged her to train her voice. On their return to Athens, Trivella enrolled in Kimon Triandafyllou's class at the Hellenic Conservatory, where she gained her diploma in 1930, winning first prize. She gave numerous recitals between 1930 and 1957, sang few roles on the stage (notably Marguerite and Butterfly), and in 1934 was taken on as an associate professor of singing at the National Conservatory. She taught there, but also gave lessons at her tiny house (which is still standing) on Hoffmann Street, toward the end of Patission Street.

Mary went to Trivella's for private lessons every day, and much less often to the conservatory. "So the days turned into months and Mary had her lesson every day," Trivella recalled in 1957. "Sometimes [she came] alone and sometimes with her mother for company. I put my heart into teaching her, out of my love of music and admiration for her voice, which was like a fertile plain. She had rare perception and musicality, and what is more she worked hard. A model student. Fanatical, uncompromising, dedicated to her studies heart and soul. She studied five or six hours a day and I was never in the unpleasant position of having to reprimand her. Her progress was phenomenal. Within six months she was singing the most difficult arias in the international operatic repertoire with the utmost musicality. And the more progress she made, the more enthusiastic I became. She had an amazing faculty for learning, and her repertoire grew more and more extensive. From time to time she would give me a hug and a kiss and say, '*I don't know how to thank you. I owe my progress to you.*' And she was always saying, in her strong Greek-American accent, '*Darling, I love you so much! I shall take you to America, I shall make you a great music teacher!*' I never believed any of her promises, I was only sure that she was extremely talented and that very soon she would be rising in the firmament and taking her place among the stars. Her exquisite voice could be heard all over the neighborhood and people would open their doors and windows to listen to her. Everyone marveled at it and asked who it was that was singing."[9]

"Every day it was the same," recalls Penelope Adali, Maria Trivella's niece. "She would arrive with her music under her arm before lunchtime and have an

Maria Trivella.

hour's lesson. Then, as her mother was hard up, my aunt would often give her lunch, either a proper meal in the kitchen or just a sandwich in the hall, outside the door of the little room where the piano was—an upright Stichel with a bronze bust of Mozart on it. After lunch she picked up her music, tucked it under her arm again, and off she went. Sometimes she came in the afternoon as well." Penelope Adali's memory of Mary, who was about the same age as her, was of "a plump but not a fat girl, a bit of a country bumpkin to look at, with a rather scowling face and very thick glasses, wearing a shapeless dress and big shoes, altogether without the least trace of elegance or taste." However, Mary was always very friendly to her: "I remember her telling me that she wasn't allowed to go out like any other girl of her age, because her mother was so strict. She had to spend a lot of her time studying and practicing, so that she would be able to go on stage as soon as possible. She never told me much more about herself, and she was rather ungracious in her manner. But she really was keen on her work and seemed to have a fire burning inside her."[10]

Meanwhile Litsa had also been trying to arrange a meeting with Yorgos Karakandas, who had recently been appointed head of the opera school at the National Conservatory. She had happened to meet his mother and would not rest content until he had been persuaded to make room in his busy schedule for an audition with Mary. "Her mother brought her to see me and asked me to give her an audition," Karakandas said in 1977. "Her voice was good but immature, and she did not make a good visual impression. In those days she was very fat, and I could not imagine how she could ever develop. The first thing that struck me was her strong desire to get somewhere, to be a good actress." In his memoirs Karakandas added, "I was excited by the fact that her voice was so well developed for her age, and although she did not have all the necessary formal qualifications I entered her in the school, with the consent of Manolis Kalomiris, as a promising youngster."[11]

So Trivella, and perhaps Karakandas too, asked Kalomiris to award Mary a scholarship at the conservatory: this would probably have been at the beginning of the academic year 1937–38 or possibly a little after, as Mary had already had several lessons by then. Years later Kalomiris wrote a note on the subject: "Since the family was in difficult financial circumstances, I readily agreed to a proposal from Mrs. Trivella that [Kaloyeropoulou] should be given free tuition. However, this was by no means an exceptional favor, because the National Conservatory always gave free tuition, as far as it was able, to exceptionally talented students of limited means." Leonidas Zoras, then a young conductor and associate professor of advanced theory, in his recollections forty years later referred to "the rather ill-favored girl with the shining face and large expressive eyes, who was brought to us at the National Conservatory by [Maria] Trivella, a modest and conscientious singing teacher. We were astonished by this exceptional voice and Kalomiris admitted her into the conservatory at once, with free tuition."[12]

—⁂—

Manolis Kalomiris (1883–1962) was born and educated in Smyrna, and it was there that he had his first music lessons. He continued his musical studies in Athens (1894–99), in Constantinople, and at the Gesellschaft der Musikfreunde in Vienna (1901–06). In 1908 he made his first appearance in Greece at a concert of his own compositions at the Athens Conservatory, where he subsequently (1911–19) taught piano, harmony, and advanced theory. A naturally ebullient man, he had grown up in what were then the three greatest historic centers of Hellenism and had lived through the triumphs of the Balkan Wars and the nationalistic fervor of Eleftherios Venizelos's short-lived dream of re-creating the Greater Greece of earlier centuries. As a composer, consequently, he more than anyone else was the embodiment of the national school in Greek music, which set out to counter the westernizing tendencies of composers from the Ionian Islands. In 1919 he founded the Hellenic Conservatory, but in 1926 he left it and founded the National. Within a few years the National Conservatory was turning out internationally recognized opera singers, like Nicola Moscona and Elena Nikolaidi, who, in 1937, were already singing at the Metropolitan in New York and the Vienna State Opera, respectively.

Manolis Kalomiris (right) with Dimitri Mitropoulos, Athens, early 1920s.

The inspiration and driving force behind the National Conservatory was Kalomiris himself, who was its principal until 1948. He admired and encouraged enterprise, especially in young musicians, and he was not as strict and fussy about the compulsory subjects as some others, such as Filoktitis Ikonomidis, the principal of the Athens Conservatory. One of his critics in this context was the conductor Andreas Paridis: "Kalomiris used to hand out diplomas to all and sundry because he believed it was better to send young people out into the world as musicians than as something else. But in that way the National Conservatory turned out a lot of half-trained students." As defined by Kalomiris himself, the functions of the National Conservatory were threefold: a "purely artistic" function (which mainly involved propagating, supporting, and giving recognition to Greek music), an "operatic" function, and a "purely educational" function. In the late 1930s around sixty of its approximately two hundred singing students received free tuition, either "on the recommendation of the City of Athens" or "by courtesy of the professors and teaching staff."[13]

In 1935 the National Conservatory had moved from its original premises to a new building (still standing) at the corner of Solomou and Tritis Septemvriou Streets. The top floor of the building was the principal's residence, where Kalomiris lived with his wife, Hariklia, his daughter Krinó, and his son-in-law Leonidas Zoras. The offices were on the mezzanine and above that were two floors, each with three or four classrooms. For special occasions, such as matinée concerts, award ceremonies, and end-of-year examinations, the partitions between the classrooms on the second floor could be removed to create a sizable auditorium with a small stage and room for two pianos. Kalomiris, who was particularly keen on vocal music (he composed five operas and many other vocal works), supervised the singing classes himself, always attending the end-of-year examinations and signing

The National Conservatory, Solomou and Tritis Septemvriou Streets, Athens.

the mark sheets. Like all Greek conservatories, the National had three grades: lower, intermediate, and advanced. At the end of each year the students went before an examining board for promotion to the next grade, unless their teacher considered that they ought to repeat the year, in which case Kalomiris tested them privately to review the teacher's verdict. Of the twenty-two teachers then employed in the school of singing, six women were full professors, the best known of them being Nina Foka, Smaragda Yennadi, and Marika Kalfopoulou. Maria Trivella, with a short career and only three or four years' teaching experience behind her, was one of the five associate professors. The students at the National Conservatory did not keep the same registration number throughout their time there; they were given a new number at the beginning of each year, and this was recorded beside their name on the mark sheet. Mary's registration number for the year 1937–38 was 891.[14]

—⁊⁊⁊—

Heartened by the scholarship and by Trivella's personal affection and professional dedication, Mary buckled down to work with a will. *"Comforted by that [scholarship], I continued studying voice and piano with a kind of fury,"* she told a journalist later. Litsa confirms this: "Never have I seen her work as she did then. She practiced day and night and sometimes forgot to eat. . . . Maria would refuse to leave her piano for meals, and I would bring them to her in her room. She would put the plate in her lap and go on working."[15] Her zeal, her determination to make her mark and reach the top, was the thing about her that everyone who knew her then remarked on with admiration, mixed with a certain bewilderment. When this rather gauche, austere, unsociable girl was still at the tender age of fourteen or so, her workaholic tendency may not yet have been regarded as an overambitious conceit but was nevertheless annoying to those around her. "At that time Maria was jealous of the other pupils at the conservatory," her own mother wrote, "and many of them disliked her for she was always asserting herself before them."[16]

Yorgos Karakandas well remembered this side of Mary: "As if she could see a vision of her future, she paced nervously to and fro, saying over and over again with deep conviction, *'Some day I'm going to make the big time!'"* In his memoirs, written when Maria was at the zenith of her career, he implies that he admired his pupil's "great zeal and strong will," but in reality it seems that he did not much like her either. Admittedly, Mary had even less liking for Karakandas, and he was probably aware of that. He later said that he had taken Mary into his class at the conservatory "against the advice of some of the senior staff," who objected to her on the grounds of her girth and general appearance. "My dear Maria, how *did* you manage to tame that filly?" he once asked Trivella. And he goes on to inform us that Kalomiris himself "could not stand her." When, on one occasion, the principal apparently ignored her singing and commented on her size, Mary was rude to him and he instantly expelled her. She went home in tears and her mother took her to Karakandas. "I told her that the only way out was for her to apologize to him," Karakandas recalled. "This she did, and she was readmitted to the conservatory."[17]

It is almost universally agreed, then, that Mary was not liked by either her peers or her elders. This is particularly true of her early adolescence, when she was even more insecure than later. All sorts of reasons could be suggested to account for the development of her prickly and withdrawn character: heredity, the family environment in her early childhood, and the pressures that arose when she came to Greece (for example, her poor Greek, which betrayed her social background, her unprepossessing and fast deteriorating appearance, and the family's straitened financial circumstances). All these would explain why, although so young and soon to be spectacularly successful, Mary was rather distant and unsociable and at the same time occasionally aggressive and even insolent, why she found it so hard to communicate, and why she was so curiously standoffish toward most of the people around her.

One thing Mary did already have in abundance, however, and that was a rare musicality. This instinctive "feel" for music is something that other people have to be taught and some never acquire, even to a lesser degree, but with her it was a divine, inborn gift. And it was because she possessed this faculty, this innate musical knowledge, that she never set a very high value on the necessity of theoretical musical studies. But whether she liked it or not, at the age of fourteen she had to learn some theory. "*Before you reach the great roles you learn music, solfège, history of music—you know, just many hours,*" she admitted in 1970.[18] In point of fact, although Mary's name does not appear in the National Conservatory's records for 1937–38 as a student of any subject other than singing, according to her classmate Yorgos Vokos (later a teacher at the National Conservatory and a music critic) she also attended music history classes in her first year. And one subject she certainly did take in her first year was acting in Yorgos Karakandas's opera class.

Karakandas always maintained in his lessons that the future of opera depended on acting. In a letter to the press in 1977 he wrote boastfully, "I taught her—and she followed my advice, which is the main reason she became famous— that the opera artist must base his or her performance on acting." However, it was also part of Karakandas's teaching that "the first genius in opera is the writer . . . and after him the composer, who, taking his inspiration from the words, embellishes and puts the finishing touches to the work in the sublime language of music." And Mary reacted instinctively against this precept of her teacher's, which later she was to reject flatly, always insisting that in opera the composer was the one who really counted. Operatic performers, she would maintain, ought to see themselves as the composer's humble servants in order to re-create what he had created: "*The first duty of a singer, of a musician, is to try to feel what the composer wanted,*" she said in 1968. Certainly the vast majority of operatic libretti are so thin, have so little literary merit, and give such a distorted version of historical facts that they will not stand comparison with the original works from which they are taken, still less with the composer's musical creation. So it would appear that, in spite of her natural bent for acting, Karakandas's opinions and teaching methods did not go down at all well with Mary from the outset: as Litsa wrote, "She actually preferred to teach herself."[19]

Besides Karakandas, Trivella also taught Mary acting. "That was the most difficult part, because at that time Mary was a lump and moved awkwardly," Penelope Adali recalls. "My aunt was small and very supple, and she tried to get Mary

Yorgos Karakandas, 1948.

to put a bit more flexibility into her body movements too. Right here in the hall she would make Mary practice falling, over and over again. 'Come on, Mary!' I would hear her say encouragingly." Maria herself still remembered this part of her training thirty years later: "*I was taught then, when I was fourteen years old, the continuous flowing of a movement. It was always this movement of the arms and hands, which means freedom. Also how to fall down. It was really something to laugh [at]. To learn how to fall well—and you can't always fall the same way—you have to completely relax yourself and forget how you are going to fall. A slight tenseness and you hurt yourself. Then you also have to learn how this woman would fall and how that one would fall, etc.*"[20] However, this and much else that she learned initially from Trivella (who also gave Mary her first French lessons, since many of the pieces she assigned her to learn were in French) Maria conveniently forgot to mention in later life, or, worse still, she gave all the credit for them to her second teacher, Elvira de Hidalgo.

Yorgos Vokos remembered Mary making the floorboards creak as she entered the classroom with her heavy tread. Whenever Rosa Zarb, the conservatory's administrator, with the "deep, masculine voice and piercing eye," remonstrated with her, Mary would answer meekly, "*Yes, Madame Rosa . . .*" Rosa Zarb, a tall woman with a forbidding presence and despotic manner, was feared by all the students. If she heard Mary talking too loudly to another student she would speak to her sternly: "Don't let me hear your voice again! Go into your [singing] class if you want to shout!" And Mary, red as a beet, would stammer, "*Sorry, Madame Rosa . . .*"[21]

Vokos also remembered how regular Mary was in her attendance at the conservatory, and how punctual she always was. But Trivella apparently used to arrive even earlier and wait for her beloved pupil in the hall. After greeting each other with endless hugs, kisses, and loud endearments under the stern eye of Madame Rosa, they would go into the classroom for their lesson. "I remember how we, younger students, often hung about in the hall and listened to Kaloyeropoulou's voice exercises," Vokos stated. "She had a brilliant ear. Whatever exercise Trivella played for her on the piano, she sang it right at the first go, almost. Even then she showed that she had some sort of musical genius in her. . . . We would hear Maria doing her vocal acrobatics—trills, runs, phrases, *legati, staccati,* scales—and every so often Trivella's voice exclaiming, 'Well done, Maria, well done!' '*But my passage-work was terrible, my trills were only half there, my legati were awful.*' 'But, Maria . . .' '*No, no, I must do it again from the beginning! I've got to satisfy myself, too. I'm sorry.*' So once more *da capo,* until Kaloyeropoulou gave it her O.K."[22]

Before long even the teaching staff was talking about Mary as a new student of exceptional promise. One thing that particularly impressed Vokos was her uncompromisingly self-critical approach to her work, remarkable in one so young: he thought in fact that she was rather stricter with herself than her teacher was. "Even in those days she was never satisfied with herself. As a young girl she worked on her voice interminably, taking care over every detail to make sure that the pitch of the note came out just so, the tone just that little bit different, always trying to inject as much musicality as possible in the way *she* wanted, the way her unerring musical instinct told her." Vokos's views are echoed by everybody else who remembered Mary at the National Conservatory in those very early days: she displayed "a vocal gigantism"; her talent was "overflowing"; she was an exceptionally quick learner; she could sol-fa at sight; she would pick up her part and devour it and almost immediately sing it note for note. But the greatest of all her qualities, even then, was the expressive power she put into her singing. On the other hand, Vokos remarked that her voice was not of the highest quality and her tone did not then have the brilliance it had later.[23]

Indeed, Vokos's very significant criticism was that Mary already had an excessive vibrato in her voice. This is a matter of the greatest importance, as the wobble so clearly audible in Maria's voice at times from the mid-1950s onward was and still is the main fault her critics have found with her art. To establish whether it was inherent in her voice from birth—or at least acquired at a very early age, and if so how and why—would help us understand the fundamental problem that affected Maria's voice later in her career, also causing her not negligible psychological stress. Opinions differ as to the causes of the wobble among those who noticed it during her early years in Greece; but most of them, especially her classmates, are agreed that the problem did exist from the beginning of her time at the conservatory. According to Zannis Kambanis, "Her voice had that wobble when she was studying with Trivella and I remember it both the times I sang with her. But she never took any notice of what anybody said." Her classmate Vyron Simiriotis, the first tenor with whom Mary ever sang a whole opera on stage, *Cavalleria Rusticana,* confirms: "She did have a beautiful voice, though I myself would have preferred it a bit mellower. Her voice in those days was very stentorian and not always the voice of a lyric soprano; sometimes actually more of a mezzo. But on her high notes she had a bit of vibrato, a ripple. It wasn't unpleasant to listen to, but there clearly was that undulating effect."[24]

—ɯ—

Why did you take up singing?

Because they made me take up singing. When you're thirteen, it's your father and mother who decide things for you. And that's what they decided. . . . No, I didn't choose a singing career. I didn't really have any confidence in [my] singing, I didn't believe I had a voice. But since my mother was so insistent, and since I didn't have any money during the war to pay a singing teacher at the conservatory, I always won scholarships, and that made me feel sure that I had talent. But I never really believed in myself. Yet there was nothing else I knew how to do.

To Micheline Banzet, Paris, February 1965

CHAPTER 11

A Crisis with
Grave Consequences

Just as Mary's life seemed to be settling down to some sort of rhythm, with her days spent almost entirely on music lessons and practicing, the landlord of the house at the end of Patission Street decided he wanted to live there himself. So Litsa and the girls spent most of the winter of 1937–38 in "a beautiful and very old house," but so cold that Mary could hardly work.[1] The exact location of this, their fourth home in Athens, is not known, but it was probably at or near the corner of Patission and Guilfordou Streets. This house was only a few minutes' walk from the National Conservatory on Solomou Street. When Mary had lessons with Trivella there, she always arranged them for about lunchtime. Afterward she would walk home and stay there until it was time for her to go back to the conservatory for the compulsory theory lessons in the late afternoon. One day Trivella introduced her to one of Kalfopoulou's pupils, a young soprano named Afroditi Kopanou, whose father had also lived in America. Kopanou remembers Mary wearing her school uniform overall with a white collar and white bobby socks. "We often went and sat on a bench in front of the archaeological museum," she recalls, "where we would buy a drachma's worth of melon seeds and talk about music and the conservatory."[2]

Meanwhile Litsa had begun to break away from her mother and her brothers and sisters. Argumentative as she was by nature, and having come to realize that she had no hope of being supported by her family, one day she picked a quarrel with Doukas which led to a full-scale row with their mother. Most probably she had been refused some more money, and the resulting argument had blown up into an angry scene. Litsa's severance of relations with her mother inevitably invites comparison with Mary's progressive estrangement from Litsa and the final breach between them. Admittedly the two cases were very different, but there was one factor common to both: Litsa's appeals for money and her conviction that it was only because of "unreasonable" meanness that she was refused financial assistance. Indeed, years later she would feel just the same about Mary. Although their final breach in 1951 would be due to complex and deep-rooted psychological factors, on the surface the quarrel would be over money matters, just as disagreements over money must have ignited the spark that led to Litsa's break with her own mother and the rest of the Dimitriadis family.[3] In both cases, each time with Litsa the protagonist, we have a fairly abrupt severance of relations between mother and daughter, a most unusual phenomenon in middle-class Greek families of that period.

Jackie was devastated at the proscription of her beloved grandmother, whom she describes as "an island of loving calm, of decent good sense in the restless tides of my mother's insatiable ambition."[4] Of the magnitude of Litsa's ambitions, mainly social but professional and financial as well, there can indeed be no doubt. However, it would be wrong to overlook the fact that at that time she was under great psychological and practical pressure. She was homeless in a strange city, practically penniless, and the responsibility for her daughters' future weighed heavily on her. So, to make ends meet for herself and her daughters, as the remittances that arrived sporadically from America were not enough for them to live on, Litsa decided to try and make new contacts that might prove useful. And there could have been no greater godsend than her chance meeting with Miltiadis and Hariton Embirikos, scions of the well-known shipowning family.

Jackie relates how they met at the office of a notary who happened to have the two brothers in to see him at the time. Hariton, the first of the two to fall for Jackie's good looks, recalled that she was "completely Americanized, but light on her feet and very beautiful, with flamboyant good looks and graceful poise." Litsa, with her nose for social status and affluence, picked the brothers out immediately as good prospects and left Jackie in no doubt as to what she thought about them. Soon Hariton invited Jackie to a *thè-dansant* at the chic Cecil Hotel in Kifissia, but he spoiled everything by making a pass at her too abruptly. Although he asked her out again, this time to Zonar's, a fashionable café-patisserie near Syntagma Square, he sent in his stead his elder brother Miltiadis, who had asked to be introduced to Jackie himself. Miltiadis, a reserved young man of thirty-two who had enough panache to drive a flashy Cadillac-Lincoln two-seater roadster, immediately captured the interest of the twenty-year-old Jackie. At the same time he "went out of his way to be pleasant to Mother, who at first acquaintance could be very charming," as Jackie puts it. Milton (as Jackie called him) soon became a frequent visitor to their house where, after witnessing minor arguments and petty family squabbles, he came to see Litsa in her true light and to realize how domineering she was with her daughters. On their drives or walks in the country around Athens both Litsa and Mary often came along too, but Mary was too young to go out with them in the evenings—with one notable exception. [5]

Incredible though it seems to us now, Mary had still never actually been to the opera. "One day," Jackie says in her book, "Milton announced that he had got us all tickets for the Lyric [sic] Theater. We were to see *La Traviata*." It so happens that this opera was staged only once in Athens that year, at a "special performance" on 2 February 1938, so the date of this highly significant moment in Mary's life

Miltiadis Embirikos, 1936.

can be fixed with certainty. It was an ad hoc production, as usual, put on by the Hellenic Melodrama at the Olympia Theater on Akadimias Street, with Michalis Thomakos as Alfredo, Vangelis Mangliveras as Germont, and Maria Drakatou as Violetta. To Drakatou, then, an otherwise unmemorable singer, goes the honor of having been the first prima donna that Mary ever saw on stage.[6] Although later, with hindsight, Jackie described the performance as "a tired old production of no particular merit, the sort of thing that puts many people off opera for life," at the time, when it was over and she turned to look at her sister, she saw "someone transformed with sheer pleasure. She was in another world. She had in fact entered her own world."[7]

Sometime in February or early March 1938, a year after her arrival in Greece, Litsa and the girls had to move for the fifth time in just over a year.[8] By this time they were in such dire financial straits that, although they had no furniture of their own, they rented an unfurnished apartment. Litsa asked Jackie not to bring Miltiadis to see them in these bare surroundings: at all costs, he should not realize that the three of them were sleeping on the floor, living out of the suitcases and trunks containing mainly what they had brought from America. Furious with the absent George and constantly railing against him for his inability to support his family, Litsa threatened her daughters with horrible punishments if they ever let anybody suspect the truth about their plight, which she was sure would lead to their social ostracism.[9] But the situation only went from bad to worse, until eventually they could not even pay the rent and were in imminent danger of being turned out into the street. Litsa was then forced to play her last card: rejecting Jackie's suggestion that they go back to America, where George would be legally bound to support them, she dragooned her daughter into telling her wealthy admirer the whole truth. This diplomatic appeal for help in saving the family from humiliation—a humiliation which would probably have spelled the end of Jackie's relationship with Miltiadis—had the desired effect.

Miltiadis went around to the apartment at once and was horrified by what he saw. "Within a matter of days tradesmen were delivering furniture, a maid had been hired, the larder was full—all at the expense of Milton Embirikos," Jackie records, omitting to mention that from then on he would also be paying their rent and settling all their bills. "Mary would have her voice; I had been offered in exchange," she adds pathetically.[10] Humiliated though she felt, Jackie was in too desperate a plight to do anything but accept, hoping that one day the situation would change. After all, she told herself, Milton loved her, he was a gentleman and he treated her generously, moving in high society and taking her to places that she had not even known existed. What was more, by following this course of action she would be helping her mother and sister, who ought to be grateful for her indirect contribution to their material well-being. And these arguments were enough to salve Jackie's conscience.

The first-floor apartment where they were living, no longer unfurnished, was at 70 Harilaou Trikoupi Street, at its intersection with Dervenion Street, in Neapolis, which in those days was something like the old Latin Quarter in Paris: it had the Institut Français and the German School at its center and the university, the polytechnic, the school of fine arts, and the Olympia Theater, the hub of the city's musical life, on its fringes. Many writers and artists lived there, and most of the houses rented out spare rooms to students. The streets were unpaved, apart from Ippokratous Street, the main artery along which the green streetcars rumbled on their way. On summer evenings, after the watering-cart had been by to lay the dust and take the edge off the heat, the women would carry chairs out into the road and sit there knitting and chatting with their neighbors, while the men went off to the "local" to play billiards or sing to the accompaniment of ukuleles. One of these establishments was the coffeehouse of Kyr-Andreas, next door to the house where the three "crazy Americans," as Litsa and her daughters were referred to, lived.

The building, then new and still standing today, had shops on the ground floor and four apartments on two upper floors. The main entrance had a short flight of marble steps and a plain iron-frame door, and inside was a marble staircase leading to the upper levels. The first floor of apartments was occupied by the Kaloyeropoulos family and by Dr. Spyros Katiforis and his wife, Christina, a phar-

The first-floor apartment at 70 Harilaou Trikoupi Street, Athens.

macist. The apartment of Litsa and her daughters consisted of three rather small rooms plus kitchen and bathroom and extended all along one side of the building, overlooking Dervenion Street. The sitting room was on the corner, with one of its windows looking out on Harilaou Trikoupi Street, while the kitchen was behind the stairwell, backing on to the Katifori kitchen. Litsa got on well with Christina and her family, with whom she exchanged visits regularly. Ismini Thiveou, one of Christina's three sisters, and Nada Tzaka, the daughter of another, have given vivid descriptions of the everyday life and atmosphere during the year and a half or so that Litsa, Jackie, and Mary spent there.[11]

—⁓—

Throughout this protracted crisis Mary took little part in coping with practical problems. Naturally, when she was at home, she helped with the housework, such as it was, but on the whole she just lived the life of a singing student on a scholarship. "That was when I learned the meaning of serious practicing and professionalism in a student," says their neighbor Dinos Petroyannis. "Her voice was so big that it roused the whole neighborhood, especially me, as I lived just a few yards away from the room where she practiced. She never stopped—exercises, vocalises, pieces from her repertoire, the lot."[12] Although her life seemed on the surface not to have been disrupted as much as her mother's or her sister's, the truth is that the threat of utter penury on the one hand, and Litsa's exploitation of Jackie to rescue the family on the other, left a mark on the fourteen-year-old's character that was to affect her for the rest of her life.

To take the money problem first, this was the first time that Mary had been so directly, almost tangibly, threatened by the specter of real poverty and perhaps even starvation. They had known hard times in America but that had been in the context of a stable family home with a much-loved father to support them, so she had never felt really threatened. Now, however, things were very different. Although she herself never talked about this critical period of her life, her memories of that time—the three of them alone in the world, sleeping on the floor of the bare apartment, with the threat of eviction and humiliation hanging over them—must have been one of the main factors behind the pathological financial insecurity that Maria suffered from throughout her life. And that insecurity was to be the cause of occasional acts and omissions which led to her being branded (sometimes unfairly) as a skinflint.

The other matter that deeply affected Mary was the fact that she was cushioned against poverty by Jackie's relationship with Miltiadis, a relationship into which her sister had been pushed by their own mother. This was to have complex consequences: much of Maria's behavior in later life can be traced back to these crucial events of her impressionable childhood and adolescence, which implanted in her a core of rigid puritanism streaked with touches of middle-class priggishness. In the first place, the acquisition of a "protector" for the family at Litsa's instigation opened Mary's eyes to the absence of moral principles in the one person who should have set her a strict example of moral conduct. Litsa, already guilty of treating George so cruelly, now stood convicted on another grave charge, that of moral elasticity. From this point on, every moral lapse of Litsa's—and there were to be others, often of a much more serious nature—aroused Mary's disgust, contempt, and hostility, which she sometimes expressed openly but mostly kept bottled up inside her, until their final breach in 1951.

Secondly, while Jackie's willingness to be used as bait for the sake of the family's economic survival may have won her mother's gratitude and admiration, it made her younger sister like and respect her less. Like most young teenagers, Mary had uncompromising ideas about propriety and had not yet learned enough tolerance to accept that Jackie's position was extremely difficult, for her sister knew that her refusal to go along with Litsa's plan would have incalculable consequences, not only for herself but for her mother and sister as well. No doubt Maria later came to understand and excuse Jackie's compliance, but to Mary, at her age then, that was impossible. She must have been extremely angry, and she does not seem to have made any attempt to hide it. "*I'm going to get to the top,*" she is said to have yelled at Jackie once, when they were quarreling, "*but I don't know what* you *are going to do. Right now, you're selling yourself to Embirikos!*" or even harsher words to that effect.[13]

More than ten years later, Mary's feelings about Jackie's "moral lapse" would still be bitter. This made Litsa—whose conscience still troubled her—come out in Jackie's defense, in a letter to Mary in September 1949, during the crucial period of her daughter's distancing process: "Your sister, the one who is so hollow, as you write, . . . offered herself solely in order to save you and me. [When] we lived [on Patission], and you were just fourteen, you kept asking me for ice cream . . . . I remember well a few words that your sister told me then: 'Mother, do search and find three drachmas, so that Mary may not yet know what misery is. It is a pity to let her know so young that we don't even have three drachmas.' How can I forget these words, my daughter . . . ? You don't remember, nor did we let you feel our worries. And Jackie was responsible for this, as was her destruction [a sacrifice] for our sake. And don't get angry, you must admit it: your sister would never have given herself had it not been for the material question [of our survival]."[14]

Mary's antagonistic attitude to Jackie had other ramifications too, in which the connection between cause and effect is harder to trace. Photographs taken of Jackie when she was approaching twenty show that she had grown into a strikingly beautiful young woman. Poor Mary, then going through the awkward stage of adolescence, only made things worse with her compulsive overeating. According to Jackie, it was about this time that Mary started stuffing herself with rich and heavy Greek food at the oddest hours, sometimes even in the middle of the night: "She had always had plump ankles and now they thickened badly. . . . As she got more and more unattractive she submerged her misery by consuming more and more platefuls of food."[15] Before long the contrast in looks between the two girls was so marked that Mary began to suffer from a severe inferiority complex, which she usually externalized in aggressive behavior.

What upset Mary most about all this was the way her mother kept comparing her unfavorably with her sister. Instead of trying to treat the two of them as equally as possible, Litsa was now always harping on the theme of Jackie's superiority, all the more so as Jackie had saved them from financial and social ruin. In material terms, after all, the future of all three of them depended entirely on the continuation of her relationship with Miltiadis, and Litsa, in her usual thoughtless and misguided way, lost no opportunity to show up her younger daughter, recalls Ismini Thiveou: "'What are *you* doing for us?' she would say to Mary. 'God knows how we'd survive without Jackie!'" And as Litsa and Mary were both quick-tempered, when either of them was under strain they would flare up over the most trivial issues. "Mary often provoked her mother," Nada Tzaka confirms, "by saying to her imperiously, *'Just go away, will you? You're bothering me. I want to practice!'*" Dinos Petroyannis also remembers frequent shouting matches between them: "They had terrible fights which were audible throughout the neighborhood, and as they didn't seem overconcerned about being discreet, people often heard things that added a bit of spice to the local gossip."[16] But these petty quarrels, rowdy though they may have been, did not matter as much to Mary as her mother's obvious partiality for Jackie.

This favoritism—persistently denied by both Jackie and Litsa but roundly condemned by all Mary's relatives, friends, acquaintances, and fellow singers—was deeply upsetting to Mary. Though not necessarily occasioned by important matters nor always put into words, it was displayed openly and at all times, and Mary found it particularly irritating when it touched on her weak points. One example of Litsa's preferential treatment of Jackie was the difference in the way the two girls dressed. This was a matter of comment throughout the time they were in Athens, and comparisons were invariably to Mary's disadvantage. "At the Athens Conservatory," says Niki Zacharopoulou, who was then a piano student there, "Jackie was the belle of the year, well dressed and well turned-out generally. Mary, poor girl, used to wear a plain black smock buttoned down the front, with a white collar that was often filthy dirty. The contrast was pitiful. Poor little thing!" Maria herself was later to remark ruefully, *"My mother had a mania for dark-colored frocks with a white collar."*[17]

Mary (left) with her mother and sister, Athens 1938 or 1939.

Most mothers, surely, would take more care over the appearance of the less attractive daughter than of the one who was not only good-looking but also had a rich man to look after her. The most convincing explanation of Litsa's attitude was suggested by Ismini Thiveou, who heard it from her sister Christina, which almost certainly means that it had originally come from Litsa herself: "She didn't dress her well in case some young man fell for her and turned her head. She was so worried that someone would seduce her away from music!" Evidently, the mother who had pushed one of her daughters into the arms of a rich suitor, deliberately kept her other daughter looking as plain and dowdy as possible, in case she caught the eye of some man who might prevent her from developing into a successful music-making—and money-making—machine. The tenor Andonis Kalaidzakis, who later gave singing lessons to Jackie and talked to Litsa about Mary, agrees that the mother deliberately neglected her younger daughter to reduce the likelihood of her falling in love and being swept off her feet. "She had an intuition that her daughter was going to be a great singer and I think that one of the reasons for doing what she did was to instill in her a desire to make a success of her career. Singing was fine, in other words, but it ought to bring her some material benefit—some money—as well."[18]

Litsa did succeed in her object at first: by the start of the academic year 1938–39 Mary was a most unattractive sight. "I don't think any man would ever have taken any notice of her," Nada comments. "She was an eyesore in those days!" This verdict is supported by some of the men who were Mary's classmates at the time. "She looked so awful that we took no notice of her," says Stefanos Chiotakis, who was a pupil of Smaragda Yennadi at the National Conservatory. Spyros Salingaros, de Hidalgo's pupil at the Athens Conservatory, shares this view: "And she gave the general impression that she just didn't care what she looked like. At the beach, in her bathing suit, she was a terrible sight, and on top of it all she bit her fingernails," he adds. Even worse, according to Jackie, "Her skin was allergic to perfumes and deodorants and in the heat of an Athens summer this caused her serious embarrassment."[19]

At first the two sisters shared a bedroom; later, what with Jackie's burgeoning relationship with Miltiadis and frequent late nights, Mary asked to sleep on her own. Even Jackie admits that the affair with Miltiadis had turned Mary against her: "She had found out about me and Milton and, prudishly shocked, was no longer prepared to accept my elder sister role as she had in the past. But then Milton paid all our expenses, as we had absolutely no money coming in," she reiterates rather truculently: "The rent, the piano, her teachers [sic], her food. Mary went short of nothing! But I think she loved me. She had nothing against me, she was just jealous." Eyewitness accounts of everyday life at Harilaou Trikoupi Street, however, leave no doubt as to the tension that was always in the air, ready to explode at any moment. "I was constantly hearing Mary having her screaming fits," says Nada. "If anybody contradicted her, she flared up immediately and started shouting. She was terribly jealous of Jackie, and so she would pick a quarrel at the slightest excuse: Jackie came in and stopped her practicing, Jackie woke her up by coming home so late at night, and so on. Then she could be heard all over the building, because when she was angry she became hysterical. Breaking glasses, ashtrays, anything that came to hand, hurling them to the floor to relieve her tension. I saw her do that in their kitchen—crash, smash!—screaming and howling as if she were acting a part on stage."[20]

Jackie, 1938
or 1939.

In an attempt to explain her sister's emotional instability, Jackie suggests, among other things, that she was "without mother love," that she wanted "the sort of success with boys" that she had, and that she was lonely. There can be no doubt that each of these factors, to one extent or another, contributed to Mary's irritable state of mind. Self-consciousness about her lack of success with the opposite sex would even have been heightened by the attitude of her sister, who admits that she occasionally behaved badly, deliberately spoiling things for Mary.[21] Such behavior would obviously have hurt and angered Mary, who was younger and less attractive and had no Miltiadis to love and care for her. Mary's complex about her weight, coupled with her self-consciousness about her fat legs and periodic recurrences of bad acne, now inflicted yet another psychological trauma on her: she felt that she was unable to attract men, unable to express and satisfy her sexuality.

Add to this the insecurity caused by her penury and her utter social inadequacy and much is explained, especially her antagonistic attitude both toward Jackie and the world in general. It was then, indeed, during and immediately following the hardships and financial pressure of 1938 on Harilaou Trikoupi Street, that the foundations were laid of Mary's obsessive competitiveness, soon to be fueled by the competition that thrives in all theater and opera companies. It was to remain a driving force throughout her life, with some positive consequences (without it she would perhaps never have risen to be a great diva) but negative as well (such as the effect it had on her manner, which was frequently taken for arrogance).

Dinos Petroyannis tells a story that illustrates this antagonistic side of Mary's character well: "Just across the road from Mary and me, there lived an amateur tenor a bit older than us called Falakras. One evening, when there was a lull in the singing and ukulele-playing from Kyr-Andreas's coffeehouse, Falakras was heard singing the popular song 'O Yero-Dimos.' The neighbors' applause had hardly died down when Mary was heard singing the same song from her apartment, accompanying herself on the piano. Obviously she wanted to show everyone how much better she could do it, and she certainly won more applause! I don't know what got into me, but I then started singing the song myself, in a piping treble. Probably because everyone was so taken by surprise, I got more applause than either of the others, which piqued Mary so much that when we crossed each other in the street the next day she cut me dead!"[22] Mary's jealousy of anybody who got more applause than she did lasted well into her early years as a professional singer in Athens, and probably throughout her career.

The stresses in Mary's everyday life were soon to be compounded by yet another problem, which was to be one of the most serious. As we have seen, apart from her music, Mary had no way of escaping from the suffocating atmosphere at home. At that time she never went out on her own or with friends, and only occasionally did she go somewhere with her mother, Jackie, and Miltiadis. By 1939, however, with the financial crisis overcome and the apartment put into shape, Litsa took to asking friends in, among them a Navy officer and a lawyer who was an amateur violinist. "That was when she also started seeing a lot of an army officer, Menis Fotopoulos," remembers Nada Tzaka. "He was an almost daily visitor, very attentive to her as he evidently adored her. He was quite a bit younger than her and it was rumored that he had once been on the verge of committing suicide on her account." Although Jackie describes Fotopoulos simply as "a family friend from Meligalas," he had apparently been seriously involved with the girls' aunt, Pipitsa Dimitriadou, whom he planned to marry until the unprincipled Litsa appeared on the scene.[23]

So within a short time of her separation from George, Litsa had started leading an independent life of her own, openly entertaining men friends at home. What was notable about her behavior was not that she had such relationships, but that she made no attempt to conceal them from her daughters. Fifteen-year-old

Mary and Jackie (wearing identical overcoats) with Menis Fotopoulos and a friend, Maroussi 1939.

Mary, whose feelings with regard to her father and Litsa's treatment of him have already been described, must have been extremely shocked and upset. Most probably she felt that it was up to her to defend the honor of her absent father, a daunting responsibility indeed, which only worsened her relations with her mother at what was already such a stressful time. From that point on, Litsa, who must have justified her harsh treatment of her husband on the grounds of George's infidelities, forfeited the only plea that her daughter could accept in extenuation of her "crime" of desertion. So the presence of men in Litsa's life, which would otherwise have been quite normal for a woman still young and attractive as she was, became for Mary extremely reprehensible. And her mother's conduct was to become even more provocative in the next few years, widening the rift between them until it was beyond repair.

—∭—

Mary reacted to the weight of this cumulative burden of stress not by sinking into depression or simply giving up, but by laying the foundations of her musical career: a herculean task for a girl of her age. Apart from the inner strength that enabled her to preserve her mental equilibrium, what saved her then was the fact that she chose the escape route she did, by deciding to devote all her energies to music. Making the most of her natural gifts, which she rightly believed to be exceptional, she realized that her voice offered her the only chance she had of escaping from her soul-destroying predicament, making her way up in the world and giving proof of her merit, her superiority. To Mary, in other words, this ordeal was a necessary evil: it was this that drove her to choose her path in life and start out on her phenomenal career. For the fact is that the traumatized, gluttonous, unsightly, unpredictable girl who was Mary at fifteen was none other than Maria Callas in embryo. *"I'm going to succeed, and people are going to talk about me!"* she would often say, with increasing self-confidence, especially if anyone questioned her ability. And sometimes, taking it one step further, she would give vent to a primitive, earthy affirmation of her angry determination: *"And I'll walk over dead bodies if I have to!"*[24]

Having reached this turning point, Mary stopped caring about what she looked like; she suppressed her sexuality and had no qualms about eating as much as she liked. The facing doors of the Kaloyeropoulos and Katiforis kitchens were nearly always open. "When they first moved in they hardly had anything to eat," Ismini Thiveou remembers. "So Christina, who saw Mary every time she came and went and was sorry for her, took to inviting her in. Mary, who adored Christina in those days, caught on immediately. *'Hello, Christina, what have you got to eat today?'* she would say. And she had lunch there nearly every day." Litsa had presumably let her neighbors know her views on keeping the voice well fed, and the other housewives in the building used to bring her food for Mary, without letting their husbands know. "She devoured anything that was put in front of her," says Ismini. "And then, to lose weight, she would sit on a woolen rug, with her legs in the air, and polish the floor by sliding her ample bottom from side to side!"[25]

Nada Tzaka describes another, even more extraordinary scene: "One day her food had been put out in the kitchen, where she usually had her meals, when suddenly from our kitchen we heard a terrific uproar and Mary yelling, *'Dirty rotten cat! It's eaten my fooooood!'* We all came running and I remember seeing Mary holding a cat by its tail, whirling it around and flinging it out over the fire escape. I was only a little girl then, and I burst into tears. The wretched creature had eaten her food, and in such matters Mary was quite capable of murder!" Nada, however, goes on to add that had Mary not been as she was, her mother would have crushed her, just as she crushed Jackie. "But Litsa couldn't make Mary do what she wanted, and that infuriated her beyond words." Although Mary was working at her music as avidly as ever, it never seemed to be enough for Litsa, who was always pestering her: "She even used to come to the conservatory to check up on what her daughter was doing, much to Mary's annoyance," says Vyron Simiriotis. "Her mother maddened her. 'Get on with it! Down to work! More!' she kept telling her," recalls Ismini Thiveou. "And sometimes she would even want to 'help' Mary with her practicing. I even saw her trying to take the part of whoever was supposed to be partnering her!"[26]

Meanwhile Jackie, who had been forbidden to find a job, was working harder at her piano. Miltiadis had provided the household with a piano, which was placed in the living room, diagonally, between the two corner windows. When Mary practiced her singing in the small, low-ceilinged room, her voice reverberated through the whole building and the windows rattled in their frames. One day, when none of the windows were open, she is said to have broken a pane with one of her high notes. "It's absolutely true," Nada insists, "and her mother shouted at her because of the cold draft!"* And every day Mary would leave home with her music under her arm, on her way to the haven of the conservatory or Trivella's little house. What is truly remarkable is that, throughout this period of intense stress and against the background of her stultifying environment, she was able to make steady progress with her work, actually preparing for her musical baptism by fire.

—ɯ—

My mother was the one who thought about selecting my clothes, and she didn't allow me to stay in front of the mirror for more than five minutes. I had to study, I couldn't "waste time with nonsense," and certainly I owe it to her strictness that now, at just thirty-three, I have vast and extensive artistic experience. But on the other hand, I was deprived entirely of the joys of adolescence and of its innocent pleasures, those that are fresh, naïve, and irreplaceable. I forgot to say that, by way of compensation, I got fat. Using the excuse that in order to sing well one needs to be hefty and blooming, I stuffed myself, morning and night, with pasta, chocolate, bread and butter, and zabaglione. I was rotund and rosy, with a quantity of pimples that drove me mad.

To Anita Pensotti (*Oggi*, January–February 1957)

---

*This account is also vouched for by Nada's nephew Angelos Papadimitriou, who heard it many times from Christina and her sisters: "After that, whenever Mary sang, her mother rushed to open the windows so that they wouldn't break," he adds. For a similar incident in 1945, see Chapter 34. In a television interview in 1969 (L'INVITÉ) Maria herself told a story about the French tenor Gilbert Duprez who, when singing with Rossini at the piano, once sang the high C from *Guglielmo Tell* with such force that the composer rushed out to see if his collection of Venetian glass had survived. Technically speaking, the phenomenon depends on the volume and frequency of the sound emitted. When the capacity of the glass to absorb energy is exceeded, the glass breaks.

CHAPTER 12

Baptism by Fire

It is doubtful whether Mary attended classes for the entire autumn term of 1937. The mark sheet for Trivella's class for that period has blanks against the name "891, Kaloyeropoulou G. M.," where there should be marks for application (awarded by her teacher for classwork) and progress (awarded by an examiner at the end of each term). It may be significant that her name comes ninth and last in the list of students in the class. By the end of six months of daily lessons of about an hour with Trivella, Mary had made remarkable progress. Jackie says in her book that Mary was always practicing: not only endless vocalises but exercises to strengthen her diaphragm as well. At first she limited herself to simple songs, and it was "only" in the spring of 1938 that she started practicing her first operatic arias. At the same time, she was studying opera both with Karakandas at the conservatory and with Trivella on Hoffmann Street. Trivella also gave her elocution lessons to improve her Greek diction and pronunciation.[1]

Mary's teacher was so pleased with her progress that she decided to put her on the stage at the annual exhibition concert of her class. Whereas the students' regular open practice sessions were held in the auditorium of the conservatory, for the class exhibition concerts Kalomiris usually rented Parnassos Hall on Karytsi Square. Besides the students' relations and friends, the audiences always included a good number of musicians, critics, and ardent music-lovers who wanted to cast an eye over the year's crop of budding talent. All in all, these concerts can be described as semi-formal but definitely public appearances at which a high musical standard was expected. For Trivella's class of 1937–38 the exhibition concert took place on Monday 11 April at 6:45 p.m. The performers were accompanied by Stefanos Valtetsiotis, highly regarded both as conductor and as accompanist, and besides Mary there were eight other young women and four men, including Zannis Kambanis, who was in his final year.[2]

Mary's excellent progress made Trivella choose her to conclude the program, following three solos by Kambanis. As Marianna Kaloyeropoulou,* she sang three

*At this time Mary was trying to decide which name suited her best. Besides Mary, which was

Near Omonia Square (Panepistimiou and Patission Streets), where Mary walked almost daily during most of her years in Athens.

solos herself, followed by the love duet from Act III of *Tosca*, which she sang with Kambanis. This was the first time she had sung to a prearranged program, with the much greater stress that that entails compared to small gatherings of relatives, friends, and acquaintances with no real musical discrimination, choosing whatever simple pieces she felt like singing at the time. Her program for that first public appearance makes interesting reading, not only because of the wide range of vocal abilities it called for but also for what it tells us about Mary's voice and Trivella's teaching. She started with Agathe's recitative and aria "Leise, leise, fromme Weise" from Act II of *Der Freischütz*, presenting technical difficulties in the *legati* at the beginning and more particularly in the rapid passagework of the second half. This was followed by an aria from Act III of Gounod's now forgotten opera *La Reine de*

---

still the most widely used, especially in the family and among close friends, she found that more and more often she was called Maria, not surprisingly. She herself, however, seems to have liked the name Marianna. In 1944 she had her first calling cards printed with the name MARI-ANNA KALOYEROPOULOU, her first stage name in Greek.

Saba, probably Balkis's cavatina "Plus grand dans son obscurité," a difficult part which Gounod wrote for a soprano "Falcon," that is a dramatic soprano with a particularly well-developed lower register.[3] Mary's third solo was the Greek love song "Two Nights" ("One frosty night in January, I held you tight in my arms…") by Ioannis Psaroudas, a pupil of Massenet, who was then the music critic of the newspaper *Eleftheron Vima*.[4] Finally—no doubt with great dramatic emphasis—Kambanis and Kaloyeropoulou sang "O dolci mani," ending with the tender words of Tosca/Mary, "Gli occhi ti chiuderò con mille baci e mille ti dirò nomi d'amor." This would undoubtedly have been greeted with tumultuous applause, but the critics completely ignored the event—not even Psaroudas wrote it up—while neither Maria nor Litsa ever mentioned it at all. Only Jackie had this to say in her memoirs: "It was terrifying, and Mother and I could hardly breathe until it was over. But when they had finished and the applause was lapping all round us and Kambanis was gesturing Mary forward to take her bow, I suddenly knew that things would never be the same again."[5]

The success of this performance must have given Mary a considerable psychological boost, and not only because it was her first quasi-public appearance. Having been such a short time in Greece, and with only six months' musical training behind her, she was still unknown in Greek musical circles. But she was already beginning to crave recognition of her talent, and many of those who knew her at that time remember her precocious "cockiness," "big talk," and "conceit," most with admiration or amazement but several with annoyance or hostility. For the fact is that Mary's self-assurance was decidedly egocentric and, coming as it did from such a young girl, it was often taken to be (and probably often was) deliberately provocative or antagonistic. It was usually manifested in a brash and insolent manner; that, at least, was the impression she gave when she expressed her absolute faith in herself, whether to young classmates or to well-established singers, teachers, and other musicians. "Mary always spoke her mind," Kambanis recalled, "even though she was so young. She was obsessed by the idea that she was great. She really believed there was no one to match her!"[6]

Now that her music lessons were giving her more liberty, more time away from her mother's critical gaze, she began spending more time with other young people and had her first taste of freedom of movement and speech, even if only in the few hours a week she spent away from home. As a result she gradually became less tolerant of Litsa's attempts to rule her life, and the explosive mixture of her own and her mother's personalities led to increasingly frequent and acrimonious fights. She decided that the time had come to defend herself and was always prepared to answer back, thus raising the pitch of their arguments. They were often heard "having rows," even "abusing each other," and young Mary's vocabulary "shocked some of the more straitlaced neighbors." Her abrupt way of speaking sounded even worse in Greek, which she still spoke with a strong foreign accent. Whether because of an American tendency toward simpler and more direct speech or, more probably, because her Greek was still not very good, she always addressed people in the second person singular and called them by their first names, regardless of their age or social standing.

Mary never showed warmth and friendliness to her peers, nor was she particularly talkative except on subjects to do with music and singing. Very occasionally she would go out with a group of fellow students, without her mother. "Generally she shunned our company," said Zannis Kambanis, who of course was fifteen years her senior. "One day I offered to take her to a little taverna where the food was good and suggested that we might sing a song or two there. '*What on earth for?*' she snapped back." On one occasion, however, she was eventually prevailed upon to go after a lesson to a taverna in Patissia, near Trivella's house. At the end of the meal Kambanis launched into "M'appari" from Flotow's *Martha*. "Well, there I was, singing the aria quite softly," continued Kambanis in 1991, humming the familiar melody in a now tremulous voice, "but before I reached the end of it Mary got up and flounced out! She pretended afterward that she'd had to go and arrange some rehearsal or other at the conservatory; but the truth of the matter is that she didn't want anyone else to be the center of attention. She couldn't bear to hear applause for another performer!"[7]

Yannis (Zannis) Kambanis, late 1930s.

Kambanis was emphatic in his assertion that Mary was not a likable person. "She was overcompetitive and argumentative. She was annoyed that Trivella seemed to like me and she used to say to her, '*Oh, for heaven's sake! Always your dear little Zannis! Why do you take more notice of Kambanis?*' Trivella would answer,

'My dear little Zannis is in a class of his own!' and Mary would go on, '*And what about the rest of us here? Are we no good?*' 'Yes, my dear, but Zannis has graduated, he's already an established singer and a voice like his doesn't come often.'" That, of course, stung Mary even more, and at times she even refused to practice with Kambanis: "*Oh, come on! Why do you want to rehearse with me?*" she would ask in a spirit totally different from her attitude to rehearsals in later life. Once, when Kambanis told her that they ought to make the most of Trivella's teaching, Mary snapped, "*You and I are proficient already! We don't need Trivella to show us!*" Kambanis was "so taken aback," he said, that from that time on he "distanced himself" from her.[8]

—⁂—

It is clear from Mary's cutting words about Trivella that she had come to realize that her teacher, however hard she tried and however fond of her pupil she might be, was not up to the standard that Mary demanded. We know of no specific reasons which led her to conclude that Trivella was "not up to it," but inferences can be drawn from the comments made about her as a musician and as a teacher by various figures on the contemporary musical scene. Taking the relatively few favorable opinions first, we find that in most cases these were hedged with reservations. One exception was Ioannis Psaroudas, who was soon to devote a fair amount of space in his columns to Mary. Writing in 1937—only a few months before Mary started having lessons with her—he thought that Trivella's musicality and her remarkable talent as an actress enabled her not only to develop the vocal abilities of her pupils, but also to pass on to them "the inspiration, sensitivity, expressiveness, and feeling which she herself has in such abundant supply."[9] Another who praised Trivella was Yorgos Vokos, who called her "a marvelous teacher, one of the élite of the old guard of the teaching profession," though he acknowledged that Mary was "a priceless gift" to her. Leonidas Zoras, while describing her as "a modest, conscientious teacher," also conceded that she was "not of the caliber" to train and develop a phenomenon like Kaloyeropoulou. As for the purely negative opinions of Trivella, they are both more numerous and more eloquent. "For Trivella, Kaloyeropoulou was a windfall," according to Elli Nikolaidi. "She was a very bad teacher and had no pupils of any real merit. And then, suddenly, along comes a voice like that!" Her view is shared by Zoe Vlachopoulou, at that time one of de Hidalgo's prize pupils, who first heard Mary sing at the Athens Conservatory in the autumn of 1938: "Maria had learned nothing at the National Conservatory. Trivella was a bad teacher. I heard several of her pupils and they all screeched." Kostas Dounias, a pupil of Kalfopoulou at the time and a member of the Greek National Opera chorus for many years later, remarked, "We all knew that Yennadi had one good voice in her class, Anna [Zozo] Remoundou, and that Kalfopoulou had Michalis Koronis. And then people started to say that Trivella—whom we didn't think much of—had Kaloyeropoulou."[10]

It is impossible to believe that the idea of moving to another teacher was put into Mary's head entirely by her mother, as Maria herself implied in 1961: "*I changed, at my mother's wish, and went to the Athens Conservatory, where Elvira de Hidalgo was teaching.*" What probably happened is that, once she became aware of the general opinion of Trivella's relative inexperience, Mary somehow let her mother know that she was worried about not being in better hands. Not long after she had made her move, she said to Vlachopoulou, "*At the National Conservatory I had everything, but they never showed me, never taught me anything. Whatever I did, they just said, 'Well done!' or 'Very good!'*" Naturally, Litsa redoubled her attempts at arranging auditions for her daughter with anyone "useful" to whom she had access. One of those was the composer and conductor Antiochos Evangelatos, who was also one of the three principals of the Hellenic Conservatory. Mary went to his house, sat down at the piano and left him almost speechless with amazement. "All you need is a little bit of luck, my girl," he said, "and you will be the greatest star in the world." As it turned out, in September 1945 Evangelatos would conduct Mary in her last performances before she left Greece.[11]

On 17 August 1938 the bass Nicola Moscona, who had just sung in Verdi's *Requiem* under Toscanini in New York and London, came on a visit to Athens.[12] Before leaving for Italy and the new season at the Metropolitan—one can imagine how deeply Mary must have been in awe of him—he was persuaded to hear her sing by his friend and agent in Greece, Manolis Hadzis. Hadzis was also a friend of Mary's uncle Efthymios Dimitriadis, and it was Efthymios who asked him to arrange an audition with Moscona for his niece, "the druggist's daughter with the great voice." An appointment was made for one morning in September 1938 at the Olympia Theater, but when they got there they found that the stage and the piano were being used for a rehearsal. Seeing Mary's look of consternation, Hadzis went next door to a fashionable modern dance school, which had a piano. He explained the urgency of the situation to the caretaker, mentioning the name of Moscona, and settled the matter by giving him a tip. On emerging into the street to fetch the others, Hadzis bumped into conductor and pianist Lysimachos Androutsopoulos; he asked him to play the accompaniment for an audition with Moscona, giving him a small "sweetener" as well.[13]

And so the audition did take place, with Androutsopoulos at the piano of the dance school on Akadimias Street. Hadzis did not remember what Mary sang, but "she sang well." What did leave an impression on him, however, was the way her voice "wobbled, wavered, was not true and clean." As for Moscona, he appreciated her "huge" voice: "If she gets it under control, she will be a great singer," he said. For the present, though, he advised "an immediate change of teacher." Evidently Moscona was impressed by Mary's innate talent and the sheer size of her voice. When he returned to Athens the following year he probably heard her sing an aria from *Aida*. He then forecast that she would be a great star within fifteen years at the most, telling Litsa that then she would "eat with a golden spoon."[14]

Nicola Moscona, 1938.

Meanwhile, Hadzis had heard from his friend the baritone Lakis Vassilakis—de Hidalgo's pupil and newfound lover—about the Spaniard's ability and experience as a teacher. So he told Efthymios that de Hidalgo was the only teacher worth having as far as Mary was concerned. Hadzis recalled that about a year later, at de Hidalgo's house where he had gone to see Vassilakis, he heard a voice that seemed familiar. "I asked her who it was and she answered in her broken Greek, 'My dear fellow, that girl's a buffalo—but what a voice!' Soon Yerasimos Koundouris, who played the piano at de Hidalgo's lessons, came out of the music room followed by Kaloyeropoulou. 'Well,' I told her, 'you sing like a nightingale—now! Don't ask me to tell you what you sounded like when I first heard you!'"[15]

Moscona also spoke about Mary's rare talent to Totis Karalivanos, the experienced conductor of the Hellenic Melodrama, as the various efforts to establish an official Greek opera company had come to be known. Karalivanos recalled in September 1977 that he had immediately recognized her potential and had been struck by such self-assurance in one still so young. He promised to help her and advised her, as others had done, to study with de Hidalgo at the Athens Conservatory.[16] It seems, however, that Mary too had been investigating other teachers, starting with those at the National Conservatory. As Vyron Simiriotis recalls, "She went everywhere. She wasn't the sort of person to be afraid or shy. Anyway, there isn't an artist in the world who doesn't 'shop around' a bit. Now and then Mary

Mary, 1938.

would go to Kalfopoulou, who I know gave her some lessons at the National. And presumably Yennadi gave her a bit of tuition too, as I happened to meet Mary at Yennadi's apartment on Heyden Street on two or three occasions." Trivella herself, who unlike many other teachers (notably de Hidalgo) was not ambitious nor possessive about her pupils, "used to encourage them to go and listen to others, and she was glad when they did," as Margarita Dalmati recollects. No doubt she never imagined where these occasional "disloyalties" would lead a spirited and ambitious girl like Mary.[17]

The recommendations and tributes to de Hidalgo's teaching ability that Litsa kept hearing must have persuaded her to make a fresh attempt at having Mary enrolled at the Athens Conservatory. She managed to find out when de Hidalgo's opera class was having its end-of-year examinations in the small auditorium on Pireos Street. That year, on 9 June 1938, de Hidalgo was putting on the first act of Bellini's *La Sonnambula*, Puccini's one-act *Suor Angelica*, and the first act of Humperdinck's *Hänsel und Gretel*. Young Zoe Vlachopoulou played both Suor Angelica and Gretel, two diametrically opposed roles, "in order to show what I could do," as she put it: "At the end of the performance, when parents and friends crowded on to the stage, a lady I didn't know came up and congratulated me, saying, 'I am Mrs. Kaloyeropoulou and I have a tremendously talented daughter aged sixteen [sic] with a wonderful voice and great acting ability. After seeing your performance I have decided she really must go to your teacher.'" When Litsa got home she told Mary how excited she was, as Mary later confided to Vlachopoulou: *"Mother went and heard you singing and saw how you acted; and she was so thrilled that she came home and said to me, 'The problem's solved. You'll go to de Hidalgo!'"*[18] And this took place the day after Mary had won a distinction in her proficiency test at the National Conservatory and received a prize from the principal—just at a time when, after only a year of formal musical studies, everything seemed to be going right for her. And of course no one, apart from the mother and daughter Kaloyeropoulou, could have had any suspicion of the plot that was being hatched.

—⁓—

Following Mary's success in the April exhibition concert at the National Conservatory, and probably under pressure from the ambitious mother and headstrong daughter, Trivella decided to enter her prize pupil for the proficiency test in June—at the end of her first year! Students called it the "pre-diploma" test, because it was an intermediate step between the licentiate and diploma examinations.[19] That year the proficiency test was held in Parnassos Hall on Wednesday, 8 June 1938, but what Mary sang on that occasion remains unknown, nor is it known exactly what she had been learning in the past few months. She was probably accompanied by Elli Nikolaidi, a highly proficient pianist, though the latter had no recollection of it. There were fourteen candidates, eleven of them women, among them Marika Papadopoulou, a pupil of Kalfopoulou and subsequently a soloist at the National Opera. She had heard a certain amount of talk about a "unique voice," a "phenomenon," but this was the first time she actually heard Mary sing. "She was wearing a white dress with lace trimmings and a colored belt round her waist, and her hair was a dishevelled mane," Papadopoulou recalls. "But when I heard her I was stunned. I don't remember what she sang, but that was no voice, it was a whole orchestra!" Nine candidates were unanimously awarded distinctions; first in order of merit was one of Kalfopoulou's pupils, the tenor Michalis Koronis, and second was the dramatic soprano Zozo Remoundou, a pupil of Yennadi. Mary was fifth. Each of the first four received a prize of 500 drachmas and each of the other five a score of the opera *To Daktylidi tis Manas* (*The Mother's Ring*) by Manolis Kalomiris.[20]

Twenty-six days later, on Monday, 4 July 1938, Mary made her official public début. Maria herself only once made any public reference to it, in an interview she gave in New York twenty years later, in 1958: *"I début'd—imagine!—for the Americans, July 4th, in Greece."*[21] We do not know how she came to be invited to sing at the American Independence Day celebrations. On 15 March 1938 she had registered as an American citizen at the U.S. consulate general, stating that she had come to Greece for the purpose of studying and that she intended to return to America within a year and reside there permanently.[22] It may have been a spin-off from this contact with the U.S. consular authorities, or perhaps Litsa had ap-

AMERICAN
INDEPENDENCE DAY
JULY 4th 1938
ATHENS

Program, Rex Theater, Athens, 4 July 1938.

PROGRAM

1. Presentation of Colors by Honor Guard of American Legionnaires.
2. American National Anthem.
3. General Nicholas Tsipouras, former Governor General of Macedonia, will speak in Greek.
4. «AMERICA». Everybody is requested to join in the singing.
5. Mr. Charles House, President of the American Farm School at Salonika, will speak.
6. Mr. E. Mangliveras, barytone of the Greek Melodrama, will sing his own selections.
7. Miss Nota N. Kamperou will sing in English and Greek.
8. Mis Mariana Kalogeropoulou will sin Greek and American songs.
9. Greek National Anthem.
10. Retirement of Colors.

INFORMAL

Note: A 4th of July/dinner will be given at the Glyfada Center of Jim & Jim, at 9: 30 P. M. Those who desire to attend are requested to make their reservations through Mr. E. Drymonas, Secretary of the Greek – American Society of Athens or direct to the Center of Jim & Jim,
Tel. 04–284

Fire works will be burned by the establishment. The microphone installation is due to the kindness of Mr. H. Petropoulos, representative of the R. C. A. in Athens.

proached the Greek-American Society of Athens, which organized the event in cooperation with the American embassy. On 4 July 1938 the temperature climbed to more than 37°C (99°F), and Mary must have felt the heat badly, what with her weight problem and the fact that the ceremony began at 11 a.m. The Rex Theater on Panepistimiou Street was packed, not with music-lovers but mainly with diplomats and high-ranking officials. The ceremony began with the presentation of the colors by a guard of honor of American Legionnaires, then the American national anthem was played, "America" was sung by all present, and the piano-accompanied concert started, led off by Evangelos (Vangelis) Mangliveras, a young but already fairly well-known baritone, who sang "his own selections." After soprano Nota Kamberou, who had studied in Germany after her Hellenic Conservatory diploma, had sang "in English and Greek," it was the turn of "Mariana Kalogeropoulou" to "sin [sic] Greek and American songs."

"This must have been the first time Vangelis met Mary," reflected Christos Mangliveras, Vangelis's younger brother, who didn't remember what she sang. One thing that he did remember, however, is that Mary sang as an encore—incredible though it may sound—the aria "Casta diva" from Bellini's *Norma*. "I remember it perfectly," he insisted, "because that was what made such an impression on my brother and me." Unless his memory was at fault, this would mean that Mary had already learned the famous aria which was to set the seal on her great career in her very first year with Trivella, when she was barely fourteen! The Independence Day celebrations closed with the Greek national anthem and the retirement of the colors, and the day ended with a Fourth of July dinner at Jim and Jim's, a restaurant in the seaside suburb of Glyfada, with a display of fireworks "specially ordered in Greek and American colors." Although we cannot be sure, it is most likely that Mary was present at the dinner—with her mother, of course, as Litsa would never have let Mary go alone, and in any case never missed an opportunity of going out and getting to know the right people.[23]

The epic move and events at 70 Harilaou Trikoupi Street described in the previous chapter, which left such a mark on Mary's personality, just preceded her first public appearances and the experience of being on stage and hearing the applause of the audience. To escape the atmosphere of financial doom, the recriminations, and the multiple pressures of that tense summer, Mary asked Trivella if she could go on with her lessons after the end of the year at the conservatory. "She insisted on having lessons through the summer," Trivella said later, "and I didn't like to disappoint her."[24] Another way of broadening her musical horizons was by listening to the wide selection of classical music broadcast on the radio. There had always been plenty of foreign radio stations which could be picked up in Athens, but on 21 May 1938 Athens Radio went on the air for the first time. In the evenings it broadcast classical music until late at night, with two or three concerts every evening. Having heard so many broadcasts from the Met in New York, however, Mary was hardly likely to be satisfied with most of what she heard now.

Evangelos Mangliveras, 1938 or 1939.

"When there was opera on the radio," says Ismini Thiveou, "she kept saying they were all singing out of tune. *'For heaven's sake, switch it off!'* she would often shout in exaggerated dismay."[25]

—⁓—

Apart from a few dips in the Saronic Gulf, and probably some evening outings with the family to open-air cinemas and the cool gardens of out-of-town tavernas, Mary evidently spent the hot summer months studying and practicing assiduously, sometimes to the point that she fell asleep from sheer exhaustion. One of the goals she was preparing herself for that summer, of course, was the audition with de Hidalgo that her mother was determined to arrange for her. Once she had made the decision, in June, Litsa worked tirelessly toward that end until eventually—we shall never know how—she persuaded de Hidalgo to give Mary an audition at her home, at 8 Codringtonos Street. It is possible that Mary approached de Hidalgo herself: "One morning a girl appeared," de Hidalgo recounted later, "asking me to audition her because she wanted to study with me." As Vlachopoulou recalls, "Apparently her mother arranged to take Mary for an audition before the start of the new year, and as soon as de Hidalgo heard her she accepted her on the spot, because when she heard talent she didn't let it go."[26] However, matters were not quite as simple as that.

De Hidalgo has left us various vivid descriptions of her feelings on first hearing Mary sing. "The very idea of that girl wanting to be a singer was laughable! She was tall, very fat, and wore heavy glasses. When she removed them she would look at you unseeingly as if from a great distance, with huge, staring, feverish eyes. . . . She had her black hair done up in two untidy plaits over her ears, with a little cap on top. She was wearing a loose-fitting schoolgirl's overall, buttoned down the front, and worn-down sandals. She sat in a corner, not knowing what to do with her hands, and began biting her nails. . . . She walked heavily, with a swaying gait. Her round face was spotted with pimples, doubtless due to overindulgence of a childish greed. . . . 'I'm not going to get anywhere with her,' I thought. And then, without a word of warning, she started singing. . . . All at once I was alert, full of tension. That voice was the voice I had secretly been waiting for, in fact I had been looking for it for years. It was as if our meeting had been arranged [by fate]." On another occasion de Hidalgo said that, "Of course her vocal technique was by no means perfect, but there was innate drama, musicianship, and a certain individuality in her voice that moved me deeply. In fact, I shed a tear or two and turned away so that she could not see me."[27]

De Hidalgo remembered that on her first audition Mary sang Rezia's aria "Ocean! thou mighty monster" from Weber's *Oberon*. However, we may be fairly sure that she did not actually sing that huge aria on that occasion. De Hidalgo was probably thinking of the aria that Mary was to sing to her about a year later, when she was officially auditioned by a panel of Athens Conservatory examiners in order to be formally enrolled.[28] That would explain why de Hidalgo remembered her "waiting for her turn" while she herself "listened with her eyes closed"; whereas the first time she heard Mary, at her home, she would most probably have played the accompaniment herself, after a fashion (for she was an indifferent pianist). But none of this detracts from the value of the rest of de Hidalgo's recollections, in which she probably was thinking of the first time she heard Mary sing, in September 1938: "It was a tempestuous, extravagant cascade of sounds, as yet uncontrolled but full of drama and emotion. . . . That voice needed to be retrained from scratch, but I was happy to have such valuable raw material to work on. . . . I was already sure I would be able to transform it."[29]

Whereas this description, made in 1958, has been quoted by most of Maria's biographers, another account of Mary's singing given by de Hidalgo in 1968 has been completely ignored: "[She had] an artistic personality like a river in flood. It is terrible what a woman like that can do. I remember she made that impression on me at once, the very first time I met her. . . . In those days she called herself Marianna Kaloyeropoulou. She was fourteen years old and a great lump of a girl. . . . I had just started my first [sic][30] year of teaching when I was approached by this overgrown girl, who asked me to audition her because she wanted to come and study with me. I must say, when I first saw her I was none too enthusiastic. She was tall, fat, and rather gauche, with a very spotty complexion. Her clothes were very ordinary, almost slovenly: she was wearing a black overall or pinafore of the kind worn by schoolchildren, . . . a white collar and a little white cap on top of her heavy tresses. Her eyes, large and deep-set, were the most expressive things about her, but they were hidden behind very thick glasses. I showed her into my study and listened to her. When she opened her mouth I was dumbstruck. Maria sang with exceptional power, she had a voice like a trombone. It was rough, but with a very individual timbre, quite extraordinary. It thrilled me immediately. All at once I felt an odd liking for that girl. It was as if her singing had touched some strange chord in me. I felt that I had to help her, and that only I could do it."[31]

Equally vivid is the description of that important moment given by one of de Hidalgo's pupils, Spyros Salingaros. "It was a Friday afternoon in autumn [probably September 1938], and after a lesson at de Hidalgo's apartment I stayed on with two other students to hear the vocal phenomenon she told us she had discovered.[32] Soon there appeared a big, fat creature wearing thick wire-rimmed glasses, with her hair almost falling in front of her eyes. She sat down on a chair, just perching on the edge of it although she was so fat, and with her hands crossed on her knees she waited for de Hidalgo to speak to her first. De Hidalgo asked her what she wanted to sing and Mary suggested a number of pieces, adding that she was quite willing to sing anything else that de Hidalgo wanted, so long as she knew it. Madame—that's what we used to call her—sat down at the piano, Mary found a place for herself facing her, and the audition began." Salingaros remembers being greatly impressed by Mary's voice and also by her interpretation as she sang the aria "O patria mia" from Act III of *Aida*, one of the most difficult in the dramatic soprano's repertoire. "Never before had I seen de Hidalgo so wide-eyed, with such a look of astonishment on her face. We were literally struck dumb!"[33]

It may well be true then, as Vlachopoulou says, that de Hidalgo wanted to take Mary on as soon as she heard her, because when she came across talent she "didn't like to let it go." But Litsa, who still decided her younger daughter's opinions and preferences for her, knew that Mary, having got into Trivella's proficiency class, could take her diploma in as little as a year and then be launched on a lucrative career; whereas if Mary were to go to de Hidalgo, she would more or less have to start again from the beginning. In other words, the problem posed by de Hidalgo's acceptance of Mary was a simple dilemma: on the one hand a better teacher but slower progress; on the other, continuation with Trivella with the possibility of starting some sort of career in as little as a year. In the end Litsa came down in favor of the shortsighted solution of going for a "quick" diploma. But wanting to keep the door that had just been presented to her open, she must have concocted some plausible pretext and asked de Hidalgo to allow Mary to attend her classes unofficially—without actually enrolling at the Athens Conservatory—while at the same time continuing with Trivella at the National for another year in order to take her diploma. Presumably, by promising that Mary would go to her next year, she persuaded de Hidalgo to agree to this arrangement. The shrewd Spaniard had obviously realized that Mary's voice was exceptional and well worth waiting for; and in any case she would be following her progress and giving her guidance—to all intents and purposes she would be her teacher—during the coming academic year of 1938–39.

—◊◊◊—

I stayed only a year at the National Conservatory. After that I went to the Athens Conservatory with de Hidalgo.

"Smentite di articolo 'Time'" (MS, in Italian, 1956)

CHAPTER 13

A Waiting Game,
with Further Progress

On 15 September 1938 the new academic year started at the conservatories. To Mary, who that year was registered as student no. 440 at the National Conservatory, the beginning of term did not mean much, as she had continued her lessons with Trivella during the summer and she was not interested in the theory lessons. Apart from singing, the only subjects in which her name appears on the mark sheets are Solfège V and Harmony I. Both of these were taught by Michalis Vourtsis, whom the students liked and considered a good teacher. On the mark sheet for the solfège class, signed by Kalomiris and Vourtsis, Mary was given 10 (out of 10) for application and 10 for progress, with the comment "excellent." The significance of this assessment is considerably diminished by the fact that no fewer than seventeen of the other twenty-seven students in her class received the same marks. However, that she was put straight into level five shows that she must have had an unusually good natural grasp of this subject, so vital for the proper study and quick learning of the music she would have to sing. In harmony, which she always found difficult and for which she was put into the first level, she again received 10 and 10, along with ten of her twenty-five classmates.[1]

For Mary, what made the new academic year so different from the previous one was that she was now unofficially attending de Hidalgo's classes at the Athens Conservatory while keeping the fact secret from Trivella. In later years Maria was always evasive about this period of her life—not only about the personal and family problems described earlier, but also about the switch from one teacher to another. It is impossible to know just what effect this hole-and-corner situation had on Mary, who was still less than fifteen at the beginning of the year. Apart from a taste of the ruthless tactics she would inevitably have to adopt if she wanted to get to the top, she probably gave little thought to the matter, if any, as her "betrayal" of Trivella was not yet total: she would not start studying full-time with de Hidalgo until the next year. Meanwhile Litsa was determined to do all she could to persuade Trivella to enter Mary for the diploma examination in June 1939.

"One morning at the beginning of the year 1938–39," recalls Zoe Vlachopoulou, "when we were all sitting in the classroom where we had lessons with de

Hidalgo, in comes a big fat girl with a great mane of black hair and large black eyes. She kept glancing around her, looking rather scared. As soon as de Hidalgo called her name I remembered her mother approaching me; and when she opened her mouth for the vocalises I realized that she was something very special. After that I always stayed on when Kaloyeropoulou was having a lesson, but we were at the conservatory together for only one year, my final year, when she was still attending unofficially." The unusual circumstances (which most of her classmates were unaware of) and the unfamiliar environment of the Athens Conservatory made Mary withdraw into herself even more than before. Considering that even in the National Conservatory, where she was now fairly well settled in, she hardly talked to anyone, it is not hard to imagine how odd and how unlikable the other students must have found "this awkward, gauche girl who had nevertheless captivated our teacher with her talent," as Vlachopoulou describes her.[2]

We do not know how often Mary went to de Hidalgo's class in the year 1938–39, nor what she worked on with her, apart from exercises, of course. Until then she had been "on the wrong track," de Hidalgo commented later: "An aspiring opera singer could hardly have done more things wrong. . . . The colors she wore were 'over the top,' and it was the same with her voice too. Gifted as she was with phenomenal breath control (she could sing a whole melodic line in a single breath) and a natural flair for dramatic inflections, she thought the right thing to do was to open the floodgates and pour out everything she had inside her. So the first thing I had to do was to put a brake on her. 'You're young,' I explained to her, 'and for the time being you must get into the habit of singing lightly: think of it as delicate embroidery. Later on, we shall see.'"[3] As regards Mary's voice then, it seems that the main problems, the ones requiring immediate attention, were how to eliminate the wobble and how to lighten the tone.

Soon Mary began to also feel emotionally dependent on her new teacher, and de Hidalgo must have encouraged this relationship from the outset. Even in those early days Mary often stayed on late at her lessons and sometimes left the conservatory with her. It is quite possible that Mary was already going to de Hidalgo's apartment from time to time, as she was later to do regularly, for private lessons which were less likely to arouse comment. All this would of course have distanced her still further from Trivella, who for a time had herself been a stabilizing influence in those areas of emotional life where Mary could not turn to her mother. The combination of de Hidalgo's personality and qualities as a teacher (not necessarily the same as her *abilities* as a teacher) seems eventually to have also turned Mary further against Litsa, who was still pressing Trivella for the diploma that would enable Mary to earn money on the stage. Litsa's ambitious schemes were probably encouraged that winter by all the press publicity about Deanna Durbin, only two years older than Mary, who was described by a Greek newspaper as "the golden voice of our century, the star who combines the youthfulness of a dynamic new generation and the charm of a precocious woman, with the voice of a prima donna and an astonishing talent as a dramatic actress." Much later Maria was to refer to Durbin's success as something that had greatly influenced her mother, who saw in her a model for her own daughter: *"It was the era of Deanna Durbin and Shirley Temple, and no doubt my mother was dreaming. Of what? Why, of glory, of course."*[4]

Litsa must have been thrilled early in 1939, when Mary was selected to play the part of Santuzza in one performance of *Cavalleria Rusticana* at the Olympia Theater. This would of course have been highly gratifying to Mary herself, but at the same time it would have encouraged her mother's more mercenary schemes, for if Mary acquitted herself well she would obviously have a better chance of getting her diploma at the end of the year. No doubt the uncertainty over her future was beginning to wear on Mary's nerves, making her more and more difficult to get on with, as by this time she had mentally written off both Trivella and the National Conservatory. She remained on bad terms with Kambanis, who already had his diploma and was loyal to the teacher who had been so good to him since 1932. "With Kambanis, in particular, she was always quarreling," recalled Stefanos Chiotakis, "because whenever they appeared together at the National or sang at Parnassos, Kambanis made more of a hit than she did. Maria took that to heart, especially at the conservatory matinées, where Kambanis always brought the house down."[5] Now there was to be an occasion for a renewal of this rivalry, if not actually face to face, as Kambanis was to play Canio in *Pagliacci* on the same evening that she was to be Santuzza in *Cavalleria*.

—m—

Kalomiris was not content merely to arrange student exhibition concerts, as the other conservatories did: he also put on full stage productions with costumes and an orchestra, and sometimes with one or two well-established singers in the cast. These performances usually took place in the Olympia Theater owned by the three Karandinos brothers, who had always done all they could to promote opera, regularly renting out their theater to the Hellenic Melodrama and to the National Conservatory. That year Kalomiris decided to show off his students in two full productions with costumes and sets, one a double bill of *Cavalleria Rusticana* and *Pagliacci*, the other *Madama Butterfly*. The first was to be directed by Yorgos Karakandas and the second by Artemis Kyparissi, a former principal soprano with the Hellenic Melodrama. Elli Nikolaidi was to be the répétiteur and Michalis Vourtsis the conductor for both productions. The leading roles in *Butterfly* were to be taken by Anthoula Mavridou and the final-year diploma student Michalis Koronis, and in *Pagliacci* by Zannis Kambanis and Zozo Remoundou. In *Cavalleria*, which was to be performed twice, Vyron Simiriotis was cast as Turiddu and Hilda Woodley, a girl of mixed Greek and English parentage from Corfu, as Santuzza. According to Karakandas himself, it was he who insisted that Mary should also sing Santuzza, after persuading the reluctant Trivella to allow her to do so. However, although everybody recognized "Maria's astonishing qualities," the first performance had to be given to Woodley because she was a graduate, as Kalomiris explained later. "That, of course, was something that a girl not yet sixteen could not understand, and naturally she felt bitter about it." As a compromise, it was eventually decided that two performances would be given so that Mary too would have a chance to demonstrate her talent.[6]

The Olympia Theater as it was in 1939, when Mary sang there twice as a student: at her first appearance on the stage (*Cavalleria Rusticana*, 2 April 1939) and at a concert (25 June 1939).

At home, Mary spent hours and hours going through the score at the piano. And, of course, besides rehearsing with Elli Nikolaidi and the rest of the cast at the conservatory, she studied the part of Santuzza with Trivella, who helped her practice her stagecraft as well. Mary's biggest problem was her heavy tread. "Walk more lightly, my dear, or the stage will give way!" Trivella would say to her.[7] Several participants remembered the production well: "One day in 1939 Kaloyeropoulou was sent to me to be coached for *Cavalleria*," said Nikolaidi. "When we rehearsed on Solomou Street, her voice wasn't beautiful, but her expressiveness was incomparable!"[8] Kostas Dounias, who sang then in the conservatory chorus but had not yet met Mary, recalled how Vourtsis told them to assemble one evening in the large hall on the second floor of the conservatory, for the first rehearsal of *Cavalleria* with young Kaloyeropoulou. "We sat down, chatting and joking in the usual way, and when I saw a great big girl wearing thick glasses, her face covered

Elli Nikolaidi, 1939.

with acne, with legs this big, and weird sandals, 'Is this the girl who's going to play Santuzza?' I asked. 'We're in for a bit of screeching!' But then she opened her mouth to sing! She had a voice that was a real dramatic soprano in the middle of her range, a mezzo in the lower notes, and a lyric soprano at the top!" Yennadi's pupil Vyron Simiriotis, who was cast as Turiddu, was a fairly light tenor who did not have a big voice but turned out well in the part. "We were coached mostly by Nikolaidi from the piano, and sometimes by Vourtsis," he says. "I remember that when we rehearsed the scene where I say to Santuzza that I am not a slave of her vain jealousy and have to throw her to the floor, the other students in the chorus used to laugh at the idea of a slip of a fellow like me pushing over the great lump that Mary was then. In the end I not only managed to do it, but I pretended to get angry with her and pushed her in such a way that the scene looked very natural. Once, in fact, Mary fell so heavily that she hurt her hand."[9]

Karakandas later remarked that Mary's determined efforts to overcome her initial timidity had wrought "a miraculous transformation" in her performance. By "bringing out her hidden self" she outshone the older members of the cast. "She was determined to win the prize and she did. At rehearsals she would listen as if in a trance, and sometimes she would walk nervously up and down the room repeating passionately to herself, *'I'll get there one day.'*"[10] The very difficult role of Santuzza, a girl passionately in love and obsessively jealous, called not only for a good voice but above all for a good stage presence and convincing acting, which obviously no one could expect from such a young second-year student. "However, Mary did have a spontaneous way of expressing herself," Simiriotis observes. "She acted with her heart and soul. Nobody had ever really taught her how to do it, but when we were together on stage I could see that she threw herself into it with great feeling, and without suffering at all from nerves." Afroditi Kopanou, who sang the role of Mamma Lucia in that *Cavalleria*, remembers an incident which illustrates Mary's precocious passion for dramatic authenticity. "Going through her big aria 'Voi lo sapete' at the first stage rehearsal with Karakandas, when she came to the line 'Priva dell'onor mio rimango' she suddenly stopped and asked me in an undertone, *'What does it mean by "honor"?'* I didn't know what to say, because I hadn't realized it meant virginity. 'It must be something really valuable . . .' I whispered back. *'But I can't just mouth the words!'* she retorted irritably. *'I've got to know what they mean!'* And she immediately turned to Karakandas, who laughed and told us to ask our mothers."[11]

Mary, who was already very nearsighted, now discovered for the first time what a serious handicap this could be to her in her work. Until then, in concerts where she sang with piano accompaniment, she had not needed to see more than was necessary to make her way on to and off the stage without tripping. It was an entirely different matter now that she was in a performance with stage sets, other members of the cast all around her, and a conductor some distance away. The consequences of her very poor vision will be discussed in more detail later: suffice it to say here that the first time she ever had to cope with the practical difficulties this deficiency caused was in the dress rehearsal of *Cavalleria Rusticana* at the Olympia Theater, probably on the very morning of the performance. However, Mary had foreseen the problem and, in her characteristically thorough and perfectionistic way, she had been practicing her movements at home, marking the exact positions and distances apart of the various pieces of furniture and other items of the scenery, either with objects on the floor or with chalk marks on the flat roof of her house.[12]

The first performance of *Cavalleria Rusticana* was given at the Olympia Theater on 19 March 1939, with Hilda Woodley as Santuzza. The second performance, again at the Olympia, was on Sunday, 2 April, at 6:30 p.m., with Mary who was then just fifteen years and four months old. That morning the daily *Proia* carried an announcement referring to "a chorus of a hundred and a large orchestra conducted by Mr. M. Vourtsis" and "Miss M. Kaloyeropoulou appearing for the first time in the role of Santuzza." More important still, *Eleftheron Vima* presented to its readers the first photo of the future Maria Callas ever to be published.[13] Mary, however, had a serious problem: *"I was in despair because my face was swollen and contorted by a tremendous toothache."* In an interview exactly twenty years later she described how, although she had learned her part by heart, she was so nervous that she felt that everything was going to go wrong. Worst of all, she was in so much pain that she went to "the director" (Kalomiris, Karakandas, or Vourtsis)

Vyron Simiriotis (above left), the first tenor with whom Maria Callas sang a whole opera on the stage; conductor Michalis Vourtsis (above right); and Afroditi Kopanou (Mamma Lucia), *Cavalleria Rusticana*, Athens, 2 April 1939.

and told him she would not be able to sing. To make her point she even seized his hand dramatically and put it on her swollen jaw. The director saw that what Mary needed just then was strong encouragement and a firm hand; so he told her sternly that she had to sing, and that if she didn't sing that night she would never sing at all. This little drama, played out behind the scenes at the Olympia, was watched by several of Mary's classmates, some of whom had hoped to step into the role of Santuzza that night. "She's afraid she'll be booed, of course," a particularly jealous one is meant to have said to the others. And Mary, who heard her, in a moment forgot all her problems, slapped the offending girl on the face, and hurried off to her dressing room to prepare to go on stage.[14]

The theater on Akadimias Street was as full as it had been for the first performance, and the audience included the prime minister, Ioannis Metaxas, and the minister with responsibility for Greater Athens, Konstantinos Kodzias.[15] For Trivella this must have been the most satisfying evening of her career as a teacher, since she had one of her pupils starring in each of the two short operas. Dressed in her finery, glowing with pride, and probably more nervous than either Kambanis

The first photo of Maria Callas ever to appear in the press, *Eleftheron Vima*, Athens, 2 April 1939.

or Mary, Trivella watched the performances from a box. The scenery and costumes were simple but adequate, although no other particulars of the production have survived apart from a description of the big aria and the final scene. Afroditi Kopanou remembers how Mary kneeled before her and sang "Voi lo sapete." Her passion was reflected in her eyes when she sang, "Lola e Turiddu s'amano, io piango, io piango!" And when Lucia murmurs, "Miseri noi, che cosa vieni a dirmi in questo santo giorno," Santuzza bemoans her fate crying out, "Io son dannata!" At the end of the opera, when the scream announcing Turiddu's death is heard, Mary, who was standing near the wings at one side of the stage, suddenly writhed and collapsed in an agony of despair, perhaps as she had been taught by Maria Trivella. The applause was long and loud.[16]

"We made quite a hit, we were both applauded," Simiriotis recalls. "The result was good and Mary remembered it for a long time afterward. She had enjoyed it." Karakandas remembered that, in spite of not having "full control of her voice," Mary "made such a dramatic impact in 'Voi lo sapete' and the Easter Hymn that one did not notice any vocal imperfections. One could not forget how this young débutante conveyed so memorably the conflict in the forsaken peasant girl, who still loves but resents her betrayer." Kalomiris, writing much later, described the performance with exaggerated enthusiasm as "an incomparable triumph" for Mary. Elli Nikolaidi's sibylline comment, however, was: "With a voice like hers, she made a great impression on a not particularly discerning audience." Maria

Mary (indicated by arrow) in the only surviving photo from *Cavalleria Rusticana*, Athens, 2 April 1939.

herself merely said, "*Everything went very well*," which suggests that her performance was perhaps not quite as successful as she had expected. Psaroudas reviewed the performances of Hilda Woodley and Mary with faint praise: "Both deserve credit for their efforts, which came off very well, because both of them sang and acted the difficult role of Santuzza with fine voices and a good understanding of the part, and they were enthusiastically applauded." The inference is that as Santuzza in 1939 Mary was not such a resounding success as some people have since claimed.[17]

The person who actually stole the show that evening, earning a storm of applause at the end of *Pagliacci*, was Zannis Kambanis as Canio. The stage went quite purple with all the bunches of violets thrown by the audience, and Kambanis was given a standing ovation. He sang something or other as an encore and then pointed to his throat, meaning that he couldn't sing any more. And the evening was a triumph for Trivella, of course, who was cheered by the audience for the performance of her two star pupils. When it was all over, Minister Kodzias asked Karakandas to introduce him to Mary. After having a few words with her in her dressing room (probably in the presence of Litsa, who would have been radiant with joy at seeing her daughter congratulated by a public figure for the first time)

Kodzias asked Karakandas if there was anything he could do for her. Karakandas, according to his own account, answered, "Send her to Europe: her future's wide open." Finally, when the excited congratulations in the dressing rooms and the wings had died down, the whole cast and crew went off to celebrate their success at a taverna in nearby Kallithea.[18]

—⁂—

"The performances at the Olympia were universally acknowledged to be a success, not only by the critics but also by the élite of Athenian society who, led by the right honorable prime minister, honored these events with their presence," said Kalomiris in his report on the year. To Litsa, however, Mary's success (limited or not) meant that she now had a new lever with which to put pressure on Trivella to enter Mary for the diploma in June. "When [Mary] won first prize for opera," Trivella wrote to Litsa in the late 1950s, "I remember that you suggested I give her a graduating diploma and that I objected. 'Let us wait one more year,' I told you. 'We have excellent material here, but we need still more work.'" Trivella's niece, Penelope Adali, has her own version of the story: "The trouble started when Mary took the proficiency test and her mother insisted that my aunt should give her the diploma. She wanted to put her to work on the stage, because they were short of money. My aunt said to her, 'I won't give her the diploma, although she's almost ready, because I want her to have a few extra notes under her belt. If I give it to her now, I'll be pushing her on too fast and ruin her voice.' But instead of doing it my aunt's way, Mary went and had her voice spoiled by de Hidalgo!" This last remark, of course, implies that Trivella had found out, though perhaps not until later, that in 1938–39 Mary was "playing it both ways," and from then on blamed Mary's vocal problems on de Hidalgo.[19]

So it was in an atmosphere of rancor and recrimination that Mary prepared for the exhibition concert of Trivella's class and the concert of graduating and top-grade students, scheduled for 22 and 23 May 1939 in Parnassos Hall. Kambanis remembers that Mary left Trivella speechless one day by saying to her, "*Just you wait and see me in a year or so!*" Once again Stefanos Valtetsiotis was the accompanist when the concert began at 7 p.m. on 22 May, with the famous barcarolle from *The Tales of Hoffmann*, "Belle nuit, ô nuit d'amour," a short piece of no great technical difficulty, sung by mezzo-soprano Anita Bourdakou as Nicklausse and Mary as Giulietta. Mary did not come on again until near the end of the second half of the program. She started with Rezia's aria "Ocean! thou mighty monster" from Act II of Weber's *Oberon*, a vocally exhausting and technically very demanding piece, with *pianissimo* and legato passages in the first part and decisive attack, rapid roulades and *fortissimo* passages in the second; altogether an aria for a dramatic soprano *par excellence*. She then sang "Ritorna vincitor" from Act I of *Aida*, another typically dramatic and technically difficult aria, and her third solo was a song by Psaroudas, "I Shan't Forget." At the end of the program Mary and Kambanis performed the final duet from *Aida,* "O terra addio." This time Psaroudas made a very encouraging remark about Mary in his review of the concert. He had found both singers in the closing duet "quite outstanding" and thought that "Miss Marianna Kaloyeropoulou has one of the finest voices in all the singing classes." However, this was followed by a caution: "I am sure that by practicing and following her teacher's instructions she will develop the absolute evenness that she sometimes lacks," though she had "a very fine voice, well worth listening to."[20]

Stefanos Valtetsiotis, who accompanied Mary at least four times in 1938 and 1939.

The concert given at 6 p.m. the next day, 23 May 1939, in the same venue, featured solo performances by eighteen students, including nine singers. The first half closed with Zozo Remoundou, and the second half with Mary singing two extremely difficult arias, quite different from each other, not only in mood but also in their technical demands on the singer: she started with a repeat performance of "Ocean! thou mighty monster" and ended with the aria from Act II of Massenet's *Thaïs,* "Dis-moi que je suis belle," which is equally dramatic but also full of sensuous passion. Psaroudas, in his review, commented that she was "excellent" in the first piece but "not quite up to standard" in Thaïs's Mirror Aria, not quite having the "great flexibility of voice, seductiveness, flirtatiousness, and a touch of hedonism" that are called for in that scene. Certainly it is hard to imagine Mary, a rather fat adolescent who had never yet experienced love, giving a convincing performance of this highly erotic aria. But the criticism that her voice was not flexible enough seems rather surprising, considering that Psaroudas himself had described Mary as "excellent" in Rezia's aria, which is much more demanding in this respect.[21]

Since Mary had undoubtedly done well in these two concerts, it is probable that Litsa seized the opportunity to exert further pressure on Trivella to enter her for the diploma examinations to be held only a few days later. Of those who had passed the proficiency test at the same time as Mary, three were to take the diploma that year, so why should not Mary be entered too? But Trivella disagreed, insisting that it was too early. Kalfopoulou was not entering Zozo Remoundou for the diploma yet, she argued, although she had been at the conservatory since the early 1930s. Litsa refused to be browbeaten and became furious with Trivella. Mary on the contrary was probably relieved as, in spite of her impatience to be finished with her studies, she must have realized by now that much more still needed to be done, under the guidance of a teacher of de Hidalgo's caliber, before she could embark on the career she dreamed of.

And so the decision to move Mary to the Athens Conservatory was finally made. Surely de Hidalgo would be informed of it, to her great joy, but not Trivella, as the move still depended on Mary's winning a scholarship to the Athens Conservatory: until that was confirmed, the option of continuing with Trivella at the National had to be kept open. And it was in this atmosphere—a mixture of relief, guilt, and uncertainty, aggravated by the serious psychological and practical problems besetting her in her home environment—that Mary prepared for the exhibition concert of the opera school classes and the official announcement of the results for the year 1938–39. This time, as it was a more formal occasion, the ceremony was to be held in the Olympia Theater at 6 p.m. on Sunday, 25 June 1939. The program would consist of ten excerpts from *Aida, Lucia di Lammermoor, Werther, La Gioconda, Un Ballo in Maschera, Madama Butterfly, Cavalleria Rusticana,* and *Faust;* none of the students would sing solos. The stage directors were Yorgos Karakandas and Artemis Kyparissi, and the répétiteurs Stefanos Valtetsiotis and Elli Nikolaidi would take turns playing the piano accompaniment.[22]

Mary sang in the last of the six excerpts in the first part of the program and in the second of the four after the intermission. The first of these, in which she was directed by Kyparissi and Nikolaidi, was an excerpt from Verdi's *Un Ballo in Maschera,* probably consisting of the last scene of Act II ("Ve' se di notte")—with Petros Hoidas as Sam, Nikos Aliprandis as Tom, and Christoforos Athineos as Renato—and the beginning of Act III, with Amelia's aria "Morrò, ma prima in grazia" and Renato's famous "Eri tu." Mary's second appearance that evening was a twenty-minute excerpt from *Cavalleria Rusticana* directed by Karakandas and Nikolaidi. It began with the scene between Santuzza and Mamma Lucia, in which Mary sang the aria "Voi lo sapete," and included the jealousy duet "Tu qui, Santuzza?", culminating in Santuzza's furious outburst "A te la mala Pasqua, spergiuro!" to the obdurate Turiddu, played by Michalis Koronis.[23] All in all a highly effective excerpt, both musically and dramatically, with a climax in which we may be sure Mary gave full expression to her pent-up emotions.

The performance was reviewed in the newspaper *Proia* by musicologist and critic Dimitrios Hamoudopoulos, a first cousin of Kalomiris and a member of the board of governors of the National Conservatory. He judged Elli Katsirelli, Zozo Remoundou, and Mary to be the best of the twenty-one singers, but singled Mary out for special mention, saying of her, "She had some really successful moments with her spontaneity of self-expression." Of the prizes awarded that evening for the year's work, a sum of 1,000 drachmas was divided equally between Remoundou

Tenor Michalis Koronis with *soprano lirico-leggero* Zoe Vlachopoulou, *Madama Butterfly*, Athens 1940.

and Mary for their achievements in the opera school. As regards Mary's progress in Trivella's proficiency class, the mark sheet shows that "No. 440, Kaloyeropoulou M." was given 10 for application and 10 for progress in each of the three terms. The remarks column—where the teacher might make a note if a student had stopped attending, been promoted to a higher class, been awarded any certificate or diploma—remained tellingly blank.[24]

Although it is undeniable that Trivella was Mary Kaloyeropoulou's first teacher, ultimately her contribution to the evolution of "the Callas phenomenon" was rather limited. There are many who maintain that if Trivella's name is known today it is entirely because she was lucky enough to have had Mary (and to a lesser extent Kambanis) among her pupils. Maria herself was partly responsible for the wide currency of this view. She rarely mentioned Trivella's name and repeatedly gave her second teacher, de Hidalgo, all the credit for her achievements. In her brief memoirs, dictated late in 1956, she remarked, *"I began studying with a teacher, probably of Italian origin, Maria Trivella,"* and immediately went on to tell how she succeeded in achieving her aim of being taken on by the "wonderful" Elvira de Hidalgo. In an interview in 1964 she stated casually, *"Before I studied with de Hidalgo, I had already had a year of French repertoire,"* and again in 1970, *"I took lessons from Maria Trivella: she taught me a method favored by the French: in basic words—you sing through the nose."*[25] Did Maria have good grounds for her low opinion of Trivella's contribution to her artistic development? Or was she being unfair to her?

Unquestionably Mary respected and liked Trivella as a teacher to start with, though it is impossible to say for how long. This is borne out by the dedication

Mary wrote in English on the famous photograph of herself that she gave to her first teacher: "*To my darling teacher, to whom I owe all.*"[26] She also liked her as a person, for Trivella had been a great help to her when she was finding her feet as a singer. Litsa, who was still monitoring Mary's progress closely, says that during the two years she was with Trivella at the conservatory, Mary "loved" her and from Trivella, who was "like a second mother to her," Mary "learned the secret of music."[27]

At this distance in time it is difficult to judge what Trivella really achieved as the first teacher of Maria Callas. Although there is no denying that she had had very little experience as a singer and as a teacher, she was by nature a gentle and thoughtful person with an innate love of learning and the arts, qualities that are always precious in a teacher; and particularly valuable in the teacher of Mary Kaloyeropoulou, still so young, a girl who had finished elementary school—and only elementary school—in New York, whose spoken and written Greek was still poor, and who came from an uncultured family background. Thus there can be no doubt that it was Trivella who first instilled in Mary the rudiments of civilized behavior and a sense of social conduct that was more than just a veneer; it was Trivella who improved Mary's Greek and gave her her first introduction to French; and it was to Trivella that Mary was indebted for her first meaningful musical experiences, her first serious musical tuition, and her crucial first real contact with singing and the world of music, not merely in a theoretical and idealized form but in all its arduous and often unpleasant reality.

Strictly as a teacher of music, it is less easy to form a fair judgment of Trivella from where we stand. The opinions of those who knew her and moved in the same circles as she did, such as Elli Nikolaidi and Zoe Vlachopoulou, inevitably carry the most weight, and, as we have seen, their opinions were decidedly unfavorable. But it would be unfair to blame Trivella for all Mary's "faults" or "bad points," least of all for the excessive vibrato that was to plague her for most of her career. Whether or not Mary possessed any physical characteristics that may possibly be thought to have caused the wobble, such as a diaphragm or ribcage too small to sustain such a big voice, the amount of evidence as to its existence makes it almost certain that she already had this flaw in her high notes when she came to Greece. The only possible explanation is that she had strained her voice between the ages of ten and thirteen. Mary herself confided to a fellow piano student in 1942 or 1943 that she had started singing "too young," adding, "*It was a dangerous thing to do.*"[28] After all, as we have seen, when she was a girl she had mimicked anything she heard and liked on the radio or phonograph, and had tried to sing arias such as "Je suis Titania." Indeed, Jackie recalled that her little sister had sung along with Lily Pons, whose voice she admired; and the roles that Pons had sung in NBC broadcasts between the end of 1931 and early 1937 were Rosina, Lakmé, Lucia, Philine, and Amina, all hopelessly unsuitable for an unformed and untrained voice.[29]

Lela Skordouli, 1939.

Another of Mary's classmates at the Athens Conservatory, Lela Skordouli, who in 1940, under de Hidalgo's tuition, was learning the notoriously difficult aria "Ombra leggera" from Meyerbeer's *Dinorah*, tells how one day she was walking with Mary from the conservatory to the Royal Theater on Ayiou Konstantinou Street. "All at once I heard her singing 'Ombra leggera' quietly to herself. 'Hey,' I said, 'I haven't even learned that myself yet, and now you're singing it!' And Mary answered, '*But I sang all that stuff in America!*' I was flabbergasted and then, of course, I understood why, ever since I first heard her as Santuzza, she had always had that wobble. If she had attempted to sing things like that all on her own when she was eleven or twelve, just hearing them on the radio and shrieking along with them, no wonder her voice had picked up problems and was not under full control."[30] Naturally, the views of Maria Trivella on this important subject—to which we shall be returning when Mary will be finally in de Hidalgo's hands—obviously have to be treated with respect. Rather surprisingly, Trivella always maintained that Mary had no wobble when she herself was teaching her. According to Trivella's niece, "She was always saying that de Hidalgo altered the range of Mary's voice, that she overstrained it and harmed her vocal cords. Mary was and always had been a dramatic soprano, and she shouldn't have been made to sing such high coloratura parts. My aunt was annoyed that this damage had been done and regretted that all her hard work on the magnificent raw material of Mary's voice had gone to waste."[31] Be that as it may, and given the fact that the wobble already existed in 1937–38, on the evidence available today it is difficult to argue that the wobble in Callas's voice was caused by Trivella's teaching.

There are better grounds for the charge that Trivella made Mary sing pieces hopelessly unsuitable for a first- or second-year student of fourteen or fifteen. Certainly the arias from *Der Freischütz, Oberon, Aida,* and *Thaïs* do not belong in that sort of repertoire, and *Cavalleria Rusticana* perhaps still less. As far as the arias are concerned, it is fair to assume that Trivella yielded to various pressures. First

To my darling teacher to whom I owe all.
Mary Anna

Mary Anna Kaloyeropoulou. Photo dedicated to Maria Trivella, Athens, early spring 1939.

from Mary herself, who was very impatient to "get on": she is reported to have said to Ypatia Louvi, "*Trivella belongs to the French school. That's not good enough for me. I want to develop my higher register.*" "If you don't have the lower notes, how are you going to get the higher ones?" Louvi asked. "*I don't want any of that stuff. I want opera, straightaway!*" But Trivella was probably pressed even more by Litsa, whom Afroditi Kopanou remembers telling Kalomiris, "She doesn't need any more lessons, give her a role on stage; Aida for example!" "And she was doing the same with Trivella," Kopanou adds, "who, in order to please, gave Mary arias from *Traviata, Aida,* and *Tosca* to sing."[32] If the honest Trivella seems to have withstood Litsa's pressure reasonably well, there is no question that she had been bowled over by Mary's ability and, being an amenable and unassertive person, it is more than likely that she gave in to her requests for an overambitious expansion of her repertoire. As for *Cavalleria Rusticana,* the fact is that it was chosen by Kalomiris and Karakandas; Trivella simply did not have the standing to block it, especially as there were many older and more experienced students taking part in the double bill.

Yet the fact remains that the way Mary and Litsa behaved toward Trivella, a woman who was good-hearted and guileless to the point of naïveté, was thoroughly reprehensible, no matter how inadequate they considered her as a teacher. What is more, it continued until the very last moment, in September 1939, when a fresh batch of candidates presented themselves at the Athens Conservatory for the annual entrance and scholarship examination. That year the examinations began on 16 September, and among the candidates, apart from Mary, was Lela Skordouli whose comments are quite forthright: "On the very day that we were taking the scholarship exam at the Athens Conservatory, Maria had lunch with Trivella, to whom she hadn't yet said a word about it! If she didn't win a scholarship she would be going back to Trivella. Word got round in the National that Maria had 'done the dirty' on Trivella." The same sentiments are expressed by Trivella's niece, Penelope Adali: "They sold her out! Such gross ingratitude! She was terribly hurt and upset about it, it almost made her ill. She realized that it was partly due to coercion by Mary's mother, prompted by shortage of money and her desire to put her out to work as soon as possible; but the way they went about it was nothing short of a betrayal!"[33]

Trivella's "little house" at 5 Hoffmann Street, where Mary took most of some six hundred lessons from summer 1937 to autumn 1939.

Voicing a very legitimate grievance, Trivella told a journalist in 1957 that she had given Mary about six hundred lessons free of charge: "[Yet] she deserted me for de Hidalgo, who started passing her off as her own 'creation.'. . . Never once has she even sent me a card, and that hurts me terribly." Finally, carried away by her feelings of bitterness, Trivella described Mary as "very ambitious, suspicious, and vindictive." When, a few months later, Maria, by this time a grown-up woman and a celebrity, came back to Athens on her first visit after an absence of twelve years, she had not forgotten Trivella. On the contrary, she had a bad conscience about her and was full of remorse. One of the first things she did was to telephone her. "*I want to come to that little house, to see that little house where I started,*" she said. "*I must see if I can fit it in.*" Trivella's niece takes up the story: "She sent my aunt a complimentary ticket for the concert at the Odeon of Herodes Atticus, and my aunt sent flowers and went backstage to congratulate her. Needless to say, she didn't stoop so low as to bring up the subject of Maria's past attitude. There were kisses, tears, it was a very emotional scene. Maria signed a photograph for her, told her that she had never forgotten her and would make sure she came to see her before she left. But she never came to Hoffmann Street."[34]

Then, in 1960, when Maria told Greek journalists that the person who had helped her in those early days was Kostis Bastias, Trivella wrote a letter to the newspaper *Ta Nea* to correct "inaccuracies" and "perversions of the truth": "Has she forgotten how I was the one who took her on as soon as she had arrived in Athens and spent two and a half years teaching her singing, elocution, opera, all free of charge, at the National Conservatory, where I got her in with a scholarship? I treated her not as a pupil but as a daughter, giving her the love and guidance that her talent deserved . . . [but] her unmindfulness and indifference have wounded me. I do not deny that Mr. Bastias helped her, but only after I had 'made' her."[35] Maria Trivella carried on with her work as a teacher—perhaps not a brilliant one, but always conscientious, sincere, and warm-hearted—in the "little house" on Hoffmann Street, surrounded by her beloved cats, sitting at the same upright Stichel piano with a small bronze bust of Mozart on it, where on an autumn morning in 1937 she had first heard the voice of the girl who was to become Maria Callas. She died of a heart attack in June 1963, at the age of sixty-nine.

CHAPTER 14

The Athens Conservatory:
Elvira de Hidalgo and Bel Canto

The Athens Conservatory was founded in 1871. In those days the only music to be heard in the Greek capital consisted of occasional performances by the military band and rare appearances by foreign musicians, mainly Italian opera companies. No other vocal music was heard beneath the Attic sky apart from sentimental ballads of Turkish origin, and even they did not often disturb the silence of the very beautiful but culturally backward small town. The government made over to the Musical and Dramatic Society (as the conservatory was first called) the former premises of the School of Arts and Crafts on Pireos Street, a building described as "crumbling" and "totally unsuited to the purposes of the conservatory." The German architect Ernst Ziller, commissioned to rebuild it in accordance with the latest thinking on conservatory design, converted the west wing into an auditorium of about 250 seats with its own entrance, a stage, orchestra-level seating, a dress circle, and excellent acoustics. The Great Hall, as this auditorium was called, was destined to play a very large part in the education of Greek musicians; and in June 1940, by then somewhat dilapidated, it was the scene of the second stage appearance of young Mary Kaloyeropoulou.

By that time the conservatory had been in existence for almost seventy years and enormous progress had been made. Greece had given the world a number of internationally recognized musicians and, after 1920, Athens had developed into a major musical center honored by many of the world's greatest soloists. The most exciting event of the 1920s was a series of three concerts and one recital by Camille Saint-Saëns in the spring of 1920, when he was eighty-four years old. These were held in the Odeon of Herodes Atticus, which open-air amphitheater thus, on 16 May 1920, was used for its original purpose for the first time in the modern era. Exactly six years later, in May 1926, Richard Strauss, himself a great admirer of ancient Greece, came to Athens and conducted three concerts of his work including one in the Stadium, which had been completely rebuilt for the first modern Olympiad thirty years earlier.

The dominating figure on the Greek musical scene was then Dimitri Mitropoulos, professor of musical form at the Athens Conservatory.[1] Between the

The Athens Conservatory, 35 Pireos Street, near Omonia Square, Athens.

autumn of 1924 and the end of 1937 Mitropoulos conducted 172 concerts, often
with quite demanding avant-garde programs. From 1927 the reconstituted Athens
Conservatory Orchestra, whose seventy to ninety members included the composer Nikos Skalkottas among the violins, gave two or sometimes three concerts
a week. But it was the next decade that was to be the great heyday of music in
Greece. The list of those who appeared in Athens during the 1930s, many of them
more than once, is impressive indeed. Among them were Emil Sauer, Alfred Cor-
tot, Artur Schnabel, Wilhelm Backhaus, Wilhelm Kempff, Alexander Brailowsky,
José Iturbi, Clifford Curzon, Gerald Moore, Pablo Casals, Zino Francescatti,
Jacques Thibaud, Gregor Piatigorsky, Georg Kulenkampff, Bronislaw Huber-
man, Alexander Uninsky, Artur Rubinstein, Adolf Busch, Fritz Kreisler, Andrés
Segovia, Nathan Milstein, Jascha Heifetz, and the conductors Karl Schuricht,
Clemens Krauss, Jonel Perléa, Jascha Horenstein, Hans Knappertsbusch, Charles
Münch, Eugen Jochum, Herbert von Karajan, Paul Paray, and Hermann Scherchen. Consequently, Athens in 1937—the year in which Mary Kaloyeropoulou
arrived and started her musical studies—though small, underfunded, and by no
means highly regarded in comparison with other musical centers, nevertheless
maintained high standards and possessed a hard core of experienced musicians,
teachers, and critics as well as a fairly exacting public.

—⚹—

On 18 April 1934 the board of governors of the Athens Conservatory appointed "the distinguished opera singer" Elvira de Hidalgo to be professor of singing and opera. Born in Val de Robles, Aragón, probably in 1892 (but perhaps in 1888 or even 1882), de Hidalgo considered Barcelona her hometown and claimed to be descended from an aristocratic family. Her teachers were Conchita Bordalba and the lyric tenor Melchor Vidal, both Spaniards, and perhaps later the Italian baritone Pasquale Amato.[2] She made her début very young, though it is not known when or where: possibly as Rosina at Teatro San Carlo in Naples in 1908. Maria was later to draw a parallel between her own case and that of de Hidalgo: *"I started very early; my teacher, de Hidalgo, started very early. She is a Spaniard and I am a Greek; so we are Mediterranean, where girls grow and mature quicker."*[3] De Hidalgo was a *soprano lirico-leggera*, with a silver-toned voice and a flexibility that earned her a great name as a *soprano d'agilità*. Her repertoire comprised all the classic coloratura roles: Rosina (in which she was said to have been unsurpassed), Violetta, Lucia, Gilda, Lakmé, Amina, Elvira, Manon. Her lower register was also very strong, and she made good use of her chest voice in zarzuelas and traditional Spanish songs. She had a reputation as a very fine actress,[4] made her name in the course of a long career in the great opera houses of Europe and the Americas, including sixteen performances (eight as Rosina) at the Met, and she sang with all the great singers of her day, such as Enrico Caruso, Mattia Battistini, Titta Ruffo, Riccardo Stracciari, Tito Schipa, and Fedor Chaliapin. Although de Hidalgo was generally talkative and not averse to publicity, she seems not to have said much about her illustrious past and did not have many old photographs or other mementos on display in her home.

For some reason de Hidalgo always said that her presence in Athens was the merest accident, maintaining that she had come to Greece just before the war, had been stranded there by the outbreak of hostilities, and had eventually had no option but to take the job at the Athens Conservatory, which she had turned down several times. However, the truth is quite different. Her first visit to Greece had been in 1919, when she triumphed in eleven performances of *Barbiere* and *Lucia* and won the admiration of King Alexander and Prime Minister Eleftherios Venizelos. In the spring of 1930, still at the peak of her vocal powers, she came back to Athens to sing in *Barbiere* and *Rigoletto*, and on that visit she met and fell in love with Panayis Karandinos, a sensitive and cultivated man who was also a capable theater manager and co-owner of the Olympia Theater. As a result, she was back again in October of that year for a production of *La Traviata* (again at the Olympia) with Petros Epitropakis as Alfredo and Yannis Angelopoulos as old Germont, both fully capable of holding their own against her.

In Athens she stayed for a while at the Acropole Hotel before moving in with Karandinos at his house, on Valtetsiou Street, in 1932. At that time she was still

Elvira de Hidalgo as Rosina,
La Scala 1916.

married to her second husband, Armand Bette, formerly Clemenceau's secretary and later manager of the casino at Ostend, and she traveled on a French passport, making frequent journeys to France, where she had some property. She then continued her career with the Hellenic Melodrama, singing mainly in Athens but also in Volos and Thessaloniki (1931, 1932, 1936), Iraklion (1932), and Corfu (1933). On 2 February 1934 she sang in a concert with the Athens Conservatory Orchestra under Dimitri Mitropoulos, and on 1 December of the same year, shortly after she had started teaching, she appeared in another production of *La Traviata* at the Olympia, in which the baritone was her old friend Riccardo Stracciari.

In the summer of 1935 de Hidalgo went on tour with her own company to Aigion, Patras, Zakynthos, and Kefalonia. The small orchestra was conducted by

Elvira de Hidalgo, Athens 1935.

Alexandros Kyparissis and the up-and-coming young conductor Michalis Vourt-sis. *La Traviata, Lucia,* and *Lakmé* were the productions taken on tour, and the principals included veteran bass Michalis Vlachopoulos (the father of Zoe Vlacho-poulou) and the young tenor Andonis Delendas, who was to be the first tenor of note in Callas's career. The pianist and répétiteur was Elli Nikolaidi, who accom-panied de Hidalgo at her practice sessions. "She was still slim," Nikolaidi recalled, "and her voice was superb—she sang like a nightingale! She practiced every day, sometimes on pieces that she no longer performed in public. But she knew only the Italian repertoire, and only opera."[5] In the spring of 1937 de Hidalgo gave two farewell performances at the Pallas under the baton of Totis Karalivanos. In *La Traviata* (20 May) she was partnered by Delendas and the thirty-year-old baritone Lakis Vassilakis, who at that time was still a pupil of hers and had just become her lover. In *Rigoletto* (22 May) the baritone was Yannis Angelopoulos who, as Rigo-letto to her Gilda, became the last man to hold Elvira de Hidalgo in his arms on stage.[6]

De Hidalgo was still a fine figure of a woman, but, as she herself admitted, her voice was beginning to feel tired. Nevertheless, when she visited Italy in 1938, "one of the most famous theaters" tempted her with offers of one of her great roles: Gilda, Lucia, or Rosina. Very wisely, she preferred not to risk a flop which would bring her career to an inglorious end. However, she did agree to make one more appearance in a concert with a compatriot of hers, violinist and conductor José de Bustinduy, at the Kimon Rallis Concert Hall in Piraeus. On 16 March 1938—just three days before the annexation of Austria by Nazi Germany—she sang an aria from one of the eighty operas by Neapolitan composer Niccolò Jommelli (probably *Fetonte*) and then rang down the curtain on her career with Lucia's great aria, which was to be one of the most stupendous achievements of her young pupil Maria Kaloyeropoulou.[7]

After retiring from the stage, de Hidalgo continued teaching at the Athens Conservatory (usually on Tuesday and Friday evenings from six o'clock) as well as giving private lessons at her home. When she took up with Lakis Vassilakis and moved out of the house on Valtetsiou Street, leaving Karandinos heartbroken, she lived for a time on Patission Street. Her next move was to a unit in a nearby apartment building still standing at 8 Codringtonos Street, on the corner of Drosopoulou Street. It was there that she first heard Mary sing and gave her her first private lessons. She later moved to a fifth-floor apartment at 79 Patission Street, on the corner of Heyden Street. In all three of these she lived with Lakis Vassilakis, a man many years her junior described by Zoe Vlachopoulou as "good-looking, good company, Jack of all trades and master of none, and a great womanizer," who was completely in thrall to the dynamic Elvira at that time.[8]

During her time in Athens de Hidalgo had a busy social life, mixing in high society in company with Greek and foreign diplomats and other admirers. She herself admired Mussolini, and in her drawing room she had a signed photograph of Il Duce in a conspicuous position next to one of Puccini. She enjoyed making public appearances and going to concerts and the theater, often dressed up in spectacular finery. Though naturally gregarious and capable of great charm, she was a cantankerous person and many considered her to have a mean character. Certainly she was very self-centered and very possessive, she loved furs, jewelry, and above all money. Although many of her pupils still remember her as a money-grubber, at least she was able to use the money from well-off students with little or no talent in order to offer reduced fees or free tuition to the more promising ones, whether rich or poor. Elli Dioridou, for example, the "nightingale with the amazing voice," never paid anything for her lessons although she could well have afforded to. Nor did de Hidalgo ever accept payment from her two best pupils, Zoe Vlachopoulou and Mary, who were also two of the poorest.[9]

It came as a surprise when, in 1934, de Hidalgo joined the staff of the Athens Conservatory, as it was a school with no tradition of teaching any kind of vocal music, least of all Italian. This was due mainly to the personal taste of Filoktitis Ikonomidis, deputy principal of the conservatory from 1925 and its principal from January 1935, who belonged to the German school and regarded Italian opera as second-rate music. When de Hidalgo took up her appointment at the Athens Conservatory on 1 September 1934, there were a mere fifteen students in the advanced voice classes, of whom only three were in her class. By 1937 the figures had risen to twenty-three and ten, respectively, and remained at about that level thereafter. The total number of voice students at the conservatory fluctuated between ninety and a hundred, of whom about a third were on scholarships. From the year 1938–39, following the departure of Loula Mafta, the only voice teachers besides de Hidalgo were Henriette Varatassi, a German who had been on the staff since 1924, and the French-trained Kimon Triandafyllou, who had been teaching there off and on since 1917. Ikonomidis himself also taught theory, solfège, and harmony (he had done so since 1910) and was adamant that these subjects be studied by all students.[10]

By the late 1930s the Athens Conservatory's premises at 35 Pireos Street were fairly dilapidated, especially the three-story main building, which had not been renovated since 1892. Behind the main building there was a courtyard with mulberry trees, a picturesque well, and a small outbuilding in which the caretaker ran a snack bar. The front door, entered by a short flight of steps from Pireos Street, led into a hall with a black-and-white marble floor. At the far end of the hall was the staircase to the upper floors, on the right the stage door of the auditorium, and on the left a square waiting room. Leading off from the back of the waiting room, from which it was separated by a glass partition painted white to prevent visitors from looking in, was Classroom 25, where de Hidalgo taught. It was a large room, with plain wooden chairs around the walls, a grand piano, and a small stage at the far end, which was used for opera lessons and rehearsals of student concerts.[11]

—⚬—

De Hidalgo's practice in teaching her pupils amounted to much more than a vocal "method": she followed a comprehensive set of precepts for training and exercising the voice, a "school" of singing that constitutes a distinct manner of performance known as bel canto. She herself was one of the last in the long line of adherents to the rules of bel canto, and she passed them on to her pupils, especially Mary, through the medium of her own experience in very much the same way as she herself had learned them around the turn of the century.

Bel canto, which flourished in the eighteenth century, is a much-ornamented style of singing that concentrates on musical expressiveness to the exclusion of all else and is thus diametrically opposed to the declamatory style of *verismo*, which displaced it toward the end of the nineteenth century and is based mainly on dramatic expression. The foremost composers of bel canto operas were Bellini, Donizetti, and Rossini, many of whose works were no longer performed for that reason, and so a large part of that repertoire had fallen into oblivion. De Hidalgo was once asked why that had happened. "We had difficulties with the singers," she answered, "because their technique was inadequate." She went on to explain that *verismo*, which is required in the works of Puccini, for example, is easier than bel

Elvira de Hidalgo's Classroom 25 at the Athens Conservatory.

canto: "If you have a good, strong voice you'll always be all right. But when there are notes calling for delicate coloring, agility, and all those difficult techniques of bel canto, you naturally need more intensive and exacting schooling of the sort that we had in the old days but has since been completely forgotten."[12]

The singers for whom Bellini, Donizetti, and Rossini wrote, as well as Verdi in his early years, were exponents of the Italian lyric tradition of the seventeenth and eighteenth centuries. The central aim of that tradition was the production of notes with a clean, even tone embroidered with *fioriture* and other ornaments (*coloratura*). Although these embellishments called for considerable vocal agility, they were intended not merely to show off the singers' technical virtuosity but to lend color to their dramatic expression. Singers went through years of arduous training to perfect their voice control, and sometimes this was carried to absurd lengths, as in the case of Caffarelli, who was made by his teacher to spend five years practicing a set of exercises written on a single sheet of paper. Operas composed in the first half of the nineteenth century made use of that style of singing—later known as bel canto—one of the essential features of which, besides the mellifluous tone in the singing of musical phrases, was the use of *coloratura*, vocal ornaments or "graces" which composers employed to express the feelings of their heroes and heroines. In time, however, the use of such embellishments became more and more debased until they ended by being mere vehicles for the display of vocal virtuosity. Maria was to return to the subject frequently in later life. In one interview she said, "*In the eighteenth century the composer would say to the singer, 'Tell me what you want in the way of a cadenza, a turn, an ornament, and I will write it for you. But don't improvise, otherwise you'll ruin the style of my opera!'*[13]

The reasons for the degeneration of bel canto and its fall from favor were complex. As orchestras grew larger from the mid nineteenth century so did the volume of sound they produced, and at the same time the role of conductors became more important. Consequently, the singers felt threatened and composers started demanding a greater volume of sound from them, so that their voices would not be drowned out by the orchestra. As a result, to the permitted dramatic freedoms —already steadily increasing in number—was added a freer "lyric" style of expression. This style, which satisfied the demands of the younger composers, in turn prompted more and more singers to concentrate on dramatic expression at the expense of vocal expressiveness. As time went on they paid less and less attention to the vocal precepts of bel canto and took to expressing their emotions by means of overdramatized declamatory outbursts, in which *legati* and *pianissimi* were replaced by hard and often harsh tones. In short, *verismo* had arrived: the tonal beauty, smooth phrasing, and fluent roulades of bel canto were now relegated to a position of secondary importance.[14]

Between 1920 and 1950 the standard of soprano and mezzo-soprano singing declined, with some exceptions of course, led by Claudia Muzio, who died suddenly in 1936, and Rosa Ponselle, who retired when still quite young, in 1937. As Rodolfo Celletti has commented, perhaps with a touch of exaggeration, "[Most singers of those days] did not know how to make the transition from their low notes to their middle register. They had one octave that was rather unpredictable and precarious and another that was sometimes almost a shriek. They were unable to support their sound production with proper breathing, they found *pianissimi* and *diminuendi* difficult and, as for technical skills, they left those to their little sisters, the coloratura sopranos." The consequence of Callas's "resurrection" of bel canto in about 1950 was that a forgotten repertoire came to be heard again and the vocal fireworks became once more "the symbol of Armida's charms, of Norma's religious devotion and explosions of rage, of Amina's purity, of Elvira's dreamy, dazed state of mind, of the diabolical evil of Abigail and Lady Macbeth."[15]

According to Maria herself, the scales, trills, embellishments, and other technical accomplishments of bel canto constitute a "schooling," a whole system of vocal training. Bel canto does not mean "beautiful singing" or "a beautiful voice": "*It's a way of singing which doesn't exist today: it calls for enormous breath control and a firm line; the ability to produce a pure flow of sound together with the fioritura.*"[16] Similarly, "*Bel canto is the method that keeps your voice light, pushing the instrument into a certain zone where it might not be too large in sound, but penetrating. . . . So these tricks—which are not tricks but rather exercises, like those of an athlete who trains and builds little by little his strength and his muscles—is exactly what they mean by bel canto. A quite complicated but most fascinating lifetime job. The trouble is that it never stops, and the more you learn, the less you know that you have learned. More problems, more difficulties, more passion, more love."*[17]

While Mary Kaloyeropoulou was busy learning bel canto, it was becoming ever more obvious that it was only a matter of time before war broke out. On the evening of 19 June 1939, about a week before Mary sang at the Olympia Theater in her third student concert in the space of a month, Athenians went up to their roofs or to Lykavittos or Philopappos Hill to watch an antiaircraft exercise with searchlights, flares, and sounds of heavy gunfire, which "sent shivers of war fever down their spines," in the words of an Athens newspaper. That same month the Athens Conservatory Orchestra was conducted at the Odeon of Herodes Atticus by Dimitri Mitropoulos and Herbert von Karajan, whose Greek family origins and name, Karayannis, was emphasized by the press. Meanwhile events in Europe were moving inexorably toward their fatal dénouement. On 23 August, in Moscow, Molotov and Ribbentrop astonished the world by signing a nonaggression pact between the Soviet Union and Germany, and a week later, on 1 September, Germany announced the annexation of Danzig and invaded Poland. And while the Soviet Union and Germany were agreeing on the "provisional" division of Poland between them and Stalin was preparing to invade Finland, Mary was concentrating all her energies on the crucial entrance examination for the Athens Conservatory.

CHAPTER 15

Working on the Voice

When Mary took the entrance examination for the Athens Conservatory behind Trivella's back, in order to be admitted officially as a student and in the hope of winning a scholarship, the auditions took place in three relays on 16 and 25 September and 5 October 1939. In spite of her exceptional talent and the influence brought to bear by de Hidalgo, the outcome was by no means a foregone conclusion as the principal, Filoktitis Ikonomidis, and perhaps some others too, were against the idea of letting her in. This was mainly because of the conservative attitude prevailing in the conservatory and the narrow-mindedness of Ikonomidis himself, especially toward students such as Mary, who was hoping to be excused the compulsory theory lessons. De Hidalgo, of course, had already done her best to convince the governors of the exceptional circumstances of the case: "I decided to present Maria's case to the other teachers and the principal of the conservatory, and I spoke up for her enthusiastically because I admired her, but they weren't interested."[1]

De Hidalgo would undoubtedly have warned Mary about the general feeling against admitting her, and that was why Mary did not rule out the possibility of continuing with Trivella if necessary. Shortly before the audition de Hidalgo raised the subject once again, speaking forthrightly in Mary's favor, but again to no avail. "That was mostly because they knew she had been studying at another school," she commented later. "Their advice to me was, 'Forget about her! She won't get anywhere, and what's more she'll create problems for you because she's conceited.' I disagreed strongly and told them Mary's voice was unlike anything they had heard before. I didn't manage to convince anyone but I had confidence in my judgment, so I brought the discussion to an abrupt end. 'All right,' I said, 'let's say no more about it. I think she's quite exceptional, and I'll take her on as my pupil at my own expense. You won't need to bother about paying me for any of the lessons I give her.'"[2]

The candidates were auditioned in the auditorium of the conservatory by a panel consisting of Ikonomidis, de Hidalgo, Triandafyllou, Varatassi, and perhaps some others. Lela Skordouli, who was in the same group as Mary, remembers that they sang one aria each and were immediately told that they had passed. According to her recollection, Mary sang "Voi lo sapete" from *Cavalleria Rusticana*,[3] but it is almost certain that what she actually sang on that rainy afternoon was Rezia's aria "Ocean! thou mighty monster" from Weber's *Oberon*, which she had sung at Parnassos Hall just three months earlier. Calm now, and thinking of the satisfaction she would have in "working on such valuable raw material," de Hidalgo would no doubt have closed her eyes and enjoyed wallowing in those cascades of sound. "I told her she was bound to be accepted," she recalled later, "and that she could take it for granted that she would be given free tuition. She then went back to her place and started biting her nails again." The examiners had a short deliberation, during which Mary waited "as if mesmerized," and then one of them informed her that she had been accepted and exempted from tuition fees. After a moment of speechlessness she "blurted out a few words of thanks" and de Hidalgo told her she was free to go, but she did not move until all the candidates had had their turns.[4]

In the Athens Conservatory student register Mary was listed as Marianna G. Kaloyeropoulou, no. 1,862; in the class register for the year she was no. 488, and no. 19 on the list of de Hidalgo's thirty pupils. She was awarded the Averoff scholarship, which she held for all four years of her studies at the Athens Conservatory.[5] She was enrolled in the advanced class but, since the theory grades from the other conservatories were not recognized, she had to do the compulsory subjects all over again, which must have annoyed her considerably. We shall probably never know how or on what terms Ikonomidis's opposition was overcome. It is interesting to note that Mary was enrolled not only for singing and opera but also for Harmony I and Solfège IV, both with Ikonomidis. She also took the eurhythmics course with Polyxeni Mattei-Roussopoulou, but the main reason for that was probably to reduce her weight and in any case she evidently attended only a few sessions: Mattei-Roussopoulou has no recollection of having taught her, and in the surviving archives of the conservatory there is no record of her ever having been enrolled for eurhythmics again.[6]

—ɯ—

Maria Callas's voice would one day be characterized by certain distinctive attributes, some good and some bad.[7] First and foremost, it had a unique timbre that made it immediately recognizable. Secondly, her range was enormous: from the A (or occasionally F-sharp) below middle C, up to the E (occasionally F) above the stave—in other words, almost three octaves. Thirdly, her upper, middle, and lower registers were so different that some critics spoke of them as being three different voices. Fourthly, from 1954 onward she had an ever-increasing tendency to wobble. Which of these characteristics were already present in Mary's voice when she started having lessons with de Hidalgo in Athens?*

---

*What makes the answer to this very important question so complex and difficult is that there

The first attribute, the distinctive timbre, was already part of Mary's voice in those early days. From then until the end of her career, when using her head voice to suit the role and the music, she would vary the timbre to make it menacing or proud, ecstatic or fragile as the occasion demanded. Not only was her voice able to cope with a repertoire ranging from the contralto to the coloratura soprano, but throughout that great range it was illuminated by marvelous tone colors. Unlike some other voices with an exquisitely beautiful tone that nevertheless becomes monotonous after a while, hers had a timbre that was not immediately pleasing to every listener; many actually found it unpleasant, but it was never unremarkable, whatever she might be singing. Perhaps Walter Legge was right when he suggested that the dark-hued and highly personal sound she produced was due to the formation of her upper palate, which he said was "shaped like a Gothic arch, not the Romanesque arch of the normal mouth."[8]

The second attribute, the great range of her voice, was something that Mary did not possess from the outset, but the potential was always there, waiting to be tapped, and she soon had full use of it, thanks mainly to de Hidalgo's exercises and correct positioning of her voice. De Hidalgo realized that Mary had the sort of raw material that would be receptive to training as a *soprano sfogato* or *soprano assoluto*, whose voice makes full use of the whole range from mezzo to high soprano. This calls for natural strength in the lower register, as was the case with Malibran and Pasta, both of whom started as contraltos. To achieve the desired result, each register of the voice is trained separately and the three registers are then joined together into a more or less unified whole, though the transition from one to another is never completely seamless.

------

are no known recordings of her voice made before 1949. Visitors to the exhibition "L'opéra secret de Maria Callas" (Musée Carnavalet, Paris, 10 Apr.–20 May 1979) were able to hear for the first time a recording of "O mio babbino caro" from Puccini's *Gianni Schicchi*, which her tardy friend Vasso Devetzi claimed to have found among Maria's personal belongings in the apartment at 36 Avenue Georges Mandel and dated to 1938–39, when Maria was at the Athens Conservatory (see "La Callas Speaks," *The Callas Circle*, no. 1, Nov. 1994). If that recording really was found by Devetzi among Maria's belongings, we have to accept that the unrecognizable, quavery, childish voice actually is Mary's. But no other recording from that period of her life is known, nor is there any evidence that it could have been made in Athens, as there were no tape recorders in Greece at that time. It is worth stressing that Maria herself said later that she had *first heard* her voice recorded on 18 September 1949: "*I don't like my type of voice, I hate it. I have a horror of it! The first time I heard myself, I was singing Stradella's 'San Giovanni Battista' at Perugia, in a very beautiful church, in 1949 I think. It was the first time it had been broadcast on the radio and there was a tape of it. I was made to listen to it between two sessions. I cried— you can't imagine how I cried—and I didn't want to go on.*" (CALONI.) But during the German occupation several productions of the National Theater and National Opera were broadcast on the radio, and the Germans also had outside broadcasting units that recorded other concerts and plays. After the war the German radio archives were taken to Moscow: they have only recently been transferred to Germany and are now kept in the Rundfunkarchiv in Frankfurt. Recent discoveries of historic recordings—such as that of Elisabeth Schwarzkopf's first broadcast performance in 1938—keep alive a faint hope that a 1944 recording of Maria Callas's voice may one day come to light, perhaps as Marta in *Tiefland* or as Leonore in *Fidelio*.

This brings us to the first of her two vocal problems. The inconsistency of tone between her "three different voices," as they were often called, was something else that Mary acquired early on, when she was studying with de Hidalgo, and it went hand in hand with the extension of her range: it was the natural consequence of extending the voice downward and upward through the use of the chest or head as a soundbox. Her transitions were nearly always audible and her tone varied from one register to another; de Hidalgo was not able to eliminate this flaw, nor would Maria ever be able to avoid it later. All they managed to do was to disguise it cleverly, at least until the early 1960s, and even then, when singing the transitional notes, Callas often produced a *tubato* effect as if the sound were coming from a separate resonating tube. On the subject of these "audible gear changes," Walter Legge pointed out that they were unnoticeable only in rapid passages, particularly descending scales, where she succeeded in "joining the three almost incompatible voices into one unified whole."*

Maria's other vocal problem, the wobble on her high notes, has already been mentioned, and we shall return to the subject again. She had certainly been troubled by it when she started having music lessons in Athens, if not before, and she had probably caused it herself, or at least aggravated it, by overstraining her vocal cords. De Hidalgo managed to improve it, and almost to eliminate it for a time, by setting her the right exercises and positioning her voice correctly. But she never succeeded in curing her of it altogether, for it reappeared in 1954 and even more after 1959, when Maria started forcing her voice again, thus overstraining her already tired vocal cords.†

---

*LEGGE; J. Amis, "Callas via Legge," *Uw Maria Callas Brief,* no. 18, Dec. 1989, 23. Quite possibly this flaw in Callas's technique may have been due to de Hidalgo's inability to teach her pupils how to breathe properly and support the voice with the diaphragm, which she herself did instinctively. The importance of the diaphragm to a singer's breath control is too well known to need emphasizing. The tenor Andonis Kalaidzakis, a colleague of Mary in her early days at the National Opera, later studied in Milan with the tenor Nino Piccaluga, who impressed upon him the importance of supporting the voice with the diaphragm: to illustrate his point, he explained that a singer has to use his diaphragm muscles in the same way that an archer pulls back the bowstring to power the arrow on its flight. "Maria's singing and breathing exercises had given her a rock-hard diaphragm, so hard that it was almost bulletproof," says Kalaidzakis. (KALAIDZAKIS). She had also developed enormously strong muscles elsewhere: "The muscles of her stomach and abdomen were like steel," comments Corinna Spanidou, her physiotherapist on Onassis's yacht *Christina* in the early 1960s. "The first time she did exercises with me she said proudly, '*Punch me in the stomach, as hard as you can!*' I punched her once, not too hard, but she wasn't satisfied and told me to hit her with all my strength, which I did. My fist felt as if it had slammed into a suit of armor. By doing breathing and diaphragm exercises, she had made her stomach muscles incredibly tough. I was amazed!" (C. Spanidou, *Onassis As I Knew Him,* Athens 1996, 145.)

†Walter Legge described the agonies that Maria went through in 1954: "Unfounded rumor that I might be looking for a deputy for Callas had magnetized several well-known sopranos, who were buzzing hopefully in and around Biffi Scala, where we habitually ate. Callas walked in as if unconcerned, pecked my wife's [Elisabeth Schwarzkopf's] cheeks and without sitting

So it is clear that Mary already had some vocal problems when she started studying with de Hidalgo, yet nearly everybody who knew her at either conservatory remembers that her exceptional talent was apparent from the first moment. In the words of Smaragda Yennadi, a highly experienced teacher at the National Conservatory, "She was in a class of her own, in spite of and because of the flaws in her voice." The first impressions of her fellow students in the class she joined unofficially in 1938 are of interest for what they have to say about her voice as it was then. Ekaterini Politou, who was with her at the Athens Conservatory, recalls that one day she heard "a stentorian voice with a terrible tremolo." When she came out she saw a tall, rather fat and shapeless girl with long, unkempt hair, wearing a tweed coat. "The next day I asked de Hidalgo what she had thought of her. 'I'll fix that tremolo of hers,' she answered. 'Just wait and see how she improves!'" Lela Skordouli, too, describes how de Hidalgo first set out to lick Mary's still unruly voice into shape: "The lower notes simply didn't go with the top notes, so she tried to lighten the lower notes to bring them into balance with the high ones. But her high notes were sometimes more like screeches, especially in the pieces from the *leggero* repertoire that she was then trying out. In the *drammatico* repertoire her notes were better shaped and controlled, because de Hidalgo was keeping Maria as a *soprano drammatico* with vocal flexibility, in other words a *soprano lirico-drammatico*, for *Norma*, *Trovatore*, and other operas of that kind." Skordouli also remembers clearly that the wobble was present in Mary's voice from the very beginning, even as early as that first Santuzza of hers in 1939, and that even then de Hidalgo was trying to straighten it out as far as possible. "I don't think de Hidalgo ever really managed to eliminate those faults," Skordouli concludes shrewdly, "but she did teach Mary to turn them to good account and make features of them."[9]

Besides occasionally having a nasal tone (which she attributed to Trivella's having taught her the French method of singing "*through the nose*"), Maria said later that her voice was always on the heavy side, more like a contralto. She also admitted that at first she had not had the "*low chest tones*" which she considered essential for bel canto "*because they build the bridge from the chest notes to the middle register.*"[10] De Hidalgo therefore started by tackling Mary's low notes, which were weak: "With Trivella her high notes were good, but her low notes were virtually nonexistent," Elli Nikolaidi recalled. "However, de Hidalgo must have done

---

down said, '*Show me how you sing top A's and B's and make a diminuendo on them. Walter says mine make him seasick.*' When Schwarzkopf demurred, Callas, ignoring the astonished diners, sang with full voice the notes that were giving her trouble, while Schwarzkopf felt her diaphragm, lower jaw, throat, and ribs. Waiters froze in their stride, while guests turned to watch and hear the fun. Within minutes Schwarzkopf was singing the same notes while Callas prodded her in the same places to find out how she kept those notes steady. After twenty minutes or so she said, '*I think I've got it. I'll call you in the morning when I've tried it out,*' and sat down to supper." (LEGGE.)

her a great deal of good, because she soon acquired a greater degree of vocal homo-geneity." According to Giuseppe di Stefano, Maria herself once asserted that her low notes had been "made" by her teacher in the space of a few days, but actually they had always been latent within her, de Hidalgo having merely discovered them and positioned them correctly. Then, in 1969, Maria said that de Hidalgo had taught her the chest voice by singing the transitional notes: "*When I went to her I had had nearly a year with a teacher of the French school, and at that time I didn't have any of the low chest notes which are so necessary for a dramatic soprano.*"[11]

While working on Mary's lower register and teaching her to use her chest voice—or very soon after that—de Hidalgo, who generally liked to lighten her pupils' voices, also pushed Mary's top notes higher. Zoe Vlachopoulou remembers having the same experience: "She used to give me *leggera* arias, even though I was a lyric soprano," she says, and recalls de Hidalgo telling them in class that she had once been offered a contract to do a lot of performances of *Butterfly* around the world but had turned it down because she did not want to sing roles that were "too heavy" for her voice: "Lighter roles, yes! So she pushed *our* voices higher, pitching our vocalises as high as she possibly could." Maryitsa Konstantinou remembers Mary doing those exercises and soaring easily to a high E, and even higher, despite having the big voice of a dramatic soprano.[12] Maria herself later touched on this topic quite frequently: "*It was my great luck to study with Elvira de Hidalgo, one of the old school, and she always kept my voice on the light side,*" she said in 1961. "*Some people say I started out as a mezzo, which is most probably right, because I did start out with a very short voice. But immediately, my high notes came—which means it was not exactly a question of study. They automatically came; they would have come anyway.*" And later she insisted: "*[De Hidalgo] always trained me to keep my voice limber,*" and, "*She knew that I was a very heavy voice, but she also knew that such heavy voices should be kept limber.*"[13]

However, the extension of Mary's voice downward and upward created new problems. "*If your middle voice is weak,*" she once said to John Ardoin, "*you make up for it on the top; but when you build a more solid middle voice, something gives on the top. What can you do?*"[14] The most troublesome consequence was the awk-wardness of the transition from one register to another. De Hidalgo indirectly acknowledged that this was virtually insuperable: "It is a very big problem—a prob-lem and a mystery, because no one can understand why it is so."[15] The problem of Maria's "gear changes" or "three different voices" was the price she inevitably had to pay in order to sing, more or less concurrently, such utterly incompatible roles as Elvira and Brünnhilde, Amina and Norma, Violetta and Aida, Lucia and Imo-gene, Armida and Isolde, Gilda and Tosca, Rosina and Elisabetta, Turandot and Carmen, Fiorilla and Medea, Ifigenia and Gioconda. At all events, the changes of register remained audible throughout her career, but she did with them what she usually did with her weaknesses, turning a natural fault to her own advantage and using it as a brilliant means of expressing her temperament and her acting talent.

Besides the undesirable but unavoidable consequences of extending the voice to such a great range, Maria's vocal faults were also essential aids to her becoming a *prima donna assoluta* in the forgotten tradition of Grisi, Malibran, Pasta, Lind, and some others. It has been aptly said that in the low register her unforced chest notes were those of a drunken sailor, that in the middle register she had the slightly veiled and hollow tone of a clarinet, and that her high notes were bright and effortless but always a bit unsteady and tending toward a shriek in dramatic passages.[16] But one must remember that this vocal diversity or "fragmentation" and the various "unpleasant" sounds inherent in the voice were also characteristic of all the legendary prima donnas of the past, who evidently used them cleverly—as Maria did—to enhance their dramatic expressiveness. Pasta sang "like an angel," according to Bellini, and Verdi described Malibran as "a prodigious artist"; but both of them had serious vocal problems: according to Verdi, Malibran's tone was "not always as pure as it might be" and her voice was "sharp and piercing on the high notes"; of Pasta, Stendhal wrote, "[Her voice] is not all molded of the same *metallo*, as they would say in Italy; and this fundamental variety of tone produced by a single voice affords one of the richest veins of musical expression." And then, as if springing to the defense of Maria Callas a hundred and thirty years before her time, Stendhal added, "No voice whose timbre is completely incapable of variation can ever produce that kind of suffocated tone, which is at once so moving and so natural in the portrayal of certain instances of violent emotion and passionate anguish."[17]

Thus from the early nineteenth century onward, the traditional and purely musical bel canto of the seventeenth and eighteenth centuries was gradually extended by the introduction of the dramatic element, which was often conveyed by the use of "different voices" and the exploitation of vocal tricks (or "faults") in various combinations and proportions. That was the climate in which Verdi worked and which led eventually to *verismo* and to Puccini; and that was the reason Maria Callas sang Bellini, Donizetti, and Rossini *and* Puccini, Giordano, Mascagni, and Boito. No doubt the great *prime donne assolute* of an earlier period would have been capable of doing no less, if the works of those composers had existed in their time. "*Let's state this plainly*," Callas once said: "*My voice has one main repertoire, that of Bellini, Donizetti, and Rossini, and it comprehends more than one of the modern categories of voices. It is soprano. Period! Pasta and Grisi did Normas and Fidelios, and I'm only doing what they did.*"[18]

—∞—

De Hidalgo's pupils remember that she would occasionally accompany them on the piano herself, but only when it was absolutely necessary ("because Madame was rather spoiled"). Being no pianist, she did not play at all well, and in any case she preferred to give her undivided attention to the singers. She therefore took care to find the best accompanists she could, and by a curious coincidence the three she chose were all Greeks from Russia. The first, her principal accompanist who was to be the cornerstone of her thirteen-year teaching career in Greece, was Yerasimos Koundouris, who had graduated in 1933 and was already teaching the piano at the Athens Conservatory. Koundouris, an unassuming and affable man, was well liked for his courtesy and breadth of learning in addition to his professional competence. The second, Klada Matsouki, had recently graduated with distinction as a pianist but also had a diploma in singing from the Athens Conservatory; she was therefore thoroughly familiar both with her job and with the way the conservatory worked. The third, who played mostly for de Hidalgo's own practice sessions and some of the private lessons she gave at home, was Elli Nikolaidi, who had been recommended to her by the conductor Alexandros Kyparissis in the early 1930s.

De Hidalgo divided her students at the conservatory into two groups: one comprising those in the preliminary and lower classes and the other those in the intermediate and advanced classes. The upper group she took herself, sharing the work with Koundouris. While she was doing voice exercises with one student, another would go into the next room and practice with Koundouris; then they would change places, and so on. Meanwhile the lower group went into another room, where they were taken by Klada Matsouki. "De Hidalgo trusted me and didn't want to get overtired," said Matsouki. "She only taught the more advanced students, and quite often I took those too. She knew nothing about the classical repertoire or lieder, but she was second to none on opera, which was all she was interested in." The teacher and her new pupil Kaloyeropoulou obviously shared the same taste: all they wanted was opera, and especially Italian opera. Anything else, however beautiful and however necessary, to them was more or less an imposition.[19]

At the beginning of each year de Hidalgo gave her pupils their set pieces to study. "She chose the right kind of music for each student's voice and capabilities, without ever offending anyone," Spyros Salingaros recollects. "Whenever she went abroad, she came back with sheet music and scores that weren't available at the conservatory. These she handed out to us, and there was no question of our asking for anything else."[20] Maria would always be grateful to her teacher for having lent her operatic scores: "*Elvira de Hidalgo used to lend me the full scores of operas, which I could not have bought. I used to learn them by heart, so as to give them back as soon as possible. This was good training of the memory, and training of the memory is good for the training of the mind.*" In fact Mary trained her memory so well that she was able to practice without the music: "*I learned, for instance, 'Norma' and 'La Gioconda' before I could ever have sung them properly. So I could rehearse them in my mind, on the top of a bus or walking in the street. There is a great deal to be done in the mind: you do not always require a piano, nor to open your mouth. . . . The poets talk of the mind's eye: there is [also] the mind's ear.*"[21] In after years de Hidalgo also touched on this subject, apropos of Mary's serious nearsightedness: "She read the notes by bringing the music very close to her face, while holding her glasses," she

Elvira de Hidalgo (in striped dress) in the Athens Conservatory courtyard with students and accompanist Yerasimos Koundouris (standing left). Behind her is Spyros Salingaros and crouching is Vangelis Lakadzis, whom Mary coached as Radamès in 1940.

once said. "Without glasses she couldn't see a meter," she stressed on another occasion. "But this physical handicap helped the development of her memory enormously. Maria Callas has performed dozens of operas on stage without ever being able to see the conductor. In order not to miss her entries she memorized the whole opera, the parts of the tenor, the baritone, the bass, the chorus, everything. When she came to me at the conservatory she was already in the habit of learning the entire opera by heart."[22]

Before the lesson started the whole class would do breathing exercises, filling their lungs with the fresh air (as it was then) of Pireos or Patission Street. Then they started on the exercises of Giuseppe Concone (Turin 1801–1861) or Heinrich Panofka (Breslau 1807–Florence 1887), two famous teachers who wrote major textbooks for their pupils. Maria often spoke about these exercises in later life: "*Today, even great singers have never heard of Panofka or Concone and other books of this kind. . . . The preparation of trills, of distances, of scales, of runs, of legati*" [1957], and "*I did have training in Concone and Panofka; that teaches you trills, the legati, the distances [intervals], the way of bel canto*" [1961].[23] She did not resent having to do these exercises, as she realized that they were essential if one was to sing the music in accordance with the precepts of bel canto. She herself confirmed years later that she had been happy when she sat down at the piano to do her beloved exercises by

Concone and Panofka: "*To me they are not dry vocalises, not frozen particles of chromatic scales or of acciaccature, mordents or trills, but fantastic embryos of melodies, sketches, shadowy jottings for pieces of music that have yet to take shape.*"[24] De Hidalgo also had her own exercises, of course, which she gave to each student according to his or her needs. She did not have them written down but sang them to the accompanist or, occasionally, played them on the piano herself. There were about twenty of these exercises, and she selected from them in light of her own experience and intuition, always asking the students not to reveal them to anybody: "C'est votre secret!" was her standard injunction.[25]

After the exercises de Hidalgo would start on opera (arias, duets, and quartets). There she felt in her element, as no doubt did Mary. The usual accompanist was Koundouris, but for student concerts or other public performances she sometimes called on the services of Andreas Paridis, a very fine pianist who had just graduated from the Athens Conservatory. Paridis was a strict critic of the students, but he also loved a joke, often necessary to relieve tension in the classroom: "If one of them sang really badly I would burst out laughing and play wrong notes on purpose, which cracked everyone up. Sometimes de Hidalgo got angry, but she was a wonderful teacher and had a terrific ear for talent. She often interrupted to correct some fault: she would explain what she wanted by singing the passage herself, and as her voice was properly positioned she sang quite naturally."[26]

Besides vocal interpretation, de Hidalgo taught stagecraft at the same time. The actress Maria Alkeou, who held a licentiate in piano performance and also had singing lessons, remembers her telling the class, "Movement must spring from the rhythm, the melody, and our feeling for the words we are singing." De Hidalgo dinned that into them all, and Mary, of course, took it in at once: "She was very good at matching her movements to the rhythm and style of the music," says Alkeou. "We started by practicing the music as such and then went on to act it out on the small stage in our classroom. Our teacher often sang the aria and 'acted' for us at the same time. That was her method." Drawing on her wealth of experience with the world's greatest directors and singers, de Hidalgo passed on to her pupils all the seemingly insignificant but invaluable secrets of stagecraft. For instance, as Zoe Vlachopoulou recalls, "We were never allowed to have an arm outstretched with the palm upward, or to keep our arms pressed tightly to our sides. When I was sitting down, I had to extend the upstage leg." De Hidalgo's fiery temperament also enabled her to demonstrate how to interpret each role convincingly. Vlachopoulou continues: "Later, when I was a principal at the National Opera, de Hidalgo sometimes had me over to her house for coaching in certain roles. In Massenet's *Manon*, for example, she put me through the scene in Act III where Manon sets out to seduce des Grieux: 'You take the tenor part,' she said, and started acting out my role for me, showing me how to put my arms around him, how to do this and that, and all the time singing my part. I am sure she must have done as much or more with Maria."[27]

—⁂—

But was de Hidalgo actually a good teacher? Most of her pupils think not, although they remember her with the utmost respect and affection. The consensus among them is that she was better at developing their performing skills than at teaching them the basics: "She improved my stagecraft no end. She was fantastic!" is the comment of Marika Papadopoulou, a pupil of Marika Kalfopoulou who had private lessons with de Hidalgo beginning in the school year 1939–40. "But she wasn't the right teacher for a beginner. First you had to position your voice and learn how to breathe, and then you could go to de Hidalgo." Arda Mandikian is of the same opinion: "I wouldn't say de Hidalgo was an extraordinary teacher. She was a very good coach, not a technique teacher. What she did for Maria and me was wrong, in a way, because when you are seventeen and eighteen it's not right for the voice to sing such heavy roles, duets from *Gioconda*, *Norma*, and *Aida*. Yet we did it, and it must have been very bad for the voice. Fortunately it didn't harm ours." What Mandikian does not make clear, however, is whether it harmed their voices in the long run.[28]

Elli Nikolaidi, too, who accompanied de Hidalgo at the piano for years, considered that her knowledge of singing was empirical only: "When Kaloyeropoulou heard her well-positioned voice she learned a lot. But de Hidalgo's only way of teaching was by example: her pupils had to imitate her. She couldn't teach them how to breathe, for example. Once I asked her how she breathed, and she answered, 'With my chest,' whereas I could see that she was breathing with her huge diaphragm. In fact she always did instinctively what was musically right!" In other words, de Hidalgo was not good at imparting to others the skills that came naturally to her. She was good at trills, for example, but she could not teach others how to do them: she gave her pupils very few exercises to develop the technique and justified this on the grounds that too much practicing of trills tends to make the voice wobble. That, in broad lines, is the opinion of most of her pupils, though with two exceptions, Mary herself and Zoe Vlachopoulou, those pupils were neither particularly talented nor very serious musicians. "Few of her pupils were really gifted," says Vlachopoulou. "Quite a lot of them had good voices, but that was not enough."[29]

Probably, therefore, the fault lay not so much with the teacher as with the students. Certainly that is the view of Galatea Amaxopoulou, who believes that de Hidalgo did all that was required of a good teacher: "She sang herself, showing her pupils how to position their voices." Spyros Salingaros agrees that de Hidalgo was an excellent teacher for those who could follow and understand her: "Most of those in our class, regardless of their vocal abilities, lacked the necessary grounding to be taught by de Hidalgo," he explains. Mary and Zoe Vlachopoulou were the two who could absorb everything she said—the two "sponges," as they were called—and so they benefited more than the others. "Yes, Zoe and Maria profited most from her teaching," Ekaterini Politou admits, "but that did not make it easy for everybody, and de Hidalgo got annoyed when we didn't do well. Sometimes she was so exasperated that she threw her books on the floor!"[30]

Be that as it may, Maria always spoke of her in the warmest and most glowing terms, both as a teacher and as a human being. *"Elvira de Hidalgo was a great teacher,"* she said in 1970. *"Not only could she teach a girl to sing, but she saw what she could sing best. That is the difference between good teachers and great teachers: good teachers make the best of a pupil's means: great teachers foresee a pupil's ends. Elvira de Hidalgo saw I would be best singing Bellini and Donizetti, partly because their kind of music appealed to me. And she orientated me toward them."* Similarly, Maria never tired of expressing her gratitude to de Hidalgo as a person, the person who had supported her more staunchly—and above all more soundly—than her own mother: *"She could say more about me than any other person, because with her, more than with anyone else, I had contact and familiarity."*[31]

It is true that there were to be temporary estrangements between Maria and de Hidalgo, starting as early as 1944; but with two such strong personalities it would be surprising if that had not been the case, and de Hidalgo was one of the few significant people in Maria's life with whom she remained on good terms to the end. De Hidalgo, for her part, was proud of her former pupil as she followed Maria's triumphant progress in Italy, and she wrote to her regularly with congratulations and words of encouragement. When she heard the broadcast of Maria's tremendous performance as Kundry in Wagner's *Parsifal*, in March 1949, she wrote: "You were great, Maria! As you see, I was quite right when I told you not to listen to what anyone said because by following my method you would one day be able to sing any opera whatsoever. Whereas others kept telling you when you were sixteen that you were a dramatic soprano, I made you sing *Cenerentola* and scales for a *soprano leggero*. That's why you are now able to amaze everybody by singing *I Puritani* and *Parsifal*. I am really proud of you!"[32]

Without ever openly expressing her displeasure, de Hidalgo later made it clear on several occasions that she resented the fact that, justifiably or not, her reputation was based not so much on her own past glories as on her identity as Maria Callas's teacher.[33] Yet it was, indeed, Maria who had rescued her from oblivion and so, on Maria's visit to Athens in 1957 and on other occasions later, de Hidalgo remained faithful and supported her unstintingly. When, on 16 September 1977, Maria was finally released from an existence that had turned sour, a photograph of her teacher was standing on the piano in her apartment on Avenue Georges Mandel. "Maria never forgot me, never lost her love and affection and gratitude for her old teacher," de Hidalgo said shortly after. "She always kept in touch with me. Not only when she had problems but also when she had triumphs. This gave me the greatest satisfaction in life."[34] She died in Milan, in January 1980, twenty-eight months after her faithful Maria.

Elvira de Hidalgo with Maria Callas, Odeon of Herodes Atticus, Athens, August 1957.

—⁂—

[Elvira de Hidalgo] tells the story of how I turned up for my lesson every morning at ten and stayed to hear all the other lessons, until six in the evening. If I know such a vast operatic repertoire, I perhaps owe that precisely to that fact, to that thirst for advice and instruction of which I wasn't even aware then.

To Anita Pensotti (*Oggi*, January–February 1957)

CHAPTER 16

"A New Exciting World"

Right from the time when she started studying unofficially at the Athens Conservatory in 1938, Mary felt closer to Zoe Vlachopoulou than to any of the other students in de Hidalgo's class. The attraction was mutual, because they had many points in common that separated them from the rest. First and foremost, they both had outstanding natural ability and both took singing very seriously. Their approach was very professional, while none of the others intended to make a career in singing, either because they were not good enough or simply because they had private means. Fortunately, too, Zoe was a *soprano lirico-leggero*, so they were never directly in competition with each other. Two other attributes they had in common were that they were both extremely nearsighted and both found it very easy to learn their parts. Maria's ability in this respect was to become proverbial, and Vlachopoulou still remembers it with admiration from their student days: "She could read the most difficult part at sight and learn it by heart. She would read it once, as if it were a newspaper, and after that she would never forget it!" De Hidalgo later described Mary's musical memory as "an extraordinary faculty of learning a page of music at just a single glance."*

Another factor that strengthened the bond between Mary and Zoe was that they were both extremely poor, whereas nearly all the other girls in the class (but not the boys) came from middle-class families, several of them being the daughters of well-to-do businessmen. It was obvious from the way the other girls dressed

---

*VLACHOPOULOU; DE HIDALGO 161. Maria herself subsequently described the occasion in November 1947 when Serafin wanted her to sing Isolde at about a month's notice and asked her whether she knew the part. *"I thanked my lucky stars because I had studied at the conservatory, because I had just looked at the first act just by curiosity. . . . So I bluffed. I said, 'Of course I know Isolde,' and I sight-read the second act—I don't know how, God must have helped me. . . . And he turned round [from the piano] and said, 'Excellent!' Thank heavens he didn't ask for the third act, because I would have died. I couldn't stand the tension anymore.* [She laughs.] *And then I confessed: 'Look, Maestro, I bluffed. I didn't know the role, I sight-read.' He was surprised and he appreciated me even more then."* (DOWNES; cf. Paul Hume, "Maria Callas, Fiery Opera Star of Dramatic Power," *The Washington Post*, 17 Sept. 1977.)

and everything about them that they were comfortably off, whereas, as Zoe says, "We usually walked home because we often didn't even have two drachmas for the streetcar fare."[1] Referring specifically to Mary, Spyros Salingaros says: "She always looked like a girl who felt that fate had given her a raw deal, who suffered from her appearance and her poverty. About the first of these she didn't seem to make any effort, while her attempts to hide her poverty simply made it all the more obvious." Inevitably, Mary realized that it was useless trying to conceal the realities of her life, and that aggravated her feeling of inferiority. "She felt—and in those days she was—too unattractive and too poor to fit in," Salingaros continues. "Consequently, feeling unable to compete with the other girls in our class, who were well off, smartly dressed, and well turned out, she withdrew into her shell and didn't mix with the others. This may have helped her to become a great singer, it's true, but she always had a serious hang-up about it."[2]

Although her classmates admired her dedication to her work and there was never any open friction, Mary seemed aloof and was rather difficult to like. While the other girls chatted and joked together, "she would keep herself to herself with a supercilious air which we could never understand," in the words of Elli Dioridou. According to Maria Alkeou, "She was brusque, and she said what she wanted to say in a tone that brooked no argument." And Arda Mandikian adds, "She was a blunt-spoken American, a very insolent girl who spoke familiarly to everyone from the first time she met them."[3] Once when Filoktitis Ikonomidis had had the nerve

Mary with her cousin Yorgos Evangelidis in the public garden of the Archeological Museum, Athens 1938 or 1939.

to criticize her, she is said to have marched into his office, banged on his desk and shouted to his face, "*Look here, Filoktitis, I won't have you sticking your nose into my business!*" The principal, so flabbergasted that he was at a loss for words, simply roared at her in fury: "Get out!" Realizing that this time she had gone too far, Mary scuttled down the stairs and made herself scarce.[4] This particular incident, if true, may have been partly due to the mutual antipathy between Mary and Ikonomidis, but she was later to behave in much the same way to others who were much older than she was and held positions of authority.

Niki Zacharopoulou and Nina Vaki, two piano students at the Athens Conservatory, felt sorry for Mary because she was so lonely and looked so awful, especially in comparison with her sister: "Jackie was always dressed and made up like a lady," comments Zacharopoulou, "and most of the students at the conservatory avoided Mary's company so as not to show up her inferiority. One day we went over and talked to her because we were sorry for her. She was always all alone and never spoke to anyone; she was fat, with a pimply face and unwashed curly black hair; and she invariably wore a school overall with a dirty collar and shoes that looked like army boots." When Zacharopoulou and Vaki first spoke to her, she seemed surprised and was very guarded. They tactfully advised her to lose weight and generally to make a bit more effort over her appearance. "The expression in her eyes changed then. She admitted she was the Cinderella of her family and thanked us, but said nothing more." Some time later, when the two girls had got to know Mary a bit better, they took her into the little outbuilding in the courtyard: "We cut her hair and brushed it out, washed her collar and even pressed it with an iron one of us had brought from home. She just looked at us with a hangdog expression, like a lost soul."[5]

By the time Mary went to the Athens Conservatory, her weight problem had worsened. She was now really fat, especially from the waist down, and although she had an attractive face with beautiful dark eyes, the effect was spoiled by acne. Her eyebrows, as well as her hair, were black and bushy. "There was black hair wherever you looked," says Zoe Vlachopoulou. When not wearing her thick glasses, she screwed up her eyes and thrust her head forward to be able to see. Her clothes were often a disgrace, and sometimes she wore long, gaudy-colored woolen stockings with her tatty sandals. "She was an awful sight," Spyros Salingaros agrees. "She had a red-and-black checked overcoat, slightly frayed at the hems. But she herself never seemed to care: her hair was always a mess and she just didn't bother about her appearance."[6]

De Hidalgo tried to pull Mary into shape: "When I asked her to wear something attractive for an examination, she came wearing clothes in bright and ill-matching shades of red—clothes which, because of their size, created a richly comic spectacle."[7] Maria was later to acknowledge the fact herself: "*My teacher bemoaned my incredible clothes. . . . Once, after having entreated me, insistently, to put on my most chic outfit, because she was going to introduce me to an important person, she saw me turn up in a dark red skirt, a blouse another shade of red—gaudy and stri-dent—and on my head, atop rolled-up braids, I had a ghastly hat of the 'Musetta' type. I thought myself quite elegant and was very crestfallen when Madame Elvira tore off that absurd headgear, yelling that she would not give me any more lessons if I didn't make up my mind to improve my appearance."*[8] Thereafter Mary started taking rather more care over her clothes, especially for the few relatively formal functions she attended. At the same time she became gradually more approachable and less snappish in her reactions. Thus her new environment did not bring her only unpleasant experiences and relationships: her productive work with de Hidalgo and her classmates' camaraderie began to have a relaxing effect on her and to make her feel that she was on the right track. And this must have given her a sense of well-being that she had never known before.

—⁂—

The summer of 1939 was very hot, with the temperature rising to 42°C (106°F) in the shade on 20 July. Miltiadis Embirikos invited Litsa and both her daughters, as well as their first cousin Mirka Dimitriadou (Efthymios's daughter), on a short outing to Corfu and back on his father's S.S. *Eleni*,[9] to celebrate his "secret engage-ment" to Jackie: secret because, even at the age of thirty-three, he did not dare to marry against his family's wishes. Jackie, for her part, had nothing to lose, as by that time Miltiadis was her lover and she was "now in love with him," as she wrote later. Also on board the *Eleni*, besides the fare-paying passengers, were Miltiadis's unmarried sisters Nina and Moscha and some friends whom they had invited along for the trip, including Sophia Destouni, who remembers Mary singing with Jackie at the piano and amazing her listeners with the tremendous power of her voice. The party spent one night at Corfu, some of them in their cabins on board and the rest in the Grand Hotel, which Litsa later described as "almost our last taste of luxury until long after the war." On the return leg of the journey, perhaps after another demonstration of Mary's vocal prowess, Miltiadis introduced the Dimitriadis fam-ily to General Ioannis Dourendis, the minister of the interior, who was among their fellow passengers: as chance would have it, Litsa and Mary were to spend a ter-rifying week cooped up with him in their apartment some five years later.[10]

Short though it was, that trip to Corfu must have left its mark on Mary. In the first place, as Mirka Dimitriadou remarks, "She must have felt unwanted and out of place." Secondly, the sight of Jackie and Miltiadis so happy together was bound to make Mary feel envious and inferior. Jackie states in her memoirs that her sis-ter was then "plainer than ever" and relates that one day a bystander was moved to shout mockingly "Laurel and Hardy!" when he saw the two of them walking down the street together. There can be no doubt that Mary's total dedication to her ambition of becoming a great singer was then the one thing to which she clung des-perately. *"My life was my work, and my work was my life,"* she said in 1970, and that was probably the period she was thinking of when she said it.[11] It was in the environment of the conservatory that she found her equilibrium, not only when working on her voice but also when relaxing with her classmates and her beloved teacher.

Mary at the beach in Kavouri, summer 1939. With Apostolos Hadziioannou (left), Manolis Hadzis, Pepi Andreadou, Spyros Salingaros (right), and Zoe Vlachopoulou (top).

Every year up to 1940 de Hidalgo would arrange one or two trips to the seaside with her favorite pupils. It was always after the examinations, in other words after the middle of June, because she maintained that sea air was bad for the vocal cords. Mary certainly went on at least one of these happy excursions in the summer of 1939, and probably again in 1940. The group would gather at eight in the morning outside the Eye Hospital on Sina Street to catch one of the large open-top buses that ran an "express" service to the beach. The seats on these buses were arranged in rows of five, each row with its own door, and there was always a fierce battle among the large crowd of waiting passengers to grab a seat. The bus then set off down Syngrou Avenue (a two-lane road in those days), turned left at the coast, and arrived at its destination in Glyfada, Kavouri, or Vouliagmeni more than an

Mary with
Lakis Vassilakis
(de Hidalgo's
lover, left),
Pepi
Andreadou,
and Apostolos
Hadziioannou.

hour later. On these "Schubertiads," as de Hidalgo called them, the teacher and her pupils all relaxed and let their hair down, led by de Hidalgo's inseparable companion Lakis Vassilakis and his friend Manolis Hadzis, who were rather older than the rest. Photographs of those expeditions suggest that wine, song, and a succession of games and charades all contributed to an atmosphere of mounting hilarity. Mary, wearing her black bathing suit, not only swam well and fast—"you could see she was in her element in the water"—but also, in spite of her bulk, joined in the acrobatics on the sand. On the way home they all sang, light songs as well as classical, which so delighted the other passengers that "they would ask the driver to turn round and do the journey all over again."[12]

On the bus journey to the seaside in 1939 Mary sat next to Zoe Vlachopoulou, who on 23 June had obtained her diploma with distinction after only two years with de Hidalgo. They talked about music and singing, as Mary could never be drawn into discussing personal or family matters. "She was not at all gossipy," says Vlachopoulou. "And I never heard her say a bad word about any of the students at the conservatory, nor about her colleagues at the National Opera later." All Mary talked about was opera: the requirements of this or that role, the problems of staging and acting, the way a good leading man could draw out the best in his partner. But one subject she never discussed was the wobble in her voice, and even de Hidalgo took care not to use the word when giving her exercises designed to eliminate the problem. "At the National Conservatory, with Trivella, she had

Mary at Kavouri, summer 1939, seated with Manolis Hadzis and Arda Mandikian; Zoe Vlachopoulou, Apostolos Hadziioannou, and Pepi Andreadou standing.

strained her voice by singing unsuitable pieces," says Vlachopoulou, "and this created problems for her when singing *forte*, especially at the top of her register. After only a few lessons with de Hidalgo, however, the wobble began to go away." On that outing in 1939 Mary and Zoe went off and sat on a rock a little way away from the others, talking about this and that. "After a while," Vlachopoulou recalls, "I started singing 'Una voce poco fa,' *pianissimo* at first. As we were by ourselves on the rock, looking out across the open sea, she joined in and sang the whole aria with me. 'Hey!' I said to her at the end, 'you're so good at the vocalises and you've got such a lovely *pianissimo*! Why don't you ever sing at less than your full volume?' I didn't say anything about her wobble, but that was what I was thinking of, of course. She didn't know how to answer, because all that volume and power came naturally. But the fact is that Maria sang much too loud in the early days: her voice was a tremendous raw mass!"[13]

Mary with Spyros Salingaros and Zoe Vlachopoulou, Manolis Hadzis in the background.

—ɯ—

Now that Mary was officially on the books of the Athens Conservatory, a gradual change came over her. She had recently appeared as Santuzza at the Olympia, even though she had only two years at the National Conservatory behind her. She was one of only eight in de Hidalgo's advanced class—and that despite being listed as a first-year student in the class register at her new school—and she was the youngest of them all. For the first time, she was now taking life fairly cheerfully and had developed a measure of self-confidence. She was beginning to see that her chosen way of dealing with her problems and getting ahead was the right one. Also, her teacher was encouraging, supportive, warm, and sympathetic, nothing like what she had to endure from her mother at home. With hindsight, it seems fair to say that the period from September 1939 to April 1941 must have been one of the happiest—or least unhappy—in her life, a conclusion indirectly supported by some of Maria's own later statements. For example: *"When you are very young and on the threshold of a career you have all the confidence in the world—there's nothing you feel you couldn't tackle and do splendidly."*[14]

Just as she had with Trivella from the very beginning, so now under de Hidalgo Mary threw herself wholeheartedly into her work. This time, however, she did most of her studying and practicing at the conservatory or at her new teacher's apartment: she had no incentive to work at home, especially as she would have had to share the piano with Jackie, and furthermore the conservatory gave her a perfect excuse to stay out of Litsa's sphere of influence. Jackie sums up Mary's attitude to work during this period as a "panic to get on," and adds: "She no longer maintained any pretence of obedience to Mother. [When she left for her lessons] Mary would just yell out that she'd be back when she chose and off she'd go, slamming the door behind her." Besides the time spent at the conservatory, where de Hidalgo only taught in the afternoons, and not every day, Mary went more and more often to her teacher's apartment for lessons: *I started going to her classes from morning till night: from ten o'clock, when she began, till we went to lunch or had a sandwich there, and then on through to eight o'clock at night—it would have been inconceivable to stay at home, I shouldn't have known what to do there. I loved to listen to all those different voices: leggero soprano, lirico soprano, and the men too. It was all new to me, you see, a new exciting world.*[15]

De Hidalgo was greatly impressed by the expressiveness with which Mary sang Italian, even when she did not know exactly what the words meant: "She put a lot of expression into her art and I was struck by the way she interpreted the pieces, because she knew very little Italian then and she was singing in Italian. She watched me all the time: she was speaking to me not only with her mouth, her big mouth, but with her eyes as well. I was struck by that. 'This is really somebody,' I said to myself." De Hidalgo also spoke admiringly of her new pupil's zeal at those first lessons: "Maria was always the first to arrive for the lesson and the last to leave. She could learn a whole opera in two weeks, whereas the others took two months. It gave me great pleasure to teach that hardworking girl, to whom the only thing that mattered was her voice. Once I tried to help her by saying, 'That was wrong!' and she dissolved into tears when we got out into the street." Reminiscing on another occasion, de Hidalgo said: "I often spoke quite sharply to her after our lessons when she was walking back home with me through the streets of Athens, in darkness because of the war. I would tug at those awful clothes she wore, criticize everything she did, take her to task for the slightest fault. And nearly every evening she would burst into tears and grab my arm, sobbing, *'But what do I have to do to make you say I am getting on all right?'*" Elsewhere de Hidalgo remarked again on Mary's insatiable appetite for work: "She took to leaving the conservatory with me, suggesting that we might walk home together as we lived in the same street. On the way she would keep pressing me for advice and information. I was quite alarmed at her manic devotion to her work: I thought it was just the initial enthusiasm of those early days, but she stayed like that the whole time." As Maria said herself, very convincingly, *"When you are young, you like to stretch your voice, you enjoy singing, you love it. It's not a question of willpower,*

it has nothing to do with driving ambition and all such nonsense that has been writ-
ten about me. You simply love your work—this beautiful, intangible thing which is
called music. . . . When one is very young, one has a driving urge to assimilate every-
thing, a sort of furie d'apprendre, which is not so much ambition as thirst to be able to
satisfy the need for self-expression."[16]

The general atmosphere in the class was disciplined and studious, but friendly too. De Hidalgo kept her pupils in order by tempering strictness with flexibility, without ever playing them off against each other. They respected and liked her and regarded her as a friend: during the summer break they would continue to see her from time to time, and some kept up with their lessons. She, for her part, fostered the camaraderie among them and gave two or three parties every year at her home, usually around Christmas and Easter. "At those parties we sang and danced," says Arda Mandikian. "Our dance partners were the boys in the class and Lakis Vassilakis, who was a permanent fixture there, of course. Salingaros and Hadziioannou were the good-looking ones. All of us danced—tangos and foxtrots—including Mary, who would be there already when we arrived because she used to go early to help with the preparations." Also present at these and other gatherings at 79 Patission Street was Gigi, de Hidalgo's terrier, who was generally looked after by a devoted Vassilakis, though sometimes Mary took her out for a walk. These and other small services Mary performed for de Hidalgo because she felt under an obligation to her. "Our teacher often invited Mary round for a meal," says Zoe Vlachopoulou. "In fact people said that she used to let her do the washing-up afterward." De Hidalgo, however, denied this in 1977: "I would not allow her to do housework," she said, "but instead encouraged her to look after her hands, her fingernails, and so forth." The future prima donna, she added, should have elegance not just in her singing but in her appearance as well.[17]

De Hidalgo once asserted that she had taught Mary Italian, "which she was speaking fluently within three months." On this point, however, she was probably claiming the credit for something she had merely encouraged. As Maria remembered it, her teacher had often said to her, "It will be useful for you, because sooner or later you will go to Italy. . . . And in order to interpret and express well, you must know the exact meaning of every word. . . . It is ridiculous to sing Italian without understanding what you are saying." So, as Maria said, "*I bet my teacher that in three months I would manage to converse in Italian with her. But I didn't know how to do it.*" De Hidalgo used to send her pupils for Italian lessons at the Casa d'Italia, where she was well known, but Mary did not want to go to "*the fascist school,*" as she called it, because it would compromise her reputation: "*My compatriots naturally would have considered me a traitor. [Anyway,] I couldn't manage the money for private lessons.*" So she worked out the solution for herself: "*At that time I had struck up a friendship with four young doctors who had studied in Italy. . . . One was half Italian, half Greek. I just started talking with them. I had them say the verbs to me, all by ear, and after two months I managed to speak Italian. . . . I had won my bet.*"[18] But despite these claims (which are not corroborated by any other source), the truth is that Mary really learned Italian in the two years from late 1941 to late 1943 when, as we shall see, she fraternized with several Italians.

Among the first assignments de Hidalgo gave Mary were Bellini's *Norma* and the scene and concert aria "Ah, perfido!" by Beethoven.[19] We know that Mary studied, or rather devoured, anything that came into her hands. However, the only evidence we have for her repertoire during those years, apart from the examination records of the Athens Conservatory and the programs or other records of productions and concerts that she took part in, comes from the recollections of her classmates or, later, her colleagues at the National Opera. In that first year, 1939–40, besides the pieces she learned for examinations, we can be fairly certain that she studied *Norma* and *Aida*. Arda Mandikian remembers that the class was taught nearly all of *Norma*: "Being a mezzo, I used to sing duets with Maria as Adalgisa to her Norma, while Apostolos Hadziioannou, who had a very good but rather harsh-toned voice, made a fine Pollione. Maria and I were the two youngest in the class, and de Hidalgo let us sing with a fair amount of freedom. She would try to lighten our voices by giving us a coloratura passage, which she would sing herself and get us to imitate her." That year de Hidalgo also took the tenor Vangelis Lakadzis out of the intermediate class to study *Aida* and arranged for him to go and practice with Mary at her home. Mary, being in the advanced class and a reasonably good pianist, on that occasion more or less stood in for Klada Matsouki who coached the intermediate and lower classes, while at the same time she had a Radamès to sing with her when she practiced her own part.[20]

Mary was also enrolled in de Hidalgo's opera class, where only four of the seventeen, including herself, were in their first year. Maria Callas often harked back to de Hidalgo's opera teaching: "*[I received] movement training, yes, mainly from my singing teacher, de Hidalgo. I was taught then, when I was fourteen years old, the continuous flowing of a movement. . . . You learn how to act: that is, one step here, you have to face the public there, and you have to turn this way.*" In later life Maria once asked de Hidalgo whether she had been good at acting from the very beginning. "*She said, 'Yes, you were amazingly so'. . . . She admired my hands even then, so it was since I was a child. Though I remember that the very first experience, when I was still thirteen years old, I didn't really know what to do with my hands.*"[21] De Hidalgo herself recalled in 1968: "When I started teaching her she was the laughingstock of the whole conservatory. My colleagues pitied me, while the other girls teased poor Maria mercilessly—and it has to be said that she was frightfully clumsy, fat, and ungainly." However, with her usual patience and persistence, she soon began to surprise even the most skeptical observers. "She never lost her temper when her classmates laughed at her," de Hidalgo continued; "in fact she did not even seem to be aware of it. She was a glutton for advice and suggestions, and made every effort to take it all in and act on it as far as she could. The results were pitiful at first, but little by little she did begin to improve."[22]

It is interesting to see how Mary came to be assigned the part of Suor Angelica for the examinations of June 1940, amid great skepticism from the other students, perhaps from de Hidalgo too. The story is told by Ypatia Louvi: "When our teacher asked the class who would like to do Suor Angelica, Mary raised her hand and said, *'I would, Madame!'* 'You?' de Hidalgo echoed in amazement. Then she turned to me, knowing I knew the part, and said, 'Well, then, you take her and teach her!' To Mary, who was just standing there saying nothing, she commented ironically that at least the nun's habit would cloak the fat she hadn't managed to lose." Louvi says that, as Mary found it very difficult to fall or even to kneel down, de Hidalgo reiterated that she would have to lose weight. She drove the point home by adding that in her own apartment, where Mary was staying at the time ("because she had had a fight with her mother"), she saw how she wolfed down everything that was put in front of her. Mary went regularly to Louvi's home on Kalymnou Street to learn Suor Angelica: "She would come in the morning, and I remember my mother would give us egg yolks beaten with sugar, the standard concoction for building up a child's strength in those days. I played the piano for her and she learned the whole of her part until she was note-perfect. I also gave her my score, which she never returned."[23]

Meanwhile the declaration of war had had serious repercussions in Greece. The gravest threat came from Mussolini's Italy, Greece's greatest rival for territorial and economic supremacy in the eastern Mediterranean and the Balkans. The media reported on the state of the war with radio broadcasts and sensational articles under banner headlines, but they adopted a more or less neutral stance in accordance with the policy of the Metaxas government, which hoped that Greece would manage to avoid becoming embroiled. Thus life went on without too much change, apart from the regular publication of "precautionary" news bulletins. Between 13 and 16 December 1939 Athenians followed the drama of the German pocket battleship *Graf Spee*, chased into Montevideo harbor by three British cruisers and then spectacularly scuttled in the River Plate. As rumors of an impending German offensive on the western front intensified, the most popular form of distraction for Athenians was the cinema; and the Kaloyeropoulos family used to go quite often because Miltiadis Embirikos kept them at arm's length from his brother and sisters and their snobbish friends. Many of the new releases of the 1939–40 season were musicals or movies about music and musicians. Besides Marion Talley and Deanna Durbin, other singers who made a hit on the screen included Marta Eggerth, Erna Sack, Beniamino Gigli, Jan Kiepura, Margherita Carosio, and Zarah Leander. Two of the Athenian box-office successes of that year were *The Prisoner of Zenda*, featuring Ronald Colman, and *Ninotchka*, starring Melvyn Douglas and Greta Garbo. As for the field of serious music, the Hellenic Melodrama was extremely active despite the problems facing it: in the last three months of 1939 the company put on no fewer than fourteen different operas at the Olympia Theater. It is not known whether Mary attended any of these productions, but on the radio she may have heard complete performances of *Faust*, *Trova-tore*, and *Aida*, as well as a program featuring recordings of Rosa Ponselle, Geraldine Farrar, and Amelita Galli-Curci broadcast on 11 November 1939. In January 1940 the Athens Conservatory Orchestra was conducted four times by Hermann Scherchen, who also gave a series of talks and master classes at the conservatory.

—⁓—

On Friday, 23 February 1940, when a blanket of snow covered most of Attica and Lykavittos Hill in Athens itself, the Athens Conservatory held a benefit concert at 6:30 p.m. in its Great Hall for its scholarship fund for needy students. De Hidalgo's pupils performed at the end of the concert, with Yerasimos Koundouris at the piano, and the last item on the program was the duet "Mira, o Norma" sung by Mary and Arda Mandikian. De Hidalgo happened to have recently heard *Norma* on the radio with Italian singers whom she had not liked at all. "So she wrote '*Brave Caloyeropoulo e Mandikian*' on our scores, the implication being that she thought we were better!" says Mandikian. The applause was thunderous and prolonged, and the treasurer of the conservatory congratulated Mary and predicted (much to her delight, no doubt) that she would soon be singing Norma at the Met in New York. When he repeated this to de Hidalgo, she told him archly not to exaggerate.[24]

About a month and a half later, on Wednesday, 3 April, at 10:30 p.m., Mary and Arda sang "Mira, o Norma" again in a musical program on Athens Radio, one of a series of "radio soirées" that were broadcast live from the station's studio at the back of Zappion Hall. This, Mary's first broadcast—of which Mandikian has no recollection at all (nor does Irma Kolassi, although her name is down on the program of the soirée, published in the newspapers of 3 April)—was probably also her last, despite the fact that her first biographical note, written in 1943, states that she had taken part in "radio broadcasts."[25] At all events, when she was again invited to sing on the radio under the baton of Yorgos Lykoudis, one of the conductors of the Radio Orchestra, probably in 1941 or 1942, she is said to have told him "quite brazenly" that she would sing something of her own choice. He "tried to make her see reason," pointing out that first they would have to see if she was capable of singing the piece she wanted. Touchy as ever, and prompted by the sense of inferiority that always possessed her when anyone questioned her capabilities, she snapped back, "*When I tell you I can, I know what I'm saying!*" Taken aback, Lykoudis told her to watch her tongue, whereupon Mary, giving him a black look, flung at him for the first time the insolent retort that she was to repeat twice more within less than six years, once to the general manager of the Greek National Opera and once to the equally flabbergasted general manager of the Metropolitan Opera of New York: "*In a few years* you *are going to be begging* me!" And she flounced out, slamming the door behind her.[26]

Although Mary did not believe that the compulsory theory lessons were really necessary, she felt she ought to attend at least some of them, especially as she would

Conductor Yorgos Lykoudis, who never forgot Mary's insolence.

not get her diploma without doing so. But she did not want to study theory with the pedantic thoroughness for which the conservatory was renowned. "So she asked me to give her private lessons to speed up her progress," recalled Kostas Kydoniatis, who had recently joined the staff as a junior teacher. "She wasn't good at harmony, but in solfège she did fine. However, she didn't work hard: she couldn't be bothered, as she already knew how to sing. Anyway, what those courses teach you is basically to read music and respect each note, which she did quite amazingly by instinct, without needing to be taught. So we just had a few lessons, only about ten in all, for which she paid me, always bringing the money cheerfully and politely." Maria would surely not have disagreed with what Kydoniatis said, for she later remarked, "*Solfeggio is a singer's most important training asset*," thus indirectly decrying the value of the other theory subjects, at least to herself.[27]

Following the German occupation of Denmark, the landings in Norway, and the internecine naval battles in the North Sea, on 10 May 1940 Germany invaded Belgium, the Netherlands, and Luxembourg. On the same day Neville Chamberlain resigned as prime minister and was succeeded by Winston Churchill. Three days after these dramatic developments Mary was plunged into the end-of-year examinations at the Athens Conservatory. The first paper she sat for, on 13 May, was Harmony I for Ikonomidis, who marked her 1-2 for application and 2-1 for progress (on a grading scale of 1, 1-2, 2-1, 2, 2-3, 3-2, 3). Not one of the eleven candidates was given a straight 1, and Ikonomidis did not award any marks for ability. The same was true of the Solfège IV examination on 17 May, in which Mary came second out of thirteen candidates with marks of 1-2 and 1. The singing examination for de Hidalgo's advanced class on Tuesday, 28 May, was judged by a panel headed by Thrasyvoulos Georgiadis, the deputy principal of the conservatory, who had succeeded Dimitri Mitropoulos as professor of musical form. In accordance with the regulations, Mary sang one aria from the "classical" repertoire ("Care selve" from Handel's *Atalanta*), two "romantic" pieces ("Casta diva" from *Norma* and one of Leonora's arias from *Il Trovatore*, either "D'amor sull'ali rosee" or "Tacea la notte placida"), and lastly Duparc's "Élégie," a song with sustained *legati* and long, flowing phrases, which she probably sang in the bel canto style that she was then learning. In the examination record, the marks that de Hidalgo noted in her own hand, as she always did, were 1 for application, 1 for progress, and 1 for ability. She subsequently spoke admiringly of Mary's success in those first examinations of hers, adding coyly, "And then all the members of the staff who had been against accepting her came up and congratulated me."[28]

Meanwhile events were moving rapidly on the western front. Belgium capitulated, and only ten days after the German offensive the Allied forces were being evacuated from Dunkirk. The Germans immediately turned on France, and on 15 June they entered Paris, while the world trembled at the triumph of German arms. That year, in Athens, the exhibition concert of de Hidalgo's opera class was held on Sunday 16 June, just a few hours before the German army's historic parade down the Champs Élysées with the swastika fluttering atop the Arc de Triomphe. In the small packed auditorium on Pireos Street, far away from those dramatic events, the program for the evening—which was to be the last of its kind for de Hidalgo and Mary—comprised excerpts from five operas (*Lakmé, Lucia, Otello, Fra Diavolo*, and *La Bohème*) and the whole of Puccini's one-act *Suor Angelica*. De Hidalgo's seventeen students performed with rudimentary costumes and minimal scenery, with Yerasimos Koundouris accompanying them on the piano. Alexandra Lalaouni, in her review of the performance in the newspaper *Vradyni*, praised de Hidalgo for "her tireless hard work" and described her class as "a disciplined ensemble . . . [especially] in the chorus of *Suor Angelica*, which, I can honestly say, could acquit itself with credit in any opera house."[29]

Mary's performance as the young nun Sister Angelica, a noblewoman who had sinned by giving birth to an illegitimate child, has never been forgotten by those who saw it. When Angelica learns of her child's death she prays (in the famous aria "Senza mamma," which Maria was to record with Serafin in 1954) to be allowed to die and join him. In her death throes, after poisoning herself, she asks for a sign of divine forgiveness and Our Lady (on this occasion in the white-robed form of Ypatia Psarra, a student in de Hidalgo's intermediate class, holding a doll representing Angelica's unhallowed child, whom God has taken into his flock) appears miraculously. On that June night in 1940, Mary acted sensationally, breathing her last while the chorus sang, "Mater purissima! Salve Maria!" Spyros Salingaros, who was singing in other parts of that evening's program, was ecstatic: "She swept the whole audience off their feet, she eclipsed all the other performers. From then on everybody at the conservatory started talking even more about 'the

ΩΔΕΙΟΝ ΑΘΗΝΩΝ
1871

ΠΡΑΚΤΙΚΟΝ ΕΞΕΤΑΣΕΩΝ   ΣΧΟΛΗ _Μονωδίας_   ΣΧΟΛ. ΕΤΟΣ 19 _39_ - 19 _40_

Τάξις _Ανωτέρα_   πρὸς

τ ῆς _Καθηγήτριας Κ.ᾶς Ε. ντὲ Ἱδάλγω_

Αὔξων ἀριθμός	Ὀνοματεπώνυμον	Ἔτη		Θέματα ἐτησίων ἐξετάσεων	Βαθμοί			Παρατηρήσεις
		Φοιτ.	Τάξ.		Ἐπιμελ.	Προόδου	Ἱκανότ.	
7	_Καλογεροπούλου Μαρ_	✓	1	_Händel_	1	1	1	
8 62				_Care Selve_				
				Bellini				
				Casta Diva				
				Verdi				
				Trovatore				
				Duprato				
				Elegie				

Ἐν Ἀθήναις τῇ _____ 19 40.

Η ΕΞΕΤΑΣΤΙΚΗ ΕΠΙΤΡΟΠΗ

Ὁ Πρόεδρος   Τὰ Μέλη   Ὁ Διδάξας

Mary's mark sheet in Elvira de Hidalgo's handwriting, Athens Conservatory, 28 May 1940.

Kaloyeropoulou phenomenon,' some with genuine admiration and others with envy." Manolis Hadzis still found himself moved by his recollection of the scene with all the nuns singing on their knees. He was so carried away that he went up to de Hidalgo after the performance and kissed her on both cheeks, while she, trying to conceal her obvious gratification, reproved him for his "forward behavior."[30]

One of those present that night, who had been cast as Mimì in the excerpt from *La Bohème* immediately before *Suor Angelica*, was Ypatia Louvi, the classmate who had helped Mary in the early stages of learning her part. "I couldn't get over how well she sang it!" Louvi recalls. "'You were terrific!' I told her. *'Well, I worked hard, I really slogged at it!'* she retorted, instead of thanking me for the compliment. Then, as she had a white hairpiece on her head, she asked me coquettishly, *'Ypatia, will I be beautiful when I'm an old woman?'"* De Hidalgo has also described her memories of Mary's Suor Angelica: "Beneath her long white habit her physical bulk didn't show, and with her height she cut a majestic figure. Even her face seemed thinner with the wimple wrapped round it, and her large, deep-set, expressive eyes, with no glasses to detract from them, were quite remarkable. She made a tremendous hit—it was a real triumph for her. 'If she manages to lose some weight when she has finished growing, she will be a very great artist,' I said then. And I was not mistaken."[31]

In the opera examination record de Hidalgo gave eight of her seventeen pupils 1 for application and 1 for progress, but only Mary Kaloyeropoulou and Lela Skordouli (who on that occasion had sung Zerlina in the second act of Auber's *Fra Diavolo*) received the same mark for ability: for all the other students she left that column blank. The only negative criticism of Mary's performance was a remark by Alexandra Lalaouni to the effect that she needed to take more care over her diction because she sang Greek with a foreign accent, which often made it hard to understand what she was saying. That is not surprising, as Mary had a slightly foreign way of speaking which she would never lose (with the *l* slightly rolled on the palate and a frequent intrusive *n* at the end of a word). Of course, having by then been three years in Greece, she spoke the language almost perfectly, though her vocabulary was relatively limited. As usual, she herself was aware of the problem: "*I wasn't happy about my pronunciation, which is most important in singing,*" she said in 1961. "*You've got to enunciate well—to put forward the word and make the public participate in what you say and feel with you.*"[32]

—⁓—

I took in more hours than necessary [at the conservatory] because I liked to watch all the other pupils. I always have had one principle in life, that even the poorest voice can teach you something.

To David Frost, New York, December 1970

PART THREE

War, Occupation, and the National Opera (1940–1943)

CHAPTER 17

The National Opera
and Early Prospects

Just four days after the performance of *Suor Angelica*, on 20 June 1940, Mary signed her first professional contract with the National Theater, represented by its general manager, Kostis Bastias. The contract was actually with the Royal Theater, as it was then called, while in the periods when Greece was a republic it was called the National Theater (and as such it is referred to throughout this book, for the sake of convenience). It had been founded in 1900, after long personal efforts by King George I, and its neoclassical building at the corner of Ayiou Konstantinou and Koumoundourou Streets was the work of Ernst Ziller, the architect who had also built the small theater of the Athens Conservatory. The document, headed "Private Contract" with the handwritten note "Contract No. 90, Opera," evidences the engagement of "Marianna Kaloyeropoulou, resident of Athens (61 Patission Street)" as a member of the chorus for one year from 1 July 1940 to 30 June 1941. Her salary was fixed at 1,500 drachmas per month, "payable in advance every ten or five days, as the Theater may decide." Under the terms of the contract, Mary was obliged to take part in all performances for which she was detailed "by the proper authorities." An additional payment of 50 drachmas would be made only for each performance over and above ten per week. Some of the other terms of Mary's first contract for stage work required her to accept any role "without argument, without exception, and without reserve," to provide herself at her own expense with costumes for any role allotted to her that was to be performed in "modern dress," and to attend rehearsals at the theater on any day of the week, including Sundays. She was also obliged to go on tour with the company anywhere in Greece, when her salary would be increased by fifty percent for the duration of any tour outside Athens, Piraeus, and the suburbs (for which there was no extra pay). Needless to say, there was a clause forbidding her to perform with any other company or to take part in any performance "not given by the Theater." If she were dismissed she would be eligible for a severance payment of 25,000 drachmas; but if she broke any term of the contract she would be liable to a penalty of the same amount and the theater would be entitled to dissolve the contract unilaterally.[1]

Ι Δ Ι Ω Τ Ι Κ Ο Ν   Σ Υ Μ Φ Ω Ν Η Τ Ι Κ Ο Ν

Ἐν Ἀθήναις σήμερον τήν   20ην τοῦ μηνός Ἰουνίου τοῦ ἔτους 1940 ἀφ' ἑνός ὁ κ. Κωστῆς Μπαστιᾶς, κάτοικος Ἀθηνῶν (ὁδός Σατωβριάνδου 44), Γενικός Διευθυντής τοῦ ἐνταῦθα ἑδρεύοντος Βασιλικοῦ Θεάτρου, ἐκπροσωπῶν ὑπό τήν ἰδιότητα ταύτην τό Βασιλικόν Θέατρον, (ἀποκαλούμενον ἐφεξῆς τό «Θέατρον») δυνάμει τοῦ ἄρθρου 4 ἐδάφ 7 τοῦ Α. Ν. 836) 1937 καί συμφώνως πρός τήν ἀπό .... ἀπόφασιν τοῦ Διοικητικοῦ Συμβουλίου τοῦ Θεάτρου, τήν προβλεπομένην ὑπό τοῦ ἄρθρ. 5 ἐδ. 5 τοῦ αὐτοῦ Νόμου, καί ἀφ' ἑτέρου ἡ δ. Μαριάννα Καλογεροπούλου κάτοικος Ἀθηνῶν (ὁδός Πατησίων 61   ), ἀποκαλουμένη ἐφεξῆς ἡ " Χορωδός ":   συνωμολόγησαν τά κάτωθι:

1) Τό Θέατρον προσλαμβάνει τήν Χορωδόν   εἰς τόν Θίασόν του διά χρονικόν διάστημα ἑνός ἔτους   ἀρχόμενον τήν 1ην τοῦ μηνός Ἰουλίου τοῦ ἔτους 1940 καί λῆγον τήν 30ην Ἰουνίου τοῦ ἔτους 1941.

2) Ὁ μισθός τῆς Χορωδοῦ   ὁρίζεται εἰς δραχμάς χιλίας πεντακοσίας (ἀριθμός 1.500.--) --------- κατά μῆνα καί εἶναι καταβλητέος προκαταβολικῶς κατά δεκαημερίαν ἤ πενθημερίαν ἀποφάσει τοῦ Θεάτρου. Τό τέλος χαρτοσήμου τῶν σχετικῶν ἀποδείξεων, οἱ ἐπί τοῦ μισθοῦ φόροι καί ἐν γένει ἡ ὑφ' οἱανδήποτε μορφήν φορολογία, κράτησις, τέλος ἤ εἰσφορά βαρύνουν τήν Χορωδόν   πλήν τῶν ὑποχρεωτικῶς βαρυνουσῶν τό Θέατρον.

Ταῦτα συνομολογήσαντες οἱ συμβαλλόμενοι συνέταξαν τό παρόν εἰς διπλοῦν, λαβόντες ἑκάτερος ἀνά ἕν.

ΟΙ ΣΥΜΒΑΛΛΟΜΕΝΟΙ

Διά τό Βασιλικόν Θέατρον
Ο ΓΕΝΙΚΟΣ ΔΙΕΥΘΥΝΤΗΣ

Marianna Kaloyeropoulou's first contract (introduction, first two clauses, and signatures) with the Greek National (then Royal) Theater, Athens, 20 June 1940.

With the foundation of the National Opera, in 1939, the effort of three generations of Greek opera-lovers was finally rewarded by Prime Minister Ioannis Metaxas, with whom Kostis Bastias, the director of state theaters in the ministry of education, had used his personal influence.[2] The main obstacle to the foundation of a state opera company, which had brought previous endeavours to nothing, was the cost of building a new opera house. Bastias got around this problem by means of a compromise, whereby the new opera company would work in harness with the National Theater. The National Opera, an opera company without an opera house for the time being, would not start life as an independent entity but would come under the jurisdiction of the general manager of the theater, who was none other than Kostis Bastias himself. And so, on 9 December 1938, Metaxas had announced the formation of the National Opera and Bastias had spent 1939 quietly getting on with the business of setting up the opera division of the theater. In Greece in the past, he said, the pursuit of the best had always prevented the attainment of the good: "We have chosen to achieve the good while waiting for the best."[3]

While the technical problems were being solved, arrangements were being made to engage the necessary staff. Three key members were brought in from abroad: Viennese conductor Walter Pfeffer,[4] stage director Renato Mordo, a Viennese of Greek extraction,[5] and Czech dancer and choreographer Sasha Machov,[6] all of whom would have had bright careers ahead of them in central Europe had it not been for their Jewish blood, which put their lives in jeopardy under the Nazi régime. The engagement of highly qualified Greek artists—author Angelos Terzakis (who was the secretary of the theater), stage designer Kleovoulos Klonis, costume designer Andonis Fokas, and chorus mistress Elli Nikolaidi—also promised an auspicious start. The general atmosphere was one of enthusiastic optimism, notwithstanding the grumbles and criticisms which (as one might expect) were to be heard on all sides.

In September 1939 Bastias announced the formation of a small appointments board to select singers for the new opera company. The board consisted of himself, Angelos Terzakis, Renato Mordo, Yorgos Lykoudis, actress and ex-singer Katina Paxinou, stage director Dimosthenis Matsoukis, and Elvira de Hidalgo. Of these, the one whose views apparently carried most weight was Mordo, followed by de Hidalgo, but the final decision of course rested with Bastias. Auditions were held in the National Theater, with Elli Nikolaidi at the piano and board members sitting in the audience. The main criterion for selection, apart from musical ability, was stage presence and general appearance, as everybody was agreed that the overall effect had to be pleasing to the eye as well as the ear, especially in that most quintessential of all Viennese operettas, Johann Strauss's *Die Fledermaus*, which had been chosen for the gala première. A total of 387 applicants presented themselves for the auditions, of whom eighteen soloists and fifty-four chorus members were shortlisted, the final selections to be made after a further round of auditions.[7]

Kostis Bastias, 1939.

Hiring singers for the National Opera presented Bastias with a grave dilemma: was he to take on the heroic stars of the old Hellenic Melodrama, who until 1943 would continue to scrape a living from the occasional ad hoc performances they arranged among themselves, or only young singers with a promising future? By siding with the future and overlooking many prominent singers who had dedicated their lives to opera in Greece he incurred a good deal of hostile criticism. In making this decision he was counting on the probability that the imminence of war, coinciding with the foundation of the National Opera, would induce many established Greek singers working abroad—such as Margherita Perras, Elena Nikolaidi, Anna Tassopoulou, Fanny Aidali, Nicola Moscona, Titos Xirellis, Vangelis Mangliveras, and Thanos Bourlos—to come and sing in Athens more often or even to join the National Opera on a permanent basis. In fact, it was partly on this assumption that the final decision to found the opera had been made, and it had already been arranged that the first production of the 1941–42 season was to be *Carmen*, with Elena Nikolaidi in the role that had recently made her famous in Vienna. In the end, although the war prevented most of these singers from coming to Greece, Bastias won general recognition for his work for the National

Opera, the appointments he made, and his firmness and fairness. He could have received no greater vindication than the fact that Dionysios Lavrangas himself, the father of the Hellenic Melodrama, dedicated to Bastias his *Memoirs*, published at that very time, in 1940.[8]

—⁓—

We do not know exactly how or when the possibility of engaging Mary to work at the National Opera was first raised. Dr. Ilias Papatestas—a neighbor with whom Mary had by this time started discussing some of her problems—was to say in 1963 that she was then very worried about the family finances and realized that she would have to find some kind of paid work while she was studying.[9] The most likely answer is that the idea of signing her on at the National Opera, when still only a third-year student, originated with de Hidalgo. According to the account the Spanish soprano gave later, one of the members of the appointments board (most probably Bastias) asked her if there was anyone she wished to nominate. Thinking of Mary's lack of money and dependence on her domineering mother, it would have occurred to de Hidalgo how useful it would be in so many ways if the girl had an income of her own. Not only would it be advantageous in practical terms and give her a psychological boost, but it would save her from the serious possibility of having to take a time-consuming menial job to make ends meet. "I have one [student] who is a genuine phenomenon, but she is very young and I wouldn't want her to sing just yet," de Hidalgo answered. "However, I am willing to introduce her to you if you promise you will sign her on immediately for the chorus." The promise was given and Mary was brought along by her teacher to be auditioned by Bastias in his apartment just behind the theater. Bastias's son takes up the story: "[De Hidalgo told him] to take no notice of Mary's appearance, adding that she had a marvelous voice and tremendous talent and needed help because she was very badly off." Elvira herself accompanied Mary on the piano, to the best of her ability. Bastias recognized her potential straightaway and, being fortunately in a position to bend the rules in a good cause, "he decided to take her on to the books so that she would have some money to live on and be able to continue her studies."*

---

*GENTE; conversation with Yannis Bastias, 23 Jan. 1995. It has also been alleged that de Hidalgo asked Bastias to come to her own apartment on Patission Street to hear Mary sing, and that once Mary had left she explained to him that if this exceptionally promising student were not taken on by the opera she would have to drop out of the conservatory and find some sort of job in an office or shop. (*Ellinikos Vorras*, 19 Oct. 1981.) A Greek newspaper article (*Embros*, 27 July 1957) alleged that, while studying music in Athens, Mary had worked for the post office, and that later on, in America, she had sold newspapers and worked as a waitress. As the author's source was probably Litsa herself, the information is not without interest. Twenty years later another article (*Opernwelt*, Nov. 1977) repeated the allegation that Mary had paid her way through the conservatory by working for the post office. No other evidence of her having had such a job has come to light, but she did sing at an Athenian nightclub in 1942 (see Chapter

Speaking about the matter on another occasion, de Hidalgo muddled the dates and placed the incident in the occupation, explaining that it had been necessary for Mary to be given employment at the National Opera because she was in trouble through consorting with Italians to obtain food: "Precisely in order to rescue her from certain dire hardships and give her a means of subsistence, one day I made the decision. I took her to the hairdresser, the manicurist, and the dressmaker. When I presented her to the other governors of the state opera, nobody recognized her. She went up on to the stage and I heard the other students saying, 'How well she moves!' The transformation was astonishing. When she had finished singing I said to the board, 'You must take this girl on to the books and pay her a chorus member's salary, but without making her do anything. She mustn't sing: she needs to spend all her time studying, but with an assured income, otherwise she will go to the dogs, singing for soldiers for a crust of bread. We've got to look after this treasure.'" In telling the story this way, of course, de Hidalgo obviously wanted to claim the credit for having "saved" Mary.[10]

Mary spent some time turning over the National Opera's offer of a job before deciding to accept it, according to Ilias Papatestas: "At first she didn't want even to consider the idea of joining an opera chorus, because she believed she was much too good for that." By then, of course, she had done a certain amount of thinking about the best strategy to pursue in order to get ahead, and had probably talked it over with de Hidalgo. Around the beginning of 1940, when Lela Skordouli had just been taken on by the National Opera as one of the first sixteen female choristers, Mary warned her, "*If you go into the chorus you'll get stuck there and never become a soloist.*" But she herself, not yet seventeen years old and with only three years of musical studies behind her, was obviously not in a position to follow the good advice she gave Skordouli. And so, when Bastias offered her a position in the chorus coupled with a firm assurance that she would not be required to sing in it, she decided to accept. After all, it was a sinecure being offered to her as a special favor; this is clear from the minutes of the board of governors of the National

---

22), and in 1946–47, about a year after leaving Greece, Maria worked in New York as an au pair in the family of the conductor Sergio Failoni. One day Failoni was astounded to hear her singing "Casta diva," and he talked about her to Giovanni Zenatello, the director of the Verona Festival, with momentous consequences. In the winter of 1946–47 Maria also worked at Asti's, a restaurant in New York City's Greenwich Village, where the proprietor employed waiters and waitresses with good voices to sing the customers' requests. The RAI correspondent in New York, Ilario Fiore, heard Maria amaze the diners there by singing "Casta diva" and "Suicidio!" (See B. Tosi, *Casta diva, l'incomparabile Callas*, Rome 1993, 119–120, and *Giovane Callas*, Padua 1997, 183, 185, 193; articles in *Gente*, 24 Mar. 1994, *Kathimerini*, 19 June 1994, and *Oggi*, 1 Aug. 1994.) Jackie now denies that Maria ever took any job, either in America or in Greece: she dismisses all such allegations as "lies," saying that Embirikos had paid for everything, so Maria had had no need to work. (KALOYEROPOULOU.) Of course, if Mary had worked and contributed to the housekeeping, or at least paid her personal expenses, this would have detracted from Jackie's own importance as the family's "sole provider"—courtesy of Miltiadis Embirikos.

Theater, which on 20 June 1940 voted to engage eighteen female chorus singers, seventeen of them at a monthly salary of 2,000 drachmas and Mary, eighteenth and last, at Drs. 1,500 (Drs. 1,402 after deductions).[11] This favor would hold the door half-open for her to join the National Opera as a soloist as soon as an opportunity should arise.

One very interesting point is that in late 1939 or early 1940 Bastias had given Mary a job in his office, as some kind of assistant. As he explained in August 1960, he was not allowed to pay her as she was not yet on the books of the National Opera, so he took her on as an assistant in his private office. This job would have involved little or no work, and Bastias probably covered himself by citing a clause in a recent board resolution referring to "the necessity of enlarging the administrative staff by engaging extra personnel on three months' probation." Once her contract as a chorus member had been signed on 20 June 1940, she kept her sinecure in a different form. "*I am grateful to Mr. Bastias,*" Maria said fully twenty years later, "*because when . . . I was being auditioned at the time of the formation of the National Opera—I was just a young girl then—he agreed with Madame de Hidalgo that the National Opera would pay me a retainer while I continued to study. In this way they showed great faith in me and helped me in my first year, when I was most in need of help.*"[12]

—m—

Besides this financial support and the consequent boost to her morale, another factor that improved the quality of Mary's life at this time was a change of home environment. Around the autumn of 1939 the family had moved from 70 Harilaou Trikoupi Street to a three-room ground-floor apartment at 5 Marni Street, just a stone's throw away from Patission Street. A few months later they were on the move again, this time to a fifth-floor unit at 61 Patission Street, an Art Deco apartment building still standing on the corner of Patission and Skaramanga Streets, one block away from the National Archaeological Museum and the same distance from Alexandras Avenue. Leading up to the tall wooden front door of the building, with its ornamental ironwork, was a flight of nine marble steps, and in the entrance hall was the elevator, an airy wooden cage enclosed in its wrought-iron grille. Emerging from the elevator on the fifth floor and turning left at the end of the corridor, one came to the front door of an apartment that extended all along the Patission Street side of the building. The other door, across the corridor and slightly to the right as one stepped out of the elevator, was the entrance to the Kaloyeropoulos apartment, which was at the rear of the building with some of its windows looking out onto Skaramanga Street.

The front door of the apartment led straight into a large room that did duty as hall, living room, and dining room combined, with a large glass partition down the middle and a french window on the right leading out onto a small balcony that overlooked the flat roof of the next house. Everything in this room—walls, sofas,

61 Patission Street at the corner of Skaramanga Street.

carpets—was blue, to suit Litsa's taste. The piano, that indispensable movable, stood against the wall opposite the front door and slightly to the left, in the darkest part of the room, where it would remain all the time the family lived there. Litsa states that the two girls had separate rooms, but according to Jackie the two bedrooms overlooking Skaramanga Street were occupied "one by Mother and one by the two of us," while the corner bedroom was to be let out to bring in a small but useful extra income; the main bath was off the corridor that led to the bedrooms. To the right of the dining area, near the balcony, there was a very small room that was occupied over the next few years by the canaries and a succession of maids and occasional visitors. On the same side of the apartment, at the back of the building, were the spacious kitchen, a pantry, and a small second bathroom. The unit had a floor area of between 150 and 200 square meters and faced southwest, so it was

The Kaloyeropoulos apartment at the rear of the building, as it appears today.

always light, a point in its favor in winter especially. All the bills—rent, electricity, and water, totalling 3,700 drachmas a month to start with (two and a half times Mary's initial salary)—were paid by Miltiadis Embirikos, who demanded in return that there be no telephone in the apartment so that Jackie's other admirers could not call her.[13]

In the spring of 1940, probably during the Easter vacation, Litsa took her daughters on a trip to the Peloponnese. After a short stop at Xylokastro they traveled down to Meligalas, where the girls met their father's relatives. As their uncle Mitsos was living in their father's old house, they went to stay with their aunt Tassia at nearby Sandani. They spent several days touring the surrounding countryside and visited the family home at Neohori. They all seem to have enjoyed their time there, to judge by the fact that three years later they would revisit Meligalas in spite of the difficulties of traveling during the occupation. Back in Athens, their contacts with the Dimitriadis family remained infrequent: Litsa never went to see her mother in Sepolia and only occasionally got in touch with her brothers and sisters, one of whom, Efthymios, was now running the Old Tourist Hotel at the corner of Voulis and Ermou Streets, near Syntagma Square. On the rare occasions when a family gathering took place there, Litsa usually went with Jackie, leaving Mary behind because, as she announced, she had to stay at home to work on her music.[14]

Litsa was on much friendlier terms with the family of Konstantinos Kambouris, her first cousin by marriage and brother of Iraklis Kambouris, who had bought the Dimitriadis family home at Stylis some thirty years earlier. Konstanti-

Mary, Litsa, and Jackie in Xylokastro, spring 1940.

nos's widow Vassiliki lived in a house at 206 Patission Street with her two sons Nikos and Panos (who were around Jackie's age) and two daughters Eleni and Anna (about the same age as Mary). Of her four second cousins, Mary was always closest to Panos, a good-looking and rather shy young man who had studied agriculture in Italy, where he had heard a lot of opera and liked it. It quite often happened that when either he or Mary would start singing an aria or duet, the other would join in, and soon the whole house would be ringing to the sound of their voices. It was Panos who taught Mary to ride a bicycle in the flagstone courtyard of the Kambouris house: "At first she couldn't keep her balance and he held her up," Anna Kambouri recalls, "but she soon learned and was very pleased with herself." The warm atmosphere of these visits and her easygoing relationship with Panos Kambouris must have given Mary some of the few moments when she knew what it was to be a carefree teenager; and this showed in her unusually affectionate behavior: "She was friendly and good-humored with everybody—a girl just like the four of us," as Nikos and Anna Kambouri agree.[15]

As for Mary's musical ambitions, for the time being they were nourished by the admiration of those who heard her sing. Even the smoldering jealousy of some of her classmates at the conservatory only confirmed her belief in her ability and made her feel strong and optimistic. Her positive outlook often made itself felt at home: she once said to Litsa, "*Mother, I'm going to be the greatest opera singer of them all. The whole world will be talking about me!*" Spyros Salingaros gives a vivid description of a similar scene: "One day we were waiting for her in the living room while she got dressed in her room, and she was singing something that reverberated through the whole apartment. 'For heaven's sake, stop!' her mother shouted, not minding that we were there. 'We've had enough, our heads are spinning, we can't hear ourselves think!' Defiantly, Mary answered from her room, *'Mother, I'm going to be the greatest prima donna in the world!'* 'Oh, get lost!' her mother retorted. The whole atmosphere in that apartment was full of tension, which any visitor couldn't help being very well aware of."[16]

Nevertheless Litsa always tried to make out that her relations with her daughters were friendly, full of lively talk, jokes, and teasing; that they lived in a warm family atmosphere no less idyllic than the picture she later painted of their past life in America. In reality, however, Litsa simply "got by" from day to day in accordance with her elastic code of conduct, while Mary had begun to give shape to her long-term aspirations and was making systematic and determined progress. If Litsa ever told her she was wearing herself out by practicing all the time and spending hours on end out of the house, she would snap back that neither Litsa nor Jackie had any serious aim in life. She herself, on the other hand, was going to press ahead regardless of anybody or anything else, as she reportedly told Litsa to her face, to her great astonishment: *"I won't let anyone stand in my way. If anyone tries I'll smash them, and I don't care who they are!"*[17] And even if she did not actually use such strong words, we may be sure that her threat was directed against Litsa herself, among others.

Although Mary was now much calmer and more self-controlled at the conservatory, many people were still put off by her single-mindedness in pursuit of her goal in life and her rather abrupt manner. Obedient, disciplined, hardworking, conscientious, virtuous, strong-willed, firm, and good-hearted, as well as conceited and self-centered, are the adjectives used most often about her by those who were at the conservatory with her. She was fairly taciturn, and many remember her entering and leaving a room without even saying hello or good-bye. Although it was probably due in part to her nearsightedness, this attitude of hers was often attributed to arrogance or "uppishness," as it would be later on at the National Opera. However, Lela Skordouli insists, "She was neither excessively withdrawn nor the opposite, but she was always cautious about personal and family matters, which she hardly ever mentioned. When we chatted on the way home, practically the only subjects we talked about were music and our future careers." On this last point nearly everyone is agreed. "She didn't join in personal conversations," says Spyros Salingaros. "She was eternally absorbed in singing: nothing else interested her. It was as if she had been told, 'You, madam, will make music your business, and nothing else. That is your destiny.'"[18]

When it came to singing, however, Mary attracted a steadily growing circle of admirers, even though she generally avoided singing at the conservatory matinées (held in the auditorium, usually on Fridays), either because she was bored with the pieces she had heard hundreds of times in the classroom or, more probably, because she was ashamed by her size and her shabby clothes. "We took her with us a few times, but we almost had to force her because she was embarrassed about appearing in public," says Niki Zacharopoulou. In spite of de Hidalgo's pressure, Mary still dressed scruffily, often in castoffs that her mother had altered; but when she sang she always created a sensation. "She was a terrific hit," Salingaros confirms. "Her standard was already very high, even then. She had no time for pieces like 'O mio babbino caro' but sang *Aida, Trovatore, Gioconda,* and *Tosca,* and then the class went wild!" Students from other classes made a point of going to hear her on her rare appearances at the matinées, even if it meant skipping their own class. By the spring of 1940 her fame had begun to spread more widely: Kostis Nikolaou, a great bass of international repute (he made ninety-five appearances in the United States between 1909 and 1922) spoke highly of her to the students in his own private musical academy and predicted a brilliant career for her.[19]

Nevertheless Mary's behavior remained odd, often antisocial, as her evolution into a star of the conservatory had inevitably provoked further rivalry. Clever and sensitive she may have been, but she was also brusque, and she would signify her annoyance by reacting aggressively if she felt she was not being valued at her proper worth. Since she had nothing to be proud of in her person or her family circumstances, in the one field in which she did excel, namely music, she expected— almost demanded—absolute and unqualified recognition. Yet, in general, she stayed on good terms with everybody, though she had no deep relationships or emotional involvements. Certainly there was never any talk of her having an affair or even a romance in the conservatory circles. Maria herself said in 1959, showing her usual tendency to exaggerate her misfortunes, *"You see, I didn't have anything to distract my attention—neither friends nor admirers."* Just occasionally she would go out with classmates to have a meal or a pastry at one of the well-known restaurants or café-patisseries. "To us she was 'Mary with the lovely voice,' the Mary who came to the conservatory like a church mouse," is how Spyros Salingaros puts it.[20]

—⁂—

The gala première of the National Opera was held at the National Theater on 5 March 1940 in the presence of the royal family, the prime minister and members of the cabinet, the diplomatic corps, and Athenian high society. Those who saw that production of *Die Fledermaus* still remember it as having been equal to the best that Vienna had to offer. With the help of glowing reviews and word-of-mouth recommendations, it enjoyed a run of eighty-nine further performances, the last being on 26 May. It is not known whether Mary saw it but it seems likely that she did, even though she was working for her examinations in May and then rehearsing for *Suor Angelica* on 16 June that year.

Six days before that memorable occasion, on 10 June 1940, Italy entered the war on Germany's side, causing grave apprehension in Greece. Metaxas decided to put the population on a war footing and made preparations for a general call-up. For some time before that, the newspapers and radio had been advising the population on civil defense and the creation of air raid shelters in buildings that had a basement suitable for the purpose, as 61 Patission Street did. For Litsa and the girls to reach the shelter they had to walk down a hundred and forty stairs, as the elevator was not to be used when there was an air raid warning. It was at this time that the first restrictions were placed on the consumption of electricity, and ration cards were issued for certain foodstuffs and basic essentials.

Mary (right) walking by the sea with Litsa, Jackie, and two friends, 1939 or 1940.

As she had the previous summer, Mary again took several trips to the seaside in 1940, for she loved swimming. She usually went with her family but sometimes with students from the conservatory. Open-air cinemas were still the most popular as well as the cheapest way of spending the evening, and the abundance of musical films continued: the highlight of the middle week of August, when Mary celebrated her name day (on 15 August, the feast of the Assumption), was the screening of the Italian film *Il sogno di Butterfly* starring the ever-popular Maria Cebotari, at the Egli Cinema in the Zappion Gardens. But the atmosphere suddenly became much more tense and anti-Italian feeling flared up strongly when the Greek cruiser *Elli*, visiting Tinos for the great religious festival on the island, was torpedoed at anchor in the harbor there. A lot of people now saw the likelihood of an Italian offensive against Greece, as it was an open secret that the submarine of "unknown nationality" that carried out the attack was actually Italian. The Kaloyeropoulos family started thinking about going back to the safety of America, a possibility which they discussed with their "adviser" Miltiadis Embirikos.[21] For the time being this was only a vague idea, but it reflected the unease and nervous tension that had suddenly entered the lives of most Athenians.

September was, as always, the time for registration for the new year at the conservatory, and Mary's scholarship was renewed without any problem. Besides singing in de Hidalgo's advanced class, the only other subjects she was enrolled for were Harmony II and Solfège V, both with Ikonomidis; but she must also have taken opera with de Hidalgo again, although there are no surviving records of it.[22] By the autumn of 1940 the looming clouds of war and the talk of going back to America must have begun to have an unsettling effect on Mary, who would probably have been against leaving Greece because it would have meant parting from her precious teacher. As she had no other outlet for the release of her nervous tension, she worked harder than ever at her music, spending most of the day at the conservatory or in de Hidalgo's apartment. This was also a way of demonstrating her independence of her mother, and she may have gained some satisfaction from seeing the reaction to her disobedience. As Jackie comments, "Mary was now [nearly] seventeen and was showing her independence in small ways clearly designed to irritate Mother."[23]

On Monday, 21 October 1940, the National Theater inaugurated its tenth season with Shakespeare's *The Merchant of Venice*, with Eleni Papadaki as Portia and Alexis Minotis as Shylock. There was a good deal of incidental music in the production, with a full orchestra under Yorgos Lykoudis playing suitably arranged excerpts from Humperdinck's *Hänsel und Gretel*. Many of the solos were sung by the actors themselves, while other numbers were performed by singers from the National Opera stationed in the wings. Although there is no evidence one way or the other, it is almost certain that Mary was one of them. She mentioned the fact to Minotis when she first met him, at Dallas in 1959: Minotis subsequently said that she had teased him for not remembering her even though she had been an extra in one of his performances. According to him (and we must remember that Minotis was married to Katina Paxinou and therefore never missed an opportunity to disparage the memory of Eleni Papadaki, who had been a more talented actress) Maria also claimed to have sung Papadaki's solos for her.[24] "That's nothing but a malicious canard," says the actress Maria Alkeou, who took singing lessons with de Hidalgo in the same class as Mary and happened to have a part in that production. "Papadaki was right next to me, and she was certainly singing the song herself. Those are slanders put about by Minotis and Paxinou, neither of whom could stand Papadaki—nor could they stand anyone else, for that matter."[25] In any event, the fact is that Mary almost certainly took part in a National Theater production for the first time on 21 October 1940, singing some of Humperdinck's

Eleni Papadaki singing, with Maria Alkeou at her feet, *The Merchant of Venice*, Greek National Theater, Athens, October 1940.

melodies from the wings as part of the incidental music. *The Merchant of Venice* was repeated on each of the next three days at 5 and 9 p.m., and again on Sunday, 27 October, the day before Italy declared war on Greece.

Meanwhile the National Opera had for some time been in rehearsal for the second production in its history, Puccini's *Madama Butterfly*. Although this opera had not been chosen for diplomatic reasons, Kostis Bastias had invited the composer's son, the lawyer Antonio Puccini, to attend the première with the idea of calming the anti-Italian feeling provoked by the sinking of the *Elli*. The Italians persisted with their acts of provocation and it was obvious that their forces in Albania were "up to something," but the Greek government continued to feign ignorance of their perfidious intentions. However, it is now known that on 15 October 1940 Mussolini had made the decision to invade Greece. In this highly charged atmosphere, that momentous première of *Butterfly*, conducted by Walter Pfeffer with Zoe Vlachopoulou as Cio-Cio-San and Michalis Koronis as Pinkerton, took place on Friday, 25 October, after consultations between Bastias and the Italian ambassador, Emmanuele Grazzi. "Even if I lived to be a thousand, I should never forget that night," Grazzi wrote later in his memoirs. "It was to be the last time in my life that I had a chance to see such a display of elegance and opulence. The king and the whole of the royal family were present, as well as Metaxas and the cream of Athenian society. A magnificent spectacle of beautiful women, jewelry, evening gowns. . . . My heart was tight in my chest and I felt myself blushing at the thought that . . . a policy both criminal and senseless was paving the way not only for a crime but also for an ignominious disaster for our country."[26]

The next day, Saturday, 26 October, there were two more performances of *Madama Butterfly* at 5 and 9 p.m. and then at about midnight everybody involved in the production went to an official reception at the Italian embassy. An unbelievable array of mouthwatering foods was offered at the buffet and the drinks flowed freely, but the atmosphere was strangely chilly and the turnout of guests disappointing. By a macabre coincidence the text of the Italian ultimatum to Greece had arrived at the embassy that very afternoon and was being deciphered while the reception was in progress. Exactly twenty-four hours after the last guests had left, and after a warm, sunny Sunday, Italy declared war on Greece, expecting its large and well-equipped army to sweep through to Athens without difficulty.

Monday, 28 October 1940, was one of the dates that were probably graven indelibly on Maria's memory. At dawn the air was full of the wail of air raid sirens, and people flocked into the streets and headed instinctively for the city center. When Mary went out she followed the stream of demonstrators to Omonia Square and probably on to the university gates and Syntagma Square. Neither the appearance of the first Italian aircraft nor the warning note of the sirens persuaded any of them to run for safety to the air raid shelters: Athens, like Rome, had been declared an unfortified city and it seemed highly unlikely that the Italians would bomb it, since that would automatically mean that the British would retaliate by bombing Rome. Nevertheless, when she came home from her outing to central Athens, where the patriotic slogans and irrepressible exuberance of the crowds had created an eerily festive mood, she would probably have dragged herself wearily down the one hundred forty marble stairs for the first time, to take refuge in the dark air raid shelter at 61 Patission Street.

CHAPTER 18

War and *Boccaccio*

F or the first two days of the war in Greece everything came to a standstill while
people read the papers and listened to the radio to find out what was happening and what emergency measures were being taken. The schools were closed and
all travel was subject to strict controls. In particular, aliens—including Mary, who
did not acquire Greek citizenship until 1966—were forbidden to travel outside
Athens without a special permit. First aid stations and several military hospitals
were hastily set up in the days that followed, but the greatest disruption to everyday life was caused by the blackout and the fact that all shops, offices, cafés, and
restaurants had to close at dusk. The people of Athens "blacked out" their windows
with thick blue paper of the sort that schoolchildren used for covering their exercise books, while car headlights and even the interior lights of the streetcars were
also painted blue. Gas was rationed, bank deposits were blocked, the stock exchange closed down, consumer spending slumped. The newspapers were full of
appeals for charitable gifts in cash or in kind and for blood donations, as well as
information about war lotteries and soup kitchens. Although most people
responded generously according to their means, there were cases of profiteering,
mostly in goods subject to rationing or price controls. Fixed prices were set for
foodstuffs and before long a black market flourished, even though martial law was
extended to cover offenses against the market control regulations. At the front, the
irrepressible Greek forces had already started routing the bewildered Italians, and
five or six Italian aircraft were shot down for every Greek loss. Greek flags flew
everywhere and the church bells rang out joyfully to celebrate every fresh Greek
victory. Before long the first Italian prisoners of war, abject and half-starved, were
being marched through the streets of Athens, where bystanders would offer them
cigarettes and chocolate that they could ill afford to give away.

The National Theater on Ayiou Konstantinou Street had to be closed as there
was no air raid shelter there, but the Army Share Fund came to the rescue by allowing the company rent-free use of the Pallas Cinema, which had a huge basement
suitable for use as a shelter. The building was converted forthwith: dressing rooms
were put in, the orchestra pit enlarged, and central heating installed, all in less

than four weeks. On 24 November 1940 the company reopened at the Pallas with a production of *The Persians* by Aeschylus, with performances seven days a week at 6 p.m. and matinées at 3 p.m. on Tuesdays, Thursdays, Saturdays, and Sundays. This schedule, with eleven performances of drama or opera per week, was to be maintained until the company moved back into its own premises on Ayiou Konstantinou Street in May 1941. While the current drama productions and the revival of *Die Fledermaus* were running, rehearsals started for new productions including the third work to be produced by the National Opera, Suppé's *Boccaccio*. As it was scheduled for a fairly long run, fully rehearsed understudies were cast for most of the roles in the near certainty that they would be given some performances to do. The two main parts, Boccaccio and Fiametta, were taken by Michalis Koronis and Zoe Vlachopoulou, with Nikos Glynos and Zozo Remoundou as their respective understudies.

Franz von Suppé wrote *Boccaccio* in 1878. It is a very slight work with mediocre music and a poor libretto, for all that it is based on the masterful *Decameron* of Giovanni Boccaccio (who appears in the operetta himself). One of the roles is that of Beatrice, the unfaithful wife of a barber and only the fourth in importance of the female characters, who has an affair with a visiting student named Leonetto, a friend of Boccaccio. She is the first woman to appear on stage, very early in the first act, pretending to have been frightened by a man in her room and calling on her husband for help. The short aria she sings at this point is musically uninteresting, though it does present some technical difficulties. Her only other appearances are in the finales of the three acts, where she sings in the *tutti*.

On 14 December 1940 the weekly theatrical review *Paraskinia* informed its readers that the rehearsals for *Boccaccio* were "continuing." Mary was involved in these, as she was Nafsika Galanou's understudy in the role of Beatrice. The idea of casting her in this minor role as an understudy had been suggested to Bastias by de Hidalgo in the summer, presumably with the object of giving her young pupil her first professional stage experience and in the hope that she might receive some small addition to her pay for taking part in rehearsals and performances as a soloist. Maria herself subsequently made only passing references to *Boccaccio*. On one occasion she telescoped the year and a half since the 1939 *Cavalleria Rusticana* into a few months: "*That first success opened the way for me to other auditions, and a few months later I was chosen to sing the part of Beatrice in the operetta 'Boccaccio.'*" And in an interview in 1968 she explained, "*They needed a Beatrice and they asked if I could break my engagement: instead of not doing anything but studying, to study and perform.*"[1]

When Mary was asked how she was feeling on the day of her first professional appearance—the precise date is not known—she is reported to have said with her usual indomitable self-confidence that she was sure she would be a great success. "*I have never felt more relaxed,*" she added.[2] The bass Nikos Papachristos, who was in the chorus for some of the performances of *Boccaccio*, remembers the occasion:

"One day we heard that Galanou was to be replaced by Kaloyeropoulou, about whom we knew practically nothing. Before she comes on she shouts "He-e-elp, he-e-elp!" from offstage. So we heard this rich voice, hysterical and terrifically alive, that swept you off your feet. We were amazed. It was an erratic sort of voice, quite different in the upper and lower registers, which appealed to you without your knowing why, a voice that was pleasing and irritating at the same time. She made her entrance in a long green velvet dress, stormed around the stage, then went off and shut herself up in her dressing room, and we never saw her again. She did one more performance, but Galanou didn't let her sing again!"[3] As Papachristos joined the National Opera as an extra chorus member on 15 February 1941, Mary's first appearance must have been after that date, when she was seventeen and three months. Her fine performance also came as a surprise to young Dimitris (Takis) Horn, later to make a considerable reputation for himself as an actor, who recalled how Galanou would come running on to the stage shouting for help in her excessive vibrato, "like a train whistling as it starts to move." Then, at a matinée, he heard the cry for help coming from a different voice—a firm, strong voice. "It sent shivers down your spine. The audience went wild. We were thunderstruck and wondered who this new Beatrice could be."[4]

Everyone is agreed that Mary only appeared in very few performances of *Boccaccio*, and most of those at matinées. The person responsible for this was Nafsika Galanou, who had no intention of letting herself be upstaged by her understudy. She had every reason to be concerned, because by this time Mary's reputation had begun to spread from the conservatory to the National Opera. "And in any case," as Zoe Vlachopoulou recalls, "Galanou would never share her part with anyone. Anyway, de Hidalgo had advised Mary to be patient as the main object in the short term was to get the extra salary." One of the singers in the chorus for that production, the tenor Andonis Kalaidzakis, thinks she sang five or six times, perhaps once at an evening performance. "But anyway," he adds, "the world had now had a glimpse of the tigress lurking inside her." Maria herself later said that operetta had done her a lot of good, "*because instead of being a stiff opera singer it taught me how to work on freedom of movements, to be supple, a certain lightness on stage.*" However, when she said this she may have been thinking not of the 1941 *Boccaccio* but of another operetta, *Der Bettelstudent*, which she sang in 1945.[5]

Boccaccio was a great success. Counting the fifteen performances of its revival in July 1941 as well as the seventy-one of the initial run from 21 January to 9 March, it was the National Opera's second longest-running production up to 1945, beaten only by *Die Fledermaus*. Four reviews were published in the press, but all of the first night, when Mary was not singing.[6] Although Jackie has no recollection of *Boccaccio*, Litsa says that Mary was "excited and thrilled" and that she was proud of her, even though she received no ovation. "She was [just] one of four girls who sang and danced in a barrel. No one was overcome by the brilliance of her performance, and I'm not sure that anyone except her family noticed her particu-

Mary in *Boccaccio*, National Opera, Pallas Theater, February–March 1941; curtain call, Mary with Nikos Glynos on her right and Athanasia Moustaka and Mitsa Kourahani on her left.

larly." Litsa also comments sourly on the small sum that Mary was paid for her part as Beatrice, "the first money she had ever earned professionally" (omitting to mention the salary Mary received for her sinecure position in the chorus), saying, "It wasn't much but Maria was delighted."[7] Certainly in the photograph of the final curtain call, in which Mary was wearing a long dress with a floral pattern and a tall pointed hat, she looks radiant with joy. In the other photographs of that performance, she gives the impression of being thoroughly at ease with herself and remarkably expressive in her movements. As de Hidalgo subsequently admitted to her, "Even I admired the way you moved your hands and your body . . . and yet I was considered a good actress and had seen the greatest. I saw that there was something different and completely your own."[8]

Those who were in every performance found their work very tiring, particularly if they lived a long way from the city center. For Mary it was not so bad: if she occasionally happened to stay at the theater for the evening performance she could walk home in less than half an hour. However, it was not pleasant walking around Athens that winter. After dark the streets were almost totally deserted and a pervasive atmosphere of desolation hung over the city. Nevertheless, the changed circumstances did bring some new experiences into people's lives. With quite a number of British soldiers in town, everybody suddenly wanted to learn English. French now took second place, and it was considered just as necessary to have an English speaker with you as to have a flashlight in your pocket. This was probably good for Mary's morale, as it gave her an opportunity to talk to Englishmen in the language that she now hardly used. A photograph of Litsa and her two daughters with three British NCOs in Pedion Areos Park probably dates from around this time, the spring of 1941.

One of the Athens Conservatory students who had been called into service was Vangelis Lakadzis, with whom Mary had recently studied *Aida* at home. Sometime between December 1940 and March 1941, she sent him a postcard at the Albanian front, written in Greek—all except the words "Maria" and "Marianna"—with only a few minor errors of spelling and grammar: *"Maria Kaloyero-poulou, Patission 61, Athens. To NCO Evangelos Lakadzis, 18th Infantry Regiment, II Machine-gun Unit, Athens 724. Dear Evangelos, At last I have time to write you a few lines. You can't imagine how much work I have had. As you know, I have now got a part in Boccaccio. I'm only sorry you can't come and see me in it. I just hope you come back soon, victorious, and that we can sing in something together. My family and Madame send you their best wishes. God be with you always, and I want you to know that we think of you constantly. With sisterly love, Marianna."*[9] One is struck by the fluent handwriting and the maturity with which she expresses her admittedly uncomplicated sentiments in a language that she had really only been speaking for three years and had presumably taught herself to write. Except for her seven-page transliteration of the recitative and aria "Celeste Aida," which she also did for Lakadzis earlier in 1940, it is the earliest known specimen of her hand-

Mary, Jackie, and Litsa with three British soldiers, Pedion Areos Park, Athens, spring 1941.

writing in Greek, predating the next earliest example (not counting signatures and dedications or notes written on photographs) by about five years.

—◦◦◦—

When Nafsika Galanou talked about Mary in 1979, she said that one day in 1940 (probably at the time of the first rehearsals of *Boccaccio* in December), while passing the door of one of the practice rooms, she heard "a crystal voice" singing "Casta diva" from *Norma*. She opened the door out of curiosity, only to find young Mary Kaloyeropoulou, who was to be her understudy as Beatrice. "I remember a plump girl with glasses and a peculiar accent," she said, adding that she had kissed Mary and told her she was a dramatic coloratura soprano, and that Mary had complained that she was being pressed to sing in a concert she did not want to be involved in. No doubt the tone of the conversation has been prettified in the telling and the reference to the impending concert may be chronologically inexact, but the fact remains that Galanou, who was notorious for her rabid antagonism toward all her fellow singers, had on her own admission had this chance to assess Mary's talents for herself and thus to weigh the threat she posed. When asked whether she

Mary's card to Vangelis Lakadzis, then fighting on the Albanian front, December 1940–March 1941.

had had the feeling even then that Mary would go far, Galanou replied unequivocally, "I have no hesitation in saying yes." Consequently, even with the work load of eleven performances a week, she took care not to let her understudy take her place. This must have annoyed Mary, who would no doubt have complained to de Hidalgo and the latter probably took the matter up with Bastias: according to Galanou, Bastias told her one day that he wanted to "give her a bit of a rest" and asked her if she had any objection to Kaloyeropoulou's taking the part at a few performances. "I agreed with pleasure," she answered insincerely.[10]

Nafsika Galanou, late 1930s.

Galanou too commented on Mary's nearsightedness, which made it impossible for her to see the conductor's movements once she had taken her glasses off to go on stage. "But the stage electrified her," Galanou continued. "Her singing and acting were so brilliant that she did not need to be able to see anyone." Galanou acknowledged Mary's "huge vocal range" but also remarked on her bad Greek diction: "Unfortunately, in operetta Kaloyeropoulou had problems with her spoken lines, especially since she was performing with actors from the National Theater. Her pronunciation, with that curious Greek-American accent of hers, had a devastating effect on the phrasing and coloring that theatrical dialogue really needs."[11] That has to be accepted as fair comment, as Alexandra Lalaouni had made the same criticism of her performance in *Suor Angelica* eight months earlier. On the other hand, several witnesses have testified to Galanou's active hostility to Mary at that time. Her attitude seems to have been absolutely uncalled-for, as her repertoire was almost all operetta and did not clash with Mary's; but in the season of 1940–41, when Mary was still virtually unknown and her prospects uncertain, Galanou felt strongly that Mary's talent posed some kind of threat and reacted with unbelievable spite. "She would gladly have scratched her eyes out," commented Elli Nikolaidi, the chorus mistress for *Boccaccio.* "She was a sharp one and, being much older, she saw Mary's talent as a threat."[12]

Galanou's main ally in this wicked war of nerves against a raw seventeen-year-old girl was Anna (Zozo) Remoundou, a dramatic soprano with a big voice and a considerable gift for coloratura, who was antagonistic toward Mary by temperament as well as through force of circumstances. Born on the island of Andros exactly six years before Mary, in December 1917, she was a true product of the National Conservatory, having been sent there at the age of twelve by a poor but ambitious widowed mother. She had started studying the piano and singing in 1932, and she had been given some small roles as early as 1934, soon becoming the favorite protégée of Manolis Kalomiris, whose most difficult roles she sang regularly to the detriment of her voice. It is generally agreed that Remoundou was not a spiteful or malicious person at heart, as Galanou seems to have been. In fact she thought well of Mary and admired her from the outset, as she subsequently confided to some of her friends and colleagues. However, in those difficult times, with the soloists of the fledgling National Opera competing for the few roles and performances on offer, any young singer had to fight not just to make headway but to survive.

Anna (Zozo) Remoundou, late 1930s.

An important witness of the running warfare waged against Mary from her first entry into the National Opera is the soprano Galatea Amaxopoulou, who was with Mary in de Hidalgo's advanced class from 1939 and sang in the chorus of *Boccaccio.* "Even in rehearsal Mary's fantastic performing ability had been obvious," she remembers, "and from then on the others started trying to find ways of preventing her from appearing. They went about it in the most awful way, insulting her whenever they had a chance: 'That American bitch that's come in, what right has she got to be here, the fat cow, taking our performances away from us?'

and that sort of thing." But it was after the success of her first appearance that the concerted sabotage campaign got under way: "They talked about her in loud voices in the corridors so that everybody could hear, saying, 'Kick the American out! A foreigner's got no business in our opera company. She'll ruin the performances with her accent,' and so on." Shocked and bewildered, Mary would creep up to her dressing room, often racked with sobs. "Don't cry," Amaxopoulou would say, "it's only because they realize how good you are and they're afraid. After all, nobody kicks a dead dog!" Mary would just go on crying, and only when she was feeling really low would she murmur, "*I'm very upset,*" in a despairing voice. All this open malice inevitably made her feel anxious and nervous, and she would still remember it in 1956, when Amaxopoulou saw her in Vienna: "*How often you wiped my tears away!*" she said then. "*Do you remember?*"[13]

Galatea Amaxopoulou, 1940.

    Another who has firsthand memories of the incessant backbiting during *Boccaccio* is Maria Alkeou: "They used to stand in the wings while Mary was singing and make remarks about her, muttering, laughing, and pointing their fingers at her. The leaders of the bunch were Galanou and Remoundou, who stood with their heads bent together, keeping up a flow of loud whispers and giggles (among others about her fat legs), until eventually Mary couldn't go on singing!" Alkeou recalls an occasion when she was in a dressing room with comic actor Michalis Kaloyannis, the understudy for Beatrice's husband, the barber: "All of a sudden Mary walked in, sat down on a divan, and said through her sobs, '*It'll kill me! I can't sing! They sit in the wings and laugh at me. I get a lump in my throat and no sound comes out! Why do they* do *it to me?*'" Then she asked Alkeou and Kaloyannis to come down and stand in the wings while she was singing. "So down we went, Michalis on one side and me on the other, and as soon as they saw us they went away—they had to!" One day, unable to restrain herself any longer, Galanou went up to Alkeou and Kaloyannis and said, "Tell her to give up the theater! After all," she added, looking as if butter wouldn't melt in her mouth, "the poor girl's never going to get anywhere."[14]

Maria Alkeou, 1940.

Almost forty years later, in 1979, Galanou herself described Mary as "a rather difficult person" but added that "she was quite good at showing respect and esteem for the right people." By this cryptic comment she acknowledged that Mary had behaved correctly toward her, while insinuating that she had tried to curry favor with persons of influence. Galanou then went on to say that Maria never forgot anyone who had done her an injury, implicitly admitting that she had been one of those who had "done her an injury" and that Maria had never forgiven her. Of this she had been left in no doubt by the coldness with which Maria, now world-famous, had treated her on her visit to Greece in 1957. On that occasion Galanou and Remoundou had of course made a point of going to the airport to meet Maria Callas, along with Mireille Fléri and Anthi Zacharatou, both of whom had also been involved in unpleasant incidents with Mary later on in her time with the National Opera. The celebrated prima donna was astonished to see all her old tormentors lined up with smiles on their faces. Her reaction was to feign total amnesia, and her belated well-wishers were left stunned. As she said in 1963, "*I never forget! Sometimes I forgive, but I never forget!*"*

Even if some of the culprits can plead in mitigation that they were provoked by Mary's aggressiveness and bad manners, it remains beyond argument that the seventeen-year-old budding star was subjected to persecution by some of the older singers at the National Opera from the time of her arrival there. The attacks made on her in that very first phase of her career have been described by many writers, with innumerable inaccuracies and exaggerations. But the fact remains that the machinations really did exist, and they must certainly have had a serious effect on the formation of her character. Until *Boccaccio* went into rehearsal Mary had only had to deal with friction in the classroom, where her unusually frank and straightforward way of dealing with her equally inexperienced classmates had made up for the disadvantages of her youthfulness, her unprepossessing appearance, her humbler social background, and her shortage of money. Now that her public reputation and future career were at stake, however, things were much more serious. Her rivals were not raw "coeds" but established soloists at the National Opera, all considerably older than she and with firsthand experience of the ruthless infighting of the theater world.

Mary's initial astonishment and timidity was soon followed by a feeling of having been wronged, a determination to defend herself, and probably a desire for revenge. As de Hidalgo once said, the concerted attacks of her so-called colleagues not only made Mary work harder, but taught her to be a warrior: "I believe that it was after *Boccaccio* that Maria learned to be a fighter and a survivor, not a victim."[15] Maria herself said (with regard to incidents that took place ten years later, in 1951), "*At first, because of the surprise, I couldn't manage to say even a single word; but then (I always rebel when I feel myself struck unjustly) I reacted very quickly.*" And in 1965 she would analyze, "*In life you have to defend yourself. There are those who are better at self-defense and those who can't defend themselves because they are weak. I was lucky enough to be able to defend myself. . . . When people say I have no ability, of course I get angry. It's my amour-propre, which is very strong in my character. One should never offend my amour-propre: I'm very touchy about that, and sometimes I get spiteful.*"[16] Yet, although liable to flare up easily, Mary was not naturally aggressive. Whenever she was involved in quarrels it was always through force of

---

*Radio interview with Michel Glotz, Paris, 25 May 1963. In 1958, in Milan, Maria said to Galatea Amaxopoulou, "*Do you know who came to the airport? Galanou and Remoundou! And Papachristos, who used to call me an old cow! When Remoundou greeted me I looked at her and asked her who she was. 'But I'm Remoundou, Zozo . . .' 'Zozo?' I said. 'I don't remember any Zozo . . .'*" (AMAXOPOULOU.) Another widely accepted version of the story is that when Remoundou came up to her, cooing "Dear Maria, do you remember—," Maria broke in: "*Yes, Zozo, I've forgotten nothing!*" Zacharatou claims to have heard this retort with her own ears (conversation with Anthi Zacharatou [not taped], 8 July 1993).

Athens, August 1957: Maria Callas surrounded by her former antagonists, the sopranos of the Greek National Opera, (left to right) Mireille Fléri, Anthi Zacharatou, and Anna (Zozo) Remoundou, while veteran tenor Ulysses Lappas holds her hand protectively.

circumstances, and others were chiefly to blame. She herself never started trouble with another singer who had not harassed or been in conflict with her. She always looked straight in front of her with what almost amounted to tunnel vision: *her* path ahead, *her* future, *her* duty. She never even thought about other people: she did not have time. That is why she has often been portrayed—not altogether unfairly—as a monumental egoist.

Mary was temperamentally incapable of ignoring provocation; she was not sufficiently pliant or sophisticated, least of all in those early days. Looking at the world from her own point of view, she always had her own idea of what was right and fair and seethed with a sense of injustice if anyone questioned or challenged her standard of rectitude. Then she could no longer restrain herself, and although she did not like quarrels, she threw herself into them with furious venom, often blowing up a trivial disagreement into a serious row. Maria herself talked about this side of her character in a 1970 interview: "*I never enjoy disagreements. My character is the kind that does not like to quarrel . . . but sometimes on stage, especially in the early years, we didn't have time to sort of have other people be persuaded that you would not be persuaded to do what they wanted, and time was running out, and so I had to play sort of very firm.*"[17] Here Maria virtually admitted that, in the early years of her career, not only was she impatient but her principal line of defense was to refuse to yield an inch. These problems were to resurface with a much more traumatic effect about two and a half years later, and still more in 1944 and 1945.

—⁊⁊⁊—

Concurrently with her professional duties at the opera, Mary was continuing her lessons with de Hidalgo and doing just enough work on theory to get by at the Athens Conservatory, where she was now in her second year as an official student. Classes resumed on 1 November 1940, running from 8 a.m. to 5 p.m., when it grew dark and the blackout regulations came into force. The board issued a press release stating that whenever the air raid sirens sounded the students and teaching staff would be taken to two designated shelters behind the conservatory. For the whole of that year the regular public practice sessions and students' concerts were suspended, and indeed music began to sound altogether incongruous in the context of war bulletins reporting on heroic victories and casualties at the Albanian front.

When Italy invaded Greece, de Hidalgo worried that the Greek authorities might deport her because of her known pro-Italian sentiments and her friendships with Italian diplomats and officials of the Casa d'Italia. For some time thereafter she refused to answer the telephone and asked some of her pupils to keep her company in the evenings, as Vassilakis had been drafted. Her photograph of Mussolini was carefully hidden away, of course, and so were her jewelry and furs: from time to time she would take the furs out and ask her pupils to help her to air them. She went to the conservatory only when she had to and gave more and more of her lessons at home, mostly to the more talented and better-off students. Mary now went to de Hidalgo's apartment nearly every day. When they were not actually working on the voice, we may be sure that they talked about music, with the young girl eager to hear the prima donna's reminiscences. No doubt, however, they also discussed personal matters, especially the problems of Mary's adolescence.

The love and admiration lavished on her sister by Miltiadis Embirikos (and by others too, according to Jackie) can only have aggravated Mary's sense of inferiority and insecurity. "She was jealous of Embirikos, but she didn't hate me and I think I helped her," Jackie claimed in 1991.[18] But Jackie's help—if Mary saw it as such—was not enough for her, and it could hardly have answered her emotional needs. So, when Litsa sublet one of the bedrooms at 61 Patission Street, Mary found a new ally in the tenant, Marina Papayeorgopoulou. Born in 1904 and unmarried, Marina was a family friend of their former neighbor Christina Katifori.

She worked at a bank and she too, like Mary, spent most of her time out of the house. She was always well dressed, wore glasses, and sometimes dyed her hair blonde. Though not particularly well educated, she was a quiet and very discreet person who quickly won the confidence of Litsa's uncommunicative younger daughter. Moreover, as her lover was killed in the Middle East soon after her arrival in the household, she was no stranger to the emotional problems of her young friend.

Mary's confidante, Marina Papayeorgopoulou.

For the last two months of 1940 Marina shared her room with her young nephew Alkis Papayeorgopoulos. When Marina was out at work Alkis stayed in the apartment, so he became almost a member of the family. "Mary was often bad-tempered and irritable and hardly ever paid any attention to me," he recalls. "Litsa I remember as being always heavily made-up, forever smoking, talking loudly, singing, and telling jokes. 'Come here,' she said to me one day. 'Everyone in this house makes fun of me. Tell me, who do *you* think is the best-looking of the three of us?' '*You* are!' I answered at once, and from that moment on she spoiled me, and continued to do so whenever I went back to visit my aunt after I had moved out." Papayeorgopoulos remembers the two girls practicing the piano separately, playing endless scales and exercises, never arias or songs. "And in the evenings, before going to bed, they would put various creams and lotions on their faces. 'Don't look at us!' they would say, giggling."[19]

Whenever Litsa and Jackie were both out for the evening with their friends, Mary would go into Marina's room and pour her heart out to that sympathetic listener. The fact that Marina lived in their house and therefore knew all about the strained relations between Litsa, Jackie, and Mary must have made it much easier for a reserved girl like Mary to unburden herself. "It was sad that she no longer turned to me for comfort and advice; we had grown apart," Jackie comments in her memoirs. In her opinion, Mary's biggest problem at that time was her unattractive appearance, which meant that men took no notice of her. "Mary was forever in [Marina's] room asking her what she should do to be attractive, begging her to tell her the secret. She vowed that she would give up everything if she could find true love. . . . She begged her to explain why I and not she was always loved. Thinking to placate her Marina reminded her that she had her voice, but this only made Mary angry. '*What is a voice?*' she cried. '*I'm a woman, that's what matters.*'" Jackie believes that her sister was missing the love of a man, not of her mother.[20]

But what Mary was suffering from then was not—or at any rate not only—the lack of a male interest in her life but rather the lack of parental and especially paternal love and affection. This meant that the only outlet for her feelings, given that she lived with a domineering mother whom she held responsible for her father's exit from their life, was to look for tenderness in a man who would also boost her self-confidence and her womanly self-respect. One man who by early 1940 had become important in her life was her dentist, Dimitris (Mimis) Doustabanis, whose clinic was just across the road from 5 Marni Street, the building in which the Kaloyeropoulos family had lived before moving to 61 Patission Street. Jackie later recalled that when Mary had problems with her teeth she looked forward eagerly to her appointments. What attracted her to Doustabanis, besides his profession, was the atmosphere of melancholy surrounding him, for he was a man of about thirty who had just been jilted by the woman he loved. He was shortish, with fair hair, blue eyes, a moustache, very good manners, and a sense of humor. But Mary's overt interest in him apparently made his life a misery, according to the account given to Jackie later by his brother. "When he bent near to examine her she would suddenly say things like, '*Oh, Dimitri, you're just the sort of man I'd like to marry.*' But it was no use, the poor man was preoccupied. . . . For Mary it was just another rebuttal to cry over with Marina. '*Why does nobody love me?*' she would moan. '*Why do they always love Jackie?*'"[21]

In general, there is nothing unusual about a young woman having a crush on her dentist, and the only point of interest in Mary's case is that she was sixteen and Doustabanis was almost twice her age. He was perhaps the first of a succession of considerably older men for whom she formed an attachment in her quest for a surrogate father. The next, not long afterward and much more important in her life, was Dr. Ilias Papatestas, a tuberculosis specialist and director of the Piraeus Diagnostic Institute, who had a private clinic on the ground floor of 61 Patission Street.

—⁓—

In those early months of the war the cinemas were open from 10 a.m. to 10:30 p.m., showing films starring such Hollywood idols as Tyrone Power, George Sanders, and Shirley Temple. Newsreels were extremely popular, of course, as the war news consisted largely of a string of Greek victories. By 3 December 1940 the Greeks had crossed the frontier and were pursuing the Italians back into Albania. Every announcement of a fresh triumph was celebrated in Athens with flags and bell-ringing. Yet beneath the surface the mood was apprehensive as the winter set in and fears of German retaliation mounted. People started hoarding food, and thirty-six soup kitchens were set up in various parts of Athens. As Jackie puts it, "Nothing tangible happened except an increasing awareness that our humiliation of the Italian fascists was not to go unpunished and that the Germans were preparing to come to their aid."[22] In fact Hitler had already decided that Operation Marita (the contingency plan for the invasion of Greece) would have to go ahead whether he liked it or not, in order to rescue his ally Mussolini from total humiliation. On 20 January 1941 (the day before the première of *Boccaccio*) Piraeus was bombed by the Italians, with many casualties. It was bombed again a few days later, and a performance of *Boccaccio* was interrupted by an air raid warning. Everybody—actors, singers, stage crew, and audience—trooped down to the basement of the Pallas, but the dull thud of the explosions, ten kilometers away, could be heard even in the suffocatingly overcrowded shelter. Meanwhile life continued: Mary may well have read for the first time then the biographies of Jenny Lind and Maria Malibran,[23] two of the greatest sopranos of the first half of the nineteenth century, which were published in the newspaper *Proia* in daily installments. At the beginning of January the first telephone connection between Athens and New York, via Berne, was opened, "with good audibility and clarity." The National Theater was doing Beaumarchais's *Le mariage de Figaro*, and the cinemas were showing *Wuthering Heights* with Laurence Olivier and Merle Oberon.

Public euphoria about the war died down as the Greek advance was hampered by severe winter weather on the Albanian front. Rumors of a German counterattack were intensifying, and the downcast Athenians looked more and more kindly upon the British servicemen who were to be seen enjoying the sunshine in the Zappion Gardens, Syntagma Square, and Pedion Areos Park. One day, somewhere near Omonia Square, when Mary was using her knowledge of English to show some British soldiers the way to Piraeus, passers-by stopped to admire her efforts and applauded her when she had finished.[24] On Sunday, 6 April 1941, the Germans invaded Greece, which of course was in no position to resist. At eight o'clock that morning Radio Athens announced that once again Greece had fallen victim to "an unjust and unprovoked attack," and soon afterward the national anthem and rousing marches were to be heard through the open windows as people turned up the volume of their radios. Before long the streets were full of men and women pouring toward Syntagma Square, where the Greek G.H.Q. was installed in the Hotel Grande Bretagne. Suddenly the specter of enemy occupation was at hand and the food shops, which opened specially for the occasion, were cleared within hours. That evening Piraeus was bombed again—this time by the Germans—and when Litsa, her daughters, and Miltiadis came up from the shelter Mary led Jackie to the piano and started to sing. To relieve the doom-laden atmosphere she chose some of the light songs from the past—a past that already seemed distant.[25]

One matter that was very much on the minds of Litsa and the girls was the possibility of escaping to the safety of Egypt. In those last few days of freedom the newspapers and radio reported laconically that the Greek army was "putting up a superb fight" and "holding" the enemy; but Miltiadis knew that the Greek front had already been broken: enemy occupation was a matter of days, or even hours. With the pressure hard upon them, they "hastily bundled some things together, handed the poor canaries over to the maid for safe keeping and set off for the harbor," as Jackie writes. There Miltiadis secured places for them all on a ship about to leave for Egypt. However, as the crowd of passengers stood on the quay waiting to embark, news reached them of the sinking of a ship and panic spread among them. In the last two weeks the Germans had spared nothing afloat in the Saronic Gulf, having sunk not only passenger ferries but two hospital ships as well. Litsa now flatly refused to go on board, ignoring the pleas of Jackie, who hoped that if Miltiadis got away from his family he would find the courage to marry her. As for Mary's feelings in those tense few hours, we know nothing at all. All she ever said about leaving Greece during the war was, "*I could have come back [to the U.S.], but I didn't feel it right or proper, I don't know, to leave my mother and my sister there, so I stayed on*," implying that her American passport would have allowed her to get out, at least until the entry of the United States in the war in December 1941.[26]

For the inhabitants of Greater Athens, the three weeks from 6 to 27 April 1941 were perhaps the most harrowing period of the war. The sky seemed to be full of bombers, which not only devastated the port of Piraeus but attacked other areas as well. Although the Germans seemed to be respecting Athens's historic monuments, their aircraft often flew right over the city center to drop their bombs not far away, for example in the suburbs of Maroussi and Nea Smyrni. For a whole week before Easter, Athenians spent practically all day and all night in their air raid shelters. Mary, who did not like the dark, felt queasy and was sometimes sick down there, despite the comforting presence of her neighbors. Litsa tells how once, during an alert, Mary started off down the stairs to the shelter but suddenly dashed back up again to get a comb for her hair. This unusual concern about her appearance was probably due to the presence of Dr. Ilias Papatestas, who was practically the only person Mary talked to in the gloomy basement.[27]

Maria was to carry memories of that month of April with her all her life. "I remember many conversations when Maria recalled the wail of the sirens, . . . blackouts, rushed trips to the cellar, and the eerie silence that followed the curfews," writes Nadia Stancioff, who came to know Maria well when working as her secretary some thirty years later.[28] On Palm Sunday (13 April) there were no fewer than sixteen air raids, one of them lasting for fully four hours in the evening. This pattern was repeated the following Wednesday and again on Holy Thursday, when Junkers and Stuka bombers hit the military hospital at Voula. With Athens in a state of near-collapse, the Easter celebrations were distinctly subdued that year. On Easter Sunday the Germans again bombed Piraeus, Elefsis, and Megara,

Germans on the Acropolis.

and British Spitfires shot down several Messerschmitts in a dogfight near Athens. By this time the Nazis were well on their way to Athens, capturing one Greek town after another. On the Tuesday after Easter, King George and the government left Athens to carry on the struggle from Crete, while the civilian population followed developments dumbfounded. Greece had fallen to the Germans and—what was really humiliating—to Mussolini's defeated but now swaggering Italians.

The morning of Sunday, 27 April 1941, dawned on a seemingly dead and deserted Athens, a city cowed into stupefaction. Doors and windows remained closed, and the few faces to be seen on the streets were drawn with sleeplessness, anguish, and deep dejection. Athens was formally handed over to the German invaders at the Café Parthenon in Ambelokipi and two tanks rumbled down Vassilissis Sophias Avenue at the head of a long motorcade of army vehicles, passing in front of the flag-bedecked German embassy and then turning left at Syntagma Square toward the Acropolis. By 8:45 a.m. the red flag with the swastika was flying over the sacred rock. Litsa has been described opening a window and provoking an outburst of patriotic fury from Mary, who stormed at her in a tone that had "something frightening about it, something that allowed no room for argument." Much more convincing is the story told by Jackie, who says that when the first German motorcyclists turned from Alexandras Avenue onto Patission Street on their way to Omonia Square, she and Mary went up on to the roof of their build-

ing: "Along with countless other people that we could see on neighboring buildings, we started spitting into the street below. Over and over—sputt, sputt, sputt
—until we were dry. I doubt if any of it ever as much as marked an enemy uniform
but it made us feel better."[29] The occupation, which was to last for three and a half
terrible years, had just begun.

CHAPTER 19

Studies in Music and Life

At first, practically everything came to a halt. Only the curious came out of their houses, the shops stayed shut, and soldiers patrolled the streets. In those early days the blackout and curfew started at six, even before the sun had set. Government offices, banks, theaters, and schools (including conservatories) were closed down again for a time. Litsa describes the consolation that she and her daughters found in going to church to light candles and washing the icons in their home with wine every Friday, according to an ancient tradition. "Mary, who was truly religious, burned candles in five churches, and using the prescribed ritual whenever she entered a church, she crossed herself and entered with her right foot first," her mother informs us, although Maria was later to say of herself that she rejected the strict formalities of religious observance.[1] On 3 May 1941 the German occupation forces staged an ostentatious parade reviewed by Marshal List and Wing Commander von Richthofen. After passing the saluting base in front of the tomb of the unknown soldier, in Syntagma Square, the Nazis marched down Panepistimiou Street in a formidable display of force. Several armored units then turned right onto Patission Street, passing directly beneath the windows of No. 61, and right again onto Alexandras Avenue. Life, however, gradually resumed its normal rhythm, and Athenians began the painful process of adjusting to the new situation.

In their efforts to impose their authority and to solve the problems of feeding and housing themselves, the occupation authorities behaved with incredible harshness and high-handedness. Cars and other valuables were confiscated, large houses were requisitioned, and property was seized from private individuals and tradesmen who were terrorized into giving their "consent" to what amounted to daylight robbery. Black marketeers and profiteers flourished, prices rose from day to day, and very soon there was a shortage—real or artificial—of basic foodstuffs. Vegetables, legumes, lemons, and garlic were among the few items that were still available in the shops, at least for a while, and artichokes with broad beans became a staple food for many Athenians. As time went on, shortages worsened and the lines at food shops grew ever longer. The little gasoline that the British had left behind

233

soon ran out, and the few cars that were seen on the roads were all equipped with special permits. The smart restaurants and cafés were now patronized almost exclusively by uniformed German and Italian officers in gleaming jackboots, and the cinemas showed only German and Italian films and newsreels full of the latest Axis victories. Shop windows remained empty, and the main shopping streets were crowded with itinerant vendors selling trash. The streetcars stopped running at ten, restaurants closed at the same time, and a general curfew was in force from eleven in the evening.

When the conservatory reopened, around the middle of May, Mary sometimes reverted to going there for lessons and to practice duets or ensemble singing with other students, but more frequently she had her lessons at de Hidalgo's fifth-floor apartment at 79 Patission Street, usually at about lunchtime. "She lived on the top floor so as not to disturb her neighbors," recalls Lola Ritsou, who started having private lessons with de Hidalgo that year. "We always went up by the stairs in case there was a power cut. When Maria came in she generally looked awkward and uncomfortable. Usually she would go straight to the kitchen and do some odd jobs. This made her feel better, as she wasn't paying for her lessons and she knew that our teacher was rather mercenary-minded. She then came into the sitting room where we all sat listening to each other's lessons."[2]

After her own lesson Mary would stay on and listen to the other students, as she had done in previous years. Her conscientiousness and appetite for work have been emphasized by most of her biographers, who make it sound as if Mary herself was having lessons or practicing for hours every day. But, however much time she might have spent practicing on her own, her lessons with de Hidalgo never lasted longer than an hour a day. De Hidalgo herself later remembered: "Maria wasn't like my other pupils, who came just in time for their lesson and then left to do whatever they had to do. Always silent, almost scowling, . . . she would sit in a corner and stay there until I finished, in other words until the evening. She was there, watching and listening while I took all my other lessons, and she learned all there was to be learned. She had a phenomenal memory and tremendous willpower. When it was time for her own lesson, she worked with me. The rest of the time she never even spoke to me but just sat there, alert and taking it all in."[3]

Mary's lessons were rewarding to pupil and teacher alike. "She was [a] perfect [pupil]," de Hidalgo remarked in 1969. "Obedient, clever, hardworking. It was quite extraordinary, I never had to repeat anything twice. She would say, '*Yes, I see.*' The next day she would be amazing. And it was always like that!" De Hidalgo then stressed what a natural musician Mary was and how much she expected of herself. "'*Can I learn picchiettati?*' [a rapid succession of staccato notes], she would ask me. 'If you go on like this, you'll be able to do anything you want—provided you continue working as you are now.' . . . And, of course, she made fantastic progress." De Hidalgo was definitely not given to flattery, but about Mary she was quite fulsome: "She was some kind of phenomenon, because her low notes were very strong and very good, so were her middle notes, and she could go really high, right up to E natural! She was the singer who had everything—voice, singing style, interpretation. On stage she was wonderful, she was lovely. Even then her hands were exquisite, in spite of the fact that she bit her nails."[4]

The increased difficulties of everyday life had the effect of making Mary work even harder at her music. Her obsessiveness for work now became even more marked. Her friend Dr. Ilias Papatestas observed her dedication to the idea of overcoming the obstacles and starting a successful career: "She practiced so hard and so intensively that sometimes it was sheer folly," he remarked in 1963. "She would often spend more than ten hours a day practicing, which left her dead tired." For reasons that we shall be looking into later, Papatestas added that her excessive practicing left her no time at all for "the usual preoccupations of girls of her age." However, although similar allegations have been made by others as well, their truth is open to question. What is certain, nevertheless, is that even in the darkest days of the occupation Mary never missed any of her lessons either at the conservatory or at de Hidalgo's. "Of this I am absolutely sure, because I was very close to her," insisted the faithful Papatestas, who would remain a close friend of hers until her death.[5]

De Hidalgo, a clever woman with a powerful intuition, became more certain every day that Mary really was the person chosen for her by fate. To this elect disciple she passed on a deep-rooted belief in the splendor of music and the musician's vocation. Under her guidance, it was not long before Mary began to feel that her musical talent was not merely a means of earning her living and proving her own value but a destiny and a duty. In addition Mary started discovering and using vocal and dramatic gifts which she already possessed but had never used. Nor was de Hidalgo merely her teacher of music: drawing on her own experience, she soon became Mary's spiritual mentor, acting more or less in loco parentis both for her overbearing and unscrupulous mother and for her absent father. She also took it upon herself to give Mary a smattering of general education, and to support her whenever her relations with her mother became particularly strained. Mary would then go and stay with her teacher for a few days, as to move permanently out of 61 Patission Street at her age would have been quite impossible.

To Mary the world of singing and of opera was not merely the whole of her daily life: for the time being, at least, it was her sole means of expressing her emotions. So her musical studies and, later on, all the rehearsals and other preparatory work for her stage performances were never a hardship to her. On the contrary, she enjoyed them and they gave her a chance to escape to the worlds of her romantic imagination. "*[Being on stage] is a delight! It's as if you had wings,*" she would remark later. At that time, however, with her chances of spending time in the theater still limited, de Hidalgo's apartment and the Athens Conservatory were the only available substitutes for a world she was beginning to love and need. It never even occurred to her to go home after her lesson. "*I've got nothing to do at home,*" was the standard answer she gave her teacher. But the story of the poor defenseless girl defying the invading forces by breaking the curfew to go to her singing lessons has to be seen in a different light, when one realizes that her dangerous unlawful journey took her about 200 meters along the pavement of Patission Street. In the summer, when Mary sang with the windows open or on the roof of No. 61, her teacher was near enough at No. 79 to hear her and recognize her voice.[6]

The final examinations at the conservatory were held rather late that year, because of the tense situation still prevailing in Athens. On 13 June 1941 Mary failed to appear for the Solfège V examination taken by Ikonomidis. On the official examination record the space opposite "No. 20, Marianna Kaloyeropoulou" was left blank. Three days later, on 16 June, she again failed to appear for the Harmony II examination, also under Ikonomidis, and again there is no comment beside Mary's name. Knowing what we do about Mary's fiery temperament, her past brushes with Ikonomidis and the latter's mentality, it is a fairly safe guess that some new quarrel had erupted and caused a serious breach between them. This supposition seems to be borne out by the fact that the next year Mary enrolled again in the same classes, but under a different teacher. Three years later she would have yet another unpleasant confrontation with Ikonomidis, and she would never forget his attitude toward her, which she considered to be one of open hostility—and so it was.

On Thursday, 19 June 1941, Mary took the annual examination of the advanced singing class. On the examination record, signed by Elvira de Hidalgo, the second-year student Marianna Kaloyeropoulou (No. 6) again received top grades for application, progress, and ability. The same marks were given to the other five students who took the examination, but Mary's program was longer and more exacting than anyone else's. Each candidate had to start with a "classical" aria (as defined by the conservatory), and for Mary, de Hidalgo had unearthed an aria from *Béniowski, ou Les Éxilés de Kamtchatka*, a three-act opera by François Boieldieu (1775–1834). After that she sang something from Beethoven's *Fidelio*, probably "Abscheulicher!" from Act I, with which aria she was to triumph three years later. For her lieder singing she chose Brahms's "Von ewiger Liebe," which she probably sang in French as de Hidalgo wrote the title on the examination record as "Les amours éternelles." And her fourth and last piece was one of Leonora's arias from *La Forza del Destino*, probably "Pace, pace, mio Dio" from the last act.[7]

—∿∿—

Although de Hidalgo did her best to give Mary some clothes sense, her pupil still dressed badly and was careless about her appearance. "*I did try,*" Maria is reported saying shortly before her death, "*but, to be frank, I never paid much attention to clothes or how I looked then.*" She ate irregularly and, inevitably, what she ate was of inferior quality and poor nutritional value. Eventually, however, de Hidalgo's

ΩΔΕΙΟΝ ΑΘΗΝΩΝ
1871

ΠΡΑΚΤΙΚΟΝ· ΕΞΕΤΑΣΕΩΝ   ΣΧΟΛΗ _Μονωδίας_   ΣΧΟΛ. ΕΤΟΣ 194_0_ – 194_1_

Τάξις _Ανωτέρα_ πρός _τῆς Καθημερίας Κας ὲ ὲ ὰὲ Ἰναζμο_

Αὐξων ἀριθμός		Ὀνοματεπώνυμον	Ἔτη		Θέματα ἐτησίων ἐξετάσεων	Βαθμοί			Παρατηρήσεις
			Φοιτ.	Τάξ.		Ἐπιμελ.	Προόδου	Ἱκανότ.	
1686	5	Μαρτινας Ἀρλα	V	2		1	1	1	
1862	6	Καρογηροπούγου Μαριάννα	V	2	Beethoven² Fidelio Boieldieu ¹ aie de Bensonthe Brahms del amour eternelles Verdi Forza del destino	1	1	1	

Ἐν Ἀθήναις τῇ _19 Ἰουνίου_ 194_1_

Η ΕΞΕΤΑΣΤΙΚΗ ΕΠΙΤΡΟΠΗ

Ὁ Πρόεδρος   Τὰ Μέλη   Ὁ Διδάξας

Mary's mark sheet in Elvira de Hidalgo's handwriting, Athens Conservatory,
19 June 1941.

pressure did at last awaken in her a certain sense of style. "She dressed very simply, usually in a blouse and skirt," says Lola Ritsou, "but when I first met her at de Hidalgo's she had her hair dyed blonde." She had evidently started experimenting with her appearance and using makeup—and no longer to cover up her acne, which was now noticeably better. Thomas Apostolou, who worked at the Minerva Grocery at 56 Patission Street since 1937, remembers Mary coming in from time to time from across the street. "She was very polite," he recalls, "and she had her hair done in plaits taken up over her head." His wife, Regina, was struck by Mary's almond-shaped eyes and loud voice: "One day she put her hand on the back of my neck and stroked and ruffled my fair hair, saying dreamily, *'Blue eyes, shifty eyes!'*"[8]

The problems caused by Mary's living in the same house with her mother and sister soon became a major issue. From the moment her links with America and her father were broken, the emotional void inside her had grown. The last news of George that reached Athens was that he was traveling around the United States selling medicines and cosmetics, with no fixed abode. Meanwhile Litsa continued to lead her own life among her own friends and Greek admirers, whose number was shortly to be swelled by officers of the occupation forces, mostly Italian. But by now Mary was approaching eighteen, and she had others to whom she could look for moral support and practical assistance. We have seen her telling her mother in the most forceful terms that she wanted to take charge of her own life, and her desire for independence was to gather strength throughout the time she was in Greece.

Mary was an early riser. After a breakfast of whatever there was to eat in those difficult times, she practiced until she had to leave for her daily lesson. The room resounded to her powerful voice, so much so that one day (if the story is to be believed) one of the canaries collapsed in its cage. "At home she practiced early and late, forgetting the enemy in her music," Litsa wrote later, adding drily, "My daughter Maria would not let a war interfere with her ambitions." Whenever Jackie wanted the piano at the same time, the two girls became quite unpleasant to each other; and they found plenty of pretexts for quarreling, not the least of them being the allocation of household chores. Mary had to do some of the housekeeping, an arrangement that would have been neither unusual nor unfair if the work had been shared equitably. But there is evidence from a number of sources that the brunt of it—or at least of the heavy work—was borne by Mary. Her classmate Mitsa Kourahani noticed one day at the conservatory that her hands were all red. "*I was washing all night, doing the washing for both of them,*" was the explanation Mary gave when asked. Jackie, however, complains of exactly the opposite: "The one thing that sometimes united my mother and me was our anger at the way Mary never helped out in the apartment—she'd eat, then off she'd go to de Hidalgo without so much as putting her cup in the sink, let alone washing it."[9]

The most convincing explanation for this petty bickering is that Jackie was exploiting the fact that she was, via her lover, supporting all three of them, indeed enabling them to keep up quite a respectable standard of living. As Litsa acknowledges in her book, "If any one person saved us, it was Jackie's wealthy fiancé, Milton Embirikos, who gave us money and food and clothing all through the war." Jackie saw this as her contribution to the housekeeping, so why shouldn't Mary contribute from time to time by mopping the floors or washing the clothes in the washtub? "[Milton] was, at the same time, fiancé, brother, and father for us," Jackie told one of Maria's biographers. "He saw my family as his own. He was rich and in spite of difficulties during the German occupation, he carried on with his money to provide us with a big apartment, food, clothes, and even a maid." The fact that being "kept" by a man who was neither a relative nor a family friend was nothing to be proud of is passed over in silence, for the purpose of refuting Maria's later statements that she had been the one who supported the family: "*I scoured the town and wore myself out trying to keep them all fed,*" Maria allegedly claimed once, while on another occasion, "*When the war came, all financial support from Callas père dried up. And who,*" she asked in the voice of a true tragedian, "*was expected to look after the family then? Me, of course!*"[10]

Statements of this kind—if reported accurately, of course—were quite untrue. The money that Mary earned during that period was indeed the only earned income coming into the household, but it covered no more than Mary's personal expenses and pocket money: "*Thanks to that contract [with the Greek National Opera], I had money which made it possible for me to buy clothes and pursue my studies, with enough left over for transport,*" she admitted on one occasion when she was feeling calmer.[11] "The story that Mary told about how she kept us all on the salary she received at the Greek National Opera is absolutely untrue. Her salary was symbolic, and I would say she spent it all to buy a lipstick, or some pastries," Jackie stated many years after Maria's death, and that was about the truth of it in those very early days. "Everything was provided by Milton. He did all this for my sake, because he adored me. . . . Mary was able to devote herself to her art without any care of how to live, to eat, to dress. Without Milton we would have starved!"[12]

The small starting salary that de Hidalgo had arranged for Mary gave her the satisfaction of knowing that such money as she had was her own and she had earned it herself. Later, however, from the beginning of 1943 and even more from April 1944, when she was a Grade A soloist, Mary would doubtless have had something considerable left over to contribute to the household budget, whereas her mother and sister were always content to rely on what others gave them. It must have been this line of reasoning that justified Maria's statements that she had supported the family; and, surely, she must have been reacting to grossly untrue statements of her mother, who would not hesitate to lie one day that Mary never supported herself in Greece, except during a month after the liberation, late in 1944! Even then, Litsa would add, it was she that had found her daughter a job with the British military command, and when Mary had handed her salary over to her she had allegedly told her that it was "a minimal advance" and that when she would be famous she would "make a statue" for Litsa.[13] Be that as it may, this was to be the theme—Mary had had to work so hard because her mother was determined to be supported by her without working herself—that Maria was to harp on for the rest of her life; and it proved to be the rock on which her relationship with her mother eventually foundered. The truth, nevertheless, about Mary's contribution to the family's survival during the occupation is clearly borne out by Litsa's words in a recently discovered letter. Writing to Mary in September 1949—just before they fell out with each other—exasperated by Jackie's steadfastly waiting for Miltiadis to marry her, Litsa wrote, "I know, my little Mary, that [Jackie] carries on about having sacrificed herself for us. Shame on her! What are you to say then, you who were feeding your family at sixteen? I am not saying that she did not save us through that man. But it would have been better had she supported us by her work and in dignity, like you."[14]

—⁂—

Late one evening, toward the end of the summer of 1941, an officer in the Greek air force brought two fugitive British airmen to 61 Patission Street, asking Litsa to hide them. At first she refused; eventually however her patriotic pride overcame her misgivings—they might all have ended up in front of a firing squad if they were caught—and the two officers were put into the little room, with the canaries. They were between Jackie and Mary in age, one—a Scot named John Atkinson—was dark, lively, and very brave, the other—an Englishman possibly called Robert[15]—was fair-haired, reserved, and cold. Jackie and Mary were glad to have someone to talk to and would keep them company, but only so long as no one else—especially Miltiadis—was in the apartment. Late in the evening, after Jackie's "fiancé" had gone and the coast was clear, the two girls would sit with John and Robert in the living room. Evidently it was not long before the extrovert John fell for the beautiful Jackie, but we do not know whether there was any particular attraction between Robert and Mary.

One day Miltiadis arrived unexpectedly when the two fugitives were talking rather loudly in their hiding place. On that occasion Mary saved the situation with great presence of mind by starting to sing an aria, probably from *Tosca*. As it happened, this turned out to be a sort of dress rehearsal for another, much more important, performance that would follow soon after. Mary also sang at nine o'clock every evening, when John and Robert switched on the wireless to listen to the BBC news. That was their only contact with the outside world during the six weeks they were on Patission Street, except for one foolhardy excursion into the city center, described by Litsa and Jackie with slight variations. After dyeing the Englishman's fair hair dark, the two girls, in one of their last moments of shared girlish exuberance and happy-go-lucky recklessness, walked out arm-in-arm with the two young officers, heedless of the mortal danger of discovery. At last the same

Greek officer came and took the airmen away with him, much to Litsa's relief. According to Jackie, a few days later they heard on the BBC (to which they would listen surreptitiously throughout the occupation) that Robert had managed to leave the country, but John had been fatally wounded just before he boarded his escape vessel at Kalamata. "I had enjoyed the episode," Jackie remarks coolly, but she continues ominously: "Would that that had been our only contact with foreign soldiers and that events had not turned out the way they did."[16]

The very day after the British officers had left, armed Italian soldiers pounded on the front door and pushed their way in to search the apartment. As the little room still contained incriminating evidence of its recent occupation by the two British fugitives, once again it was Mary's presence of mind that saved the situation: she quickly ran over to the piano and started singing. "Never had I heard her sing better than she did that day—a girl of seventeen singing for her life," Litsa recalled. Listening to the young Tosca (probably singing "Vissi d'arte"), the Italians sat around the piano speechless with amazement, enjoying the unexpected recital of familiar music, probably in their own language. Full of admiration, they left without having searched anywhere and came back the next day, not with hostile intent but to bring presents for signorina Maria the soprano, their new friend. "They heaped loaves of bread, ham, and macaroni on the piano as though these gifts were burnt offerings to a goddess, and again she sang to them," Litsa relates. Jackie, however, who happened to be out at the time, accuses her mother of "transforming this into part of the Maria mythology." When she came home, she writes, "They looked like two scared females rather than heroines of the resistance."[17] And this might be closer to the truth.

Most events in a person's life are linked by a chain of cause and effect. One thing leads to another, an incident that at first sight seems trivial gives rise to another that is more significant, and so on. Hiding the British airmen led to the intended search of the apartment; the visit of the Italian soldiers caused them to hear and admire Mary's voice; and their admiration and the way they expressed it —by bringing food—had an enormous effect not only on Mary herself but on her mother too. Litsa, of course, was quite aware that soldiers of all ranks—and Italian soldiers in particular—were skirt-chasers. Doubtless she also knew that they used to tempt the girls with the most enticing bait they had to offer, namely food. So severe was the shortage of basic essentials in 1941 and 1942, and so unbearable the hunger, that pasta, rice, cooking fat, coffee, chocolate, sugar, flour, and other staples were used as substitutes for money in a kind of barter trade that the more straitlaced citizens condemned as being no better than prostitution. The soldiers had a good time, but for the Greek girls it was often a matter of life and death, for themselves and their families. So when Mary, before the very eyes of her hard-pressed and none too fastidious mother, showed that she could purchase with her voice what other girls could only purchase with their bodies (prostitution actually multiplied fivefold from 1941 to 1945), it did not take long for Litsa to decide that her daughter could serve a useful purpose by offering her family a higher standard of living.

Litsa was later in the habit of saying how much she liked the Italians. However, this was a sentiment that developed after she had met a number of Italian officers whom she liked on a personal level (one of whom became her lover) and for reasons of relative patriotism, once the Germans had shown how much more brutal they could be in trampling on the human dignity and pride of the Greeks. A liking for the Italians was no part of her makeup at the start of the occupation, and still less in June 1941, when the Italians had just taken over from the Germans in Greece to allow the latter to serve the Reich more effectively in Russia and elsewhere. At first the Italians were regarded by the Greeks with the utmost contempt, a sentiment which was shared by their German allies. The Greek government had earnestly entreated the German authorities not to allow the Italians to take over in Athens, but Mussolini, suffering from badly hurt pride after the humiliating defeat of his army in Albania, pressed Hitler to agree to an arrangement which suited his plans anyway. The Germans established a puppet Greek government in order to ensure administrative continuity in a country they had conquered only through force of circumstances. At the end of May they completed their conquest of Crete after a bloody campaign, while King George and his government fled to Cairo. Eventually Greece was carved up between the Bulgarians, the Germans (most of Crete, Piraeus, the Turkish frontier zone, and the islands of Lesbos and Chios), and the Italians, whose jurisdiction covered most of the islands and mainland (including Athens).[18]

A Greek journalist wrote in 1963 that one day Mary came home to see an Italian officer's cap on the hall table and her mother sitting with the officer in the living room. When the officer had gone, Mary turned on her mother in fury and demanded an explanation. *"No one is ever again to set foot in our house!"* she stormed. "I'm the one who decides who comes into my house, not you!" retorted Litsa. To which Mary growled, *"Then as soon as they come, I go!"*[19] If Mary did react with hostility to the presence of Italians in her house in the early days, soon her attitude changed. In the latter part of 1941, when the Italians were all over Athens, she came to know quite a number of Italian servicemen and made friends with several of them. Sometimes, no doubt, she met them through her mother or de Hidalgo, who had good connections in the Casa d'Italia, but others she must surely have met independently. And, as one of her first biographers wrote with stinging irony, "Italians being a singing nation through thick and thin, an improvised concert of arias would always bring an additional supply of spaghetti, butter, and sugar."[20]

Little has so far come to light about particular Italian or German friends or acquaintances Mary had during the occupation, and even less is known about specific occasions when Litsa exerted pressure on her daughter to exploit her voice or her feminine charms. Many insinuations have been made, and it has even been alleged that Mary went to Italy during the occupation!* Needless to say, at no stage in her life did Maria herself speak openly on this subject. Litsa, on the other hand, while not casting discretion to the winds, did talk about foreign men who came to the apartment and admired Mary, actually naming some of them, including her own lover, Colonel Mario Bonalti. Jackie, too, gives some interesting information in her memoirs, especially about Mary's "first real romance" with Major Attilio De Stasio. One very valuable source of information, overlooked until quite recently, is the testimony of de Hidalgo on the subject, but what is even more illuminating is the disclosure of concrete facts and names in the written memoir of an Italian who was friendly with Mary at that time.

The various stories that have appeared in print over the years may contain a kernel of truth, but most if not all have almost certainly been embroidered with figments of the writers' imagination. One of her best-known biographers, Arianna Stassinopoulou, describes Mary's "friendship" with an Italian soldier who heard her singing as he passed her open window on Patission. But the apartment had no window on Patission Street; nor can the fifth-floor balcony, beneath which her Italian admirer is supposed to have expressed his feelings, actually be seen from the street. Be that as it may, Mary and the soldier are said to have met several times in one of the parks nearby, where they sat on a bench, and she sang him her favorite arias while he wept with emotion. Before they parted he always gave her some food he had saved from his rations, and on her way back Mary would hide in a doorway, tear the parcel open and eat the food then and there. "Her mother was furious that she hardly ever brought anything back," the overimaginative biographer continues, with cloying sentimentality, "but Maria was too hungry, too lonely, and feeling too unloved to share."[21]

The only other evidence to corroborate to some degree this story of Mary's "first wartime friendship" comes from the painter Yannis Tsarouchis through some recent reminiscences of Franco Zeffirelli. "Her mother wanted her to go off and sing for the military every evening in return for food. Mary realized at once that these soldiers were not interested in music but wanted something else from her. She tried to tell her mother how the land lay, but her mother refused to believe

---

*Such allegations, which were later regularly exploited by jealous professional rivals, were put about by people who were basically ill-disposed toward Mary: they would say what they wanted to say and then immediately hedge their statements with reservations and qualifications. Ypatia Louvi, for example, said, "And what about that time when she went to Italy with a German during the occupation? She worked a lot of fiddles like that to further her career, and she succeeded. But I didn't witness any of that myself." (LOUVI.) Manolis Hadzis was at pains to make the same point: "They got her out to Italy, to hear her sing. In 1942 or thereabouts she spent five or six months there, and that wasn't the only time she went. I can't say any more, I'm not sure, I only know that the Italians got her out. Some senior officer had fallen in love with her and all his subordinates helped." (HADZIS, who added quite openly, "I didn't like her. I never tried to get to know her better, I just didn't like her as a person—not for any particular reason.")

it. Every afternoon there were terrible rows between them. 'No, I shan't go!' Mary would shout in tears. But Evangelia would push her out of the house, telling her not even to think of coming back without any provisions." Tsarouchis also told Zeffirelli that he had once seen Mary leaving her house, slamming the door behind her, having been sent out by her mother to get food for the family by making friends with Italian servicemen. However, Mary only went to the square nearby and waited there for a young Italian soldier to whom she was secretly engaged. According to Zeffirelli, "They sat there chatting, and from time to time Maria sang to him. 'It was a very touching scene,' Tsarouchis told me. Later, when I was a friend of Maria, I mentioned it to her. She flashed me an angry look. '*How do you know that?*' she asked. '*Do you know that soldier?*' 'No, a neighbor of yours saw you from his window,' I replied. Maria looked thoughtful and then said, '*You pervert! You were spying on me even before you met me!*' And after a while she added, '*Now you know a secret that nobody else knows.*'"[22]

Elvira de Hidalgo, who was certainly one of Mary's close confidantes, never mentioned any names, but she did state unequivocally that her pupil had yielded to the temptation of singing for virtually anyone who was in a position to remunerate her handsomely with food: "From time to time some officers would come round to pick up my girl pupils and take them not only into Athens but sometimes all the way to Thessaloniki or Volos. They got them to sing for the soldiers and rewarded them with kilos and kilos of pasta, butter, sugar, and cakes." In 1968 de Hidalgo elaborated: "The Italian soldiers were mad about singing. On Sundays, and often on weekdays as well, they used to organize concerts. They would come to pick up the girls from the conservatory, take them out for a walk and get them to sing, rewarding them with gifts of spaghetti, bread, jam, and other food. Maria did the rounds with the rest of them and sang for the soldiers to get something to eat. I was extremely concerned. It would be disastrous for her, because she was still too young and oughtn't to overstrain her voice. I didn't know which saint to pray to."[23] In these overlooked interviews, de Hidalgo mentioned only the danger to the voice of her star pupil and said nothing about love affairs or romantic attachments. However, it would appear that Mary's friendships with these Italian music-lovers were not always confined to the musical sphere.

In the late 1960s the Italian journalist Renzo Allegri struck up a friendship with Elvira de Hidalgo, who declined to make any sensational revelations (Maria being still alive then) but did disclose a good many hitherto unknown facts. "In that article of mine," Allegri wrote in a personal letter in 1994, "I did not reveal everything that de Hidalgo had confided to me. However, I do know that during the war Maria was strongly encouraged by her mother to make friends with servicemen in order to earn payment in kind, in the form of food. And soldiers, of course, are not known for their delicacy of feeling and manners. De Hidalgo told me that Maria was in danger of coming to grief with the soldiers. She made it quite clear that her pupil had really let herself go and at times had been completely infatuated, which would have been fatal for her career."[24] Allegri discovered that one of the Italians who had been particularly friendly with Mary was a young officer or NCO from Verona, who may well have been the Pierro with whom Mary had some kind of liaison. Litsa was later to reveal that Pierro, a regular visitor to 61 Patission Street, came from northern Italy and was tall, dark, and handsome.[25] Allegri also unearthed some information about a group of Italian paratroopers who had served in Athens and had known Mary. "We had fun with her, as we did with the other girls," one of them told Allegri, while another claimed to be Mary's fiancé (*fidanzato*) and apparently told some friends of his that he was having an affair with her. However, this story belongs to the summer of 1942 and we shall be returning to it in a later chapter, together with the question of Mary's relationship with Attilio De Stasio.[26]

—⁂—

On the subject of Mary's attitude to sex during her adolescence, Litsa wrote that her daughter was "rather less interested in boys than most girls of her temperament," although she was "aware of the opposite sex and liked to flirt and giggle with the fuzzy-cheeked boys of her age." Litsa, however, tells us that in those days young men were more interested in their own survival than in romantic love, and in the theater Mary met older professionals, with different moral standards from those that she had been brought up with in the public schools and Greek Orthodox church of Washington Heights. In Litsa's opinion, "Maria came through both these periods of adjustment without too much inner turmoil," and despite the admission that her daughter never "poured out her soul" in times of mutual confidence, she concluded with the questionable generalization that Mary was more interested in opera than in men.[27]

Maria herself confessed much later that she had been initiated into the facts of life at about this time, in late 1941 or early 1942. She was eighteen when she "*first learned how a baby is born*," she told her accompanist Robert Sutherland in 1974. When he asked her how she could have been in opera since the age of thirteen and not have learned from her colleagues, Maria answered: "*Greek girls must remain chaste till they are married*," adding that she was too busy working and, anyway, she was "*not particularly interested*."[28] People usually remember how and when they discovered the facts about sex, so there is no reason to doubt the truth of this statement, which Maria made when she was over fifty. What is interesting is that the age at which she acquired this knowledge coincides with the time when she was out and about with members of the Italian occupation authorities. So, whether she acquired the knowledge empirically or theoretically, it seems almost certain that some Italian soldier or soldiers played some part in her sexual enlightenment. And the same applies, at around the same time or a little later, to her neighbor, Ilias Papatestas.

In light of all this, and despite Litsa's assertion that the first man in her daughter's life was her husband, Meneghini, it is clear that Mary did have relationships of some kind—whether simple acquaintances, friendships, or love affairs—with several Italian soldiers. According to Allegri, who talked to de Hidalgo about this subject, her mother not only knew what was going on but encouraged it. She used her daughters (for she is widely alleged to have done the same with Jackie as well as Mary) as "bait" to effect an introduction to Axis officers (Italians for the most part), whose friendship she believed would be highly beneficial to them all, and certainly was to herself. What was the difference, she must have reasoned, between being supported by gifts from Jackie's "fiancé" Embirikos (who, after all, had no intention of ever lowering himself so far as to marry her) and accepting gifts as a quid pro quo for the company and impromptu recitals that Mary offered to Italian or even German opera-lovers? The fact that the quid pro quo (usually food) came from members of an enemy army of occupation evidently did not bother her: she was to demonstrate that by taking an Italian lover herself, a colonel who happened to be a fine man but was nevertheless an enemy of her country at the time. Litsa took people as she found them, judging them by their character and their potential usefulness to her. She would probably not actually have advised her daughters to bestow their favors promiscuously on anyone who offered them presents, but rather to be "realistic" about it. And as Mary's voice was winning more and more admirers among the Italians, while Jackie was preoccupied with the possessive Miltiadis, Mary was the one chiefly affected by Litsa's "maternal" guidance.*

It is probably no exaggeration to say that whereas until then Mary's feelings about her mother had been ambivalent, resentful, and probably unloving, from about this time she must have begun to hate her, perhaps even consciously. That was the opinion of her husband, Meneghini, who would no doubt have had long conversations with her on the subject, since her final stormy breach with Litsa occurred in 1951. Shortly before he died, Meneghini confided to Allegri that Maria's hatred for her mother dated from the time of the occupation: "She didn't want to go out with the soldiers in the evenings, but her mother made her. There were times when she was reduced to tears, but she had to obey her mother and go."[29] In 1969 Maria herself confided to Giulietta Simionato that her mother encouraged her "even to go with various men": "Maria resisted because she had no

---

*According to the journalist Vassos Vassiliou, who knew Mary at that time, the Kaloyeropoulos household was "ruled by the theory of *la dolce vita*," and Litsa, who was supremely interested in having a good time, saw her daughter's musical accomplishments as a means of improving the standard of living for the whole family. Vassiliou maintained that Mary "fought tooth and nail against the 'bargain sale' mentality": she was given lectures on the theme that in order to succeed she had to place a lower value on her feminine taste, her youthful passions, and her overambitious musical aspirations. (VASSILIOU.) Another Greek journalist, Stamatis Tsoutis, wrote: "Attempts were made by a member of her family to introduce her to Italians, to see her through the hard times. Maria refused angrily, and there were many occasions when she quarreled over the matter with her mother, who was one of the advocates of such ideas." (TSOUTIS.) The "member of her family" was probably Litsa herself, whom Tsoutis (writing in 1963) avoided mentioning by name for fear of a libel action.

inclination to this sort of thing," Simionato said. "Even when Maria was fat, she was attractive and very playful, and this was often mistaken for coquetry. But she was not like that. In fact she confided to me—and I believe she was telling the truth—that even with the men her mother wanted her to go with, she managed to remain untouched. In tears she would tell them her story and they would give her money without touching her. Do you understand? Maria took the money to her mother, who thought that she had given herself to them. That way the mother practically pushed her daughter into prostitution!"[30]

In her memoirs, of course, Litsa says with her usual air of disarming honesty, "Occupation soldiers and officers who admired Maria's singing . . . smuggled food to us or shared their rations with us." And then, in an obvious attempt to discredit Maria's accounts of what she had suffered during the occupation, she concludes: "I would say that on the whole Maria's wartime lot—and her sister's and mine as well—was considerably easier than most Athenians', because music-lovers among the officers of the occupation forces went out of their way to show their admiration for her." Double-edged words these, intended to give the unenlightened reader a false impression of family unity and relative happiness. And although Jackie insists that Litsa knew nothing about Mary's personal friendships or the people she spent her time with, there is no doubt that Litsa was often well aware of it all, having on one occasion even gone so far as to have a surreptitious affair with an Italian whom Mary was smitten with at the time. As Litsa later confessed to Afroditi Kopanou, one of Mary's old classmates, early on in the occupation an Italian had fallen in love with Mary and declared his willingness to do whatever she wanted of him: he was happy to be her lover or her husband, and he would also be her manager and get her an engagement at La Scala one day. "Thrilled, Mary lost no time in telling her mother, who slapped her on both cheeks, as Litsa told me herself," Kopanou relates, "and retorted that it was too early for anything like that, that her voice still needed a lot of work, and more in the same vein. But when she discovered that Mary was still seeing the Italian, she followed her, went to see him secretly and— believe it or not—stole him from her own daughter and started an affair with him herself! Madame Litsa then told me that Maria had never forgiven her for this and was still trying to get her back."[31]

No matter the extent of Litsa's involvement, however, some responsibility for Mary's actions must be borne by Mary herself, even allowing for all the miti- gating circumstances, including the fact that her salary was suspended from July 1941. Considering the determination with which Mary advanced her career and her own interests, it is not unlikely that she herself coolly calculated that certain relationships might enhance her musical prospects. In particular, she must have seen the advantages of maintaining a good relationship with the Casa d'Italia, which functioned as a propaganda machine throughout the occupation by organ- izing concerts in several of which Mary sang, probably on the recommendation of de Hidalgo. So it is quite possible that Mary sometimes consorted with the Italians on her own initiative, and possibly with the knowledge of her teacher. This would surely have been the case when she lost her heart to one of them and was perhaps introduced to pleasures of the flesh which she had never experienced before. Considering her age and the circumstances of her life at the time, she should certainly not be condemned for weaknesses of this kind. But there must have been other occasions when she did what she did for motives unconnected with her emotions, and for those she must bear at least a certain measure of responsibility.

In the troubled times of the occupation it was certainly not easy to follow the dictates of one's conscience as regards consorting with the enemy. Some people managed to stick to their patriotic principles; for others personal interest came first; and there were many who were forced to compromise out of sheer necessity. Throughout the occupation this dilemma was particularly acute for the members of the one and only opera company in Greece, which was state-run: they could hardly refuse to sing when there were high-ranking Italian or German officials in the audience, nor at special public or even private functions organized by officers of the occupation authorities. Most Greek actors and musicians, including nearly all the principals of the Greek National Opera, sometimes performed for the enemy during the occupation. No less a person than Sophia Vembo, who came to be known as "the singer of Victory" because of her invaluable services in providing entertainment for the Greek people and the forces at that time, sang at an all-German soirée in June 1942.[32] Vembo did not even belong to a company controlled by the state (and therefore by the enemy), yet nobody would ever make such accusations against her. "We simply didn't have the option of refusing," insists Andreas Paridis, voicing the view expressed today by nearly all the musicians who started their careers during the occupation. "But that has nothing to do with being collaborators or traitors. Quite the opposite, in fact, because our music made the Italians or Germans treat us less harshly as our conquerors. Most of them loved music and admired us."[33]

It would be easy to digress at length on the social, patriotic, philosophical, ethical, and other implications of this subject. But the point to be made here is that opera singers in those days had three absolute priorities to consider. First, they had to keep body and soul together, in other words to eat. Secondly, they had to keep their careers going, in other words to sing. And thirdly, they had to stay alive, which meant that they had to toe the line laid down by the enemy army of occupation, at least as far as their work was concerned. These were problems which they all faced in accordance with their own individual standards of judgment, their own principles and beliefs, their own needs and circumstances: even whether they were asked to perform or not influenced their action and attitude toward colleagues. "No Greek singer is known to have turned down any engagement offered by the company at this time," writes Stelios Galatopoulos. "Those who were not asked to sing became pseudo-patriots through misfortune rather than choice." As for their invectives against Mary, they were more fierce "because she was young, bright, exciting, and above all successful."[34] Indeed, the stance taken by Mary Kaloyeropoulou has been the subject of endless distortions, exaggerations, and calumnies. But even so it cannot be denied that, for one reason or another, she frequently did have, as it will become obvious, both professional dealings and personal relationships with enemy servicemen, mostly Italians, and also that, after the Italian withdrawal in September 1943, she would be backed professionally by the German propaganda and cultural authorities.

In evaluating these relationships and the benefits they brought her, to see whether she is rather to be condemned or excused, one has to judge each case on its own merits, taking into account the circumstances, the amount of choice she had in the matter, her motives, and of course her mentality and outlook, both in general and in each particular case. Unfortunately the available evidence is limited and it is difficult to arrive at any firm conclusions. What one has to remember, anyway, is that Mary was following her mother's advice and example, that she had an unshakable faith in her own musical ability, and that she was a political innocent who saw nothing reprehensible in transactions or relationships that might assist her survival or her professional advancement. Since she was unaware of the gravity of some of her actions and underestimated the moral implications of the assistance or personal support given by the occupation forces, she invariably reacted to criticism of this kind, often violently. Admittedly, sometimes she must have had an inkling that the criticism was well-founded, but usually she appears to have resented what she heard as an unfair and opportunistic attack on her.

De Hidalgo's role in this delicate matter was also ambivalent. She was later to claim the credit for having "saved" Mary, as we saw, but the truth may not be so "pure" and creditable. As a foreigner she was able to consort freely with Italian diplomats, musicians, and artists in Athens and with Italian officers who showed musical knowledge and taste. Moreover, she held musical soirées at her home from the beginning of the occupation, with Italian officers prominent among her guests and Mary as her star soloist. On some of those occasions, Ioanna Yennaropoulou —who was then married to the tenor Dionysis Thanos, a pupil of de Hidalgo— thinks that her intention was to launch Mary and perhaps to prepare the ground for a future career for her in Italy. "I accompanied her two or three times in 'Casta diva' for very small groups of Italian officers, although I don't remember that it ever caused any great stir."[35] This, nevertheless, suggests that de Hidalgo's subsequent deprecation of Mary's friendships with Italians was a later conception, and that her possible reaction had been prompted more by her personal disapproval of the men in question than by concern over the risk of Mary's being accused of collaboration with the enemy.

After a time, probably when Mary was in a panic over some unpleasant incident which may even have endangered her life, she evidently realized that the situation was becoming too risky. It is possible, as de Hidalgo once mentioned, that Mary had even been pushed to accept a job in an Italian military office.[36] Whether

because her Italian "friends" were not socially or otherwise top-drawer, or because the Greek resistance movements were beginning to make threatening noises, she saw clearly that she was getting into a situation that she would find hard to get out of. And so, as her mother was leading her literally to destruction, Mary had to confide in her teacher, who stepped in promptly. "Those were really difficult times," de Hidalgo told Allegri, though she kept quiet about the fact that she herself might have been partly responsible for leading Mary into dangerous friendships. "I saw that poor girl suffering and weeping in silence. I was terribly worried. She was only eighteen then. I had to rescue her from that situation before it was too late, otherwise I was sure she would be lost forever."[37] It is doubtful how far de Hidalgo did succeed in restraining Mary, who from the middle of 1942 was again going out regularly with Italians, fortunately without the evil consequences her teacher was afraid of.

Mary must have suffered a good deal in those dark days. *"And so we arrive at the most painful period of my life, the very, very sad war years, of which I don't like to speak even with the people closest to me, so as not to irritate wounds that have not yet healed. I remember the winter of 1941 . . ."* she would say in 1956.[38] Such love and respect as she still might have had for her mother had now evaporated. Her mother's altogether utilitarian and ultimately downright unethical attitude toward her throughout the occupation was indeed the last straw. On top of all the problems already mentioned—Litsa's attitude to George, her pushing of Mary's vocal talents, the glaring immorality of her personal life in Greece, her generally overbearing manner, and her profoundly amoral outlook on life—Mary now had to cope with the fact that her mother was unscrupulously exploiting her by thrusting her into the company of men who were potentially dangerous to her, however much they may have liked music. There is practically no doubt that Mary's Italian "friends" from the summer of 1941 onward were older men with an alien mentality, hardened military types who behaved with the arrogance of conquerors. The belated opening of her eyes to the mysteries of sex, whether in practice or merely in theory, must also have contributed to her sense of oppression. With no real guidance on these agonizing new problems, without emotional support at home, traumatized by her mother's attitude, stripped of her salary from July 1941, feeling the need for warmth and affection, and perhaps with an occasionally calculating eye on her musical future, it is no wonder that the eighteen-year-old Mary was drawn into a labyrinth of personal relationships built on thoroughly rotten foundations.

—◊◊◊—

No matter how much money they gave you, you could never find food on the market—or on the black market, where no money was enough. So I asked for any kind of food: rice, milk, macaroni, meat. And that, I remember, after a year's practical starvation on tomatoes, without oil or anything. . . . And I finally had my first rice and spaghetti and meat.

To Norman Ross, Chicago, 17 November 1957

CHAPTER 20

"*Devouring Music*"

O ne of the first things the occupation forces did was to place people they could rely on in the top posts in government services and state-controlled bodies. The man appointed by the prime minister to be general manager of the National Theater—"unpaid"—was the journalist Nikos Yokarinis,[1] who replaced Kostis Bastias on 8 May 1941. All the existing contracts of employment were annulled with effect from that date, and Yokarinis informed the staff that the theater was to be radically reorganized in accordance with a policy of "restoring freedom of thought." However, he added, he had no doubt that the members of the company would continue to serve their art "as loyal soldiers, no matter how great the sacrifices." The true nature of the new régime became apparent when, "for reasons of general expediency and consequent upon representations made to us," one of its first actions was to "request" Renato Mordo and Walter Pfeffer—both Jews—"to cease performing their duties."[2]

The tone was formally set a few days later, on 19 May, when the main auditorium of the theater on Ayiou Konstantinou Street was filled to overflowing with German officials for a variety evening organized for the Wehrmacht by the Propaganda-Kompanie (PK), a corps destined to play an important part in Mary's career. Among the items on the program were an aria from *Figaro* sung by Nafsika Galanou, the love duet from *Butterfly* sung by Zoe Vlachopoulou and Michalis Koronis, an excerpt from Goethe's *Iphigenie* read in German by Eleni Papadaki, and some Greek dances performed by Loukia Kotsopoulou and Yannis Fléri. This was the first taste of what the new situation would mean for members of the state theater companies, especially those of the National Opera, who did not have the option of working for an independent company. It was the opera singers who were most often compelled to give special performances for the occupation forces, whether they liked it or not. For some of them it posed no moral or practical problem, and often they were well remunerated; but there were a few who invented excuses to avoid doing something they considered humiliating, which might also lay them open to the charge of collaborating with the enemy. The official policy of Greek-German "cooperation" was manifest not only on public buildings, where the two countries' flags flew side by side, but also in concert programs, which generally included works by Greek and German composers. Concerts at the Olympia Theater resumed as soon as the risk of bombing was over, and on 11 May Ikonomidis conducted a program of works by Sklavos and Petridis along with Wagner and Beethoven.

In June 1941, after revivals of the now famous production of *Die Fledermaus* and the historic *Butterfly* of 1940, the contracts of all the National Theater's actors and singers were reviewed. In the National Opera, fifteen soloists and thirty-five chorus members had their contracts renewed until 31 May 1942, but Mary was not among them. Although she had acquitted herself well as a probationary soloist in *Boccaccio*, she was not even re-engaged to sing in the chorus, perhaps because she had not yet got her diploma, perhaps because of opposition from the other singers, but most probably because the company did not happen to need her at that stage. In actual fact it appears from her payroll record that in July 1941 "Marianna Kaloyeropoulou, chorus member" received a payment of Drs. 750 (an additional half-month's salary, her contract having expired on 30 June) for the two-week summer season of *Boccaccio*: in other words, she was merely taken on as a temporary extra, again as Nafsika Galanou's understudy in the small role of Beatrice. What is more, as the deductions from her pay amounted to Drs. 532 to cover an outstanding debit balance, she received only Drs. 218 net: a ludicrous sum, just enough to buy two or three loaves of bread at that time. And only recently, some time before 31 May, she had been so hard up that she had had to take an interest-free loan of Drs. 3,000 from the theater.[3]

Early in June 1941 it was announced that the National Theater had rented what had been an open-air cinema in Pedion Areos Park, just 500 meters from Mary's home, to present its first-ever summer opera season. A deeper stage with an orchestra pit was hastily constructed, some basic redecoration was done, and the Park Theater, as it now was, proudly announced itself as "the coolest theater in Athens." On 23 June Germany and Italy declared war on Russia, a decision that was to rebound on them as disastrously as it had on Napoleon a hundred and thirty years earlier. Ten days later, on 3 July, as the German armored divisions rolled toward Moscow, in Athens the summer season opened with *Boccaccio*, which ran until 15 July, a total of fifteen performances. According to Polyvios Marchand, Galanou took no part in these, or at most sang at a very few of them, as she was in rehearsal for Lehár's *The Land of Smiles*, the next production of the season. But there must be serious doubts about the number of times Mary actually sang. Beatrice is a small part presenting no real difficulties, *The Land of Smiles* did not start until the end of July, and it is quite likely, considering what we know of Galanou's character and the attitude she had taken in the winter season, that she did not allow Mary to do more than a few performances, if any. What is more, the musical director, Leonidas Zoras, makes no mention of having conducted Mary in those performances of *Boccaccio*, although he is sure she attended the rehearsals at the Park in June 1941.

Zoras had just returned from further studies in Germany and had little or no experience of conducting operas or operettas. He had been taken on to replace Walter Pfeffer, however, and, on hearing Mary again (having known her as a pupil of Trivella), he found that she had developed "a wide tremolo on her high notes— a wobble, as it is called." Evidently he talked to Mary about it, for she is said to have been angry with him and complained to de Hidalgo, who stormed off to see Zoras "like a lioness whose cub has been wounded": she told him to his face that, as Kalomiris's son-in-law, he "belonged" to the National Conservatory, on which Mary had turned her back, and that was why he was criticizing her. However, according to Zoras himself, de Hidalgo came up to him at one of the rehearsals for *Boccaccio* shortly afterward and apologized, admitting that he had been right. He also recalled that de Hidalgo had "withdrawn her pupil from participation in pub-lic performances" because of that problem. "Maria, to be sure, did have vocal problems," de Hidalgo said later. "Even then her striving for dramatic expression was considerable and at that time her vocal technique was not sufficient to meet this challenge all the time."[4]

This may perhaps explain why Mary did not sing again with the National Opera until about a year later, though it seems more likely that her "disappear-ance" simply had to do with the repertoire for those twelve months, which con-tained nothing suitable for Mary's voice as it then was.[5] Another possible expla-nation is that after her success in *Boccaccio* the soprano soloists felt her to be too much of a threat, so they conspired to have her dropped by constantly carping about her wobble and her American accent. "Everybody realized that they were dealing with a real phenomenon. They used every trick in the book to try to sab-otage her and ruin her career," Galatea Amaxopoulou insists. And by this time, of course, Mary's protector, Kostis Bastias, had been summarily dismissed from the National Theater. However, a more convincing explanation for her being passed over in 1941–42 is quite simply that she was a young and unknown singer being paid to do nothing and with only one very minor part as an understudy to her credit. As Elli Nikolaidi put it, "She was a young chorus member with a sinecure who had not had a chance to make her mark by the time Bastias left, and pre-sumably Yokarinis dropped her mainly for the sake of economy."[6]

Nothing of interest is known about Mary's private life during the rest of the summer of 1941. From 25 June the Italian flag was flying provocatively alongside the German swastika on the Acropolis, because the Italian army under General Carlo Geloso had taken over the administration of Athens. More parades, more restrictions—and also more opposition to the braggarts who had so recently been routed on the Albanian front. On 27 August the offices of the Benito Mussolini Fascio (the local Fascist organization in Athens) were opened in the Casa d'Italia. Prices soared: a new pair of shoes now cost more than 1,000 drachmas, a loaf of bread more than 50, but as long as the summer lasted there were at least plenty of tomatoes and other vegetables to be had. Fires ravaged the forests on Mount Hymettos and Mount Parnes and the arsonists sold the burned trees for firewood, plying their trade openly on the pavements of central Athens. Open-air cinemas provided Athenians with some relief from the heat, while the summer season at the Odeon of Herodes Atticus opened with two performances of Gluck's *Orfeo ed Euridice* on 6 and 7 June, conducted by Filoktitis Ikonomidis with Zoe Vlacho-poulou as Amore (a role she was to sing again six years later at Glyndebourne, with Kathleen Ferrier as Orfeo).

—⚭—

As from the academic year 1941–42 the Athens Conservatory ceased publishing annual reports, so the surviving documentary records are even more limited. A total of twenty-one students were enrolled in de Hidalgo's singing classes, of whom eight (all girls) were in the advanced class.[7] The opera class had only six students, all girls. Besides these two subjects, Mary—No. 317 in that year's class register— was again enrolled for Harmony I and Solfège V, now being taught by conductor Theodoros Vavayannis. She was also enrolled (for the first time) for the first-year course in music history under Yorgos Sklavos and the intermediate piano class of Tassia Filtsou. This clearly shows that in that transitional period, when faced with so many problems and having lost her contract with the National Opera, Mary decided to go all out for her singing diploma at the conservatory, for which she needed to have completed the piano course at the intermediate level.

Mary also had some private lessons with Vavayannis, as she had done with Kostas Kydoniatis. "What astonished me," Vavayannis said in 1963, "was the ease with which she learned. . . . She was a remarkable musical phenomenon. . . . As a person she was very clever. Nothing escaped her eye, and in her thinking she tried to see into the mind and thoughts of the person she was talking to."[8] Tassia Filtsou's classroom was on the first floor, left at the landing and first door on the right. Filtsou was over fifty and had been teaching since 1921. Although she was not a great teacher and tended to be over-fussy about technique, she was certainly good enough for Mary's requirements. Jackie also had lessons with her as a fifth-year student in the intermediate class, and another of her pupils was Katie Makriyanni, who had lessons in the afternoon, immediately before Mary. "Maria loved the piano," says Makriyanni, "and was always in good spirits when she came for her lesson. *'If I didn't have a voice, I would have taken the piano seriously,'* she once said to me. Although she didn't practice much she had terrific dexterity, an amazing touch, and a great memory. And, of course, incredible musicality." Mary had big hands, not well cared for, with short fingernails (but no longer bitten down to the quick). When she did not know the notes by heart, "she would frown and lean right forward to get closer to the page," even with the thick glasses she wore.[9]

A great deal has been written and said about Mary's piano-playing ability, much of it contradictory. Several of her classmates, who were probably not very good pianists themselves, have said that she was "great" and that her playing was "amazing." The fact is that in addition to her other musical talents she had a natural gift for the piano, though she never thought of working harder at it than she needed to in order to help her with her singing. As with the other compulsory subjects, she did hardly any work on it at home. What is more, she made no secret of the fact to her teacher, who liked her and gave her a lot of help in her lessons. "She used to come for her lesson without having practiced at all since the last one," Makriyanni continues, "and yet she played better and better every time. Her technique left something to be desired, but you could see she had ability. She wasn't much good at Czerny, but she played Bach beautifully." Among the pieces she is known to have played at that time were Beethoven's First Sonata (Op. 2, No. 1, in F minor) and some of Schubert's impromptus. "She wasn't very advanced, she didn't spend time on the piano," Jackie confirms. "She had merely reached a standard that helped her to practice her singing."[10]

In the year 1941–42 Mary was still "a very serious girl." Unlike the other female singers, she gave the impression of being "an integrated human being," in the words of Katie Makriyanni, to whom Mary once said, "*I can't find anybody who takes her studies seriously enough to be a close friend.*" Of course, that may have been an excuse for the fact that some of the other girls avoided her company. Some thought her a musical snob because she looked down on those who did not work as single-mindedly as she did, or were not at any rate reasonably competent musicians. Others quite simply did not like her, like Ypatia Louvi, who maintains that "she was very self-centered and thought she knew everything when in fact she knew nothing." There were also some who started giving her the cold shoulder when they heard that she was seeing Italians, and particularly when her mother's relationship with the Italian colonel became known. "That sort of thing could not be kept secret in the small-town atmosphere of Athens," says Margarita Dalmati, a young harpsichordist who had been on the Athens musical scene since 1937 and lived a little way further along Patission Street. "When enemy officers went into anybody's house, the news got around immediately."[11]

The adverse publicity created by such fraternization can easily be imagined from the description of a scene witnessed by Yorgos Lazaridis, a theater critic who was then a neighbor of Mary's. One evening, he relates, a large black German limousine drew up outside the building where the Kaloyeropoulos family lived, and out of it stepped Litsa, Jackie, and Mary, who was wearing a long white evening gown and holding a bouquet. A German officer bade them good-bye by "chivalrously kissing their hands, clicking his heels with a snap that reverberated like a gunshot through the deserted street." Lazaridis goes on to say that he heard the local grocer warn his customers *sotto voce*, while doling out rationed beans: "Be careful what you say in their hearing, because they may be Gestapo spies." From that day on all the neighbors cut them dead in the street, and once when Mary asked Kitsa Damasioti, a young soloist with the National Opera, to come to her apartment to help her with some harmony exercises (which she never managed to do unaided), Damasioti refused because her husband would not let her go "to that house." Besides, Mary was always "unsmiling and frowning" and so gave the impression that she was angry about something, which was sometimes the case. "She would storm into the conservatory, storm out again and pay no attention to anybody," Makriyanni recalls. The fact that she was fat also weighed against her and provoked ever-growing hostile mockery. Dalmati described the situation well: "In that climate of tacit conspiracy [during the occupation] it was only natural that Kaloyeropoulou should be disliked. All of us, or at any rate most, were reduced to skin and bones by shortage of food, and it just didn't make sense to see someone as stout as she was—there was something repulsive about it. . . . She wasn't liked. She was isolated by her plumpness, the handicap of her nearsightedness, and her home environment, cut off as she was from the gloomy atmosphere of occupied Greece."[12]

Mitsa Kourahani had come to de Hidalgo at the conservatory in 1940, though not in the advanced class to start with; she too was one of the first to be taken on by the National Opera to sing in the chorus. Like Arda Mandikian, she often partnered Mary in class in duets for soprano and mezzo. Together they sang all the duets from *Norma* and *Aida* in 1941–42 and from *La Gioconda* the following school year. Kourahani maintains that Mary's voice in those days was totally different from the voice that the world came to know later. She agrees, however, that all her vocal problems were apparent even then: "First of all, the wobble, already quite noticeable—it was criminal to let her sing Santuzza so young. And then the difference between the registers, so marked that you would have thought it was one person singing the lower notes and someone else on the high notes. Thirdly, the very obvious transitions from one register to another." In Kourahani's opinion, de Hidalgo helped Mary most of all on the personal level, by engineering her first contract with the National Opera and encouraging her to believe in herself; on the musical level her main contribution was to develop Mary's interpretative abilities and introduce her to a large and exciting new repertoire. But Kourahani is adamant that de Hidalgo did not help her vocally except by teaching her some points of technique, "which, of course, were important in enabling her to produce the sound her vocal cords were capable of."[13]

Mary evidently did not realize at the time that de Hidalgo's teaching left something to be desired, nor did she ever suggest in later life that her teacher might have been to blame for any of her vocal problems. The gratitude she felt for her counseling caused her to overlook any deficiencies she might have had as a teacher. What counted most for Mary then was that de Hidalgo showed her sympathetic understanding and affection. As she put it in her dictated reminiscences in 1956, *"It is to this illustrious Spanish artist, I repeat, with a moved, devoted, and grateful heart, that I owe all my preparation and my artistic formation as an actress and musician. This elect woman who, besides giving me her precious teaching, gave me her whole heart as well, was a witness to my whole life in Athens, including both my art and my family."* Forever after, in fact, she kept emphasizing the importance of the technical training she had received from de Hidalgo: *"Technique must be learned in one's very early years. . . . The surprises that I could have I can deal with now, because during my early days I learned all the possibilities. And that is why you study."*[14] De Hidalgo did a great deal to lessen the wobble in Mary's voice, and indeed eliminated it temporarily. "Yes, there was some unsteadiness in some of her notes," says Lola Ritsou, "but de Hidalgo did a lot to correct it, without ever mentioning the word 'wobble.' Once she had identified the problem she gave her some special exercises. But Mary's wobble was not nearly as noticeable as it was to become fifteen or twenty years later. We only noticed it when de Hidalgo kept on setting her those exercises. And you could see that the problem immediately faded or even disappeared altogether."[15]

As regards training in opera, that is to say, acting, Kourahani says that they had very little from de Hidalgo, at any rate from 1941 onward: "To all intents and purposes we had no tuition in acting, and what we did learn we picked up by ourselves, by instinct." Mary herself once said that she went to the opera whenever she could, in order to compensate for this: *"I could see how awkwardly many singers moved on stage with disastrous consequences for their interpretation of the role, and I swore that that would never happen to me."* She also disclosed that the dreadful antics she had seen on stage had once prompted her to buy a big mirror in which she would watch herself practicing, scrutinizing her every movement from top to toe and making sure she did not overact. The fact remains, however, that the exigencies of wartime, the frequent air raid warnings, and, not least, the absence of male students discouraged the teaching of opera at the conservatory. Nevertheless, as Lola Ritsou remembers, de Hidalgo taught Mary how to act during the lessons at her apartment: "She would get up from her chair, take her by the hand while she was singing, and guide her through the movements she should perform while singing an aria or a whole scene."[16] Naturally, one area in which de Hidalgo was unable to help Mary was the correct diction and pronunciation of Greek. When Mary was learning a piece privately or for the conservatory she usually sang it in the original language, but when she was learning a part for the National Opera she had to learn it in Greek. Having already had two unfavorable reviews on account of her bad pronunciation, she was working hard in her own time to eliminate her American accent and improve her diction. In her everyday life she not only spoke Greek like a native but also wrote it fairly well, apart from some (often quite glaring) spelling mistakes.

As in her other years at the conservatory, so too in 1941–42 we do not know precisely what pieces Mary learned to sing. There is evidence that she studied excerpts from Handel's *Messiah*, Bach's *Saint Matthew Passion*, Purcell's *Dido and*

Aeneas (probably the part of Belinda), Pergolesi's *Stabat Mater* (which she was to sing in a complete performance at a public concert in April 1943), Rossini's *Stabat Mater*, Mozart's *Requiem* and Great Mass in C minor (K. 427), Pizzetti's *I Tre Canti Greci*, and several *arie antiche*, Handel arias, and unspecified lieder by Schubert and Brahms. Naturally she would have concentrated mainly on bel canto operas assigned to her by de Hidalgo, and to Lord Harewood she herself said in 1968 that in Athens she had studied *La Traviata*. We also know she studied *Die Entführung* (late 1941) and *Tosca* (from the spring of 1942), as well as isolated arias such as "Bel raggio lusinghier" from Rossini's *Semiramide* and Maddalena's aria "La mamma morta" from Giordano's *Andrea Chénier*. "*I have done everything I could lay my hands on, more or less well, but one helps the other,*" Maria said in 1968. "*If you do Purcell, it helps I do not know whom; if you do Verdi it helps Bellini, and vice versa. Every music gives you more maturity and more inner views.*"[17]

De Hidalgo considered *Norma* ("which we studied so lovingly," as she recalled in a letter to Maria in 1949[18]) to belong to the "light" repertoire. "*Norma . . . was used by de Hidalgo as an exercise,*" Maria explained in 1968. "*So I remember I started learning 'Norma' at the very early years of my schooling in music, many, many years before I sang it, at least ten or twelve. That was just before and all during the war.*"[19] In 1955 de Hidalgo said of Maria, "She put such force, such sentiment, such wonderful interpretation into all she sang. She would want to sing all the most difficult coloraturas, scales, and trills. Even as a child, her willpower was terrific. She had a phenomenal memory and could learn the most difficult opera in eight days." Maria herself has described the mentality then prevailing among the good students, or at least among those who were concurrently embarking on a career in the National Opera: "*We were more technical then in our work. We went to do music in a rather cold way. It had to be that way, and we had to reach the note well done, regardless of a certain [lack of] conscientiousness. . . . I feel that I was more of an athlete. I wasn't ready yet and didn't have the time. I was busy making a career performing. . . . I was growing, I suppose.*"[20]

Besides expanding her repertoire, Mary was also taking steps to overcome various technical problems. "*I was taught in my younger days . . . that there are some tempi that are not all that slow, but [seem slow] so long as you take them with a slower attitude. . . . I can take a very slow tempo and give it an agitating quality or color or pace without budging at all from the rhythm or the tempo.*"[21] This was the quality Luchino Visconti was referring to when he said, "Maria has timing in her blood, it is absolutely instinctive." But there is no doubt that her instinct for rhythm and tempo was greatly helped by her teacher. "De Hidalgo's tempi were amazing. You felt as if you were working with a maestro," commented Elli Nikolaidi, and Lola Ritsou summed it up when she said, "De Hidalgo—like Maria—had a sense of the rhythm within the rhythm."[22] As regards embellishments, Maria was to return again and again to the subject of those "graces" that she had been taught by de Hidalgo, while crediting Tullio Serafin alone with teaching her what she knew about the interpretation of *recitativi*.* All in all, her appetite for learning everything there was to be learned knew no bounds: "*I didn't give much time to the people who taught me,*" Maria said in 1961, "*because I was always so anxious to foresee what they wanted to tell me. It was some sort of—not exactly a game—but at any rate I felt very upset if I didn't see what point they were going to make almost before they said it. When they started to tell me how I should sing a certain phrase, I always prided myself on being able to say, 'I know what you mean. May I show you?'*" In the same interview, but in a different context, she said, "*I like such anticipation—it makes you feel like quicksilver, vibrant, alive. To me it is a sign of energy, of youth.*"[23]

As for her eyesight, in her last years Maria had nearly seven degrees of myopia in each eye, not to mention incipient glaucoma. Even as a teenager she could hardly see without glasses. Yet this serious handicap actually had some positive consequences. Her inability to establish eye contact with the conductor ("*No, I can't [see the conductor's beat]. I do it all through my hearing and my world of music, because in music you don't have to pick the rhythm, you feel it.*") and the difficulty she had in moving about the stage (where she could not wear glasses, of course) strengthened her innate musicality and sense of timing, and her hearing also became progressively sharper and more finely tuned. "*My hearing is very good,*" she said once, "*because, you see, I do not see the director, so I suppose nature has made my hearing more acute and I am very annoyed if I hear during my performances another noise. . . . It gives me another rhythm and it abstracts me from my own world.*"[24]

Beyond a doubt, it was in those years that Maria Callas's multifaceted artistic personality was formed and developed. When she spoke about her studies in later life, she invariably stressed their enormous importance. "*[Training] creates the spinal cord,*" she told Lord Harewood in 1968. "*It's like a child that's well-bred from the beginning. If you learn how to read and write correctly, that will bring you along during and throughout your career. . . . I learned the secrets and the ways of this bel canto, which is not 'beautiful singing': it is a way of making music. It is a sort of straitjacket which you are supposed to put on whether you like it or not. . . . If you don't have the bel canto you cannot sing any opera, not even the most modern. . . . I was fascinated by listening to all the pupils singing the various repertoires, . . . even tenors, and it was most interesting. . . . Even [de] Hidalgo was amazed and frequently asked me, 'Why do*

---

*To John Ardoin, for instance, she said: "*There cannot be an embellishment just for the sake of glamour or fireworks. For example, trills are necessary and they have to be well performed. . . . Verdi was very fond of his trills and I found that with words he always used a trill if he wanted to express fear, happiness, joy, insecureness. . . . Bellini used to use a one-tone embellishment, three or four notes' embellishment, whereas Rossini used the half-tone.*" (Conversation with John Ardoin, Dallas, 13 Sept. 1968. Maria went on to describe how, when Serafin gave her a private audition for the part of Norma in 1948, he told her: "Go home and talk these phrases [the recitatives, which Serafin also described as 'recitar cantando'] over to yourself. In other words, sing them as though you were talking. . . . You have to talk with notes and then these notes always have a rhythm.") She discussed these matters the same year with Edward Downes. (DOWNES.)

you stay here?"' Mary's answer to that question had been that everybody can learn from other people: a classical ballet dancer, for example, can learn a lot from a cabaret dancer. And she continued: *"[The classroom] was where I also heard many operas, many arias, which I took up and enjoyed later on in my career . . . . I was devouring music then, whatever it was and in any form, for ten hours a day. For me it was not heavy work, it was really an amusement."*[25]

—〰—

After you've learned the music rhythmically, then you say: "Right: now this is the tempo of Bellini. Donizetti would have felt it this way. Wagner would have felt it another way." They might all write allegro or adagio, but each composer has his particular rhythm, and that is too elusive to put on a metronome (I never use a metronome).

To Derek Prouse, London (*The Sunday Times*, 19 March 1961)

CHAPTER 21

Wartime Diet and the
Weight Problem

The constant gnawing hunger, the biting cold, and the appalling misery to be seen everywhere in Greater Athens in 1941 and 1942 have remained etched on the memories of all who lived through that time. Between October 1940 and October 1942, out of a population of 1,125,000, approximately fifty thousand people died of starvation or the consequences of malnutrition. The famine was caused initially by the cold-blooded looting and confiscation of all stores of food in Greek homes and warehouses, which were taken as spoils of war. This was followed by systematic commandeering of agricultural produce, not only for the maintenance of the Axis armies but also to feed the populations back home. From the autumn of 1941, when the death rate suddenly rose fivefold, handcarts as well as the municipal rubbish carts were pressed into service every morning to clear away the bodies of those who had died in the streets during the night. By the summer of 1942 the only things available to eat were marrows (a type of gourd), eggplants, artichokes, beets, chicory, and wild greens. Malnutrition reduced the people's resistance to illnesses, chiefly respiratory, circulatory, and of course intestinal complaints. The scarcity of soap (one of the most expensive luxuries on the black market, along with olive oil) led to widespread lice infestation, especially in the poorer sections of society, and was another contributory factor to the spread of germs and diseases. Ill health assumed the proportions of a plague, with about 350,000 people in Greater Athens suffering from one sickness or another. The commonest complaints were ulcers and perforations of the stomach or intestines, hernias due to enteroptosis or atrophy of the muscles, enteritis, diarrhea, typhus, and even certain types of malaria. But most of the deaths were due to edemas caused by malnutrition and to tuberculosis, which was rampant throughout the occupation.

"*When the war began, I knew real privation. We were then both poor and miserable, for we lacked clothing and food, which became more scarce daily. It was then that I suffered,*" Maria said in 1956, and she often spoke in that vein about the years 1941 and 1942, which she once described as "*the most painful period of my life.*"[1] "People were dying of starvation in the streets," de Hidalgo recalled. "I myself had

Collecting corpses on the streets of Athens, a very common spectacle in the winter of 1941–42.

to give lessons [to carabinieri] for a piece of bread, but Maria's position was worse. . . . Two or three times a week she would walk many kilometers out into the country to bring home a basket of tomatoes or something else to eat."[2] Maria later exaggerated the extent of her suffering from hunger, mainly in an attempt to rebut the charges of having had close friendships with Italians and to explain the reasons for the stinginess systematically imputed to her: "*For all the rest of my life I will never be able to spend money needlessly and will suffer—it's stronger than I am—at the waste of food, even if it's a bit of bread, a piece of fruit, or a little bit of chocolate*," she said in 1956. "*For the whole summer I had eaten only tomatoes and boiled cabbage leaves, which I managed to obtain by covering kilometer after kilometer on foot and begging the farmers in the neighboring countryside to spare me a few of their vegetables.*"[3]

Litsa later accused Mary of ingratitude, alleging that it was she, Litsa, that had worn herself out scouring the streets for potatoes and cabbage leaves, running the gauntlet of German army patrols in her determination to hunt down some extra food. In her memoirs she is at pains to point out that Mary never went alone to the black market "in the mountains, a long way from Athens . . . although she did sometimes accompany me to help with the loaded string bags of food we brought back." With or without Mary, Litsa had to travel in *gazogènes*, which she describes as "little old box-like cars drawn by wood-burning locomotives that often broke down," to buy vegetables, scrawny chickens and rabbits, and occasionally (if she was lucky) a little veal or a few eggs.[4] Jackie, however, wishing as always to emphasize her own contribution to the family's survival thanks to Miltiadis, maintains that neither Mary nor Litsa ever went anywhere for food: "Mother wrote that afterward, to claim that she too had provided something. But God bless Embirikos, who brought us everything!" In her memoirs she describes him making long trips into the country to bring back "olive oil, figs, nuts, anything to keep us from starvation," once even enduring the humiliation of being struck across the face by an Italian soldier who searched him and found the food he was carrying.[5]

Although specific incidents such as this are probably authentic, it is easy to see that every statement on the subject serves the interests of the person making it, not necessarily the cause of truth. Less plausible than most is the story told by "one of Maria's close friends," who asserted that during the famine Mary "literally ate out of garbage cans."[6] It hardly seems possible that with Miltiadis Embirikos looking after the 61 Patission Street household, with Litsa having a generous Italian colonel as her lover, and with Mary winning fervent admiration from the Italians and soon to become a star of the National Opera with a respectable income, the Kaloyeropoulos family (or even Mary alone) should nevertheless have been reduced to eating scraps out of a trash can. Nor are these the only grounds for believing that Mary survived the famine conditions of much of the occupation more than adequately in comparison with most Athenians, even if it did involve her in some difficulties and perhaps some dangerous escapades.

In the first place Litsa and her daughters went to see their better-off relatives quite often (in fact quite regularly, it seems) in the hope of being asked to stay for a meal. Among them were the Kambouris cousins from Stylis who, having had a bumper crop from their olive trees in the winter of 1941–42, were in a position to help not only their friends but the Food Supply Commission as well. So when the Kaloyeropoulos family turned up at 206 Patission Street they were invited to stay and eat with them, said Nikos Kambouris, who still remembered the way the younger generation (including Mary, of course) used to raid the kitchen, where the cook was producing fried potatoes that usually disappeared before reaching the table. Sometimes Litsa and her daughters called on another cousin, Alexandra Evangelidi, who had two children, Yorgos and Maria, and occasionally they would go to Maria Evangelidi's house on the corner of Patission and Lesvou Streets for a chat and a bite to eat. "On the whole," considered Nikos Kambouris, "their relations with the extended family were superficial and self-interested."[7]

Then there were others who really did help them. When a journalist asked Maria in 1957 whether she had been given food by Greeks as well as Italians, she answered without hesitation, "*Yes, they did. I remember, they deprived themselves.*" She remembered Miltiadis bringing oil, cornstarch, and potatoes to their house in the winter of 1941–42, to their "incredulous stupefaction," and it is hardly possible that this surprise visit was the only occasion on which he helped them to keep the wolf from the door.[8] Another Greek who helped them out with food was Yorgos Goudelis, who had been working since 1928 in the ordnance inspectorate with Litsa's elder sister Sophia and was described as "more than just a friend" of hers. Before the collapse of the Greek front, the farsighted Goudelis, then serving as an officer at Yannitsa in northern Greece, had managed to send a whole boat-load of wheat and other foodstuffs to Athens by way of Thessaloniki and Halkis. These he had hidden in the storeroom of a house on Ipponaktos Street, in the suburb of Neos Kosmos. Being a generous man and genuinely fond of Sophia Dimitriadou, he invited her, her mother, and two of her sisters, Kakia and Pipitsa, to go and live with him on Ipponaktos Street for the duration of the famine of 1941–42. As soon as Litsa heard about the secret hoard in Neos Kosmos she started sending Mary on visits there, ostensibly to keep in touch with her grand-mother and aunts but really in order to bring food back to 61 Patission Street. From home or the conservatory it was a two-and-a-half-mile walk along Athinas and Eolou Streets, through the Plaka, down Syngrou Avenue to the Fix brewery and up into Neos Kosmos. Then, after filling some bags with food and sitting for a while with her relatives, she would set out on the return journey, this time heav-ily laden. Goudelis sometimes went with her as far as Syngrou Avenue to give her a hand. "She used to come on her own and was always very well-mannered and seemed grateful," he recalled.[9]

Maria herself said later that every so often she managed to obtain fairly large quantities of meat, offering the disingenuous explanation that her "emaciation" had stirred the pity of a man who admired her voice. As luck would have it, this opera buff happened to be a butcher whose shop had been requisitioned by the Italians! What is more, this soft-hearted, music-loving butcher introduced Mary to the official in the Italian commissariat in charge of distributing provisions to the troops, who, in another inspiring example of magnanimity, sold her ten kilos of meat every month "for a paltry sum." Hardest of all to swallow is Maria's descrip-tion of her return journeys from these shopping expeditions: "*I strapped the pack-age to my shoulders and walked for an hour under the sun . . . as lightly and happily as if I were carrying flowers,*" she says, leaving us to wonder how she escaped being lynched by starving Athenians on her way home. At all events, we should proba-bly accept the gist of her story, namely that in one way or another, until Septem-ber 1943, she managed to obtain regular supplies of meat from the Italians in large enough quantities to have some over for resale: "*We didn't have a refrigerator and so we couldn't keep it. But it was resold to our neighbors and with the proceeds we could get along by acquiring indispensable things.*"[10]

Later in the occupation Mary was to display her commercial acumen in another way. Walking home from the Olympia Theater one day with Marika Papadopoulou, a fellow singer at the National Opera, before their ways parted she asked her companion to go with her into a shop selling wartime confectionery. Papadopoulou gives a vivid description of the scene: "'*Now watch!*' says Mary. And she goes into the shop with a fistful of complimentary tickets for the opera—goodness knows how many she had managed to pick up—and barters them for sesame seedcake and other awful ersatz stuff. 'Have you no shame?' I say to her.

'Not a bit!' she answers cheerfully. *'And if you can't bring yourself to do it, give me some tickets and I'll trade them in for you!'*"[11] This particular incident is probably to be dated to 1944, by which time Mary had become more assertive and altogether more self-confident. Its significance lies in what it tells us about her enterprising business sense and her keen eye for a profit, even at that relatively early age. Although in later life this side of her character was to come out in dealings that cannot strictly be called commercial, such as her handling of contract negotiations (with Meneghini's guidance) and the investment of her money (with advice from Onassis), she was to remain money-conscious all her life. This tendency of hers probably owed its origins not merely to the poverty and hunger of the occupation but more specifically to her experience of reselling the meat obtained from the Italians.

It seems safe to say, then, that except in certain periods of real shortage such as the severe winter of 1941–42, probably the first months after the departure of the Italians in September 1943, and the terrible month of December 1944, Mary generally managed to eat fairly well during the occupation and that Litsa is right when she says: "Our sufferings [in the war] were considerably less than those of many others. Food and clothing were indeed scarce, particularly in the early months of the occupation, but thanks to Jackie's Milton, to other friends, and sometimes even our enemies, we usually had enough to eat and wear. I can still remember how well Maria ate during those unhappy years. Not until the twenty dreadful days of the civil war [in December 1944] . . . did either of us know what I call *real* suffering, and even then we were better off than many others." Jackie's recollections of the time are similar, if somewhat exaggerated: "In fact [Mary] never ceased to eat. We kept the supplies Milton brought us in a special closet and when she returned from her practice the first thing Mary did was to raid this larder. My most telling memory of the occupation is of Mary bent double, reaching for handfuls of figs or nuts, her fat backside filling the doorframe."[12]

—⁓—

When Mary left America in 1937 she was simply a well-built girl with a big frame, and she put on a lot of weight as soon as she arrived in Greece. Her weight gain at that time was caused by a classic case of psychological disturbance—an anxiety neurosis—with symptoms of depression as well, resulting in compulsive overeating. On this subject, Maria's own testimony is of particular interest. Stung by the calumnies published in *Time* magazine in October 1956, she wrote out—in her own hand, in Italian—some autobiographical notes refuting the charges made in the article, including the following about the fact that she was not fat when she left America: *"I grew fat in Greece after going on a diet of beaten eggs and suffering from a hormone disorder, for which my mother did not even take me to see a doctor."*[13] The brevity and bad wording of this note make it ambiguous: clearly a diet of beaten eggs (which was apparently recommended by some of Litsa's relatives) could not have been intended to help Mary to lose weight. If anything it suggests the reverse, that Mary was suffering from some kind of debility. The most likely explanation is that beaten eggs were prescribed as a remedy for—or at least a precautionary measure against—the disease that raged most fiercely in Greece during the occupation—tuberculosis.

In 1945, when applicants were being considered for work in the public sector, fifteen out of every twenty girls between the ages of eighteen and twenty were found to have suffered from tuberculosis. The characteristic symptom of the first stage of the illness was swollen glands, for which the treatment prescribed before the war was a healthy diet and fresh air: hence the proliferation of sanatoria in the mountains of western and central Europe, to which those who could afford it were sent to recover their health. And what was the standard tonic for people who were afraid they were suffering from tuberculosis? Why, beaten eggs with plenty of sugar, of course. So it would seem that something of this kind was troubling Mary: as a result of the depression caused by the family's abandonment of her beloved father in America, the shortage of money, and all the side effects described above, she was in a permanent state of stress. This in turn had probably impaired the functioning of her thyroid gland, leading to what Mary called a "hormonal disorder." Malfunction of the thyroid can take the form of overactivity, which generally results in weight loss, or (as in Mary's case) underactivity, in which case one not only puts on weight but may also suffer from skin complaints of which the visible symptoms may be acne or allergies. Mary's hypothyroidism would presumably have made her worry that she might have tuberculosis—thus her diet of beaten eggs. Litsa, probably because she did not want to call these ailments by their names, attributes the dermatological problems to the starchy foods that Mary ate in such large quantities, asserting that in those days Mary was allergic to starches. Indeed, she tried to cure her daughter's dermatological complaints, which often led to outbreaks of boils, with homemade ointments and other nostrums which she may have remembered from the days when George Kaloyeropoulos was making his patent medicines.[14]

The diagnosis given above matches what we know of Mary's appearance in those years. Even the slight exophthalmia (protuberance of the eyeballs) noticed by some people at the time and visible in some photographs was probably due to her thyroid disorder. But besides investigating the psychological and physical causes of her various complaints, one has to consider *when* she gained and lost weight, and by how much. The few surviving photographs of her taken during that period— she generally avoided the camera precisely because she was fat, or at least she felt she was—provide the most reliable evidence of those fluctuations. For about two or three years, from 1938 to 1940, she was fatter than at any other time in Greece, but by the time of *Boccaccio* in February–March 1941 she had already lost some weight and thereafter she became progressively slimmer—intentionally or not— as a result of the extreme food shortage during the occupation. In *Tosca* (summer of 1942) she looks almost slim except for her legs, which were to remain a problem for her. After that she put on some weight, though it is hard to say exactly when or why, and in 1944, the year of her triumphs in *Tiefland* and *Fidelio*, she can fairly be described as rather fat, even stout. In other words, the photographs prove the falsity of the standard allegation that she was always terribly or even grossly overweight.

This extravagant description of the young Mary was supported not only by Jackie, who did so mainly out of personal vanity, but also by Maria herself after she had slimmed down dramatically in 1954. From then on the prima donna habitually assented to exaggerated reports of her former bulk or even initiated them herself (without placing them in their chronological context), simply because she was so delighted at having transformed her appearance. Consequently, although she had once been correctly described as fluctuating "from plump to rather fat" during her time in Greece,[15] her obituaries published all over the world in 1977 stated that she had weighed 90 kilos (198 pounds) as a young girl and that at twenty, that is to say in 1943–44, her weight had risen to 105 kilos (more than 230 pounds)! These exaggerated figures are disproved by contemporary photographs and the testimony of reliable witnesses. The truth is that as a young girl in America Mary never weighed more than 60 or 65 kilos, and in Greece, having reached her final height of 1.73 meters (5 feet 8 inches), she almost certainly weighed not more than 90 kilos even during the period of her compulsive overeating (1938–39), not more than 70 to 75 kilos from 1941 to 1943, and definitely not much more than 75 or at the most 80 kilos from 1943 to 1945.

The catalog of inaccurate or tendentious statements about Mary's weight is endless. At best she is described as "fat, but not as fat as other people say," but the generally accepted image of her is based on descriptions that make her out to have been a bloated mass of flesh. An admirer of hers, not wishing to be rude, compared her to "an elephant that had swallowed a nightingale,"[16] while the more opprobrious descriptions of her include such terms as "whale," "full-sized cow," "monster," "unsightly creature," and adjectives such as "enormous" and even "repulsive." With such epithets attached to her, it would be surprising if she had not acquired the reputation of having been indescribably, revoltingly fat before 1954, especially as Maria herself was later to cultivate this image of her former self, partly to emphasize her mother's responsibility for the wretchedness of her childhood and adolescence and partly to draw attention to her magical transformation into a sylph.

Nor should it be overlooked that at 5 feet 8 inches Mary was very tall by the Greek standards of the time; and it is also important to remember that from 1941 to 1944 (the period when the exaggerated descriptions of her size started to circulate, for that was when she started performing in public), Athenians were eating much less than usual and the average Athenian woman's weight had fallen dramatically. Amid the terrible hardships and oppressive atmosphere of the occupation Mary's tall, well-covered figure was more than usually conspicuous and aroused hostile feelings. In the words of Margarita Dalmati, "You can't just cut yourself off from the age you live in: everybody exists in the context of other people and of time. We have to envisage this plump girl surrounded by emaciated creatures of skin and bone, for that is what we had all been reduced to by the shortages and famine of the occupation."[17] In comparison with most other women in those grim years Mary looked huge, whereas at other times and in other places the most one could have said was that she was a well-built, fairly tall, healthy young woman.

The consequence of her enforced diet starting in 1941–42 was that at the time of *Fidelio*, though already fairly fat again at 75–80 kilos, she was not to be compared even with the Maria of 1946, who had been devouring "junk food" (chiefly hamburgers and ice cream) after her return to America. "*When I got back to America, I was hungry as you are hungry when you have not had enough to eat for a long time,*" she recalled ten years later. "*I ate and ate, even to a quart of ice cream at bedtime. I got fat.*" She may then have gone to more than 90 kilos but, as she herself pointed out, "*By the time I left America [in 1947] I had been on a slimming diet and had gone from about 100 kilos to 75 or 80.*"[18] Allowing for some doctoring of the figures for the sake of effect, we may be fairly sure that by the time she left America for Italy she had lost a considerable amount of weight. This is corroborated by a very open and friendly letter she wrote to Vangelis Mangliveras in January 1947: "*Everything else is going fine. I have lost quite a bit of weight and (if I may say so) I am quite a bit prettier. My legs have slimmed down a lot and I am very pleased.*"[19]

Thus it is clear that from 1942 to 1945 and even from 1946 to 1948, Mary/ Maria was nothing like as fat as she had been from 1938 to 1940 and was to be again from 1949 to 1952. In the latter period she was to grow to over 100 kilos, as is evident from photographs taken of her as Norma at Teatro Colón in 1949 and at Covent Garden in 1952. As Maria herself explained, when she was in Italy in 1948 (the year of *Turandot*, *Tristan und Isolde*, and *Norma*) her weight was down to about 70 kilos, but after having her appendix removed in December 1948 she went back up to 80 kilos and in 1950 and 1951 she started putting on still more weight "*for no reason.*"[20] To sum up, her weight must have been approaching 100 kilos around 1939 or 1940 and more than 100 kilos only from 1949 to 1952; her final slimming bout started in December 1952, by which time she was already down to 92 kilos, and within sixteen months she was down to 64 kilos. The lowest weight she ever reached, in the mid-1950s, was a mere 53.5 kilos (118 pounds).[21]

—m—

On 3 October 1941 the general manager of the Royal Theater, Nikos Yokarinis, informed the new board of governors that he intended to separate the opera company from the theater company. His proposal met with some opposition, but on

14 October the National Theater signed a contract with the Karandinos brothers, leasing the Olympia Theater on Akadimias Street for the use of the National Opera for the 1941–42 winter season. On 25 November Ulysses Lappas was appointed a governor of the National Theater and Yokarinis, welcoming him to the board, said that the assistance of the great Greek tenor, who had "bonds of friendship with the occupation authorities," would be invaluable in those difficult times. On 16 December Lappas presented the board with his proposed list of productions for the remainder of the season: among these he had included *Tosca*—presumably in collusion with de Hidalgo—with the intention of casting Mary Kaloyeropoulou in the title role.[22]

The National Opera's first productions of the 1941–42 season were *The Gypsy Baron* by Johann Strauss and revivals of *Madama Butterfly* and *The Land of Smiles*. On 12 December, a week after the 150th anniversary of Mozart's death, there was a gala performance of *Die Entführung aus dem Serail* at the National Theater on Ayiou Konstantinou Street: this was the first all-Greek full production of a Mozart opera. It was conducted with great success by Walter Pfeffer (from 18 December at the Olympia), on condition that his name not appear in the program. The most interesting point about that production, however, is the testimony of Dino Yannopoulos, the stage director, revealing that although Mary was not listed as the official understudy for the soprano Frangiska Nikita, she learned the part of Konstanze so as to be ready in case she were needed: "I first saw Maria Callas in November 1941, when she was understudying Nikita in *Die Entführung aus dem Serail*. This arrangement was kept secret as far as possible in order to avoid arousing the jealousy of the others. De Hidalgo had requested it and Pfeffer had supported her. I heard Maria practicing the part in a classroom, not on stage, and she was great!"[23]

In the end Mary was not called upon to sing Konstanze. Apart from her learning the role and perhaps having some voice rehearsals in private, nothing came of this move, nor are there any records of it in what remains of the National Theater's archives. Nevertheless it does tell us certain things about Mary's development as a singer. First, that de Hidalgo and Lappas, both of whom were well in with the occupation authorities and the National Opera, were doing their best to get Mary back into the company. Secondly, that some of the female soloists were ill-disposed toward her, as Yannopoulos's words clearly imply. Thirdly, that de Hidalgo, who knew that Mary was making trouble for herself by getting involved with Italian soldiers, felt that it would be good for her to have a responsible and remunerative job. And lastly, that Mary, aged barely eighteen, was already sufficiently well-developed vocally and technically to be able to sing one of the standard roles in the coloratura repertoire: indeed, Konstanze's two main arias, "Ach, ich liebte" and "Martern aller Arten" (which Maria was to sing on stage only at Milan in 1952, in the first *Entführung* in the history of La Scala), are technically difficult and vocally very demanding.

On 16 October 1941 large areas of Athens had been flooded in a cataclysmic cloudburst that left the streetcar lines choked with mud and rubble. The biggest problem, however, was the shortage of food and the resulting boom in the black market. Toward the end of 1941 the occupation authorities arrested black marketeers for mixing sugar with sand and earth, butchers for selling dog meat, and even doctors for filching food intended for their patients. Despite the situation, in the first week of December there were various events commemorating the 150th anniversary of Mozart's death, among them a concert conducted by Franz von Höslin at the Olympia and a performance of the *Requiem* at the same venue conducted by Filoktitis Ikonomidis on 7 December. On that very day, on the other side of the world, the Japanese air force struck at Pearl Harbor and by doing so brought the United States into the war. When Hong Kong fell to the Japanese two weeks later, the official Athenian newspapers headlined Hitler's statement that Germany had done everything in its power to avoid war and von Ribbentrop's denunciation of President Roosevelt as responsible for its expansion to the Far East. Meanwhile, the Axis armies were advancing victoriously in North Africa and Russia.

That winter was extremely severe, making the food shortage bite still harder. In the last days of December 1941 the mountains surrounding Athens were blanketed with snow and a few flakes fell on the city itself. The New Year was ushered in with a stoppage of public transport. No buses, no streetcars: the only way of getting about was on foot or by the ingenious but slow and unreliable *gazogènes*. Prices now soared out of the public's reach. In March 1942 the profiteering tribunal tried several more fraudulent butchers who made a business of stealing donkeys and selling the meat as beef. Simply to stay alive, most Athenians were reduced to selling their most precious belongings "for a mouthful of bread." This was the time when clever entrepreneurs and collaborators acquired huge collections of art and other valuables, buying them up for derisory prices from their starving owners. At the National Opera, Ulysses Lappas had to ask the board to restrict its performances to four a week, so as not to exhaust the undernourished singers.[24]

From about the spring of 1942 an important person in Litsa's life was Mario Bonalti, a middle-aged Italian colonel from Verona. "Overt friendliness [with the enemy] was considered wrong. Everybody knew this . . . except Evangelia Callas," Jackie comments caustically in her account of how her mother first met him at an open-air café in Kifissia. "'Our Colonel,'" as Litsa describes him in her memoirs, "was a charming, cultivated man and a fine pianist." Her romance with Bonalti developed into a full-blown affair in the summer of 1942, when Mary would sing for the Italian army in Thessaloniki, just before triumphing in *Tosca*. When Bonalti found out about Mary's musical talent he took her under his wing: he would often accompany her on the piano and he would share his rations with her and bring her small presents. "He was my good friend, and to the two girls he was almost like a father," is how Litsa describes the relationship.[25]

For some time Jackie took a stand against allowing this kindly Italian into the apartment at 61 Patission Street, mainly because Miltiadis Embirikos had once happened to meet him there, had objected angrily, and had warned her of the likely consequences for all of them when the occupation was over. From Jackie's accounts of her quarrels with her mother, who had begun to dislike Miltiadis because he refused to marry her daughter, it is clear that the atmosphere in the house had become even more unpleasant than usual. There was a terrible reckless naïveté about her," Jackie remarks of her mother. "I tried to point out . . . that she could as well see him outside [the home]. . . . I had forgotten how perverse she could be. . . . 'Are you to be the only one allowed to have a gentleman friend?' [Litsa snapped] . . . 'Just because he *helps* doesn't mean to say he can control whom I choose to invite.'" Miltiadis's attempts to persuade Litsa that she was setting Mary a terrible example achieved nothing: little did he know that Litsa was actually encouraging Mary to consort with Italians "bearing gifts." "She was unstoppable and if she decided to ruin us all there was nothing I or anyone could do about it," Jackie concludes.[26]

Litsa's liaison with Colonel Bonalti lasted about a year and a half, right up to the time of Italy's capitulation and the break-up of the Axis alliance. To avoid being separated from Athens and Litsa he had refused promotion to the rank of general, and when the Italians were overwhelmed by the vicious German retaliation against them, in the summer of 1943, the good Bonalti disappeared and Litsa believed him dead. On discovering later that he was in a concentration camp, she managed to send him two food parcels, but by the time he was released by the Russians he was paralyzed from the tortures inflicted on him: in Litsa's words, "He had been starved, beaten, forced to sleep in mud and water—all the classic refinements of Nazi torture." He went home to Verona in a wheelchair, and in 1947 was not even able to write to Maria when he heard that the girl he had accompanied on the piano only four years earlier was appearing at the famous Arena in his hometown. According to Litsa, he then sent his brother to her with a message begging her to go and see him: "In the war Colonel Bonalti had been incredibly kind to us all and he had loved Maria as a daughter. I can still see him entering our living room at Patission 61 in Athens, holding in his hand a little packet, his day's sugar ration, which he had saved for the sweets-loving Maria." Mario Bonalti died early in 1949 without ever seeing either Litsa or Maria again.[27]

Presumably Litsa's intention in giving this moving description was to paint a picture of Maria as a hard, heartless person. Certainly the likelihood is that Maria did not go straightaway to see the kindhearted colonel. But to Maria, who was then just beginning to spread her wings, Mario Bonalti was a powerful link with a past that she now wished to forget. So, what with her work commitments and the assiduous attentions of Meneghini, whom she had just met, she kept putting off the visit until eventually Bonalti died before she could see him. There is no doubt that she had been intending to call on him from the moment she arrived in Verona

Colonel Mario Bonalti.

on 29 June 1947,[28] for Meneghini says in his first letter to her, written on 2 July, "I am sending you yesterday's local paper with the mention of your arrival in Verona. . . . You will have to tell me the name of the colonel again for me to locate the information you want." Litsa chooses to ignore this although she must surely have known about it. Jackie too, in her memoirs, criticizes her sister for her callousness in not answering the plea from this figure from the past who was paralyzed and bedridden "not far from Mary's new home in Verona."[29]

But let us return to Athens and to May 1942, when "Marianna G. Kaloyeropoulou" was taking her end-of-year examinations at the Athens Conservatory. It appears from the surviving records that only twenty-six of the ninety-four students passed in music history, and Mary was not one of them. Her classmate Lela Skordouli gives a vivid description of their oral examination with Yorgos Sklavos: "We went into the room together and sat side by side. Every time he asked her a question, any question, she didn't know the answer. In fact she kept protesting, saying things like '*I don't know Greek, I can't read, everything I know is just what I've picked up by myself.*' So Sklavos started addressing his questions to me, but by that time I had caught her nervousness and he failed us both, telling us we'd have to re-sit in October."[30] For piano Mary was marked 1-2 for application and 1-2 for progress, and she was the only one of Tassia Filtsou's fourteen students to be given 1 for ability. Next came the two subjects in which she was examined by Theodoros Vavayannis. In Solfège V three candidates were marked "excellent" and four, including Mary, "very good." In Harmony II, her worst subject, she received 1-2 for application and 2-1 for progress, while none of the thirteen candidates were given marks for ability. These grades put her in third or fourth place overall. In opera there were no examinations that year: on the mark sheet de Hidalgo gave

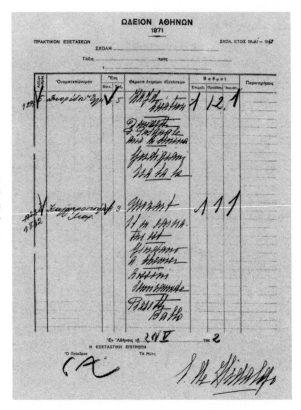

Mary's mark sheet in Elvira de Hidalgo's handwriting, Athens Conservatory, 29 May 1942.

Mary 1 for application, but no other marks. Finally, the singing examination was held on Friday 29 May. Mary started with the "Et incarnatus est" from Mozart's Great Mass in C minor, K. 427; her second piece was "La mamma morta" from *Andrea Chénier* by Giordano; then the aria "Bel raggio lusinghier" from Rossini's *Semiramide* (which she had been learning for the forthcoming concert in Thessaloniki); and her fourth and last item was Ildebrando Pizzetti's song "Il Ballo." Once again she had sung four pieces to everyone else's three. As usual, she received straight 1s for application, progress, and ability.[31]

On the very next day, 30 May 1942, Mary, chaperoned by her mother, left with four other singers and an accompanist for a concert in Thessaloniki.

CHAPTER 22

Thessaloniki and a
Summer Adventure

According to the received version of Callas's life story, the trip to Thessaloniki followed Mary's performance as Tosca and was a result of her success in the role. In reality, however, the two events were entirely unconnected and they actually took place in the reverse order. Most probably the celebration of the 150th anniversary of Rossini's birth was the idea of Colonel Mario Alberici da Barbiano, the "arts officer" of the Italian occupation authorities. He was a cultivated middle-aged aristocrat whose main job was organizing concerts, not only to entertain the Italian forces but also to promote the arts as part of Italian propaganda in Greece. He also wrote musical notes and reviews for *Il Giornale di Roma*, the occupation authorities' daily newspaper published in Athens. "He wore a uniform, of course, but he was deeply interested in music and was very polite. Wherever he saw talent he supported it, and he took an interest in Maria and in me," recalls Andreas Paridis, who was chosen to go to Thessaloniki as accompanist for that concert.[1]

Litsa opens her account of the trip by saying how difficult it was for the singers to avoid performing for "our conquerors." Although the likelihood is that she herself, through Colonel Bonalti, arranged for Barbiano to include Mary in the party, in her book she says that it was the commander of the Italian occupation army, General Geloso, who asked the other singers and Mary to go to Thessaloniki. "It was a command we dared not disobey," she adds. Once Mary had been picked for the tour, Litsa decided to seize the opportunity to go with her to Thessaloniki, where she had relatives. Playing the part of the overprotective mother, she asked "a Fascist officer named De Stasio" for permission to travel with Mary as her chaperone. De Stasio (who was to play an important part in Mary's life, especially after her return from Thessaloniki and her success as Tosca) at first refused Litsa's request, but when she threatened to withdraw her daughter from the company he relented, either so as not to upset Bonalti or because he had in the meantime met Mary personally.[2]

It is a measure of the pull that Litsa, and perhaps Mary herself, must have had with the Italian authorities that such a young and untried soprano, with only student performances and the insignificant role of Beatrice in *Boccaccio* behind her, was picked to join that select group of National Opera soloists. Considering that she now had no contract, her inclusion could only have been due to favoritism on the part of the Italians. The other members of the company besides Mary, who was described as a dramatic soprano, included the lyric soprano Mireille Fléri (b. 1907), the coloratura soprano Fanny Papanastasiou (b. 1912), the tenor Petros Epitropakis (b. 1894), and the bass Spyros Kaloyeras (b. 1904). The accompanist was Andreas Paridis (b. 1916), a pianist who had several years' experience of accompanying the advanced classes at the Athens Conservatory. "They sent us a message from the Casa d'Italia via the National Opera," Mireille Fléri remembered. The travel permit (Durchlaßschein N. 6203) was issued on 29 May by the German Kommandantur in the name of "Pietro Epitropakis and 7 companions" for a return journey from Athens to Thessaloniki. The actual date of departure was probably Saturday 30 May; the train was very slow, and as a safety precaution it traveled only by daylight. The party was personally escorted by Count da Barbiano, who passed the time in friendly conversation with the musicians and Litsa. Mary did not talk much: "The one who chattered away nonstop was Fléri," recalls Paridis. "Litsa was very amusing and so was Epitropakis, who teased all the women and cheered us all up."[3]

The journey was very tiring, lasting three days, with overnight stops at Lamia and Larissa or Katerini. The party arrived in Thessaloniki on Tuesday 2 June, and it is not certain whether they all stayed in a hotel not far from the White Tower Theater (as Fléri remembered), or whether Litsa and Mary were put up by their Moundouris cousins on Lassani Street but spent most of the rest of the time with the others. They all had breakfast and lunch together at "a big school" (perhaps the local Y.M.C.A.) and enjoyed walking about the town, usually along the waterfront and around the White Tower. "In the mornings we had our rehearsals and then we might go for a walk," Fléri recalled. In the evenings they dined at the well-known Olympos-Naoussa restaurant, always with the Italians, who were paying all the bills. Litsa paints a picture of the whole party (including Mary, of course) "stuffing themselves" at breakfast, lunch, tea, and dinner with "food such as we had almost forgotten existed."[4]

The concert, on Sunday 7 June, was organized by the inspectorate of the Fascist organizations in Greece and its inspector, Major Attilio De Stasio. The local secretary for Thessaloniki, Professor Piccoli, had arranged for it to be held in the Pallas Cinema on the waterfront, which seated about five hundred. It had been advertised in the previous day's newspapers as a "grand concert" arranged by the Italian Institute and the Thessaloniki Fascist Club, with a program comprising "the finest arias and songs." By 6 p.m., when the concert started, the hall was full to overflowing. Sitting in the dress circle were the Italian consul general, senior Italian and German officers, Greek officials, and other distinguished guests; the orchestra was packed with members of the local Italian community and Italian and German soldiers, but numerous Greeks as well. After a short introduction by Piccoli, Barbiano gave a talk on Gioacchino Rossini and then the concert started.[5]

Thessaloniki, very near the White Tower. Mary crouches in front of (left to right) Petros Epitropakis, Fanny Papanastasiou, Litsa, Spyros Kaloyeras, Mireille Fléri, and Andreas Paridis, who accompanied Mary's most important concerts and recitals in 1942 and 1943. The Pallas, where the concert took place on 7 June 1942, can just be seen above Fléri's hat.

The singers, wearing evening dress—"shabby and unstylish but with a touch of pre-war glamour," as Litsa notes—performed Rossini arias and duets, and perhaps the odd quartet. We may be sure that the program included excerpts from *Il Barbiere di Siviglia*, *Semiramide*, and *La Gazza Ladra*. Fléri remembers Mary singing "Bel raggio lusinghier" from *Semiramide*, and Paridis has a mental picture of her singing Rosina's aria "Una voce poco fa" from *Il Barbiere*, though on that occasion it would almost certainly have been sung by Fanny Papanastasiou. All the items were enthusiastically applauded, Athenians were informed by *Il Giornale di Roma*. The audience demanded numerous encores, the consul general congratulated the performers, and the leading ladies were presented with bouquets. "Miss Kaloyeropoulou, making her first appearance at a very early age, but already well prepared for an outstanding career, was received with affectionate warmth and well-deserved applause." The fact that Mary attracted special notice is also apparent from the prophetic review that appeared in Thessaloniki's *Nea Evropi*: "Miss Kaloyeropoulou was a real revelation. She has a voice of rare quality and very soon she will win a pre-eminent position for herself in our National Opera."[6]

Litsa's recollections of the trip to Thessaloniki are full of inaccuracies. One thing is sure, however: she enjoyed every minute of it. "It was just what she wanted out of life," Jackie wrote later: "her daughter's success, with herself in the wake enjoying all the praise, the glory, the attentions of the admirers and, of course, all the salami and prosciutto the Italians paid the singers with."[7] Indeed, the Italian consulate asked the musicians whether they would prefer to be paid with money or food. All agreed that they would rather have food, which they would never be able to obtain in Athens, no matter how much money they were paid. The Luigi Razza Fascio in Thessaloniki arranged for the food to be delivered to them, altogether 374 kilos (90 of wheat, 9 of raisins, 57 of rice, 90 of dried beans, 90 of lentils, and 38 of potatoes). Shared among the six performers it came to more than 60 kilos per person, which meant that Mary and Litsa had to carry over 30 kilos (about 70 pounds) each.

On 10 June the consulate issued the travel warrant for the return journey to Athens, as well as a note addressed to the Italian and German authorities asking them to provide the party with every comfort en route. The warrants were date-stamped on Friday 12 June, the day of their departure from Thessaloniki.* The return journey seemed to take even longer and was even more exhausting to everybody. By the time they reached Athens, on Sunday 14 June, they were all covered with soot from the engine. "The terrible thing was that the food was too heavy to lift and we had to carry it ourselves, on foot," Fléri remembered. "Litsa, Maria, and I found an old man with a handcart. He loaded it on, but we had to do the pushing! As we were walking up Ipirou Street we collapsed with exhaustion and sat on some steps on the pavement. Covered with soot as we were, passers-by thought we were beggars!"[8] So the last leg of the journey may have been a grueling experience, but ultimately all of them—and their appetites—must have been very well satisfied.

—◊—

It must have been immediately after her return from Thessaloniki that de Hidalgo told Mary that approval was expected imminently for a summer production of *Tosca* in which she might be given the leading role. In spite of the sweltering heat —on 20 June the temperature rose to almost 42°C (106°F) in the shade—and the usual summer distractions (less accessible that year, since there were no buses to take people to the seaside), Mary threw herself into the task of learning the part she was hoping for. Another story told by Litsa which has passed into the Callas

---

*The following is typical of the sort of slander that Mary and her mother had to endure during and after the occupation—quite apart from the accusations that were justly leveled against them. According to Mireille Fléri, when a permit for the transport of the food was needed from the German authorities, "Her mother took Maria by the hand and marched her into the Kommandantur." When asked what she meant, Fléri answered, "She left her in there for hours, to get the permit. Maria, of course, was extremely unwilling. But she was in there for so long— what could she have been doing with a Hun all that time?" When Andreas Paridis heard this insinuation, he exploded: "Just listen to who's talking! Maria wasn't that sort of girl! Shame on Fléri, saying such things!" (Documents from the Petros Epitropakis papers, property of Stathis Arfanis; FLÉRI; PARIDIS.) On Mary's serious clash with Fléri, see Chapter 31.

mythology dates from that summer of 1942: the occupation authorities had issued a proclamation ordering Athenians not to make any noise, even in their own homes. Thereupon, according to Litsa, "At my suggestion, we pulled Maria's piano up to the door of her balcony, and she would sit there singing with door and windows wide open. When she sang Tosca, a man some distance away would answer her singing the part of Mario, and they would sing together across the Athenian rooftops. . . . We never learned his name." This scene, we are told, was re-enacted several times, and it is certainly highly romantic: here is the Parisian *vie de Bohème* transported to Athens under enemy occupation. But the only point of any significance is that Mary, who had already studied the part of Tosca four years earlier with Trivella, was now relearning it with de Hidalgo. What is more, she was now learning it in two languages, Italian and Greek, which is not as simple as it sounds. "*'Tosca' was put on for me, and moreover we rehearsed it for more than three months*," Maria said in 1956, adding that the director, Dino Yannopoulos, could confirm it.[9]

Maria's insistence on this and her exaggeration of the time spent in rehearsal (which in fact was not more than six weeks) were presumably prompted by the untrue stories in circulation to the effect that she had made a traumatic first appearance as Tosca in July 1941. According to those stories, the soloist who was to sing Tosca fell ill before a performance and within twenty-four hours Mary, whom de Hidalgo had immediately suggested as a stand-in, was ready to go on stage. The original soloist—identified by one biographer as Zozo Remoundou and by another as Mireille Fléri—annoyed at being replaced (but why, if she was ill?), was said to have sent her husband to guard the door of the theater and physically prevent Mary from entering! Another version placed the husband in the audience, sitting in the orchestra. And when this fantastic story first saw the light of day in *Time* magazine, in October 1956, he was in the wings: according to the article, Mary was backstage, before the show, when she overheard a man remark, "That fat bitch will never carry it off." Enraged, she leapt at him, shrieking, tearing his shirt and giving him a bloody nose. Maria performed that night with a swollen eye, "but she got raves from the Athens critics." The facts? Suffice it to say that the only operas performed in Athens in July 1941 were *Boccaccio, Madama Butterfly*, and *The Land of Smiles*, and that *Tosca* was staged for the first time in August 1942. Maria herself stated categorically, "*It's all quite untrue, all that stuff about a torn shirt and me with a black eye and bleeding nose.*" And that was nothing but the truth.[10]

The board of the National Theater had authorized Nikos Yokarinis to renew the contracts of the opera soloists, which expired on 31 May every year. Knowing nothing about the personalities involved or the theater's requirements, Yokarinis had sought the help of Ulysses Lappas, one of the governors, who agreed "to engage the most suitable members for the summer opera season." De Hidalgo and Lappas were good friends, and the latter had been much impressed by Mary's talent and progress: we have already seen how he had tried to cast Mary as Nikita's understudy as Konstanze in *Die Entführung* in 1941. This time, probably with the backing of music-loving officials in the Italian forces, with whom both he and de Hidalgo were on good terms, Lappas continued to press for *Tosca* with Mary in mind for the main role. Louisa Terzaki, the widow of Angelos Terzakis, then secretary of the National Theater, takes up the story: "One day Kaloyeropoulou came into Angelos's office on Ayiou Konstantinou Street. I remember she was wearing a straw hat with flowers, so it must have been the spring or early summer of 1942. *'What about me? Aren't you going to give me a part?'* she asked him in that strange manner she affected with everyone. Lappas had probably told him something about her, and it was in the cards that she might sing Tosca. However, as Mary had no previous experience, Angelos felt he had to ask de Hidalgo's opinion first. Once she had assured him that Mary was able to manage it, the matter was put to the board and it was decided that she should be given the part."[11] This decision was indeed reached on 10 July 1942, and three days later Mary's name appeared for the first time in a framed advertisement of the National Opera's summer program in the Athenian press.

Particulars of the renewed contracts and the extra personnel engaged on Lappas's recommendation are no longer to be found in the National Theater archives. Mary's contract (which has disappeared, along with the whole of her personal dossier) presumably stipulated, among other things, that she was required to attend all the rehearsals and appear in all the performances of Puccini's opera to be given by the National Opera in August and September 1942. For those two months she was to be paid a total of 40,000 drachmas, a fairly large sum of money in those days.[12] Although there can be no suggestion—especially with hindsight—that the choice of Mary was unfair or partial, her engagement and its terms must have aroused some hostility among the older soloists on regular contracts. At that stage, however, they could say nothing against her, except perhaps that she lacked experience and her selection was hard to justify. Nevertheless, quite apart from the fact that the other possible candidates for the part of Tosca had prior commitments (Fléri, for example, was cast as Violetta for a July production of *Traviata*, immediately before *Tosca*), Mary had the necessary talent (guaranteed by de Hidalgo) and was the only available soprano capable of singing the whole opera in both Greek and Italian, as the Italian authorities wanted.

—⁂—

Yet, though everything seemed to be going well for Mary, the summer of 1942 was actually not an easy time for her. It is a fact, hitherto unknown, that until less than a month before the triumphant *Tosca* that was to set her firmly on the road to success, Mary was singing at a nightclub near Omonia Square frequented exclusively by officers and men of the occupation army. The tenor Andonis Kalaidzakis, then in the chorus of the National Opera, is the only person to have admitted that such things were done, by himself and by others whom he did not name: "They forced us to sing to the occupation forces and at night spots in Athens. . . . For these performances they would give us a biggish parcel of food. . . . Among other things, I had to sing 'Piccolo bambino innamorato.'"[13] We do not know the name or location of the nightclub, nor how long and on what terms Mary had been working thus. But one wonders what could have led her to take such a drastic step. It is possible, of course, that she did it because she enjoyed showing off her voice, practicing in public and being paid for it at the same time. To have done it under pressure from the occupation authorities seems rather improbable, particularly with her high level contacts. To have done it on her own initiative, simply to make ends meet, cannot be excluded. That her mother pushed her into it, however, so as to reduce the burden of their maintenance, then carried exclusively by Miltiadis Embirikos, seems much more likely.

The latter view is corroborated by Maria's later statement, which until now sounded exaggerated, to the effect that Litsa was exploiting her: "*She had even tried to destroy my career, by pressing me to become a singer in clubs, as in that way I would earn money faster.*"[14] Maria also spoke about this to her colleague and friend Giulietta Simionato during their last meeting in Rome in 1969: "First she told me quite openly about her mother's encouragement of contacts with members of the occupation forces in order to contribute to the household necessities. And then she told me that she had sung in a sordid club for the military that could be described as a brothel [*postribolo*], and that she sang exactly this sort of music, Arditi's 'Il Bacio,' Leoncavallo's 'Mattinata,' etc."[15] Presumably we shall never be quite sure about what exactly happened, but the fact remains that at the age of about eighteen Mary had a secret second pseudo-artistic persona. Not only was she practicing as hard as ever during the day, but in the evenings she was under some kind of contract to sing in a completely different environment, where she could not help being exposed to all sorts of hazards.

In late July 1942, in the course of her nightclub work—which Jackie denies, repeating that she did not need to work since Milton took care of everything— Mary met and evidently fell seriously in love with an Italian paratrooper named Angiolo Dondoli, from the Maremma region of Tuscany. Forty years later Raffaelle Doronzo, who had served in the same unit as Dondoli and had been a close friend of his, published the following illuminating story.*

---

*Raffaelle Doronzo, "Il meglio e il peggio," in E. Vannozzi and T. Bryk Ovi, *Storia del paracadutismo in Maremma, 1946–1987*, Novara 1987. Doronzo was unwilling to provide any further information, but Vannozzi gave me permission to make use of the text as I saw fit. Although Doronzo does not mention his friend's name (he calls him "il maremmano"), Vannozzi wrote to me that, before he published his text, Doronzo revealed to him that "the man from the Maremma" was Angiolo Dondoli. Dondoli was born in the Maremma in 1917, so when he met Mary he was about twenty-five, six or seven years her senior. He had already served on the Albanian front and would later fight in Africa. Soon after the war he settled in

"The 9th and 10th Battalions [of the Folgore Division] left the Grottaglie area by train on 15 July [1942]. Postumia, Belgrade, Karlovac, Salonika, and finally Tatoi, about 20 kilometers out of Athens. We arrived on 27 July and pitched camp near the airfield. But here the matter becomes a bit more complicated, because you have to realize that at that time Greece, and especially the big cities, were suffering from famine—and I mean real famine. People really were dying of hunger. I didn't see it myself, but I believe trucks went around Athens early every morning picking up the dead bodies, and it did not take long for us to realize that with half a piece of army biscuit we could lay the most beautiful women. I said the matter became more complicated because I am now going to touch on a topic that needs a word of introduction. There we were, about a thousand of us paratroopers, young and healthy . . . and, as far as women were concerned, armed with implements (if I may call them that) that you could hang buckets of water on! But the trouble was the language. 'Kalimera, kalispera' was about as far as we could go. And I do believe that grappling with a Greek woman was the first thing (perhaps even the only thing!) we all intended to do. . . . Every year at the end of July I see myself back there with all those wartime friends of mine, giving rusks and biscuits to young children who begged us for bread in our own language. They used to wait at the station and offer to take us wherever we wanted to go, or even just to polish our shoes. I even remember one little brat, hardly out of his rompers, saying to me, 'Wanna girl?'

"Anyway, on our first evening, there we are in Athens: me, him [the Maremmano] and two others from the 27th. That cabbagehead of a Maremmano had been in the Balkans [fighting on the Albanian front] before becoming a parachutist, and he could manage a few words of Greek. So where do we go? We're in Omonia Square, and there, in the pavement arcade, we see a nightclub with a small orchestra.[16] The four of us do a quick check to see how many drachmas we've got, and in we go! The place is packed with Italian and German soldiers. I think the only local people in there are the staff and the girls. But girls there are in plenty, and all quite good-looking, I must say. We find room at a table where some Italian officers are already sitting, right next to the stage. A few glasses of red wine—and a good look around to see if there are any chicks worth plucking. Well, there we are, when suddenly, after a waltz, on comes a little dumpling who is greeted with thunderous applause. But what's this? Even ordinary mortals like us can tell at once that this voice is something phenomenal. How well I remember! She sang 'Il Bacio' by Arditi, she was fantastic and all eyes were riveted on her.

Castiglione della Pescaia in the province of Grosseto in the Maremma, where he dedicated himself to agriculture and fruit production. When I tried to contact him, in September 1995, his wife informed me that his failing health and memory would not allow him to add anything to Doronzo's reminiscences. I also spoke to the wife of Camillo Curini, another officer in the Folgore Division, who knew Dondoli. Signora Curini described Dondoli as a *contadino* (peasant) with no interest in art or literature, adding that he was a tall and very good-looking man.

"So there we are, the four of us, just two or three yards from the stage, while she bombards us with these heavenly high notes, and she never stops looking in our direction. Well, so maybe she does weigh in at a couple of hundredweight, but it certainly makes us feel important—especially me! I mean, even a doorkeeper can see she's taken a fancy to us. The dirty looks we're getting from the spaghetti-eaters at our table make it quite clear that they don't like the way things are going one little bit. And paratroopers, at that! The customers demand an encore, and the little dumpling sings a Greek song. . . . But by this time yours truly has realized that he might as well be a stuffed dummy. The singer's eyes and words are directed at none other than the Maremmano. And what can I do about it? He has the features of an Etruscan, the physique and bearing of a grenadier. Me, I'm more like a foot soldier, so I'm not in the least surprised when the dumpling steps down from the stage at the end of her turn, comes over to our table and asks him (in good Italian) if he really liked her singing. Well, I knew just how strong the Maremmano was on the subject of music, and I can't imagine how he managed to get himself out of that fix, preoccupied as he was with a bunch of Italian and German bores who were crowding round our table. Anyway, sooner or later we pay for our drinks and out we go. At moments like this, it's your duty to leave the way clear to who-ever has got the bird in the bag . . . and then, ciao, ciao, we take the low road, they take the high road!

Paratrooper Angiolo Dondoli.

"We stayed a week in Athens, and every evening we descended on Omonia Square like hawks. The Maremmano and the little dumpling were inseparable. Her name was Maria, she was about our age and under contract to that night-club. She was being supported by a high-ranking officer in our army, and the Maremmano told me about the stratagems he and the girl had had to think up to get that food supplier out of the way. On the evening of 3 August we both went back to Omonia Square, but because of a small problem over an unpaid bill I thought it more prudent to stay out of the nightclub. The Maremmano wanted to say good-bye to the girl. 'Go on, you go in! I'll wait for you.' . . . Ten minutes later, out they both came. The girl was sobbing her heart out, it was a pitiful sight, and he didn't look any too happy either. . . . On 4 August the Folgore Division left Tatoi. I remember that departure well. Reveille at four, the platoons marching, boarding the G12s, and then a last bird's-eye view of that incomparable city with the Acropolis, already bathed in sunlight, standing guard over it."

In 1955 or 1956 the author of this narrative was idly scanning the publicity about Maria Callas singing at La Scala in Milan. In one of the many photographs of her, he recognized in her face (though not in her figure or her fashionable clothes) the "little dumpling" who had fallen in love with his friend Angiolo Dondoli in Athens in the summer of 1942. As one of his colleagues at work was a professional claqueur at La Scala, he asked him to try to arrange a meeting with Maria. Only about a week later he received a message via the claqueur, asking him to meet her at seven o'clock that evening at the Café Savini, in the famous galleria in the city center. After fourteen years, Doronzo felt strangely nervous about meeting the transformed Maria, to whom he remembered offering his army blanket on their parting evening of 3 August 1942 in Omonia Square.

"Ah, here she comes! True, she's no longer the 'dumpling' she was then, but an extremely elegant and—how shall I put it?—rather aloof lady. To my greeting of 'Ciao, Maria, how is everything?' she responded with the faintest of smiles and didn't seem to notice my outstretched hand, which was left hanging there in midair—and you can imagine how pleased I felt about that, in front of so many people. She had come with another woman, very polite, also Greek and presumably a friend of hers. It's a hard thing to admit, but there at the Café Savini, in the Galleria in Milan, I felt just like the stuffed dummy I had been that first evening, when the Greek singer's eyes had first met those of the Maremmano in the Athens nightclub. For at least a quarter of an hour she bombarded me with questions: *'What's his surname? Where does he live? Is he married?'* . . . And what answers could I give her? The Maremmano seemed to have vanished, I hadn't found anyone who could give me news of him. As for me, she didn't even ask me how I was. I think she was convinced that for some reason I didn't want to tell her anything, because after a time she suddenly pushed her cup of tea unceremoniously away from her, stood up and made it quite clear to her friend that she was ready to go. She did at least say 'Good evening' to me! Then, after a word or two with her friend, the woman who was now a world-famous opera star went out of the door of Savini's and disappeared from view."

Doronzo's narrative ends with a postscript: "I mentioned that the singer exchanged a few words with her friend before leaving Savini's. Well, I don't know a word of Greek, but the claqueur is a bit of a polyglot, so, as you can imagine, I asked him, 'What did she say?' 'Well, I understood her to say that with the paratroopers not even your ears were safe. What did she mean by that?' 'Don't you worry about that,' I told him. '*I* know!'"

The two paratroopers did not meet again until 1978, a year after Maria's death. Angiolo Dondoli talked to Raffaelle Doronzo about his wife, daughter, and granddaughter, but not a word did he say about "the Greek girl." He died in late 1995, aged seventy-eight, without ever having spoken about his youthful adventure with the future prima donna. Did he remember those Athenian days of August 1942, strangely sweet but hard and miserable as well? When he left Mary Kaloyeropoulou, still under nineteen years of age, she consoled herself by immersing herself in the final stages of the preparation and the rehearsals of *Tosca*. She would interpret her first important leading role in Italian as well, the language of Angiolo Dondoli, who had sent her emotions into such turmoil in the one week that their paths had crossed.

—⁓—

I could never live without music and without love!

To Giulietta Simionato (*Gente,* 2 November 1992)

CHAPTER 23

Tosca: A Star Is Born

The early rehearsals for *Tosca* in the summer of 1942 were held with piano accompaniment in the main auditorium of the National Theater on Ayiou Konstantinou Street. "From the very first rehearsals [Mary] was outstanding for her musicality and virtuosity, and she astonished us all because she was only eighteen," the tenor Ludo Kouroussopoulos recalled in 1977.[1] The two casts, one singing in Greek and the other in Italian, rehearsed alternately, but Mary rehearsed with both, benefiting doubly but also tiring her voice twice as much—especially considering that when the orchestral rehearsals started in the open-air theater in Klafthmonos Square she never held back to save her voice. It is not known whether she was advised to adopt this practice or whether she herself felt it was what she had to do, but from then on she stuck to it unfailingly throughout her career.

Besides the support and guidance of Elvira de Hidalgo, from now on Mary also enjoyed the appreciation and admiration of Ulysses Lappas. Being a former colleague and still a good friend of de Hidalgo, Lappas was able to follow Mary's development. "He went crazy about Kaloyeropoulou, talking about her to anyone who would listen," Elli Nikolaidi recalled; and Andonis Kalaidzakis adds, "Having sensed the promising future ahead of her, he treated Mary like a great singer, even though she was so young and he was choosy about the people he made friends with." Lappas was also seen with her in public, having coffee with her at the Loumidis Café (a favorite haunt of artists and musicians), and he would often walk with her from there to nearby Klafthmonos Square or the Olympia Theater. In later years he took pride in Mary's fame, calling himself her "old friend from Athens, and godfather in art." *"Thank you, Odysseas,"* Maria declared publicly in 1960. *"Thank you, and I have not forgotten how when I was young you taught me how to walk, how to stand, how to hold my staff [in 'Tosca']."*[2]

With her insatiable appetite for learning and her perfectionism, Mary studied her part privately with the musical director of the production, Sotos Vassiliadis, and with her Scarpia, the baritone Titos Xirellis, a well-established singer who was also an excellent musician and a composer.[3] Like Lappas, Xirellis gave Mary valuable help in those early days of her career. At the Hellenic Conservatory on Fidiou

286

Street, where he was on the teaching staff and had a classroom always at his disposal, he taught her how to play the difficult scene with Scarpia in Act II, a lesson which must surely have left its mark on all her subsequent performances right down to 1965. Xirellis made no attempt to conceal his admiration of Mary, with the result that his wife, who was a member of the chorus, resented her balding forty-two-year-old husband's attentions to the eighteen-year-old "beginner," going so far as to make a scene about her in the conservatory one day.[4] Nor was she the only woman who was jealous of Mary, a girl unjustly described by all her biographers as having always been fat, plain, and devoid of sex appeal. Haris Vassiliadou, the wife of the conductor of *Tosca*, viewed Mary with a jaundiced eye for the same reason, namely that she had persuaded her husband to devote extra time to coaching her in her part.

Sotos Vassiliadis, a former director of the Thessaloniki branch of the National Conservatory and a teacher of the violin and theory of music at the National and Hellenic Conservatories in Athens, had little conducting experience and had never conducted opera before.[5] Several of those involved in the production of *Tosca* commented on the fact that he had been taken on by the National Opera, despite his left-wing views, thanks to his pull with a government minister. This aroused widespread resentment and created a strained atmosphere, with some unpleasant incidents, though Mary refused to be a party to them. She knew that Vassiliadis was to be her conductor, and that was what counted with her just then. Later she was to refer to him as "*il mio primo maestro*" and he stated in writing that he had been given an inkling of her future by her regular attendance at rehearsals, her disciplined and serious approach to music, her quickness at learning, and her ready compliance with all his suggestions.[6] Mary did, of course, have a special reason for wanting to work in close collaboration with him, and that was her terrible myopia: "*In my early years I always . . . asked when the maestro would have his readings with the orchestra, because I am nearsighted and I cannot depend on cues given to me by the conductor himself or the prompter. . . . So I used to assist to his readings [to attend the conductor's rehearsals with the orchestra].*"[7] Vassiliadis's widow remembered that time: "She was the one who asked my husband to rehearse her at her house. She was very conscientious, so much so that he got fed up with her. 'You have no idea what a nitpicker she is!' he used to say. 'She drives you up the wall, always pestering you about the most trivial details. "*Shall we go through it once more, Maestro?*" Then she makes a circular movement with her hands and, whether you like it or not, she makes you do it all over again! Whereas with the others you only have to mention the word "rehearsal" and they start looking at their watches.'"[8]

Haris Vassiliadou, a very young woman who had studied the violin with Vassiliadis, mistrusted her husband because she knew he was "quite a womanizer." At first he went to Mary's on his own, but one day when she accompanied him to 61 Patission Street she happened to see him hugging and kissing Mary as he left. Sotos had calmed her down by saying, "Don't worry! The one person you needn't be afraid of is Mary." And Haris felt reassured, "not because Mary was overweight and had big fat legs, but because she was a very virtuous girl," she explained, though she admitted she never was quite sure what went on between her husband and his young prima donna. After the working sessions they would both sit down with Litsa and her daughters to eat: "We even had spaghetti dishes, which were an untold luxury in those days." Presumably the family larder was still well stocked with the provisions Mary had earned by the concert in Thessaloniki.[9]

Haris also misinterpreted Mary's professionalism, which made her throw herself heart and soul into her work from the moment rehearsals began: "She was standoffish and discouraged any attempt at communication. There were times when she didn't even speak to me, didn't even look at me, and I was the wife of her conductor. She did herself no good in that way, in fact she put people right off her." Worse still, when Haris went to her husband's dressing room during the first intermission on opening night she found the door locked, and when Sotos opened it for her she saw Mary doing her hair or freshening her makeup in front of the mirror. On being confronted later by his wife, Sotos explained that Mary had locked the door so that no one would come in and disturb them: "She had gone there to ask him to hold the orchestra back a little longer at some point in the second act, to give her time to take a breath for a sustained note." If that is true, it shows how Mary went on taking trouble over the details of her part right up to the last minute, because she knew she could not trust herself to see the conductor's baton. And Vassiliadis kept telling his wife not to worry, "because even if I tried something with her she wouldn't have any of it."[10]

Although one cannot help wondering how Vassiliadis had arrived at this conclusion, it seems most likely that Mary's involvement with him was a figment of his wife's imagination. But at the same time it does show that Mary, so often represented as a monster with no femininity, actually possessed certain qualities that made her desirable to men. The picture of her as an unattractive, sexless creature reflects the miserable conditions of life in the occupation and the hostility of some of her rivals. It also derives from various statements made with ulterior motives, such as the testimony of Ilias Papatestas, intended to show how implausible it was that Mary had had close relationships with Italians and Germans: "She was a young girl without the least trace of femininity, whose looks could not possibly arouse any man's interest," he said in 1963, in the certainty that he would not be offending his old friend (then at the height of her fame), as he himself had once proved by his actions that exactly the opposite was true.[11] Although Jackie maintains that there was not a breath of sexuality about her sister, their mother admits that this was not the case: "Men did like Jackie, who was slim and quiet and sympathetic whereas Maria was plump and aggressive, but they also liked Maria. She has never lacked the quality known as sex appeal, and some men were more attracted to her than to her sister." This is corroborated by a colleague of Mary who was then a young man, Andonis Kalaidzakis: "Yes, she may have been rather fat, rather slatternly and thick in the leg, but she certainly excited interest in men! She didn't do it deliberately: it was just her manner, the way she moved. She had a good waist, and when it was held in, it emphasized her bust. And on top of everything else she had a fire burning inside her, and there was no hiding that!"[12]

One woman who was not jealous of Mary was Xenia Kouroussopoulou, soon to be the wife of the tenor lead in the Italian performances of *Tosca*. She first met Marianna (as she says Mary liked to be called in those days) at the rehearsals in the National Theater, and she remembers her as "a cheerful, pleasant girl with fat legs and a rather bad complexion, though it doesn't look so bad in photographs."[13] What is interesting about these photographs, taken by Xenia herself during rehearsals on stage, is that they show a noticeably slimmer Mary with a new hairstyle and an air of greater self-confidence, no longer a child who did not care about her appearance. The rehearsals in Klafthmonos Square were held in the relative cool of the late afternoon, before the evening performances of *La Traviata* with Mireille Fléri and Nikos Glynos. The stage there was so small that Dino Yannopoulos had suggested very simple "modern" sets consisting mainly of drops and curtains, but the idea had not been acceptable to the conservative-minded Lappas.*

Mary also got on well with Yannopoulos and they occasionally saw each other outside their work. As his mother was American and relatively well-placed at the time of the famine, Mary often went to her house, where the two of them would talk about America and the older woman would always give Mary something to eat. But that was not the only reason for her visits, for she secretly found Dino attractive as a man, as she admitted to him more than ten years later: "In 1954, in Milan, I was in a box at the opera with Walter Legge, Elisabeth Schwarzkopf, Richard Tucker, and Jerome Hines, and at one of the intermissions Callas walked past quite near me without recognizing me. 'Don't you know each other?' said Tucker. *'Oh, Dino, what's happened to your good looks? You've put on so much weight . . .'* 'Whereas you, Maria . . .' and so on and so forth, because she really had under-

---

*In those days the stage directors had not yet overtaken the actors in importance. Maria was to refer to the subject toward the end of her life, by which time the situation was reversed: *"In the old days it wasn't the stage directors who directed: we did it ourselves, in consultation with the other singers and the conductor. We would say to one another, 'Right, you enter from over there,' and so on, and we produced triumphs and marvels, because it is the opera singers who make the show, not the stage director. Directing is like setting a beautiful jewel, a ruby, in its mount; but it is the stone that counts, not the mounting. Well, we singers are the gemstones of the show. Apart from the music, we are the ones who make the show: directing simply provides a good setting."* She continued with a tirade against the recent vogue for altering the periods and locations in which operas are set: *"Opera can't be done like that. You often hear it said nowadays—it's very much the in thing—that opera belongs to the people. Well, yes, it does belong to the people, but it's an art, a sumptuous art, and people like a bit of sumptuousness. . . . Opera is made up of details, and if an opera is staged in a Palais des Sports all the details are lost, because the scale is too big. A hundred or a hundred and fifty years ago La Scala used to put on thirty or forty performances of the same opera, and then everybody could go and see it. But not five performances in a Palais des Sports."* (CALONI.)

Leonidas Zoras conducting a rehearsal of *La Traviata* at the open-air theater of Klafthmonos Square, Athens, August 1942.

gone a transformation. Then she turns to me and says in Greek, '*Do you know how much in love with you I was?*'"[14]

The heat of August in Athens must have been a sore trial for the singers, and not least for Mary. She referred to it in a talk she gave in 1960: "*I don't usually sing in summer, not because I'm so high and mighty but because, like everybody else, I suffer from the heat and my throat gets dry. I need humidity, like most singers.*"[15] Before she left Greece, of course, Mary often had to sing in the heat of summer, and to sing roles that she would not have chosen for herself. "*I did everything under the sun,*" she said in 1958, "*because, you see, when you do become great, then you can do what you want, but at the beginning you just take what they give you and try to make the best of it.*"[16] Although *Tosca* was to be the springboard for her rise to stardom, the fact that she had learned it as early as 1938 with Trivella and then again on stage for the summer of 1942 left her with no great enthusiasm for that particular Puccini opera or its heroine. She had actually found the experience very tedious, as she later admitted: "*I promise you, if you keep on practicing a role for six months, you can't stand it.*"[17]

As opening night drew near, Mary doubtless felt tired but fully prepared for the appearances that she had long been waiting for. Confident of her success, she overcame her timidity to call on her "stuck-up" relatives to invite them to the performance. One was the well-known obstetrician Nikos Louros, Litsa's second cousin. "She came to invite me to go and hear her in *Tosca*," Louros wrote later.

Director Dino Yannopoulos with mezzo-soprano Mitsa Kourahani, Athens 1943.

"She was then a fat, unattractive girl, but her mouth and eyes sparkled with intelligence and charm. . . . Two fiery eyes and a very wide mouth with dazzlingly white teeth and an enchanting smile."[18] At the age of eighteen and three quarters, Mary was to see the dreams she had cherished for years come true: at last she would demonstrate her worth as a prima donna in the title role of *Tosca*, one of the best known and most popular operas in the repertoire, and she would do so at the first-

Rehearsing *Tosca*, Athens, Klafthmonos Square open-air theater, August 1942, with baritone Lakis Vassilakis and prompter Manolis Xynidis. Bass Petros Hoidas can be seen in the back and the head of conductor Sotos Vassiliadis in the foreground.

Rehearsing *Tosca*, Athens, Klafthmonos Square open-air theater, August 1942, with tenor Ludo Kouroussopoulos.

ever production of this opera by the National Opera before a packed audience of Greek as well as foreign music-lovers and opera buffs.

—៧៤—

On the day of the première and the following day, the headlines of the Athens newspapers, which were censored and controlled by the occupation authorities, were dominated by news of German bombing raids on military targets in southern England, Italian raids on Malta, and the Russians' plea to the British and Americans to open a second front in Europe. Subsequently, and throughout the run of *Tosca*, the main news reports gave detailed accounts of "heavy losses by the Bolsheviks," the German advance into Russia, and the murderous street-fighting in Stalingrad. But in Athens the tickets for the first night and most other performances were sold out. The presence of such a young and unknown singer in the title role had aroused interest and curiosity. In the words of a contemporary, "Rumor carried word of conflicting opinions among the experts. Some spoke of a strange voice, others of a voice that was every kind of voice in one and had not yet settled to its final timbre, some maintained that there was no voice at all, and so on and so forth." When the curtain rose the front rows were full of Italians and Germans, most of them wearing colorful uniforms, medals, and plumed hats. Behind them were the Greeks, public figures and socialites, all wondering about the quality of the production they were about to see.[19]

About ten minutes into the first act on that Thursday, 27 August 1942, the people in Klafthmonos Square realized that the new prima donna was someone to be noticed. "When she came on stage it was as if she took the audience by the scruff of the neck and said, 'Now hear me! I've got something to tell you!'" Dino Yannopoulos said later.[20] And certainly the first entrance of that Floria Tosca remained imprinted forever on the memories of many of those who witnessed it. Her voice could be heard in the distance as she approached the church where her lover, Mario Cavaradossi, was busy at his easel. "Mario, Mario, Mario!" Mary called, offstage and moving nearer, before making her entrance wearing a tight-waisted ruby-red dress and matching hat and holding a long staff. She burst on to the stage with tremendous panache, as she always would do in this scene, and launched straight into the flurry of lovers' talk with Andonis Delendas, mingling sweet nothings with outbursts of jealousy. Andonis Kalaidzakis, a member of the chorus that night, says, "I remember that 'Mario, Mario, Mario!' It sent a shiver down your spine! It was a cry that came straight from the heart. That voice of hers was strange, there was a natural sob in it that projected you straight into an atmosphere of drama. The sound was a bit throaty, but attractively throaty, like the sound of a string instrument when not played absolutely true. It became crystal-clear only on the high notes."[21]

Many of the features of that production of *Tosca* were to be retained and re-used by Maria later in her career, when she left her personal imprint on the role.

Mary (Floria Tosca)
with Andonis
Delendas (Mario
Cavaradossi), Athens,
August 1942.

Besides the cry of "Mario, Mario, Mario!" and the aria "Vissi d'arte," the scene where she stabs Scarpia was spine-chilling thanks to the "business" devised by Yannopoulos and brilliantly executed by Mary on that occasion. As Scarpia sat at his desk writing the safe-conduct Tosca had asked of him, she backed diagonally downstage toward the table. "On the table was the dagger, with the hilt toward her," recalled Stefanos Chiotakis, another member of the chorus. "Closer and closer to the table she moved, walking rather unsteadily, and we, knowing she couldn't see, were on tenterhooks. Would she put her hand on it, or . . . ? But she, having measured her paces to perfection, arrived at the table and picked up the dagger with absolute precision, without even turning her head. That really froze the blood in your veins! It was as if there were a magnet drawing her hand toward the hilt!"[22] Then, when Scarpia bore down on her, snarling "Tosca, finalmente mia!", she stabbed him furiously, screaming "Questo è il bacio di Tosca!" A few moments later, watching him struggling helplessly on the floor, she urged passionately, "Muori, dannato! Muori! Muori! Muori!" And after she saw him motionless and uttered the famous "E avanti a lui tremava tutta Roma!", Andonis Kalaidzakis recollects with emotion how Mary let the dagger drop from her hand and placed a candle on either side of the dead tyrant. At that point she had to lift Xirellis bodily and move him a little way away. "At the first performance, carried away by her excitement and youthful verve, she hoisted him up quite roughly—we were all thin, especially in those days—and dropped him unceremoniously on the floor," as Yannopoulos still remembers. "His head hit the boards with a hollow thud, which sent a brief ripple of amusement through the audience."[23]

However, everyone in the audience felt a tremendous thrill of excitement when Mary extracted the note clutched in the dead Scarpia's hand. And then she made her exit with another clever piece of staging by Yannopoulos, walking off at stage right, trailing her cloak behind her, while the curtain was drawn across from stage left to bring the scene to an end. Many people still remember the silent tension of that moment when, with the ermine cloak thrown over her shoulder and trailing on the floor, Mary turned round to look back at the dead Scarpia. No less a director than Luchino Visconti acknowledged that he had admired that ingenious touch of the trailing cloak and had used it in his own productions.[24] Another who borrowed it was Franco Zeffirelli, the stage director of Maria's last *Tosca* in London and Paris in 1964 and 1965: some of the photographs of that production, almost a quarter of a century later, show a marked resemblance to the same scenes from the Athens production during the Axis occupation.

The performance was frequently interrupted by bursts of applause, sometimes in places where silence is called for. When Mary hit a high note, the chorister Kostas Dounias recalls, Ulysses Lappas stood up in the auditorium and shouted "Brava! Brava!" Even at the performances in Greek there were so many Italians in the audience and their enthusiasm was so vociferous that Mary always had to sing an encore of the famous second-act aria, "Vissi d'arte," in Italian. "At the end of

Tosca, second act, Mary with Titos Xirellis (Scarpia), Athens, August 1942.

that aria she would utter a sob of the kind favored by some tenors at the end of 'Ridi pagliaccio,' which drove the audience wild," Mitsa Kourahani remembers. That was something Mary had probably learned from Lappas, a disciple of the old school who always followed the standard precepts of *verismo*.[25] Later in her career Maria said she did not like "Vissi d'arte" because she felt that it broke the flow of the action. Moreover, in light of her subsequent statements to the effect that applause ought to be kept to the end of each act (for example: *"I wish they would manage to eliminate applause in opera until the end, as they do in the theater. I find it disturbs the atmosphere . . . and you have to rework to re-create it."*[26]), it seems that the summer of 1942 was probably the first time she was made aware of how applause can ruin the atmosphere of a performance by dragging the singer out of the ambience of the dramatic action.

In the last act, after Cavaradossi's famous aria "E lucevan le stelle," sung by Andonis Delendas,[27] and Tosca's tender love duet with him, came the execution scene. "I can still hear Maria's final cry as she falls on Cavaradossi's body and realizes he is dead," says Kalaidzakis. And the Spoletta of that production, Nikos Doufexiadis, describes how, having discovered that Scarpia had been murdered, he came on stage to arrest her, crying, "Ah, Tosca, pagherai ben cara la sua vita!", whereupon Mary gave him a push (which in the first few performances knocked him flat, as she was much bigger than him), uttered the dramatic words "O Scarpia, avanti a Dio!" and leapt from the battlements.[28] Although the Italian and German officers in the front rows gave her a standing ovation and Spyros Salingaros says that on the first night she took seven curtain calls, it is by no means certain that the audience as a whole applauded Mary more than Delendas. According to one member of the audience, "The public gave ovations to the well-known singers but was rather reserved toward Maria. We looked at each other questioningly and cast furtive glances at the musical experts in the audience to see whether they felt the same way as we did." Evidently Mary's own reaction to the applause was quite modest, as her habit of self-criticism was present in her even at those early appearances. "After one performance I went up to congratulate her on her way back to the dressing room," Kalaidzakis recalls, "but she just shook her head without saying a word, as if she mistrusted the applause and had doubts about her performance."[29]

In the second run of *Tosca*, starting on 8 September 1942 and sung in Italian, the front rows presented an even more colorful array of uniforms, medals, and plumed hats. So many Italians tried to get in, even though the tickets were sold out, that the wooden barrier collapsed and many watched the opera standing. Xenia Kouroussopoulou remembers Mary putting on her makeup that evening in her makeshift dressing room. Because of her bad complexion she relied fairly heavily on cosmetics and was already quite expert at applying them. Consequently, whenever she made her entry costumed and made up as Floria Tosca she looked very striking and was often described as a beautiful woman.[30] As the dressing rooms were very small, at the end of each performance people used to wait in the auditorium or out on the pavement to congratulate the soloists when they emerged. "And then we would set off on foot—Ludo, Maria, and often her mother and sister, also carrying bouquets and basketfuls of flowers," says Kouroussopoulou. "On the way home we would discuss the performance, and Maria was usually happy and in high spirits. To have a hit like that was quite something for such a young girl."[31]

What aroused the most admiration, however, was not Mary's voice but her powerful characterization of Floria Tosca. "If you heard her sing without seeing her, you would think it was three different people singing," says Kouroussopoulou. "She had difficulty with the transitions from one register to another. When she hit a high note cleanly her voice didn't wobble, but on an upward portamento it did. However, she had such a big vocal range and such warmth of tone, and above all her acting was so good, that those things were forgotten. The whole effect was so vibrantly alive that it made you jump out of your seat." Nikos Papachristos, who was in the chorus, concurs: "She made a terrific impression on us. As in *Boccaccio*, we were baffled and taken aback by her voice. It had so many different tone colors that it lacked homogeneity: a high voice, a middle voice, and a low voice, all quite distinct. But there was tremendous fluency throughout, and she acted so naturally on stage that you overlooked her vocal flaws." Someone whose opinion of Mary's first performance in a leading role carries special weight is her stage director, Dino Yannopoulos: "She was marvelous, and I had recently seen plenty of performances in Vienna and Salzburg to compare her with. Only she was still a bit wild, unbridled." And Litsa, while summing up Mary's *Tosca* as "no spectacular success," did admit that her daughter's acting was brilliant. This she attributed to two causes: the influence of the films Mary had been seeing and the inherited histrionic talent of her father![32]

It may be true that Mary's acting transported her audiences into the world of the character she represented on stage, as has often been said, but the person who really did enter another world was Mary herself. "*You no longer belong to yourself,*" she said in 1965. "*You feel huge, big enough to fill the whole theater . . . but sometimes you feel very small, so small that you want to disappear because you are ashamed of what you are doing.*"[33] Once, when asked whether she thought her Greek background had anything to do with her acting ability, she said that after singing in *Iphigénie en Tauride* and *Alceste* at La Scala she had seen many of the very same movements she had made being taught to young actresses for a performance of Greek tragedy. So she said she was sure that being Greek had helped: "*There must be something in the blood. . . . Who taught me those things? Nothing but instinct! Because in Greece I had not gone to see any play—I was too young and did not have energy and time, and it was during the war—and I had not seen those movements.*" In 1956 Luchino Visconti wrote to Maria: "It's a bit like the touch of orientalism in you, which adds so much mystery and so much strength to your temperament as an artist and as a woman." And in 1969 he said of her, in her presence: "Maria Callas is Greek, she has tragedy in her blood, she has in her blood the ability to express herself. . . . I should very much like to see Maria acting in a tragedy by Euripides or Sophocles at Epidavros." Indeed, the last time Yannis Tsarouchis went to see her in Paris, a few months before she died, Maria was enthusiastic about his idea that she should play Euripides's three Trojan heroines (Hecuba, Andromache, and Cassandra) at Epidavros.[34]

Nafsika Galanou recalled that during one of the intermissions of *Tosca* she went to congratulate Mary and asked her if she had stage fright. "Maria gave me a wide-eyed smile and said, '*What does that mean?*'" But Zoe Vlachopoulou thinks otherwise: "Maria always had stage fright, perhaps a different kind of stage fright in those days. Galanou was way off the mark. I expect Maria was pretending to be unaffected by nerves so as to demoralize her." And Maria Alkeou supports Vlachopoulou: "Maria must have said that to Galanou deliberately, to give her a complex." Alkeou agrees that Mary was always nervous: "At first it would have been nervousness caused by youthful self-doubt, not the nervousness of the artist who feels the weight of responsibility." She had seen evidence of this one evening when Mary had gone to Alkeou's dressing room to get ready for the performance: "While she was making up she kept examining herself critically in the mirror and voicing her anxiety about how it would go. I mean I *saw* her nervousness, I'm not guessing!" De Hidalgo, on the other hand, who must have been in a good position to know, maintained that in the early days Mary was not really nervous: "And the extraordinary thing is that I didn't feel nervous myself when she was about to sing. I had a feeling of tranquillity which my other pupils didn't give me. I felt sure of her, so sure that I was actually pleased when she was going to sing: 'Ah, at last I can relax!'"*

---

*Michalis Payidas, interview with Nafsika Galanou, *Acropolis*, 1 July 1979; VLACHOPOULOU; ALKEOU; L'INVITÉ. Maria herself talked about this subject several times, usually asserting that when she was young she had had no stage fright, or hardly any, but that her nervousness had progressively increased thereafter because of her sense of responsibility to the public. Thus: "*I never did [have stage fright] in the beginning, and now [I have] terrible,*" and, "*The more I grew in reputation, the more frightened I got.*" In one interview she admitted that even in the early days she had felt nervous, but not very: "*At the beginning of my career I had very little stage fright.*" (Radio interview with William Weaver, Paris, 10 Apr. 1965; P. Dragadze, "My Lonely World: A Woman Looking for Her Voice," *Life*, 30 Oct. 1964.) Then in 1965 she discussed the matter more fully: "*When you are young you think you're entitled to everything by right. We thought it was the duty of life to offer us all the opportunities in the world. I wasn't at all scared, I couldn't have cared less! Whereas now, of course, it's very different. . . . But it's not fear of the public, it's fear of oneself: the fear that you might not do justice to the great destiny, the great obligation upon you.*" And on another occasion she described what form that fear took in her later: "*You count sentences in your head, you lose your lucidity, your heart starts pounding, you're like a frightened animal, you feel ill at ease with yourself, you want to run away.*" (BANZET; interview in *Elle*, 9 Feb. 1970.) Many of the greatest performers have suffered from stage fright; as the great violinist Isaac Stern once said, "Only children and idiots don't have it." Among the common symptoms of stage fright are a heightened perception of colors and objects, heavier perspiration, icy hands, and a memory lapse caused by the increased flow of adrenaline. Nearsighted people, of whom Maria was one, grow tense and their blood flow accelerates.

—⁓—

As Sotos Vassiliadis wrote many years later, the day after the première of *Tosca* Mary received a note "from the Italians" congratulating her and inviting her to "come and collect a number of food parcels for distribution among those responsible for the success of the production." That the Italian authorities should thank the prima donna of an opera which they themselves had requested and give her some precious food parcels is eminently reasonable. What strikes one as odd is that they should have asked Mary to convey congratulations and remuneration in the form of food to the other members of the company, considering that she was comparatively unknown and easily the youngest of the soloists. Be that as it may, Vassiliadis described her as being "clearly overjoyed" when she rushed in to tell him the news, implying that she was the one who had done most to win "this valuable gift for the company."[35]

Of much more interest than this semi-official accolade are the reviews that appeared in the papers on the two days immediately following the first night. The 1956 *Time* article claimed that the Athenian critics had given her rave reviews, but she herself denied that they had been complimentary: she actually wrote, "*They have never spoken well [of me].*"[36] In reality, the critics of that *Tosca* production were divided into two camps, some full of praise and others distinctly unimpressed. Seven reviews were published altogether, three on Friday 28 and four on Saturday 29 August. Alexandra Lalaouni, who had noticed Mary in the same composer's *Suor Angelica* two years before, this time wrote a fulsome eulogy in the newspaper *Vradyni*: "A girl of eighteen, practically a child still, . . . does not merely carry the part tolerably or unexceptionally: she lives the part, she feels it to the depth of her being, and she conveys the most profound emotion to her audience. She is a real marvel." Lalaouni described Mary's voice as rich throughout the range, crystal clear and homogeneous, which she had no reason to say if it were not so. In fact not one of the critics contradicted this view, and Dimitrios Hamoudopoulos also commended the homogeneity of her voice. So it seems that her work with de Hidalgo had already paid off in that it had noticeably lessened her wobble and her problems in changing register, in other words her unevenness. Lalaouni, who had earlier criticized Mary's Greek, now praised her for "her faultless breath control, articulation, and pronunciation." Nor was this all. Having complimented her on her innate musicality, her exceptional sense of theater, her outgoing personality, her intelligence ("quite remarkable for her age"), and, not least, her looks ("full of beauty and grace"), she concluded: "It is not at all surprising that the audience gave her a thunderous ovation."[37]

Sophia Spanoudi in the *Athinaika Nea* was much less effusive. She did acknowledge that Mary, though "still young and lacking in experience, . . . did not make any real mistakes from start to finish of this very big role." She also commended her for her fine stage presence, good looks, and rich voice, but added that the voice had yet to crystallize into that of a dramatic soprano. She concluded, "Miss Kaloyeropoulou is not yet a Tosca, of course, but already she shows every promise of becoming one." The next day, 29 August, four more reviews appeared. Petros Koulmassis, in the *Deutsche Nachrichten in Griechenland*, wrote: "Visually she made a pretty picture, which won the audience over and gave her credibility both as a desirable woman and as a renowned artist." Commenting on her voice, he noted her "variations of tone" and the vocal power that enabled her to rise easily above the orchestra. Hamoudopoulos in *Proia*, after remarking that Mary's performance in her début had aroused the well-deserved admiration of the audience, complimented her on the homogeneity and range of her voice, while her acting, he said, was of a standard "not found even in experienced performers." His only negative comments referred to a certain "hardness" of her voice and some exaggerated gestures with her hands.[38]

Two who were much more critical of the production in general and of Mary in particular were Ioannis Psaroudas in *Eleftheron Vima* and the anonymous music critic of the *Proinos Typos*. The latter acknowledged Mary's "remarkable musical and vocal talents," but he considered her to be a lyric soprano rather than the dramatic soprano that the role of Tosca calls for. Because of this she forced her voice and very often her intonation was imperfect, especially on the high notes. In his opinion she had not "got into the part" in spite of her good acting, and even there he found fault with her for "some excesses."[39] Psaroudas, still more disparaging, described the performance as below par vocally with the sole exception of Andonis Delendas. As for the "likable" Miss Kaloyeropoulou, Psaroudas wrote that she had "overextended herself by making her début in an opera that is both vocally and dramatically very demanding." Her voice, though "a little harsh," and her "fairly relaxed manner" promised well, but only "for the not too distant future." For the time being, Psaroudas felt that Mary did not have the maturity required of Sardou's heroine. He judged her "good, though slightly affected" in the first act and "outstanding" in the third, which he considered the best. In the second act, and especially in the scene with Scarpia, he judged her "vocally substandard."[40]

No doubt these two very unfavorable reviews remained etched on Maria's mind. Her overriding memory of that *Tosca*, however, was of pride in her success and her undisputed overnight rise to stardom. Nothing can diminish the magnitude of her achievement: born in New York and educated at an American school, she had sung her part in one foreign and one virtually foreign language when still not nineteen years old. The performances, which started at 7 p.m., when it was beginning to get dark, generally alternated day by day with Mireille Fléri's *Traviata*. The first six were in Greek, the first night of the Italian version was on 8 September, and then came eleven more performances, only two of which were in Italian, making a total of fifteen in Greek and three in Italian.[41]

That production of *Tosca* in the summer of 1942 was a memorable event— doubly so, in fact. For the National Opera and operagoers in Athens it marked the emergence of a new star: "That was when Maria suddenly took wing and the world of opera went wild. It was something new, and it was much needed," as Elli Niko-laidi put it. Secondly, it was a turning point for Mary herself. Her success boosted her self-confidence and equipped her to cope with her personal and family problems, as well as the first complications in her professional life; for the sudden transformation of an almost unknown teenager into a prima donna naturally aroused the alarm and hostility of some of the other, mainly female, singers in the country's only opera company. After all, to use the apt metaphor of Nikos Papachristos, "That was no little pebble that had dropped into the still waters, but a great big rock!"[42]

—m—

The rehearsals [for "Tosca"] lasted more than three months, without interruption, and I got so tired that even today that opera occupies the last place on my scale of preferences.

To Anita Pensotti (*Oggi*, January–February 1957)

CHAPTER 24

The Consequences of Success

Success—the applause of the crowds and the congratulations of the "experts"—had a catalytic effect on Mary. True, although many people subsequently claimed to have seen the stamp of greatness on her even then, many others admit that they did not foresee the future triumphs of "that unbridled eighteen-year-old girl," as Dino Yannopoulos still remembers her.* But by the standards of 1942, Maria's performance as Tosca was a tremendous hit, not least because it came as a surprise. "She was very good, no doubt about it," comments Lela Skordouli, "but the thing is, it was so unexpected!" What made the greatest impression, of course, was her acting. Here was a major new singer with real personality, with a "presence" of a different kind: more theatrical, more alive, more expressive. "She acted with every fiber of her being," as Xenia Kouroussopoulou puts it, and it was this that came as a shock to a public used to the then prevailing view that an opera star's job was to sing, and little more.[1] Success, however, with the first taste of public recognition and a certain amount of admiration expressed, was bound to have a serious effect on Mary's character, and this transformation, this metamorphosis of the chrysalis into a butterfly, inevitably had repercussions on her behavior and her relations, both private and professional.

---

*Yannopoulos was to direct Maria again in *Tosca* at the Met in 1956 (with Dimitri Mitropoulos conducting, in his one and only collaboration with her). On that occasion, during a rehearsal with the piano which Maria was observing without taking part because of a cold, Yannopoulos was standing in for Tosca in a scene with Scarpia. "I saw her signaling to me at one point," he recalls, "so I went over and, as she had been ordered by the doctor not to open her mouth, she handed me a note telling me that I had done something or other two bars earlier than we had agreed in the Athens performance! I was so astonished that the next day I asked her how on earth she could remember. Her answer was that she had not done *Tosca* so many times that she had forgotten the one in Athens. Yet that had been fourteen years earlier! Her memory really was phenomenal." (YANNOPOULOS.) It is worth noting that in those fourteen years Maria had sung Tosca again in Mexico City, Bologna, and Pisa in 1950, Rio de Janeiro in 1951, Mexico City in 1952, and Genoa in 1954, though the total number of those performances came to only eleven.

Mary had always had a tendency to act spontaneously and express her feelings openly: she had been quick-tempered and belligerent when her honesty was impugned or she was treated unfairly, persistent to the point of stubbornness in coping with difficulties, impatient and argumentative when she was sure of what she wanted, aggressive when slighted. Having decided some years earlier that she would use her musical talent to cover up and surmount her problems and insecurities, now that she seemed to be proving herself she became calmer and more optimistic. At the same time, however, her newfound self-confidence manifested itself not only in tactlessness and indiscretion (to both of which she was always prone) but in a burgeoning arrogance and provocativeness. And the first people to become aware of this change were, naturally, her mother and sister in their daily life with the "new" Mary.

The relationship between Mary and Jackie was now one of jealousy on both sides, but for different reasons. Mary envied Jackie her good looks, social graces, and success with the opposite sex, while Jackie envied Mary her talent, her fine record at the conservatory, and her engagement at the National Opera. After Mary's success in *Tosca*, these differences became more pronounced. While Mary had made a plan for her future and was already reaping the first fruits of her labors, Jackie was bogged down, both in her private life and in her musical activities. With Miltiadis, besides providing the family with support they could hardly have done without, she had a good relationship; but, as long as his father disapproved of the match, her "fiancé" did not dare marry her. As for music, in which she insisted on competing vainly with Mary, after five years she had only just been provisionally accepted into the advanced piano class and had given up singing after sounding out her prospects in that direction. Describing her own rather sad plight, Jackie cannot resist the temptation to take some nasty digs at her sister. When Mary became well-known "in occupied Athens," she says, people started referring to Jackie as "the sister of the singer." She now realized that she could never make a career in the musical world. In order to survive there, one needed not only talent but also "the instincts of a killer"; and Mary possessed those instincts, according to Jackie: she had "mastered the art of upstaging other performers, of using all the tricks that can win over an audience—and not merely on stage." What is more, Mary knew how to get her own way in the company, she says, where there were few new productions each year and few parts to be had. This astonishing talent for infighting was the result of "Mother's 'lessons' in selfishness and ill-temper, which had given Mary an unflinching desire to get her own way at all costs." Mary had inherited the martial genes of her Dimitriadis ancestors, Jackie concludes, while she herself was a true daughter of George Kaloyeropoulos.[2]

As far as Mary's relations with her mother were concerned, the main consequence of the *Tosca* success was that Mary became even more independent. Litsa had taken advantage of the Thessaloniki trip and the *Tosca* production to make herself as helpful as possible in the hope of winning back her daughter, who was slipping daily further away from her. She had been firmly ensconced in Mary's dressing room before and after every performance and during the intermissions. "Mother was everything to her," Jackie remarks, "a nursemaid, a confidante, someone to build up her courage in those nerve-racking moments before she ran on stage." Litsa was to remember these occasions for the rest of her life as some of the very few oases in the desert of her relationship with Mary. "I always chaperoned her at the theater and waited in her dressing room when she was not on stage," she says, describing herself as Mary's shadow. "I would fan her with a towel as though I were a prizefighter's second. . . . In those days she demanded much of me, and I was happy to give her what she wanted." Litsa was to offer her services for the last time at Mexico City in 1950: "Maria . . . wanted me to act as her dresser, as I had done in Athens," she would write. "Each night when she came back to the hotel, tired and exhausted, I rubbed her with alcohol and put her to bed as I had done at Patission 61."[3]

In spite of this, relations between Litsa and Mary in Athens remained very strained. "Her mother continued inviting Italians and Germans home, and in the summer would have parties on their roof terrace," says Marika Papadopoulou, who lived about 500 meters from 61 Patission Street. She remembers one evening hearing a voice singing "Vissi d'arte" in the distance: "I immediately recognized Mary's voice and, next day, I asked her what had been going on. *'Oh, the usual thing. There was a crowd of them there and I had to sing,'* she said."[4] Another thing that continued to annoy Mary was her mother's protective attitude toward Jackie. Whenever Sotos Vassiliadis was about to say anything complimentary about Mary, Litsa would cut him short. "By raising her eyebrows she would signal him not to say too much about Mary's voice and successes, because it upset Jackie," recalled Haris Vassiliadou. She believed that Litsa took this line in order to act as a buffer between the two girls: "Maria was a very strong character, unruly, willful, and self-centered. When she became successful she had a way of tormenting her sister, who couldn't defend herself. And in this case Litsa, who was equally unable to impose her will on Maria, naturally supported the underdog. To Mary's vainglorious and infuriating predictions of her own future stardom she would snap, 'Who do you think *you* are? Don't be so swell-headed!'"[5] Perhaps the main cause of their friction was now Mary's emotional attachment to Attilio De Stasio. Litsa's own affair with Mario Bonalti, however, left her in a weak position to take a stern attitude toward her daughter, and that must have been extremely irritating to such a quick-tempered and domineering mother as she was.

Apart from the rare occasions when Mary's teachers Elvira de Hidalgo and Tassia Filtsou were invited to dinner ("in order to impress them," according to Jackie), Mary was unhappy with the home environment at 61 Patission Street. She once talked to Filtsou about the constant comings and goings of visitors, who would often sit up smoking until very late in the night: *That's not a real home, a place where you can sit down and do some work,"* she told her according to Katie

Makriyanni, who also had lessons with Filtsou. One day Makriyanni saw for herself what it was like at Mary's home: "We were going toward Omonia Square when Mary got something in her eye. It was terribly painful, her eyes were streaming and she couldn't see. We walked there arm in arm, went up by the stairs, and let ourselves in with her key. There was her mother at the far end of the sitting room, with her hair dyed bright blonde—and that was something people noticed in Greece in those days—playing cards with three or four men in a cloud of smoke. She looked up and must have seen that something was wrong with her daughter, as she was leaning on my arm. But she just went on playing without a word, as if nothing was the matter. *'You see what sort of mother I've got?'* Maria whispered to me. We went to the bathroom, she washed her eye out and then I left."[6]

Ever since the bombing raids of 1940–41, when they would talk together in the darkness of the air raid shelter, Mary's sense of security had been bolstered by her friendship with Dr. Ilias Papatestas. Papatestas was about twice her age (he was born in 1906), he was shortish and unprepossessing to look at, but a well-educated and pleasant man, with a beautiful deep voice. He belonged to a well-off Piraeus medical family, had studied in Paris, and worked in Swiss sanatoria. He loved music, was sociable by nature, dressed well, and, being a doctor, still had a car.[7] Papatestas's circle of friends included Alekos Xakoustis and his sister Kiki, who, like all the rest of them, came from a well-to-do background. Kiki Xakousti, a good-looking and clever young widow, lived with her mother and daughter on Skaramanga Street, directly opposite the windows of the Kaloyeropoulos apartment. "In the corner building on the other side of the street I could see the bedroom where the two sisters slept," she recalls, "and there were times when Mary and I would call across to each other from window to window." Kiki remembers her as a pleasant, cheerful, and talkative girl, who fit in quite well with the rest of the group. The friends often gathered at the Xakoustises' apartment for a card game or just for a chat, but Mary would usually only watch for a while and then go home. "She never poured out her personal or family problems, nor did she speak out against her mother or sister. What we saw and heard, well, that's a different matter . . ." says Xakousti. As for her singing, "Mary talked optimistically about her career prospects. And even in those days she kept saying that people were fed up with seeing enormous prima donnas. *'I'm going to be a sylph!'* she would exclaim."[8]

Some people view Mary's relationship with Ilias Papatestas as one of "amorous friendship" at the most. Kiki Xakousti, for example, insists that Papatestas was simply a friend whose shoulder Mary could lean on, that theirs was "a great friendship"—which, after all, lasted for the rest of Maria's life. But Xakousti's opinion is probably biased, since she herself had an intimate liaison with Papatestas that seems to have suffered from the appearance of Mary on the scene. Others think that the amorous feelings had the upper hand, especially on Mary's side: "Perhaps partly out of gratitude for his help as a counselor," says Marika Papadopoulou,

Dr. Ilias Papatestas teases Mary on the day of her departure from Athens, 8 August 1957.

who knew Papatestas then. But she remembers "a terrific age difference" between them and qualifies the way he talked about her as "affectionate rather than amorous."[9] As for those who talk about the relationship as a "love affair," among them Ismini Thiveou knew "for a fact" from Christina Katifori (the former neighbor from Harilaou Trikoupi Street who was a close friend of Marina Papayeorgopoulou and of Litsa) that "Mary loved the doctor, who was her first lover." She insists that Litsa expressed her consternation over this to Christina: "Have you ever heard anything like it? Her with a man of *his* age!" And when Thiveou's attention is drawn to Litsa's assertion that Maria was a virgin when she married Meneghini, "No way!" she exclaims. "First she had the doctor, then an Italian, and then Mangliveras." The same inference is to be drawn from a snappish outburst of Jackie's in conversation: "She went with Papatestas, who was fifty [sic] years old to her nineteen! All those old men, for God's sake! She was always with him, and I don't believe in simple friendship between a man and a woman."[10]

In deciding on the nature of Maria's relationship with Ilias Papatestas, much more significance is to be attached to the testimony of Lalaki Kamara, a young woman who was a friend and a patient of his early in 1941: "Almost every time I was sitting in his waiting room, Mary would appear and we'd have a little chat. I knew they were very attached to each other, of course, and so I was always a bit reserved with her. What struck me, though, was the cool way she would just walk into the consulting room, even if Ilias had a patient in there. One day, annoyed by her manner, I told her it was my turn next. *'Oh, I'm not here as a patient,'* she replied, and went on in. Another time she went into the consulting room just when Ilias was giving me an intravenous injection. 'You can see the doctor's busy!' I said. *'Don't worry,'* she rejoined airily. 'Patients seeing a TB specialist don't want anyone else in the room with them,' I pointed out to her on another occasion. *'You mind your own business!'* she snapped back. She always spoke insolently, that was her way. But Ilias, who had a very soft spot for her, hardly ever reprimanded her or told her to wait outside. And she would sometimes tell jokes that made him laugh, using words that were considered shocking in those days. In fact you could say that her language was rather coarse."[11]

Every summer, to escape the worst of the heat, Papatestas spent July and August in a rented house on Georganda Street in Kifissia, which he shared with his brother Nikos or his friend Alekos Fifas and their wives. Various friends and relations would often visit them, among them Lalaki Kamara, who saw Mary several times there. "We would have lunch on the veranda and then sit around talking. On those occasions Mary didn't give herself airs because of the presence of the others, especially Ilias's brother. I don't know if she ever stayed in Kifissia overnight, but I don't remember ever seeing her at similar gatherings in the evenings." According to Kamara, however, Mary's relationship with Ilias was unquestionably a sexual one as well. "I think Mary was in love with Ilias, and even he, an inveterate womanizer, had no other lady friends at that time and was devoted to her. She was certainly his mistress even though she was a gawky, hefty lump and slightly pigeon-toed. Ilias evidently found her attractive in spite of that, and he was not the sort of man to 'respect' her just because she was a young girl. In fact, considering that their affair started in 1941, he may well have been the first man in her life." Asked what she thought about Litsa's statement that Meneghini had been Mary's first lover, Kamara retorts, "Don't you believe it! Mary was in love with Ilias and he was as good as a husband to her. He came from a good family, was well respected, well educated, an attractive man, and not only well-off but generous with it. Quite possibly he helped Mary financially as well."[12]

The relationship, whatever its nature and although not necessarily exclusive of others, lasted until 1944. "If Ilias's friend Alekos Fifas hadn't made him marry his wife's sister, I think Ilias might well have kept up his affair with Mary even longer," concludes Lalaki Kamara. It is hard to imagine what effect the continuation of this liaison would have had on Mary's career. Be that as it may, however, Ilias remained her lifelong friend. During her unhappy stay in Athens in 1957 she saw him frequently, dining out with him quite openly at least twice, and it was he who took her to see the ENT specialist Solon Kotsaridas when her voice went hoarse just before her first concert at the Odeon of Herodes Atticus.[13] When Papatestas talked about Maria in 1963, by which time she was the constant companion of Aristotle Onassis, he was particularly concerned to clear her of the charges of having consorted with Italians during the war. He described the accusations as a wicked and malicious fabrication and attempted to put all the blame on Litsa, referring to her "fairly intimate dealings" with Italians. Mary, he said, had loathed this "sick state of affairs" and had done everything in her power to prevent it, but Litsa had persisted stubbornly in her ways. Allowing himself to be carried away into blatant exaggeration, Papatestas asserted that Mary could not stand the sight of Italians and Germans, whom she saw not as human beings but as conquerors. Such was her "disgust and loathing" of her home environment that, when the Axis officers left, she would open the windows to let in the fresh air and get rid of the smell of them. She had tried to bring her mother around to her point of view, he insisted, but had been brushed aside. "You mind your own ways and don't meddle in my life," Litsa is said to have retorted. "You're too young to see things as they really are."[14]

According to Papatestas, when undesirable visitors came to the apartment, Mary would go out to friends' houses—more often than not to his place. Whatever her reason for going there, the fact is that in those days Mary did spend a good deal of time in Ilias's clinic on the ground floor of 61 Patission. Whether it was a convenient place for her to wait until she could go back up to the fifth floor, or she simply enjoyed his company, or she was initiated by him to the secrets of sexual love—in any case it is beyond any doubt that she did pour out her heart to the paternally protective doctor. So it is not surprising that what started as friendly affection developed, as it seems to have done, into sexual love and—as far as Mary was concerned—a lasting emotional dependence. In 1963 Papatestas said: "I really loved that young girl. To me she was a very good friend and a very good companion in the tough times of the occupation." He described Mary as "a little girl without the least trace of femininity" who could not possibly arouse lust. "I am not trying to suggest that Mary was incapable of emotion," he added, in an attempt to shield her from the persistent scurrilous charges, "but it came out only in true love, not in sexual desire."[15] We shall never know just what sort of relationship Mary did have with Ilias, nor whether he was for sure "the first man in her life." One thing that cannot be denied, however, is that Dr. Papatestas, then approaching forty, was the first considerably older man who played a really important part in her private life, and in whom Mary was subconsciously looking for the father she had been deprived of.

—⁂—

In the professional environment of the National Opera Mary was not really different from the person she was at home and in her private life. The picture of her that generally prevailed was of a quiet, unassuming, ordinary girl who, when somebody annoyed her, questioned her value, or provoked her, became uncontrollably aggressive and antagonistic. Already in the preceding three years Mary's sense of insecurity in her personal, family, social, and financial affairs had caused her to behave toward others in a way which made her generally disliked. She was not by nature a tactful person, and, in any case, it would be unreasonable to expect a young girl to behave with restraint at the very moment of her triumphant début and first experience of public acclamation. Her feeling of undisguised self-satisfaction first became apparent in a tendency to be generally more extroverted. While it may be true that Mary did not meddle in other singers' business and certainly did not actively try to outshine them, she became even more liable to fly at anyone who questioned her ability or opposed her interests. In the words of Dino Yannopoulos, "She was a difficult person. In those days it was impossible to have a quiet conversation with her. She was a dynamic personality who struck fear and terror into the other singers. She was always right. You couldn't argue with her."[16]

To Mary, who had now proved on stage that her artistic egocentricity was no vain conceit, the fact of her superior ability was perfectly natural and reasonable. Anyone who happened to go against this "inescapable reality" was bound to provoke her fury and indignation. Not only were her opinions dogmatic but she was in the habit of speaking her mind bluntly, sometimes even rudely. In the words of Andonis Kalaidzakis, "Her bluntness was shocking and unnerving. She was very direct. And heaven help you if you offended her! She would listen to criticism, but she didn't like you to make it sound like a final judgment. She had to give her own critical faculty time to work on it."[17] Every little difference of opinion was eventually blown up into a full-scale row, a vicious spiral in which Mary was often responsible for the escalation. Unsophisticated though she was, she considered the traditional theatrical conventions to be a waste of time and the ways of the older singers, whose languid expressions and movements recalled the era of silent films, to be outmoded, not to say ridiculous. So it was not long before Mary found herself the target of covert hostility and slander, which would keep her in obscurity for more than a year. At first the older singers kept their irritation to themselves, as Mary's laurels were still very fresh, and anyway the bumptious young upstart had no more parts in the new winter season, nor did she even have a contract. From the beginning of the 1943–44 winter season, however, when she would start making her presence felt in the National Opera once again, that hostility would come out into the open. Mary would then find herself at the center of much backstage infighting, some instances of which are described in the following chapters.

Although she herself never initiated any of the intrigues, she felt obliged to defend herself, and in her view attack was the only means of defense. To the end of her life this daughter of Litsa, with Louros blood in her veins, never managed to pass over a challenge without fighting back, often with savage ferocity and intemperate rage. She declared in 1961, "*I hate the nervous mental confusion [fights and quarrels] engender. But if I have to fight—I'll fight!*" According to a Greek journalist who, like many others, failed to understand the psychological processes that sparked off her aggressiveness, "In the National Opera she conveyed an impression of unbelievable brazenness, always ready to take up the cudgels with anyone, to devour anyone who stood in her way." Mary provoked so many incidents, we are told, that in the end "she made enemies of everyone and aroused nothing but antipathy, hatred, and jealousy."[18]

Although this version of events makes out the exceptions to have been the rule, there certainly were some unpleasant occasions when Mary had no hesitation in defending herself with ferocity, sometimes even with physical force. Her anger set her tongue working faster than her brain, her fiery youthful temperament allowed her no time to think before acting (or reacting). *"If I have stepped on some people at times because I am at the top, it couldn't be helped,"* she snapped in 1958, *"What would I do if someone gets hurt—retire?"* Even in later life Maria never acquired the wisdom to accept hostility as the necessary price of success and happiness, let alone the maturity to turn the other cheek to her adversary. Onassis advised her that instead of reacting to this sort of behavior from her colleagues she should go out of her way to be nice to them, while leaving them in no doubt that she was well aware of their hostile designs. But she was never able to take such a mature attitude. *"That woman's got her knife into me, and you expect me to help her? I'm not crazy!"* she fulminated on one occasion.[19]

Most of Mary's opera colleagues thought she was older than she said she was. It was partly her physical development that gave them this impression, but more than that it was her manner, her readiness with a pertinent retort, her remarkable air of savoir-faire. It was also her aggressive way of speaking, perhaps partly due to her American upbringing, which may have been intended to cover up a sense of inferiority but which most people took as unpleasant insolence. Elvira Mataranga, who was then in the chorus, remembers that once, when Yokarinis was offering *halvá* (a great luxury in those days) to some of the singers in his office, Mary suddenly turned to the general manager and said, *"Come on then, Niko, get up from there and let me make a few phone calls!"* "Yokarinis looked at us and tapped his head with his finger to suggest that she wasn't quite all there, but he got up from his chair!" Mataranga says. Later, too, Mary used to address Kalomiris by his first name, using the familiar second person singular: *"Listen, Manoli, please, just go outside, will you?"* Mitsa Kourahani agrees that Mary didn't behave in the least like the child she still was, and she still wonders at her effrontery: "How could she have the nerve to talk like that to general managers, directors, and older colleagues?"[20] In other words, one of the main reasons why Mary was always quarreling was that she had none of the social graces, had not learned how to avoid pitfalls, shrugging off the sort of provocation that was as much a part of life in Greece's National Opera as in any other theater in the world.

However, as it will become clear, those who had serious differences with her, either because they could not stand her as a person or because they saw her as a threat to their careers, were not very numerous. When she first came up against professional hostility during the production of *Boccaccio*, we saw her being upset, surprised, and angry at first. From then on she started viewing everybody as a potential enemy and, as Elli Nikolaidi said, "Feeling bitter about the few people who really were hostile to her, she imagined that everybody was against her." Even in those days in Greece Mary was cultivating the idea that the hostility toward her in the National Opera was more general than it really was. Feeling unfairly persecuted, she often hinted at a conspiracy against her, reinforcing her allegations by alluding to instances of hostility or latent rivalry toward her. She may also have sensed that it could be useful to make herself out to be a victim of mediocrities banding together—as mediocrities always will—to suppress real talent, a casualty of the conflict between the good and the bad, the competent and the incompetent, the guileless and the sly. The long wait until her recognition in 1944 put a considerable strain on her, and in later life, when she needed to explain it away, she exaggerated the importance of everyday rivalries and petty squabbles, which were thus accepted without argument into the Callas mythology. However, this feeling of being surrounded by enemies clearly suited Mary's temperament. She took the greatest pleasure in surmounting an obstacle, never letting a difficulty get her down: "*I like challenge*," she admitted with a laugh in 1968, and already in 1956 she was quoted as saying, "*When I'm angry I can do no wrong. I sing and act like someone possessed.*"[21]

For the time being what mattered was that, despite her success as Tosca, Mary was not taken on to the payroll of the National Opera. All her biographers have repeated Litsa's statement that in 1942, after *Tosca*, Mary was made a leading soprano at a monthly salary of 3,000 drachmas, a sum so paltry that it all went on ersatz wartime sweets and ice cream. Facts, however, are quite different. At the beginning of the 1942–43 season the basic salaries of the twenty soloists ranged from 5,800 to 16,000 drachmas, and they were very soon increased. After the Drs. 40,000 that Mary was paid for her appearances in August and September 1942, the next salary she received was a sum of Drs. 59,000, again for two months' work (January and February 1943) as one of seven extra choristers in Kalomiris's *O Protomastoras*. Not until March 1943, however, fully six months after *Tosca*, does her name appear on the regular payroll of the National Opera. Her monthly salary then was Drs. 30,000, the highest rate on the payroll, also paid to eight other female soloists. By then, however, the rate of pay had become of purely nominal significance. "Inflation was running so high that our salary lost its value from one day to the next. In the end it just about covered the price of a pair of stockings," says Marika Papadopoulou. So, from the beginning of 1943, singers were paid the price of a daily meal at the soup kitchens, as well as "a cost of living allowance" of Drs. 260,000 per month! And before long this too would be overtaken by inflation, with the result that in August 1943 the allowance would be doubled.[22]

But we are getting ahead of the story. It is still late 1942 and Mary, bursting with energy and self-confidence, is to all intents and purposes temporarily out of work. She is continuing with her studies at the Athens Conservatory as a matter of form, and of course she is still having lessons with de Hidalgo, who is giving her as much help and support as she can. De Hidalgo was to say later that she had found Mary a job with the Italians, without specifying where, when, or what kind of work. There is no evidence to corroborate this statement, and it seems unlikely to have been a regular job. Litsa complains in her memoirs that de Hidalgo did not find any work for Mary, with the Italians or with anyone else. She concedes only that de Hidalgo did send Mary one pupil so ungifted that she herself had refused to teach him (or her).[23] With de Hidalgo's help, however, Mary did her best to go on appearing in public so that her name would continue to be heard in musical circles. In this she was greatly aided by her teacher's contacts with highly placed Italians working in the Casa d'Italia, especially Mario Alberici da Barbiano, the "arts officer" of the Italian forces and music critic of *Il Giornale di Roma*, and Attilio De Stasio, inspector of all the Fascist organizations in Greece and their various cells.

—◊—

Numerous concerts and other artistic events were organized by the Benito Mussolini Fascio of Athens, the Gabriele D'Annunzio Fascio of Piraeus, and the Dopolavoro delle Forze Armate, Grecia, for Fascist party members and the officers and men of the Italian 11th Army. Some were held in various cinemas or the open-air marble Stadium, but most concerts and lectures were given in the auditorium of the Casa d'Italia at 47 Patission Street, where the Italian Cultural Institute still has its premises today. In those days it was run along the lines of the Fascist Dopolavori (recreation centers) as a sort of club for the Italian community in Athens. Unfortunately the records of the Casa d'Italia were destroyed when the building was sacked by furious mobs after the liberation, so we do not have particulars of all the concerts at which Mary sang in 1942 and 1943. However, it is beyond dispute that she performed there quite a number of times, as did many other well-known Greek singers.

Needless to say, in using her entrée to the Casa d'Italia, de Hidalgo gave preference to her pupils. Spyros Salingaros recalls an occasion when Mireille Fléri was to give a concert at the Casa with Andonis Delendas. Fléri fell sick a day or two before, and de Hidalgo asked Mary to take her place at the last minute.[24] Mitsa Kourahani relates that "sometime in 1942 or 1943" the Casa sent a note to the National Opera asking for a tenor, a soprano, and a mezzo-soprano to sing in an oratorio in Italian. On this occasion Delendas, Mary, and Kourahani were sent and, on the day before the concert, the person in charge (probably Barbiano) realized that the oratorio was not long enough for a full concert program. When he asked the singers to throw in the love duet from *Madama Butterfly*, Delendas turned to Mary and asked her if she knew it. "*No, but never mind, I'll learn it,*" she answered. "But the concert's tomorrow!" "*Never mind, I'll learn it!*" she insisted. To continue in Kourahani's words: "We went straight off to Delendas's house, where he showed her some of the points to be careful of, and Mary took the score home with her. The next morning we went to the Casa for the final rehearsal, and after the oratorio the organizer asked for the duet. The way Maria sang it—with the music in front of her, of course—was just amazing! Delendas turned to her and said, 'Hey, that's fantastic! You're really going to be a great singer!' '*I am!*' Maria retorted, thumping the piano with her fist. And she picked up her music and stormed out, leaving us all thunderstruck." There was a distinct touch of theatricality in Mary's excessively self-important reaction. No doubt she had been stung by the use of the future tense, implying that she was not already a great singer. Eventually she apologized to Delendas and admitted to Kourahani that she was "*a bit nervous.*" The concert was an unqualified success. After the oratorio Mary sang "Vogliatemi bene" with Delendas, reading from the score, and both were loudly applauded. Instead of being paid in cash, the soloists and the pianist left their names and addresses, and the Italians sent them food, in accordance with the usual practice.[25]

There were three other concerts at the Casa d'Italia in which Mary definitely sang: on 9 January, on 21 April, and on 16 May 1943. On 19 December 1942 Barbiano repeated in Athens the lecture he had given in Thessaloniki in June for the celebration of the 150th anniversary of Rossini's birth. The Athens talk was followed on 9 January 1943 by an all-Rossini concert. Stefanos Valtetsiotis and Andreas Paridis accompanied in turn the five soloists: Mary, soprano Mary Tambassi, mezzo Mitsa Kourahani, tenor Michalis Kazandzis, and bass Yorgos Moulas. In his review of the concert in *Il Giornale di Roma*, Barbiano wrote that the large audience included senior officers and cadres of the fascio led by De Stasio, while the singers included some "very young and well prepared, who might be called promising newcomers if they had not already given examples of their very considerable talents at public concerts and stage performances." Among them "Signorina Maria Calojeropulo" [sic], who in the quartet ["Sancta Mater"] and duet ["Quis est homo"] from the *Stabat Mater*, the rondo from *La Cenerentola*, and the cavatina from *Semiramide* "reconfirmed the admirable vocal and expressive gifts which we had already noted when we heard her in other concerts and the National Opera production of *Tosca*." Barbiano also commended the "uncommon quality" of mezzo-soprano Mitsa Kourahani, "whose voice blended perfectly in intonation and tone with that of Signorina Calojeropulo, thanks to their excellent training at the same school under Elvira de Hidalgo."[26]

The second concert at the Casa d'Italia in which Mary took part was on 21 April 1943, which was the Wednesday of Holy Week in the Orthodox Church and one day before the concert at the Italian Cultural Institute, at which she sang in a performance of Pergolesi's *Stabat Mater*. The Casa concert, advertised as "vocal and instrumental," was part of an out-and-out Fascist celebration of the "birth of Rome," that is to say, the anniversary of the city's foundation in the eighth century B.C., for which the hall was decked with the flags of the Axis powers. It was attended by Italian Consul General Nuccio and Major De Stasio, as well as delegations of Italian Fascists and their Greek sympathizers. The proceedings started with introductory formalities, culminating in a full-throated acclamation of the king-emperor and Il Duce. The music was organized as usual by the Dopolavoro of the Athens Benito Mussolini Fascio. Most probably the accompaniment was provided only by a piano, but the pianist remains unknown. The tenor Lambros Mavrakis sang "Che gelida manina" from *La Bohème*, followed by Mary who sang "Ritorna vincitor" from *Aida* and the song "Il Ballo" by Pizzetti. She was followed by Petros Epitropakis in *romanze* by Tosti and Penino (probably the well-known "Pecché?"), and then mezzo-soprano Lysimachi Anastasiadou sang "O mio Fernando" from *La Favorita* and a *romanza* by Tosti. While the applause was still reverberating, Andonis Delendas continued with two arias from *La Fanciulla del West* and *La Gioconda*, and finally soprano Mary Tambassi sang "Ernani involami" from *Ernani* and a song by Arditi (probably the famous "Il Bacio"). "These artists, already well known and highly regarded by the public for their vocal and interpretative prowess," commented *Il Giornale di Roma* next day, "were acclaimed with tumultuous applause at the end of every piece. At the end of the program the artists sang one more piece each, most of them choosing Italian folk songs or *romanze da camera*. Finally the large audience of comrades crowding the auditorium of the Casa d'Italia showed its enthusiasm with a fervent display of devotion to Il Duce."[27]

The third of Mary's known appearances for the Benito Mussolini Fascio at the Casa d'Italia was at the celebration of "Italians Around the World Day" on Sunday, 16 May 1943. At about ten o'clock that morning the official guests were greeted by a guard of honor of the Fascist Youth of Greece (GILE) at the marble steps leading up to the main hall. This was again decked with Italian and German flags and it was soon packed to overflowing, with generals, staff officers, Italian diplomats, and officials of the Fascist organizations occupying the front rows. Professor Bianchini, secretary of the local fascio, delivered the opening address in honor of the king and Il Duce; next, Consul General Nuccio paid tribute to the ten million Italian colonists and other expatriates around the world; then Professor Ferrarino, director of the Italian Cultural Institute in Athens, gave a speech on "Italy and Africa" with readings from the poetry of Gabriele D'Annunzio. In the first half of the concert that followed, the "virtuoso" violinist Giovanni Battista Dantone—Mary's personal friend—played Paganini and Beethoven and conducted a string orchestra in pieces by Handel and Mascagni. After the intermission, Valtetsiotis accompanied at the piano Lysimachi Anastasiadou, Andonis Delendas, and Mary who sang "*romanze* and duets from Italian operas," according to the review in the *Deutsche Nachrichten in Griechenland*, "with prolonged applause after each number."[28]

From the purely musical point of view, those concerts enriched Mary's repertoire by the addition of the duet from *Madama Butterfly*, the duet "Quis est homo" and the quartet "Sancta Mater" from Rossini's *Stabat Mater*, and the aria "Nacqui all'affanno" from *La Cenerentola*. The last of these and the aria "Bel raggio lusing-hier" from *Semiramide* were showpieces of vocal virtuosity that were to remain in her repertoire when she was at the height of her career. However, these fairly detailed descriptions are of interest not so much as records of Mary's musical progress as for what they tell us about the atmosphere of the concerts outside the National Opera at which Mary sang during this period. The first point to note is the number of Greek singers who took part, although the events were organized by the loathed enemy. Even those with leftist political views seldom missed such oppor-tunities to make a public appearance, to further their careers and be rewarded for their services, usually with food that could not otherwise be obtained at any price. Of course there was no question of their being accused of collaboration. The case of Sophia Vembo, the Greek equivalent of Vera Lynn, who could equally be said to have compromised herself by singing at a German musical soirée, has already been mentioned. No one held that against her, any more than they blamed Epitropakis or Delendas for these or other appearances at the Casa d'Italia. So there is no justi-fication for singling Mary out as a collaborator on these grounds alone.

In her case, however, her accusers have concentrated much more on her social intercourse with Italians (making no distinction between her own and her moth-er's friendships) than on her "collaboration" in the field of music. It need hardly be said that there is an important difference between the two. In the matter of giving musical performances for the enemy, Mary can be absolved of all guilt and so can all the other musicians who did the same, except in a few cases where the collaboration was unnecessarily regular and motivated by sheer self-interest. But where personal relationships are concerned, matters are far less clear and each instance has to be considered in light of circumstances, having particular regard to the motives and intentions in each case. In Mary's case it is beyond question that she did have close friendships with a number of Italians on a clearly personal basis. We have seen how dangerously she seems to have exposed herself in the winter of 1941–42 and her subsequent traumatic love affair with the paratrooper Angiolo Dondoli. In these cases—for which the available evidence is very meager—she cannot be considered entirely blameless, although each case must be judged indi-vidually. Certainly the fact that she was encouraged by her mother to fraternize with the occupying forces does mitigate her guilt to some extent, but by that time she had won a considerable degree of independence and was largely responsible for making her own decisions in her private life. We have also seen that she had per-sonal contacts in the Italian commissariat whence she regularly obtained meat and other foodstuffs. And from the summer of 1942 Mary had acquired "a high-rank-ing officer provider of food," who was probably none other than the all-powerful Attilio De Stasio, inspector of the Fasci in Greece.

According to Jackie, it was at a concert at the Casa d'Italia, sometime during 1942, that Mary attracted the notice of a senior Italian army officer, whom she calls *di* Stasio and describes as "no ordinary major but something shadowy in the intelligence sector of the Italian command. In other words a man to be avoided at all costs." Her sister had found an admirer, Jackie adds, "a man who religiously attended all her concerts and who had quickly made himself known to her." Now, as she generally does when asked about her sister's love life during the occupation, Jackie clams up, and about De Stasio she only says that "he admired her and brought her flowers." Yet in her book she is less cagey: "Finding it impossible to emulate my successes with men," she remarks, re-emphasizing her own superiority in this respect, "she had only Mother's example to copy and at the moment that was a particularly bad example."[29] The fact that Litsa had an Italian lover herself made Mary unwilling to take any criticism of her own behavior. Kyriakos Papayeorgopoulos, the brother of Marina, who rented a room in the Patission Street apartment, once found himself caught in the crossfire between mother and daughter when he was visiting his sister there. *"You mind your own ways and don't meddle in mine!"* he heard Mary shout. And when Captain Papayeorgopoulos (as he then was) remonstrated with her sharply, she turned to him defiantly and retorted, *"What goes on between us is nothing to do with you. We'll settle our differences by ourselves. Would you please mind your own business!"*[30]

Mary's new admirer, Attilio De Stasio, had his office at the Casa d'Italia, only a few steps away from 61 Patission Street. He may have been an army officer, but when his name is mentioned in the press—where he is often ranked next in order of precedence after the minister plenipotentiary, the consul general, and the commander in chief of the Italian forces in Greece—he is referred to simply as *camerata* (comrade), a term of address used then by the Fascists.[31] It is practically certain that De Stasio met Mary in May 1942 or thereabouts, probably in connection with the Rossini celebrations in Thessaloniki. We know that Litsa approached "a Fascist officer named De Stasio" to ask to be included in the party herself. She never mentions him again, though her reference to "the Italians who loved Maria [and] welcomed her back to Athens by bringing her more food" may well allude to him. What is more, Litsa tells us that at about then Mary started showing an interest in fortune-telling, which Litsa practiced by reading coffee grounds or cards.[32] Knowing what we now do about Mary's brief but very deeply felt attachment to Angiolo Dondoli at that very time, there is a fair chance that her interest in knowing the future was due to the emotional confusion his presence had caused in her. On the other hand, since Dondoli had vanished as suddenly as he had appeared, quite possibly Mary was concerned about her relationship with Attilio De Stasio.

Jackie maintains that De Stasio—"an old man, at least twice Mary's age," which would still make him about forty or forty-five—was her "first real romance." Mary herself kept quiet about it at home until she found it impossible to go on hiding her emotions and her excitement. In the smug and suggestive words of her sister, "I knew too well what poor dumpy Mary wanted; she just longed for someone to be nice to her, to flatter her and tell her all the things she believed as a woman she had a right to hear. If di Stasio had realized that, then he would have everything he wished. Of course I tried to talk to her about it but by then it was useless. '*Jealous, are you?*' she retorted." In Jackie's view this attitude summed up Mary's complexes, described selectively as her desire to be loved and to compete with her older and more beautiful sister.[33] So, taking no notice of her sister's advice and probably hoping to annoy her mother, Mary now spent even more of her time away from home, not only at her lessons with de Hidalgo but also having regular clandestine meetings with Attilio.

Nothing is known about the precise nature of Mary's relationship with De Stasio, except from Jackie's assertion that she fell in love with him and her insinuation that her sister suffered when he eventually stopped reciprocating her feelings. "In her usual pressing way with men, Mary chased him mercilessly, sometimes waiting for hours outside his office, until she realized that he had left from the back door in order to avoid her!" Nevertheless, the relationship lasted several months at least, and perhaps until the Italians were driven out of Greece by the Germans in September 1943. With their precipitate departure, which also took Bonalti away from Litsa, "the Italian situation resolved itself," as Jackie puts it, since both De Stasio and Bonalti disappeared overnight. No matter how upset Mary may have been, however, she still did not confide in her sister. "This sudden, even violent, end to her first real romance . . . must have been a terrible time for her," Jackie thought, adding rather tartly that it did not take Mary long to get over the blow: her musical commitments soon came to dominate her life again, which showed "how much the theatrical life had already replaced the world of real emotions for her."[34]

—⁕—

That's been the trouble with my career, I've always had to fight. But I don't like it. . . . Up to now I've generally won, but never with any feeling of elation. They are bleak triumphs, simply because it was necessary to fight in the first place. When I fight, it's almost always my fundamental beliefs—my artistic credo—which are at stake.

To Derek Prouse, London (*The Sunday Times*, 2 April 1961)

CHAPTER 25

Sporadic Appearances and Serious Developments

At the end of October 1942 the British launched their offensive in Egypt. The El Alamein front was soon broken and the Germans went into retreat. On 28 October, the second anniversary of Metaxas's historic "No!" to the Italian ultimatum, flags and wreaths appeared as if by magic on the trees and marble busts in front of Athens University. Spirits soared as protest marches converged from several parts of the capital on the tomb of the unknown soldier; but the marchers were eventually dispersed by tanks, Italian cavalry, and fire hoses. When news of the blowing-up of the Gorgopotamos railway viaduct reached Athens toward the end of November, unseen hands started painting resistance slogans on the walls, while roadblocks and body searches in the streets were intensified. Power shortages did much to make life miserable for Athenians, who had a gloomy Christmas. Shops closed at four o'clock, the streetcars now stopped running at six, and such food as there was to be found was priced out of most people's reach. Yet against this background of general misery a faint hope of liberation had begun to glimmer. It was kept alive by the news from North Africa and Russia and by the resistance movements, which were gathering strength in the Greek mountains and gradually making some headway in the cities as well. In February 1943 it was rumored that the collaborationist government was about to declare civil mobilization and EAM, the civil arm of the communist resistance movement, responded by staging protest meetings and strikes. Now the occupation forces no longer had any scruples about firing on demonstrators at random, but the civil mobilization order was eventually suspended, and on 7 April 1943 Ioannis Rallis, an experienced and widely trusted politician, was sworn in as the new prime minister.

Against this troubled background, at the end of 1942 the National Opera had started rehearsals for its new production, a musical tragedy by Manolis Kalomiris entitled *O Protomastoras* (*The Master Builder*). The libretto, adapted from the play of the same name by Nikos Kazandzakis, deals with the legend of the bridge of Arta, which will not remain standing until the master builder's true love is immured alive in it. Since no woman can be found who answers this description, the local ruler decrees that the master builder himself must be sacrificed, where-

319

upon the ruler's daughter Smaragda comes forward and declares that she is the fated victim. Her despairing cries can be heard to the very end of the opera from inside the foundations, where she has been buried alive.[1] This was Kalomiris's first opera, written thirty years earlier, in 1913, a milestone in the history of modern Greek music. The composer made no secret of the fact that he was strongly influenced by Wagner, giving the orchestra a prominent part and making extensive use of leitmotifs and other devices borrowed from the Wagnerian music drama.

In the rehearsals for *O Protomastoras*, directed by Leonidas Zoras, Mary made her reappearance with the National Opera after nearly four months' absence. But this time she was not cast as a principal. Between the two acts a double chorus of peasant and gypsy women—corresponding to the chorus in ancient Greek tragedy—sets out the dilemma facing the master builder: the choice between transitory happiness and moral duty. To help in this technically difficult Intermezzo, Kalomiris decided to reinforce the chorus with seven female soloists (Kitsa Damasioti, Eleni Kokkori, Irma Kolassi, Mitsa Kourahani, Frangiska Nikita, Aliki Zografou, and Mary), who sang virtually *in camera*, half-hidden behind a transparent curtain placed across the stage. The peasant women encourage the master builder: "Harden your heart like steel, do not bend. You did not come into the world to enjoy yourself in idle revelry: you came to lay foundations, to build." To which the gypsies answer, "What are all the bridges in the world, compared to one kiss?" *O Protomastoras* was given its first performance at 4 p.m. on Friday, 19 February 1943, and ran until 20 March. The critics were unanimous in their praise of the production as a whole and of the select chorus for the Intermezzo in particular. Friedrich Herzog, the new arts editor of the *Deutsche Nachrichten in Griechenland*, called it an important artistic event and reserved special praise for the choruses which play such a large part in the action. This was the only time that Mary appeared on the stage of the National Theater on Ayiou Konstantinou Street.[2]

In the midst of political ferment, and while *O Protomastoras* was still in the early part of its run, Mary took part in a benefit concert in support of student soup kitchens and other charitable activities of the Hestia of Nea Smyrni. It was held on Sunday morning, 28 February, at the Sporting Cinema in Nea Smyrni, about four kilometers south of the center of Athens. With her in the concert were two other National Opera soloists, Petros Epitropakis and Kitsa Damasioti, and a male chorus. The pianist was Yerasimos Koundouris, de Hidalgo's class's main accompanist, and Mary was on in the first half, singing an aria from *Aida* (probably "Ritorna vincitor") and Floria Tosca's "Vissi d'arte." She was listed as "Mary Kaloyeropoulou (soprano)" in the program of this "special grand concert," printed in Greek, German, and Italian.[3] At exactly the same time on that sunny winter Sunday, not far from where Mary was singing, Greece was paying its last respects to the great poet Kostis Palamas, in a spontaneous fervor of patriotic enthusiasm.

"On this bier lies Greece!" cried the poet Angelos Sikelianos, and the thousands of people that had gathered at the main Athens cemetery bade farewell to Palamas by singing the national anthem.

It was probably in March 1943 that Mary announced to her mother and sister that she was going to sing in Pergolesi's *Stabat Mater* on Holy Thursday, 22 April, at the Italian Cultural Institute (Istituto di Cultura Italiana per la Grecia). The institute, situated on Zalokosta Street near Syntagma Square, was a propaganda organization founded in 1932, with a library, a record collection, and a lecture hall. That Easter concert was organized by the institute in collaboration with the Italian commissariat for Greek broadcasting, and the *Stabat Mater* was to be broadcast on the radio. "I begged her not to do it but she was by then beyond control," writes Jackie in her memoirs, meaning that Mary was then so infatuated with De Stasio, one of the organizers of the concert, that she could not see that her involvement in an event of this kind could damage her reputation. The contralto part in the *Stabat Mater* was to be sung by Arda Mandikian, who insists that she was coerced into taking part—an attitude adopted all too easily by those who wish to defend themselves from stigmas which they do not hesitate to hurl at others, in this case at Mary. One day, she recalls, de Hidalgo marched into the classroom and announced: "Calojeropoulou et Mandikian, vous allez chanter le *Stabat Mater* de Pergolesi!" On being told they were to sing at the Italian Cultural Institute, Mandikian protested but was overruled by her teacher: "Qui croyez-vous être? Calojeropoulou chante, Delendas chante, tout le monde chante!" de Hidalgo snapped back at her in front of Mary, "who had already agreed," Mandikian adds, implying that she was less willing than Mary to accept.[4]

Be that as it may, the rehearsals were held at the Athens Conservatory (including a few with the orchestra in the Great Hall) and at the homes of de Hidalgo and Mandikian. The concert was attended by a fair-sized audience of about a hundred and fifty persons, most of them senior Italian officers. One of the few Greeks present was the budding composer Manos Hadzidakis, then an eighteen-year-old student at the Athens Conservatory. He was so impressed by Mary's singing on this occasion that he became a devoted follower of hers from then on. According to Psaroudas, the performance was "truly something out of the ordinary" and the two soloists "left the audience genuinely moved by the musicality, deep understanding, great expressiveness, and perfect articulation with which they sang these prayerful words." Jackie notes that Mary seemed well pleased with herself afterward, but the two soloists came in for a good deal of criticism, especially in the Athens Conservatory: "Their name was mud. After all, what business did they have singing for the Italians?" comments one who was a piano student at the conservatory with Mary. Of course, it is always easy for outsiders to criticize and, as we have seen, matters were not so simple for the singers concerned: not only was it very difficult for them to refuse, but they often met Italians and Germans who were genuine music-lovers.[5]

Singing Pergolesi's *Stabat Mater* with Arda Mandikian under Yorgos Lykoudis, Athens, 22 April 1943.

Jackie maintains in her memoirs that the *Stabat Mater* concert was arranged on the initiative of De Stasio, implying that Mary's appearance was the determining factor. Although it is true that Mary generally did have her interests in mind, it seems unfair to accuse her of pursuing her relationship with De Stasio for ulterior motives. She was, after all, nineteen years old, and what must surely have mattered most to her then—besides her career—was to find a man who made her feel fulfilled as a woman and boosted her self-confidence. She would always be susceptible to admiration and flattery, even at the height of her fame; how much more so now, in the time of her greatest insecurity about her physical self as a woman? Moreover, in conversation Jackie herself insists that this was the theme running through all the daydreams Mary had been forced to suppress: "She wanted to get married and have a family, she wanted it like mad! And she said the same to her confidante Marina Papayeorgopoulou: '*I want a family, I want to get married! Why don't they want* me? *What's Jackie got that I haven't?*' 'But you've got your voice,' Marina would answer. '*I don't want my voice! I want a family, I want a man of my own!*'"[6]

There is, however, good evidence to suggest that even if young Mary really did feel such a strong desire for marriage and a family, her success in *Tosca* made her begin to think of her singing as a substitute for emotional fulfillment. Now that she had had her first real taste of professional success and having glimpsed the career prospects that were opening up before her, she was more self-sufficient and selective in her personal relationships. Another major factor behind this change was, naturally, the experience of her first amorous involvements and love affairs. Papatestas, Dondoli, and De Stasio (and perhaps others too), each in his own way, must have helped to make Mary's magical dream come true, by giving her answers to fundamental questions and allaying some of her deep-seated insecurities. Admittedly her unsatisfied desire for children was to be a sorrow to her throughout her life. "*Where did I fail?*" she would ask rhetorically in her last interview, in 1977. "*Why, I failed to fulfill myself as a woman, because what I always wanted, even more than success, was to be a mother and have lots of children. If I could start out all over again I would have at least six children, four boys and two girls. We Greeks put our family life before everything else.*"[7] But from 1943 onward, when Mary/Maria was building her career, she was less and less willing to sacrifice her artistic future to her personal life.

The factors that carried most weight with her now were the demands of her career and her ever-increasing dedication to her professional future. Things would change again only after her marriage and when her career had taken off. "*I have to make a confession. I want so much for us to have a baby. I also believe a baby would be good for my voice and my bad skin,*" she would write to her husband from Mexico City in 1950, as her desire for motherhood resurfaced. But at about the same time she would confess to her mother: "*I can't have children, and I'm so unhappy! If I could have twins and die the next day, I would be happy!*"[8] Jackie says that Mary had started menstruating at the age of ten, and according to Stelios Galatopoulos Maria herself later confided that she had begun to have menopausal problems even before she was thirty, that is to say, before 1953. Meneghini himself would confirm later that Maria was unable to have a child because she displayed symptoms of premature menopause, adding that malformation of the uterus had been diagnosed and that she had refused an operation which held out little hope of success. Meneghini never believed Maria's pregnancy by Onassis, who is said to have persuaded her to have an abortion in 1966. "Knowing her character and her great yearning for motherhood," he wrote, "I am also certain that if she *had* become pregnant, she would never have agreed to an abortion, for any reason in the world."[9]

—⁂—

For the remainder of the 1942–43 opera season, approval was given for the staging of Ponchielli's *La Gioconda* and Donizetti's *Lucia di Lammermoor*, and Mary was being prepared for the title role of *La Gioconda*—a part which she had already learned with de Hidalgo. One day, as the bass Nikos Papachristos was passing the door of the soloists' practice room at the National Theater, he heard Andonis Delendas, Vangelis Mangliveras, Yorgos Moulas, Kitsa Damasioti, and one other soprano, whose voice he did not recognize, rehearsing *La Gioconda*. "I thought it was Zoe Vlachopoulou, she was singing so lightly," he recalls; "but then they came out and I was surprised to see Kaloyeropoulou."[10] So, after rehearsing for Konstanze in *Die Entführung* at the end of 1941, we find Mary doing the same for another opera that she did not perform until quite some time afterward: indeed, in the end *La Gioconda* was not performed in 1943, but Maria was to make her historic début with this role just four years later at the Arena in Verona.

The stage director of *Lucia* was Elvira de Hidalgo, and the production had already gone into rehearsal when the Italian embassy announced that Italian soloists and an Italian conductor were to come over for several performances of Donizetti's opera and of Cilèa's *Adriana Lecouvreur*, which they asked the National Opera to add to its repertoire. The soloists who came to Athens were sopranos Augusta Oltrabella and Rina Pellegrini, tenor Mario Filippeschi (with whom Maria was to sing *Tosca* in Mexico City 1950 and record *Norma* in 1954), baritone Carlo Togliani (who was to sing Ping in her *Turandot* of Udine in 1948), and bass Corrado Zambelli. We may be fairly sure that Mary went to performances and perhaps to rehearsals of *Lucia*, directed by her own teacher, and of *Adriana Lecouvreur* with the renowned Augusta Oltrabella (1898–1981), who had made a great name for herself at La Scala in the title role. While in Greece Oltrabella was also to give a series of recitals, and de Hidalgo, who had once sung with her in Lisbon, asked her to allow a pupil of hers to sing with her.

Telling the story in about 1980, Oltrabella said that on meeting Mary she had been horrified to see how fat and charmless she was, besides being terribly nearsighted and obviously desperately poor, for her shoes were torn. However, Oltrabella acknowledged that Mary had revealed "a stunning coloratura": "Why, oh why did she not stick to the coloratura repertoire?" she asked in exaggerated astonishment. "In that she was truly sensational, but the rest of the voice was simply manufactured," she said referring to Mary's later career. In 1943, though, she was happy to have her share her programs.[11] Oltrabella's testimony prompts a number of thoughts. In the first place, it is a good example of how people's ideas—and even their memories—were influenced by later reports of Mary's weight problem, which could surely never have been bad enough, especially in those days of chronic food shortage, to justify Oltrabella's description of her as "a whale of flesh." Secondly, it confirms that de Hidalgo never missed an opportunity of pushing Mary's interests. Thirdly, it provides evidence that at that time Mary's voice was strongest in the upper register and her fluency in coloratura passages was already impressive. Lastly, it is pleasing to imagine Mary Kaloyeropoulou at the age of nineteen singing with the then celebrated Oltrabella; but no evidence has yet been found that this actually occurred.

In the context of their cultural propaganda and rivalry, the Italians and the Germans offered occasional scholarships to talented young musicians to study in their respective countries. They usually approached the music schools and asked permission for their best students to be auditioned by "experts." Few young Greek musicians, however, were willing to accept the stigma attached to such scholarships. The conservatories, of course, did not have the option of refusing the cultural authorities' requests; but most of the young musicians who received offers, flattered and tempted though they may have been, found some pretext either for evading the audition or for turning down the offer without suffering any adverse consequences. One of those who was offered an audition before a panel of "experts from Milan" was Mary. The story was told in 1963 by Galatea Amaxopoulou: "Mary and I were awarded scholarships for higher studies in Italy. Needless to say, neither of us accepted the scholarship. We both said we were prevented by family commitments." Amaxopoulou recalled that out of all the people who had been auditioned the only one who was criticized was Mary, and that, she said, was for reasons of professional rivalry. She did not deny that Mary, "like nearly all the musicians," had performed at parties and other functions for the Italians, but she pointed out that Mary had sung for a fee, unlike some others who had offered their services free and had been on friendly terms with the Italians. According to Amaxopoulou, who does not appear well informed, this was never the case with Mary.[12]

Besides the concerts at the Casa d'Italia and the musical soirées organized by de Hidalgo at her apartment, Mary did sing in some other private concerts around the first part of 1943. The concerts were combined with parties at private homes, where the musicians earned some extra income and presumably mixed socially with officers of the occupation forces. One of those houses was by the sea and belonged to a Greek whose daughter was having lessons with de Hidalgo. "She took us there to sing," Lela Skordouli recollects, "but she also let us know that we would get a good dinner." Considering the scarcity of food and the enormous prices of the little that was available, it is easy to see that the offer of a good free meal was an irresistible temptation. De Hidalgo's "troupe" traveled in two cars to perform at the house by the sea, two or three times, with Koundouris as their accompanist. De Hidalgo herself selected the singers, nearly always from among her best pupils, but once Andonis Delendas was included as well. Skordouli remembers singing something from Rudolf Friml's operetta *Rose Marie*, to which de Hidalgo had added *fioriture* of her own. The other singers in what was evidently a program of "classical pops" included Lakis Vassilakis (of course) and Mary. On one occasion, when the young people had sung and taken their bows, de Hidalgo herself sang Mary's old favorite, "La Paloma."[13]

In May 1943 Mary took her last end-of-year examinations at the Athens Conservatory. The only subjects she is known to have sat for were piano (in Filtsou's intermediate class) and singing on Tuesday and Thursday, 25 and 27 May, respectively. In the piano examination, for which there were ten female candidates and one male, Mary (No. 7 on the list) played a prelude and fugue in F minor by Bach and the scherzo from Beethoven's Sonata No. 3, Op. 2, in C major. Alone of all the candidates, she was marked 2-1 for application, 1-2 for progress, and 1 for ability, a sure sign of her great potential as a pianist. In the singing examination two days later she started with an aria from Gluck's *Orfeo ed Euridice* (probably "Che farò senza Euridice?"), followed by the "Et incarnatus est" from Mozart's Great

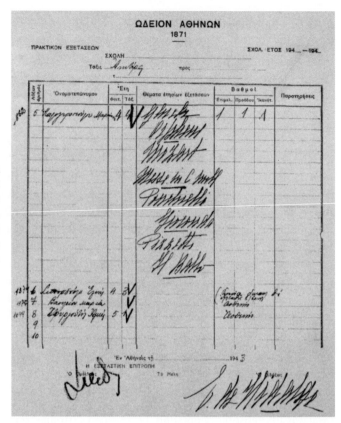

ΩΔΕΙΟΝ ΑΘΗΝΩΝ
1871

Mary's mark
sheet in Elvira
de Hidalgo's
handwriting,
Athens
Conservatory,
27 May 1943.

Mass in C minor, K. 427. Then, more in her element, she sang the grand aria "Suicidio!" from Ponchielli's *La Gioconda*, and ended with Pizzetti's "Il Ballo," which she had sung the previous year. Once again she received straight 1s for application, progress, and ability. Nevertheless, "Callas never managed to take the diploma examination at the Athens Conservatory owing to the strict regulations in force there," as Achilleas Mamakis wrote in 1957, "because she had no progress record in harmony and had failed to attend classes in that subject."[14] Encouraged by her success in *Tosca*, Mary decided to give up her formal studies at the conservatory and to abandon her efforts to obtain a diploma. From now on she would continue her private lessons with de Hidalgo, and a few months later, as her friendship with Vangelis Mangliveras ripened, she would start having occasional lessons with him too.

Even after she was no longer registered as a student at the conservatory Mary continued to go there from time to time, usually to meet de Hidalgo. The latter, openly proud of her disciple, spoke of her to younger pupils as a paragon of industry and dedication to music. "She adored Kaloyeropoulou," says Frangiski Psacharopoulou, a former pupil of de Hidalgo. "Her wish was de Hidalgo's command.

Our teacher would ignore all the rest of us and we would sit there like idiots, listening to her teaching Kaloyeropoulou. She started with a warm-up and some exercises and then sang her piece. She was really awe-inspiring to listen to. It wasn't so much her voice as the way she acted her part and brought it to life. She was fantastic!" Yorgos Patriarcheas, then a very young pupil of de Hidalgo, who first set eyes on Mary one day in 1943, corroborates: "We heard all the time that Kaloyeropoulou was the hardest-working of all the students. We were expecting to see a goddess but, when she came one day, we were surprised to see an ordinary girl wearing a simple blouse and a long skirt which concealed her legs. She was rather stout with a bosom to match, but her waist was small, so it didn't matter that she broadened out below. When she first met you she would look straight into your eyes as if she were X-raying you!" On that occasion, after introducing Mary personally to all her pupils, de Hidalgo asked her to sing something for them, to which she readily agreed, and Klada Matsouki accompanied her in Delibes's "Les Filles de Cadix," a standard showpiece for vocal virtuosity. Naturally, her young listeners were left speechless.[15]

—⁂—

An invitation from George Kaloyeropoulos's sister Tassia, probably in early June 1943, asking Litsa and her daughters for a visit to Meligalas, arrived just when all three of them were in need of a change. The prospect of eating well, as one could still do in the Greek countryside, especially fresh fruit and vegetables—which Mary adored—made the invitation all the more attractive. They traveled by train via Corinth and Tripolis, and as Jackie remembered forty-five years later, her mother spent the whole journey talking to Mary about her career, advising her how to deal with jealous rivals and other obstacles standing in the way of her rise to stardom. At Meligalas station, where twenty years earlier Litsa had started out on the long journey to New York with her husband, George, and their six-year-old daughter Yakinthi, they were met by aunt Tassia, who took them to her house in nearby Sandani. Jackie found Meligalas dirty and very run-down, while their old house was now unoccupied and derelict. After a holiday of several days, about which nothing else is known, they had to return home for Mary to prepare for her first recital in Athens and the revival of the previous year's success, *Tosca*.[16]

On 12 June 1943, the new board of the National Theater had its first meeting with Prime Minister Rallis in the chair. Whereas the theater had hitherto come under the jurisdiction of the ministry of education, it was now placed under the administrative supervision of the prime minister's office, and the prime minister of the day was to be ex officio chairman of the board. The governors with primary responsibility for running the National Opera were Manolis Kalomiris and Ulysses Lappas, as before. But Angelos Terzakis, as the new general manager of the theater, also had an important say in its affairs, and the playwright Theodoros Synadinos, who was nominated to the board by Rallis himself, became more and more

Mary Kaloyeropoulou, studio shot, Athens, June 1943.

Another of the series: Mary with her mother and sister, Athens, June 1943.

actively involved. The decision to revive *Carmen* and *Tosca* was not made until 17 June, on a motion proposed by Kalomiris. This meant that from 20 June the two revivals were in rehearsal concurrently, on alternate days. The first performance of the new run of *Tosca* took place at the Klafthmonos open-air theater at 7:30 p.m. on Saturday 17 July, with Vassiliadis again conducting, Delendas as Cavaradossi, and Xirellis as Scarpia. Full of unreserved praise, Alexandra Lalaouni wrote of Mary that, "Both her voice and, even more, her marvelous, natural, spontaneous talent rivet the attention and sweep the audience off its feet."[17]

Tosca was performed only twice more, on Wednesday and Saturday, 21 and 31 July 1943, respectively. The rest of the run had to be canceled because serious clashes took place in the streets of Athens on 1 August and the ensuing German reprisals included the closure of all theaters. Reviewing the second performance, when the wind was so strong throughout Act I that it "blew the sound back into the singer's mouth," as the critic Mary Halkia noted in *Kathimerini*, Mary, "a young singer of precocious artistic maturity," had stirred the audience's emotions by the power of her remarkable dramatic talent as well as her vocal gifts. Friedrich Herzog complimented Vassiliadis on his efforts to prevent the orchestra from drowning the voices, Xirellis on his commendable performance in the difficult role of Scarpia, and Delendas for the polish and glowing warmth of his tone, though he thought his sobs and some of his other theatrical tricks were rather overdone. But it was for the Floria Tosca of Mary, whom he had not heard before, that he reserved his highest plaudits: "Her voice possesses youthfulness, harmony, sweetness, gentleness, and roundness of tone, and with these qualities she imbued the title role with a high degree of expressiveness, which gives operatic singing great fluency and a radiant airiness. She showed talent in her acting, too, although at times she seemed to me rather immature; but this is only natural in view of her youth," Herzog concluded.[18]

Before the decision to revive *Tosca* was made, Mary had already booked her first recital, for Wednesday, 21 July 1943. She was to sing only in the first half of the program, the second half being a violin recital by Nikos Dikeos. Both soloists would be accompanied by Andreas Paridis, who has only a faint memory of that concert. Whenever he had to rehearse with Mary he would pick her up from her house and take her down to the Athens Conservatory on Pireos Street. Zoe Vlachopoulou remembers that Mary had no evening dress. "*What am I going to do? How am I ever going to appear on stage for the concert?*" she wailed, until Vlachopoulou suggested that she should wear her costume from the second act of *Tosca*. Mary was delighted and kissed her gratefully.[19] But the most serious problem arose when, at the last moment, the second performance of *Tosca* was scheduled for the very same day at 7:30 p.m., exactly one hour after the advertised time of the concert. This meant that Mary would have to cut her program short and race from Mavrommateon Street to Klafthmonos Square with her heart in her mouth (but her voice well warmed up), in time to put on her costume and run on to the stage looking for Cavaradossi in the church of Sant' Andrea della Valle.

The program, a long and ambitious vocal tour de force, was printed before the conflict with *Tosca* was known. Mary had intended to begin with "Care selve" from Handel's *Atalanta* and continue with the grand aria "Abscheulicher!" from *Fidelio*, followed by one of Konstanze's arias from *Die Entführung* (probably "Martern aller Arten"), the aria "Nacqui all'affanno" from Rossini's *La Cenerentola*, an aria (either "Tacea la notte placida" or "D'amor sull'ali rosee") from *Il Trovatore*, an aria (almost certainly "Io son l'umile ancella") from Cilèa's *Adriana Lecouvreur*—a choice that may have been prompted by Oltrabella's recent performance—and finally, as if all these were not enough, two Greek songs: "The Cemetery" by Menelaos Pallandios and "My True Love's Getting Married" by Nikos Lavdas. From this truly exhausting program Mary eventually decided to cut the arias by Beethoven and Mozart and the song by Pallandios. Even so she would hardly have had time to draw breath between the other five pieces, if she was to get through them all in little more than half an hour.[20]

In this concert Mary won glowing reviews, particularly for the breadth of her repertoire. "Once again Kaloyeropoulou enthralled and captivated her audience with the incandescent power of her voice," wrote Friedrich Herzog. He and Alexandra Lalaouni admired her "pastoral style" and "restrained classical line" in the Handel, her "crystal-clear tone" and "the effortlessness of a light soprano in all the intricacies of the Rossinian acrobatics" of *La Cenerentola*, her "dramatic expressiveness" and "the inestimable nobility of her tone" as Leonora in *Trovatore*, the passion and "the limpid, refreshing lyricism" of her Adriana, her fire and "fine understanding of the folk-singing style" in the Lavdas song. Lalaouni, who had perceived more clearly than any other critic Mary's burning dedication and the future that lay before her, wrote with unfeigned enthusiasm, "It is not only the beauty and richness of Kaloyeropoulou's voice, nor only her technical brilliance—her astonishing breath control, her unbelievable effortlessness and accuracy in the most difficult *fioriture*—that captivate and enthral the listener. Above all it is her natural, inborn talent, her musicality, the presence of a sacred flame burning in the soul of this young girl." But Lalaouni warned that care was still needed with Mary's diction and with her low notes, which she found "not completely homogeneous" with the rest of her vast range.[21]

In this comment about Mary's problems with her low notes we have additional confirmation of the fact that, although she had started out with a very "dark" voice and had been described as a potential mezzo-soprano, the work done by de Hidalgo—putting her voice into a higher register, lightening her tone, and giving her bel canto exercises—had not only expanded and settled her upper register and developed her coloratura capabilities but had actually ended by weakening the lower reaches of her voice. Indeed, Mary was to tackle this problem in the next three or four years by working more on her lower register. Another point that emerges from all this is that, in spite of the difficulties of life under enemy occupation and the rarity of her appearances with the National Opera, Mary was beginning to promote her own image as a talented young singer. In the next five months she was, indeed, to appear in at least three more concerts and recitals, starting with one in Thessaloniki, a city that she recalled fondly from the previous year.

—m—

While Mary was rehearsing for the revival of *Tosca* in that hot summer of 1943, Greece learned of the Allied invasion of Sicily. Combined with the German retreat in Russia, the news encouraged most Greeks to believe that the balance had finally tilted in favor of the Allies. In those early weeks of July there were frequent air raid warnings, though the people of Athens knew that the Allies would never bomb their city. All in all, the atmosphere was tense and the occupation authorities were very jittery, as the Germans and the Italians would by the end of the month have to settle the differences arising from the fall of Fascism. Also, the Athenians had launched a more widespread campaign of mass protests and strikes, and on 22 July, the day after the second performance of the *Tosca* revival, German tanks were deployed in the city center to halt a large crowd of demonstrators marching up Panepistimiou Street to the university, singing the national anthem. The tanks fired at random into the crowd, killing more than twenty and wounding a hundred. The Germans, who by this time had more or less brushed the Italians aside, punished the Athenians—on this occasion by closing all café-patisseries, cinemas, and theaters until 29 July.

This grave crisis caused the cancellation of two performances of *Tosca* scheduled for 23 and 25 July. For Mary, however, the troubles went much deeper, because the fate and continued presence in Athens of Attilio De Stasio, whom she still loved according to Jackie, depended on the outcome of the German confrontation with the Italians. The same applied to her mother, who was in danger of losing her good Colonel Bonalti. Jackie, on the other hand, viewed the situation with relief, as it would put an end to her mother's and sister's dangerous liaisons. On 28 July the news of Mussolini's fall from power filled most Greeks with feelings of exhilaration, which it is by no means certain that Mary shared unequivocally, for purely personal and emotional reasons. We do not know for sure whether she was still in touch with De Stasio, but in any case the pull-out of the Italians and the growing hostility of the Germans—who were in the process of taking over the occupation of Athens and adopting a much tougher approach, setting up roadblocks with barbed wire, sealing off parts of the city, and patrolling the streets regularly—must have made Mary extremely anxious. The situation would become much worse in September, after Mary's return from Thessaloniki, where she would spend the whole of August. So it is most probable that she never saw De Stasio again, and nothing more has been heard of him since.

Before leaving for Thessaloniki, however, Mary demonstrated her precocious professionalism by going to the offices of the *Deutsche Nachrichten in Griechenland* to introduce herself in person to Friedrich Herzog and thank him for what he had so recently written about her. Although Herzog's account of Mary's visit to the offices of the *Deutsche Nachrichten* on Kolokotroni Street did not appear until sixteen years later, it is to all intents and purposes her first-ever portrait and press interview.[22] "When I first saw my visitor, a strapping young girl wearing a sort of dirndl and holding a pair of glasses in her hand," Herzog wrote, "I did not recognize her as the Tosca I had recently heard." Speaking half in Greek and half in French, without a trace of inhibition, Mary told him about her obscure life up to that time. She started by revealing to him that she had an American passport and was worried about the possibility of being arrested and interned. Herzog assured her that her fears were groundless, as the military commander of the Athens district, Air Marshal Wilhelm Speidel, who loved music, would never stand for such a thing. At the end of July 1943 the real reason for Mary's anxiety would no doubt have had more to do with the fact that, while the Italian Fascist régime was collapsing, she was surely known to the Germans as having been on friendly terms with several Italians, and with De Stasio in particular.

Mary then talked to Herzog about her father, from whom she said she had not heard a word since the beginning of the war. She told him, quite untruthfully, that she was in Greece with her mother and sister because the outbreak of war had prevented them from returning to America after her father had sent them to Greece for a holiday. And then she spoke to Herzog about singing and her first appearances with the National Opera. "As soon as she started talking about her art, she flared up in a towering rage," Herzog noticed. She described how she had had to fight every inch of the way to win the part of Tosca, because the older singers always "pulled rank" and did their best to prevent any of the younger ones from stealing the limelight. Even Elvira de Hidalgo, using the influence she had with the National Opera, had not managed to get her any more parts, Mary said, and that was why she was now seizing every opportunity to make public appearances, as in the recent recital at the Moussouri Theater that Herzog had praised.

In that overlooked 1959 article Herzog made a statement about Mary which was evidently intended to catch the reader's eye, as part of the sentence was spaced and used as part of the title: "Since Maria could not expect any help from her compatriots, who regarded her as an interloper (and she herself showed no inclination to compromise), *German officials, especially members of the Propaganda-Kompanie, frequently took an interest in Maria Kaloyeropoulou.* Their efforts on her behalf were crowned with success."[23] Pausing to analyze the meaning of this statement, taken together with the implications of the two German operas (*Tiefland* and *Fidelio*) that Mary was to perform in 1944, one is led to the conclusion that from that point in time Herzog, who was himself a member of the Propaganda-Kompanie (noncombatant army personnel responsible for German propaganda, including publishing newspapers, running radio stations, and arranging film showings, theatrical productions, and concerts), promoted her career through his contacts with senior officers and the cultural departments of the German occupation authorities.

This view is shared in an article about the PK that appeared in *Die Welt* in 1970, containing the unsupported and untrue allegation that Mary owed her "discovery" and rise to stardom in the Greek National Opera almost entirely to the Germans. Two photographs of Callas—one in *Tiefland* during the war and one of her dancing in 1958—were published side by side above the caption "PK-Stimme Maria Kalojeropoulou ([aged] 17), Star Callas ([aged] 45)." According to this article, when Mary came to the attention of the PK she was completely unknown, but the PK decided to demonstrate her talent once and for all to the German military and the Greek public: "Maria Kaloyeropoulou needn't have worried. The German PK held a protective arm over the quick-tempered foreign girl. By the time the German forces withdrew in 1944 their young protégée was already very popular. There was no longer any obstacle on her path to stardom." At the end of the article the writer wondered tartly whether Maria, the *prima donna assoluta*, still remembered from time to time the protective arm of the PK. He did acknowledge, however, that the "numerous" Greek actors and musicians who collaborated with the forces of occupation and the PK had no alternative: "What else could they do? The country was starving. Only the German conqueror could guarantee to provide actors, singers, and musicians with their daily bread."[24]

Another short magazine article entitled "Discovered by German Soldiers," which appeared in Germany in the late 1950s, followed a similar line, reiterating the same exaggerations and distortions of the facts, obviously based on the Herzog material: "Maria Callas was a fat, gauche, ambitious teenager when she was discovered by German soldiers in an open-air theater in July 1943. She was singing the part of Tosca to make some pocket money and was ignored by the Greek press. She had come on a visit from New York with her mother and sister, and they had been caught by the outbreak of war. Her mother had gone hungry to pay for her education, and the family was surviving on what could be bought on the black market. The Callas trio were living on respectable Patission Street, in a dilapidated house heated by coal fires, with iron bedsteads and rickety chairs. Maria, with her Bavarian-style dirndl dresses and thick-rimmed glasses, looked like a chunky peasant girl. The German occupation authorities presented her with several good opportunities, and her first orchestra was put at her disposal by Wilhelm Speidel, the brother of the present NATO general. At that time Maria was still called Kaloyeropoulou."[25]

In the midst of these factual errors, which are too obvious to need correction, there are some statements that come close to the truth, the most important of them being that Mary was helped by the German authorities in the last year of their occupation of Greece. Of course it would be wrong to suggest that Mary's visit to the offices of the German newspaper was necessarily prompted by the ulterior motive of winning German support. But it is quite reasonable to suppose that in view of the collapse of Fascist Italy, Mary, who had fraternized with senior Italian officials and enjoyed their patronage, now seized the opportunity afforded by Herzog's favorable review to enlist German backing. Most probably, however, her purpose in going to see Herzog was simply to further her career. When she told him how she had been passed over at the National Opera as a result of backstage scheming, Herzog, who had already formed a favorable opinion of her, naturally offered to help her. In her precarious and dangerous position, it would have been unreasonable for Mary not to seize the opportunity, and she accepted. The support she received was given discreetly, off the record, and was destined to remain unproved and unprovable. But given it undoubtedly was—in the course of the following year Mary would sing the leading soprano role of four operas, among them *Tiefland* and *Fidelio*, the first two German operas to be staged by the Greek National Opera—and it was to earn her the wrath of some of her colleagues during 1944 and especially after the liberation.

—∿—

No one who has not experienced the miseries of occupation and famine can know what liberty and a tranquil and comfortable existence mean.

To Anita Pensotti (*Oggi*, January—February 1957)

CHAPTER 26

Waiting for Recognition

In the summer of 1943 Mary traveled out of Athens again, after the family excursion to Meligalas, this time on her second trip to Thessaloniki. Considering how keen her mother was to further her professional career, it is quite possible that Litsa had the idea of combining a recital there with a visit to their distant cousins Dimitris and Koralia Moundouris. Having enjoyed their first stay in Thessaloniki fourteen months earlier, and knowing that life there was considerably easier than in Athens, they would both have felt that the change was bound to do them good and might, with luck, turn out to be useful as well. In her memoirs Litsa says that this time they went to Thessaloniki "for fame and, we hoped, for money," looking forward to a repetition of the previous year's success.[1] Anyway, the trip came at a time when mother and daughter were both feeling upset and anxious, as their relationships with Colonel Bonalti and Major De Stasio had just come to an abrupt end. We shall never know whether they ever sought mutual consolation by confiding in each other, perhaps while crossing the Thessalian plain in the baking heat of August.

The Moundouris family lived in a fairly large second-floor apartment centrally situated near the cathedral, at 5 Lassani Street, between Mitropoleos Street and the waterfront. Maria Moundouri, then aged twelve, was studying piano at the Thessaloniki Conservatory, and Mary practiced on her young cousin's instrument. Otherwise, when at home, she usually sat talking with the rest of the family and in general she seemed cheerful, laughing a lot and eating well. From time to time, in the afternoon or on a Sunday morning, Mary would say to Maria, "*Let's go for a walk, it will do us good,*" and together they would go down to the waterfront, Mary wearing her usual summer outfit of a light blouse and a wide skirt of darker color, "she taking one step to every two of mine," as Moundouri remembers. "She was pretty, very pretty, even though she was fat from the waist down," she adds.[2]

On these walks Mary would almost certainly have passed the White Tower Theater, where she was to sing: with the help of the governor general of Macedonia, whom Litsa had once met, it had been arranged that Mary would give one or two recitals there. "This officer was of great assistance to us in Salonika. He helped me find a theater for Maria's recitals and sent German officers in their private cars to attend them," Litsa states in her memoirs.[3] The White Tower Theater had featured prominently in the city's life between the wars. It had some eight hundred seats and an outside balcony facing the White Tower, about 100 meters away. It stood not far from the Royal Theater, which had been opened in June 1940 by Kostis Bastias. The waterfront road then ended at the Thessaloniki State Conservatory, and about 200 meters from the sea was the Third Army Corps Club, which also had a small auditorium. In 1943 Mary sang only in the White Tower Theater, but two years later she was to perform in all three of these theaters, of which only the Royal now survives.

Contemporary Thessaloniki newspapers contain not a word about Mary's recital or recitals there in the summer of 1943. The only sources are a brief report in a German-language newspaper, Litsa's memoirs, the reminiscences of Maria Moundouri (whose chronology is vague), and the testimony of just one person who attended a recital of hers that year. The anonymous correspondent of the German paper wrote that Maria Kaloyeropoulou "gave great enjoyment" to her audience in lieder by Schubert and Brahms, without specifying the pieces she sang. The only other items on her program were two arias from Rossini's *Otello*. She made a strikingly theatrical choice, starting with one of Othello's arias (presumably "Ah! si, per voi già sento," which he sings on his first entrance) wearing a long red stole, which she then reversed so that the white lining was showing to sing Desdemona's better-known third-act aria "Assisa a piè d'un salice." She sang Rossini's two arias (the first written for a tenor and the second better suited to a mezzo than a soprano) "with innumerable embellishments," and she "made them sound familiar."[4]

This recital must have taken place on Wednesday, 1 September (or perhaps Tuesday, 31 August) 1943. Two pieces of circumstantial evidence suggest that she may perhaps have made another appearance in Thessaloniki before that date, though we do not know when or where: one is Litsa's reference to "two recitals," and the other is the comparison drawn by the German newspaper correspondent between the way Mary sang the two Rossini arias and the way she had "recently sung the *Stabat Mater*." One can only guess whether the latter was referring to the Pergolesi *Stabat Mater*, which Mary had sung at the Italian Cultural Institute in Athens in April 1943, or to the excerpts from Rossini's *Stabat Mater*, which she had sung at the Casa d'Italia in January 1943. It is, of course, most unlikely that a whole *Stabat Mater* had "recently" been performed in its entirety in Thessaloniki, as that would surely not have gone unreported.

On the other hand it is quite possible that Mary did give another recital on that visit to Thessaloniki. Andonis Kosmatopoulos, a journalist, publisher, and theater critic, went to a recital of hers at the White Tower Theater, but he has no recollection of what she sang or who accompanied her; so we do not know whether it was the recital described above or a different one. One thing Kosmatopoulos does remember is that she was wearing a long black dress, which does not tally with Litsa's account: "For these performances [Mary] wore a dress lent her by one of my mother's cousins. It was made of pink tulle with pink polka-dots . . . and was very becoming to her." More interesting, Kosmatopoulos also remembers that she sang to an almost empty hall: "There weren't more than about fifty people in the audience all told." After the performance he went to congratulate and encourage the young girl and walked back to Lassani Street with her and her mother. They sat on the second-floor balcony for a while, over a cup of coffee, and Kosmatopoulos remarked that Mary was calm but "rather disappointed by the small turnout." Litsa, for her part, concludes her account philosophically: "She was a great success artistically but not financially. Maria left Salonika for Athens poorer in wealth but richer in fame."[5]

Mary returned to Athens to find the situation more tense than ever. A fresh round of strikes by public sector employees, blue-collar workers, and the self-employed had virtually paralyzed the whole country. Every day the newspapers carried public warnings from the German Kommandantur that strikers and "troublemakers," as well as persons buying or otherwise obtaining arms from the Italians (who were now being ruthlessly pursued by the Germans) were liable to be executed or sent to labor camps. On 8 September news of the Italian capitulation reached Athens, and the people could not contain their joy. The hated "pseudo-Romans," the "coxcombs," who had been humbled in the field by little Greece but had taken their revenge by bullying and oppressing the Greeks in the protective shadow of the Germans, had at last surrendered unconditionally. The very next day the Germans started rounding up the Italians and disarming them, a process that led to some inexplicably overlooked war crimes. Although facing the ever more certain prospect of defeat, the Germans now took over the administration of the whole of Greece, while Allied planes continued to bomb military targets in Attica to the great delight of the Athenians who, instead of running for cover, watched the spectacle from their balconies and rooftops.

Against this grim background Mary now started preparing for her next appearance, at a charity concert benefiting Greek students from Egypt stranded in Greece by the war. The festival was arranged with the support of a committee of prominent public figures headed by Archbishop Damaskinos, with the Alexandrian writer and publisher Marios Vaianos as its organizer and artistic director. Vaianos produced a commemorative issue of the magazine *Orizontes* containing the program of the festival and biographical notes on all those taking part. The one on Mary Kaloyeropoulou was in fact her first published biographical note, probably written by Vaianos on the basis of particulars supplied by Mary herself.[6] The festival, held in the Olympia Theater on Sunday 26 September, starting at 10:30 a.m., was a major event: those taking part included such well-known figures as the poet Angelos Sikelianos, the actors Emilios Veakis, Dimitris Myrat, Yorgos Pappas, and Eleni Papadaki, and the dancers Yannis Fléri and Angelos Grimanis.

Mary's lengthy contribution in the second half of the program started with Leonore's great aria "Abscheulicher!" from *Fidelio*. Her accompanist, Kostas Kydoniatis, speaking shortly before his death, had only a faint memory of the occasion: what he remembered best was the impression made by this difficult aria, "which had never been heard before in Greece."[7] It was followed by the "Et incarnatus est" from Mozart's Great Mass in C minor, K. 427, an aria requiring great vocal flexibility, which Mary had already sung twice at the end-of-year examinations of the Athens Conservatory, in 1942 and 1943. Next came the dramatically challenging Mirror Aria ("Dis-moi que je suis belle") from Massenet's *Thaïs*, which she had sung in Parnassos Hall at the concert of graduating and top-grade students of the National Conservatory four years earlier. Her next piece, dramatic in a different way, was "Ritorna vincitor" from *Aida*, with which she had so impressed de Hidalgo at her first audition in the autumn of 1938, when she was not yet fifteen. She ended with two songs, Turina's "Canciòn Española" and a love song by Nikos Lavdas, "My True Love's Getting Married," which she had sung at her recital in the Moussouri Theater two months before. There was a festive atmosphere in the Olympia Theater, and the audience applauded all the performers enthusiastically. The critics had nothing special to say about Mary, apart from Mary Halkia, who wrote, "She gave some splendid demonstrations of her excellent voice, which gains so much from an indoor acoustic," and singled out her rendering of "Ritorna vincitor."[8]

—⟶⟵—

According to her sister, Mary prepared for and sang in the concert at the Olympia in a state of emotional turmoil due to the sudden disappearance of Attilio De Stasio. What is certain is that the ousting of the Italians had a serious consequence for the whole Kaloyeropoulos household, in that it deprived them of several sources of food. So the winter of 1943–44 must have been worse for Mary in this respect, even though she was to be frequently invited out to dine with a new friend and admirer at some of the smartest restaurants in wartime Athens (as the next chapter relates). The stories written about Mary's gnawing hunger are not always reliable, but they do contain some vivid descriptions of the desperate circumstances of her everyday life. One such story tells how in December 1943, having just been paid by the opera and wishing to spend her money before inflation made it worthless, she joined the line at the soup kitchen in her neighborhood, where for two days the bakers had been unable to produce even the bread ration. She had almost reached the front of the queue when the stallkeeper announced with malicious glee that nothing was left, and the waiting crowd turned on him in fury, ready to lynch him. Mary had just managed to push her way out of the mob when two German patrol cars arrived on the scene, and she saw their occupants lashing out indiscriminately with their rifle butts at the half-starved wretches. She arrived back home "exhausted, frightened, and hungry."[9]

Following the example of her mother's scrounging from relatives, Mary often used to go to friends' houses in the hope of being given something to eat. One of these continued to be 21 Amerikis Street, the home of Dino Yannopoulos's well-to-do American mother. Although Yannopoulos himself was away "in the mountains"—since that autumn he had been serving as a liaison officer with Allied undercover agents—Mary now went "nearly every day" to keep his mother company and, of course, to taste the cookies that came with the tea. This period must also have been the setting for the incident that Mary is said to have related to Ilias Papatestas, when she came home one day "terribly upset" and "trembling all over": "*I saw a man dying of starvation in the street. . . . He was walking along as if nothing was the matter, when all at once I saw him sway slightly and then suddenly keel over. The passers-by near him looked at him for a few moments and then carried on as if nothing out of the ordinary had happened. I just stood there, horrified. I covered my face with my hands, and then I stopped the first person who passed me. 'Don't worry, love,' he said. 'He's gone, done for. Ah well, his troubles are over. I expect it will be our turn one day.' Then he walked on without doing anything about it, without even glancing at the poor man lying dead of starvation in the street. It was terrible.*"[10]

Contrary to what has been said and written about Maria's self-centeredness and meanness—acquired characteristics whose roots lie deep in the hardships of her life in Greece before and during the war—young Mary often went out of her way to see that other National Opera singers had enough to eat. We have seen how she gave food to Sotos Vassiliadis, the conductor, after her first concert in Thessaloniki. "She had feelings and was kindhearted," comments Vassiliadis's wife, Haris, who recalls how Mary once used her influence with the Italians to get them to give food to the members of the Greek Railways choir, which Vassiliadis conducted. Eleni Mangou, who played the piano for the National Opera ballet, remembers her sharing chocolates with some of the dancers. One of Nikos Zachariou's earliest memories of his time with the National Opera, probably dating from the spring of 1943, is of Mary, "a plump, bespectacled girl with a spotty complexion who was already regarded as a vocal phenomenon," standing on a cart surrounded by loaves of bread. Every morning at ten o'clock the Italians used to bring bread for the opera employees, one day's ration for each, and the member of the company deputed to distribute it on their behalf—because she knew the language, and perhaps also because of her connections—was Mary. So for a time she was to be seen standing on the cart outside the theater every morning.[11]

Andonis Kalaidzakis spoke in 1988 about the fearsome shortage of food in the occupation: "From time to time some sacks of raisins would be brought to us [at the opera] and we would line up, bowl in hand, waiting to be given a cupful each. . . . The money we got was a paltry sum: it cost us half a month's salary to buy a medicine-bottleful of olive oil, which we would then measure out drop by drop."[12] Once when the chorus was "on strike" for two cupfuls of raisins per rehearsal instead of one, Mary, who was on good terms with most of them, tried to help them. Not only did she go to the Italian authorities as the leader of a delegation of musicians and chorus singers, putting her Italian to good use, but some of the delegation remember her picking up a heavy sack of flour and loading it onto a cart. "She was a plucky girl," says Kostas Dounias, "and she was also a good person to work with. She didn't join cliques and we never heard her say a bad word about any of the other singers." When mezzo-soprano Lela Stamos, the first winner of a Maria Callas scholarship, joined the Greek National Opera in the early 1960s, she found that many of the singers and stage crew still had vivid memories of Mary "coming to the rescue" or "saving lives" when the food shortages were at their worst. "Once she even managed to bring food for a soup kitchen. A big cooking pot was found and Mangliveras was one of those who served the food out with a big ladle," according to Stamos.[13]

More remarkable still is the story recounted by Stefanos Chiotakis to the effect that Mary once went "on her own initiative" to see Hermann Neubacher, the all-powerful former burgomaster of Vienna and now Reichskommissar for financial affairs in Greece and the Balkans, and "got him to issue a food warrant for the singers of the opera." What Chiotakis could not know is that Mary had a personal contact not with Neubacher himself, who was hardly ever in Greece, but with the anti-Nazi Hauptmann Paul Kemp, then serving in the Armee Begleitungslager in Piraeus, through her industrialist friend Takis Sigaras. Chiotakis's memory of the episode was that Mary went with somebody else (and we shall probably never know who it was) to a German food warehouse in Piraeus. In his own words, "They loaded a wheelbarrow with oil, sugar, cheese, lentils, beans, and I don't know what else, and pushed it up Pireos Street all the way from Piraeus to Ayiou Konstantinou Street [in the center of Athens]. There they were met by other singers from the opera, including me." He remembered seeing her "barefoot, holding her heavy rubber-soled shoes in her hand, with torn and bleeding feet." Another member of the chorus, Ermis Troizos, undertook to distribute the food.[14] Yet, while not a word has been written or said about Mary's "heroic" errand of mercy, every story about her stinginess, her relations with Italians and Germans, and any behavior considered disloyal to her fellow singers has been retailed uncritically and often maliciously.

What is more, although her ill-wishers have consistently maintained a blanket of silence on the subject, Mary apparently worked for a time with EAM, the Greek communist resistance movement. Until well into 1943 even the BBC was urging the Greeks to join EAM, and many apolitical or even right-wing patriots collaborated with it before they became aware of its communist roots and the ulterior motives of its leaders. Mary, who always avoided committing herself politically in spite of her instinctive leaning to the right, was one of those: she offered her services to an EAM "victualling squad." According to an anonymous article written in 1983, "One of the most tireless members of the team was Maria Kaloyeropoulou, whom everyone remembers traipsing about in her clodhoppers to find a bit of food for the families of imprisoned theater employees." In view of the nature of the work, this was not widely known, but there is no reason to doubt that Mary was active in this field for a while, not out of political conviction but stirred by the wave of patriotic feeling then sweeping through most young people. "Nearly all the actors were in EAM, so most probably Maria was too," says Maria Alkeou. "In fact, considering how she always reacted against her mother, that alone could have been enough to push her into the arms of EAM." Margarita Dalmati agrees that Mary probably worked with EAM before it showed its face openly: "Yes, she would have done it—not for political motives, of course, but because she was a good-hearted person." Moreover, left-wing actress Aspasia Papathanassiou states in her memoirs that Spyros Patrikios, the president of the Association of Greek Actors, "had appointed the future Maria Callas to be one of the guards at the soup kitchens [of the EAM survival committees] on account of her imposing physique."[15]

Mary was a much misunderstood person according to Stefanos Chiotakis, who explained that the other singers were jealous of her, either because they sensed that she was destined to eclipse them all or because she had helped them, and everyone knows that there is no surer way of earning a person's dislike than by doing him a favor. Of the hundred and seventy or so musicians and dancers then employed by the National Opera, Chiotakis reckoned there were only about thirty who felt kindly toward Mary.[16] The antagonism of some of the singers is well illustrated by the case of Cypriot mezzo-soprano Lysimachi Anastasiadou. Anastasiadou, who occasionally had private lessons with de Hidalgo, had appeared in some lesser Italian opera houses shortly before the war and also in some Hellenic Melodrama productions, her greatest success being as Amneris opposite the Aida of Mary Tambassi and the Amonasro of Vangelis Mangliveras. Toward the end of 1941 she had worked with Kostis Bastias's short-lived Athens Theater, and ever since then she had been doing her best to get into the National Opera. Eventually she was taken on in July 1943 as a Grade B soloist under the opera's "philanthropic" hiring policy at a time of great social unrest, when Mary was singing in the revival of *Tosca* and giving her first Athens recital. When Anastasiadou's protest claiming Grade A status was rejected by the board, it only aggravated her natural aggressiveness.[17] So it is hardly surprising that, sooner or later and for no particular reason, a frost set in between Anastasiadou, well into her thirties and believing herself to have been unfairly treated, and Mary, not yet twenty and already a rising star. The older woman disputed Mary's worth and, conveniently overlooking the fact that her own presence in the company was due to an act of charity, spread rumors that Mary had been taken on "through the back door" while "real artists" had been left out: this was presumably an allusion to Bastias's offer of a sinecure to Mary in 1940, when established singers (among whom she included herself) had been omitted. Furthermore, as Anastasiadou was a left-winger, the gossip circulating about Mary and her mother—malicious in intent but not unfounded—would no doubt have increased her antagonism.

Soprano Lysimachi
Anastasiadou (left)
with Vangelis
Mangliveras and
Fanny Papanastasiou,
Rome 1939.

One day around the middle of October 1943, when several of the singers were sitting chatting in the staff cafeteria of the National Theater and Anastasiadou was holding forth to her juniors Zozo Remoundou, Anita Bourdakou, and Anthoula Mavridou, Lakis Vassilakis heard her saying that Kaloyeropoulou had no talent, that her voice was "vulgar" and that she would soon lose it. Rallying to the support of his mistress's prize pupil, Vassilakis told her not to talk like that about a colleague. Someone else remarked that even Andonis Delendas had praised Mary's voice, whereupon Anastasiadou flared up and yelled that Delendas had a "lousy" voice, adding for good measure that it was "a proven fact" that Zoe Vlachopoulou had no talent either. Later, when she came to give evidence to the disciplinary board, Anastasiadou said with an air of wide-eyed innocence that they had been talking about *Manon* and she had simply "expressed the view that Miss Kaloyeropoulou's voice might be a bit too hard for the part of Manon."[18]

When Mary heard about the altercation (probably from Vassilakis), she was too incensed to take Anastasiadou's insults lying down. Always touchy about any criticism of her ability, she marched down to the National Theater to have it out with the obnoxious mezzo. In her own statement to the disciplinary board Mary said that when she met her at the entrance to the theater she simply told her to keep out of her affairs. Anastasiadou, whose description of the encounter is probably closer to the truth, maintained that Mary stormed in, "beside herself with rage," and abused her roundly, "screaming with fury" in the presence of the junior staff, calling her "a Cypriot courtesan" (doubtless a different and more offensive word was used) and other rude names, and uttering threats. But Anastasiadou was surely being economical with the truth when she said, "I forbore to reply but reserved the right to report the incident to the management of the theater." To get a better idea of how she really reacted we have to rely on Mary's statement, according to which Anastasiadou "went wild," threatened her with physical violence, and swore at her like a fishwife, insulting her family, casting aspersions on her private life, and calling her mother "the arch-bawd of all Greece." According to the official summary of her statement, Mary cleverly avoided specifying the abusive words thrown at her: "Confronted with the wild fury of Mme Anastasiadou, Miss Kaloyeropoulou went to the management of the theater and reported the incident without having answered the torrent of insults of Mme Anastasiadou, many of which she did not fully understand."[19]

The scene could hardly have lasted more than two or three minutes, but apparently it was extremely acrimonious and the protagonists very nearly came to blows. Anastasiadou's reference to Litsa and her use of the word "arch-bawd" tells us a lot about the slanders put about by Mary's foes in the company. "The immoral mother who hired her daughter out to enemy soldiers" was evidently a standard taunt among those singers who could find no other way of dealing with Mary's talent. "I heard a lot from other singers; in fact they used to say that her mother pushed her into the arms of Italians and Germans," recalls Marina Krassa, who subsequently married Leonidas Zoras.[20] Nor is she the only person who remembers the petty backbiting of some of the other singers, who found an easy justification for their stance in the undeniably discreditable conduct of Litsa, and of Mary too, to a lesser degree. However, Mary's fraternization with the occupying forces was on a much smaller scale and less flagrant, and it would never have received so much publicity had it not been for Litsa's provocative behavior. It is easy to see then how and why Litsa's way of life at this time was bound to alienate Mary. Not only had she seen her mother acting recklessly over a fairly long period, but she was now beginning to realize that those reckless actions were having a very adverse effect on her own life and career. As we shall see, her friendship and serious discussions with Vangelis Mangliveras, as well as the political developments of

1944 and 1945, following the liberation (when the atrocities of Nazism and Fascism came to light, showing up the gravity of her mother's—and to some extent her own—amoral behavior), opened the windows of her conscience. And so, little by little, this heavy and traumatic burden led to her irrevocable estrangement from the mother whom, deep down, she had come to hate.

—⁓—

Whereas the number of soloists in the National Opera had stood at twenty (eleven men and nine women) in the first few months of the 1942–43 season, by early 1943 it had risen to thirty and by August 1943 to forty-five (twenty-two men and twenty-three women), the highest total ever up to that date. This huge increase was due to a decision of the board of the National Theater to pursue a "philanthropic policy," which meant that besides engaging well-known singers who would be useful but had been passed over for one reason or another, they would also give contracts to others who were not really needed at all. By 2 July 1943, however, a curb had already been put on this spate of new hirings and talk of "streamlining the staff of the National Opera" was in the air, for on that date the board set up a committee (composed of Angelos Terzakis, Manolis Kalomiris, and Ulysses Lappas) with instructions to draw up a list of "those who are to form the definitive, permanent framework of the company." The implication is clear: in anticipation of the full independence of the National Opera, it was henceforth to be treated as a separate entity from the National Theater with the reins of power held by Kalomiris, designated as its first general manager. Kalomiris, known for his pro-German leanings in music, enjoyed the backing of Prime Minister Ioannis Rallis. Besides Lappas, who was basically pro-Kalomiris, the other person who did well with the new arrangement was the playwright Theodoros Synadinos, who was active beneath the surface, preparing the ground for his own general managership. On 7 July 1943 the board had to double the salaries of the soloists and conductors, and the turbulent situation forced an indefinite postponement of the planned "downsizing." On 24 September the board approved the renewal of all musicians' and dancers' contracts until 31 May 1944, but, thereafter, a certain number of soloists were laid off, so that by January 1944 their number had declined to thirty-four.[21]

It should be emphasized that the soloists' salary scales were by now virtually meaningless except as a matter of personal prestige. From a purely financial point of view the differences between the grades were irrelevant: the nominal basic salaries of Drs. 20,000, 25,000, and 30,000 were of purely symbolic significance, as they were hugely outweighed by the food and subsistence allowances that were paid in addition. From July 1943, the first month in which salaries doubled, they soared and kept on soaring, either in the form of percentage increases or in extra hardship allowances, in a vain attempt to keep up with galloping inflation. Whereas Mary's basic salary remained unchanged at Drs. 30,000 per month, her total remuneration amounted to Drs. 580,000 in July 1943, 890,000 in October, 1,228,000 in November, 1,752,000 in December, 2,553,000 in January 1944, 3,331,000 in February, and 4,456,000 in March. Finally in April 1944, when the economy collapsed for the first time, although her basic salary had been reduced to Drs. 20,000 she actually received Drs. 19,000,000![22] Inflation continued to spiral out of control (by July 1944, when Mary was receiving 40 or 50 million drachmas a month, a good seat for a first night at the opera cost Drs. 3,000,000) until the economy collapsed completely in September 1944.

On 26 July 1943, Terzakis, now general manager of the National Theater, had submitted to the board his proposed schedule for the newly independent National Opera's delayed 1943–44 season. The opening production in the refurbished Olympia Theater[23] was to be *Rhea* by Spyros Samaras, followed by three one-act operas by Marios Varvoglis, Yorgos Sklavos, and Dionysios Lavrangas, and then *La Gioconda, Manon,* Edmond Audran's *La Mascotte,* Smetana's *The Bartered Bride,* Auber's *Fra Diavolo, Don Carlo,* and *Der fliegende Holländer.* The few surviving papers in the archives offer no clue as to whether Mary was cast or even considered for any of the soprano parts of these extremely disparate works, though she may have hoped to be cast as La Gioconda, a part she already knew, and perhaps also as Senta in the Wagner. Be that as it may, quite out of the blue, on 18 October 1943 Terzakis proposed to the board that *Tiefland* by Eugen d'Albert, one of Hitler's favorite operas, should also be included in the 1943–44 repertoire. The board approved this suggestion forthwith.[24]

We do not know whether this extraordinary choice of opera was ordered by the Germans, whether Kalomiris, Lappas, and Terzakis decided on it with German "prompting," or whether they put it forward on their own initiative to silence German complaints that they were consistently giving preference to Italian operas. Litsa states categorically, "The Nazi Kommandantur asked or ordered the director of the Athens Royal Theater to produce *Tiefland* . . . [as] it was high time that the repertory included some serious German music." And Jackie, discussing the changed situation following the disappearance of the Italians, says that one of the first things the "arrogant and interfering" Germans did was to announce that there would be a production of *Tiefland,* "a choice that had even our experts running to their books to find out why." According to Jackie, "[Mary] confessed that she rather liked the new sense of discipline that had been brought into the workings of the opera house." While many of the singers "quietly withdrew," Mary, "a fanatical professional . . . [who] was already notoriously sharp with anyone who fell below her own exacting standards, . . . found a little Germanic discipline very much to her own working tastes."[25]

Although Jackie's assertion that other singers in the National Opera withdrew (quietly or otherwise) is untrue, Maria did once say, when talking about the "German period" of 1943–44, "*The only time the Athens Opera functioned professionally was during the occupation, under the Germans. The rest of the time, it was*

total chaos, a disaster!"[26] Yet her favorable comment about the Germans in the
context of the National Opera was not entirely due to German influence, nor yet
to the competence of the then general manager, Kalomiris, but to a combination
of circumstances: German coercion (of course), the personalities of those involved,
the inefficiency of Kalomiris's predecessor, Yokarinis, and of his successor, Synadinos. Nothing Maria ever said, however, should be interpreted to mean that she was
pro-German in her sentiments. When, in 1958, she quarreled with Rudolf Bing,
the Austrian director of the Metropolitan Opera, she branded him "a German
sergeant"; and although she might have prolonged her career when her voice was
failing by going over to German lieder, she persistently refused to sing in that language, let alone learn it: *"I hate the German language,"* she once said. *"It reminds me
of the rough time the Nazis gave us in Athens during the war."*[27]

Once they realized they had as good as lost the war, the Germans in Greece
behaved with appalling brutality. Admittedly they were faced with mounting
resistance in the cities and the country, but the methods they used—indiscriminate
reprisals, killings of hostages, massacres of civilians, torture and other horrific ways
of extracting information—left an indelible impression of cruelty on the minds of
most Greeks, and therefore of Mary too. The notorious Höhere SS und Polizeiführer Jürgen Stroop, fresh from his exploits in wiping out the Warsaw ghetto,
launched a vicious pogrom against the Jews in Greece as well. Even Berlin considered his use of force excessive and, in October 1943, he was replaced by Walter Schimana who proved, however, hardly less brutal than his predecessor. The
Rallis government's strict measures against food hoarding and profiteering were
certainly necessary, but on 25 October the German authorities raised the stakes by
publicly hanging two black marketeers from trees on Patission Street, just a few
hundred meters from where Mary lived.

If *Tiefland* was selected by the Germans, as seems most likely though not
absolutely certain, those involved in the decision—besides Friedrich Herzog and
perhaps some of his colleagues in the PK—would have been the music-loving Air
Marshal Wilhelm Speidel, military commander of the Athens district, the chargé
d'affaires Dr. Kurt Fritz von Grävenitz, and perhaps the cultural attaché at the
Reichskommissariat. So it is reasonable to suppose that, after Mary's visit to Herzog in July 1943 and his promise of support, it was he who brought the subject up
with his superiors, suggesting *Tiefland* as the ideal choice both for the current situation and for Mary, who would take the soprano lead as Marta. Precisely when
Mary was told she had been given the part is not known, but it must have been
before the end of October, as rehearsals began on 2 November. No doubt she was
thrilled and immediately started learning this unknown and difficult part, either
on her own or with de Hidalgo, with whom she was still having lessons.

On Sunday, 12 December 1943, pianist Maria Cheroyorgou and six singers
from the National Opera (Frangiska Nikita, Loukia Heva, Kostas Persis, Dimitris
Efstratiou, Michalis Kazandzis, and Mary) gave a charity concert at the Rex The-

ater in aid of insurance workers suffering from tuberculosis. They were directed and accompanied by Lysimachos Androutsopoulos, who had accompanied Mary at her audition with Nicola Moscona in 1938. This time Mary's program was fairly short and included no new additions to her repertoire. In the first half she sang "Abscheulicher!" from *Fidelio* and "Bel raggio lusinghier" from *Semiramide*, in the second, the aria of Leonora's from *Il Trovatore* that she had sung at the Moussouri Theater in July 1943 and Turina's "Canciòn Española." The only published review of this concert was by Psaroudas, who found fault with Mary's rendering of the Beethoven, saying that she failed to get "the appropriate style, or rather the right mood." However, he praised the "marvelous *soprano leggero* qualities" she had displayed in the Rossini and suggested that for the time being "this likable and excellent singer" ought to stick to purely lyrical rather than dramatic roles. Finally, after expressing reservations about "a certain harshness of the voice, especially on the high notes," he came to the obvious conclusion that Miss Kaloyeropoulou was "a singer to be watched."[28]

Lysimachos Androutsopoulos, late 1930s.

The review made no mention of the pieces Mary had sung in the second half of the concert, which leads one to suspect that its critic may have left during intermission. There had been other occasions when Psaroudas, the president of the Association of Greek Theater and Music Critics—a short, slight, erect, red-headed man, cutting an old-fashioned figure with his goatee and ornamental cane—had been caught writing reviews of concerts he had not attended, and even of concerts that had been canceled! Similar stories about other critics, as well as rumors of their being manipulated or even occasionally "bought," caused musicians and knowledgeable music-lovers to mistrust what they wrote. Musicians in particular, even while seeking the critics' favor, secretly laughed at them because everybody knew who liked whom and could predict fairly accurately what each critic was going to write. Mary, too, was skeptical about them: it annoyed her that, although her talent was universally recognized, the critics always seemed to demand something more of her before they would give her their unqualified praise. Suspicious by nature and made more so by circumstances, she could not accept their less favorable comments as honest, constructive criticism but attributed them to "suspect motives and scheming cliques." And so, as time went by and articles proving her skepticism to be well-founded appeared with increasing frequency, she "vented her spleen in a stream of florid but unprintable epithets" directed at critics in general, to quote the journalist Vassos Vassiliou.[29]

Learned though Psaroudas was, his opinions carried relatively little weight. He was not at home with bel canto, and so he remained to the end a severe critic of Mary, acknowledging her talent but finding her interpretations either exaggerated or ill-suited to the character of this or that composer. Whereas Psaroudas was considered an ill-natured person who lacked objectivity as a critic, the always elegant Alexandra Lalaouni had a reputation for sternness. However, she knew her business and, although some thought that even she was not above bias, musicians respected her opinions on the whole. This being so, the fact that she—with Friedrich Herzog—was the most complimentary of all the critics at the time and was openly enthusiastic about Mary and her prospects, must surely have carried some weight in Athenian musical circles. Lastly, the flamboyant Sophia Spanoudi—a colorful personality with her physical bulk, her hats and scarves, and her fund of anecdotes and witticisms told in her very nasal voice—also possessed profound musical knowledge and experience and was certainly an influential figure on the contemporary musical scene: she sat on the governing bodies or artistic committees of various conservatories and theaters and, shortly afterward, of the National Opera as well. Yet, especially during this period, she was considered over-susceptible to social and other temptations which slanted her critiques and diminished their authority. About Mary she was at first rather lukewarm, and not until shortly before Mary left Greece did Spanoudi praise her warmly and without reservation. Later she was made out to have been the driving force behind Mary's first steps up the ladder, largely on the strength of her own and her daughter Athina's radio broadcasts on musical topics. At all events, Mary herself apparently took more notice of her opinions than those of other critics, and for that reason the complimentary reviews that Spanoudi would belatedly give her in 1944 and 1945 must have pleased her and boosted her self-confidence.

—⚉—

It is so much hard work, so much love and so much devotion . . . but other people around you don't see that, they think everything is just given to you.

To David Frost, New York, December 1970

CHAPTER 27

A Romantic Interlude

In the last months of 1943, after the departure of the Italians had left such a gap in the lives of those at 61 Patission Street, Mary found consolation in the company of Takis Sigaras.* She had met him a year earlier at a surprise party, a form of amusement that continued even during the occupation among the gilded youth of Athens. We do not know how Mary happened to be invited, but the fact that she was shows that she was not altogether a social outsider. "It must have been toward the end of 1942 that we first met," Sigaras recalled, "and from then on we started going out together, though not often in the early days. We used to go to parties given by friends of mine. *'Come and dance with me,'* she would say, and we would get up and dance, usually slow waltzes and foxtrots. But she wasn't a good mixer, she didn't really like the company of my friends. Whenever I suggested going out with anyone else she reacted like a scalded cat: *'No, I don't want to! Let's go out on our own!'* And when we were out together and anyone came up to us, she would say, *'Let's go!'* And we would go somewhere else."

Takis Sigaras, the son of an industrialist, was then thirty-two years old, "fabulously rich, clever, a womanizer, and always well dressed," in the words of Zoe Vlachopoulou.[1] His father's textile mill, which had been requisitioned by the Germans, produced blankets for them throughout the occupation. He had had business dealings with German companies before the war and still had a good many German contacts, whom he made use of from time to time. Besides having money, he also enjoyed certain privileges, such as a firearms license and exemption from the curfew restrictions. He drove a black Adler with a white hood, in which he had

---

*The only sources for Mary's relationship with Takis Sigaras are Sigaras himself and his wife, pianist Maria Cheroyorgou-Sigara, who arranged for me to see her ailing husband and gave me all possible help during my interview with him. Although Sigaras's memory was still very sharp, even for factual details and conversations, his chronology was muddled and he refused to talk about purely personal matters, usually deflecting questions with a curt "No comment" or "A gentleman never talks." At the end he admitted he had told me only about a third of what he could have said. Maria's words have been transcribed verbatim from the tape-recording of our conversation. Takis Sigaras died on 12 April 1995.

a serious collision with a German vehicle on his way home from a party one evening in the autumn of 1943, just after dropping Mary off at her house. While he was confined to bed after the accident, friends often came to keep him company at his house on Alexandras Avenue, and one of his most regular visitors over a period of three weeks was Mary, who would stay patiently with him for hours at a time: "That was when we came to know each other better," Sigaras recalled.

Being an extremely eligible bachelor, Sigaras attracted a bevy of female admirers, spoiled little rich girls with haute couture dresses and all the snobbery of their kind, so when he introduced Mary into his circle they sulked and gave her the cold shoulder. Their air of social superiority and affluence irritated Mary, who knew she was not as well educated or as good-looking as they were, with the result that she developed a chip on her shoulder and became more aggressive. *"I'll get even with those bitches! One day they'll come and bow down before me!"* she would say to Takis. *"I'm glad your mind doesn't work the same way as theirs. All they think of is what they can lay their hands on, what they can get out of you. Mind they don't get you in their sights!"* "Oh, come on, Mary, what's it got to do with you? Do you think I can't look after myself?" *"Look, you're too gullible, too kindhearted, you don't treat them the way they deserve."* But Takis just advised her to restrain herself because she lived in Athens and it was no good trying to pretend that Athenian society didn't exist.

One day, at a friend's house, one of Takis's snobbish girl friends said to him straight out, "Why have you brought that fat girl here again? What do you expect us to do with her?" Whereupon Sigaras left without another word, taking Mary with him. "I was really angry, and I didn't go to any of their parties ever again," he remembered. That evening he took Mary to the Femina, a well-known nightclub on Voukourestiou Street almost directly opposite the Pallas, the scene of her first professional appearance barely two and a half years before. "We went and enjoyed ourselves there for a while, and then, as we hadn't eaten, I took her to Adam's, next door to Yannaki's Patisserie at the corner of Panepistimiou and Kriezotou Streets. It was the first time we had been to such an expensive restaurant and Mary asked me if I had enough money. So I opened my briefcase and showed her about twenty million—inflationary drachmas, of course, but still equal to several months' salary for her." From that day on their relationship became much closer. "For a time we saw each other almost every evening. I would drive down Alexandras Avenue, usually between six and seven, and go up to her apartment. She was always ready and waiting, but before we went out her mother and Jackie liked me to sit and talk to them for a while. One evening I received a very cold reception when I arrived, because Mary had just had a row with her mother and sister and was still holding forth in the middle of the living room. I tried to calm them down as tactfully as I could, even taking Litsa's side on some points, but Mary yelled, *'You keep your nose out of it, because you don't know what goes on in my family!'* And then she added, *'Please go away now and come back in an hour.'* When I went back Mary came downstairs by herself, still fuming, and said, *'Sooner or later I think I'm going*

Takis Sigaras in the late 1930s.

to walk out on my mother and sister and get out of here.' Then she told me about some system they had for keeping accounts, with each of them paying her own share. She didn't get on well with them, they were always shouting and quarreling, she said. So after that unpleasant scene she would always be at the window, waiting for me to drive up Patission Street on my way from the mill, and when she saw me she would come downstairs on her own."

Mary went out with Takis almost every day in the winter of 1943–44, and less often for the rest of her time in Greece. "She was the one who usually decided how we would spend the evening. We would drive up Alexandras Avenue and turn right at some point, toward the city center. Sometimes we didn't go straight to a restaurant but stopped off first at the bar of the Hotel Grande Bretagne. On the whole she avoided cold foods. She might drink a bit of wine, but never beer, and she then preferred desserts to ice cream." Although some people remember seeing Mary with a cigarette in her hand later on—when she was going out with Mangliveras, a heavy smoker—she never smoked with Takis, even though he too smoked like a chimney. Sometimes, but not often, instead of going to a restaurant they would call on a friend, for example "a certain conductor" (whom Sigaras did not name) "who used to entertain officers of the occupation forces in his house." According to Sigaras, who was doubtless exaggerating and referring to people in his own circle, "Half of Athens used to entertain Italians or Germans in their homes in those days. If you went to a friend's house in, say, Psychiko, you were pretty sure to find some Germans or Italians there. Most of the ones that came to Greece were cultivated men who played the piano: the Italians, in particular, were mad about music and great opera-lovers. So it was only natural that they should admire Mary. Some of the high-ranking officers would go up to congratulate her and would kiss her hand. '*They're all just flattering me because they want me to sing for the Wehrmacht,*' she would say."

Usually, however, Takis and Mary went out on their own, and he would take her to restaurants and nightclubs which were so expensive that she would never have dreamed of going there otherwise. Besides the places in the Syntagma area there was a recently opened restaurant run by an Austrian behind the Fix brewery, and sometimes they would go to a seaside restaurant at Varkiza, the Très Joli: "It was a popular place with courting couples and it served fresh red mullet, but its specialty was meatballs—God knows what sort of meat they were made of—which made your mouth water just to smell them cooking." One day, when Takis picked Mary up from home rather earlier than usual, she said, "*I want to go to the sea! Where will you take me?*" Sigaras takes up the story: "I drove down through Kallithea until we came to the end of the road at Dzidzifiés. We crossed over the streetcar lines and parked right by the sea. '*It's so lovely and romantic here. I'll sing for you!*' Mary exclaimed, and she launched into an aria." Sigaras admitted he knew very little about music and did not like opera. While Mary was singing he went to have a look at the wheels of the Adler, which were half-sunk in the sand. "That annoyed Mary, of course, and she told me again (as she often did) that I was a philistine. My usual response was to ask her when *she* had ever managed to pick up any general education, which she agreed was not altogether unfair, though she would add, '*But I'm not a jackass like you!*'" That day at Dzidzifiés, while Mary was filling the air with some sustained high notes, along came some children to see what was afoot, shattering what remained of the romantic atmosphere she had been trying to create. "Let's go, or people will think we're at each other's throats," said Takis, and they jumped into the car and drove off hurriedly.

Takis often gave Mary little presents. From the hens that he kept on the grounds of the mill he might bring her a fresh egg or two—a rare treat in those days. Once he gave her a two-piece black suit made of material from the mill, only to learn later from her mother what the sequel had been: "My dear fellow," Litsa said to him, "what on earth made you give her that outfit? They fought over it like cats! Eventually Jackie took it from her and had it altered to her own measurements." But Takis never gave Mary either jewelry or money. "Although I had money to throw around, I never gave her any," he affirmed. "Nor did she take advantage of our relationship in any way. Embirikos gave them money, but I helped Mary personally in other ways, mainly by giving her clothes and accessories such as shoes and nylons, which were terribly expensive at that time. Sometimes I also gave her things to eat, such as fritters that I got from the Germans. She often said, '*Who told you to bring me that stuff? I don't want it!*' But in the end she would take it, even though she had her pride and found it hard to accept the smallest favor. '*I don't want to be under an obligation,*' she would say."

When Mary went out with Takis, and especially when they went to the expensive places around Syntagma Square, she dressed quite smartly. She wore her skirts slightly longer than was then fashionable, presumably to hide her legs. Once, when Takis asked her to raise her hemlines a bit, she snapped back, "*I see! So now I have to become a dressmaker to please you!*" But at any rate she had at last started taking some trouble over her appearance. She always preferred darkish colors, which made her hips look smaller, and she avoided high heels. She still had to wear glasses, of course, but now she favored frames that were not so dark and heavy. Mary used makeup, cared for her hands (she no longer bit her nails), and took great pride in her hair, which she dyed from time to time (she even went to the hairdresser's, sometimes at the suggestion of Takis himself, who would go with her and fret impatiently while he waited). The shade she usually favored was a very light brown, much lighter than her natural hair color, and she occasionally experimented with other colors from peroxide blonde to auburn. Maria Cheroyorgou, the pianist who subsequently married Sigaras, remembers Mary at that time as being "just a tall, plump girl with rather fat and ugly legs but a pretty face that was often lit up by a smile. Her hair was very light brown, not dark." For a man's view we must turn to Sigaras himself, who, while admitting that she was "not well favored by nature," insisted that her personality more than made up for these shortcomings: "She had almond-shaped eyes, slightly protuberant, and she was fat and walked and moved awkwardly. Jackie was beautiful and very attractive, but so what? Mary was the one who, when you got to know her, really made an impression on you. And she was full of life—she was terrific!"

—⁓—

Although Takis Sigaras refused to be specific about the nature of his relationship with Mary, the inference to be drawn from what he did say is that not only was it something more than mere friendship but for a time it probably was real love. When she once confided her dreams to him and told him that she believed she would be a great prima donna, he asked her what made her so confident. "*You'll see!*" she insisted. "*You'll be proud of me one day!*" "I don't know about being proud of you," he rejoined, "but I tell you now that you'd better not become a prima donna, because if you do we'll be going our separate ways." This exchange and several other conversations they had on a variety of subjects point to an easy intimacy between them that can hardly be described as mere friendship. Yet Sigaras implied that Mary was still somewhat lacking in femininity: "Now and then there was something hard, even severe, in her manner, that made me realize she was not right for me. She was a very nice girl who was susceptible to emotion, but she didn't let her emotions show. We both knew that what we felt for each other was love, but neither of us ever said so. You could say that we were united by a sort of amorous friendship, but we did not have a full relationship because I didn't want to get too involved." Even so, there were times when Takis, for all his determination to remain levelheaded and undemonstrative, found that the situation was threatening to get beyond his control.

Like many sons of rich but uneducated parents, Takis Sigaras had problems with his father, who resolutely opposed the idea of his marrying a girl who was neither well-off nor of any consequence socially: "I had told my father that Mary was a nice girl who didn't go out with just anybody, but he would not accept her. Mary was still an outsider in Athenian society." Miltiadis Embirikos was in the same position with Jackie, and the fact that Mary was "one of those theater people" could only make it worse for Takis. He himself had been put off the idea of marriage by the nagging of his father and the recent death of his mother, and being unmusical he would have found it hard to hold his own against the ambitious young opera star. "I remember her saying to me, *It's impossible for you to enter my world. I move in a different orbit, an artistic orbit, whereas you are a manufacturer.* 'Does that prevent us from sharing our lives?' I asked. *No, far from it! With you I find comfort and love,* she answered." Yet the fact that Takis was a stranger to the world of music and had nothing to do with Mary's work put the future of their relationship in doubt. What is more, by that time Mary herself had stopped setting such a high priority on marriage as her sister says she had done earlier. After her success in *Tosca,* as we have seen, it had become her overriding aim to do well in her career. "*Art and marriage are incompatible,*" Takis remembered her saying in 1943 or 1944. "If anyone so much as mentioned marriage to Mary in those days, she wanted nothing more to do with him. Nor did she ever talk to me about marriage. Never! She would never even have considered the idea, and all that stuff that's been written about my proposing to her is pure imagination."[2]

Nevertheless, when Takis's father died suddenly just at that time, it is possible that the subject of marriage was thought about and perhaps discussed. It may have arisen again in 1945, and Takis may actually have proposed marriage then, even though by that time Mary had already decided to leave Greece as soon as possible. Several Greek journalists have suggested as much. According to one of them, Yorgos Roussos, at the time of the liberation "[Mary] found love, real love. An industrialist fell well and truly in love with her and eventually proposed to her. This marriage would have set her up both financially and professionally. . . . And yet she turned down this splendid proposal. *I don't belong here,*' she told her suitor, *'I am cut out for greater things.*' 'Maybe you are, but how will you make ends meet?' *'I don't know, but I'll manage.*'" An anonymous article in 1961 revealed what it described as a practically unknown page in Callas's life: "The other legend most journalists keep trotting out is that Callas never made any conquests in her youth. . . . Conquests she made in plenty. In fact she turned down something that to other girls—richer and better-looking girls—was the dearest dream of their lives: a well-to-do young man, a 'good fellow,' a husband. . . . This was at the end of the occupation. Marianna Kaloyeropoulou was then a twenty-year-old singer at the National Opera, fairly promising but considered immature both vocally and artistically. . . . Disappointment seemed to be awaiting her, when into her life came a fairly well-off young man with whom Maria got on well. One day the great moment arrived and he proposed to her. . . . Instead of falling into his arms . . . Maria calmly explained to him that although she loved him she was not cut out to be a housewife." And in 1963 Stamatis Tsoutis wrote: "But nothing could keep her in Greece, not even a proposal of marriage. Among the flowers in her dressing room [at a performance of *Der Bettelstudent*, in September 1945] were some from a well-known manufacturing tycoon who knew her. Two days later he proposed." There follows a surely imaginary conversation in which the industrialist tries to persuade her not to go to America—in other words, to all intents and purposes, to give up her career—but she turns him down, thanking him for the compliment and explaining that she definitely intends to go away "because singing is my life."[3]

Although Takis Sigaras expressly stated that their relationship was never consummated ("Anyone who says that Mary was my lover then is lying"), he admitted, "I loved her as a woman, and she loved me. When I took her home at the end of an evening we would kiss in the car, but Mary didn't give in. She simply didn't want it, she wouldn't let you." She actually explained her attitude by saying that her mind was on other things, in other words her career, in which she was going to rise "very high." And then, piqued, Takis would say, "Only if *I* let you! And I may fall for you, head over heels, and not let you!" All these exchanges between them, of course, attest to a very close and intimate relationship which, even if it was never consummated, seems to have been very loving.

Maria Cheroyorgou too believes that at some stage Takis and Mary were truly in love, and she tells two stories that tend to support her opinion. In July 1957, before her recital at the Odeon of Herodes Atticus, it had been arranged that Maria Callas would go and practice at Cheroyorgou's piano in the apartment where the pianist lived with Takis Sigaras, to whom she had been married for several years. At the last moment, however, Maria did not go: according to Athina Spanoudi's description of the scene, when Maria heard that the piano was in Sigaras's apartment she exclaimed in horror, *"Oh, then I'm not going!"* without explaining why. The next day Cheroyorgou received a bouquet of flowers from Callas with a card thanking her for the offer of the piano. Knowing of her husband's past friendship with her, Cheroyorgou asked Takis to telephone her and thank her. But when he called, Maria pretended not to remember him. "Don't you remember your friend from the occupation?" *"I don't know, I can't remember . . ."* she stammered, perhaps because Meneghini was within earshot and she would have found it embarrassing to have to explain to him what Takis had once been to her. "Oh well then, if you've lost your memory—sorry to bother you. Good-bye."

The second incident occurred in the early 1960s: Takis Sigaras happened to be coming out of the Asteria nightclub in Glyfada, very long past midnight, just

Mary,
Athens,
early 1944.

as Maria was going in with Onassis. This time it was Takis who pretended not to see Maria, but to his astonishment he heard her call out, "*Taki, come here!*" "She gave me her hands, which were ice-cold, like the hands of a corpse," Sigaras recalled with emotion shortly before he died. "Then she turned to Onassis and said, '*Aristo, if it hadn't been for this man I might have died of starvation in the occupation. This is my good friend Takis Sigaras.*'"

We women are scheming creatures, and that's not nice. We are very sharp-tongued and we open our mouths without stopping to think. That applies to me too, I'm no exception. . . . Women have one great strength which they don't make enough use of: femininity. . . . If we were able simply to be women, we would have the world at our feet.

To Micheline Banzet, Paris, February 1965

PART FOUR

Success, Liberation, and Civil War
(1944)

CHAPTER 28

Tiefland: The Promise Confirmed

When the cast list for *Tiefland* was announced, Mary must have been glad to see that the tenor playing opposite her as the simple peasant Pedro would be Andonis Delendas once again. The tyrannical landowner Sebastiano was to be Vangelis Mangliveras, whose path she had crossed only once before in 1938. Now she would get to know the thirty-five-year-old baritone who had sung in France and Italy, had appeared with Elvira de Hidalgo and Ulysses Lappas on his return to Greece, and was already a prominent figure on the operatic scene, thanks partly to his charismatic and dynamic personality. Mangliveras applied his irrepressible energy to everything he did, both in his private life and in his work, and made an impression on everyone who met him with his impulsiveness and his passionate dedication to whatever he was doing. However, being someone who expressed himself bluntly without pausing for reflection, he inevitably made enemies as easily as friends. "Obstreperous he certainly was," says Spyros Salingaros, "but there was no malice in him, and if you had a row with him he would suddenly say, 'Oh, what nonsense this all is,' and put his arm around your shoulders." And Andonis Kalaidzakis speaks of him in the same spirit: "Vangelis was an honest fellow with a good heart."[1]

Evangelos Mangliveras was born in Athens in 1909. From a very early age he showed a leaning toward the arts, not only singing but writing and painting as well. His vocal talent was discovered by Dionysios Lavrangas, the father of the Hellenic Melodrama, who arranged for him to give a series of recitals accompanied by Stefanos Valtetsiotis when he was still only seventeen. A year later, in 1927, he married his music teacher Artemis Vrassivanopoulou (Diane Vrassy), a woman about ten years his senior, with whom he went to live in Paris. There he studied with French singer Albert Gebelin and the Spaniard Miguel Fontessia, and he made a successful début under the name of Evan Manglivera in 1931, singing in a number of French towns such as Cannes, Aix-les-Bains, and Trouville, as well as Paris where, on 17 March 1934, he sang the title role in *Rigoletto* with no lesser partners than Lily Pons and Jan Kiepura. His first critical notice in the Greek press appeared in January 1933, when he was hailed as a rising talent who brought credit upon Greece. At about this time he fell in love with a Greek dressmaker working in Paris, Kalliopi Vrettou, and returned to Athens with her toward the end of 1934, appearing soon afterward as Amonasro in *Aida* at the Olympia Theater. The critics wrote then that he "took Athens by storm," and that it was not surprising that Bruno Walter had called him "a rare artist."[2] Between 1935 and 1938 he sang in Greece with the Hellenic Melodrama and with other troupes which he formed himself, and which usually lost him money. He was particularly admired as Amonasro, Rigoletto, Escamillo, Scarpia, and Tonio, and he appeared with Ulysses Lappas, Margherita Perras, Elena Nikolaidi, Nicola Moscona, Elvira de Hidalgo, and many younger singers. In 1939 he went to Italy, where after enrolling in the local fascio (because "without that no artist had any chance of getting ahead in Mussolini's Italy"),[3] he sang at a number of opera houses, scoring his greatest hit as Tonio in *Pagliacci* at Ancona's Teatro delle Muse. He was scheduled to sing at the Bari Opera in the 1940–41 season, but the outbreak of war between Italy and Greece forced him to return to Athens in November 1940. The National Opera did not take him on immediately, however, and he had to wait until June 1943 before signing a one-year contract.

It was above all in his relations with women that Mangliveras was larger than life. While he lived with his considerably older wife at 21 Dionysiou Areopagitou Street, at the foot of the Acropolis, he maintained a second household in the seaside suburb of Faliro, where Kalliopi Vrettou lived with their daughter and, in early 1944, was expecting a second child by him. Besides these two, Vangelis loved every woman who took his fancy. "He loved both his wife and his mistress and was devoted to his children, but he was quite capable of loving thirty other women at the same time," says Elvira Mataranga, a member of the National Opera chorus who was having an affair with him at that very time. "I shall never forget the magical feeling I had when he once sang the whole of 'Eri tu' *sotto voce* into my ear, sitting in a crowded café. It was a dream!"[4] Having two women and two households to maintain, Mangliveras was chronically short of money. He was a spendthrift, he smoked heavily (up to three packs a day) from boyhood to the end of his life, and he ate too much. So in the early years of the occupation, when he was not receiving a salary from the National Opera, he seized every opportunity to make a bit of extra money. One such opportunity was presented to him by two friends, who wanted to take advantage of his fluent Italian by employing him as their agent in selling old copper and lead to the Italians for their munitions factories. With the money he made in this and other ways, later added to his salary from the National Opera, he lived tolerably well during the occupation but, like Mary, he therefore came in for some sniping about his dealings with the Italians.[5]

Mangliveras's personality stamped itself equally strongly on his professional activities. In his very first contract with the National Opera, for example, he tried to include the condition that no other artist should have a higher salary than his, and that his monthly salary should automatically take first place, even over subsequent appointments or salary increases.[6] Although he had been on the payroll for nearly a year, the abandonment of the 1943–44 season (including productions of *Der fliegende Holländer*, *Il Barbiere di Siviglia*, and *Pagliacci*, in which he was to have taken the baritone lead) meant that he would be making his first appearance with the National Opera as Sebastiano in *Tiefland*. Yet he had been reluctant to accept the part because he considered it too insignificant. "Having always been accustomed to directors and impresarios who described me as a star, both here and in western Europe, I was surprised not to be given a production of my own," he wrote to the board.[7] "He was flamboyant as an actor and as a singer," recalls Maria Alkeou, who had lived in the same neighborhood as Mangliveras in her childhood. Irma Kolassi, who accompanied him when he was learning *Tiefland* in 1944, has similar memories of him: "He was another great personality—a male Callas!" Whereas Yannis Angelopoulos had the tone of a cello, Mangliveras's voice was full of chiaroscuro, and it was big, "sometimes excessively big," according to Andonis Kalaidzakis. Xenia Kouroussopoulou contrasts the velvety tone of Mary's voice with that of Mangliveras, which "had a certain roughness of tone." However, nobody denies that he made a powerful impression on anyone who heard him. Elvira Mataranga, who makes the point that he never saved his voice but always used it unstintingly, says: "He would come on stage, open his mouth, and eclipse all the others."[8]

For want of more suitable premises, the early rehearsals for *Tiefland* were held in various rooms at the National Theater on Ayiou Konstantinou Street, usually with Yerasimos Koundouris at the piano. "As soon as the rehearsal schedule was posted, Maria took her score and disappeared until the first rehearsal," said Zoe Vlachopoulou in 1963. As usual, Mary went home and spent all her time learning her part. The unfamiliar and difficult role of Marta was a huge challenge to her, but when, on 2 November 1943, she turned up for the first rehearsal in a state of exhaustion, "She put her score down somewhere and stood waiting with the rest of us," as Vlachopoulou recalls. "We all had our music in our hands, and when Zoras asked her what she had done with hers she told him in a matter-of-fact tone that she didn't need it and was ready for the rehearsal to begin. We were all amazed, especially as her part was so very difficult, and we discovered afterward that she had shut herself up in her room, refusing to open the door to anyone." Kalaidzakis remembers Litsa telling him that from time to time she had gone in to take Mary a hot drink or something to eat, "and often she would find her fast asleep on the carpet with the pages of her score scattered round about her."[9]

Early in January 1944 (Mary having meanwhile also started rehearsing for *Cavalleria Rusticana* on 17 December) the *Tiefland* soloists were eagerly waiting for the Olympia Theater to be completed so that they could start learning the staging under the direction of Renato Mordo. Most of the singers of that era are rather disparaging about their stage directors—and about their conductors too, for that matter. "We picked up what we could and did whatever came into our heads, relying on our own instinct," says Mitsa Kourahani, and Zoe Vlachopoulou agrees: "The stage directors used to read through the libretto with us without going into much detail, and hardly ever giving us any direction. They would come up to us and say, 'Now you're happy' or 'You're very sad' or 'Now you have to cry' or 'Show this or that emotion.' That did have its good side, of course, as it allowed a singer with acting ability, like Mary, to expand on these basic instructions a lot."[10] But Mordo, who was to direct Mary in four productions altogether (*Boccaccio, Tiefland, Cavalleria,* and *Der Bettelstudent*), must have given her a good deal of useful advice when she was still very short of stage experience, especially in *Tiefland,* where she was unable to learn from de Hidalgo. As a result, Mordo was one of the few fellow artists of her Greek period whom Maria mentioned later by name: "*Renato Mordo . . . said two things that stuck to my mind: one, never move your hand unless you follow it with your mind and with your soul. It's a strange way to put it, but it's so true. . . . The second thing he said was that when your colleague sings his role to you, . . . your reaction must be as though you had never heard what he is saying and it's all first reaction.*"[11]

The stage rehearsals of *Tiefland* started on 20 March 1944. Until then the only work Mary had done on her part was to learn the music and the interpretation, while concurrently rehearsing for *Cavalleria.* Because of her bad eyesight, she also took great pains to learn the steps of the dance that Sebastiano makes her perform in the second act. Eleni Mangou, the National Opera pianist, describes how she went about it: "To perfect her act and make sure she would not stumble and fall, Kaloyeropoulou organized a full rehearsal. She arranged for us to go to the home of the choreographer, Loukia Kotsopoulou, where we practiced the steps and then the whole dance. She was such a perfectionist, so strict with herself! Anyone else would just have done a few steps without really bothering."[12] Mangliveras, now working closely with her for the first time, must have been as impressed with her as everybody else was. In the course of their study sessions from November 1943 onward the two charismatic artists, thrown together by chance in an exacting theatrical production, discovered that they had much in common and immediately felt a special affinity with each other in character and temperament.

Under the influence of Mangliveras's personality and charm, Mary now gradually drifted away from de Hidalgo. Carried away by the euphoric atmosphere of the rehearsals and the encouragement (perhaps the over-encouragement) she received from Mangliveras, she started "doing her own thing" for the first time. This was probably what she had in mind when she said, many years later, "*I kept on working with [de Hidalgo], but I also worked on the stage. You can call that experience, but it is not good work on stage, because you can make a lot of mistakes and create bad habits. You undo those at school (at the conservatory, I mean) and when you are at home. Then you really have to work by yourself: the teacher can't teach you everything. If you really want to pursue the matter, you find these things by yourself.*"[13] Nevertheless, the work Mary did on *Tiefland* in 1944 did much to develop her maturity and was the first step on the road to emancipation from her teacher.

Whereas in the 1942 *Tosca* de Hidalgo had helped to get Mary the part and had known how to teach her, d'Albert's work was unfamiliar to her and not her kind of opera. Moreover, there were personal factors on both sides contributing to a cooling of relations between them: first, Mary's liaison with Mangliveras, and secondly the rocky state of de Hidalgo's relationship with Lakis Vassilakis, who had started an affair with the much younger Mireille Fléri. "In 1944 and 1945 de Hidalgo was feeling fairly depressed, so naturally her teaching was not what it had been," says Mitsa Kourahani, who left de Hidalgo and started taking lessons with Marika Kalfopoulou at about that time.[14] So it would be wrong to suggest that the cooling of Mary's relationship with de Hidalgo by 1945 was entirely due to her own "defection" and her infatuation with Mangliveras.

—⁘—

On 11 January 1944 Allied planes carried out a devastating bombing raid on Piraeus and its docks, causing heavy casualties among the civilian population. A week later Athens was thickly blanketed by the heaviest snowfall since 1905. The war-weary Athenians now had running water on Tuesdays, Thursdays, and Saturdays only, and the government conveniently blamed the British for all the country's woes. The resistance movement blossomed and the government attempted to mollify its many opponents by formally announcing that King George II would never be able to reclaim his throne. Throughout the last week of January the Athenian papers were full of reports of the relentless bombing of London. The people of Athens, nevertheless, simply carried on with their own daily struggle for existence, and while, on 13 February, Filoktitis Ikonomidis conducted the Greek première of Berlioz's *Requiem* at the Pallas, Mary gave of her best during the preparation and rehearsals of *Tiefland*.

In late February 1944 Prime Minister Rallis promised the government's support for Nikolaos Laskaris, the new general manager of the National Theater, on condition that he abandon its "philanthropic" hiring policy and clear the dead wood from its payroll. Rallis declared bluntly that the theater must cease to be "a hotbed of subversive elements" and, in a move directed against the pro-communist majority in its ranks, he closed it down for two weeks until 16 March. A few days later, when the stage of the Olympia was at last ready, the prime minister seconded Kalomiris from the ministry of education to his own political office and appointed him general manager of the now-independent Greek National Opera (henceforward referred to as G.N.O.). After remaining closed for the past five and a half months, the renovated Olympia was officially opened on 1 April 1944 with the twentieth production since the foundation of the National Opera, the opera *Rhea* by Spyros Samaras. The next three months were later described by Kalomiris as "a period of redoubled efforts and hard work by the entire artistic, technical, and administrative staff of the Greek National Opera." Indeed, in the space of seventy-eight days there were sixty-seven performances of nine different operas.[15]

Interior of the Olympia Theater, restored for the use of the Greek National Opera in 1944. Mary sang here twice in 1939, once in 1943, ten times in 1944, and four times in 1945.

One of the first acts of the new general manager was to have discussions with the conductors, the stage directors, and the artistic committee (Kalomiris plus Synadinos, Terzakis, Psaroudas, and Lappas, who was replaced on 21 April by Spanoudi) on ways of rationalizing the composition of the opera company. And when the artistic committee recommended on 24 April, two days after the triumphant première of *Tiefland*, that ten singers (five men and five women) should be classified as Grade A soloists with a monthly salary of 30 million drachmas each, Mary's name was among them. Not only was this a promotion for her, but it meant that she received a bigger salary increase than any of the other nine (Vlachopoulou, Galanou, Nikita, Fléri, Glynos, Delendas, Epitropakis, Koronis, and Mangliveras). Laskaris protested that the National Theater had made much more drastic cuts, but he was overruled by the prime minister, ex officio chairman of the board of governors, who explained that the opera singers had to be given a salary raise "because it would be immoral for the government to take advantage of the fact that they are unable to find work elsewhere" (unlike the actors of the National Theater).[16]

It is interesting that Mary's appointment to the top rank of G.N.O. soloists coincided closely with the behind-the-scenes German string-pulling to have her cast as Leonore in *Fidelio*. In light of this, the possibility cannot be ruled out that her promotion was suggested to Kalomiris by officials of the Propaganda-Kompanie and the German embassy. Unfortunately, owing to the disappearance of her personal dossier from the G.N.O. archives, we cannot know whether Mary's contracts contained any special terms and conditions. The leading actors and opera soloists, who knew that their services could not be dispensed with, usually tried to have special clauses included in their contracts and often succeeded. The actress Eleni Papadaki, for example, had won the right to choose what roles she would play, while in the opera Nafsika Galanou had once pressed for a clause releasing her from the obligation to accept any role that was offered to her. All we know about Mary's contracts—and that quite by chance—is that she once succeeded in having a clause inserted to the effect that she would not be replaced in any of her roles without her consent. This meant that, once she had been allotted a part and had accepted it (if she had any choice in the matter), the management could not give it to anybody else.[17]

In fact, though, this condition and any other special terms that might be negotiated would almost certainly have been agreed verbally, or at any rate separately from the contract proper. Not one of the contracts of the leading soloists of that period includes any such exemptions or special conditions: the only variations relate to the duration of the contract, the maximum number of obligatory performances per week (if specified), and the rate of pay (regular salary, allowances, and sometimes bonuses for extra performances), which varied from one singer to another. In general, the standard terms and conditions of the contracts with the National Theater, and from 1944 with the G.N.O., were essentially the same as those of the first contract Mary had signed in June 1940. Naturally enough no mention was made of tours or performances outside Athens during this period: these only reappear after the end of the war. Also, because of the galloping inflation, salaries were variable, being linked to a basic ticket price. And the advent of the radio had led to the insertion of a clause stipulating that whenever the G.N.O. was paid a fee for the broadcasting rights to its performances, sixty percent of that money was to be paid to the artists involved—but only subject to the approval of the chairman of the board, in other words the prime minister himself.[18]

Jackie still remembers Mary "working frantically" to prepare herself for *Tiefland*, asking for extra rehearsals and begging the conductor to go through her part with her privately. Maria herself once said, when asked what the word "luxury" meant to her, "*To me it means having a conductor who undertakes any number of rehearsals so as to produce a performance of high quality, and having musicians who work hard, without fixed hours. That's the way people used to work once upon a time.*"[19] Leonidas Zoras was a conductor who worked hard, and most of the singers tried to avoid his overconscientious rehearsals, except for Mary who was "always nagging him for more work," according to Marina Krassa, his third wife. Zoras was then living at 8 Trikorfon Street with his second wife, Tatiana Varouti, the prima ballerina of the National Theater and the G.N.O., and quite a number of singers including Delendas and Remoundou used to go there for private sessions with him in addition to their rehearsals with the orchestra. From early 1944 Mary, too, would go to Zoras's house to work on the part of Marta just as she had studied *Tosca* privately with Titos Xirellis and Sotos Vassiliadis. "I shall never forget my private rehearsals with Maria, who was always after me to give her more and more of my time," Zoras said in 1977. "Every note, every phrase was studied in depth for its musical, vocal, and interpretative content until we arrived at the nearest thing to a perfect result."[20]

Conditions were far from favorable for any kind of study. "We worked by the light of little kerosene lamps," Zoras continued, "and the kerosene was watered down, so the wick needed decarbonizing every ten minutes. Blow out the lamp, trim the wick, light it again. And so it went on all the time, with Maria showing inexhaustible patience." Maria recollected those times years later: "*We were rehearsing for d'Albert's 'Tiefland'... and because of the fear of bombing we had to perform in semidarkness that was diffused by acetylene lamps.*"[21] Worse still, famine stalked the streets of Athens in February 1944, and the singers of the G.N.O. were no less liable to debilitation than anyone else. "We used to line up for a hunk of currant bread to keep us from collapsing out of sheer exhaustion," Elvira Mataranga remembers. It was at about that time that the Propaganda-Kompanie donated nearly 400 liters of olive oil to be shared among the artistic personnel, and because of the frequent power cuts, the ministry of finance kept the G.N.O. supplied with kerosene, which often had to be used to provide light for rehearsals. What with the shortage of food and the intensity of her work, Mary was so exhausted that one day she almost fainted at one of her sessions with Zoras, who had nothing to offer her except a few carobs to chew and half an orange, which she wolfed down, peel and all, and felt a bit better. Although Tatiana Varouti and Marina Krassa admit that Zoras respected and supported Zozo Remoundou, they both insist that he also admired Mary and never favored Remoundou at Mary's expense. In 1977 Zoras described the young Mary as "a forceful but nice girl," and indeed there is no reason to doubt that that was what he really felt, as she always remained on good terms with him.[22]

As she was to do all her life, from the very first orchestral rehearsal Mary sang and acted her part as if she were doing an actual performance. Both she and Mangliveras did everything with such verve that the other soloists were astounded. Kourahani, who was playing one of Marta's four gossipy women friends, remembers how impressed she was by the great scene in Act II where the tyrannical landowner Sebastiano orders her to dance in front of everybody, urging her rhythmically with his guitar. This follows straight on from another powerful scene with stirring music, in which Marta has just decided to walk out on Sebastiano and

Rehearsing *Tiefland* with Vangelis Mangliveras (Sebastiano), Greek National Opera, Athens, April–May 1944.

run away with Pedro. At the first rehearsal, vividly described by Kourahani, Mary was dressed in "the simplest peasant garb imaginable," with motley stockings and enormous clodhoppers, wearing her thick glasses and with her hair then dyed in three different shades. "Mordo had me standing on a table, playing the tambourine and urging Mary on. I shall never forget what I witnessed then. As the orchestra and Mangliveras started playing the music for her to dance to, Mary went and stood right at the edge of the stage, tensed her muscles, raised an arm, composed her features in a heavenly expression and started dancing. If only somebody could recapture that movement of hers today! It was amazing—she swooped and fluttered just like a bird! Marta was forced to dance though inside she was grief-stricken and on the verge of tears, and Mary instinctively found a way of expressing that emotion in her graceful movements. I was so carried away that I completely forgot what I was doing, until suddenly I heard a voice roaring at me, 'Kourahani! This is a rehearsal!' So on I went, jingling my tambourine."[23]

—ɷ—

Eugen d'Albert (Glasgow 1864–Riga 1932), a pupil of Liszt, was considered one of the greatest pianists of his day and an outstanding interpreter of Beethoven's music. A very competent composer, he wrote *Tiefland*, the best known of his operas, in 1902 on the shores of Lake Maggiore, inspired by his visits to nearby Monte Rosa. It was hailed as the most important non-Italian contribution to *verismo* and was first performed at Prague in 1903, then at the Metropolitan in 1908 and Covent Garden in 1910, and in the 1920s and '30s it was a staple item in the repertoire of most German opera houses. D'Albert's music is an amalgam of Wagnerian and post-Wagnerian idioms and tools. The Prelude's opening English horn theme, for example, is very reminiscent of the theme given to that instrument in Act III of *Tristan und Isolde*. The use of leitmotifs helps the listener to follow the development of the plot, the dramatic and musical elements are closely interwoven, the action is nonstop, and the orchestra provides a constant melodious backing for the singing and acting.

Tiefland is set in the Pyrenees and the action takes place in a low-lying plain that symbolizes the lower emotions and instincts, in contrast to the high mountains, which are the home of the simple-minded shepherd Pedro. Sebastiano, a wealthy landowner and livestock dealer, has long been the lover of Marta, a homeless orphan. For financial reasons he has to marry a rich woman, so he decides to marry Marta off to Pedro. But he wants her to continue to be available to him, even on her wedding night. Although at first Marta wants nothing to do with Pedro, an unpolished peasant, the honesty of his feelings eventually wins her over and she decides to run away with him "to the high mountains." The dramatic climaxes between the three principals are extremely effective, culminating in the death of the tyrant, who is strangled by Pedro. "Compared with this drama, *Cavalleria* is harmless fun and games," as Psaroudas commented drily.

Altogether there were four dress rehearsals at the Olympia, each one starting at 4 p.m. and running straight through "under strict performance conditions." This latter condition was insisted upon by the prime minister's office at the suggestion of "the German department concerned," namely the cultural section of the embassy and perhaps the Propaganda-Kompanie, which for the first time were taking a close interest in the preparations for a new opera production. *Tiefland* was given a great deal of advance publicity in the Greek and German newspapers, so the opening was eagerly awaited. "We had all been led to believe that this production was something special," Maria Cheroyorgou remembers. "In fact it was rumored that at one rehearsal Mary had broken the glass of the opera house chandelier with one of her top notes."[24]

Tiefland, with Andonis Delendas and Vangelis Mangliveras, Greek National Opera, Athens, April–May 1944.

Meanwhile the war was running its course. In March 1944 Berlin and Nuremberg were bombed, on the Italian front the fighting raged around Monte Cassino, only 100 kilometers from Rome, and in Greece the sorely tried inhabitants of the cities and towns continued to suffer from the ravages of cold weather, disease, and famine. But the most striking feature of the period when *Tiefland* was in rehearsal was the hardening of the German reaction to any form of resistance. On 9 March fifty "communists" were taken before the firing squad and many more were executed thereafter, whenever even a minute cause allowed it. Needless to say, so far from suppressing resistance, the policy of brutal reprisals fanned the flames of anti-German feeling all over Greece. And while Athenians were celebrating Easter in a far from festive mood, the Germans were preparing to celebrate Hitler's fifty-fifth birthday four days later, with a big parade presided over by the military governor, Air Marshal Wilhelm Speidel.

Just two days after the parade, on Saturday, 22 April 1944, Speidel was graciously pleased to attend the first night of *Tiefland*. Wartime austerity notwithstanding, first nights were still gala occasions when evening dress was worn, and in spite of the conspicuous presence of enemy officers, mostly high-ranking, the atmosphere was always festive. Also present on that great occasion, besides opera-lovers and the cream of wartime Athenian society, were the prime minister and other officials of the occupation authorities, including Dr. von Grävenitz, the German chargé d'affaires, and General Schimana, the Höhere SS und Polizeiführer. At the end of the performance "[the audience] burst into tumultuous applause and brought all the performers back for innumerable curtain calls." Mary had several distinguished visitors in her dressing room afterward, including the prime minister and the actress Eleni Papadaki, who, being a competent singer herself, congratulated her with genuine warmth.[25]

To ensure a high standard of performance, Zoras had taken care to choose established singers, even for the smaller parts. Kourahani, Bourdakou, and Remoundou were cast in the minor roles of three of Marta's friends, while the biggest of the minor roles, that of Nuri, Marta's closest friend, was sung by Zoe Vlachopoulou, already well known as a soprano lead. Vlachopoulou, who shared a dressing room with Mary, has an interesting story to tell about what happened shortly before the curtain rose on opening night: "Mary was unlucky enough to have a cold, and that day she went to the Olympia before anyone else and locked herself into our dressing room. When I arrived she refused to open the door, and I called Kalomiris, who asked her to let me in. '*I can't, I won't open it!*' 'But, my dear girl . . .' '*Will you please leave me alone, Manoli?*' 'But the performance is about to begin!' '*I've got a cold.*' 'That's just too bad, open up!' When she finally opened the door, I saw that her nose was running, her eyes were swollen from crying, and she was shivering all over with fever. I sat at my dressing table and asked her what the matter was. '*Can't you see?*' she answered brusquely. '*I've got a cold and a temperature and a runny nose all at once, I can't swallow and I feel as if there were a nail in my throat. How can I sing?*' 'When you go out there you'll forget all about it, and even your nose will stop running!' '*Do you really think so?*' she asked disbelievingly. 'You wait and see, we're going to give a terrific performance!' I answered encouragingly."[26] Sure enough, although she was not feeling at all well, Mary astounded the audience with her acting that night. One of her greatest moments was in the final scene where she hurls at Sebastiano that she now loves Pedro and is no longer the feeble Marta she once was. Sebastiano, realizing that he has lost her, tries to kiss her and sends her sprawling on to a pile of sacks ("Ich zwinge dich zu Boden!") where she continues to sing with passion, almost lying down, calling for Pedro's help. A dramatic photograph of this scene, taken at a rehearsal, was published on the cover of the weekly *To Radiophonon*: this was Mary's first-ever magazine cover.*

That Mary gave an impressive performance as Marta, everybody, save one critic, agreed: they only varied in the degree of their enthusiasm. Those who looked only at the surface remarked rather tartly that this was an ideal role for Mary, "because she plays the part of a peasant girl and her heavy tread and stout figure are just right." Others, such as Elli Nikolaidi, attributed her success in the part to the *verismo* of the opera, "in which the acting is more important than the singing, so it did not matter that she screamed and sang rather raucously at times." Quite possibly Mary really did identify with Marta to some extent, knowing what it was like to be oppressed and forced to accept compromises that were sometimes humiliating. "The role of Marta suited her perfectly," Vassos Vassiliou wrote later. "She was playing herself. . . . It was as if she was inspired by the symbolism of the libretto: a girl being 'sold' but now wanting to redeem herself, severing her links with base materialism, eager to get out of the low plain." Indeed, for whatever reason, the dramatic role of Marta must have stimulated Mary's histrionic talent.[27]

It was Mary's identification with her stage role, even at that early stage in her career, that gave her acting such impact. As Vlachopoulou remarks, whatever she was singing, she really lived the part on stage. Interestingly enough, considering that Mary was to all intents and purposes fatherless herself, one day when Vlachopoulou was standing in the wings, watching her sing Marta's big aria ("Ich weiss nicht wer mein Vater war"), she saw tears come into her eyes: "Real tears running down her cheeks!" And Vlachopoulou knows as well as any singer how difficult it is to sing when one is at such a pitch of emotion. The magnetism and tension of Mary's stage presence was also described by Leonidas Zoras in 1977: "Whenever she came on stage, so powerful was her personality that everybody's attention was concentrated entirely on her." So even in 1944, presumably by instinct, Mary had that way of coming on stage that was later described as a *sospiroso entrare*, "causing all eyes to be turned on her, and her alone."[28] She was already like that at the age of twenty in *Tiefland* when, responding as a woman and as an opera singer to the presence of Vangelis Mangliveras, she gave free rein to her innate talent for the first time.

Although the rare quality of her stage presence had already been apparent in her first major role as Tosca in the summer of 1942, it was in the performances of *Tiefland* at the Olympia that her ability to live her part—"not to throw it over her

---

* *To Radiophonon*, no. 46, 7–13 May 1944. *To Radiophonon* was the first magazine to publish a picture of Mary, a small portrait photo that appeared in its second issue (4–10 July 1943), just before her first recital at the Moussouri Theater; the next was in the magazine *To Theatro* (6 July 1944).

ΤΟ
ΡΑΔΙΟΦΩΝΟΝ
ΕΒΔΟΜΑΔΙΑΙΑ ΕΠΙΘΕΩΡΗΣΙΣ

ΓΡΑΜΜΑΤΑ • ΤΕΧΝΗ • ΘΕΑΤΡΟΝ

7-13 ΜΑΪΟΥ 1944

ΑΡΙΘ.
ΦΥΛΛΟΥ
46

The first magazine cover featuring the future Maria Callas, rehearsing *Tiefland* with Vangelis Mangliveras, *To Radiophonon*, Athens, May 1944.

shoulders like a cloak but to enter into it, to wear it," in the words of Eugenio Gara—became obvious to all. Talking about this with Maria some ten years after *Tiefland*, Gara referred to her *sonorità psicologica* and quoted the dictum of French tenor Gilbert Duprez, "Enfin, qu'est-ce qu'un son, sinon un moyen d'exprimer une pensée? Qu'est-ce qu'une note, sans le sentiment qu'elle colore et dont elle est animée?"[29] He pointed out how apposite this was to her own operatic outlook and asked her what she thought of Diderot's well-known aphorism, "C'est l'extrême sensibilité qui fait les acteurs médiocres; c'est la sensibilité médiocre qui fait la multitude des mauvais acteurs; et c'est le manque absolu de sensibilité qui prépare les acteurs sublimes."[30] And although Maria agreed it was true that a good actor must escape from the tyranny of his private feelings—must depersonalize himself, so to speak—she denied that good interpretation could be achieved by cold, mechanical, basically cerebral execution: "*Yes, it is true that we study meticulously every inflection of the voice, every look, every gesture. But woe betide us if the imitation of our ideal model is not transformed into a different way of living and feeling once we are on stage.*"[31]

Those who saw Mary in *Tiefland* were struck by the fact that she did not watch the conductor's baton but often sang with her back to him. "The reason for this, of course, was that she was nearsighted and could not wear her glasses on stage," says Zoe Vlachopoulou, who was also very myopic. "We often talked about it, because we couldn't see the people in the audience at all. Just a dark blur! We could barely see the conductor, so we couldn't rely on him to bring us in. I used to tell her that it didn't bother me, and she agreed, because it meant that we learned our parts by heart, and that gave us a great feeling of security in case one of the other singers made a mistake. In that way we always knew exactly when to come in, and Mary agreed that that was a great advantage. She made the point that by not being dependent on any conductor's baton we acted and moved more freely on stage. When you are preoccupied with watching the conductor's beat, your acting goes to pieces, all feeling is lost, you are no longer immersed in your part."[32]

Maria often talked about her terrible nearsightedness, precisely because the brilliance of her stagecraft excited so much admiration. "*I'm as myopic as a mole. When I walk on a stage, I don't see anything,*" she admitted to Meneghini soon after she met him, and in 1956 she told an interviewer, "*I have never been able to see the conductor . . . . I can't see the people in the audience who are scratching their heads while I am lost in my role and giving everything I have to the drama.*" In 1969 Luchino Visconti said publicly, in her presence, "Maria can't see very far. That's a great asset to her, because she feels as if she's in a sort of great big aquarium. She can't see, she can't see a thing! She feels immersed in a sort of world of her own."[33] Of course it is not easy to decide how much, and in precisely what way, her nearsightedness affected her artistic development and performance; but it would seem that its overall effects were beneficial, and it was only in her private life that it posed problems. Sometimes it caused her to move awkwardly, and besides that there must have been times when she was accused of being "stuck-up" by people whom she had not even seen. "Everybody who is very nearsighted is clumsy and often gives offense unwittingly," says Margarita Dalmati apropos of Callas's myopia, "but there are some parts of the world where birds have their eyes put out to make them sing better!"*

To return to 1944 and *Tiefland*, the success of the production can be judged from the adulatory tone of the reviews, and without a doubt it was, with *Fidelio*, Mary's most impressive achievement in Athens. "What a performance! Unforgettable!" mused Elli Nikolaidi, the chorus mistress, who had coached Mary for her very first stage role in 1938 and was soon to coach her again for *Fidelio*. And indeed all those who saw Mary in *Tiefland*, performers as well as members of the audience, were equally lavish in their praise. "Astonishing," "superlative," "magnificent," "unrivaled" are some of the adjectives used again and again to describe the performance as a whole and the scenes that each person found most impressive. In particular, the scene where Sebastiano makes Marta dance is universally remembered for the dramatic tension of Mary's acting. "How on earth did that woman manage to dance like that wearing that long black skirt?" wonders Nikos Papachristos. "They were all fantastic—Mangliveras was, and so was Delendas, who sang a high C lying on some sacks on the floor and thrilled everyone with his dramatic passion when he strangled Mangliveras on a wooden table." Mitsa Kourahani noticed that Mary was amazingly light on her feet when she danced in the performances, as she had been in rehearsal, and that she sang the whole of her tragic role "with that plaintive sob that she had in her voice." And Marika Papadopoulou sank into a reverie, remarking that she could not have imagined anybody with Mary's figure moving so beautifully: "Those arms of hers! She was like a swan!"[34]

Elvira Mataranga, a member of the chorus in *Tiefland*, who until then had been close to Mangliveras, obviously resented seeing the romance between Vangelis and Mary blossoming before her eyes. All she will concede today is that Mary's acting was "sensational" and that her own teacher, Smaragda Yennadi, who saw the performance from the orchestra, had said so. "Zozo Remoundou admitted it too, and from then on we nicknamed Mary 'the God-given' and used to tease her by saying to one another, 'Here comes the God-given!' That was what Lalaouni had called her in her review two days after the première." When the cho-

---

*DALMATI. Contact lenses were not widely used until after 1950, and in any case Maria could never wear them with comfort. That is why she continued to wear glasses, though she never liked being photographed with them on. When Victor de Sabata was conducting the dress rehearsal of Verdi's *I Vespri Siciliani* in early December 1951 (the first time that Maria was to open the season at La Scala), a momentary discrepancy in rubato between her and the orchestra occurred. De Sabata stopped immediately and shouted at her, in front of the audience of critics and invited guests, "Callas—watch me!" But Maria, putting on her most seraphic smile and wagging her forefinger at him, answered, *"No, Maestro, you watch me—your sight is better than mine!"* (LEGGE.)

rus was not on stage Mataranga's colleague, the tenor Nikos Doufexiadis, often slipped out to watch the performance from a box. "It was superb! How well I remember Mangliveras ordering Mary to dance, and chanting the words rhythmically to keep her at it!" One day, seeing her reading by herself somewhere in the theater, Doufexiadis went and bought two cheese pies, gave one of them to her and said, "You're going to be very great!" These spontaneous words, even coming from a chorus singer, must have been very gratifying to Mary. She had matured since the time, a year and a half earlier, when she had been jealous of Delendas for having more curtain calls than she. Now she longed for sincere compliments and the support of her fellow musicians, and this longing was to remain with her all her life. On 15 November 1956, before the first night of *Tosca* in Maria's first appearance at the Metropolitan Opera (with Mitropoulos conducting and Yannopoulos as stage director), George London, her Scarpia, went to her dressing room to wish her luck with the traditional wish, "In bocca al lupo." Years afterward London remembered how Maria had taken his hand in both of hers, deeply moved: "She later told me that this insignificant courtesy had meant a great deal to her."[35]

—⁓—

Mary's undisputed success in *Tiefland* seemed to have gone to her head. A few days after the première, the mother of her classmate Arda Mandikian told her: "Mary, you were wonderful!" "*Oh, yes, I was!*" Mary answered smugly, and then, irrepressibly, "*And tell me, Mrs. Mandikian, who else in the world today can sing Marta as I can?*"[36] The intoxication of success also led Mary into what is perhaps the only known instance of prima donna behavior on stage. The story is told by Leonidas Zoras: "There was one high final note which she sang beautifully, but she held onto it after the orchestra had stopped playing, to show off. . . . I asked her not to let it happen again. She agreed, but at the next performance she did it again. When I reproved her, she said, '*I'm sorry, Maestro, I forgot.*' I don't know whether she was doing it deliberately or whether her temperament was getting the better of her. Anyway, next time I kept the orchestra playing under her high note until she ran out of breath and the note just died. Nobody said anything, but after that she didn't make the same mistake again."[37] When she had acquired greater maturity, Maria said once, "*A high note cannot just be stupidly held,*" and on another occasion, "*The better a musician you become, the less you should push your voice to your advantage, in other words for easy applause. At the beginning of your career you can't get away with what you want: you have to give the public a little bit of your desire, in other words a very long held note, this sort of thing.*"[38]

The rave reviews in the press and the tumultuous applause in the theater, where the audience gave the soloists a prolonged standing ovation, gave Mary a first taste—on a smaller scale than what came later, of course—of the publicity that would follow her throughout her life. On 23 April Lalaouni in *Vradyni* described the performance as "the most polished opera production we have ever seen in

Athens." In a tribute to Zoras, who does seem to have done a truly excellent job on *Tiefland*, she praised the rich tone colors of the orchestra. After also complimenting Delendas and Mangliveras, she had this to say about Mary: "Kaloyeropoulou is one of those God-given talents that one can only marvel at. How does this twenty-year-old girl come to have that dramatic expressiveness, that truth, that honesty, that conviction? She sang and acted the part of Marta like an established artist, and there were moments—in the recitatives, for example—when she stirred you to the depths of your being." The next day *Kathimerini* also carried a highly complimentary review of the "excellent" production, noting that Kaloyeropoulou had entered into the character of Marta "with a degree of expressiveness, honesty, and passion astonishing in one of her age" and commenting on "the extremely convincing and thrilling tones" of her beautiful voice.[39]

On 25 April, when the front pages of the newspapers were full of the bombing of Bristol by the Luftwaffe, Psaroudas's review was published in *Eleftheron Vima* and Spanoudi's in the *Athinaika Nea*. Psaroudas obviously did not feel at home with this genre of opera: "Miss Kaloyeropoulou," he wrote, "a sort of Santuzza but in a much more tragic role that is at the same time infinitely more difficult and unrewarding, displayed uncommon dramatic qualities. Vocally it is impossible to judge her because, except in a duet with Mr. Delendas in the last act, based on the most trite elements of the bad Italian *lirico-drammatico* school, she has to scream and weep all the time." Spanoudi, on the other hand, was for the first time full of unqualified praise: "The dramatic soprano Miss Kaloyeropoulou is an extremely dynamic artist possessing the rarest dramatic and musical gifts. . . . She is beginning to become fully aware of all her potential and arouses the wholehearted emotion and excitement of the audience. In the depressing and musically thankless role of Marta she triumphed all along the line."[40] Naturally, a long critique by Friedrich Herzog was published with three photographs in the *Deutsche Nachrichten in Griechenland*. Herzog described Mary as a Marta of unaffected naturalness, adding, "Things that other singers have to be taught—the instinct for drama, taut acting, spirited interpretation—these things she possesses by nature." Commenting on her voice, he drew attention to her "penetrating metallic strength" on the high notes and complimented her on her ability to "reveal all the tone colors of her precious, youthful soprano voice possessed of an inborn musicality."[41]

The one generally negative review appeared in the weekly *To Radiophonon*, even though it did put the photograph of Mary and Mangliveras on its cover the following week. The only member of the cast to escape the lash of its critic Konstantinos Ikonomou was Mangliveras, who was deemed to be "better than all the others vocally" and to have got well into his part. All the rest were dismissed as mediocre, from Vlachopoulou, who he said was over-affected, to Delendas, who sang with "a strangulated, tremulous tone . . . as if he had dumplings in his larynx." Of Maria, Ikonomou said that she had not managed to convey the gradual shift of her feelings from the "ballad of the wolf" in the first act (in which Pedro shows his honest goodness but Marta still reacts negatively) to the burgeoning of sympathy and love in her breast toward the end of the second. "She should have started to show the change [more gradually]. She had not worked out the evolution, the course of the action, and the overall development. All in all, she had not gotten into her part." Ikonomou also declared that her vocal registers had not evened out and that in the words spoken over the orchestra her voice was not melodious: "She speaks, she declaims, she shouts, or else her voice gets lost on the low notes. Only on the high notes does she achieve something, and even then there is a certain harshness in her voice."[42] Vangelis Mangliveras, who had been a contributor to *To Radiophonon* for a time, wrote a counterblast to Ikonomou, in defense of the singers and of Zoras and Mordo. The conductor, he said, had succeeded in conveying the spirit of the work to the performers and had inspired them; and in his opinion Renato Mordo was the only stage director worthy of the name currently working in Greece. After defending each of the singers in turn, he wrote of Mary: "The singer who took the part of Marta, that new star in the Greek firmament, with a matchless depth of feeling, gave a theatrical interpretation well up to the standard of a tragic actress. About her exceptional voice with its astonishing natural fluency I do not wish to add anything to the words of Alexandra Lalaouni: 'Kaloyeropoulou is one of those God-given talents that one can only marvel at.'"[43]

Tiefland also gave Mary her first international publicity. The Amsterdam newspaper *Deutsche Zeitung in den Niederlanden* carried a dispatch from Herzog saying much the same as his Athens article. A piece that made a much greater impact, however, was a two-page illustrated feature about the success of *Tiefland* in the *Wiener Illustrierte*, where Mary was described as "the foremost and most popular opera singer in Greece today."[44] As a result of this fulsome praise, the German authorities in Athens suggested that the G.N.O. give a series of performances of *Tiefland* at the Staatsoper in Vienna. That would of course have been extremely gratifying from a purely musical point of view, but compromising in every other way. The performers, or at least the majority of them, therefore decided to scotch the plan, "some citing health reasons, others family commitments and other excuses," as Zoras later wrote.[45] Nothing is known about Mary's reaction to the proposal, nor about that of her mother.

Litsa, who kept a scrapbook of press clippings about Mary, names *Tiefland* as her daughter's first major success. Yet, surprisingly, she says practically nothing about the role of Vangelis Mangliveras in Mary's life. The only time she mentions his name (in connection with a photograph of Mary and him in the *Wiener Illustrierte*), it is to say that the "sinister-looking" Sebastiano was played by a "splendid actor-singer . . . who is now dead." In 1944 Mangliveras's closeness to Mary made it impossible for Litsa to sit in her dressing room for as long as she liked, as she had done two years earlier in *Tosca*. What is more, Mangliveras, a married man and almost penniless, must have seemed to her not only a most unsuitable companion for her daughter but also someone who stood between her and Mary, exerting a bad influence on their relationship, which had already gone from bad to worse. Whenever she went to see Mary at the opera house "there were scenes," according to Vassos Vassiliou. Consequently, in her memoirs Litsa all but ignored the man she held responsible for this further alienation.[46]

Tiefland had a run of eight performances, all at the Olympia and all starting at 5 p.m. They were conducted by Leonidas Zoras and, because of the very heavy demands made on the performers' vocal resources and acting abilities, an alternate cast was out of the question; especially for the three main roles and most of all for Marta, a part which was beyond the capabilities of any other soprano then in Greece. So all the soloists sang at every performance, except Zoe Vlachopoulou who was replaced as Nuri by Galatea Amaxopoulou in the last three. The reason *Tiefland* had to be taken off so soon was the bad design of the scenery store at the Olympia, which made it impossible to have more than three operas on the stocks simultaneously. So when the time came for *Manon* to be performed, while the double bill of *Cavalleria* and *O Pramateftis* was still running and *Lucia* was in rehearsal, *Tiefland* had to close, very prematurely in view of the interest and acclaim it had aroused.[47]

—∞—

In Greece during the war, it took six months of rehearsal, morning and evening, to get an opera ready for the stage. Eventually you reached the point where you couldn't take any more, but at least you were well prepared. Whereas nowadays . . . young singers are thrown out onto the stage just as they are, without preparation, without knowing the opera well. [After a few engagements, they] don't take time to reflect: they immediately think they are great and famous, and that's the beginning of the end.

To Micheline Banzet, Paris, February 1965

CHAPTER 29

"Éducation Sentimentale"

Mary's liaison with Vangelis Mangliveras was probably the most important love affair of her life before she met her future husband some three years later in Verona. Working on *Tiefland*, an unfamiliar opera that turned out to be a surprisingly satisfying experience for all concerned, had provided the ideal conditions for their love to flower. "It was then, in the rehearsals for *Tiefland*, that they got together," many of the other singers remember, and Mitsa Kourahani adds that he would throw his arms round her in a very forward and intimate way that set tongues wagging. In photographs of those rehearsals all faces seem to be glowing with a feeling of enjoyment most inappropriate to the wretched conditions of daily life at that time: this is especially true of Vangelis and Mary, who must have been feeling exhilarated not only by their work but by their love as well. "*When you are working well, life can be sublime, but when you are not it can be torture,*" Maria said in 1961. "*My psychological situation must be perfect, otherwise I don't find certain passages easy to execute. Whereas if you sing out of pleasure and enjoyment, things come beautifully. It's like getting drunk—only from pleasure, the pleasure of doing something well.*"[1] That is approximately how Mary must have felt during the rehearsals and performances of *Tiefland* seventeen years earlier.

Besides having a similar artistic temperament, Mary and Vangelis were also well matched in their acting ability. On his return to Greece in 1934 he had brought a powerful breath of fresh air into the world of operatic acting. Whereas Yannis Angelopoulos definitely belonged to the old school, Mangliveras's way of acting was freer and made a more direct impression on the audience. "Mary, who soaked everything up, could not help being influenced by watching him and singing and acting with him," says his brother Christos. "Each of them inspired the other: they were better when performing together than with other soloists." Spyros Salingaros adds that, in *Tiefland* especially, the character traits they shared were brought out even more strongly by Vangelis's love: "His impassioned acting was due to his love for Mary, and she too performed better for the same reason." Certainly it is true that Mary's superb histrionic ability was revealed not so much by her *Tosca* in 1942 as by her *Tiefland* in 1944, with Vangelis Mangliveras.

Mary in love. With maestro Zoras, director Mordo, and Vangelis Mangliveras, at a rehearsal break of *Tiefland,* Olympia Theater, Athens, April 1944.

"When they met at rehearsals their friendship was immediate, and Mangliveras taught his young singer friend various important points of stagecraft," wrote one of her earliest biographers.[2]

 With her colleague Mangliveras Mary also shared the problems of a career in opera. Both of them had the same obstacles to overcome, not only to ensure their professional advancement but also to cope with the hostility of their rivals in the G.N.O. In the older, experienced, extroverted, and often aggressive Vangelis, Mary had found not only an open-minded adviser to whom she could pour out her heart but also an able defender. Not all the lessons she learned from Vangelis were necessarily constructive: though such arrogance and aggressiveness as he displayed never spilled over into her professional conduct—or at least, not to the same degree—in later life she did have the reputation of being an extremely tough negotiator.[3]

Mangliveras's presence by Mary's side and his feelings for her strengthened her position vis-à-vis her colleagues. "He recognized her worth and helped her with his advice as much as he could," says Galatea Amaxopoulou. "'Don't worry about anything,' I heard him say to her one day as we were coming down toward Kaningos Square together." In fact there were some who believed, or insinuated, that at least in the beginning Mary had shown interest in Vangelis "because she knew he was strong, and so it would be to her advantage," as Terzakis's widow Louisa puts it. According to violinist Vyron Kolassis, the concertmaster of the G.N.O. orchestra at the time, "The story then going the rounds was that Kaloyeropoulou had attached herself to Mangliveras and used him to help her get ahead." And Lela Skordouli, Zozo Remoundou's close friend, maintains that the main reason Mary approached Mangliveras, even though he was married and had children, was to make sure she got the part of Marta, "just in case he said he didn't want her as a partner."[4] But the fact is that, although some of her fellow singers and other musicians at the G.N.O. were annoyed by his backing for Mary and continued to slander and intrigue against her, Vangelis's support made her rise in the esteem of most.

Sometimes Mary waited for Vangelis at the corner of Akadimias and Harilaou Trikoupi Streets, where there was a good basement restaurant, the Helmós. When they wanted to get away from the people they worked with, he would buy her a drink at the Inomena Voustasia, an established up-market patisserie near Omonia Square, where in fine weather the waiters in their dinner jackets and aprons would put the marble café tables and Viennese-style chairs out on the sidewalk. Many of the other opera singers often saw them sitting there or walking away hand in hand. Salingaros talks about the pervasive air of loving intimacy between them: "Whereas all the rest of us called him Vangelis, Mary called him Evangelos, and he was very attentive to her. They didn't trouble to hide their feelings much, and she would hug and kiss him in front of us in a way that was more than just friendly. In other words, the general impression was that their relationship was a full-blown affair, though there is no way of confirming that." And Nikos Papachristos tells of an occasion when a member of the chorus was good-naturedly teasing the two of them, and Vangelis suddenly launched into an extravagant eulogy of her fiery nature. "Apparently Maria was a very passionate lover, a really volcanic temperament!" Papachristos concludes.[5]

Mary's ideas about men and her relations with them were molded gradually by life, her environment, and her growing maturity, but the foundations of her attitude to the opposite sex must have been laid then, in Greece: not only by her own experiences (although these were more numerous than was once thought) but more particularly by what she saw and heard around her at the age of transition from girlhood to womanhood. Most of all she must have been influenced by her mother, who always lived a free life at home, without bothering in the least about appearances, and was constantly giving Mary advice about how to treat men. Then there was the notoriously "liberated" atmosphere of the theater and the

Mary as Marta and Vangelis as
the evil Sebastiano, Athens,
April 1944.

presence of so many older males in the opera company. Litsa's comments in her memoirs, for all their exaggerations, are nevertheless informative: "[Mary] was pretty, and although some of the men whispered that she weighed too much, they looked at her with an interest that had nothing to do with music. . . . The men in the company found my chaperonage a nuisance. I was in their way to arrest their roving eyes, obstruct their animal magnetism, and thwart what they considered their male prerogatives and the normal processes of nature."[6]

Litsa also informs us that Mary was not much interested in these "frustrated Lotharios," as she calls them, nor even in the male animal. She compliments herself on having given her daughter a good moral upbringing, generously conceding that, "Like all girls, she had 'flirts' with whom she laughed and innocently enjoyed herself." She adds, however, "But I am positive that she had no lover nor wanted one." And then, painting Mary as a loveless and ungrateful daughter, she remarks bitterly, "Even then, before she was twenty, Maria cared more for her career—for fame and money—than for love." Litsa's tardy moralizing is decidedly provocative, considering all that has been said (and will be said) in these pages about her own behavior and mentality. According to Yannis Tsarouchis, she actually urged Mary not to waste time while she was still young but to find a rich old man who would set her up as his mistress. Yet when she came to dictate her memoirs, by which time she was so distraught at her abandonment by Maria that she was almost hysterical, she insisted that Mary's "first lover" was her first husband, Meneghini. However, as this book shows, Mary had already had several men friends in Greece, and Maria herself later said, "*I haven't had many experiences, but I am the kind of person that goes either all the way or nothing.*"*

---

*LITSA 58–59; P. Dragadze, "Parla la madre di Maria Callas," *Gente*, 15 Oct. 1977; FROST. Nevertheless it should not be imagined that Mary had a very active clandestine sex life. Deep down inside her, and even more in public, she was always rather puritanical, largely in reaction to her mother. "*Let's face it,*" she said later, "*I am honored, adored, venerated, just a woman out of nothing, not going to bed with one and then the other, on the contrary saying 'No' to everyone. It is a miracle that I made a career.*" (ARDOIN 45.) Then on another occasion, to muddy the waters (as was her way), Maria came out with a statement that implicitly corroborated what her mother had said: "*It's better to have friends. It's not the ideal life. . . . One would like to belong to somebody. . . . I don't give myself so easily. . . . In the end, the right conclusion is that my private life could never have been more important than my work.*" (*L'Express*, 19 Jan. 1970.) Renzo Allegri also maintained that Meneghini was the first "real man" in Maria's life (ALLEGRI 82), but in 1994 he expanded on that statement in a letter: "When I say in my book that Maria 'felt herself to be a woman' only when she met Meneghini, I don't mean that only then did she start to have a full sex life. . . . I mean that from the time of their first meeting Meneghini wooed her with great style, he laid siege to her in accordance with all the traditional rules of romancing, taking her out to grand restaurants and dining with her by candlelight, sending her sentimental letters and flowers. In other words, Maria—who had been the Cinderella of her family since childhood; who had felt unattractive and unwanted at the conservatory; who during the war had found a certain amount of affection only from servicemen looking for excitement; who in America, in 1946–47, had had to endure the flattery and advances of Bagarozy, an unscrupulous lawyer who tried to take advantage of her and had a relationship with her under the nose

Although some people believe that Mary's relationship with Vangelis Mangliveras was no more than a close friendship and others that it was a passing fancy based on sex, the consensus of opinion is that for a certain unspecified length of time the two of them were deeply in love with each other, lovers in every sense of the word. Others again take the view that Vangelis was more in love than Mary, who was chiefly concerned with her own interests and her future. Mary even refused to marry Vangelis, because she had "no love in her, except a love of music," as has often appeared in print over the years. We have already seen what rumors and opinion were current at the time of the liaison. Furthermore, Arda Mandikian told Stancioff in the mid-1980s that Mangliveras had been very unhappy about the outcome of his affair with Mary and had his proposal turned down on the grounds that he was too old. Mandikian also accused Mary of behaving very badly toward Mangliveras, saying that later on, when he was ill and had asked to see Mary, she had refused. Finally, in 1998 Stelios Galatopoulos wrote that Mangliveras had "declared himself willing to leave his wife and children in order to marry her."[7] But none of these nonattributed and rather superficial comments can be accepted without more detailed analysis and interpretation, considering how strongly they color our ideas about Maria Callas's personality, character, and moral identity.

In the first place, how sure can we be that Vangelis Mangliveras really did propose to Mary? The first person to make such an allegation in print was Friedrich Herzog, the critic of the *Deutsche Nachrichten in Griechenland,* who was living in Athens in 1944 and had met Mary and most probably Vangelis too: "Mangliveras loved Maria to distraction and was frantically keen to marry her, but she kept saying no." This statement, however, appeared only in a rather obscure local magazine in Germany, in 1959, and it is doubtful that Galatopoulos, the next writer to suggest that Mangliveras had proposed to Mary, knew about it. It was probably from his first book on Callas, published in 1963, that other writers took the story and repeated it, and not one of them—nor even Galatopoulos himself—mentions the source of the information.[8] If the source actually was Herzog, the allegation may have some foundation in fact. It is true that Mangliveras was already married and had a second woman in his life, with two children by him, but it is possible that he may have proposed to Mary in the hope of keeping her with him after she had told him of her desire to leave Greece. If he did, two obvious questions arise: would the lovesick Vangelis have been able to get a divorce from his wife—which he did not manage to do until just before his sudden death, eight

---

of his own wife—this Maria felt for the first time that she was a real woman, a lady, besieged in broad daylight by a rich and influential man who showed her by his words and actions that he was in love with her. Meneghini fell in love with Maria at their first meeting on 29 June 1947, the day she arrived in Verona. He fell in love with the woman herself, not with her voice, her musicianship, her possible career. And that must have been very gratifying to Maria, who, I repeat, felt for the first time in her life that she was being treated as a real lady, a person of some importance." (Letter from Renzo Allegri to the author, 9 Feb. 1994.)

years later—and, if so, would he have married Mary or the mother of his two children? In the circumstances, however much she loved him, Mary could never have taken a proposal from Vangelis seriously, even if she had wanted to accept a proposal that would have upset her plans and slowed the progress of her career.

Some say that the liaison between Vangelis and Mary did not last more than two or three months. Others speak in terms of a year, while some, including Christos Mangliveras, believe that it came to an end only with Mary's departure from Greece. The likeliest answer is that after a period in which they were deeply in love, starting with the rehearsals for *Tiefland* and probably lasting until their next collaboration in *Fidelio* and perhaps until the liberation in early October 1944, their feelings for each other must have cooled off somewhat. In October and November 1944 Mary had a brief romance with a British officer, as we shall see, and then came the violent eruption of civil strife in December 1944. This means that Mary would have been able to see very little of Vangelis, if she saw him at all, until February 1945, when the G.N.O. reopened and they started preparing for a revival of *Tiefland.* On the other hand there is no doubt that the basically good relationship between them was maintained until Mary's departure in September 1945, and even after, by correspondence. But it could not have remained a happy love affair, as it had been in 1944: Mangliveras was still in the doldrums, both in his private life and professionally, and he was tied fast to Athens by his heavy family commitments, while Mary was thinking about nothing but her future career.

Seeing Mary about to sever her ties with him and with Greece in search of a future that he too must have longed for, and being unable to follow her, Vangelis must have felt a resurgence of his love for her—all the more so, perhaps, after the renewal of their partnership in *Tiefland,* in March 1945. Given the irrepressible exuberance of his feelings, it may be that he swept her off her feet all over again and they relived some of the moments of the recent past, with Vangelis playing in real life the part of Sebastiano trying to persuade Marta to stay with him. This time, as it had been with the golden-hearted Pedro, the ideal of the "high mountains" was the lure of an international career. And that was a rival that neither Mangliveras nor anyone else could compete with, least of all at so critical a time as this. According to Galatopoulos (who again does not, however, mention his source), Mary "felt that there was only room for music in her heart," but Vangelis continued wooing her, writing her passionate letters. "*You must not ask of me my life,*" she answered. "*You are the finest of men but you are not free. Even if you were, my answer would have been the same. I can only be married to my art for the moment. You will always be a wonderful friend and that is really more important.*"[9]

So Mary was the one who broke off the affair by her determination to leave Greece as soon as she could, a determination that was strengthened by the persecution she was to suffer in the G.N.O. after the liberation. Christos Mangliveras remembered her trying to persuade the lovesick Vangelis to leave too and pursue his career abroad, a prospect which his family commitments made utterly unthinkable for him. Putting self-interest first, he therefore tried to change her mind about going away. No doubt one of the arguments that Mary threw at him to justify her inflexibility was that his wife, his mistress, and his children were all so unhappy. In her first letter to Vangelis, written in early 1946, she stated her case quite plainly: *"You see, you can say what you want about me and you are right to accuse me of perhaps not having behaved with absolute sincerity toward you (if those feelings of yours were sincere!) But I did not stop considering you my best friend and loving you as such. I do hope that you don't hate me much, and that you love me as you did before! . . . You knew well, Evangelos, that our lives were different. You had so many obligations and I could never live happily, even though I loved you, to the detriment and the misery of two women who have done me no wrong. So don't be angry with me!"* And in her 1945 Christmas greetings she had written, *"May you be happy always and forgive your little Mary if she has ever caused you to feel bitter. Fame and happiness be always with you. Mary."*[10]

The reasoning behind Mary's decision to end the relationship and leave Greece as planned was entirely justified. Vangelis was obviously unable to follow her—that was probably why he accused her of insincerity—and he was seriously ill with typhus when she left. So, in her first messages from New York, now heading for new horizons and perhaps suffering from remorse, Mary reiterated her arguments against prolonging a hopeless relationship, asking him to forgive her and to continue loving her as a friend.

Mary was acquainted with Vangelis's wife, Artemis, a discreet, petite woman then in her late forties, and she probably used to go to their house to practice on the piano there, alone or with Vangelis. She had also met Vangelis's children and their mother, Kalliopi Vrettou, not when she and Vangelis were passionately in love but later, when love had given way (at least on Mary's side) to warm affection. In fact she must have been on reasonably good terms with both the women in Mangliveras's life, as she often sent them her love in her letters from America.[11] So one has to conclude that what Mandikian told Stancioff about Mary's "very bad behavior" toward Mangliveras is not true. The fact is that Vangelis and Mary eventually separated very amicably and kept in touch with each other until the middle of 1947, when Mary went to Italy and met Meneghini. The whole tone of her letter to him, dated 12 January 1947, is very affectionate indeed:

> *My dear Evangelos,*
>
> *I have received all your letters—with my mother—and I am glad, because I thought you had forgotten me and were not writing to me any more. Now I am satisfied. I see you will never have it easy—always worries and trouble. That makes me sorry, because you deserve a better life. Ah well, God is great and He will reward you one day. § My news, dearest, is that I am getting ready for my première at the Chicago Opera House in Turandot and Aida. May God give me the health and strength to succeed—as I want to. § Everything else is going fine—I have lost quite a bit of weight and (if I may say so)*

I am quite a bit prettier. My legs have slimmed down a lot and I am very pleased. § Well, Evangelos, that's my news. I shall have more—I hope—after the 27th. I'll write and tell you all about it. My voice, thank God, is in splendid form and is getting steadily deeper. I am almost a mezzo-soprano now. § Please write to me at once with all your news—you write so well—it does me good. Write and tell me about your life and your flirts. Do you love any of them? § I send my love and wish you all the pleasant things life has to offer. § Give my love to Artemis and Vrettou—and to your children. § Regards from my mother. § Send me a long letter at once.

With my love always,
Mary

P.S. Give my regards to the chorus, don't forget!! How's your voice?[12]

About Mangliveras, as about De Stasio, Jackie prefers to say nothing. In her memoirs she refers him as a tenor with whom Mary was "very close" and who had given her the benefit of his stage experience. She also tells us that Miltiadis Embirikos was amazed at Mary's choice, as Mangliveras was not only short but also twenty-five years older than Mary! And she mentions that Mangliveras died of a heart attack shortly after *Fidelio*, adding that Mary showed no sign of grief at his loss. "My sister, supposedly unloved and in search of deep affection, was turning out to be a butterfly," she comments.[13] Quite apart from the caustic tone, the factual errors in her statements are astonishing: Mangliveras was a baritone, then only thirty-five years old and at the peak of his vocal powers, and he died in October 1952, of a perforated gall bladder. Indeed, the way Jackie and Litsa gloss over Vangelis's role in Mary's life is to be deplored, all the more so considering that they both knew him well from Patission Street, where he had been a regular visitor. In a letter to him from New York, toward the end of 1945, Maria asked Vangelis to continue visiting them: *"They'll be so pleased. They love you!"* she said. Litsa was still sending Vangelis her "regards" from New York in 1947, having even brought her daughter several letters from him from Athens. Yet all that did not prevent her—or Jackie, for that matter—from giving Vangelis no more than a few misleadingly bland lines in their memoirs. As for Maria, when Galatopoulos asked her about Mangliveras shortly before her death in 1977, she apparently remembered him "fondly, but only as a very good artist, and a marvelous colleague and friend."[14]

—⁂—

Let a man think he's the one who gives the orders, when it's exactly the other way around! It's great fun being a woman, I find it delightful!
That's very Machiavellian . . .
It's just fine, and I'm convinced you men like it that way.

To Philippe Caloni, Paris 1976

CHAPTER 30

Cavalleria Rusticana and
O Protomastoras

The recognition of Mary's talent in *Tiefland* had various consequences, in the same way that important consequences had followed from her "discovery" in *Tosca* twenty months earlier, and were to follow from her emergence as an established soloist in *Fidelio* five months later. In the first place, it gave her great satisfaction and reinforced her self-confidence, especially as a singer. Inevitably, her enemies reacted to this like a bull to a red cape, each one for his or her own reasons. "They now started cutting her dead: not talking to her, not congratulating her, not even saying hello when they met. You could see they perceived her as a threat—well, naturally they did, it was so obvious that the future was all hers," says Tatiana Varouti. One evening at a taverna that spring of 1944 Mary is reported to have said, in answer to a friend who asked her when she would sing again, "*Not for some time. I made such a hit that I can't possibly make another appearance just yet. . . . They've all got their knives into me as if I had done them the most terrible wrong. . . . They can't stand me. . . . But wait and see! The time will come when they'll be begging me to sing in Athens, and then I'll think about it.*"[1]

The self-assurance that Mary gained from her relationship with Vangelis Mangliveras provided further grounds for antipathy in certain quarters. This was another important consequence of *Tiefland*, for it was there that she had become close to someone who loved and protected her and boosted her morale when necessary. This relationship must surely have increased the self-confidence of Mary as a woman by giving her a taste of hitherto unknown pleasures. All this was bound to provoke jealous ill-will, to which Mary reacted, as usual, creating a vicious circle. Another negative consequence of Mary's relationship with Mangliveras was that she started having lessons with him and not bothering to keep up with de Hidalgo. De Hidalgo was extremely upset: not only did she have good grounds for concern about the effects this might have on her pupil's voice, but in addition she was by nature possessive of those she saw as her own "creations." One way and another, the new situation was bound to cause Mary to distance herself from de Hidalgo, with fairly serious consequences.

As might be expected, Mary's relationship with Takis Sigaras also cooled down considerably. According to the testimony of Ilias Papatestas, possibly based on his own experience, Mary was single-minded in her affections, and, "despite the environment into which her career had thrown her, she was scathingly critical of any illicit relationship."[2] This disapproval she continued to express regardless of the amoral environment of her home, just as in later life she would moralize about others, blithely overlooking the nature of her own liaison with Onassis. Be that as it may, the fact is that when her affections swung sharply in another direction she started drifting away from Sigaras, who recalls that he once appealed to Mangliveras to leave her alone, but to no avail. Yet Mary's relationship with Sigaras did continue, though probably in a somewhat strained and emotionally fraught atmosphere, right up to the time she left Greece: they continued to spend time together, and as we shall see it was he who provided vital help in arranging her passage to America.[3]

Another fairly serious consequence of Mary's emergence into the limelight by her performance as Marta was that she won the admiration of a German officer. "En masse we loathed the Italians and Germans but we did not hate them all as individuals," Litsa says in her memoirs. "We even grew to like some of the Germans, those who were human beings instead of strutting clockwork figures in Nazi uniforms. When in 1944 some of these more sympathetic officers asked Maria . . . to sing the *Stabat Mater* at one of their services, she did so." Nothing more is known about this service, but after the first night of *Tiefland* Mary was sent a bouquet by an officer and a few days later—"to our astonishment," according to Litsa—a tall, well-dressed man of twenty-four appeared at their door, introducing himself as Oskar Botmann. They all liked him, he in turn was entranced by Mary, and Jackie remembers the "charming" German officer with his highly polished jackboots and Nazi insignia, describing him as "an extremely gentle and cultivated person." The photograph that Litsa kept and published in her book shows that Botmann really was a handsome man: blond, blue-eyed, with long fingers and well cared-for hands. Mary and Botmann went out together a few times, "but that was all," according to Jackie, who adds complacently, "He was much weakened by his wounds and his only real interest in her was a deep admiration for her voice."[4]

But once again it would seem that things were not as Jackie describes them and that Litsa is probably hinting at much more when she says, "Sometimes I wonder if Maria ever thinks of this young enemy officer who admired her and whom we all liked or if she has forgotten him as she has forgotten so much of her Athenian past." It is true that Maria in her days of glory would give the impression of having forgotten much of what happened to her in Athens; but in reality, of course, her apparent amnesia was a cover designed to blot out a past filled with painful memories, largely because of Litsa's attitude and example. *"I don't know what to do. My mother wants to marry me off to a German! Just so that we won't*

Oskar Botmann.

starve!" With this cri de coeur Mary vented her feelings to Maria Alkeou, who had been so supportive when the other singers in *Boccaccio* first began to let their jealousy show. The inference is that, once the Italians had gone, the opportunistic Litsa started urging her daughter to have an affair with a German officer, or even to marry him. And although it may have been true that "our dear Oskar . . . hated what his countrymen were doing to the Italians in Greece," as Litsa puts it, nevertheless he did wear the uniform of an officer in the occupying German army, a detail to which she clearly attached no importance. Of course, for the question of marriage even to arise, Mary must have spent quite a lot of time with him and presumably he must have given her some kind of hint, perhaps actually proposed to her, or even fallen in love with her. "There was a German who had fallen in love with her, and her mother was thinking of marrying her off to him," Maria Alkeou insists. "Maria talked to me about marriage, in so many words."[5]

Mary's feelings for Vangelis Mangliveras may have been the reason her relationship with Oskar Botmann (whatever that may have been) did not develop any further. However, Jackie doubts whether Maria ever had a liaison with him: "Yes, all right, she flirted with him, but I don't think they had an affair, that he found her exciting as a woman. And the question of marriage definitely never arose. That was always her grievance." However, Jackie is confusing the early years of the occupation, when Mary did nurse that "grievance," with the last years, by which time she had changed and hardly ever revealed any of her personal problems to her mother or sister. Whatever the truth of the matter, a few months later (probably just before the German withdrawal from Greece) Botmann paid one last visit to 61 Patission Street to say good-bye to the three women: then he simply vanished overnight from Mary's life. After the war Miltiadis Embirikos heard that her unfortunate admirer had reached Germany safely but had died soon afterward, possibly from his old wounds—without ever suspecting that his name would be preserved for posterity by that one encounter with the girl who was to become the prima donna of the century.[6]

—◊◊◊—

Once Mary had been picked for *Tiefland,* Kalomiris had no option but to back Zozo Remoundou for the role of Santuzza so as to maintain a fair balance. "There was some discussion about who was to have the soprano lead," Totis Karalivanos once told a journalist, referring to the casting for the first night of *Cavalleria Rusticana* which he was to conduct. "I suggested Kaloyeropoulou, but I encountered opposition. 'For heaven's sake, we've got other, more experienced sopranos,' they kept saying. But I put up a determined fight and I got my way."[7] Eventually it was decided that Mary would sing at the first night of *Cavalleria Rusticana,* which meant that Remoundou would be Smaragda in the première of the forthcoming *O Protomastoras* "as of right." However, Mary was to take the part in some of the performances of *O Protomastoras,* a choice that appears unjustified, as she was quite unfamiliar with Kalomiris's music. The explanation was revealed in Friedrich Herzog's article fifteen years later: "The fact that [Mary] took the soprano lead in *O Protomastoras* by Kalomiris, the general manager of the G.N.O., was due to German intervention."[8] By that time Herzog knew her fairly well: whenever Mary happened to meet him in the street, her first question was always, *"Quelles nouvelles?"* "Despite her success she felt imprisoned," Herzog wrote, "because she wanted to get out into the world."[9] However, all this, especially the covert German support she was presumed to be receiving (even if it was not given openly), was to provide the basis for the unpleasantness she had to endure until she left Greece, and even after.

The rehearsals for *Cavalleria Rusticana* started on 17 December 1943, while *Tiefland* was still in rehearsal. Pending the completion of renovation work on the Olympia Theater they were held in various places, with Dimitris Michailidis as the principal assistant accompanist. But right up to the last minute, apparently, it was uncertain who was to sing on opening night. "They were betting on whether Kaloyeropoulou or Remoundou would do the first night," remembered Vyron Kolassis. "You see, it was the first nights that counted, and Homeric battles were often fought over them." Several of Mary's contemporaries at the G.N.O., including Anthi Zacharatou, make the point that Remoundou usually avoided direct confrontation in her running war with Mary: she preferred to get at her behind her back through third parties, notably Kalomiris, for she was the best singer of his music and more or less forced him to pick her. "Kalomiris invariably supported anybody who sang his music," says Andreas Paridis, and Remoundou had been performing his work regularly for years. So, when she found that she would be sharing the lead with Mary in *O Protomastoras,* she was tearful with indignation.[10]

Elvira Mataranga, who had known Kalomiris from the time when her mother was caretaker of the National Conservatory, once asked him why he had snubbed his faithful Zozo. His answer is revealing: "My dear girl, if I don't give parts to my enemies, who am I to give them to? My friends?" As far as possible, he always tried to combine the creativity of an artist with the businesslike approach of a professional manager and the duties of a civil service administrator. This meant that his feelings and principles always had to be weighed against his social and professional ambitions—a precarious balancing act. One of those who suffered from his maneuverings was Mary, who never knew where she stood with Kalomiris. She had fallen out with him badly when she was still at the National Conservatory; he had then given her a helping hand in her early years (1937–39), but she had "betrayed" the National Conservatory by switching her allegiance to its greatest enemy, the Athens Conservatory. Although Kalomiris seemed to have got over this act of treachery, it is unlikely that he had forgotten it.[11]

In the circumstances, and in light of what we know of Kalomiris's and Mary's characters, it is hardly surprising that at the time of *Cavalleria* and *O Protomastoras* in 1944 this smoldering resentment flared up again. The cause of the quarrel is not known, but it must have been connected with the rivalry between Mary and Remoundou. The incident is recalled by Mitsa Kourahani, to whom Mary turned for sympathy one day in a terribly distraught state. "*He needled me so much and he was so unfair to me that it was all I could do to stop myself throwing the inkwell at his head!*" Mary told her. She may have stayed her hand, but it is unlikely that she held her tongue. Whatever it was that she said or did, Kalomiris threatened to report her to the state committee that issued actors their licenses. "So she comes to me, seething with rage, and says, '*Mitsa, what am I to do? That monster is going to report me to the committee, which means I'll lose my permit!*' Knowing that the actors' representative on the committee was Delendas, she asked me to go with her to his house. Delendas greeted us with a smile, Mary told him the whole story, and he calmed her down by telling her that he would support her to the hilt, even if it meant he had to resign from the committee. In the end Kalomiris took no action, perhaps because Delendas had a word with him, and so Maria got out of her scrape."[12]

The fact that Mary was also chosen to sing Smaragda naturally intensified Zozo Remoundou's hostile feelings toward her. People who knew Remoundou personally or were connected with Kalomiris and the National Conservatory considered her a more polished artist than Mary, not just "Kalomiris's pet." Though her friends maintain that she was above petty rivalry, we have seen how she behaved in *Boccaccio* in early 1941, and those who insist that she seethed with resentment against Mary are overwhelmingly in the majority. In 1977, when Remoundou was still alive (she retired in 1962 and died in 1982), Zoras commented that some rivalry between them was only natural, although Mary had "only had good words to say" about Remoundou and had "never tried to steal a march on anyone." Yet her rivalry with Remoundou was well known and sometimes quite open, especially after 1944, a year in which it happened four times that they were both in the same production. "There was terrible antagonism between them. You could hear and feel it at rehearsals, behind the scenes, in the general gossip, and at performances," Nikos Zachariou says.[13] Eventually the time came when Mary's restraint snapped. Perhaps she jeered that her rival had been given the part "on Kalomiris's back." Whatever the cause, the result was that Remoundou brought her arm up and gave Mary a slap in the face.[14] The incident was to be re-enacted in reverse not long afterward with Mireille Fléri, when the latter insulted Mary and Mary slapped Fléri. And although Mary had to endure "frame-ups, obscenities, cheap tale-telling, and gratuitous hostility" and "soon learned that art is a battlefield," as Vassos Vassiliou has pointed out,[15] she cannot be absolved of all responsibility for some clashes that went beyond the bounds of propriety. She would later maintain that she had learned to ignore bad manners, but the fact remains that at least then, in Athens, she was unable to let provocation go without retaliating.

—❦—

The final preparations for *Cavalleria Rusticana*, as with *Tiefland*, took place in an atmosphere of gloom. The third anniversary of the German entry into Athens was celebrated by the occupation authorities on 27 April 1944, the day of one of the performances of *Tiefland*. Meanwhile news was coming through of the bombing of Munich, described by the German-controlled press as "brutal" but greeted with feelings of vengeful satisfaction by most Greeks. In reprisal for the killing of a German policeman on 25 April, a hundred "communists" were executed; and on 2 May the press carried a statement by Höhere SS und Polizeiführer Walter Schimana announcing that the murder of two German officers had been punished three days earlier by the summary execution of 110 villagers and the "radical destruction" of the village of Kyriaki in Boeotia. "Any such further attempt at murder will be punished in the same way," the shameless statement concluded. On 9 May, in a pathetic attempt at making amends, the authorities distributed one oke (1,280 grams) of chickpeas and 80 milliliters of kerosene to every inhabitant of Athens, followed ten days later by 320 milliliters of olive oil.

The three dress rehearsals of *Cavalleria Rusticana* were followed by nine or ten performances, all starting at 5 p.m., in a double bill with *O Pramateftis* (*The Pedlar*) by Petros Petridis. The first night and all the other performances except one (under Lysimachos Androutsopoulos) were conducted by Totis Karalivanos. Mary sang opening night, on Saturday 6 May, with Andonis Delendas (Turiddu), Mitsa Kourahani (Lola), Anita Bourdakou (Lucia), and Takis Tsoubris (Alfio).[16] The day before the première Totis Karalivanos happened to meet "a teacher at the Athens Conservatory" and advised him to come to one of the performances to see a new talent. "What, maestro!" he retorted. "You want me to see the columns of the

Temple of Olympian Zeus singing on stage?" (alluding, of course, to Mary's fat legs). Karalivanos adds that that teacher subsequently became a governor and managing director of the G.N.O.[17] Now, the only members of the Athens Conservatory teaching staff in 1944 who went on to be managing directors of the G.N.O. were Yorgos Lykoudis, the pianist Spyros Farandatos, and Filoktitis Ikonomidis. The one who was so rude about Mary was probably Ikonomidis, who persistently refused to see any talent in her, but it may also have been Lykoudis, who had never liked Mary since her display of prickly temperament in the radio studios in 1941 or 1942.[18]

Not many memories of that production of *Cavalleria* seem to have lasted to the present day. We are told that in one scene, when Andonis Delendas kissed Mary, some of the rouge from his makeup brushed off on her nose. He discreetly signaled the fact to her, she turned her back on the audience for a moment and wiped the tip of her nose, and then turned back with hardly anyone noticing what had happened.[19] One thing about the production that is clear, however, is that Mary did not live up to the expectations raised by her triumph in *Tiefland,* and the contrast was all the more striking because the first night of *Cavalleria* came between two performances of *Tiefland.* "The transitions from one register to another were very obvious, whereas Remoundou's voice was smooth and even, and she was good in the part of the simple, wronged peasant girl," says Mitsa Kourahani. As for Elli Nikolaidi, echoing her own verdict on Mary's Santuzza of 1939, she thought that in 1944 too, although Mary had sang beautifully, her voice was "often hardening." But the story of Mary's outright "failure" appears to have been put about deliberately by Remoundou and her friends, to emphasize her own superiority. One of those friends is Elvira Mataranga, who says that, "Maria stole the first night from Zozo, but she was a flop and after that she never again sang Santuzza on stage." And so an unexceptional, perhaps even mediocre, performance came to be remembered as a great failure.[20]

It is hard to judge from the available evidence how far Mary was a success or a failure in a role that she knew well, was to record brilliantly in 1953, but would never sing again on stage. Several people who remember the production considered it a success for her, and a list drawn up by the stage manager, Kostas Pomonis, shows Mary as having sung a second performance after the première. Yorgos Patriarcheas, then an assistant stage designer, also remembers her second performance. She had her hair done up in a bun at the back and was wearing a white blouse with a long, tight-waisted black skirt that emphasized her bosom but also her broad hips. He was struck by how much she had changed in the year since he had met her at the conservatory: "By this time she was already a personality," he recalls, "and her Santuzza was not really bad, as many people have said. It was merely good, in the context of a generally mediocre performance. When I went up to congratulate her she was surrounded by a crowd of admirers, thanking them all with the same modest disclaimer: '*I try, I do my best.*'"[21]

However, it would appear from the reviews that as Santuzza in 1944 Mary really did overdo the histrionics at the expense of vocal homogeneity and diction. The only critic who gave her unqualified praise was Friedrich Herzog, who referred to a "storm of applause" and innumerable curtain calls for all the principals: "Maria Kaloyeropoulou was a Santuzza with instinctive temperament," he wrote. "The drama of her singing unfolded effortlessly and sensitively with broad, melodramatic movements, often accompanied by a sob in the voice." But all the Greek critics were generally in agreement in their strongly negative comments. Sophia Spanoudi was particularly scathing, so much so that one can only wonder how Mary managed to remain on good terms with her: describing her as "a talented débutante," she said she feared that Mary must have been led to believe that she was already a full-fledged artist. She needed to control her powers, which she was allowing to control her, Spanoudi continued, adding that, "She ought to use her beautiful voice to sing with, not to screech all the time."[22]

Other critics, too, noted similar faults in Mary's performance. "Miss Kaloyeropoulou overstepped the bounds of moderation in dramatic expression," wrote Hamoudopoulos, who maintained that these "excesses" and her "continual, unnecessary hypertension" had been detrimental to her in all departments. Psaroudas too commented that Mary was sometimes carried away by the size of her voice, which he described as "rather harsh." He conceded that "she acts with great skill and stirs the audience's emotions," but he thought she ought to "restrain the ardor of her musical temperament." Even Lalaouni, Mary's staunch admirer, felt she had gone "over the top": "Both Santuzzas, Kaloyeropoulou on the first night and Remoundou yesterday, fell into this error. The difference was that Remoundou managed to hold her voice on an even line and thus display its full beauty, whereas Kaloyeropoulou spoiled her singing by forcing her voice, which often lost its evenness as a result. As for enunciation, again I have to complain: you couldn't catch a word Kaloyeropoulou sang."[23]

—⁂—

In the three and a half years of the occupation, from 27 April 1941 to 12 October 1944, the main concerns of the occupation authorities, Italian as well as German, were to keep the administration going, to maintain law and order, to fight inflation and stamp out profiteering (which undermined the economy), to ensure food supplies (primarily for themselves but also for the debilitated Greek population), and to fight the ever-growing resistance movements. Compared with these high priorities, the arts were obviously a long way down their scale of importance. "The disturbed situation and unprecedented inflation had made it impossible to maintain normal cultural relations," according to a deposition made in 1946 by Dr. Alfred Six, the head of the cultural policy department of the German foreign ministry. That only a rudimentary cultural policy was pursued in occupied Greece was confirmed by Dr. von Grävenitz, the German chargé d'affaires in Athens from

1943 to 1944: "The [local] German military, police, and party authorities certainly were not concerned about musical life in Greece." They generally limited themselves to arranging concerts and other events, mainly for the purposes of cultural propaganda. As for the Italians, they were even less interested in cultural affairs than the Germans, and most of the few events they did organize were arranged by the political and party authorities, not by the military.[24]

Nevertheless, the occupation authorities encouraged Athenians to take an interest in the arts, mainly in the fields of music and drama, chiefly in order to fill the gap left in many people's lives by the suppression of political and other activities. The cultural scene therefore remained quite lively, with frequent concerts and other events that attracted good-sized audiences. Besides the state-run National Theater and National Opera, several independent theater companies were still operating, there was an average of about six concerts a month, as well as a fair number of solo recitals, and the radio also bombarded the listening public with arts programs including a great deal of vocal music of all kinds, from operetta to Wagner (from Bayreuth) and frequent broadcasts from La Scala.[25] The performers in the concerts and recitals broadcast live from the Zappion building, usually at 7 p.m., included almost all the best-known Greek musicians but not Mary, perhaps as a result of her row with Lykoudis. The German army radio station (Wehrmachtsender Athen), which was on the air for several hours a day, also broadcast a lot of classical music, including all the concerts given by its own radio orchestra, founded in October 1942 and conducted by Hans Hörner from mid 1943. After the Italian withdrawal, and especially in 1944, there was a heavy preponderance of Beethoven, Bruckner, and Wagner, with a good sprinkling of chamber music and German lieder, and most of the performers were German.

On the lighter side, the best-known stars who performed on German radio were Rosita Serano and Zarah Leander. The Wehrmachtsender sometimes put out live broadcasts of light music from the Zappion, light music was played at military concerts in the Stadium, and the Wehrmachtsender also broadcast music played by its light orchestra, composed of a nucleus of about twenty Greek musicians with an occasional importation of players from various military bands for light classical works. Then there were concerts of light music or popular ballet conducted by Georg Grohrock-Ferrari, Ekkehard Vigelius, or Georg Albert Keck, usually at the requisitioned Kentrikon Theater (Wehrmachttheater) near Syntagma Square, but sometimes in the open air, at the Egli Patisserie in the Zappion Gardens or elsewhere, with music by German and Austrian composers. The performers for these were often brought out specially from Germany or Austria by the Nazi organization Kraft durch Freude, which also staged theatrical performances with soldiers taking most of the parts ("Soldaten spielen für Soldaten").[26]

One of the events arranged by the occupation authorities for the purposes of public entertainment or cultural propaganda (which, according to Herzog, "built an enduring bridge of understanding between Greeks and Germans"[27]) was a big gala performance in aid of needy actors and musicians, organized by Achilleas Mamakis for the German radio station in Athens. It took place at 10 a.m. on Sunday, 21 May 1944. Being in aid of such a worthy cause, this was a trap that was bound to catch the entire Greek theatrical and musical world, and so it proved: no fewer than four orchestras and six conductors were involved. The second half of the program opened with Vangelis Mangliveras in the Prologue from *Pagliacci*. Then, after the overture to *Die Fledermaus*, the sixty-strong G.N.O. orchestra conducted by Leonidas Zoras accompanied Mary in her first public performance of "Casta diva" from Bellini's *Norma*. This was followed by arias sung by Andonis Delendas, Kitsa Damasioti, and Nafsika Galanou, and then the orchestra played one of Skalkottas's Greek dances (under a German conductor, Hans Hörner) and an eighteen-man jazz band directed by Yannis Spartakos played some "modern songs" of his own composition. The program also included excerpts from plays, with all the best-known actors in Greece, and ballet with the best dancers. "The entire Greek theater" was present in that one performance, the program note claimed, and it was true.[28]

Nevertheless there were some who singled Mary out for criticism for having taken part in this gala event, conveniently ignoring the fact that more than fifty other Greek actors and musicians were also present. One such accuser was the journalist Yorgos Roussos, who wrote thirteen years later, attacking Maria during her turbulent 1957 stay in Athens: "For the shows that [the Germans] organized, they invited all performers to take part. Some went, and first among them was Maria Kaloyeropoulou. Later, making excuses for her complaisance, she snapped, '*I wasn't the only one! Anyway, I'm not like the others. I had to go first—I couldn't go at the tail end.*'"[29] Her reaction as described by a German journalist seems more plausible: "*When someone sings at a charity concert in aid of the Red Cross [sic], that is not collaborating with the enemy. Anyway, others took part, too,*" she is reported to have said. According to this unsubstantiated account, Mary was twice invited to sing at performances for the Germans during the occupation: "She was urgently in need of money, her family was on the brink of starvation and those engagements were well paid. Another thing that counted with Maria was that she would be making another appearance on stage. So she allowed herself to be persuaded to collaborate. She was to rue it bitterly, because after the war she was accused of collaboration with the Germans."[30] In an attempt to dispel these bad impressions as late as 1977, Leonidas Zoras referred to that charity event as "one of those soirées we had to perform for the occupation authorities," adding that he had had the honor of coaching and conducting Mary in "Casta diva," an experience he would never forget. Conduct her he certainly did, but it is more likely that Mary was the one who coached him in "Casta diva" that time, as she may have studied the aria as early as 1938 and had learned it properly with de Hidalgo in 1939–40. In the only review of that event that mentions Mary by name, Friedrich Herzog wrote in the *Deutsche Nachrichten in Griechenland*: "Maria Kaloyeropoulou's soprano, which, despite all her vocal training, still radiates the untouched naturalness of youth, gave to the famous aria 'Casta diva' from Bellini's *Norma* a full measure of vocal brilliance and felicitous expressiveness."[31]

—⚉—

Meanwhile, according to the cast list posted on 31 January 1944, *O Protomastoras* was to be conducted by Leonidas Zoras, with Yerasimos Koundouris and Dimitris Michailidis as his répétiteurs. Rehearsals started in May at the Olympia Theater, but toward the end of June Zoras fell out with Kalomiris, who then decided to conduct his opera himself, with Lysimachos Androutsopoulos as assistant musical director.[32] When the weather grew too hot the rehearsals were transferred to the Odeon of Herodes Atticus, which lacked even the most basic facilities. Eventually, in June, the G.N.O. asked the Feldkommandantur to install electric lights and a telephone, and plans were drawn up for the construction of a wooden barrier behind the stage to give the performers some privacy. To move the whole company and stage crew from the Olympia to the Odeon, transportation by privately owned *gazogènes* was arranged and, at the end of each rehearsal or performance, the members of the cast had to return to the Olympia in these inefficient wood-burning vehicles, still wearing their costumes. On the gentle uphill gradient near Hadrian's Arch a *gazogène* sometimes broke down: as Nikos Papachristos recalls, "One day, after trying unsuccessfully to push-start it, we walked through the streets of Athens dressed as peasants and shepherds with crooks, and everybody stared at us and laughed." Casting her mind back to those really rather tragic times, Elvira Mataranga agrees that it was "like carnival time."[33]

The Odeon, built in 143 A.D. by Herodes Atticus at the foot of the Acropolis, as it was during the war, before the restoration of the upper section of the seats. Mary sang at the Odeon thirteen times in 1944.

Kalomiris on the podium, *O Protomastoras*, July–August 1944.

The hardships of the occupation, especially the shortage of food and the constant fear, were now afflicting everyone badly. Punitive executions of innocent citizens were now daily occurrences, and from 26 May the water supply was limited to three hours every other day, from six till nine in the morning. But still, some of the news coming through gave fresh courage and hope to the population: on 6 June Hitler ordered the evacuation of Rome, and on 7 June the newspapers announced with feigned equanimity that "the expected Anglo-American invasion" had been launched the previous day in Normandy. Five days later, by which time Germany had started terrorizing southeastern England with their V1 flying bombs, Ektor Tsironikos, the Greek deputy prime minister, publicly deplored the Allied invasion to the Athenian press: "Unfortunately," he declared, "the Anglo-Americans have still not opened their eyes to the danger facing European civilization and have become the blind tools of Stalin and the Jewish clique surrounding them." On 22 June news reached Greece of the failed attempt on Hitler's life, prompting the prime minister to send a message congratulating the Führer on his deliverance.

O Protomastoras was staged while desperately fought battles were raging in Normandy and south of Warsaw and the Allies were tightening the noose around Florence. Six performances were given, all at 6 p.m.: on Saturday 29 and Sunday 30 July and 1, 3, 5, and 6 August 1944. They were seen by about seven thousand people.[34] The first night (with Zozo Remoundou as Smaragda, Andonis Delendas as the Master Builder, and Vangelis Mangliveras as the Archon) was conducted by Kalomiris, as were all the others except one or two which were conducted by Androutsopoulos. Mary sang Smaragda on the second night, the only other change being that Michalis Koronis replaced Delendas. It was probably on this occasion that she was criticized by Alexandra Lalaouni as being "vocally not up to her part, as she was very unwell," though Lalaouni did admire "the innate theatrical talent of this very young singer." Hers was the only critical write-up of Mary's Smaragda. According to Nikos Zachariou, who was in the chorus of these performances, Mary recovered and on 5 August "gave her best, both vocally and dramatically," with Delendas as the Master Builder and Christoforos Athineos as the Archon.[35]

Apparently Kalomiris himself asked Remoundou not to sing at all the performances, saying, "Let's give the young one a go, too!"[36] In accordance with his personal "code of conduct," as outlined earlier, after his unpleasant confrontation with Mary he then gave her his support, not only by keeping her on as one of the ten Grade A soloists and giving her the first night of *Cavalleria*, but also by further appeasing her at Remoundou's expense and so being more evenhanded with his favors. However, the role of Smaragda presents considerable technical problems: Kalomiris made no allowances for the fact that the human larynx is subject to certain laws of nature. Moreover, de Hidalgo had taught Mary a completely different repertoire and, more importantly, a different way of singing. Yet, although "Kalomiris's music did not suit Kaloyeropoulou and those huge intervals were alien to the precepts of bel canto," as Andonis Kalaidzakis puts it, Mary saw *O Protomastoras* as a challenge, and more particularly as a chance to outshine Remoundou. So once she had been offered the part, if only as second string, she could not refuse it. But in Elvira Mataranga's opinion Mary's performance as Smaragda, like her Santuzza, was a fiasco: "She insisted on singing the part, but she couldn't do it, it was too much for her." The last and most difficult aria ("Three sisters are we, all three cursed by fate"), sung when Smaragda is being immured in the bridge, was almost beyond her. "She was ready to give up in the middle of the performance, but Man-

Manolis Kalomiris, the composer of *O Protomastoras*, surrounded by (standing from left) Manolis Doumanis, Mary, Andonis Delendas, Vangelis Mangliveras, Anna (Zozo) Remoundou, and (below) dancer Tatiana Varouti, conductor Leonidas Zoras, and Nafsika Galanou, during one of the early rehearsals at the Odeon, late June 1944.

Vangelis Mangliveras as the Archon, *O Protomastoras*, Odeon of Herodes Atticus, Athens, July–August 1944.

Mary as Smaragda in *O Protomastoras*, with Christoforos Athineos as the Archon, Odeon of Herodes Atticus, Athens, August 1944.

gliveras, standing nearby in the foundations of the bridge, urged her on and gave her the courage to go through with it."[37]

Even so, the public did not think Kaloyeropoulou a failure any more than they had in *Cavalleria*, and she was warmly applauded. Nor were the singers in the chorus aware of her difficulties. "When Mary was singing walled up in the bridge, the whole set shook with the power and vibrancy of her voice," Spyros Salingaros said in 1963, and even quite recently he still remembered the intensity of her performance: "When we were walling her up in the bridge and she was singing, her voice was so loud that it hurt our ears." Mataranga, on the other hand, influenced by her friendship with Remoundou and perhaps bitter about the fact that Mangliveras had jilted her for Mary, is adamant in her view: "That was that, and we never expected her to sing Smaragda again! Yet the next day, when we expected her to have disappeared off the face of the earth, she turned up as if she had been cheered to the rafters. You would think she would have been self-conscious about such a flop, but she behaved as if nothing had happened!" And Remoundou, who naturally was not going to miss the opportunity to get at Mary, told everybody that if she had been in Mary's shoes she would not have shown her face there again.[38]

Mary with Andonis Delendas (Master Builder), *O Protomastoras*, Odeon of Herodes Atticus, Athens, July–August 1944. Mary's resemblance to the future Maria Callas is striking.

Considering the huge range of Mary's voice, it is likely that her vocal problems in *O Protomastoras* were partly due to bad luck or ill health. But in part they were due to the natural flaws in her voice, especially as it was then. This is a rather important point, and it raises the question of how much Mary was influenced by Vangelis Mangliveras, who had started giving her lessons when they were preparing for *Tiefland*. "When she got together with Mangliveras, her voice started going to pieces," Elli Nikolaidi believed. "She was in love with him and he with her, and he gave her exercises and lessons. Unfortunately, all singers think they know everything and set themselves up as teachers. Mangliveras had a very fine voice but he sang too loud, he bellowed. And so, as it suited her own ebullient temperament, he taught her to sing too loud—go on, louder, louder still! He pushed her voice until she was shrieking too, while de Hidalgo was tearing her hair out: 'What are you doing? You'll ruin yourself!' she would say in despair." As we have seen, nearly everyone who heard Mary then agrees that there was a certain amount of wobble in her voice from the time she first started singing lessons, but Nikolaidi, who coached her for the student production of *Cavalleria Rusticana* in 1939, always maintained that until 1944 this wobble was minimal and had been kept under control. "Even before she went to de Hidalgo, Mary sang too loud, but not to the extent that her voice wobbled," she insisted. "It was just that she got carried away, giving vent to her feelings without restraint, to satisfy the passion within her. But with Mangliveras she started really wobbling, and that can never be put right. When the voice begins to wobble, that's the end!"[39]

In the words of Bruce Burroughs, written in 1989, "Pre-Callas, an incipient wobble was cause for alarm. The usual consequence was a long vocal rest, a period of repair, diligent work on the breath, and reevaluation of repertory. . . . Post-Callas, a wobble is worn almost as a badge of honor by the wobbler, and we, the hapless 'wobblees' . . . have unaccountably taken up the belief that vocal stress is in itself dramatic."[40] After a certain point in Maria Callas's career, around 1960, the wobble in her voice was undeniable, with undulations of pitch due partly to extraneous factors, particularly the tensions in her private life. However, the extent of the problem and its causes are still uncertain today. An attempt has already been made to explain it on the basis of testimony referring to the period from 1937 onward. The conclusion seems to be that the problem existed from Mary's early childhood: either (as Mireille Fléri believed) "it was a natural characteristic of her voice, not acquired through singing," or else she brought it on herself by over-straining her voice as a child and in her early lessons in Athens. With her experience and technical accomplishment, de Hidalgo succeeded in reducing Mary's wobble considerably, but it may have become worse again when Mangliveras was encouraging her to force her voice. At all events, in mid 1944 Mary's voice did have a wobble, "but very little compared with later" according to Irma Kolassi, who accompanied her when she was learning *Fidelio*. Whatever the extent of the problem—and it is impossible to say now precisely how bad it was then—the wobble must have been further reduced in Maria's early years in Italy, when she was having lessons with Ferruccio Cusinati. According to Elli Nikolaidi, Cusinati was a very experienced teacher and répétiteur, and "he managed to soften her voice, which began to broaden out so that she no longer put so much pressure on her vocal cords as she had done under Mangliveras's tuition, but rather on her diaphragm."[41]

At this point it is worth quoting the few references that Maria herself made to the subject of her wobble and its causes. In a moment of great exasperation, at Mexico City in 1950, she confided to Giulietta Simionato: *"During the war [sic] [my mother] insisted on showing me off like a clown to the first-class passengers and officers on cruise ships. When I was fourteen [sic] she pushed me on to the stage to sing 'Cavalleria Rusticana' and 'Tosca'—and then they criticize me because my high notes wobble!"*[42] Whether or not Litsa was actually to blame (and in this case it would appear that Maria was being unfair to her), it is highly significant that she vented these feelings less than five years after her Greek period, by the end of which her wobble had been temporarily eliminated. Her outburst at that time makes it clear that the problem had existed before, and that it was still very much on her mind.

She once asked Simionato, "*But how do* you *explain the fact that my voice has this problem, about which I have already asked de Hidalgo and others? Why do my A-natural and A-flat always wobble?*" To which she received the answer: "I think it is because you have sung powerful operas like *Cavalleria* and *Tosca*; and not only that, but you sang them too young." Simionato remains convinced that Mary had damaged her diaphragm so badly that it was no longer capable of supporting her breath: "When the diaphragm loses its elasticity, nothing can be done, nothing helps: neither rest nor practice, nor anything else. Maria would protest, '*But you know why that happened. My mother used to say, "You must! Since you've got a voice, go on, sing!" And I obeyed.*'"[43]

In 1964, by which time the problem was worse and Maria was virtually at the end of her career, she reverted to the subject again: "*I had a big wobble in my voice two years ago but now it's out. . . . I had to completely forget expression and art for two years and cope with purely technical problems.*" In 1973, at the start of her recital tour which revealed how acute her vocal problems had become, she admitted again that she had "created bad habits": "*I have acquired a sort of wobble, as they call it, on the high notes, which is a pulsation, and I managed to improve that. Now, during the concerts, I will improve even more the whole status of the voice.*" And in 1977, shortly before she died, Maria spoke out about the problem yet again, trying to explain and perhaps also to understand it. In short, she may not have spoken often about the wobble in her voice—precisely because it was painful to her and she realized it was more or less incurable—but she was certainly well aware of the affliction that plagued her and caused her secret anguish all her life.[44]

—⁂—

I never lost my voice, but I lost strength in my diaphragm. . . . Because of those organic complaints I lost my courage and boldness. My vocal cords were and still are in excellent condition, but my "sound-boxes" have not been working well even though I have been to all the doctors. The result was that I over-strained my voice, and that caused it to wobble.

To Peter Dragadze, shortly before her death
(*Gente*, 1 October 1977)

CHAPTER 31

Growing Pains of a
Budding Prima Donna

We have Friedrich Herzog's word for it that the idea of putting on a second German opera, Beethoven's *Fidelio*, came originally from the German authorities. "In the summer of 1944 the idea of putting on an opera festival at the Odeon of Herodes Atticus was discussed at the German embassy," he wrote. "*Fidelio* was agreed upon and an invitation was sent to the stage director Oskar Walleck, the general manager of the Prague Opera." It seems then that, although *Fidelio*, an opera on the theme of liberty, was a rather risky choice in the circumstances, the decision was made by the Germans alone. The discussions, however, at which Herzog himself may have been present, took place in April and not in the summer. This we can safely assume because Manolis Kalomiris informed the board of the National Opera of his intention to propose Beethoven's *Fidelio* for the coming summer season as early as late April 1944. He then formally proposed it to the board on 1 May 1944, together with his own opera *O Protomastoras* and Gluck's *Iphigénie en Tauride*, another German work that was probably also selected by the Germans. The board, which really had no choice in the matter, formally approved the two German operas (together with *O Protomastoras* as a sop to the Greeks). They were to be conducted by Dr. Hans Hörner, the leading German maestro in Athens at that time.[1]

Shortly before he died, Takis Sigaras told a related story which, though vague in places, is of interest: "Knowing that I had contacts at the Kommandantur, Mary told me one day that she wanted to sing at the Odeon of Herodes Atticus and asked me to arrange it with them. So I asked the Kommandant to give his permission, and I remember we talked about putting on a German opera and chose *Fidelio*. I know that the Germans didn't pay Mary, but I told her that I would pay her myself, as I was the one who had negotiated with Neubacher's A.D.C. [aide-de-camp]."[2] Unless Mary gave a solo recital for the Germans with a program that included excerpts from *Fidelio*—a hypothesis for which no documentary evidence of any kind has been found—Sigaras's hazy recollections probably refer to the discussions mentioned by Herzog. It is reasonable to assume then—but difficult to prove—that the idea of an opera festival and the discussions about it at the German embassy were prompted by Mary's request to be allowed to sing at the Odeon of Herodes Atticus, which Sigaras passed on to Neubacher's A.D.C. via the Kommandantur. That the Germans chose *Fidelio* with Mary in mind is therefore a possibility, but it is less likely that they agreed to pay Mary themselves, as she would be paid under her contract with the G.N.O. anyway. Be that as it may, when, about 20 April, Kalomiris was instructed to include *Fidelio* in the G.N.O.'s summer program, the Germans had not yet openly asked that Mary be cast as Leonore. As a result Kalomiris told Mireille Fléri that she would be taking the title role. However, after Mary's marvelous performance as Marta in *Tiefland* during that same week, the Germans must have informed Kalomiris of their "wish" that she should also be Leonore in *Fidelio*. Kalomiris was in no position to argue, and it may be that on reflection he considered Mary's voice better suited to the part than Fléri's. At all events, he decided not to make a formal announcement of the change until he had found an indirect way of letting Fléri know that Mary was to sing in her place.

In her written petition to the G.N.O. board of governors, on 3 June 1944, Fléri wrote: "When it was decided to stage *Fidelio*, the general manager summoned me to inform me that I would have the lead in the said production. A few days later, however, it came to my notice that the general manager had changed his mind and decided to give my part to Miss Kaloyeropoulou. Faced with this unforgivable *volte-face*, all I could do was to go and see him in person and protest as forcefully as I was able." At their meeting Kalomiris naturally did not tell Fléri that the decision had been imposed on him from above; instead, he tried to justify his tergiversation on the grounds that it would be more correct to choose between the two sopranos. Fléri herself conceded later that Kalomiris had told her that the part of Leonore would be given to "one of the two." In her petition, however, she wrote that Kalomiris's decision was bound to provoke the most preposterous rivalry between herself, "a world-famous prima donna," and Mary, "a youngster who has only recently made her operatic début." After listing her accomplishments of the last ten years and more (she had, indeed, sung at the Royal Opera in Rome with singers of the caliber of Gigli, Malipiero, and Cigna, and under the baton of Tullio Serafin), she requested that the "wrong" done to her be righted. The board had to reject her request, of course, whereupon Fléri, to save face, told Kalomiris and Hörner to give Mary the part "because it was too heavy for her own voice," as she admitted shortly before she died.[3]

It is interesting to see what Maria herself had to say on this subject in 1957: "*In the summer of 1944 I had my first scrapes with colleagues. They were going to put on 'Fidelio' and another prima donna had put herself out a great deal to get the part and had succeeded in getting it, but she was entirely too busy to learn it. Since the rehearsals had to begin immediately, I was asked whether I could replace her, and I naturally accepted, because I knew the score to perfection.*" And in an interview in 1958 she said rather condescendingly, "*So I suppose it so happened I got on my colleagues'*

nerves. They were older people, I don't blame them. I was so young, they couldn't under-
stand why I was chosen for certain roles. I suppose I could explain that very easily: it was
just that I was always ready. Instead of gossiping and going around trying to get parts
from other people, I just studied and was ready when the good time came. Which is
always my weapon, always being prepared. It's not a weapon used for fighting, it's just
conscientiousness and love of my work."[4] It is true that Fléri had moved heaven and
earth to get herself cast as Leonore, even though she did not know the part—
which was not surprising, as her voice was not right for it. Mary, on the other
hand, had sung the recitativo and the grand aria "Abscheulicher!" at two recent
concerts, which means that she had most probably studied the rest of Leonore's
part and all the other parts as well, in her usual way.

One point on which there can be no argument is that Mary was the person
best qualified for the part, not only because her voice was better suited to it than
anybody else's but also on the grounds of her acting ability. Mezzo-soprano Irma
Kolassi, who was then a répétiteur at the G.N.O., openly admits that Mary was
never a particular friend of hers; nevertheless, she believes that Mary won the part
on merit, "thanks to her voice and her personality." Several others take the more
apologetic view that Mary got the part by default, because there was no one else
who could sing Leonore as well as she could. But there is also a body of opinion,
containing at least a kernel of truth, which maintains that Kalomiris (who was
proud of the fact that Mary had started out at his conservatory and had recently
included her among the ten Grade A soloists in the G.N.O.) was the person chiefly
responsible for her being given the part of Leonore. According to Achilleas Mamakis, Kalomiris "had to overcome the opposition of other singers [that is to say,
Mireille Fléri] who thought they had a prior right to the part on the grounds of
seniority." One thing Mamakis did not write (although he must have known it, as
he was close to the German officials who had "selected" Mary) was that Kalomiris
had won his battle before it had started.[5]

On 3 June 1944, the very day that the board dismissed Fléri's request for
"reinstatement," the two cast lists for *Fidelio* were put up on the notice board. The
first, traditionally the stronger of the two, was headed by Kaloyeropoulou, Vlachopoulou, Delendas, Mangliveras, Moulas, and Epitropakis, while the second
had Remoundou, Amaxopoulou, Koronis, Efstratiou or Xirellis, Persis, and
Kalaidzakis or Kokkolios in the principal parts. Although Remoundou might not
have been singing at all had it not been for the friction between Kalomiris and
Fléri, the fact that she was in the "junior" cast sparked off a fresh burst of sniping
at Mary. In Amaxopoulou's words, "Remoundou wanted to be in the première of
Fidelio and kicked up a fuss to get what she wanted." Vlachopoulou is much more
censorious: "Remoundou hated Mary as much as she me," she asserts, "because we
were often chosen in preference to her. But anyway, how could they possibly cast
her as Leonore, even though she did have a big voice? Her figure was all wrong,
and her legs looked like matchsticks poking out of the top of her boots." Even so

it is interesting that Oskar Walleck, the director, had mixed feelings on the subject because the fragile figure of Remoundou was closer to his idea of Leonore.* In the end the choice of Mary for the first night was probably made by Hans Hörner, the conductor: "Hörner was startled to see Kaloyeropoulou close her score at the third or fourth rehearsal," recalls Remoundou's friend, the chorister Elvira Mataranga. "That was where the 'God-given talent' mentioned by Lalaouni showed through, though we hadn't the wit to see it in those days. Sometimes, nevertheless, when Remoundou and I were alone together she would say to me, half seriously, half in jest, 'Could it be that there *is* something divine and we haven't realized it?'"[6]

It is clear from all this why, in her brief memoirs, where she made no mention of any earlier friction and implied that there had been none, Maria did remember the bad time she had had with her colleagues in the summer of 1944: obviously the troubles she went through after her success in *Tiefland* were much worse than anything she had gone through before. Kolassi still has memories of Mary quarreling with Remoundou, Fléri, and others: "I remember them screaming at one another like fishwives, hurling vulgar abuse at each other," she says. Several incidents occurred in front of the chorus when the preparations for the production of *Fidelio* moved from the Olympia to the Odeon of Herodes Atticus. "On one occasion a spiteful remark from Remoundou made Kaloyeropoulou retaliate like a tigress," remembers Yorgos Patriarcheas, who was told afterward by Michalis Koronis, one of the two Florestans, that the incidents were constant during the rehearsals. As Tatiana Varouti remarks, "They couldn't admit that she had something they hadn't got, and they made her life an absolute misery."[7]

Tenor Andonis Kalaidzakis too has memories of the highly charged atmosphere of these days: "Mary quarreled one day with Fléri in the courtyard of the Olympia and they almost came to blows," he says. "There was quite a row going on until Fléri's husband, tenor Glynos, stepped in and gave Mary a tongue-lashing. It was something to do with the allocation of parts, the usual sort of thing."[8] But that particular row, which must have taken place at the very end of May or the beginning of June 1944, was by no means the sort of thing that happened every day. Antigone Salta, who was then a member of the G.N.O. chorus, remembered how, one day in the theater, "In came Fléri, weeping tears of rage and exclaiming,

---

*Sometime in 1950 Kalomiris happened to mention that Walleck had asked him what had become of "that Leonore," meaning Remoundou, and someone passed the story on to Maria. It was just at this time that Kalomiris was in Rome trying on behalf of the G.N.O. to persuade Maria to come to Athens for a recital, two performances of *Tosca*, and two of *Tiefland*. Maria, who had shown interest, suddenly sent a cable canceling all the arrangements. Quite possibly her change of heart was partly due to Walleck's innocent question, for she apparently had flown into a rage when she was told about it. For years afterward, whenever she was asked if she was coming to Athens she would answer sarcastically, "*But you don't need me, you've got Remoundou!*" (Letters from Kalomiris to Synadinos, Rome, 2 and 4 Oct. 1950, ELIA; KRASSA.)

'Never in my life has anyone slapped me—and now to get a slap in the face from Kaloyeropoulou!'" The incident had occurred in Kalomiris's office at the Olympia, and it was "to do with a part that Fléri was to sing." Having been a well-established singer long before the G.N.O. was founded, Fléri was still regarded by many of her colleagues as an outsider. She often felt frustrated and in consequence had the reputation of being sharp-tongued. On this occasion, frustrated by Mary's selection and the rejection of her petition, she appears to have said something rude to Mary, who retorted: *"You can think what you like, but I'm going to sing in that production!"* We may be fairly sure that in the heat of the moment Fléri alluded to the "means" Mary used in order to "take roles," referring tartly to Mary's and Litsa's close friendships with Italians and Germans. According to Salta, "Fléri insulted Mary, who responded by giving her a tremendous slap in the face."[9]

When asked about this episode, shortly before she died, Fléri hotly denied it. "It's all lies!" she exclaimed. "I never slapped her, nor did she slap me!"—though she sounded noticeably less emphatic when she spoke the last five words. But in another conversation she described Mary as "a good-for-nothing" who was "always quarreling and extremely aggressive" and "very free with her fists," adding immediately though that she herself had not actually seen Mary hit anyone. If Fléri is to be believed, Remoundou could not stand Mary, and Mary felt the same way about Galanou, "a vicious woman, a terrible viper, who would have gouged Mary's eyes out if given half a chance." She herself claimed to have admired Mary, though she did admit that Mary once called her "an old hag." Fléri attributed Mary's hardness mainly to the influence of her mother, "a terribly unpleasant woman, utterly detestable—a monster, and very jealous!" as she recalled in 1995. But then, returning to the attack, she said of Mary: "Her manners were deplorable. She had no consideration for anyone, she treated everyone as trash!" Clearly there was no love lost between Mireille Fléri and Mary Kaloyeropoulou in those days.*

—⁂—

Mary's row with Fléri over the role of Leonore had some even more unpleasant consequences. Fléri was then married to the tenor Nikos Glynos, who would naturally have been hostile to Mary and, like her, would flare up at the slightest provo-

---

*Telephone conversation with Mireille Fléri, 9 Feb. 1995; FLÉRI. Toward the end of her life, Mireille Fléri seems to no longer have harbored unkind feelings about Maria Callas. In conversation she mentioned, among other things, that she had helped her in practical ways during the war. "She had nothing to wear! *'Dear Mireille, please . . .'* she would say. I gave her all sorts of things—clothes, underwear, stockings. In 1957 she asked me to write to the papers saying that I had given her clothes, so that she could defend herself against the accusations that were being leveled against her. But I never wrote the letter . . ." When, in the early 1950s, Fléri was doing *Tannhäuser* for RAI (singing Venus to Renata Tebaldi's Elisabeth), she remembered being struck one day by Tebaldi's remark about her arch-rival Callas: "E tanto buona, questa vipera greca!" ("She is really good, that Greek viper!")

cation. So, once Fléri had been passed over in favor of Mary and Mary had slapped Fléri, the stage was set for a major eruption. Fléri herself admitted that the serious clash between Mary and Glynos probably occurred "because he always had a belligerent streak," and not only because he would naturally have taken her side. Glynos was only waiting for a pretext, and this was given him on Wednesday, 19 July 1944, when Mary was talking to her first Scarpia, Titos Xirellis, somewhere in the National Theater, in the presence of several other singers.

According to Mary's own account of the incident,[10] Glynos happened to be passing nearby when she was saying to Xirellis that it was "*not right to double up the parts in these operas.*" As she wrote in her statement to Kalomiris, "*The tenor Glynos butted into the conversation, telling me in a sarcastic tone that I had such a high opinion of myself that I objected to sharing my part with anyone else, and that it was by knowing the right people and pulling strings that I managed to sing at the premières. I told him he was wrong and said that I had got where I was on merit, and merit alone.*" Quite apart from the grave slur on Mary's character, we may be sure that Glynos's tone of voice was not just sarcastic but willfully provocative; and that Mary, who was easily stung by accusations of this kind, must have answered him more pugnaciously and in stronger terms than those she used in her statement. That is the only possible explanation for the eruption that followed: "*In reply, that cur called me a wh*** and said that I ****ed Italians and Germans, and that was why I had the highest salary in the company.*" At this point Mary, taken aback and affronted, must have answered him back, no doubt acrimoniously, and perhaps also insulted him as he had insulted her. To which Glynos responded with more foul language and threats of physical assault: "*In tears, I told him to go to hell, but he became even more violent and hurled vulgar abuse at me, trying to hit me at the same time.*" Presumably the bystanders held him back and, perhaps by common consent, accompanied Mary and Glynos to the general manager's office. All we know about what passed in Kalomiris's office is that Glynos "*pounded the desk with his fist, again calling me a dirty slut in front of you.*" "*The rest you know,*" Mary wrote—and ends her account there.

Kalomiris would most probably have tried to reach some sort of compromise, which was his preferred method of dealing with such disputes, but his already delicate task was made more difficult still when Glynos spoke rudely to him too, as he almost certainly did, unable to stifle his feelings of rancor against the one whom his wife accused of trying to diminish her professional prestige. Mary's next step would certainly have been to ask Mangliveras, who had some experience of disciplinary proceedings, for his advice. The very next day, 20 July, she sent the general manager her written account of the incident, ending with an ultimatum very similar in tone and wording to those presented in such cases by Mangliveras himself: "*For these reasons I have been forced to the irrevocable conclusion that I cannot stay on in the same theater with bad-mannered, obnoxious, vulgar colleagues such as Glynos unless, as I hope, you take appropriate action.*"[11]

History does not relate what arguments Kalomiris used or what promises he gave Mary to pacify her and persuade her to sing in the two productions that were now ready for performance, *O Protomastoras* and *Fidelio*. On 25 July "that cur," the "bad-mannered, obnoxious, vulgar" Glynos (strong words to use in a written statement—so strong that we may be fairly sure they were dictated by either Mangliveras or Litsa) sent in his own account of the incident, which has unfortunately been lost. Kalomiris referred the case to the disciplinary board with a covering note in which he requested "that appropriate action be taken against the offending singer, Mr. N. Glynos." On 17 August, three days after the première of *Fidelio*, the disciplinary board sent word to Mary, Glynos, and nine witnesses, summoning them to appear for questioning on Tuesday 22 August, only a few hours before Mary was due to sing Leonore at the Odeon of Herodes Atticus. Unfortunately the minutes of this meeting have not been found, and all we know is that the very next day Kalomiris requested "that the singer N. Glynos be brought before the disciplinary board once again." Thus it is clear that the case did have some repercussions for Glynos, though we do not know what the eventual outcome was.[12]

As far as Mary is concerned, the imbroglio with Fléri and Glynos brings into sharp focus the fact that by 1944, when she had begun to make a name for herself and had been given four leading roles in five months, she was having to face much fiercer competition—so fierce as to amount to open war. She was generally talked about by her colleagues as "the wh*** who ****s Italians and Germans," or words to that effect, and she was sometimes so called to her face. Being very touchy on the subject, and with reason—since she firmly believed that she had got where she was purely on her own merit, and that any backing she might have had from Italians and Germans had been no more than she deserved as an artist—she rose to her own defense with unfeigned indignation and a deep-rooted faith in the rightness of her cause. Her reaction to Glynos's obscenities was to counterattack with the dogged determination of one who knows she is in the right and will give no quarter to her attacker. Mary was then under the influence of Vangelis Mangliveras; evidently it was from him that she learned not only to aspire to the highest salary in any opera house where she was to sing (and later, with Meneghini's encouragement, to demand it as of right), but also to exert pressure that almost amounted to blackmail, while leaving a door open for negotiation. All of which, of course, were essential weapons in the armory of the future international prima donna.

Meanwhile, on 19 June 1944, the board of the G.N.O. had approved the program for the 1944–45 winter season. The opening production was to be *Le Nozze di Figaro*, followed by *Der fliegende Holländer*, *Martha*, *Fedora*, *Rigoletto*, *Mignon*, *Pagliacci*, and *Lestenitsa* by Yorgos Sklavos, in that order, as well as several revivals of past productions, including *Tiefland* with Mary in the lead. The program was officially announced on 1 July together with the names of the conductors and stage directors, who were asked to submit their proposed cast lists within ten days. On 28 August it was announced that in *Der fliegende Holländer*, which

Mary in a public park, probably the Royal Garden, Athens, summer 1944.

was to be conducted by Zoras and directed by Walleck, Senta would be sung by Mary (with Mangliveras, Moulas, Koronis, and Kokkolios) and by Remoundou in the second cast. In other words, not only would it be a production in the same mold as *Tiefland* and *Fidelio* but it would have much the same cast.[13] As a result of the civil strife that erupted in December 1944, the G.N.O. program was completely disrupted and *Der fliegende Holländer* was not staged until after Mary had left Greece. But it is an intriguing thought that in the latter part of 1944 she knew that she had been given the part of Senta and had perhaps started learning it. Events in Greece in 1944–45 eventually prevented her from performing a role in which all the indications are that she would have been brilliant, and which, in the event, she was never to sing. She did, however, later sing the other part in which she was cast for the 1944–45 season at the G.N.O., that of Fedora, one of her very few roles that was never recorded. The cast for Giordano's opera, to be conducted by Karalivanos and directed by Triandafyllou, was announced on 8 September 1944. This time Fléri was to sing the title role at the première, in preference to Mary who was in the second cast with Amaxopoulou, Epitropakis, and Tsoubris.[14] The prospect of further successes for Mary in these roles must have made her rivals even more exasperated than they were already, and this may partly account for the renewed wave of hostility that broke out just after the liberation. By that time, of course, fuel had been added to the fire by her resounding triumph in *Fidelio*, which confirmed her standing as a prima donna.

All this occurred when *O Protomastoras* and *Fidelio* were both in rehearsal. Feelings were running high throughout the company, a state of affairs that reflected the extremely tense political situation. The massacre of two hundred Greeks at the Kaisariani rifle range on May Day was still fresh in the memory. Arrests, executions, round-ups, betrayals, and clashes between rival resistance groups, all aggravated the miseries of a famine so widespread that people were still dropping dead in the streets every day. It is true that many of these occurrences, taken in the context of the news coming in on the BBC, signaled the imminence of the German withdrawal from Greece; but at the same time they created a situation which made civil war inevitable. Fifty further Greeks were shot by the Germans on 10 August, four days before the première of *Fidelio*, and the execution of Greek patriots and collaborators who had outlived their usefulness was destined to continue until the Germans finally left, about two months later. One can only marvel at the way twenty-year-old Mary managed to learn her parts in four very difficult operas and to face all the other demands of her work, when she had so many troubles to cope with. Considering all the pressures upon her, it is hardly to be wondered at that her performances in *Cavalleria* and *O Protomastoras* were relatively unsuccessful, or at best indifferent. "*The first essential to one's best work [is] the hardest to achieve—freedom of the mind*," Maria told an interviewer in 1961. "*To attain the highest expression of one's talent calls for relaxation of the spirit.*"[15] It is more than likely that when she spoke those words she was also thinking of everything she had endured in 1944 and again, as we shall see, in 1945.

In later years Maria the opera singer, being her own severest critic, grew more and more unsure of herself as a singer, until eventually her stage fright became unbearable. However, at the time of her early triumphs in Greece things were completely different. As a woman she still had reason to feel unsure of herself, especially before 1942; but as a musician her success in *Tosca* had given her a remarkable degree of confidence in herself, her ability, and her future. Many people who knew Mary in Greece, including de Hidalgo, have described her as a girl who was riddled with complexes about everything except her voice. Being full of energy and drive, she was not content to sit back and bask in the glow of her youthful professional self-confidence. On the contrary, she worked harder and more consistently than any of her fellow singers, with a dedication and persistence that laid the foundations of the Callas mythology. "She had set herself a goal, and she believed that the secret of success was the unremitting pursuit of that goal," wrote Vassos Vassiliou, the Greek journalist who seems to have known her well during those crucial formative years.[16] Sustained by her steadfast faith in herself and working with indomitable persistence, she survived the various trials and tribulations of the first three years of the occupation. She then managed to overcome the professional problems that arose in the difficult conditions of 1944 and of 1945, following the liberation and the reorganization of the National Opera. And having overcome them, the budding prima donna had only to apply the lessons she had learned at such a high cost.

—⁊⊠⁊—

I learned long ago to ignore bad manners. I am not, however, either docile or placid . . . . When I have really said or done something, I take full responsibility . . . . I am not an angel and do not pretend to be. . . . But I am not a devil either. I am a woman and a serious artist, and would like to be so judged.

"I Am Not Guilty of All Those Callas Scandals"
(*Life*, 25 May 1959)

CHAPTER 32

Fidelio: The Making of a Diva

Unlike the other productions in which Mary had been involved until then, *Fidelio* had Michalis Vourtsis as the chorus master. This time Elli Nikolaidi was delegated by Kalomiris to coach some of the soloists in collaboration with the official répétiteur, Irma Kolassi. When Mary was given the part of Leonore she went off to find Nikolaidi at the Hellenic Conservatory on Fidiou Street, where she would be going in any case to work with Kolassi. Nikolaidi played through Leonore's part just once, from beginning to end, analyzing it as she went, while Mary listened without saying anything. The following day Nikolaidi was all ready to start the next study session in the usual way, going through each scene several times. "I started playing, but to my utter astonishment I discovered that Mary already knew the whole part by heart! And she wasn't even looking at the music!" Talking about it just after Maria's death, she said, "It wasn't only her voice and her acting that set her in a class apart so early on: she put such meaning even into her *colorature*. . . . It wasn't mere technical virtuosity, she knew how to make music of them." Having followed her progress since her second year at the National Conservatory, Nikolaidi described admiringly how, although Mary was quite a hulking girl, her movements on stage were light and airy: "Those hands of hers, how marvelous they were when she moved them! And I remember how she would stand on tiptoe and raise her right arm on the high notes, and then, when they came to an end, bring them off by closing her fingers."[1]

Irma Kolassi also has vivid memories of the time she spent preparing Mary for *Fidelio*: "When Kaloyeropoulou was coming I knew it was her from her heavy tread, which made the whole floor shake in that dilapidated old building." Kolassi, who coached the soloists by herself in the early stages, remembers how cooperative and conscientious Mary was and how she shared her mania for getting the details right: "She was very meticulous, she left nothing to chance." As Maria once remarked, "*You need a pianist that is very, very particular in teaching you, reminding you of the exact value of notes, not letting one slip you.*"[2] The rehearsals would be transferred to the Olympia Theater only when all the soloists had learned their notes. Then, to start with, the répétiteur accompanied them on the piano with the musical director conducting and giving his instructions. So as soon as Mary was ready, Kolassi informed Hörner, who gave her the tempi and coached her in the interpretative nuances he wanted. *"If the tenor or the baritone was there sooner [before the orchestral rehearsals started], I used to ask him to come to my rehearsals or I to his,"* Maria said later. *"If not, we waited for the maestro and then we would combine. . . . Things do change from piano to orchestra rehearsals: certain maestros change the rhythm quite a lot, others not."*[3]

The Greek singers and instrumentalists who performed under Hans Hörner, the conductor of the German radio orchestra, are unanimous in their high opinions of him. "He was no genius, but a very good, reliable conductor, and he was a nice person, not at all like the other Germans who were here then," says Andreas Paridis, who played Beethoven's First Piano Concerto with the Athens State Orchestra under his direction on 13 March 1944. The forty-one-year-old maestro, who wore the uniform of a major in the Wehrmacht, "was always trying to show you, to help you," Zoe Vlachopoulou agrees, "and he was a good person, extremely polite." Everyone was struck by his modesty and good manners. He never behaved like a representative of the Herrenvolk and he always unbuckled his pistol holster at rehearsals. Most of the time he spoke French, without ever raising his voice, and he was the same when conducting. The Greek critics commended him for his "highly musical" conducting, his sure musical sense, his strongly rhythmical tempi, the surges of passion when circumstances required, the "stirring expressiveness" and "restrained simplicity and absolute rightness" of his gestures.[4]

Irma Kolassi maintains that with Hörner, who was much better at getting his way than Greek conductors, Mary always did what she was told: "He wouldn't let her do whatever she wanted—no braying on the low notes, no screeching on the high notes—and she sang very musically in those days." Here Kolassi is being unfair to Mary, who had worked very well with all her previous conductors too, even though most of them had been mediocre musicians.[5] Indeed, Maria always showed great respect for her conductors: *"Conductors for us, once upon a time especially, were gods,"* she said in 1970. *"We went to the theater on tiptoes—it's like going to church, really. That's how we were brought up."* Her only known clash with a conductor at work—and that very discreet, as we have seen—was with Zoras in *Tiefland.* But it does seem that Mary had already acquired a personality and an air of assurance on stage by the time she was twenty. It is unlikely that her mother, who sat through some of her rehearsals, was being untruthful when she said that Mary would sometimes display her temperament by yelling at the orchestra; but she would never yell at the conductor.[6]

Many years later, describing the process of preparing a production, Maria said that the first step was to analyze her own stage character in relation to the libretto, the music, and the composer's directions. Then came an analysis of the character of the music, which had to be studied in detail and in depth, in combination with dramatic interpretation. At the orchestral rehearsals, which followed, she always sang in full voice. This had been her standard practice ever since the 1942 *Tosca*, and she still believed it was absolutely essential: "*There is one thing that you really must do: that is to sing in full voice at the very first orchestra rehearsals, for your own and your colleagues' sake, for they too dose their performance according to your coloring, and the conductor also and the stage director. The main thing is to test your own possibilities.*"* Next come the stage rehearsals with the director and the chorus, Maria continued, and finally everything is put together: stage, colleagues, orchestra, chorus, and costumes. The last working rehearsals usually involve a lot of quarreling between the conductor and the stage director, who are always at loggerheads.[7]

In *Fidelio*, however, the collaboration between Hörner and the stage director, his compatriot Oskar Walleck, was extremely smooth: in fact Hörner was always helping Walleck by translating his instructions into Greek, with the assistance of Zoras, who was to conduct the performances with the alternate cast. Walleck did not arrive from Prague until early August, by which time the musical preparations were complete. Everyone was immediately impressed by his profound knowledge of music and the way he showed the soloists the precise moment when they should move, so that the dramatic action should tie in perfectly with the music and with individual instruments in the orchestra. The way he asserted his will and deployed the various groups on the cramped stage of the Odeon of Herodes Atticus was also an eye-opener. "Walleck was a great director, a dynamic director," Zoe Vlachopoulou recalls. "He could make you understand what he wanted even though I could tell only by watching his expression, as he spoke only German."[8]

The last stage of all is that of the final rehearsals, all performed without interruption, as far as possible like a public performance. In Athens in those days it was customary to have three or four *prove generali* for a new production, of which the last two were dress rehearsals, and that was the case with *Fidelio*. "Mary and I always sang and acted as if it was a proper performance, unlike many others, who needed to be jogged by the conductor or stage director," Vlachopoulou recalls. But later Maria was to go further, talking about the real, solid work that begins after the first performance, when the blanks can be filled in and the details perfected: "*There is nothing like stage performances in front of an audience. . . . Then you work the role as the years go by, if you care to really work hard.*"[9]

---

*HAREWOOD. Maria's habit of "squandering" her voice and tiring her vocal cords in this way must not, of course, be confused with the loss of vocal powers often experienced by singers as a result of bad technical training. When Maria sang in a concert with Beniamino Gigli at San Remo in December 1954, the great tenor told her that a singer should always "sing on his interest, not his capital." Maria took the lesson to heart and referred to it frequently thereafter, confident that she had accumulated ample "interest," that is to say technique. "*What [Gigli] meant was that we work on technique, rather than on mother nature, because mother nature, like an athlete, finishes very young,*" she explained in 1970. "*I don't know, twenty-two, twenty-four, twenty-five is the limit of a singer if you sing on sheer strength. . . . From then on you really last on your own technique.*" (FROST.)

Preparing *Fidelio* at the Odeon, August 1944. Hans Hörner (left) with Oskar Walleck (in white), Zoe Vlachopoulou, and Leonidas Zoras.

The preparatory work on *Fidelio* started at the end of April or the beginning of May 1944, which for Mary meant immediately after *Tiefland* and *Cavalleria Rusticana*. On 19 June Kalomiris informed the board of the G.N.O. that in Hörner's opinion the production would be ready by 20 July. By then the conductor would have to go to Germany for one reason or another (including fetching the orchestral parts) and Ulysses Lappas asked for a deputy to be appointed in case he was delayed or had an accident. The board opted for Filoktitis Ikonomidis, but Hörner returned in good time and so the alarming scenario of Ikonomidis having to work with Mary was averted.[10] Even so, it was the prospect of Mary's appearance on the historic stage of the Odeon of Herodes Atticus in an opera by Beethoven that led to the final breakdown of relations between them. Talking to Takis Sigaras one day in Mary's presence, Ikonomidis said quite bluntly, "This girl's no good for Beethoven." As Sigaras recalls, "Maria then turned and snapped at him, '*Listen, Maestro, whether I'm any good or not is none of your business. But I tell you, one day you'll be groveling to conduct me!*' And from that day on they never spoke another word to each other." Sadly, there is no denying the depth of Ikonomidis's hostility. Even allowing for the natural antipathy that would be aroused in any respected teacher and conductor by the uncouth behavior of a girl hardly more than a third of his age (and perhaps also by the fact that she happened to have no

Mary with Hans
Hörner, Athens,
August 1944.

use for his theory lessons), he seems to have taken it to extremes. Besides the fact
that he did not really like opera, least of all the kind of opera Mary was best at, this
was clearly a clash between two characters and mentalities that were poles apart.
"He couldn't stand that sort of prima donna," his widow Kalliopi explained. "His
way of thinking was central European, whereas Kaloyeropoulou's was Italian. My
husband had a very practical mind, he never let himself be carried away by sentiment. So he and Kaloyeropoulou were quite incompatible."[11] And as Mary could
never ignore provocation, especially of the kind that Ikonomidis gave her, the two
of them were bound to fall out.

Throughout the occupation—even after Mary had begun to make her name
at the National Opera, having left the conservatory and given up the idea of taking her diploma—Ikonomidis consistently refused to accord her any recognition:
this was his indirect way of fighting to block her progress. As Achilleas Mamakis,
the then director of the Athens Festival, wrote in 1957, "[Maria] insisted that the
general manager of the [Athens] State Orchestra [Filoktitis Ikonomidis], when
asked about her, always used to say either that he knew no one by the name of
Kaloyeropoulou or that he had never had a chance to see if she had a voice, even
though he had attended some of her performances." In this article, written a few
months before the visit to Athens by the now great Maria Callas, Mamakis records
her bitter account of the way Ikonomidis had behaved toward her, ending with biting sarcasm: "*I do not mind being directed by a Greek conductor in Athens, if you*

Filoktitis Ikonomidis in the
early 1950s.

want. Any Greek conductor. But it would be better if Mr. Ikonomidis, in particular,
were in the auditorium with the rest of the audience. Then he will at last have a chance
to see whether I really have a voice."[12] Ikonomidis's antipathy to Maria was to surface yet again on this occasion, for he was the only member of the Athens Festival
organizing committee who objected to the amount of her fee. Having failed to
carry the rest of the committee with him, he resorted to underhanded tactics, passing on various facts and figures to the management of the opposition newspaper
Ta Nea. The matter was scandalously exploited by the political parties, giving rise
to a huge outcry against Maria Callas, who naturally found herself growing disgusted with her countrymen all over again.

—◊◊◊—

Jackie describes Mary as having been "even more obsessed" during the rehearsals
for *Fidelio* than she had been with *Tiefland.* She also states that their grandmother,
Frosso Dimitriadou, died at about this time, though in fact she died in 1956: perhaps she was seriously ill in 1944. Be that as it may, it gives Jackie an opportunity
to lament the fact that their mother had broken off all contact with Frosso and her
other close relatives, which she says Litsa "would live to regret bitterly." When
Litsa took her daughters to pay one "last" visit to their grandmother, the atmosphere in the house was cold and depressing, though "Mother seemed hardly bothered and treated the situation as if we were visiting a distant acquaintance in a

strange hospital." Mary was kept busy by her work, but Jackie paid frequent visits to Frosso "until she died," she tells us, adding, "It took all Mother's skills as an actress manquée to shed a tear at the funeral." That may well have been true, but it was not to be put to the test until twelve more years had passed.[13]

The mood in Athens in that summer of 1944 was variable. On the one hand there were roadblocks, arrests, executions, fear, and a general feeling of insecurity; on the other, rejoicing—still suppressed, but coming more and more out into the open—over the news reaching Greece from the various war fronts. Having landed in Normandy, the Allies were advancing toward Paris; and on 15 August (Mary's name day, and the date of the second performance of *Fidelio*), while the fighting still raged around Caen, there were more Allied landings between Toulon and Cannes in the south of France. The first advertisements for *Fidelio* appeared in the newspapers of 8 August; two days later the press commissioner in the prime minister's office issued the license for the performance of Beethoven's opera, a spectacle deemed "unsuitable for children under the age of fourteen"![14] Litsa came to some of the last rehearsals to show a mother's support for her working daughter. "She kept rushing out in the evenings, even when she was not well, to bring Mary home after the rehearsals," says Jackie, who considers that Mary ought to have been more grateful for those tokens of affection, "and never mind if Mother *was* hoping to reap some of Mary's glory for herself." Litsa's friend Pepi Garofalidou, who went with her to a rehearsal at the Odeon of Herodes Atticus one day, later said that even as she and Litsa tugged at the laces of Mary's corset, just before the performance, Mary herself, feeling peckish, was actually having a bite to eat.[15]

By the time *Fidelio* was in its final rehearsals with chorus and orchestra, Mary appeared to have calmed down at last. For the first time in months, after being involved in a series of rows, she stopped behaving aggressively. After the terrible strain of preparing *Tiefland* and her rather uninspiring performance in *O Protomastoras*, the prospect of *Fidelio* evidently gave her the feeling that she was finally about to win her reward for all her persistence and hard work. The unbending and often insufferable rigor with which she applied herself to her work had begun to abate, disclosing to the world a new Mary, amiable and open-hearted, though sadly this phase was to be all too brief. "With the chorus she was very affable and friendly," recalls Thodoros Veroulis, who was in the chorus at the time. "'*Oh God, look how fat I am!*' she would say. '*I must go on a diet!*' . . . Unlike the other female soloists, she did not make us chorus singers feel shy or overawed. It is a myth that Mary was unapproachable, certainly in those days." Her good relations with the chorus are confirmed, as we saw, in her January 1947 postscript to Mangliveras: "*Give my regards to the chorus, don't forget!!*"[16]

Elvira Mataranga, who was also in the chorus for *Fidelio*, remembers hearing a voice singing "Caro nome" (from the first act of *Rigoletto*) before one of the performances. She went to see who it was and found Mary warming up for the dramatic role of Leonore by singing Gilda's famous coloratura aria! "'My dear girl, what *are* you doing?' I asked her in amazement. '*It's good for me, it lightens my voice*,' she explained." Mataranga believes—and she may well be right—that Mary was not doing this just because she felt like it, but because de Hidalgo had suggested it to her. Be that as it may, five years later, in Venice, Maria would be overheard warming up with Elvira's vocalises before singing Brünnhilde's hojotohos. "Her teacher's bel canto was so deeply rooted in her way of singing," Mataranga continues, "that when she went on stage as Leonore and sang her first phrase, 'Wie gross ist die Gefahr,' in the well-known quartet, she produced a portamento that was all wrong for Beethoven." When Mataranga asked her teacher Smaragda Yennadi what she thought of it, she was told: "However unorthodox her way of singing may be, the results are fine!" In other words, having learned to sing in a different way, "Kaloyeropoulou did what she felt inside her, and the final result was perfectly acceptable—in fact it was divine!"[17]

Mary's great moment came about half an hour after the end of the overture, after she had sung in the quartet, in which each singer expresses their conflicting feelings, and in the trio with Yorgos Moulas (Rocco) and Zoe Vlachopoulou (Marzelline). Alone on the stage, dressed as a man in dark blue velvet with a white collar, and wearing high boots, the first Greek Leonore leaned back against the ancient wall of the Odeon of Herodes Atticus and uttered the dramatic cry "Abscheulicher!", thus opening the great aria wherein Leonore tries to screw up the courage to go through with her impulsive scheme for the rescue of her falsely imprisoned husband. At that moment, voicing her own longing for love and liberty, Mary rose to truly great heights of interpretation. She herself once told a German journalist, "*The only time I was moved to tears on stage was in 'Fidelio' in the open-air theater of Herodes Atticus in 1944 . . . when, as I was singing 'Komm, Hoffnung, lass den letzten Stern der Müden nicht erbleichen!', the evening star shone out through the clouds of the Greek sky.*"[18]

In the turbulent atmosphere of Athens at that stage of the war, *Fidelio* was a work highly charged with meaning. Besides extolling conjugal love, Beethoven's opera is a hymn of praise to freedom and the overthrow of tyranny, and its relevance was instinctively realized by the audience from the very first performance. Thereafter the news spread rapidly, even in nonmusical circles, that here was a chance for a spontaneous display of anti-German feeling in front of a German conductor and high-ranking German officials. And so the remaining performances were attended not only by music-lovers but by ordinary Greeks who, after years of enemy occupation, were given an opportunity to demonstrate their love of liberty. When the prisoners emerged on to the stage in near-darkness, like primitive beasts, singing in hushed voices ("Sprecht leise, haltet euch zurück!")—hesitantly at first, but gaining in confidence as they went on—the audience sang along with them, generating a buzz of patriotic excitement which the Germans pretended not to notice. "We were singing of the freedom of Greece," recalls Nikos Zachariou, who was one of the prisoners emerging on the stage from the gloomy

Fidelio, Mary as Leonore in the first-act trio, with Yorgos Moulas (Rocco) and Zoe Vlachopoulou (Marzelline), Odeon of Herodes Atticus, Athens, August 1944.

"Abscheulicher!",
Fidelio, Odeon of
Herodes Atticus,
Athens, August 1944.

dungeon and coming face to face with the high-ranking German officials in the front row, including the notorious General Schimana. "We felt it inside us, and excitement was at fever pitch. 'O Himmel! . . . O Freiheit!' . . . For us it was a patriotic rebellion, and no one got up to stop us." Spyros Salingaros has similar memories of the occasion: "We shouted out the word 'freedom,' all of us, including the stage crew, and gradually the audience joined in. Whereupon Kalomiris came backstage, quaking with terror, and said, 'What are you doing to me? They'll send me to the firing squad!' The place was in an uproar!"[19]

There were some who criticized the trio in the first cast (Kaloyeropoulou, Delendas, Mangliveras) "for singing too sweetly, too lyrically, and not at all in Beethoven's style," Christos Mangliveras recalls. Mitsa Kourahani, however, remembers Mary's "relaxed" singing and "very well settled" voice (whereas the tiny Remoundou was "dreadful" in the part, especially visually, being "swallowed up in her boots") and Delendas's vocal and dramatic excellence (Lalaouni compared him with the "unforgettable" Leo Slezak), while Mangliveras was "out-standing, always the star, wherever he sang, helped by his big voice and his fiery temperament that conveyed his own hypertension to the audience." In 1957, at the height of the outcry against Maria, one Greek journalist wrote of her Leonore, "She stood on the stage with her legs wide apart and yelled, you might almost say howled, like a woman in labor," and Kalliopi Ikonomidi, who had been at the first night with her husband, says that Mary was "like Puss in Boots" and her whole manner was quite wrong for Leonore and "a bit of a joke." However, these are isolated criticisms and probably reflect their authors' biases: the overwhelming consensus of opinion was very complimentary for Mary. Nikos Zachariou says he has never heard any accomplished Leonore who had the "freshness" and the "spon-taneity" of the young Callas, while Elvira de Hidalgo, who at the time was not on the closest terms with her pupil, said later that Mary's portrayal of Leonore was not a mere "accomplished exercise in vocalization" but contained "convincing and moving" expression; despite her age and relative inexperience, she concluded, Mary had succeeded in a role that established singers take years to master.[20]

The six Greek critics who reviewed that first Greek production of *Fidelio* praised it to the skies. Even the crusty Psaroudas rated it higher than the produc-tion he had once seen in Paris. All raved about Walleck's directing and compli-mented Hörner and the orchestra on their well-judged, precise reading of the score, though Lalaouni remarked that Hörner's unorthodox decision to play the *Leonore* Overture No. 3 at the beginning of Act I made it sound "like a separate piece not leading into anything," not to mention the fact that it gave the late-comers time to take their seats, the result being that the opera started "without any atmosphere having been built up first." The critics' unanimous verdict on Mary was that she had given an excellent performance. Spanoudi thought her "extremely well disciplined in the purest Beethoven style" and "an excellent incarnation of Leonore" as regards her general appearance, her musical sense, and her perform-ance. In the words of Psaroudas, "This time Miss Kaloyeropoulou has found a role that suits her. She gave us a dramatic, expressive, and moving Leonore." Lalaouni, however, though "truly moved" by Mary's proven talents, commented, "Much still remains to be put right in her voice, much remains to be learned." Some "unevenness in the voice" and "deficiencies in the enunciation" were also noted by "Fafner" in *Kathimerini*, while Hamoudopoulos likewise mentioned some "undulations in the voice" and "a slight insecurity of intonation."[21]

Friedrich Herzog wrote a rave review (his last article written in Greece) in the *Deutsche Nachrichten in Griechenland*, which had previewed the production in a full-length article with photographs. Mary and Delendas he rated "equally good" at getting right into their parts: in particular, he was impressed by the inner ten-sion of Leonore's every movement and by the suppleness and sonority of her voice. In 1959 Herzog wrote again about Callas and the 1944 *Fidelio* ("the last grand manifestation of German art in Athens before the bitter end"): "The Greeks per-

„Fidelio" in Athen

Ludwig van Beethovens „Fidelio" erstmalig in Griechen'and aufgeführt

Im Theater des Herodes Attikus zu Füssen der Akropolis erklang zum ersten Mal unter griechischem Himmel Beethovens „Fidelio", das Hohelied der Gattenliebe und -treue, das sich in dem grossartigen Chorfinale zu einem Jubel steigerte, der die vielen tausend Zuhörer mit in seinen Bann riss. Generalintendant Oskar Walleck, einer der führenden deutschen Opernspielleiter, gab der Darstellung den monumentalen Aufriss und eine Stilhoheit von grossartiger Geschlossenheit. Unter der Stabführung von Dr. Hans Hörner vereinigten sich die hervorragendsten Sänger der Griechischen Staatsoper zu einer Wiedergabe, die schon in dem berühmten Quartett des ersten Aktes ihren ersten Höhepunkt fand. Unsere Bilder zeigen: Generalintendant Oskar Walleck während der Probe (oben rechts); Anton Delendas als Florestan (oben links) und die Quartettszene (unten) mit Maria Kalojeropoulou (im Vordergrund links) in der Titelpartie. Eine ausführliche Besprechung von Werk und Aufführung, die als künstlerisches Ereignis von Rang besteht, folgt. Der Beifall war stürmisch und begeistert.

Aufn.: Kemmerich (3)

Friedrich Herzog's piece on *Fidelio*'s première, *Deutsche Nachrichten in Griechenland*, 15 August 1944.

ceived very clearly in *Fidelio* the idea of the overthrow of tyrants and the victory of liberty over despotism. When Maria Kaloyeropoulou's Leonore let her soprano soar out radiantly in the untrammeled jubilation of the duet 'O namenlose Freude!' with the tenor Anton Delendas, she rose to the most sublime heights. . . . Here Maria Kaloyeropoulou scored her greatest triumph. Here she gave bud, blossom, and fruit to that harmony of sound that also ennobled the art of the prima donna." Indeed Mary sang ecstatically in the arms of Andonis Delendas. It is quite probable that one of the performances of *Fidelio* was broadcast by the German radio station in Athens, in which case it may perhaps have been recorded. The very thought of such a discovery awaiting us is enough to bring a frisson of excitement not only to Callas devotees but all true opera-lovers.[22]

Between 14 August and 10 September 1944 Mary sang at eleven of the fourteen performances of *Fidelio*, all in Greek (as were all the roles she sang in Greece).[23] Some performances between 22 and 31 August were canceled because of bad weather. To get to the Odeon of Herodes Atticus, the spectators walked up Dionysiou Areopagitou Street at about 5 p.m. The performances began in daylight and ended after dark, at about 9 p.m.; the inefficient lighting in the theater was supplemented with flaming torches. In all Mary's performances, Zoe Vlachopoulou sang Marzelline and Yorgos Kokkolios sang Jaquino. At ten of the eleven, Vangelis Mangliveras sang Don Pizarro and Yorgos Moulas was Rocco (at the other, the parts were taken by Dimitris Efstratiou and Kostas Persis, respectively). Mary's Florestan was Andonis Delendas eight times and Michalis Koronis on the other three occasions. Mary was always directed by Hans Hörner, who, conducting without a score, enjoyed a personal triumph at his last appearances in Athens: it is probably no exaggeration to say that those performances were the highlights of his rather undistinguished career. Altogether 15,861 tickets were issued, of which 13,293 were for Mary's performances and 2,568 for the three performances with Remoundou and the alternate cast, conducted by Zoras.[24]

Litsa remembered Mary singing in *Fidelio* "as I had never heard her sing before." At the final curtain she basked in the warmth of her daughter's "first real ovation," while an excited German officer sitting next to her took photograph after photograph of Mary. When Litsa told him the prima donna was her daughter, he kissed the proud mother and predicted that Mary would one day be famous. Jackie, too, comments that "for the first time [Mary] was unreservedly magnificent" and admits to having felt insignificant among the thousands staring down at her sister while she, alone on the stage, had shown everyone that she "would be great."[25] When it was all over, audience and performers alike streamed out to make their way home as best they could. One evening Thodoros Veroulis was starting for home when he realized that Mary had no transport, so he offered her a ride on his big German bicycle. "She accepted quite calmly, sat on the crossbar, and off we went down Dionysiou Areopagitou Street," he recalls. "We turned into Amalias Avenue, but I don't remember where I dropped her off."[26]

BEETHOVEN "FIDELIO"

Conductor Hans Hörner and the singers of *Fidelio* during a rehearsal break, Odeon of Herodes Atticus, Athens, August 1944. From left to right, around Yorgos Kokkolios (Jaquino): Yorgos Moulas (Rocco), Zoe Vlachopoulou (Marzelline), Hans Hörner, Mary (Leonore), Vangelis Mangliveras (Pizarro), Andonis Delendas (Florestan), and Thanasis Tzeneralis (Don Fernando).

Hans Hörner conducting *Fidelio*, Odeon of Herodes Atticus, Athens, August 1944. Photo dedicated to Mary in Hörner's handwriting.

Besides the purely musical satisfaction of her successes in *Tiefland* and *Fidelio*, Mary now began to feel the more egoistic but entirely natural gratification that comes with public recognition. Every day she gained new admirers, even outside the narrow confines of the musical world, and sometimes she was recognized by strangers in the street. She herself remembered later that Greek sailors and officers had told her father in New York how they had walked all the way up from Piraeus, braving German patrols and roadblocks, simply in order to hear her sing. *"In those years . . . I thought only of studying and of earning a living, taking advantage of the natural gift of my voice, without even realizing that in the meantime fame and the public's favor had risen around my name,"* she added complacently. However, as so often in that period of her life, every step forward provoked opposition and jealousy, which hindered or delayed her further advancement. This was true of her success in *Fidelio* too, after which her rivals exploited Hans Hörner's statement that young Kaloyeropoulou was "up to the standard of the Berlin Opera" by quoting it in support of the well-worn charge that she was collaborating with the enemy.[27]

By this time, however, Mary had greatly strengthened her position and there was no stopping her, despite the further embittering experiences that lay in store for her. "She had made up her mind to be the greatest singer in the world," her mother says in her memoirs, "and she was not going to let anything stand in her way—not even the women of the Royal Theater repertory company. They did their best," Litsa goes on in her usual snide tone, "but she pushed past them, stealing scenes, seizing any chance for applause as she has always done." At all events, she comments sneeringly, after *Fidelio*, when Mary had become "famous in Athens," her own family grew less critical, although the "olive oil" cousins still ignored them. None of Mary's relatives—the most notable offenders being the Louros family, who considered themselves socially superior, and the Kambouris family, who were probably tired of Litsa's demands—came to see any of Mary's performances in those years.[28]

—⚇—

I would have loved it if the public and the critics were able to follow many of our rehearsals, not only in the hall, rehearsals in the room, how we go about learning a part, how many months of preparation before we even eventually come before the first piano rehearsal—how many sacrifices!

To Lord Harewood, Paris, April 1968

CHAPTER 33

Liberation, Romance, and
Three Weeks of Terror

In the brief interval between the last performance of *Fidelio* and the liberation Mary enjoyed the taste of success. "After *Fidelio* she was fairly well known," said her friend Takis Sigaras, "so much so that people noticed and recognized her wherever we went." Litsa in her book recalls that in Athens her daughter "walked in glamour . . . showered with flowers and applause, known and recognized in shops and restaurants and on the street."[1] So that period of four or five weeks must have been one of the times in her life when she felt on top of the world, all the more so in view of the near certainty of an early end to the occupation. She may well have started now on the preliminary study of her next roles, too, as the prospect of productions of *Der fliegende Holländer* and *Fedora*, in both of which she was to take the lead, would certainly have boosted her optimism and sense of security.

The conditions of life in Athens, however, remained extremely difficult. The few services still functioning were paralyzed by the first rains of autumn and a torrential downpour on 5 September 1944 turned Patission Street into a river, bringing masses of mud and debris down from Lykavittos Hill. With the press choosing to ignore the "fall" of Paris and the Allied advance into Belgium, the Greek economy finally broke down completely on 11 September. Meanwhile the price of an English gold sovereign had risen from Drs. 12,000 in June 1941 to 100,000 in the same month of 1942 and 430,000 a year later, before soaring to 175 million in June 1944 and the astronomic sum of Drs. 117 trillion in November 1944. Gold sovereigns (already widely used in Greece for large transactions, especially in real estate) were by then the only currency with which one could buy anything in the foodstuffs market, where prices had soared to 250,000 times their 1940 level. Naturally enough, the collapse of the economy created still more problems for the employees of the G.N.O., whose salaries no longer bore any relation to the rocketing prices. At the end of the summer season at the Odeon of Herodes Atticus, the soloists, led by Vangelis Mangliveras, resigned in protest en masse, and on 16 September the management agreed to raise all salaries of up to 40 million drachmas per month to six billion, and all higher salaries to nine billion. Just ten days later the fortnightly salaries of G.N.O. usherettes were raised to fifteen billion virtually useless drachmas.[2]

By now the forces of ELAS, the communist resistance army, were moving into their positions encircling the capital, but Athenians still heard the news regularly on the BBC, which they listened to with little attempt at concealment. The Germans were being forced back in Flanders and the Netherlands, around Aachen in Germany, in Latvia and Estonia, and in Italy north of Florence. On 1 October 1944 British forces landed in the southern Peloponnese, and five days later the Germans began withdrawing from Greece, to the joy of the Athenians, though their jubilation was as yet fairly muted. On 6 October, during the intermission of a performance of *The Merry Widow* (which had succeeded *Fidelio*), somebody in the balcony of the Olympia Theater announced through a megaphone that the British had already reached Megara, only twenty-five miles from Athens. The outburst of cheering among the audience was complemented by Lehár's melodies, and the singing of Galanou and Epitropakis created an unprecedented atmosphere. On the morning of Thursday, 12 October 1944, the German flag on the Acropolis was lowered for the last time and the last German unit to leave Athens placed a wreath on the tomb of the unknown soldier before heading north to the accompaniment of general rejoicing and bell-ringing. People poured out onto the streets, almost delirious with joy, and streamed toward the city center carrying flags, laurel wreaths, and even palm fronds.

Needless to say, that historic day also had its less attractive moments, in which the most fanatical and the most oppressed elements came to the fore, with buildings being occupied and looted and personal scores being settled. The lawful administration of the G.N.O. was ousted by a "trade union deputation" of EAM supporters composed of orchestral players and a few ballet dancers and solo singers: one conductor (probably Karalivanos), one singer, one dancer, one chorus singer, and one stage technician called early one morning at the National Conservatory, where Kalomiris was still living, and stripped him of his office, having first subjected him to an insolent tirade.[3] The administration of the G.N.O. was taken over by a Soviet-style troika, and there followed a period of chaos, total indiscipline, and political fanaticism. Greece, ravaged by years of enemy occupation, was now sharply divided into two bitterly hostile camps, the conservative rightists and the radical leftists, and the situation was the same in microcosm at the G.N.O., where the artistic, technical, and administrative personnel were split down the middle. The only extant official document of that period relating to the G.N.O. is a single unsigned page from the handwritten minutes of a meeting of the ousted board of governors on 21 October 1944, recording the protest lodged by a deputation of the artistic personnel against "the arbitrary ousting of the general manager on the day of the liberation." Kalomiris agreed only to stay on as the temporary acting general manager, submitting his resignation to the new government and declaring that he would not take sides in the "differences of outlook and ideology" among the personnel.[4]

Litsa, writing about the first days of the liberation, describes the crowds in Syntagma Square singing, dancing, and flinging their arms round strangers. The churches were full of worshippers, she says, and adds, "Maria, Jackie, and I prayed with them," glossing over the anxiety she must have felt about the repercussions of her recent friendships with enemy officers. To complete the picture of carefree rejoicing, she tells how she and her daughters tore up the now valueless green-and-white "occupation money" and threw the pieces out into the street like confetti, to the accompaniment of Mary's joyous singing. Jackie, however, gives a much more levelheaded account of the day of the liberation, reflecting that each one of them had survived the war in her own way, making whatever compromises she had thought necessary: "None of us had really considered where we would go next, and this sudden void that opened before us left us curiously untouched by the general air of relief everyone else was experiencing."[5]

Mary, on that great day, was brought up short by a very unpleasant experience which abruptly snuffed out her euphoria of the last few weeks. With Jackie she hurried to Syntagma Square, where, amid the jubilant crowds, they ran into American journalist Larry Newman, who was to become a friend of theirs. After a while, however, she took herself off and walked to the Olympia, where she saw a crowd of her fellow artists, most of them left-wingers, gathered in the forecourt. Under the leadership of a union member who was handing out placards and rehearsing his colleagues in slogans backing EAM, the political arm of the communist resistance movement, the G.N.O. group was getting ready to join the endless circular march that went from Omonia Square up Stadiou Street to Syntagma Square, then back down Panepistimiou Street and so on for most of that day. "When Maria appeared in the forecourt we gave her a pretty hot reception," Elvira Mataranga recalls. "We set upon her, venting all the hatred we felt for the people who had collaborated with the enemy. At that moment the very sight of her, or a few others like her, was a red flag to many of us, because of their dealings with Fascists, Nazis, colonels, and so on. Feeling was running extremely high, and anyone who had as much as said good morning to an Italian or German was automatically in our sights."[6]

Mataranga was one of those who attacked Mary with particular fury. "What business have *you* got here?" she spat at her with a wealth of innuendo in her tone, throwing in a few colorful epithets for good measure. As we have seen, Mary was not one to let insults go unanswered. Whether she responded with no more than a verbal retort or actually struck the first blow herself, Mataranga no longer remembers. "At any rate, she was quite unabashed. She answered back equally rudely and we came to blows. She hit me, I hit her, and she lost an earring, which both of us then looked for on the ground." Mataranga admits that her own hostility may have been influenced by the fact that Mary had "stolen" Vangelis Mangliveras from her. "Anyway," she continues, "violent though it was at the time, by the very next day the incident had been forgotten. But that morning Maria had to run

Elvira Mataranga (left) with her friend Anna (Zozo) Remoundou, 1941.

away like a scalded cat. Needless to say, she did not join in the march, and from that day she disappeared for quite some time—literally vanished from the opera!"[7]

This episode must have given Mary a nasty shock. Until the previous day, in the jubilant atmosphere of the last week before the liberation and the euphoria induced by her own recognition as a singer, most of the singers now raging so furiously against her had treated her, if not with affection, at least with courtesy. The sudden, cold-blooded revelation of so much virulent hostility, ostensibly motivated by patriotism, would surely have taken her aback and wounded her deeply. Although the personal attack on her by Mataranga would soon be forgotten, the memory of that collective hatred would last a long time: in fact Maria was to make a cryptic allusion to it in her memoirs: "*Immediately after the performances of 'Fidelio,' which were given in the marvelous amphitheater of Herodes Atticus, came the 'liberation,' and then began the attacks against me on the part of my colleagues. . . . In the meantime, finally, the administration of the Royal Opera House granted me three months of vacation, and my mother, without losing any time, immediately found a job for me at the British headquarters, where I was assigned to the office of distribution of secret mail.*"[8] There is no other evidence concerning Mary's three-month leave of absence from the G.N.O., so we do not know whether it had already been granted to her at the end of the run of *Fidelio* or whether (as seems more likely) it was dreamed up by the pro-EAM de facto management as a way of getting her out of the opera, perhaps on the specious pretext of the physical attack made on her on 12 October.

On 3 November 1944, the very day when the newspapers carried a government press release announcing the temporary closure of the National Theater and the G.N.O. "to permit radical changes to be made," the unlawful administration of the G.N.O. organized a gala event advertised as a "Festival of Freedom." Almost all the members of the G.N.O. company took part, with the conspicuous exception of Mary Kaloyeropoulou and Leonidas Zoras and his wife, dancer Tatiana

Varouti. Having studied and lived in Germany, Zoras was systematically abused by his enemies in the company for allegedly "taking improper advantage" of his knowledge of German. Although he had no malice in him and was not active politically, after the liberation the left-wingers in the company accused him and his wife of conduct "prejudicial to the profession and contrary to the interests of his colleagues," without any clarification.[9] As for Mary, no charge seems to have been laid against her in writing and the likelihood is that she was simply not invited to take part in the "Festival of Freedom." Alternatively, it is possible that she herself refused to have anything to do with it or that somebody else, perhaps Vangelis Mangliveras, advised her not to expose herself to the risk of public disapprobation.

Around 10 November the conservatives in the company decided to make a move to restore the pre-liberation régime. Having collected 114 signatures, including Mary's, on 18 November they submitted a petition to Kalomiris in which, describing themselves as "right-thinking," they declared that they would not attend any meetings not convened by Kalomiris, "for fear of a repetition of the coup to take over the management by violent means and [a recurrence of] the chaotic state into which the theater was plunged in the first days after the liberation." In the belief that "it is impossible for an artist to be also a politician" because then "he retrogresses and becomes a tool of one political faction or another," they then called upon their colleagues to dedicate themselves to the interest of the G.N.O., "casting their personal disputes into oblivion." Kalomiris, however, was afraid to take sides and reiterated that he had no intention of meddling in disputes among the personnel: his only response was to advocate "affection, concord, unity, fraternity, and hard work."[10]

The new government headed by Yeoryios Papandreou had been formed on 23 October with the declared aims of completing the processes of liberation and national rehabilitation, consolidating unity, and rebuilding the nation from the ruins. The Germans were retreating in disorder, destroying everything they could; Larissa was liberated on 24 October and Thessaloniki on the 27th. On 28 October the British foreign secretary, Anthony Eden, arrived in Athens to attend the fourth-anniversary celebrations of the Greek rejection of Mussolini's ultimatum. He toured the city with the prime minister, greeted everywhere by cheering crowds, went up to the Acropolis, and attended a gala performance in his honor at the National Theater. On 11 November a new currency was issued: every 50 billion old drachmas were replaced by one new drachma, whose parity was fixed at Drs. 600 to the pound sterling. But the government's most immediate concern was to restore law and order, as 780 common criminals had recently escaped from prison and the settling of private scores had become an everyday occurrence. The prime minister appealed vainly to the Greek Communist party to put an end to provocative demonstrations, such as parading the bodies of slain collaborators and black marketeers through the streets. While Greece slid rapidly toward civil war, fighting continued in the other theaters of war. On the eastern front the Russian army was now nearing Budapest; on the western front a massive bombing raid flattened Düsseldorf and six Allied armies advanced into the heartlands of the Reich; in the Far East B-29 Flying Fortresses bombed Japan, where Admiral Nimitz and General MacArthur won decisive victories. And on 7 November fifty million American voters demonstrated their faith in President Franklin D. Roosevelt by electing him to a fourth term.

Meanwhile Mary was working in the British G.H.Q., going every morning to her office near Syntagma Square. Though it would be wrong to underestimate the importance of the unprecedented attack made on her by the EAM-controlled opera company, the real reason she took such a job at that time was financial. If she was going to be on three months' "leave," probably unsought and almost certainly unpaid, she needed to find work for practical reasons: "*[I did that work] not because it was interesting, but because I knew that would make it easy for me to get enough to eat*," she explained in 1959.[11] In addition, Litsa must have been well aware of the risk of ostracism hanging over herself, and to a lesser extent over Mary too, on account of their fraternization with officers of the occupation forces, and for this reason she would doubtless have been all in favor of Mary's taking a job which, besides bringing in money, would spike the guns of their enemies. Employment with the British army in a confidential post would help to clear their names (or at least Mary's name) because, as Ilias Papatestas argued later, no matter how good Mary's English was, and quite irrespective of her U.S. citizenship, the British would never have taken her on if they suspected she might have been a collaborator.[12]

The office where Mary started work shortly after the middle of October was on the first floor of the Army Share Fund building, a big office block generally known as the Tameion building.[13] This had entrances on Stadiou and Panepistimiou Streets, a continuously moving paternoster elevator, and a very good cafeteria, the atmosphere of which was heavy with the characteristic smell of Virginia tobacco smoke. It was shared by the Greek army and various British agencies including the British Information Service, which issued bulletins on the progress of the war elsewhere in the world as well as reports on the political situation in Greece and the movements and intentions of EAM/ELAS, which were becoming daily more threatening. Mary was employed by the B.I.S. as an interpreter and/or translator and to help with the filing of confidential documents. "*We started work at eight, but I had to get up at six-thirty because in order to save money I made the whole trip on foot*," she recalled later. She also went home on her midday break to share her big lunch with her mother, although the fairly long walk to 61 Patission Street and back left her little time to eat her own share of the meal.[14]

—⚬⚬⚬—

The first British units reached Athens on Saturday, 14 October 1944. One man who arrived within the next few days was the twenty-four-year-old Welshman Raymond George Morgan, from Mountain Ash in Glamorgan, a lieutenant in the Royal Corps of Signals. It is mainly through the eyes of Morgan, who met Mary later that month in 1944 and had a brief but very close friendship with her, that we shall follow the events of the ensuing weeks, both in Mary's life and on the political scene.[15]

Lieutenant Raymond George Morgan,
early 1940s.

"We had docked at Piraeus, entering the front door of Greece as the Germans politely left by the back door, northwards," Ray Morgan wrote some fifteen years later. "We hardly felt an invasion force, especially as we entrained at the metro terminal in Piraeus, and even less as we drew into the underground station in Athens. We came up into the sunlight in Omonia Square. In those days the center of the square held flower stalls and parading prostitutes." Morgan remembers the warmth and effusiveness of the people, who thrust bunches of flowers into the hands of the British soldiers as they marched up Panepistimiou Street. At Syntagma Square they turned left up Vassilissis Sophias Avenue to their barracks in the area where the Athens Concert Hall, the statue of Eleftherios Venizelos, and the American embassy now stand. Vassilissis Sophias Avenue and the usually dry bed of the River Ilissos then marked the outermost limits of Athens proper: on the far bank of the Ilissos were only a few scattered houses, while the few roads crossing the river led out to Pangrati, already a residential area, and to the new "suburbs" of Nea Elvetia, Vyron, and Kaisariani, which were settlements of makeshift housing built by refugees after the Asia Minor disaster of 1922.

Like the Germans and Italians before them, the British servicemen took every opportunity to go down to the city center for some fun in their time off. One of the best-known places of entertainment was the Argentina, a nightclub in a basement at 15 Filellinon Street, off Syntagma Square. Young as he was, Morgan was already a seasoned campaigner, having served in Italy and North Africa. He had then spent some time "lotus-eating in the flesh-pots of Cairo, Alexandria, and Tel Aviv," as he puts it, so he felt quite blasé about nightlife in the cities. He was soon on good terms with the manager of the Argentina, Alekos Parissis, who invited him one day to a "very respectable" party being given the following night by a Dr. Prapoleros at 10 Pireos Street, near Omonia Square. Surprise parties had been in fashion in Athens for some years and were still very much the thing: the Greek hosts provided the venues, domestic servants, music, and usually fruit and wine, while their British guests brought canned foods of various kinds, cigarettes, and, most important of all, their much-valued presence, which only heightened the heady atmosphere of newfound liberty.

By the time Lieutenant Morgan arrived, the sweet Samos wine had already created a relaxed atmosphere; soon after, the old phonograph began playing dance music and couples took to the floor. After a while Alekos, who was the moving spirit of the party, leapt toward the door to greet a young woman who had just arrived. "'Mary, Mary, *agapi mou*,' then a volley of Greek," as Morgan recalls the scene. "The reply was in English, perhaps for our benefit. It was perfect English. An English girl, here? I had not seen an English girl, let alone spoken to one, since Cairo many moons before. Not only was she English, she was good-looking. Conventional greetings over, I plied her with questions. . . . Now I became aware of an accent, a nasality on certain words. I realized that she was, in fact, not English but American. She was as eager to talk as I was. She spoke perfect Greek but clearly missed using English. The questions and answers flowed between us. She had been caught on holiday in Greece by the German invasion; was not able to return to America. Yes, she had work; was a singer with the Royal Opera Company. She lived with her mother not very far from where we now were. She was overjoyed at the arrival of the Allies, but was uneasy at some political developments."

The very next day Mary was with Ray again, delighted to have been noticed and asked out by a young, good-looking, well-mannered English officer. "Her joy at the freedom that had come to Athens seemed to me to epitomize the joy that infected the whole city. . . . That evening Mary and I were part of the eventide stroll, part of the huge ambling crowd that, gesticulating and conversing at maximum output, created a strange deep chorus of sound that resonated in the canyon of buildings in Panepistimiou [Street] near Omonia." Quite suddenly Mary jerked Ray's arm, which was linked in hers, and commanded him, "*In here!*" She took him to a small bar in an arcade. "'*Something unusual*,' she said . . . and handed to me a small pale yellow drink. '*Go on, try it.*' . . . It was a banana liqueur."

Ray observed Mary with genuine interest. "Much of her appeal lay in her unaffected warmth. As she leaned on that little bar top, perched on a high stool, her eyes glistened. They had that unfocused dreaminess that comes from extreme nearsightedness, but she never wore glasses when she was with me. The eyes were slanted slightly upward, exotically almond-shaped. In her full relaxed face they suggested voluptuousness, but, made-up and with intensity of purpose, they could be very dramatic. When she smiled, she was all innocence. It was a fine, generous mouth drawn at each corner into a mobile quirk, and the smile framed good, white teeth. . . . [Some people] remarked on her buxomness. I never once noticed. Indeed she was graceful; she had gawkish delicate movements like a large kitten. Yet she was taller than I, and I felt uncomfortable. The next time we met I broached the subject, reluctantly. 'Mary, would you object to wearing low heels when you come out with me?' She laughed heartily. . . . From that day on she very sweetly wore flat-heeled shoes whenever we were together."

On the first Saturday after their meeting, Ray took Mary to the Argentina. Alekos found them a table, even though the place was packed, mainly with British army, naval, and air force officers escorted by smart, beautiful girls. "We chatted; we drank; we danced. Sitting out one of the dances in the half-light we were joined by Aleko. He leaned over Mary and whispered in her ear. The dance finished. Instead of the house lights brightening they disappeared completely. A blinding white spot speared our little table. . . . I was suddenly aware that Mary was on her feet, that the piano was striking up something classical. She struck a pose, opened her mouth, and a powerful mellifluent caravanserai of notes reverberated around the building. I stared up at her. Gone was the simple, vulnerable young girl. This was an imposing, confident artist. Even her physique seemed expanded. . . . Unexpectedness had me stunned. Her work had been something we had never discussed, I had even forgotten that she had told me she was an opera singer. I would not have imagined her to be of this caliber anyway. Compounded with surprise was self-consciousness at my own role in this lime-lit tableau. I cringed with embarrassment and sank down into my chair. The tension was such that to this day I cannot remember what she sang. Was it an aria from *Tosca*? Or *Aida*, perhaps? I shall never know. The nightclub listeners were not so bemused. Applause erupted and continued for ages after she had sat down. Immediately she was herself again. As if she had come offstage, she switched back to the Mary I had got to know. Only I was not quite the same again; I had glimpsed the prima donna."

From then on, until a few days before 3 December, Ray and Mary went out regularly. He would go on his army motorcycle, always in uniform, to meet her either at the bar of the Acropole Hotel, near her house, or at Jimmy's Bar at the corner of Voukourestiou and Valaoritou Streets, a place that was popular with the smart Kolonaki set. "I went around on a motorbike but never took Mary on it," Morgan says. "We never went outside Athens. I don't even remember going to a taverna with her, although we must have done. Mostly, however, we stayed at the bars." When asked if Mary drank or smoked, Morgan replies, "She must have drunk a little but I don't remember her smoking, although everybody smoked in those days." Sometimes, too, they went to one of the ever-popular surprise parties. One such was in a penthouse belonging to the sponge merchant Yorgos Kindynis on fashionable Anagnostopoulou Street, on the lower slopes of Lykavittos Hill, with a panoramic view of the Acropolis and the Saronic Gulf. Ray and two other officers, Jock Bruce and John Lowcock, arrived laden with bottles of wine and some cans of corned beef. Mary was already there, making sandwiches with the other girls, while the phonograph filled the night with the strains of pre-war jazz, to which the guests would soon be dancing.

The atmosphere changed abruptly when Captain Spike Moran came in with several officers of EDES, the right-of-center resistance organization led by Napoleon Zervas. Captain Moran, Zervas's British liaison officer, had met Ray in Cairo. His friends, rugged, gauche, and out of place in that setting, with deeply tanned faces and long black beards and wearing heavy boots, joined in the fun, drinking, dancing, and filling the room with their presence. Mary too entered into the spirit of the party, and Ray remembers her "bouncing about like a lively young foal" with the burly resistance fighters. The host winced in agony as his parquet floor was ruined by the hobnailed boots of those enthusiastic new initiates into the ways of city life. Eventually, with tongues loosened by wine, the talk turned to politics and it was not long before the EDES officers were arguing fiercely with those who were less right-wing than they: one of those was Lina Sariyanni, the republican niece of General Ptolemeos Sariyannis. Mary tried to placate the antagonists with soothing words here, sympathetic understanding there. She was an exception among Greeks, a person with no strong political convictions, though by instinct and circumstance she leaned to the right.[16] But the mood had been spoiled by the flare-up of political tension, and Ray and Mary left the party together soon afterward.

The main issue that aroused passionate feeling at that time and was to lead to the outbreak of civil war in Greece was the formation of a regular army. This could not be done until the resistance groups, mainly ELAS on the left and EDES on the right, had been disbanded and disarmed. On 6 November the government had announced that on 10 December "the guerrilla formations of the resistance" would be disbanded, but the fanatical intransigence of both sides, the atmosphere of mutual mistrust, and the right-wingers' fear that the left would seize power by force made it extremely difficult for an agreement to be reached. On 22 November the prime minister called on the leaders of ELAS and EDES to consent to the disbandment of their forces, declaring optimistically that the machinery of state would be back in working order by the end of the year and a plebiscite would then be held to decide on the eventual return of King George II and the country's postwar constitution. Zervas did indeed come to Athens on 24 November (bringing with him, among others, the stalwarts who danced with Mary at the party on Anagnostopoulou Street) and declared that he would lay down the "honorable arms" of EDES; but the very next day Stefanos Sarafis, the ELAS leader, publicly refused to give the same undertaking on behalf of his forces. By now gunfights were continually breaking out in the center of Athens between rival bands of armed resistance fighters or between ELAS guerrillas and the police, and the rattle of gunfire filled the city.

Ray Morgan was well aware of the deteriorating political and military situation, as he was the third-ranking signals officer in the 23rd Armoured Brigade, the main British operational force in Greece. "Basically," he says, "it was a struggle between the communists who were flexing their military muscles, and the center and right who were supported by the British, and, less categorically and at a distance, by the Americans." On 27 November 1944 Churchill made a speech in the House of Commons in which he said, to the cheers of the members, "When we were driven out of Greece in 1941 we promised we would come back. The Greek people have never lost faith in that promise . . . and we have come back!" Many Greeks with political affiliations ranging from the center to the far left were suspicious of the British government's motives, and not without reason. They believed not only that the British were primarily concerned with their own interests, but also that they were preparing the way for the return of King George II. The government did concede six ministries to the left, and the vital ministry of war was given to a general who was acceptable to both sides. "The trouble was that the 23rd Armoured Brigade had gone into Greece to occupy a vacuum, not as a fighting formation," Morgan says. "We began to feel a bit precarious . . . [knowing] that the roads leading into Athens from the countryside were filled with columns of ELAS *andartes* armed to the teeth. . . . Strategic points in the city were being infiltrated. We still moved about unarmed."

The communist presence was particularly menacing after dark. "Mary and I found ourselves on one of those nights leaning against the marble base of the statue [of King Constantine I] that graced the square near her home on the edge of Pedion Areos Park. It was a still, cold night . . . no sound of traffic or trolleys, no footsteps, no voices, only an indefinable susurration, the body functionings of a city holding its breath. Then, from over the hill behind us, came a long, eerie, disembodied call. . . . A phrase was repeated over and over again. 'What does it say?' I whispered. '*Kappa, Kappa, Epsilon. The initials of the Greek Communist party,*' she breathed back. Just then, from the blackness of the trees in the park behind us, came another of the calls, hoarse, heavy with threat, unearthly. I felt my skin crawl into gooseflesh. Mary shuddered. We cuddled together, each lending the other the comfort of closeness." Among the memories that haunted Maria in later years, one of the most spine-chilling must surely have been the sound of that menacing voice through the megaphone, a sound that curdled the blood of so many Athenians in those grim days.

Although Mary and Ray were obviously very fond of each other, it is hard to tell precisely what the nature of her feelings for him was, or how deep those feelings were. "She must have been quite keen to go out with me, because she was always ringing me up at the mess," Ray says now. But he thinks she was also attracted by his position in the army, which gave him an aura of glamour and, she hoped, the ability to pull strings on her behalf. As for him, before his relationship with Mary had had a chance to progress very far he met and fell head over heels in love with Maro Sariyanni, the daughter of the general who on 25 November was appointed minister of war. Ray remembers that on the evening of Friday 1 December he and his friends gathered again in Yorgos Kindynis's penthouse at 21 Anagnostopoulou Street. He and Mary arrived when the party was already in full swing. When he discovered that Maro Sariyanni was there, Mary must have seen his state of excitement. He tried to keep a balance by dancing with both girls, but Mary's feminine intuition made her jealous. Later in the evening, when the radiogram had broken down and Ray was on his knees trying to mend it, Mary came up behind him and playfully heaved him off his heels, sending him rolling across the floor, to shrieks of laughter and a good deal of mocking banter. "I don't remember ever quarreling with her. The party push she gave me was a normal reaction, covered as a joke, at the presence of a competitor," Ray Morgan concludes.

That same day six of the seven left-wing ministers had resigned in protest against the order given by Major General Scobie, the officer commanding the British forces in Greece, for the disarmament of the ELAS militia. As that issue was inseparable from the overall military question, Maro's father, General Sariyannis, also resigned as minister of war the next day, 2 December, being unwilling to serve as a stooge taking his orders from the British. Scobie then issued a statement declaring that he would protect the Greeks and their government against any attempted coup "or other violent or unconstitutional act." At this critical juncture, as if determined to force a complete breakdown of negotiations, the Greek Communist party reneged on its commitment to a last-ditch compromise solution to which it had earlier agreed. At the same time the central committee of EAM requested permission for a popular rally to be held in Syntagma Square the following Sunday morning and called a general strike starting on the Monday. "Confrontation was imminent," Morgan recalls. "Everybody was expecting the communist coup and we were frightened to death. . . . There seemed to be no doubt that, unless we reacted, Athens, and so Greece, would become communist almost overnight."

Civil war, with all its bloody implications, finally broke out the very next day, Sunday 3 December. "[That evening] all commanders were called together at our officers' mess. The brigadier [Arkwright] was promoted immediately to major general and put in charge of operations. . . . It was, perhaps, a historic night. Certainly our general played it that way. He even used the phrase, believe it or not, 'Gentlemen, we are about to take the glove off the mailed fist.' . . . The emotional temperature jumped a few taut degrees. The general outlined the situation. He began to dispense orders. . . . So, a tense, electric atmosphere. Then . . . the telephone rang. It stood on a little sidetable a few feet from where I was sitting. A hush. The general strode across. He lifted the receiver. 'Yes!' he snapped. Over the wire, as clear and distinct as a bell, came a feminine voice, saying, '*Oh, can I speak to Ray—to Lieutenant Morgan?*' Surely it wasn't . . . Surely they hadn't put her through? It was—and they had. Mary was on the line. The general glared. I muttered a few incoherent words of excuse into the phone. . . . Well, that was it, the last time, in Greece, that I spoke to Mary. . . . But was that telephone call a cri de coeur? Was she about to beg me to go down to Patissia and rescue her from what was developing into a terrifying situation? Had I cut her off when she was desperate? Perhaps. Certainly, that area, like all of Athens except for the center, and the road to Phaleron, was in the hands of the communists."

When Mary had told Ray that she was an opera singer, he had not responded, so she must have realized at once that he was not interested in opera. Quite possibly one of the things that had drawn her to him was the very fact that he was just an ordinary man, sensitive but unconnected with her immediate professional problems, a man who might be able to take her out of the oppressive atmosphere of cut-and-thrust between musicians and the whole set-up at the G.N.O. But what else had attracted her to him? "Well," he reflects, "you may not think so now, but in those days I was a handsome fellow. And, of course, remember that we were the first British soldiers to be seen in Athens, which gave us a special aura. . . . And also the fact that she could, after quite a long time, speak English. She must have enjoyed that too . . . she was garrulous, if anything." Morgan agrees that it must also have pleased her to be with someone who, being a foreigner, knew nothing about her family, her social background, or her conduct during the occupation. Then again, it must have flattered her feminine vanity that he showed so much interest in her, and lastly she enjoyed dancing with such a "marvelous dancer" (as he describes himself in his youth). "We went to various places," he says, "both clubs and private parties, specifically to dance."

And what about Ray's feelings for Mary? "She was more attractive to me than just a casual encounter. . . . I found her a very sweet person and also responsive. . . . I think I found her quite sexy in a way. . . . That's why it annoys me to hear people say she was fat and ugly. She wasn't at all so! . . . If she had been fat and ugly, I wouldn't have been interested." Asked about the nature of his relationship with Mary, Ray says only that he did not fully commit himself to her. "Perhaps because I wasn't sufficiently attracted to her or because I switched to Maro, whom I married in 1946. And Mary knew it, she discovered it. I must have told her—I told her something, and she reacted, saying that I was going to marry a snob. She felt that Maro belonged to another class." Ray did not try to find her after the fighting broke out in December. "I had lost interest in Mary, which, to be honest, I feel very guilty about, because I should at least have tried to find out what had happened to her," he says. "I should add, however, that it was the exigencies of war rather than the vagaries of love that, at the time, brought a halt to our meetings. For the army every step in the open risked a bullet from a sniper, and they were all around."

Ray continues, "Gradually the situation deteriorated until we heard from the civilian sympathizers that an attack on the barracks was imminent. It was 13 December. I took charge of my signalmen in their hut next to the perimeter wall. Around midnight there was an almighty bang. It was an explosion that blew down a section of the wall behind us, and *andartes* swarmed through the gap. We engaged them hand-to-hand until we were surrounded and overwhelmed. We were taken prisoner and found ourselves in the basement of the hut. As the night wore on we began to realize that the band of *andartes* was trapped by gunfire from the officers' mess building (situated exactly where the American embassy stands today). The bearded, bandoliered *Kapetanios* that led them became very agitated, thrust his gun in my ribs and threatened to shoot me. However, the upshot was that, by dawn, one of our tanks rattled up, freed us, and took the communists prisoner. To say that it had been a hectic night would have been putting it mildly."

All those December days of 1944 were unremittingly tense and dangerous, and indeed not a time for romantic musings, or notions of derring-do, White

British troops engaged in street fighting, Athens, December 1944.

Knight rescues. "The news of the attack on the barracks spread far and wide, and I'm sure Mary must have heard what happened. In the end she bore me no grudge, as she showed when me met up again a few years later," concludes Ray Morgan. One thing that still annoys him is that Mary is generally made out to have been cold, timid, and shy, with strong moral inhibitions and no social graces. "She was not inhibited, not at all! We became quite close almost immediately. She wasn't all that innocent either; she knew all these places like Jimmy's Bar quite well. She knew a hell of a lot of people, and she was well known herself in the small Athenian society of those days. And she was no different in 1952, when she saw Maro and me backstage at Covent Garden. She jumped on us and embraced and kissed us both. She was as warm as anything. That is why, when I read what they wrote about her, about this 'tigress' and this 'selfish woman,' I don't even recognize the person they are talking about."

—⁂—

Maria was once asked whether it was true that in the war she had been an undercover British agent. "*Yes, it's true. They were rather dramatic days,*" she answered, presumably referring to the period immediately after the occupation, as her connection with British intelligence, such as it was, did not start until after the German withdrawal. "*When the civil war broke out I wanted to go back to the red zone,*" she went on. "*Athens was divided into a white zone, where I worked, and a red zone, where I lived. And I couldn't leave my mother alone, of course, so I was brought back by jeep. They told me, 'It's your responsibility now if anything happens to you,' because I handled top secret letters and all that.*" And in early 1957 she said, "*On December 4 [sic], 1944—I remember it very well because it was my birthday—civil war erupted in Athens. As I have said, I was then working for the British command and my superiors recommended that I not leave headquarters, because, having occupied such a delicate post as that of distributing secret mail, I would undoubtedly be a victim of communist reprisals and subjected to inevitable torture. But our house was located in the zone occupied by the Reds, and I did not want to leave my mother on her own. For that reason I had myself taken, in a jeep to Patission Street.*"[17] Mary probably did not see the demonstrators or hear the gunfire that signaled the outbreak of open warfare between right and left. Those events took place in Syntagma Square, only about 200 meters away from where she worked, but as it was a Sunday morning, 3 December 1944 (the day after her twenty-first birthday), she was probably at home. It was that very evening that she made her last call to Ray Morgan. On Monday morning, before ELAS encircled and isolated the city center, Mary walked to work as usual, but when she found out about the situation she was taken back home in a British army jeep.

"When the street fighting started, Maria and I were safe at Patission 61 with a friend, Rina [Marina Papayeorgopoulou], who was living with us," Litsa states in her memoirs. She mentions that Jackie was not with them, but she says nothing about an ill-advised visit to Miltiadis Embirikos's father, which was the reason for her absence. Before the storm broke, Litsa had been to talk to Yorgos Embirikos about his son's intentions with regard to Jackie. According to Jackie, her mother went with the object of ending the liaison which she herself had engineered and whose fruits she had enjoyed for years. Old Mr. Embirikos, having listened patiently while Litsa gave him an insolent lecture, had politely but very firmly turned her out of his house. Jackie had then decided that she could not go on living at 61 Patission Street and the weak-willed Miltiadis had found a room for her in a hotel on Ayiou Konstantinou Street, between Omonia Square and the National Theater. He had been to see her as often as he could, and the two of them had been cut off from the others by the fighting on 3 December. The outbreak of civil war and the circumstances in which she found herself naturally made Jackie re-examine her feelings for her mother and sister. "'Just think,' I said to myself, 'remember what they have done to you.' . . . Just for a moment I was almost glad that terrible civil war had broken out, because it was a just punishment for [Mother's] arrogance." Mary had been just as much of a victim as she herself, Jackie reflected, and she felt sorry for her being stuck in the apartment without any food.[18]

The three women cooped up at 61 Patission Street (Litsa, Mary, and Marina) really were in a spot, and their plight grew worse as time went on. When the electricity was cut off they were no longer able to cook, they had no heat, and in the evenings they lived in darkness, as their few candles were soon used up. The only way they could warm themselves or heat up some water for a tepid cup of tea was by burning rags soaked in gasoline, of which Litsa fortunately had a good supply. "Our faces and hands were always black and greasy from smoke and benzene fumes," writes Litsa, describing those days of wailing sirens, explosions, and the cries of dying men, the rattle of machine guns, and stray shots which sometimes smashed into the wooden blinds or the walls: one burst of machine-gun fire annihilated the canaries and their cages. "Those poor tiny creatures who had been part of our lives in America, who had been with us all through the years of war, who had been Mary's constant inspiration, had been murdered," says Jackie, although of course she was not present when the slaughter occurred. Poor Mary sobbed inconsolably over their pathetic remains.[19]

For about a week out of the three that they were confined to their apartment, the three women had an unwanted guest: this was Ioannis Dourendis, the retired general who had been minister of the interior in the Metaxas government until the Germans invaded. He was a friend of the Embirikos family, and Litsa had met him aboard the S.S. *Eleni* on the return trip from Corfu in 1939. The presence of the garrulous and terrified Dourendis was very wearing on the nerves, and there was a fearful risk that he might be discovered by the communist caretaker of the apartment building. The caretaker, who naturally knew what Litsa had been up to in the last few years, took a sadistic pleasure in terrorizing the three women by scrawling dire messages on the walls of the building and threatening to blow their brains out. "Every day Maria and I washed out these chalked messages with a sponge; the next day they would be back again."[20] So the atmosphere in the apartment grew daily more oppressive, and the food shortage more and more worrying. "I soaked [beans] in water and doled them out—from six to ten beans at a time—to each of us," Litsa informs us. But Maria was to attribute her own survival, at least, to the generosity of their neighbor, Ilias Papatestas: "*I couldn't even think of procuring provisions for my mother and myself, and I might have died of starvation (many people died of it at the time) if I hadn't had the help of my friend Doctor Papatestas, who brought me some of the little food that he had at his disposal.*" Eventually Litsa felt obliged to ask Dourendis to move on: "For Maria's sake I dared not shelter him any longer. The communists knew no mercy. I don't believe they would have spared us even if Maria had sung *Tosca* to them as she had done for the Italians." And Litsa is probably telling the truth when she says that on the night of Dourendis's departure they all cried with emotion and pent-up tension: not only she and Mary but the general too, who had shaved off his luxuriant beard to avoid recognition.[21]

One day around 20 December a small, thin boy turned up at 61 Patission Street with a message urging them to run for safety. Although Jackie asserts that he was sent by Miltiadis, according to Litsa and Maria he had come from the British G.H.Q. "*At a certain moment I received a visit from a pale and poorly dressed boy— he looked like a coal vendor—who asserted that he had been charged with a mission concerning me by an official of the British command. Terrified, suspecting a trap, I tried to chase him away in a rude manner; then, since his insistence had become unbearable and nearly rabid, I resigned myself to listening to him. He was in reality a secret agent whom the British had sent to beg me to return to headquarters, because they feared for my life and were amazed that the communists had not yet arrested me. The fellow found it very hard to convince me; but at last he persuaded me that it was absolutely essential for me to go back to the British zone, and without wasting time I called Doctor Papatestas to entrust my mother to him.*"[22] Mary went off on her own with the boy, and it took them twelve hours to reach the Tameion building, a distance of less than one and a half kilometers. "*When I think of [Patission Street],*" she recalled later, "*I always see it in my imagination as I saw it that morning, literally covered with broken glass and all sorts of wreckage that had fallen out of windows as a result of the constant machine-gun fire: gray and silent. A tremendous, unnerving silence that would last sixty seconds, to be broken, once a minute, by the communists' terrible 'blind volley,' shots at regular intervals that could hit anyone and had the specific aim of wearing down the populace's nerves. Even now I can't explain to myself how I could have run desperately through the midst of that devastation, under fire, and arrived safe and sound at British headquarters.*" A few days later Mary was reunited with her mother, who had also been helped to escape from the communist zone. Together they went to look for Miltiadis and Jackie, and they moved into Jackie's hotel on Ayiou Konstantinou Street.[23]

It is probable that Mary went on working at the British headquarters, though we do not know what her job was nor how long she stayed.[24] On being told by her colleagues there that the British prime minister, Winston Churchill, and his foreign secretary, Anthony Eden, had arrived in Athens for consultations, Mary hurried off to see them at their only public appearance, in Syntagma Square on 27 December 1944. When she got back to the hotel she told her mother and Jackie how thrilled everyone had been when Churchill had given his famous "V" sign to the cheering crowd. The gleam of hope given by that gesture to all right-of-center Athenians in those days—grimmer than most days of the war against Nazism— was a most welcome and consoling Christmas present.[25] Mary could hardly have imagined then that fourteen years later she would be having a friendly chat with Churchill aboard the private yacht of a certain Aristotle Onassis. We can only guess at whether and what she told him about her memories of that winter's day in 1944, when she had been just one among hundreds of Greeks cheering him in Syntagma Square, anonymous but very much alive and full of hope.

—⁄⁄⁄—

Really, I still haven't understood why and how they didn't come after me.

To Hy Gardner, New York, February 1958

PART FIVE

Problems and Departure from Greece (1945)

CHAPTER 34

Problems at the National Opera

The cessation of hostilities on 12 January 1945 brought no great relief, because the situation was still fraught with fear and anxiety. Countless hostages had been taken by ELAS and were missing without trace, including at least two senior members of the opera company, Mireille Fléri and Leonidas Zoras, who both survived by eating snow; and every day brought new revelations of atrocious crimes, often committed for no other motive than political fanaticism or a desire for personal revenge, usually by underprivileged individuals with a chip on the shoulder. One such was the savage murder of the actress Eleni Papadaki: to this day many questions remain unanswered about the passive attitude of certain communist actors who did nothing to save her. Another casualty closer to Mary was her youngest uncle, Filon Dimitriadis, who went missing after being involved in the resistance in Athens and then leaving for the mountains and joining ELAS.[1] Nevertheless life did slowly return to normal. In late January some newspapers resumed publication, Athens Radio came back on the air, and electricity was restored, which meant that the streetcars and the metro could start running again.

While the Allies kept up their relentless bombing raids on Germany and converged on Berlin from all sides, in Athens the cafés, restaurants, nightclubs, theaters, and cinemas reopened (one movie theater reran *Robin Hood* with Errol Flynn and Olivia de Havilland). Food, however, was still a problem in the capital: even after the annihilation of so many thousands of Greeks all over the country, the population of Athens had been swollen by about four hundred thousand refugees from the provinces (where law and order had broken down) and Piraeus (where many people had been bombed out of their houses). The daily ration of bread, which had been less than 125 grams, was increased, but only to about 300 grams; a handout of 625 grams of sugar per person was made possible by the arrival of a shipment from America, and there were distributions of 1,280 grams each of pasta, dried beans, and salted herring. Other foodstuffs, including olive oil, remained scarce, and the black market continued to thrive. The shortage of both soap and water kept the general standard of hygiene low and aggravated the perennial problem of lice. The streets were filthy, and it was difficult to pick one's way through

Athens street scene
in the wake of the
December 1944
fighting.

the piles of rubbish and the rubble of buildings blown up by the communists to make roadblocks.

The new government headed by General Nikolaos Plastiras, the hero of the 1922 Asia Minor campaign, entered into negotiations with the Greek Communist party, with the regent, Archbishop Damaskinos, mediating between the two sides. The talks ended with ELAS agreeing to surrender its arms, and the accord was enshrined in the Treaty of Varkiza, signed in early February 1945 in the presence of Harold Macmillan, the British government minister concerned. However, the political skies remained overcast, and those first moves to reconstruct the stricken country were plagued by backstage infighting, cynical self-interest, and foreign intervention. Argument over the postwar constitution and the question of King George's return were to be the central issues of all political debate during the coming months. And on 21 February—while rehearsals were in progress at the G.N.O. for a revival of *Tiefland*, again with Mary in the lead—the trial of collaborators got under way, reopening fresh wounds and stirring up scarcely buried hatreds.

In November 1944 the Papandreou government had decided to take steps to restore order at the National Theater and the Greek National Opera, but the outbreak of civil war had prevented any action and everything had come to a standstill for six weeks. On 3 February 1945 the new Plastiras government put the G.N.O. back under the jurisdiction of the ministry of education, and Theodoros Synadinos, a friend of the prime minister, was appointed its new general manager. Synadinos was a prolific playwright and essayist, who had been involved in the theater since about 1910 and had served several terms as a governor of the National Theater. For the past two years he had had his eye on the general managership of the opera and had been doing his best to undermine Kalomiris's position. The consensus of opinion in the G.N.O. was that whereas Kalomiris veered like a weathervane in his political affiliations but was basically a nationalist and a patriot, Synadinos, who liked to be thought of as left of center, was first and foremost an opportunist. Although he had been mixing with the so-called progressives in the theater and the arts for years, he was also well in with the moneyed Kolonaki set and the palace. With these "qualifications" and his skill as a trimmer, he was well equipped to cope with the challenges of his new post; but he started with the disadvantage of being strongly disliked by many members of the company he was so keen to administer. He also came under fierce attack in the right-wing press, which inveighed against the "astonishing scandal" of the appointment of a leftist general manager when the correct course would have been to purge the G.N.O. of all those who had "gone on the rampage," sacking Kalomiris "under the law of EAM" and turning the opera into "a shambles."[2]

On 16 February 1945, the day after assuming his duties, Synadinos called on his "colleagues and fellow workers" to rise to the task facing them, in order to raise the G.N.O. to "its rightful place." The main products of Greece, he said, were tobacco, currants, olive oil—and good voices. The crisis in the company's finances naturally entailed the cancellation of planned new productions, including two (*Der fliegende Holländer* and *Fedora*) in which Mary was to have taken the lead. By the time Synadinos took over, the preparations for *Martha* and *Mignon* were already well advanced and he decided to go ahead with them "because the public is beginning to get tired of a constant succession of revivals." Even so, he could not resist sniping at Kalomiris for having chosen these two operas on the grounds that during the occupation, when he was "close to the Germans," he had had every opportunity to select and obtain the scores of any other operas he liked.[3] While maintaining a veneer of politeness, Synadinos persisted with his underhanded tactics. He made an extremely bad impression on his very first day in office by appointing his son Nikos as general secretary of the G.N.O.; he promoted him shortly after to a highly salaried personnel manager position. From then on, no matter what he did, the new general manager was always open to the charge of nepotism and of scandalously favoring the clique of his own friends.

The 1944–45 winter season opened on 24 February with Massenet's *Manon*. During the following two months the G.N.O. gave seventy-one performances of seven operas (*Manon, Barbiere, Lucia, Cavalleria, Tiefland, Die Entführung,* and *An Afternoon of Love,* a one-act by Marios Varvoglis), two operettas (*The Merry*

Theodoros Synadinos, the first post-war general manager of the Greek National Opera.

Widow and *The Land of Smiles*), and one ballet. On Wednesday 14 March, after about three weeks of preparatory work and rehearsals, there was a revival of the hit of the 1943–44 season, d'Albert's *Tiefland*. It was staged with the same principals (Mary as Marta, Andonis Delendas as Pedro, and Vangelis Mangliveras as Sebastiano, with Leonidas Zoras conducting), but no reviews were published in the press. The revival of *Tiefland* was very low-key in comparison with the excitement surrounding the original production, which had been due not only to the excellent work done by the singers and all the others involved, but also to the ballyhoo created by the German propaganda machine. Nevertheless, the 1945 production did bring Vangelis and Mary together again for a while, stirring up his feelings more than hers, as Mary was by now preoccupied with the thoughts that would lead eventually to her departure from Greece. There were just two more performances of *Tiefland*, on 15 and 24 March, and the total number of tickets sold for all three performances was only 1,058.[4]

Between the second and third performances of *Tiefland* Mary sang at an English Musical Afternoon at the Olympia Theater. Being unable to put on any new stage productions without state subsidy, Synadinos had decided to organize a series of "musical afternoons" devoted to the music of the Allied countries, starting with that of England, followed by Greece, France, Russia, America, Spain, and Hungary (the last three never took place). Unfortunately, most of the singers and

Program for the English Musical
Afternoon at the Olympia Theater,
Athens, 20 March 1945.

Programme

FIRST PART

1

Speech by the General Director of the National
State Opera

Mr. TH. N. SYNADINOS

2

Indroduction on English Music, by

Col. M. C. LUBBOCK

3

a) The Greek National Anthem
b) The British National Anthem
    THE ORCHESTRA WITH THE CHORUS OF N.S O.
c) Rule Britannia

CHORUS

4

a) Dido and Ænias
    1st Air of Dido (When I am laid   *H. PURCELL*
    in earth)   *(1658-1695)*
b) Think not strange   *E. NIMEY - E. JORNEY*
c) Cherry Ripe   *C. G. HORN - L. LEHMAN*
d) To Julia   *R. QUILTER*
    * To daisies op 8 No. 3
    * The bracelet op No. 1

Mrs. K. DAMASIOTIS

5

a) As Cupid roguishly one day   *J. ECCLES*
     (1668-1785)
b) Music from Shakespeare
    * And let me the Canakin clink (From «Othello») *ANON*
    * King Stephen was a worthy peer   *ANON*
    * Hamlet's Letter   *R. S. R. STEVENS*
    (The Song of Polonius)

Mr. S. KALOGERAS

6

a) My lovely Celia
b) The happy lover
c) When daisies pied   *Dr. ARNE*
    From «As you like it».

Mrs. Z. VLACHOPOULOU

7

Old Dances   *H. PURCELL*
THE BALLET WITH THE ORCHESTRA

SECOND PART

8

a) Sigh no more, ladies   *R. J. R. STEVENS*
b) Auld lang syne   *SCOTTISH AIR*

THE CHORUS

9

a) Willow - willow   *ANON*
    (Desdemona's song)
b) Love, I have won you   *L. RONALD*
c) On Wenlock Edge   *V. WILLIAMS*

Mrs. M. KALOGEROPOULOU AND QUINTET

10

Primitive Dance   *C. SCOTT*
From the «Jungle Book»

Mrs. L. KOTSOPOULOU AND ORCHESTRA

11

a) Kashmiri-Song   *A WOODFORDE - FINDEN*
b) Prelude   *L. RONALD*
From « The Cycle of Life»

Mr. A. DELENDAS

12

a) Till I wake   *A. WOODFORDE - FINDEN*
b) The Temple Bells   *A WOODFORDE FINDEN*

Mrs. M. FLERY

13

Popular Sailors Dance
THE BALLET WITH THE ORCHESTRA

Ten minutes interval between first and second parts.

CONDUCTOR:	Mr. T. KARALIVANOS
CHORUS MASTER:	Mr. M. VOURTSIS
BALLET:	Mrs. L. KOTSOPOULOU
PIANO:	Mr. KOUNTOURIS

FOLLOWING PROGRAMMES: *FLOTTOW:* MARTHA — *G. VERDI:* RIGOLETTO — *A. THOMAS:* MIGNON — *G. VERDI:* TRAVIATA dancers showed no enthusiasm for these concerts, which would bring no financial or professional benefit to the artists themselves. Synadinos was therefore obliged to enforce his will by posting up mandatory orders with the names of the performers and the works to be included in each program, selected in consultation with the legations of the countries concerned. In the half-empty theater,[5] at 4:30 p.m. on Tuesday, 20 March 1945, after an introductory speech by Synadinos, English musicologist Colonel M. C. Lubbock gave a talk on English music and then both national anthems were rendered by the G.N.O. orchestra and chorus under Totis Karalivanos. With Yerasimos Koundouris at the piano, the first half of the program comprised songs sung by Kitsa Damasioti, Spyros Kaloyeras, and Zoe Vlachopoulou and a dance suite performed by the G.N.O. ballet. The performers in the second half were Mary Kaloyeropoulou, Andonis Delendas, and Mireille Fléri, the G.N.O. chorus, the dancer Loukia Kotsopoulou, and the corps de ballet. Mary, accompanied by a quintet, sang the folk song "Willow, Willow," "Love, I Have Won You" by Landon Ronald, and "On Wenlock Edge" (or part of the cycle) by Ralph Vaughan Williams, hard though it is to imagine her singing this kind of music, which was so alien to her usual repertoire. In the event, the English Musical Afternoon was a success, or at any rate enough of a success to be noticed by the critics, though none of them went into detail.

Little is known about the conception of the idea for "A Nite of Stars," in which Mary made her next appearance ten days later, on Friday 30 March at the 1418th American Air Force Base at Ellinikon, near Athens. The concert was organized by Sergeant Ralph H. Michaels for the European division of air transport command. Numerous performers took part and the G.N.O. was heavily involved: Zoras conducted its orchestra, and its singers and dancers filled the whole of the first half of the program. Mary's contribution consisted of "Vissi d'arte" from *Tosca* and "Casta diva" from *Norma*, and the other singers were Vlachopoulou (*Traviata, Butterfly*), Fléri (*Manon Lescaut, Ernani*), and Koronis (*Carmen, Rigoletto*). The main point of interest about this event (about which nothing else is known from a musical point of view) is that it was the first time that Mary used the name Callas: not yet Maria, but Mary Callas.

It was at about this time that an incident occurred which was witnessed by Miltiadis's brother, Hariton Embirikos, who, after serving as a midshipman in the British navy, was back in Greece with a British commission to arrange for the rewards to be given to those who had helped Britain in the war. Hariton asked Mary to sing at a small reception being given at a friend's house on Alopekis Street, Kolonaki, in honor of Sir Jock Pease and the leader of the commission, Lord Sands. "I don't remember what she sang," Hariton recalls, "but her voice was so resonant that a window broke! Admittedly, window glass was very thin in those days, but the power of that girl's voice was fantastic." This was the second time that Mary reputedly broke a windowpane with her singing, and on this occasion there was a reliable eyewitness present.[6]

Program for "A Nite of Stars" at the 1418th American Air Force Base at Ellinikon, 30 March 1945.

———※———

The G.N.O.'s financial difficulties were due primarily to the desperate state of the Greek economy, but the problem was made much worse by the excessively tough approach of the finance minister, Yorgos Sideris, and some of his advisers, who were totally uninterested in the arts. They thought it quite wrong that in the recent past the National Theater and the G.N.O. had been put under the direct jurisdiction of the prime minister, who had given them aid in the form of "loans." The ministry of finance had therefore taken steps to have both institutions reassigned to the ministry of education, and a new law had been passed stipulating that the contracts of all their employees—performing artists, administrative staff, and technicians—would be terminated on 31 May 1945. When, however, the ministry of education had decided to close down the National Theater and the G.N.O. for reorganization, the ministry of finance had objected to the prospect of so many persons enjoying sinecures indefinitely. This meant that from the time Synadinos took over as general manager of the G.N.O., the threat of a suspension of salary payments had been hanging over the heads of its employees like a sword of Damocles.

At that point there really was a grave risk that the G.N.O. would lose all its state funding and so be forced to close down altogether, for the minister of finance showed no sign of relenting. To placate him, the minister of education, Konstantinos Amandos, had ordered the G.N.O. to reopen, and it had given its first performance of the new season on 24 February, as we have seen; but he had protested that a cultural institution raising the quality of life could not be judged by the standards of business, where the goal is to equate revenue with expenditure. He admitted that the G.N.O. workforce would have to be reduced from its present level of 311 employees, but he believed it would be better for the company to be disbanded immediately than for it to struggle on with a skeleton staff, staging such works as it could "ad hoc, with meager funds." Thus the financial imperative confronting the G.N.O. just then was to raise the funds necessary to enable it, first, to put on new productions that would boost its ticket sales, and secondly to cover its payroll costs and other operating expenses. To achieve the first of these objectives, on 13 March Synadinos requested an advance of Drs. 7,500,000, to be repaid in installments over approximately two years by nonpayment to the G.N.O. of the entertainment tax levied on its behalf. The problem of operating expenses, especially payroll costs, was both more immediate and more serious: in fact the shortage of funds had already caused organized protests in pursuit of pay rises. The protesters certainly had right on their side, because the minister of finance had just set a minimum monthly salary of 14,000 drachmas for actors in the independent sector, yet the performers and conductors of the G.N.O. were still being paid from 6,400 to 7,200 drachmas.[7]

At that time the G.N.O. had contracts with sixty-five chorus singers, fifty-seven orchestral players, twenty-one dancers, and forty-one solo singers, who between them accounted for sixty percent of the employees. By the time of the first board meeting, on 4 March 1945, Synadinos had arranged for notice of termination to be given to all employees, to make it easier for the company (and the rest of the staff) to be cleared of deadwood. Those who would no longer be employed in the slimmed-down G.N.O. would continue to be paid until 31 May, while those whose contracts were to be renewed would be paid higher salaries with immediate effect, which it was hoped would encourage them to work with a will and not waste their time on union meetings and strikes. On 15 March the board appointed an artistic committee (composed of the two senior conductors, Zoras and Evangelatos, and the two stage directors, Mordo and Triandafyllou, with Synadinos as the chairman) to decide who among the performing staff would be let go, and a restructuring committee to do the same for the administrative and technical staff.

On 29 March, with the ministry of finance still refusing to do anything at all for the G.N.O., Synadinos was informed that the solo singers had decided to take action. Never had a general manager been in such a difficult position, he told the board, even though things had started well and a measure of discipline had been restored. He laid the blame squarely on the ministry of finance, which persisted in treating performing artists as civil servants and ignored the fact that their salaries, even after the increases so grudgingly awarded, barely covered their costs of traveling to and from work.[8] The next day, 30 March, thirteen soloists with center-right political affiliations (Vlachopoulou, Kaloyeropoulou, Papanastasiou, Fléri, Androulis, Vassilakis, Glynos, Delendas, Koronis, Mangliveras, Moulas, Tsoubris, and Nikita [by proxy], who were joined in the next few days by Remoundou, Molotsos, and two leftists, Athineos and Efstratiou) went to see Synadinos in his office and warned him bluntly that, if their "paltry and ignominious" salaries were not increased to their satisfaction, they would stop taking part in performances as from 3 April, though they would continue to attend rehearsals of forthcoming productions. Synadinos told them that if their demand—which he admitted was reasonable—were presented in the form of an ultimatum, there was a risk that the government would treat it as extortion. Cancellation of performances would simply play into the hands of those philistine civil servants who regarded the existence of the G.N.O. as a luxury: if the soloists carried out their threat, the opera might well be closed down altogether, and they would be held responsible. He therefore asked them to wait for the decision of the cabinet, which was to discuss the matter the very next day, 31 March.

The deputation of singers, including Mary, came out of the meeting with fresh hope, but having heard nothing by 6 p.m. on Sunday 1 April, they went back to Synadinos and told him they had no option but to stand by their decision to go on strike. Synadinos responded unwisely with aggressiveness and threats, warning them that if they went ahead they would in effect be terminating their own contracts, their pay would automatically be stopped, and their work permits would probably be revoked. Though it is true he was under pressure from various quarters, his tough stance was uncalled-for and unfair to the soloists, as his talk about waiting for the cabinet's decision had proved to be humbug. The striking singers then sent a petition to the board (one of the signatures being that of "M. Kaloyeropoulou") asking to be granted an audience because the general manager had been "unhelpful." On 6 April, when the ministry of finance had just instructed the board to resolve the G.N.O.'s financial problems, a three-man deputation of singers (Glynos, Delendas, and Koronis) appeared before the board and explained that they had two basic demands: that singers' salaries should be equated with those of actors, whose jobs were much less insecure, and that the singers should have two representatives on the artistic committee. However, now that notice had been given of the termination of contracts—the long-awaited new law was promulgated on 2 April, opening the way for streamlining the workforce and more equitable rates of pay for those soloists who were kept on—the strikers would go back to work on Monday 16 April, pending the signing of new contracts.[9]

So the fortnight's strike by the seventeen soloists achieved exactly nothing, except to further embitter the strikers' relationship with the management. One thing we may be sure of is that Mary threw herself into the protest heart and soul, fighting passionately for what she believed to be right. Her participation would not have gone unnoticed by Synadinos, who must in any case have been irritated by her maverick ways, her manner, and her close association both with the arch-troublemaker Vangelis Mangliveras and with her teacher, the forceful Elvira de Hidalgo, who belonged to the faction opposed to him. From then on, whenever it suited him, Synadinos would cite the strike as an example of the troubles that had plagued the first two months of his term of office.[10] The responsibility for defusing the situation fell upon the artistic and the restructuring committees, which were deputed to streamline the workforce. The story of that streamlining process (as it affected the solo singers) is of considerable interest, not only because for the first time the soloists were unofficially graded "according to merit" but also because it resulted in a decision greatly to Mary's detriment. That decision, which left her feeling deeply embittered, has gone down in the Callas literature as being the main reason for her leaving Greece, but in reality it merely hastened her departure.

—m—

Synadinos had been waiting since the end of March for the recommendations of the artistic committee on reducing the number of solo singers, and he had also asked the conductor Lysimachos Androutsopoulos to make recommendations for the ideal personnel structure of the G.N.O. On 4 April 1945 Androutsopoulos submitted a detailed report in which he proposed that only 145 performing artists should be kept on and the technical staff cut still more drastically. Regarding the soloists, he recommended re-employing twenty-one principals and seven junior principals, making a total of twenty-eight as against the existing forty-one, and he considered all seven of the sopranos (Fléri, Galanou, Kaloyeropoulou, Nikita, Papanastasiou, Remoundou, and Vlachopoulou) to be indispensable. On the basis of his proposals, the board recommended that the total number of soloists be kept between twenty-six and twenty-eight and awaited the report of the artistic committee. However, each member of the committee was afraid of revealing his opinion to the others; so Synadinos eventually asked every member to deliver his verdict separately, in writing, classifying his selected soloists in specified grades.[11]

Leonidas Zoras was the only one who set out his opinions in detail. Lamenting the necessity of reducing the size of the company at all, he had initially listed forty-three soloists whom he considered indispensable, but "under duress" he had later cut this number to thirty-two. In a pinch, he said, he would be prepared to let two of those (Kazandzis and Kalaidzakis) be demoted to the chorus, but if he were forced to cut two more, to reduce the figure to twenty-eight, he declared that he would waive his salary—assuming, of course, that he was kept on himself.[12] Evangelatos also listed thirty soloists, while Mordo, Triandafyllou, and Synadinos proposed twenty-seven, twenty-nine, and thirty, respectively. In the end Synadinos had his way over the composition of the top grade, which comprised the five who had received A grades from all the committee members (Delendas, Galanou, Fléri, Koronis, and Vlachopoulou) plus Epitropakis (graded B by Mordo) and Mangliveras (graded A/B by Evangelatos and Triandafyllou). Mary found herself demoted to the second grade on a purely arbitrary ruling by Synadinos, since she received A grades from Evangelatos, Mordo, and Triandafyllou and A/B from Zoras and Synadinos himself, and therefore had exactly the same point count as Mangliveras, who was kept in the top grade.[13]

The report of the artistic committee, suitably "edited" by the general manager, was presented to the board and considered at its meetings of 16 and 18 April, just after eighty-five members of the administrative and clerical staff had been re-employed (including Synadinos's son, again as general secretary and personnel manager). To sugar the pill for those who had been demoted, Synadinos renamed the top category Grade AA, the second A, the third B, the fourth C, and the fifth D, instead of A, B, C, D, and E. At the board meetings some of the governors disagreed with the rankings of some of the soloists, but the composer Petros Petridis was the only one who indirectly demurred to the injustice done to Mary.[14] The soloists' monthly salaries were initially set at Drs. 40,000 for the seven in Grade AA, 35,000 for the eight in Grade A (Damasioti, Glynos, Kaloyeropoulou, Moulas, Nikita, Papanastasiou, Persis, and Remoundou), 30,000 for the three in Grade B (Efstratiou, Kaloyeras, and Vassilakis), 25,000 for the five in Grade C (Tzeneralis, Heva, Hoidas, Kourahani, and Papadopoulou) and 20,000 for the two in Grade D (Amaxopoulou and Papachristos). Within the next few days some of the twenty-five soloists submitted petitions requesting to be upgraded, but Mary was not one of them, even though she had been wronged more than any of the others.

The board announced that the matter was now closed, except for the consideration of possible future additions to the staff, but some irregularities did inevitably take place: for example, the veteran bass Kostas Persis, who hardly ever actually sang, was soon promoted to Grade AA as a special favor. So the process of "rationalizing" the workforce turned out to be a travesty; and Mary, who had been demoted and had her salary cut ostensibly for reasons of economy, had good cause to be resentful when she saw more and more persons with the right connections being added to the payroll.[15] Although the so-called expenditure cuts had been acknowledged to be necessary when they were announced, the management in general and Synadinos in particular were accused by the press of basing their actions on "suspect and erroneous" criteria. In the end very few of the staff were let go (the most prominent victims being the baritones Xirellis and Doumanis and the conductor Vassiliadis, all of whom were soon re-employed), and the main reason for even those few dismissals was to make room for others who had friends in the right places, as every general manager—and Synadinos more than most—had his hands tied by the political situation and the persons who had appointed him.

The question that remains to be answered is why Mary, who had received no B ratings (unlike Epitropakis) and had no more A/B ratings than Mangliveras, was demoted by Synadinos. Was he motivated by personal prejudice, or was his hand forced by Mary's enemies? Maria herself later talked about the matter at some length, but in general terms, without mentioning dates: "*We are at 1945: the time had come to renew my contract with the Royal Opera House, but I found out from a maternal uncle, a doctor at the Royal House (Professor Konstantinos Louros), that Rallis [sic], then the head of the Greek government, had received my colleagues en masse. They had gone to protest to him, threatening a full-dress strike in the event that I were again engaged as a prima donna at the Royal Opera House. It was a disgrace, they railed, that a girl of twenty-one be compared to artists of their talent and their age. . . . The director of the Royal Opera House was very embarrassed when he had me summoned to explain to me that I would no longer be engaged as a prima donna. I allowed him to stammer out a bunch of excuses, then announced to him that I was leaving for America, adding, 'Let's hope that you won't have to regret this one day.'*" And in 1959 she said, with a patronizing smile, "*I never forgave them*," adding that she had gone straight to a travel agency and booked herself a ticket on the first ship leaving for America, at the lowest price available.[16]

Maria's anger fifteen years after the event was basically justified, because the subject reminded her of all the troubles she had endured in those years at the G.N.O. However, the accuracy of the facts as she describes them is open to question. In the first place, no other source corroborates her statement that her fellow singers went en masse to see the prime minister (who, in any case, was not Rallis then but Plastiras). If the matter really had been taken up to that level, somebody would be sure to remember the fact, and there might well be some written record of it. Yet none of the singers who were in the opera in those days says anything about a mass protest to the prime minister, nor even to the general manager of the G.N.O. Although one cannot rule out the possibility that Synadinos may have spoken to Plastiras about the problems he was having with the singers, the issue was surely too trivial to justify a formal protest to the prime minister. Lastly, it seems unlikely that at that particular juncture, when Mary had allied herself with the strikers, Remoundou or Fléri or Glynos—or even Galanou—would have employed such underhanded tactics against her. It is therefore hard to believe that there was any organized movement to have her downgraded. The most plausible explanation is that Synadinos had had pressure exerted on him or had been visited by a person or persons with a grievance of the usual kind and, following his own inclinations, had deliberately tried to have Mary downgraded by giving her an A/B rating himself. Then, when this proved insufficient to do the trick (since Mangliveras had exactly the same ratings), he had made an arbitrary decision to move her down to the second grade, probably to placate some of the "prima donnas" in the company while gratifying his own personal dislike of her at the same time. But there is no written or verbal evidence to support this or any other interpretation.

Maria's accounts of this episode—like her accounts of other long-past slanders and attacks on her, which she subsequently exaggerated—were probably not actually made up but merely embroidered and distorted so as to overdramatize them and make them seem more important. By taking liberties with facts and personalities and elevating the "conspiracy" against her to prime ministerial level, she inflated her own importance and magnified the part she played in the affairs of the G.N.O. in those early days. Not that she was not persecuted in 1945, nor that she was not unfairly demoted and forced to take a cut in salary. But the situation was never as dramatic as she later made it out to have been. Certainly she must have been very worried, certainly she must have felt herself to be the victim of backstage scheming by her small-minded rivals: in fact she talked about her troubles at the time to several people, some of whom saw her in tears about them. However, the untoward events of 1945 did not in themselves have any crucial bearing on her future, as she later implied they had. Mary did not leave Greece because Synadinos had his knife into her: that is just part of the Callas mythology, to which she herself contributed a good deal of material, sometimes unwittingly but sometimes deliberately. The anger that manifested itself over her "humiliating" treatment by the G.N.O. should probably be seen as the cumulative outcome of years of tiring work, hardship, and adversity combined with the psychological stress she felt in 1945, a watershed year when she had to make decisions that would be crucial to her future life and career.

—w—

So they went on a strike and they went to the prime minister and said that if Kaloyeropoulou is not brought down from first soprano to second, well, we just won't sing with her, she'll have to sing alone. And of course the prime minister, who was a very dear friend of my uncle's, told him so and said, "Well, Maria can do just what she thinks, but I can't do otherwise, because of course she can't sing by herself."

To Harry Fleetwood, New York, March 1958

CHAPTER 35

Easter Concerts in Thessaloniki

In the early years of her career, from 1940 until the end of the war in Greece, Mary had not achieved the sort of distinction that might have entitled her to demand special treatment. However, pay differentials had been relatively small and so, although younger and less in demand than the "big names," she had already had a salary equal to or not much lower than theirs. Now, after a spell during which she had triumphed in *Tiefland* and *Fidelio* and her rivals had had no comparable success, she had been demoted to the second grade, which meant that Fléri, Galanou, and Vlachopoulou had all been ranked above her for no good reason. What mattered about her demotion was not so much the financial loss as the blow to her prestige, for even at that early age she is known to have been very touchy on the subject. In that atmosphere of political feuding—coming as it did after the previous year's disturbances in her private life and friction at work, not to mention her de facto ejection from the G.N.O. on the day of the liberation—she took her reduction to a lower grade as a personal challenge and a professional slight.

Mary may have sought relief by talking the matter over with Vangelis Mangliveras, who would no doubt have encouraged her natural tendency to fight back against anything that annoyed her. We may be fairly sure that she did speak very aggressively to Synadinos, in her fury blurting out that she had already decided to leave Greece in any case, and perhaps telling him insolently that he—or at any rate the G.N.O.—would live to regret it. *"I'm not staying here!"* she is once alleged to have said. *"People in Greece are petty-minded and vindictive."* But it is not true that she went straight to a travel agency and booked a passage on the first ship leaving for New York, as she herself wrote later.[1] Immediately after her demotion she probably began to talk openly about her intention of going to America, but no more than that. The news of her impending departure was first reported, still with no mention of a date, in a Thessaloniki newspaper on 26 April 1945, about ten days after the new gradings were announced, and in the Athens papers in early June. Evidently Mary was waiting to see what came of her attempts to negotiate a better contract with Synadinos before deciding when she would leave. In the meantime, she merely set about the preliminary business of applying for a passport and finding out sailing dates and ticket prices.

Having decided not to sign the new contract she was offered, Mary suddenly found herself with no job, no income, and uncertainty surrounding the continuation of her career. The G.N.O. had become an unpleasant place to work, with a general manager who was not a musician and was uninterested in, if not positively hostile toward her; so the idea of pursuing an international career was bound to have been very much in her thoughts just then. The obvious course, for which de Hidalgo had been preparing her for years, was for her to go to Italy, the land of opera and bel canto, to which she was so well suited. But she was still strongly influenced by rosy memories of the Metropolitan Opera in New York, the city where she had grown up and her father was living. Balancing these two options—the prospect of living a solitary life with no money in the unfamiliar environment of Milan, or alternatively going back to her old haunts in New York, where she would be sure of a roof over head and the moral (and, she hoped, material) support of her beloved father and her kind godfather Leonidas Lanzounis—she naturally came down strongly in favor of New York, both for practical and sentimental reasons.

With these thoughts milling about in her head, Mary decided to go once more to Thessaloniki with her mother. Easter was coming, spring was in the air, and there was nothing to keep her in Athens: in fact she felt the need to escape the scene of her recent traumas. On Thursday, 26 April 1945, the Thessaloniki newspapers *Nea Alithia* and *Makedonia* informed their readers that "the famous dramatic soprano of the Greek National Opera Miss Kaloyeropoulou, an American by nationality," was arriving in the city "before the end of the week" (that is to say, between 27 and 29 April) to give a recital over Easter. *Makedonia* added that she was paying a last visit to the Macedonian capital "at the request of music-lovers in our city" before leaving for America.[2] It is not known whether the idea of going to Thessaloniki and giving a recital there had originated with Mary or her mother, nor how they traveled, although at least one leg of their journey (the outward leg, according to Litsa) was by sea, despite the danger of unswept mines. Photographs taken on board show Mary and Litsa with three unidentified men, one in civilian clothes and the other two in the uniforms of Greek army officers. Mary, who has a cross on a chain around her neck, is smiling and looks very serene and prettier than ever before: a plump, attractive girl with a placid expression, a clear complexion, and beautiful hair. One of those snapshots, showing her in a pensive pose on the deck of the ship, she liked so much that she sent a copy to her father, with the words *"To my beloved father, with infinite love, Marianna"* written on the back in Greek.[3]

At that time the Thessaloniki papers were full of gruesome photographs and reports of recent massacres, looting, shocking murders, discoveries of mass graves, exhumations of headless bodies, and round-ups of "traitors," profiteers, and collaborators. The front page headlines, of course, were all about the last days of the

Mary with her mother and two friends on their way to Thessaloniki, late April 1945.

war in Europe. "Adolf Hitler Slain Yesterday in the Chancellery," screamed the newspaper *Fos* on 2 May, and two days later *Makedonia* announced, "Hitler's Body Vanishes!" On Orthodox Easter Sunday, 6 May, *Makedonia* reported Patton's advance into Austria and the capture of Salzburg, and two days after that (on the day before Mary's first recital in Thessaloniki) it proclaimed VE Day and announced Germany's unconditional surrender. Sharing the page with the advertisement for Mary's recital was a photograph of Mussolini's body, strung up by the feet, with a description of his death by the man who killed him.

In Thessaloniki Litsa and Mary again stayed with the Moundouris family in the familiar surroundings of the apartment at 5 Lassani Street. Maria Moundouri was now fourteen and has clearer memories of this occasion than of her cousin's previous visits: among other things, she remembers her father asking Mary to sing the Ave Maria and Mary going cheerfully to the piano to oblige him. As soon as they arrived, mother and daughter set about making the arrangements for the recital. Not only did they need to hire a hall but they had to find a pianist as well. Tonis Yeoryiou recalls with emotion how he picked up the telephone one day and heard a voice saying, "This is Mrs. Kaloyeropoulou. I would like you to accompany my daughter, the rising star of Greece. May we come and see you?" Yeoryiou had heard on the radio that a certain Kaloyeropoulou had been making a name for herself in Athens with her impressive performances in *Tiefland* and *Fidelio*. The

Mary on her way to Thessaloniki, late April 1945.

very same day Litsa and Mary came to call on him, accompanied by a "virile-look-ing" general in plain clothes.[4] For the practical arrangements, including the ques-tion of his fee, Yeoryiou addressed himself to Litsa, but he discussed the program and other purely musical matters with Mary herself and agreed with her that they would do most of their rehearsing at Lassani Street. They hired the small audito-rium of the Third Army Corps Club on d'Espérey Street, and on the Monday before Easter, 30 April, *Nea Alithia* announced not one but two forthcoming recitals by "the dramatic soprano Marianna Kaloyeropoulou, a soloist of the G.N.O.," on Wednesday 9 and Thursday 10 May at 8 p.m.[5]

Yeoryiou and Mary spent the whole of Holy Week practicing together. Yeor-yiou, then aged thirty-one and newly married, was already an experienced soloist and accompanist. In 1926, when only twelve years old, he had accompanied the up-and-coming Nicola Moscona at a recital in Thessaloniki. He had then spent nine years in Vienna studying with Emil Sauer, who had been taught by Liszt and d'Albert, the composer of *Tiefland*. Although he had been a regular visitor to the Staatsoper, where he had heard all the great singers of the day, the impression made on him when he first heard Mary sing on Lassani Street was to remain indeli-bly engraved on his memory. At that first rehearsal session, after the ritual cup of coffee, Tonis sat down at the piano and opened his music. "I remember the first piece we tried was that aria of Donna Anna, where she asks Don Ottavio to take vengeance on Don Giovanni. So I play the chords of the recitative, in which Anna voices all her conflicting feelings, and then Maria launches into 'Or sai chi l'onore.' As soon as she starts, I feel something welling up inside me, blocking my throat and clouding my eyes—they were completely misted over. I had to stop, my eyes were so wet that I couldn't see the notes. '*Go on! What's wrong?*' she said in English, almost without stopping singing. '*Go on!*' That only made the tears start streaming even more. 'I can't! I can't see!' I said. Then at last she realized what was happening and said gently, '*Come on, Tony, come on!*' We waited a bit, and after I had got over it we went on." At the end of the aria Tonis turned to Mary and said impulsively, "What on earth are you doing *here*? You can have a great career abroad! Forget Athens, forget Thessaloniki, you're wasting your time here! Get up and go, girl!" And Mary told him quietly, "*Well, I am leaving. I'm going to America to see if I can set myself up abroad.*"[6]

Tonis Yeoryiou, who accompanied Mary in Thessaloniki, May 1945.

Tonis went to Lassani Street two or three times, and sometimes Mary went to practice at his house on Dimosthenous Street. "She wanted everything to be perfect," he remembers. "She would keep stopping me to discuss some little point of detail. We worked very well together, very constructively." When they rehearsed at Tonis's house, his young wife, Eleni, was also present. She had studied the piano herself, having grown up in a musical household where family friends used to drop in to listen to classical music on her father's radio, one of the first in Thessaloniki. Her mother played the violin and was a friend of Margherita Perras, the internationally renowned soprano. Eleni, who often turned the pages for Tonis, was in a good position to observe Mary at close quarters. "She was very plump but very pretty too, with a lovely face and a clear complexion. She was very modest and said very little, and until she opened her mouth to sing it would never have occurred to you she was a singer. Although I had heard plenty of great voices from my childhood on, when I heard Mary I was absolutely bowled over! It's hard to imagine today, but her voice then was much more beautiful than what you hear in her recordings."[7]

One evening when they had finished practicing, Tonis and Eleni went out with Mary and Litsa to have a Lenten dinner at the Olympos-Naoussa, on the waterfront. Then Holy Week drew to an end with the Epitaphios ceremony on Good Friday and the celebration of the Resurrection at midnight on Holy Saturday, probably at the nearby cathedral, which was followed by the traditional breaking of the fast with *mayiritsa* soup and red-dyed eggs. Tonis and Eleni could not help noticing how different Mary was when she was with her mother: "When she was on her own and in her element, in other words when she was singing, her whole personality glowed, but with her mother by her side playing the great lady and the great beauty, Maria was practically invisible." Eleni later visited Mary in Athens, and had the opportunity to confirm that Litsa was only interested in music insofar as she could get something out of it for herself. The sort of person she was can be judged from the opinions she sometimes expressed quite openly. "One day she turned to me," Eleni recalls, "and said, 'It's all very well to have a husband, but have a lover as well! That way, when you quarrel with your husband, you'll have something to fall back on!' And that was to a newly married girl of nineteen, in front of her own daughter, who wasn't more than two years older than me."[8]

—✳—

The auditorium of the Third Army Corps Club was not full, but those who heard the recital on Wednesday 9 May (Tonis Yeoryiou is not sure whether they in fact repeated the recital the following day) were impressed and applauded Mary very warmly. "She wore a long, black, sleeveless, off-the-shoulder dress. But the way she looked was nothing to the way her personality shone through," Tonis comments. "She had very striking almond-shaped eyes that gave her almost an Indian look, but what you really noticed about her was her artistic presence. You were aware of the superhuman potency of her talent even before she started singing, from the expressive movements of her arms and hands." The audience reacted with spontaneous enthusiasm, and word of her prowess spread rapidly in musical circles. "She made a great sensation and the whole of the Thessaloniki musical world was talking about her," says Eleni Yeoryiou. "She was more radiant and more cheerful, but even that night, after her triumphant recital, she was in the shadow of her mother." After the recital Tonis and Eleni again went out to dinner at the Olympos-Naoussa with Mary, Litsa, and Litsa's general.[9]

The exact program of that recital—and of the other recital with Tonis Yeoryiou (for there was at least one more, with a different program) and of the orches-

tral concert at which she sang before returning to Athens—is not known. Tonis
remembers eight pieces that Mary sang but admits that his memory may be shaky.
Besides "Or sai chi l'onore," they had practiced "Ah! fors' è lui" from *Traviata*, the
Jewel Song from *Faust*, the Bell Song from *Lakmé*, "Una voce poco fa" from *Barbiere*, "Abscheulicher!" from *Fidelio*, and two more arias to be sung as encores, "O
mio babbino caro" from *Gianni Schicchi* ("The sonority of her voice when she
was singing the little girl's lines was astonishing!") and "O mio Fernando" from *La
Favorita*, an aria written for a mezzo-soprano. Further information about the programs of Mary's concerts comes from Kyriakos Patras, the principal viola player in
the Thessaloniki Symphony Orchestra. Patras remembers her singing pieces from
Weber's *Oberon* (presumably "Ocean! thou mighty monster," in which she had
made such an impression back in 1938) and *Der Freischütz* ("Leise, leise, fromme
Weise," another piece she had sung in 1938), and also—most interesting if true,
but unlikely—the Liebestod from *Tristan*.[10] But two arias that she definitely did
sing at the first recital on 9 May (and perhaps again on 10 May) were "Ritorna
vincitor" from *Aida* and "Casta diva" from *Norma*, because those were chosen by
Patras for the Thessaloniki Symphony Orchestra concert at which he suggested
Mary should sing.[11]

After the German withdrawal from Greece, the members of the Thessaloniki
radio orchestra, which had been well organized by the German conductors Artur
Hartmann, Otto Fricke, and Albert Yung,[12] decided to stay together and applied
to the state for official recognition and a subsidy (which were not formally granted
until 1959). Patras tells how one afternoon, when some members of the orchestra
were playing chamber music in the Thessaloniki State Conservatory (very near
the Third Army Corps Club), the cellist Manolis Kazambakas suggested going
across the road to hear a song recital by someone called Kaloyeropoulou. Patras was
reluctant but eventually agreed to go, and that only because Tonis Yeoryiou was
the accompanist. "We arrived just as this big girl with fat legs but plenty of self-
assurance was coming on stage. As soon as she started singing I grabbed Kazambakas's arm and whispered, 'It makes me proud that Greece can produce something like this!' I was absolutely thrilled." When Patras went around afterward
with Kazambakas, the violinist Kostas Tryfonidis, and one or two others to congratulate Mary, it occurred to him that on the coming Sunday, 13 May, the
orchestra was giving its second concert of the season at the National Theater and
could not afford to move a piano from the conservatory, just 500 meters away.
Carried away by his excitement, and swayed also by the thought that a piano
would not be needed, he asked her on the spur of the moment if she would be able
to sing with the orchestra in four days' time. "'*I'll be here*,' she told me. '*I'm staying
with my aunt on Lassani Street. Have you got the orchestral parts?*' 'Yes, we have,' I
lied. '*What parts have you got?*' 'The pieces you sang,' I said, and mentioned
'Ritorna vincitor' and 'Casta diva,' the two I had liked best in her program. '*All
right, then. When do you rehearse?*'"[13]

The next day, 10 May, Kyriakos Patras told the board of the Thessaloniki Symphony Orchestra about the possibility of Mary's singing in the second sub-scription concert under the baton of Evripidis Kotsanidis. Nobody knew any-thing about Mary Kaloyeropoulou, of course, but Patras clinched the argument by pointing out that they would be saved the expense of moving the piano. He then rushed straight to Lassani Street to inform the new soloist. Once they had agreed on a token fee, he went and fetched the conductor to meet Mary. "Kotsanidis was flattered to be conducting a soloist from the G.N.O.," Patras continues. "He also considered himself something of a connoisseur of beauty, so he was pleased by her attentiveness and her youth, which made her likable and attractive." On Fri-day 11 May, the newspapers *Nea Alithia* and *Dimokratia* reported that for the forthcoming Sunday concert the management of the orchestra had secured the services of the "distinguished" and "renowned" dramatic soprano from the G.N.O., Marianna Kaloyeropoulou, who would be singing "various composi-tions, including 'Casta diva' from Bellini's *Norma*." Meanwhile Patras was work-ing hard to orchestrate three arias (two programmed items and one encore) and copy out the parts for every instrument in the orchestra. "There were no orches-tral parts," recalls Kiki Chrysafi, a Thessaloniki-based soprano, "so when Kaloyero-poulou agreed to sing I gave my piano scores to Kyriakos for him to orchestrate." Patras, his brother, Kazambakas, and Tryfonidis spent two whole days and nights copying out the parts by hand, several times for the first violins, a few less for the cellos, and so on for each instrument.[14]

Evripidis Kotsanidis, who was highly regarded in Thessaloniki,[15] was on the podium when the orchestra had its one and only rehearsal with Mary in the National Theater, most probably on Saturday 12 May. "We distributed the hand-written orchestral parts and started with the aria from *Aida*," Kyriakos Patras recalls. "After only a few bars, in the well-known theme of the Nile scene, Kalo-yeropoulou (whom I had let into the secret that there had been no orchestral parts and I had only just managed to orchestrate the arias in time) turned to me and said, '*Maestruzzo, you've got it wrong. It shouldn't be the oboe there.*' 'I thought the oboe was the most appropriate instrument for this exotic scene,' I explained. '*No, it should be the clarinet.*' And she picked up several more mistakes with that fantas-tic ear of hers. For example, I had the double basses doubling the cello part, and as the double basses are clumsy movers—the elephants of the orchestra—she turned to me at one point and said, '*Those basses of yours are making quite a racket here, Maestro!*'"[16]

Actually, on the day of that solitary rehearsal it seemed likely that the concert scheduled for the following morning would have to be postponed. The British forces had requested permission to use the National Theater for a victory celebra-tion, one of many to be held all over Europe on the morning of Sunday, 13 May 1945. Mary had apparently expressed annoyance at the prospect of having to stay on in Thessaloniki, and so it had been decided that the concert would go ahead as planned, but in the Pallas Cinema. According to the newspaper *Makedonia*, the concert could not be postponed "because of the participation of the distinguished singer Marianna Kaloyeropoulou, a soloist of the G.N.O., who cannot put off her return to Athens." But this involved a risk that the concert would be a flop, both musically and commercially, and so at the very last minute—on the Sunday morning, when the papers carried banner headlines proclaiming the victory celebration and the sirens sounded for the last time (in a "victory howl," as the *Fos* reporter put it)—it was announced that the concert would after all be postponed to the following Sunday, 20 May.[17]

Mary in the company of Greek soldiers, possibly in Thessaloniki, May 1945.

So, in the end, Mary chose to stay on for her concert with the Thessaloniki Symphony Orchestra, which would be her first appearance as soloist on her own with full orchestra. The enforced delay led her and Tonis Yeoryiou to decide to give another recital, encouraged by the success of the first and hoping to make some money out of it. This time they booked the White Tower Theater for Thursday 17 May at 8 p.m., advertising the recital in *Nea Alithia* and *Makedonia* only on Tuesday and Wednesday. "That time Mary wore a mauve gown with something that half-covered her arms," remembers Tonis. "I think she repeated Marguerite's Jewel Song, Rosina's 'Una voce poco fa,' and Leonore's 'Abscheulicher!' The last of these I had heard in Vienna with Lotte Lehmann, who was exhausted at the end, whereas Maria sang it all effortlessly and very beautifully."[18] This recital, too, was a great success, partly because of the favorable reports circulating about the first one and partly in anticipation of the Sunday orchestral concert.

No reviews were published of any of Mary's appearances in Thessaloniki. However, the press did at least give plenty of advance publicity for the second subscription concert of the Thessaloniki Symphony, for thirteen announcements appeared in various newspapers between 16 and 20 May. *Nea Alithia* spoke of the forthcoming appearance of the "outstanding" and "distinguished" dramatic soprano Marika Kaloyeropoulou (the only time her name was given in this form in print), and added, "According to experts who heard Miss Kaloyeropoulou at her recital, she is a vocal and musical phenomenon." Evidently Mary really had made an impression in her two recitals. On the day of the concert an article in the organ of the Greek Communist party, *Laiki Foni*, reported: "The soloist will be the dramatic soprano Marianna Kaloyeropoulou, a vocal phenomenon by Greek standards, who has won more admiration and applause from our music-loving public than any other singer."[19] If Mary really had collaborated with the enemy during the occupation as traitorously as some people maintained, we may be sure that the official Communist party newspaper would not have praised her in such terms.

After two or three more rehearsals the concert took place at 11 a.m. on Sunday, 20 May 1945, in the large auditorium of the National Theater. Though the governor general of northern Greece and numerous prominent public figures were present, the house was not full: it never was, except when a well-known soloist from Thessaloniki was performing. After Beethoven's Fourth Symphony, with which the program opened, Mary came on wearing a long wine-red gown. "I still remember the view I had of her well-covered backside from my place in the orchestra," Patras chuckles. "First she sang 'Ritorna vincitor' from *Aida* and then 'Casta diva.' Her performance certainly went down well and she got a lot of applause." Encouraged by the audience's enthusiastic response, Mary then sang her encore, Leonora's aria "O mio Fernando" from *La Favorita* by Donizetti. "In the concert I could watch her closely, as I wasn't playing," says Tonis Yeoryiou. "I remember being very struck by the movement she made as she started on the aria from *La Favorita*. It was as if she were about to take off: she held her arms out like wings, but quite low down, at the same time leaning forward. There was a tremendous sense of motion about her, as if *she* were bringing the orchestra in for that aria."[20] After the intermission Kotsanidis conducted the orchestra in the *Danse macabre* by Saint-Saëns and the *Capriccio italien* by Tchaikovsky.

Twelve years later Kyriakos Patras would be playing with the Athens State Orchestra in Maria Callas's recital at the Odeon of Herodes Atticus in Athens, and again at Epidavros in *Norma* (1960) and *Medea* (1961). However, being a modest and reserved man, he did not try to talk to the famous diva on any of these occasions. "I didn't dare to introduce myself to her. Perhaps I might have done if I had known that she had asked a Thessaloniki journalist, '*How are those enthusiastic youngsters in Thessaloniki getting on?*'"[21] If Maria still remembered those "enthusiastic youngsters" after so many years, she evidently had very happy memories of that third visit to Thessaloniki. After all, her appearances there gave her a few moments of relief from her troubles with the G.N.O. and the serious decisions facing her. Yet in her memoirs Maria never once refers to any concerts in Thessaloniki, while Litsa erroneously dates the visit to October 1944, immediately after the liberation. One of the main purposes of those concerts, if not *the* main purpose, was to raise money to finance Mary's future plans. That is why Litsa, who states that Mary gave "a series of concerts" in Thessaloniki, ruefully admits that yet again they had returned to Athens "without the riches we had hoped for."[22]

CHAPTER 36

Reasons and Preparations
for Leaving

S ince at least the spring of 1941, when Greece was occupied, Mary had had no contact with her father nor even heard any news of him. We do not know how much she had thought of him in the intervening years, the only information on the subject being her mother's statement, "Sometimes Maria spoke of him." Litsa says she had not heard from George since 1938, when he had gone to Los Angeles to open a drugstore, and had no idea where he was "or even if he was alive." George was still alive; for some time he had been living in San Francisco, working at the Golden Eagle Pharmacy at 251 Third Street. As soon as he heard that the Germans had left Athens he wrote to ask for news of his daughters and Litsa. In that letter, which probably arrived in November 1944, he asked if they were intending to come back to America and reminded Mary that her American nationality might come in useful, as the U.S. authorities were arranging transport for the repatriation of American citizens from around the world. To help them he enclosed a hundred dollars, which gave Litsa a pretext for arguing later that the money had been the reason for Mary's delight at receiving the letter.[1]

The oft-repeated story that Mary received no news of her father until about the summer of 1945 is clearly part of the Callas mythology. After two months of total disruption caused by civil strife, communications were again working more or less normally in Greece from February 1945, and her affectionate message on the back of the photograph of the Thessaloniki trip makes it clear that she was in touch with him again and had begun to miss him badly. Though we do not know what Mary wrote back to her father, she must surely have told him about the high-lights of her musical career so far and perhaps about some of her traumatic experiences as well. She also sent him photographs of two of her most successful performances, the 1942 *Tosca* and the more recent *Fidelio*, both with messages written in Greek on the back.[2]

Nevertheless, the main factor behind Mary's decision to leave Greece was a natural desire to make the most of her ability and talent. The idea had been matur-ing for some time, and opportunities for voicing her thoughts of an international career came mostly in her conversations with her teacher. Elvira de Hidalgo was meanwhile cultivating her contacts to prepare the way for Mary to go to Italy when the war was over, and the young rising star, encouraged by her comments and those of other experts on her promising future, quickly came to take it for granted that sooner or later she would be going in search of international recognition. Ilias Papatestas remembers that during the occupation she was already making plans to go to America, when no one else was even thinking about such things. And Dino Yannopoulos confirms that while most people had altogether different priorities, Mary was the only person who boldly asserted, "*Whatever happens, I am getting out of Greece!*"[3] So in this sense Mary's musical ambition was the decisive factor underlying her decision to leave Athens, where, in spite of the praiseworthy efforts and fine qualities of many musicians, the war had made it impossible for her to develop her career commensurately with the magnitude of her talent.

But although Mary had already reached a final and irrevocable decision to go abroad, it is not true to say that she started making preparations to leave as soon as the occupation was over. The preparations did not begin until several months later, by which time she had experienced some of the horrors of the vicious street fighting of December 1944 that had led Greece to the brink of civil war. Moreover, by that time the atmosphere at the G.N.O. had become increasingly unpleasant, and Mary's relations with her mother had deteriorated further because of the resurgence of her affection for her father. "*A mother must be a good mother to her children, yes or no? There is no going away from that. It's her responsibility. She is not doing anything special. It is her duty,*" Maria said angrily in 1968. "*There is nothing extraordinary about how wonderful a mother is. She has got to be wonderful, otherwise don't have children. But if you do, be a good mother and don't expect anything in return!*"[4]

The phrase "anything in return," which she used often, has hitherto been understood to refer to Litsa's demands for money after her daughter had become famous; but what Maria was actually aggrieved about was what Litsa had encouraged and expected of her during the occupation. She held her mother chiefly responsible for her own discreditable conduct and for giving her a shortsighted, egocentric outlook on life, for which she, the daughter, had paid dearly: in practical terms in the infighting and insults that Mary had had to endure at the G.N.O., and on the moral plane, in the remorse and anger that she must soon have started feeling. "*You know, my career was just for the money,*" Maria is reported saying in 1972. "*Mother was going to be the grand lady while I had to keep shoveling it out, screaming my guts out to get it. . . . She always kept after me until I was nothing more than a goddamned singing machine making money.*"[5]

Although Litsa and Jackie in their memoirs attach no importance to the traumas inflicted on Mary by her mother's attitude and behavior, those traumas actually provide us with the key to understanding the personality of Maria Callas. Having "discovered" her daughter's vocal talent, Litsa thought she was entitled to lay down the law on everything, even the direction of Mary's career. "She was always determined to bring up her daughters to be what *she* wanted," Jackie says even now, while in her book she remarks, "Since [Mary's] arrival in Athens aged thirteen, Mother had done everything possible to suppress any normal human reactions and to instill in her daughter those selfish, aggressive qualities that she believed would enable her to claw her way to the top." While not having been a spotless innocent herself, Mary had, as we have seen, been urged by her mother to show "tolerance" so as to reap some benefit from contacts and friendships with members of the occupation forces. On this crucially important question, although Jackie does not deny her mother's reprehensible conduct, she does deny that Litsa put pressure on Mary or caused her any anger or distress. However, while insisting that Litsa never pushed Mary into doing anything discreditable, she admits that when she subsequently told her father about the Italian "suitors," her father's response was, "You should have got out of the house and left the two of them to deal with the Italians on their own." Jackie says she felt sorry for them because they would have been left without a roof over their heads. "'What's going to happen if Milton ever finds out?' I asked them, and their answer was, 'You go off with him and leave us alone to do what we want!'"[6] Although Jackie uses the plural, it is evident that her interlocutor was Litsa. And even if Mary concurred in this instance, she often acted independently and has to bear a good deal of the responsibility for choosing the path she did. There can be no doubt that the example and the "advice" she received from her mother throughout this period must have gnawed at her like a canker, strengthening her desire to get away.

As for Mary's longing to see her father again, the most convincing evidence comes from the pianist Tonis Yeoryiou, talking about the work they did together for the recitals in Thessaloniki in May 1945. One day, when Mary had gone to his house by herself, he told her again that she would be wasting her talents if she stayed in Greece. As they had got to know each other quite well by this time and Litsa was not present, she at last unburdened herself: "She told me she had been very upset by the break-up of her parents' marriage and was longing to see her father, for whom she had a very soft spot. *'I want to go to America to be with him,'* she burst out, *'but I don't know if I can, and it's all my mother's fault because she won't let me go.'*" That summer Tonis and his wife went to Athens and called on Litsa and Mary at 61 Patission Street. At one point Tonis asked Mary straight out whether she had finally made up her mind to go to America, whereupon Litsa snapped, "Let's not hear any more of that, if you don't mind. There's no need to stir up that old story!" Jackie tried to calm her down, but a few minutes later Tonis heard Litsa saying to Mary in the kitchen, "You and your father! I told you, I don't want to hear another word about that!" Tonis and Eleni, feeling uncomfortable in that strained atmosphere, made their excuses and left, wishing Mary "all the best." They would never see her again in Greece.[7] Litsa, of course, felt that Mary's determination to go to New York was due not only to a sentimental longing to see her father again but even more so to a desire to break away from her. But Litsa could do nothing to stem the natural consequences of the way she herself had thought and behaved for the last twenty years or so. In the end, therefore, she pretended to be in favor of Mary's going back to America, and later she would even claim that it had been her own idea.[8]

By this time Mary was in most respects independent of her mother, whose conduct she regarded with deep contempt and loathing. In July 1947, one of the first things she told her husband-to-be about her past life was that Litsa had gone off to live in Greece, taking her daughters with her and "dividing the family." Naturally she could not talk to Meneghini, whom she hardly knew, about her mother's—and her own—compromising relationships with officers in the occupation forces, particularly as Meneghini was himself an Italian. However, she did tell him that she "never had anyone whom she could confide in or go to for advice." When he expressed surprise, she looked at him with a sad smile and said, *"But who would be interested in me, with my shape? . . . I'm not in the habit of kidding myself."*[9] All at once the weight problem that had bothered her at times in Athens was transformed into a problem that had always existed and had always been a burden to her. And, at a stroke, Papatestas, Mangliveras, Sigaras, De Stasio, Dondoli, Morgan, and perhaps others too in Athens—not to mention Eddie Bagarozy in America and a Swiss admirer who had followed her to Italy to hear her in Verona—were casually written off, as if they had never been her admirers and perhaps her lovers. It was at this time that Maria began to construct, perhaps subconsciously at first but before long consciously as well (when it suited her), the picture of the fat Cinderella who had found her Prince Charming in the person of the middle-aged Veronese manufacturer of bricks.

—⁋—

The most powerful interest group in Greece (as everywhere else)—that of mediocrity and self-advancement through string-pulling—simply ignored or tried to "bury" Mary, whose talent was seen as a threat. Although there were already some people who admired her vocal and dramatic prowess, they were confined to the ranks of enlightened and unprejudiced music-lovers. "Most of those involved in the world of opera and the most prominent figures in Greek musical life ignored her or refused to acknowledge her qualities," Achilleas Mamakis wrote in 1957. So Mary had good reason to feel that staying in Athens would be a soul-destroying experience, besides holding out little prospect for the advancement of her career. Granted, she could expect to be given starring roles from time to time with the G.N.O., but she would never be more than a big fish in a small pond and would have to live in an atmosphere of interpersonal friction and general bad blood, as well as constant protests and strikes. Of the 311 persons on the G.N.O. payroll, the 199 who were offered new contracts were very soon joined by many others taken on for "humanitarian" reasons (that being then the standard euphemism for nepotism) and the whole "streamlining" process turned out to be a farce, as before long the payroll had grown again to 278. In the end Synadinos merely managed to shore up the finances enough to keep the G.N.O. going temporarily, and then only by intervening personally with the prime minister.[10]

Illustrated article on Greek opera personalities, *Aera*, Athens, July 1945. Clockwise: Fanny Papanastasiou, Yorgos Moulas and Zoe Vlachopoulou, Nafsika Galanou, Mireille Fléri, Nikos Glynos, Michalis Koronis, Mary Kaloyeropoulou, Petros Epitropakis, Frangiska Nikita, and Lakis Vassilakis.

Meanwhile, several of the soloists continued to protest against the new gradings, but the board flatly refused to reconsider decisions once they had been made. Mary's name does not appear anywhere in the minutes of that period as one of the protesters, but Synadinos informed the board on 7 June that "Miss Kaloyeropoulou is the only one of the soloists not to have renewed her contract with the G.N.O., because she is leaving soon for the United States."[11] This is the first and only reference in the surviving G.N.O. records to Mary's decision to go abroad. Having finally made up her mind about it, almost certainly when she was in Thessaloniki in May, she probably mentioned the fact in Athens toward the end of the month in the hope that it would persuade the management to promote her to Grade AA. In any case, before she could go she had to find the money to pay for her ticket and the time to put her personal affairs in order, especially her relations with people such as Takis Sigaras and Vangelis Mangliveras. More than anything else, perhaps, Mary wanted to fight one last battle with the G.N.O. and force the general manager to step down, so that she could leave with her head held high. Such, no doubt, were her preoccupations and thoughts in May and June 1945.

The bitter winter that had followed the end of the occupation was fast becoming a bad memory, and Athenians were beginning to stretch their limbs and to circulate once more. Those who wanted to go out of the center of town, however, still had to beware of land mines, and the newspapers published lists of danger areas. Since the failure of the communist putsch, the right-wing forces that had fought against it had gone off the rails, and some rural areas were now in the grip of a new brand of terrorism. Even in Athens, so many people were being arrested every day that one wing of the emptied Archaeological Museum was being used as a prison! On 4 June the court set up to try collaborators handed down life sentences to two former prime ministers, Rallis and Logothetopoulos, and five days later the killers of forty-three policemen and of Eleni Papadaki (who, as a special favor, had been shot, whereas the others had been hacked to death with axes) were condemned to death and executed. Similar cases, with horrific descriptions of crimes of the most appalling nature, were reported in the press almost every day. Yet life had to go on, and on it went. In Kifissia the well-off started their summer social round, while in Athens there was a sudden proliferation of nightclubs, such as the Chez Nous on Skaramanga Street, with its "hanging garden" right under the windows of the Kaloyeropoulos apartment. And while Mary still did not know whether she would sign a contract with the G.N.O., in San Francisco the charter of the United Nations was signed on 26 June to secure the fruits of victory and peace. The next day *To Vima* commented, "It rests with the good will of all parties to translate words into deeds."

On 23 June 1945 the newspaper *Vradyni* reported, "The National Opera soprano Maria Kaloyeropoulou will be leaving shortly for America." With this public reminder of her imminent departure and the announcement of a farewell recital to be held in a few days' time, Mary played the last card left in her hand to persuade Synadinos to offer her some concession. If he did not, she would have to make up her mind whether to hold out against her demotion or to humiliate herself by signing the contract on his terms. Five days later, on 28 June, the journalist and playwright Dimitris Evangelidis wrote an article in *To Ethnos* lamenting the sorry state of the G.N.O.'s affairs and berating Synadinos for keeping "a whole lot" of superfluous employees on the payroll instead of streamlining the personnel as he was supposed to have done. Answering criticism from Synadinos's supporters, Evangelidis said, "Some time ago a special committee was formed to reduce the number of G.N.O. personnel. How many have been fired? Not one! The only person who has left is the young soprano Miss Mary Kaloyeropoulou—who happens to be an excellent singer—and even she refused to renew her contract of her own accord because she was not offered the top salary rate. If they *had* offered it to her, she too would have stayed on! Enough of charity. If they can find a social security fund to take them on, well and good; if not, too bad. Such heartlessness is necessary."[12]

To put still more pressure on Synadinos and the board, Mary then went on to arrange her farewell recital. The idea was a good one because, apart from anything else, the ticket sales would help to raise money for her voyage. She booked the Rialto Theater on Kypselis Street for Tuesday 10 July, and a press release appeared in the papers as early as 2 July: "The singer Miss Mary Kaloyeropoulou, so well known to the Athenian public, who is about to leave for America, will give a very interesting recital at the Rialto Theater on Tuesday 10 July at 7 p.m."[13] However, on 7 July the recital was postponed as, with the start of the G.N.O. summer season not far off, it would seem that some compromise was finally reached between Mary and the management. Nothing is known about the negotiations that produced this result, and the only sop that Mary may have been offered was the role of Laura in Millöcker's operetta *Der Bettelstudent*. This was a curious choice, as the part was thoroughly out of keeping with Mary's career up to that point. The real reason Synadinos gave her the part (with the approval of Antiochos Evangelatos, who was to conduct) was that no other soprano was capable of doing it: "*They were obliged to entrust it to me because no one else could sing it*," Maria admitted later. As for her audacity in taking on the fairly difficult *leggera* role of Laura after the dramatic Tosca and the even more dramatic Marta and Leonore, she evidently believed she would astonish and silence her enemies. As she put it in her memoirs, "*I wanted to give a last sample of my skills and I sang Millöcker's 'Der Bettelstudent,' an operetta as difficult as anything for a soprano.*"[14]

And so, on Saturday, 7 July 1945, the opening day of the summer season with Zoe Vlachopoulou starring in *The Gypsy Princess*—which means that Mary was probably under great pressure to make up her mind—"the G.N.O. soloist Miss Maria Kaloyeropoulou, who had fallen out with the management of the state opera house and had not renewed her contract, finally consented to sign a new contract," as Achilleas Mamakis reported in *To Ethnos*. At the same time the press announced that "the distinguished singer's planned departure for America" had been canceled and that her recital at the Rialto had been postponed "owing to a slight indisposition." If Mary's contract of July 1945 could be found, it would of course tell us whether a compromise was reached, but the board minutes make no mention of her having been given special terms. Also, the Greek word translated as "consented" in Mamakis's article strongly implies that Mary had to accept the terms offered to her. Like all the contracts of that period, Mary's would have taken effect (retroactively in her case) from 1 June 1945 to 31 May 1946, her salary would have been payable every ten days, and she would have been obliged, like all Grade AA and Grade A soloists, to take part in up to six performances and six rehearsals per week, if required.[15]

Mary's self-esteem must have been badly wounded when she signed the new contract, which obliged her not only to accept the salary of a second-grade soloist but also to sing in operetta. She would never forgive Synadinos for this humiliation (for that is how she saw it), and it would not be long before she paid him back. One reason for her capitulation no doubt is that she otherwise would not have had enough money for her ticket to New York. For that she really needed her G.N.O. pay, even the second-grade salary of 35,000 drachmas a month, and apparently it had not yet entered her mind to ask her friends and acquaintances to help out; nor was there the remotest likelihood of any assistance coming from her mother, who was still living a parasitic life at Miltiadis Embirikos's expense. As for the cancellation of her departure reported by Mamakis, it is probably to be explained as a deliberate piece of misinformation put out by Mary herself, because she could hardly sign a contract valid until 31 May 1946 while simultaneously stating that she was about to leave Greece. Evidently, when she signed, she kept quiet about her plans for going abroad or actually denied having any such intention, although the decision to leave was definite in her mind and only the date of her departure remained uncertain.

The announcement of the forthcoming production of *Der Bettelstudent* with the names of those taking part was made on 18 July, just days after Mary had signed her new contract. It was to be conducted by Antiochos Evangelatos and directed by Renato Mordo, with sets and costumes designed by young Yorgos Anemoyannis. The soloists were to be Koronis, Epitropakis, Kokkolios, Damasioti, Papadopoulou, and, in the words of Mamakis in *To Ethnos*, "the soprano Mary Kaloyeropoulou, recently re-engaged by the state opera house, who will take the female lead." Needless to say, rehearsals started at once (the soloists' rehearsals were still being held in the Hellenic Conservatory) and after only three weeks, on 9 August, Synadinos informed the board that the production was ready to be staged. However, the sets and costumes had not yet been made owing to the shortage of funds, and so *The Gypsy Princess* would continue its successful run until they were ready.[16]

Mary's next moves were to book a hall for her farewell recital, announcing her departure date at the same time, and to settle pending formalities about her U.S.

citizenship that would allow the issue of her passport. It has often been asserted that she was in danger of losing her U.S. citizenship, but that is an exaggeration, of course, as she was an American citizen by birth. Her registration as a U.S. citizen having expired on 4 June 1942, she had renewed it at the U.S. consulate on 28 March 1945, explaining that her protracted foreign residence had been due to special circumstances and to the war: *"I arrived in Athens, Greece, where I am now temporarily residing, on March 6, 1937 . . . . I came to Greece for two purposes. First, to visit my relatives, and second to start my career as an opera singer. In 1939 [sic] the Royal Opera in Athens, engaged me and this delayed my departure for the U.S."* The American consul, recommending the approval of her application for the renewal of her registration as a U.S. citizen for one year, noted that Sophie Cecelia Kalos, as she signed her name on the affidavit, was an American by birth, had come of age just four months earlier, and wished to return to the United States as soon as possible to rejoin her father, now living in San Francisco. Her registration was approved by the State Department on 21 June 1945.[17]

Then, on 23 July, Mary swore the oath of allegiance in the presence of the U.S. consul and applied for a passport, declaring that she was returning to live permanently in the United States. She named her father, George Kalos, as her next of kin, to be notified in the event of her death or disability. On 4 August the consulate issued her a passport valid for only six months.[18] With her usual talent for dramatizing events when it suited her, without always scrupulously sticking to the exact truth, Maria later said, *"Since there's always a beneficent God to help those who travel the straight and narrow and never do any harm to anyone, when I least expected it, the American consulate offered me a ticket to America. I would repay the money, I was told, when I could."* As we shall see, Mary's fare was actually paid by Takis Sigaras, but that did not prevent her from saying on another occasion, *"It was just the time that the Americans were shipping back their Americans, and I took advantage of that and came back to the States."* In this latter interview Maria also made the misleading suggestion that her decision to leave Greece was connected with her renewed friction and irrevocable rift with Synadinos, though that did not occur until August 1945, only a few days before her departure.[19]

—⁂—

Several people who knew Mary at that time have remarked on how depressed and worried she was feeling in the spring and summer of 1945. One of those is Maria Alkeou, who had kept in touch with her even though professionally their ways had parted. "One day she came to my house," Alkeou remembers, "and told me she was thinking of going abroad. When I encouraged her, she opened up and said unhappily, '*Here I just can't make myself not mind what people do to me. Going away will either make or break me!*' Her morale had sunk so low that she had actually lost all her self-confidence." Alkeou takes the view that Mary was a terribly vulnerable person who had been deeply hurt by the campaign waged against her

Form No. 213
FOREIGN SERVICE
(Corrected March 1942)

K. 6-7

AFFIDAVIT BY NATIVE AMERICAN TO EXPLAIN PROTRACTED FOREIGN RESIDENCE
~~AFFIDAVIT BY NATURALIZED AMERICAN TO EXPLAIN PROTRACTED FOREIGN RESIDENCE~~

This form should be used by any native or naturalized American citizen who has resided abroad for two years or more.

The form *must* be used by a naturalized citizen who has resided for two years in the territory of a foreign state of which he was formerly a national or in which the place of his birth is situated. It *must* also be used by a naturalized citizen who has resided continuously for five years in any other foreign state. In cases of naturalized citizens the exact periods and places of foreign residence since naturalization should be stated.

The form *must* always accompany applications for extension of passports which have been expressly limited in validity.

I, ___Sophie Cecelia KALOS___, a { native ~~naturalized~~ } American citizen, born at

___New York___, ___N.Y.___, do solemnly swear that I ceased to
(City)　　　　　　　　　　　(Country)

reside in the United States on or about ___February 16___, 1_937_; that I have since resided at

___Athens, Greece___; and that I arrived
(Countries)

in ___Athens, Greece___, where I am now { ~~permanently~~ temporarily } residing, on ___March 6,___
(City and country)

_1937_, my reasons for such foreign residence being as follows: [1] I came to Greece for two purposes. First, to visit my relatives, and second to start my career as an opera singer. In 1939 the Royal Opera in Athens, engaged me and this delayed my departure for the U.S. I now wish to return to the U.S. as soon as possible to rejoin my father, and to continue my career there.

Since establishing a residence abroad I have made the following visits to the United States:

From _____, 19____, to _____, 19____ From _____, 19____, to _____, 19____

From _____, 19____, to _____, 19____ From _____, 19____, to _____, 19____

I have { never ~~not since my naturalization as an American citizen~~ } obtained naturalization in a foreign state; taken an oath or made an affirmation or other formal declaration of allegiance to a foreign state; entered or served in the armed forces of a foreign state; accepted or performed the duties of any office, post, or employment under the government of a foreign state or political subdivision thereof; voted in a political election in a foreign state or participated in an election or plebiscite to determine the sovereignty over foreign territory; made a formal renunciation of nationality before a diplomatic or consular officer of the United States in a foreign state; been convicted by court martial of deserting the military or naval service of the United States in time of war; been convicted by court martial or a court of competent jurisdiction of the commission of any act of treason against, or of attempting by force to overthrow, or of bearing arms against, the United States [2]

I maintain the following ties of family, business, and property with the United States:
George Kalos (Kalogeropoulos) Golden Eagle Pharmacy, 251 3rd St., San Francisco, California. My father runs a pharmacy in the U.S.

I { do ~~do not~~ } pay the American Income Tax at _____

I intend to return to the United States permanently to reside within _____ { months years } or when [3] _____ as soon as possible

Sophie Cecelia Kalos
(Signature of applicant)
Sophie Cecelia Kalos
#61 Patission St., Athens, Greece.
(Address)

AMERICAN CONSULAR SERVICE AT ___Athens, Greece___

Sworn to before me this ___28th___ day of ___March/1945___.

[SEAL]
(No fee prescribed)

Malcolm P. Hallam
___Vice Consul___ of the United States of America.

(SEE INSTRUCTIONS PRINTED ON REVERSE SIDE)

[1] Executing officer will indicate whether the above is the affiant's independent statement. If not, officer should state extent to which he has prompted affiant and reasons therefor. Officer should also state whether or not affiant's statement has been translated from a foreign language.
[2] If any of these acts or conditions have been performed the affiant should set forth the facts fully in a supplementary statement which should be affixed to and made a part of this affidavit.
[3] This statement should be as clear and definite as possible.

16—21750-1

Affidavit explaining protracted foreign residence (dated 28 March 1945) and oath of allegiance sworn in Athens on 23 July 1945 by Mary Kaloyeropoulou (Sophie Cecelia Kalos) as a native American.

I solemnly swear tha, the stateme   made on pages 1 and 2 are true, and that the   otograph attached is a likeness of me.

OATH OF ALLEGIANCE

Furthe, I do solemnly swear that I will support and defend the Constitution of the United States against all enemies, foreign and domestic; that I will bear true faith and allegiance to the same; and that I take this obligation freely, without any mental reservation or purpose of evasion: So help me God.

(SEAL)

Fee for passport, $9.00.
Fee for administering oath
and preparing passport
application, $1.00.
No fee for registration.

Service No. 3677

Sophie Cecelia Cecilia Kalos (Signature in full of applicant) KALOS

SWORN to before me this 23rd day of July 19. 45

Oliver M. Marcy
Consul   of the United States at Athens, Greece

DESCRIPTION OF APPLICANT

Height: 5 feet 6 inches.
Hair brown   Eyes brown
Distinguishing marks or features ─

Place of birth New York, N.Y.
Date of birth Dec. 2, 1923
Occupation Opera singer

EVIDENCE OF CITIZENSHIP AND IDENTIFYING DOCUMENTS

Passport No. 367557 issued on Feb. 16, 1937
by Dept. of State, Washington
to applicant.
+40   SUBMITTED.
(State name and relationship)
State disposition of passport Canceled and returned to applicant.
Other evidence of citizenship and identifying documents submitted, as specified below: (Indicate whether sent to the Department, retained in files of office, or returned to applicant.) Reg. Appl. ex. March 28, 1945, valid to Mar. 28. 1946

The following should be filled in if this application is for a PASSPORT:
Countries to be visited: United States   Purpose of visit: permanent residence
Port of departure: Piraeus   Date of departure:
Name of ship: Is the ship an American line? ("Yes" or "No")

REFERENCES

George KALOS (Kalogeropoulos) (father) Golden Eagle Pharmacy, 251, 3rd St.
(Name)   San Francisco, Calif. (Address)

AFFIDAVIT OF IDENTIFYING WITNESS

I, the undersigned, solemnly swear that I am a citizen of the United States; that I reside at the address written below my signature hereto affixed; that I know the applicant who executed the affidavit hereinbefore set forth to be the person he represents himself to be, and that he is a citizen of the United States; that the statements made in the applicant's affidavit are true to the best of my knowledge and belief; further, I solemnly swear that I have known the applicant personally for   years.

(Signature of witness)

(Residence address of witness)

[SEAL]   Waived.

SUBSCRIBED AND SWORN to before me this   day of   , 1
If no American citizen is available, an alien known
to the consulate may execute the affidavit.

Consul   of the United States of America at

The applicant requests that the following person be notified in the event of his death or disability:
George KALOS (father) Golden Eagle Pharmacy, 251 3rd St. San Francisco, Cal.
(Name)   (Address)

Additional data: Location of real and personal property, nature and place of investments, location of will, et cetera. (It is entirely optional with the applicant to give this information.)

Registration {approved / disapproved} by the Department of State on June 21, 1945
(Date)

Certificate of Identity and Registration}
Card of Identity and Registration   issued to the applicant on

(Initials of consular officer)

The Department will assume that the consular officer forwarding the application to the Department for authorization for issue of passport is fully satisfied as to the applicant's identity, unless a notation to the contrary appears hereunder.

REMARKS

by her fellow singers, whose own ears and eyes told them how much better she was than they. Confirming this, shortly before he died in the mid-1980s, Yerasimos Koundouris, the cultured and courteous pianist who was de Hidalgo's class accompanist, spoke of the last memory he had of Mary in Athens, in the spring of 1945: "I happened to bump into her one day and, as we walked along, she told me all about the injustice done to her by the G.N.O. She was in tears."[20]

Even more illuminating is a conversation Mary had with Ludo Kouroussopoulos and his wife, Xenia, only a few hours before she left Greece. "We met her outside Schliemann's house, on Panepistimiou Street," Xenia recalls. "She was wearing a wide-brimmed hat with lace trimmings, and she was in tears! She told us she was leaving because she couldn't stand the G.N.O. any longer. She felt she

Mary walking down Panepistimiou Street with her faithful friend, accompanist Yerasimos Koundouris, Athens, summer 1945.

had been unfairly treated. 'Hold on a bit longer,' Ludo advised her. 'There is a pecking order and other people are ahead of you. You can't just brush them aside.' *'Yes, but I'm the best! I can't wait that long, because I know what I'm worth!'* she answered. She was in a hurry, that girl: she wanted to have her way and get a top salary. Then Ludo asked her about her affair with Mangliveras. She was not happy about leaving him, because she was genuinely fond of him and knew she was hurting him. But she told us she wanted to go back to her father and was thinking first and foremost of her future: *'I shall be looking ahead, at my career. Here I'm just wasting away.'*"[21]

It is not clear how strained Mary's relations with de Hidalgo were at that stage, but it would seem that she did have lessons with her in 1945, after their estrangement of the previous year. Presumably the problematic nature of her liaison with Mangliveras, particularly once she had begun preparations for her farewell recital and departure, had aided Mary's rapprochement with her teacher. Certainly de Hidalgo had been worried and very annoyed when Mary was being coached by Mangliveras, and naturally, when she was told that Mary had said, "*I owe the way I sing to Mangliveras,*" she felt offended and angry.[22] It is of course very doubtful whether Mary did ever say that, however much she may have been blinded by love at the time. What seems far likelier is that she said something much less emphatic—perhaps that she was grateful and indebted to Mangliveras—and her words were distorted by the malice of one of her rivals before they reached de Hidalgo's ears.

As already mentioned, if anything happened to weaken the loyalty of one of her pupils, the possessive de Hidalgo often reacted viciously. Something has also been said about her personal problems, her abandonment by her much younger lover, the baritone Lakis Vassilakis, and the effect that had on the standard of her teaching. Therefore we shall never know whether Mary's estrangement from her was due mainly to Mangliveras's presence in her life or to her teacher's personal problems, or to both. In any event, when Mary left Greece her relations with de Hidalgo were still somewhat frigid. This is hinted at in a letter written by de Hidalgo from Ankara in January 1949, in which she congratulates Maria on her successes in Italy in the autumn of 1948 and especially on her *Norma*, which they had "so lovingly" studied together. "I was absolutely right about you," she adds, "and what you decided to do at the end of your time in Athens, without my approval, did nothing at all for you except to slow down the headway you were destined to make in Italy." Nevertheless, de Hidalgo always had great faith in Mary's talent. "In the six years that I had her as a pupil," she wrote to the newspaper *To Ethnos* in August 1957, "I saw very clearly the potential of her voice, with its astonishingly wide range, and I appreciated better than anyone else her extremely conscientious approach to music."[23]

The prevailing atmosphere during Mary's last weeks in Athens was one of political tension punctuated by frequent strikes. At the end of July 1945, while the

Potsdam peace conference was under way and Japan was beginning to flinch under seaborne assaults and heavy bombing raids, public opinion in Greece was shocked by the news of Churchill's defeat in the British general election. Greek republicans, however, hoped that the new Labor government would stop supporting the return of George II to the throne. And while the trial of the eighty-nine-year-old Marshal Pétain opened in Paris, in Greece the trials of collaborators went on and rural areas continued to be terrorized by armed bands of right-wing and left-wing extremists. Mary, however, was busy arranging her recital, and she must have been very pleased when she managed to book the large Rex Theater, which she already knew from appearances there in 1938 and 1943. It was the only theater in Athens that stayed open through the heat of the summer thanks to its cooling system. Litsa says that the owner of the Rex "lent" it to Mary, but others maintain that she rented it and indeed had to put down a deposit in advance. Be that as it may, it was a great feather in her cap to be giving a solo recital at such a well-known venue. The recital was at first arranged for Friday 27 July, but at one day's notice it was postponed until Friday 3 August at 7:15 p.m.

Come the evening of 3 August 1945, the Rex Theater was full of Mary's admirers, friends, and acquaintances as well as adversaries, skeptics, and the merely curious, for "the farewell concert of the soprano Maria Kaloyeropoulou" (as it was billed in the newspapers) had aroused a good deal of comment. A few days before Mary is alleged to have said to a group of friends, *"I've got to show them who I am! They've fought against me, they've slapped and punched me in the theater several times, but now that I'm on my own I'll put all their noses out of joint! I'll make sure that they never forget me and spend their lives dreading the day I come back!"* No doubt the scorching August heat made her even touchier than usual, for on the day of the recital, as a terrible forest fire raged through the foothills of Mount Parnes, the temperature rose to 40°C (104°F) in the shade. It therefore comes as no surprise to be told that Mary wore a plain short white dress, and it is hard to believe her mother's statement that she also had a black velvet bolero trimmed with sequins. Just before the recital began, Mary peeped out through a gap in the curtains to see who was in the audience and noticed many of her former classmates at the conservatory and several of her fellow singers at the G.N.O., including some who disliked her. *"They have come to gloat over my failure,"* she is reported to have said, *"but they are the people I shall be singing for, not my friends. I'll make them eat their words and remember me for many years to come!"*[24]

With Aliki Lykoudi (the wife of the conductor with whom Mary had quarreled in the radio studio some three years earlier) at the piano, the program opened with Zerlina's aria "Batti, batti, o bel Masetto" from *Don Giovanni*, which Mary was singing for the first time in her life, and probably the last too. The first round of applause boosted her morale, and she continued with "Bel raggio lusinghier" from *Semiramide*, which was much more demanding but had been in her repertoire for some time. The third item was one of Aida's two well-known arias, probably "Ritorna vincitor," which was followed by one of Leonora's two arias from *Il Trovatore.* To end the first half Mary gave yet another performance of "Ocean! thou mighty monster" from *Oberon,* ignoring the advice de Hidalgo had given her seven years before. The second half consisted entirely of songs: some Spanish (one may well have been Turina's "Canciòn Española," a favorite of de Hidalgo's) and some Greek, by Thodoros Karyotakis and Yorgos Poniridis. As the evening progressed the audience grew more and more animated, and Mary sang two English songs as her encores, probably selected from the ones she had recently sung at the English Musical Afternoon at the Olympia.[25] The recital was a great success: she was enthusiastically applauded, showered with bouquets, and complimented even by people who disliked her. Her admirers were wild with excitement, none more so than Andonis Delendas, the very fine tenor who had shared in all her triumphs up to that time, who applauded her with tears in his eyes, cheering loudly.[26]

Two reviews of Mary's farewell recital were published in the Athens dailies, one of them full of praise, the other critical but very cautiously worded. The first was by Sophia Spanoudi, who this time came out wholeheartedly in Mary's favor, describing her as "a dynamic singer . . . with many exceptional gifts" who had put her voice at risk in the last three years by singing overdemanding roles too early in her career. In view of the "brilliant promise" Mary had shown in that very varied recital, Spanoudi felt confident that in America she would "surely rise to the heights for which she is destined." She described Mary's voice as "having a dual nature, brilliant and dark in its dramatic nuances . . . an out-and-out Falcon soprano" and concluded her eulogy with the prediction that her "superabundant musicality" and "incomparably winsome stage presence" would lead her on to international triumphs.[27] In contrast, Ioannis Psaroudas's review was distinctly cool. After expressing his "great liking and respect" for Mary's "fine talent" and "vocal and dramatic accomplishments" and commenting obliquely on her G.N.O. demotion (her accomplishments, he said, "could have put her into the front rank of singers at the National Opera"), Psaroudas expressed the fear that she had "strayed somewhat from the right path" on which she had been set by de Hidalgo, "whose pupil she had the good fortune to be." He professed not to know why and how this had happened, perhaps because he did not want to mention the bad influence of Mangliveras, but he noted that Mary, whom he called a "likable" singer, had acquired "some faults which she must do all she can to overcome."

Whatever one may think of Psaroudas's opinions, what makes his review particularly interesting is his technical appraisal of Mary's voice as it was at the very end of her Greek career. Psaroudas, who had received most of his musical training in France, more or less acknowledged that Mary was already a rare instance of a dramatic soprano coloratura: "The great intensity and range of her voice and the ease with which she, a genuine *soprano lirico-drammatico,* vocalizes in pieces written for light sopranos such as the aria from Rossini's *Semiramide* (trivial music, which nevertheless requires exceptional technical virtuosity) are qualities that are not often found together in one person." To him, the four pieces that stood out in her program, which he described as "very difficult" and "daunting even for accomplished singers," were the arias from *Aida* and *Semiramide* and the two English songs. However, "with the exception of the coloraturas," the arias from *Oberon*, *Trovatore*, and *Don Giovanni* were "not what they should have been": "If it had been another, less interesting singer, I could say I considered them reasonably well sung, but in the case of Miss Kaloyeropoulou I cannot allow myself to insult her ability by being indulgent to her. . . . After all, why did she have to put in all those unspeakably vulgar portamenti, those fermatas, acutas, and long-held high notes, causing the harshness that inevitably results when a singer strains his or her voice for no good reason? How could a genuine artist like Miss Kaloyeropoulou be so misguided as to employ such inartistic gimmicks?" Psaroudas asked, before sugaring the pill by declaring in conclusion that, in America, Mary would hear great singers, among whom he was confident that "we shall soon be able to number her."[28] If nothing else, these serious reservations about Mary's technique, coming after Psaroudas's warm praise of her Leonore and only a few days before that of her Laura in *Der Bettelstudent*, testify to the fact that in her farewell recital she yielded to the temptation to indulge in excessively showy tricks and vocal fireworks in order to impress those who questioned her ability and talent.

—⁂—

I have known since my childhood that the people around me didn't have judgment, so I had to either do what they did or do what I knew I was supposed to do. And if you manage not to be pulled down, that's all to your credit. But then you are criticized. You're hard, you're cruel, you're egotistical. That hurts. There is no defense. . . . You try to get used to it, if anyone can. This has gone on and on since I was a child, since I can remember.

To John Ardoin, Dallas, September 1968

CHAPTER 37

Der Bettelstudent and Departure

"The means of splitting the atom has been discovered and has been used against Japanese bases at Hiroshima." As if he were describing the plot of a science fiction film, the reporter for *To Vima* informed readers laconically on 6 August 1945 that the atomic bomb, two thousand times more powerful than the biggest bomb ever made before, had caused a hundred thousand casualties. Possession of the bomb automatically thrust the United States into a position of world hegemony, and President Truman declared that America would not allow a third world war to break out. Thereafter events moved swiftly and on 15 August Japan surrendered unconditionally, which news was reported with the comment, "Fascism has been crushed for good." Of more immediate concern to Athenians and to Mary, however, must have been the most recent heat wave, now into its third blistering day.

The journalist Stamatis Tsoutis, whose serialized biography of Maria Callas cannot be dismissed out of hand although much of it needs to be treated with extreme caution, wrote in 1963 that when Mary collected her share of the net proceeds of her farewell recital she found that it would not cover the cost of her ticket to America and other necessary expenses. She wept tears of despair and rage, Tsoutis continues, but "the secret became known to her friends," who "passed the hat round" and raised "a fairly satisfactory sum of money." To avoid wounding Mary's pride, they gave it to her in the form of a loan, which she accepted with considerable reluctance.[1] The gist of this story is indirectly confirmed by Jackie, Ilias Papatestas, and Mitsa Kourahani. In the end, useful though this money must have been, it was not used to pay Mary's fare to New York.

Litsa informs us that the fare was paid by the U.S. embassy and repaid later by Maria in installments of twenty dollars a month. Jackie's version of events is more convincing: according to her, when the American authorities advertised in the newspapers that there would be places on the first boat out of Piraeus for American citizens wishing to be repatriated, Mary put her name down on the waiting list. Maria herself wrote that before going to Mexico in 1950 she had repaid two thousand dollars to the federal authorities *"for my return journey from Greece and for money lent to me by the state, which I naturally passed on to my mother for household expenses.*"[2] Hard though it is to believe that Mary borrowed money from the federal government to pay her fare, let alone that she then passed it on to her mother, it is a fact that when she left America for Italy in June 1947 she owed the U.S. Treasury $718.25, which had been given to her as a "repatriation loan." To make it possible for her passport to be renewed, the repayment of this sum was then guaranteed by her father, who (in accordance with what seems to have been his standard practice) never repaid it.[3]

If Maria always insisted that at least part of her debt was related to the cost of her ticket to America, that was probably because she wanted to hide the truth, which was that her fare had been paid by her rich friend Takis Sigaras. As attested by Sigaras himself, "When Maria heard that a woman I knew was leaving by boat for New York, she came to me and said, '*So you help other women and you don't help me!*' 'Fine,' I said, 'I'll help you too. What is it you want?' So she told me she wanted to go to New York as soon as possible. It was very difficult to get a place on a ship at that time, but a friend of mine who was the local manager of Thomas Cook's successfully got me a ticket with full board."[4] When Sigaras gave her the ticket, Mary was delighted and very grateful. She now had a firm departure date in mid September, and the only thing she had to do before then was to settle her affairs with the G.N.O.

The atmosphere in the G.N.O. in the summer of 1945 was increasingly tense, and the pay demands of its personnel threatened to spark off a fresh crisis. Around 20 August, in an attempt to increase the company's meager revenue, Synadinos proposed to the board that ticket prices be raised. In accordance with a fundamental condition in the employment contracts, this would automatically lead to an increase in the employees' rates of pay, but Synadinos asked all members of the staff to waive the pay hike: this was seen as an attempt to cut their real salaries in order to patch over the holes left by his own bad management. The waiver was signed by all the solo singers bar three: Andonis Delendas, Vangelis Mangliveras, and Mary Kaloyeropoulou.[5] Meanwhile, after fifteen performances of *The Gypsy Princess*, Zoe Vlachopoulou suffered a bad cold and was replaced on 25 July by Anthi Zacharatou, a pretty blonde of twenty-three in the chorus, who was a great favorite with G.N.O. management. Thanks to her intimate relationship with Theodoros Synadinos, Zacharatou leapt to stardom overnight. She took the lead in thirty-five performances of Kálmán's operetta, in which she was an undoubted success, but her instant elevation from the chorus line to the soprano lead inevitably stirred up considerable opposition, as other members of the chorus and some of the soloists were worried about the influence she might wield through her friendship with the despotic general manager and his son, the general secretary and personnel manager, whom she later married.

Anthi Zacharatou's position and reputation in the G.N.O. in that summer of 1945 hold the key to the last serious row in Maria Callas's Greek career. Mary's refusal to accept the general manager's proposal to formally waive her right to a salary increase was her first act of retaliation against the humiliation of being demoted, and evidently it infuriated Synadinos. Seizing on Mary's act of defiance as a good pretext, he arbitrarily gave the role of Laura to Zacharatou, with whom he was "well and truly infatuated," as many of her contemporaries still remember. The cast list that caused all the trouble, with Mary's name conspicuous by its absence, has not been found in the G.N.O. archives nor in the Synadinos papers, but presumably it was dated between 23 and 25 August 1945. Coming as it did only a few days before the première, this snub was clearly an act of personal revenge against Mary who, by joining in the strike of the seventeen soloists and refusing to waive her pay rise, had turned Synadinos's dislike of her into anger. And it was this that led to the final violent clash between them.

Unfortunately Anthi Zacharatou would not be drawn out on the subject, pleading that she does not want to say anything that might be detrimental to the Callas legend. When asked about the specific incident and the audition that followed, she professed complete ignorance and her reactions varied from surprise to mild annoyance. Yet the incident did happen, and not only is it still remembered by many of the singers who were there, but it was referred to by Achilleas Mamakis in *To Ethnos* at the time: "A change in the cast has been announced, and the young singer Madame Zacharatou will appear in place of the well-known soprano Miss Mary Kaloyeropoulou. The change has been made because Miss Kaloyeropoulou is to leave soon for America and the management of the National Opera considers it preferable not to have her singing on just a few nights of the new production but to use Madame Zacharatou, who had originally been cast as her understudy, straightaway."[6] It need hardly be said that the announcement was greeted with astonishment not just by Mary but by most other members of the company, who were incensed at Synadinos's latest act.

The situation became still more tense when, at the fiftieth and last performance of *The Gypsy Princess* on 28 August, Zacharatou responded to what was probably an obscene taunt by slapping the face of one of the men in the chorus. The very next day the entire chorus demanded "that satisfaction be given to the offended chorister and that the newly elevated soloist be punished." Needless to say, the general manager rejected this demand, and the affair was referred to the state committee that issued work permits.[7] On 30 August, amid the general indignation directed at Synadinos and his protégée, Mamakis reported: "Mr. Synadinos had decided, on the pretext that Miss Mary Kaloyeropoulou is due to leave for America on 15 [sic] September, to give her part in *Der Bettelstudent* to the heroine of the day before yesterday's incident, and when announcing the change in the cast he claimed that it was for financial reasons, so that two costumes would not have to be made for the same character."[8]

Mary was not the sort of person to take such an insult lying down, least of all at a time when the general manager had made himself so very unpopular and her own relations with him had been so acrimonious for the last six months. "However, Miss Kaloyeropoulou protested strongly against the injustice done to her," Mamakis continued, "and came to the rehearsals from the day before yesterday [28 August], claiming the right to take the part herself. It now appears, following the resultant dispute, that Mr. Synadinos will not insist that Zacharatou is to appear in the contentious role on the first night and that the part will definitely be given to the person rightfully entitled to it." Mamakis was to return to the subject of this serious incident in 1957, referring to it diplomatically as a "misunderstanding" and commenting ironically: "She who now triumphs at La Scala, the Metropolitan, and the Vienna Staatsoper was detailed to appear as a *substitute* for the other singer!"[9]

None of the versions of the affair given by those who were there is complete or entirely accurate, but taken all together they recapture the prevailing mood of rancor. In 1963 Spyros Salingaros gave an account of the incident, which he described as a "coup" that drove many of the singers to mutiny against Synadinos. To make sure that the general manager's arbitrary action did not set a precedent, those who belonged to the still unofficial singers' union gave notice of a strike, but left a loophole open for a compromise by proposing a special joint audition for Kaloyeropoulou and Zacharatou, confident that Mary would be vindicated. "Everyone was angry," Salingaros recalls. "We went in a body to Synadinos's office and raised a great hullabaloo, shouting that it was outrageous, that we demanded to hear the two of them sing, and so on and so forth. Soon he came out and started saying something, but we threatened him with strike action and he was forced to give in to our demand for an audition, which he announced would be held the next day [between 28 and 31 August]." Stefanos Chiotakis also remembered Synadinos's autocratic attempt to install Zacharatou and the protest delivered to him by a deputation of singers. "The first reaction of Tricky Theo, as we called Synadinos, was to say, 'How could anybody pay good money to see a tub of lard like Kaloyeropoulou?' But we stuck to our guns and eventually he was forced to back down."[10]

And so the next day at about 11 a.m., all those involved in the rehearsals for *Der Bettelstudent* and anybody else who wanted to compare Mary, the "rightful" holder of the role, with her challenger Zacharatou, gathered at the open-air Alexandras Avenue Theater (now the Metropolitan). Feelings were running high: Antiochos Evangelatos was particularly angry—so much so that he threatened to resign—because he was sure that Synadinos's diktat would ruin the quality of the production he was to conduct. "The crucial audition took place in the heat of the August sun," says Elvira Mataranga. "Sitting in the front row were the choreographer, Loukia Kotsopoulou, and the stage director, Renato Mordo, who was muttering irritably under his breath. We listened to Mary and Anthi, and of course the difference between them was enormous. So peace was restored, but I remember Mary being very much on edge, constantly walking in and out of her makeshift dressing room and asking in a worried voice what was happening."[11]

That unprecedented Sängerkrieg in the hottest days of the summer is still remembered by Spyros Salingaros. "There were at least thirty of us sitting together in the orchestra," he says. "With only the piano for accompaniment, Zacharatou sang first and then Mary, whom we applauded furiously, shouting "Brava!" as loudly as we could. She thanked us warmly and embraced some of her supporters, while Zachatarou disappeared. In the circumstances, naturally, Synadinos had no alternative but to reinstate Kaloyeropoulou." The acid test that finally confirmed Mary's superiority was the scene in Act I with Laura's great aria "Doch wenn's im Lied." Twice the soprano has a long cadenza, at the end of which the orchestra comes in, and the singer stands or falls on the accuracy of her pitch and timing. "In that aria Maria was unbeatable," Mitsa Kourahani affirms. "She always sang with tremendous accuracy and ended at exactly the right pitch when the orchestra came in, whereas Zacharatou was usually two or three tones out, either above or below." Nikos Papachristos adds that Mary sang the whole cadenza in one breath, while Anthi had to take a breath in the middle.[12]

Anthi Zacharatou in the 1950s, when she was married to the son of Theodoros Synadinos.

Now, however, Zacharatou denies everything and asks, "Is, anyway, one aria really enough to judge a singer's fitness for a role? Just because of some coloraturas?" And although she admits that Mary was "very good" as Laura and that "the part was absolutely right for her," she insists she knows nothing about any special audition. "*I* never had an audition, at any rate," she says, and adds challengingly, "I don't know what Maria may have done to try and persuade her friends . . ." In fact Zacharatou goes so far as to assert that she had originally been down for the part until Synadinos told her one day that Kaloyeropoulou would sing at the first few performances—"so that she can have one more role to her credit before she goes abroad"—and that she had accepted this substitution without demur! What is beyond doubt, however, is that the part was officially given to Mary (probably under the terms of a compromise settlement between her and the management, as we have seen) with Zacharatou as her understudy: this is apparent from the original cast list written in Synadinos's own hand, which is preserved in his papers.[13]

—⁂—

The composer of *Der Bettelstudent*, Karl Millöcker (1842–1899), is to be numbered with Carl Zeller and Franz von Suppé among the most prominent successors of Johann Strauss the younger, the real creator of classic Viennese operetta. *Der Bettelstudent*, a light and frothy entertainment set in German-occupied Poland in 1704, makes no intellectual demands on the audience; its success is owed to some tuneful melodies, waltzes, and mazurkas and a fairly well-crafted plot.[14] Although the stage of the Alexandras Avenue Theater was small for a work involving numerous principals, chorus, ballet dancers, and lavish sets, Yorgos Anemoyannis directed *Der Bettelstudent* as "a phantasmagorical Singspiel," as he put it, dividing the three acts into nine scenes and dressing the ladies in billowing crinolines, especially rich and large for the three principals, Kitsa Damasioti, Marika Papadopoulou, and Mary Kaloyeropoulou. On 19 August *To Vima*'s society column—which happened to be written by Synadinos's wife—gave a detailed description of the costumes of the principals, including the "new discovery" Anthi Zacharatou, who was named (even before the cast change had been announced by the G.N.O.) as the singer who would play Laura in the forthcoming production. In the first act she would be wearing a turquoise brocade with a multicolored floral print, and in Act II a white brocade "to set off her fair-haired beauty." Obviously the same costumes would in the event be worn by Mary, who, Anemoyannis remembers, "pleaded" to be given long sleeves to cover her plump arms and a high neckline so as not to accentuate her bosom. *"Oh, please, do what you can about these things!"* she begged him as she stood in front of the mirror at rehearsals.[15]

The soloists had learned their parts in practice sessions at the Hellenic Conservatory and a few orchestral rehearsals were held at the Olympia, but there were only two full dress rehearsals on the stage of the Alexandras Avenue Theater. The date of the opening night was not decided on until 27 August, when it was scheduled for 1 September, but the sets were not ready in time and it had to be postponed to Wednesday 5 September at 8 p.m., the hour of nightfall. By then everything was ready at last, and the première was attended by the cream of Athenian society, government ministers, and diplomats. Marika Papadopoulou remembers that, while she herself was a bundle of nerves, Mary showed not a trace of stage fright. *"For God's sake, stop that! I can't bear to look at you!"* Mary snapped at her at one point. *"How nervous can you get? If you go on like that, I'll catch it from you!"* The dressing rooms were so small that when the ladies wanted to put on their crinolines they had to go out into the corridor, which was only just wide enough. The predominant memory of those involved in that production was of Mary's relaxed

The center pages of the program for *Der Bettelstudent*, Greek National Opera, Alexandras Avenue open-air theater, Athens, September 1945. From left to right: conductor Antiochos Evangelatos, director Renato Mordo, Mary, stage and costume designer Yorgos Anemoyannis, and choreographer Loukia Kotsopoulou.

manner on stage. "Her ordinary walking gait was clumsy and heavy," says Elvira Mataranga, "but she moved incredibly gracefully when she was singing, especially in that 'Doch wenn's im Lied.'" *Der Bettelstudent* was an enjoyable spectacle, and it played to an almost full house every night. "It was a terrific hit," Stefanos Chiotakis recalled, and the three leading ladies were highly complimented on the verve they put into their performance. They strolled about the stage with a handkerchief which they passed from hand to hand, while their footman (Thanos Tzeneralis) followed them holding a little parasol over their heads. Mitsa Kourahani—as the officer Richthofen, the aide-de-camp to Colonel Ollendorf (Petros Epitropakis)—had a retinue of three NCOs (the basses Hoidas, Papachristos, and Stefanidis, who was replaced later in the run by Nikos Zachariou). The tenor lead, playing opposite Mary in the role of Simon, the eponymous "beggar student," was the ubiquitous Michalis Koronis.[16]

The critics all raved about the production. Great admiration was expressed not only for the performances of the singers but also for the sumptuous sets and costumes, though these were rightly criticized for being too lavish for a time of general austerity, and especially for a work of minor musical merit. Mary was unanimously hailed as the star of the show and nearly all the critics lamented the fact that

The final curtain call, *Der Bettelstudent*, Greek National Opera, Alexandras Avenue open-air theater, Athens, September 1945.

she would be leaving Greece in a few days. The day after the première, Mamakis in *To Ethnos* called her "an artist of high caliber, whom the National Opera should make every effort to keep." Sophia Spanoudi, in *Ta Nea*, wrote that Mary had performed her big aria "superbly" and commented that it was a misfortune for the G.N.O. (though a godsend for her) that she was leaving Greece. "She is a dramatic prima donna of high caliber with a dual nature both vocally and musically, like Cornélie Falcon," Spanoudi continued, "who has the matchless gift of being able to bring to a light role all the allure of a lyric soprano, following the unforgettable dramatic performance she gave in *Tiefland*." And Psaroudas, in *To Vima*, expressed the view that Miss Kaloyeropoulou had found "her best role" and had sung her big aria "marvelously, with taste, brio, and intelligence." Without reserve this time, he noted that this was "quite a feat for a dramatic soprano, a feat largely due to the good training she has had [from Madame de Hidalgo]." The production was a great success, and almost five thousand tickets were sold for the seven performances in which Mary sang, on 5, 6, 7, 8, 9, 11, and 12 September.[17]

—m—

It had been known ever since Mary gave her farewell recital that she was soon to go abroad but, according to Marika Papadopoulou, "It was only during the run of *Der Bettelstudent* that she told us when she would be leaving." Though she did not

Marika Papadopoulou
in 1945.

say good-bye personally to all the members of the company, she did to those who were singing with her in Millöcker's operetta. "One day Mary was much more expansive with us than usual. *'I am going to join my father, and once I am there I shall see about my career,'* she told us," recalled Antigone Salta, who was surprised by her open and friendly manner. The tenor Michalis Kazandzis (Casimir in that production) remembered that at her last performance, "when she brought the house down with her big aria, as she always did," it was already known that she was to sail in two days' time, "and some people made fun of her conviction that she would make it to the top in her new home."[18] But Mary can hardly have been giving much thought to her future in those last eventful days. She still had unfinished business with the management of the G.N.O., and she had decided to close that phase of her life with a grand exit that would satisfy her injured self-esteem.

Mary's bravura showdown most probably took place the day before she sailed, when for all practical purposes she had parted company with the G.N.O. By then she had come to see the general manager, who had unquestionably been prejudiced against her, as the personification of all the wrongs she had suffered and all the opposition she had encountered at the National Opera since 1941, and especially in the last two years. Knowing she no longer had anything to lose, she stormed into the Olympia Theater where Synadinos had his office, shortly before lunchtime that day, 13 September 1945, determined to give vent to all her pent-up fury. "*Come and watch!*' she called out to us," says Spyros Salingaros, "and she marched to the general manager's office. Entering without knocking, she inquired curtly of his astonished secretary, '*Is Thodoros in?*' and, before he had time to stop her, she opened the door and went in. Everything she had had buried inside her for so many years she flung at him in the space of a few minutes. Having rubbed Synadinos's nose in the dirt, she tore up her contract before his eyes and flung the pieces in his face." Salingaros still remembers how Mary was shaking all over when she came out. "*I let him have it!*" she kept muttering; and to the secretary, who scurried after her entreating her to calm down, she snapped repeatedly, "*Shame on you all! Shame! Shame!*" According to the version of the story that later went the rounds, Synadinos had risen to his feet in amazement, and Mary, after venting her fury at him, had taken the contract out of her handbag, ripped it up and thrown it on to his desk. Thirteen years later Maria still remembered the scene vividly: "*I tore [the contract] up and I told them, I am sorry, but I hope they won't be sorry for this kind of treatment. But of course, then I said it as a bluff. I was most unhappy and couldn't believe that such a thing was happening. Only sometimes we keep a front, as we say, and I said these words never even dreaming that they would come true.*"[19] The last performance Mary was to have given that night was canceled. Heavy black clouds had been gathering since the afternoon and, like Mary, they erupted in a furious thunderstorm that evening, ruling out all possibility of a performance in the open-air theater.

Not much else is known about Mary's last days in Athens. Of the few people who remembered their farewells to her, the most significant was Takis Sigaras: "The last time we went out I said good-bye on the steps of her house. I told her 'Look after yourself, Mary' in English (we often spoke English together). I warned her to beware of flatterers and wished her godspeed. She leaned forward and kissed me, and I kissed her too and said again, 'God be with you!' The next day she telephoned me, sounding rather stilted and having no particular reason for calling: perhaps she felt under an obligation to me for having paid for her ticket. After that we wrote once each, and that was all until the incident of 1957 and our chance meeting in the presence of Onassis in the early 1960s."[20]

The story that Mary casually informed her mother that she was going to America as she was serving the coffee one April morning is probably a fiction. But at all events, once Litsa realized that she could not dissuade her from leaving, she fell in with the plan and helped Mary to get ready. Jackie tells us that Litsa used her skills as a dressmaker to make sure that her daughter had some decent clothes to wear when she went to New York, although she had not bothered much about that until then. Although Mary was glad to be going and assured her mother she was not worried about traveling by herself, Litsa professes to have been sorry for her because she was an inexperienced young woman and did not even know how to find her father. This, of course, is nothing but a cheap sentimentalism written long after the event. The truth of the matter, as Maria made clear later, is simply that she had not written to let her father know her exact date of arrival in New York, and even that had been on her mother's advice: "*I hadn't written my father that I would be arriving; my mother had advised against it; I don't know why. Or perhaps I do, but there's no need for me to state it,*" she said in 1956. Jackie's relations with her mother also remained extremely strained: Litsa had not stopped pressing Miltiadis to make his intentions clear, and the unhappy Jackie was grateful for all the fuss about Mary's impending departure, which left Litsa little time to nag her. However, the relationship between the two sisters had by now lost all its warmth and descended almost to a purely formal level.[21]

To say farewell to the departing prima donna of the National Opera, a luncheon was given in Mary's honor by the mayor of Piraeus, a friend of Ilias Papatestas. Though she herself later thought that it had taken place on the day she left, it must actually have been the previous day, perhaps immediately after her showdown with Synadinos. Litsa remarks peevishly on the fact that Papatestas was present at the luncheon whereas she and Jackie were not: "We weren't invited. Maria refused to let us come to Piraeus with her. '*I'm going alone, Mother,*' she said when I asked her to let me come to the ship with her." Jackie repeats this allegation, commenting on the "cruel blow" to Litsa, of being left to sit at home on her own while her "precious daughter" was being fêted by the mayor. However, this version of the facts directly contradicts what Maria had said in her own memoirs three years before Litsa wrote hers: "*My mother and my sister refused to accompany me to Piraeus. They said they wouldn't have been able to stand the commotion.*"[22] And since it would have been so out of character for Maria to fabricate a lie like that, we have to conclude that Litsa really did refuse to see her off on the boat, which shows what bad terms she was on with Mary until the very end.

Another person who is said by some of Callas's biographers to have gone down to Piraeus to see her off is Elvira de Hidalgo; Maria, however, never once mentioned the fact and she would surely not have failed to do so if it had actually happened. Presumably they must have said their good-byes in Athens shortly before Mary left for the port, probably at de Hidalgo's apartment. Mary's refusal to heed her teacher's advice to go to Italy has been taken by most of her biographers as the reason for their falling out, but that interpretation originated with none other than de Hidalgo herself, who once said: "I explained to her, 'You must go to Italy, that is why you have learned the language. Once you have become somebody in Italy, the rest will follow naturally.' But Maria took no notice. . . . On the evening [sic] of her embarkation she telephoned me from Piraeus and said, '*My last words are for you. I shall always remember you with great gratitude. Please tell me you forgive me.*' 'You must not go,' I told her again."[23] As we have seen, the real reason for the cooling of relations between them was Mary's recent "defection" from de Hidalgo under the influence of Vangelis Mangliveras. That is also why, when Mary asked for some letters of introduction to people in America, de Hidalgo was reluctant at first and suggested cuttingly that she should apply to Mangliveras. "De Hidalgo told me so herself," says Lela Skordouli, "even though she was quite capable of treating all her other pupils unfairly for Mary's sake. '*You* know whom she has to thank for her training!' she remarked, piqued at what Mary had once reportedly said in favor of Mangliveras."[24]

In the end de Hidalgo did give Mary at least one letter of introduction, to Rosa Ponselle's teacher, Romano Romani. But several years later, despite her affection and admiration, she could not refrain from describing her pupil as "a very clever schemer."[25] Nevertheless, in 1945 de Hidalgo was very well aware of the practical and sentimental reasons that led Mary to insist on going to America. As she herself said later, "When the war was over Mary wanted to go to America to be with her father, from whom she hoped to find some affection at last, and also to start her career over there." And she admitted that if Mary had gone straight to Italy, success—which would have come to her in any case—would merely have come rather sooner. As she had already said in 1945 to a Greek who, apparently, offered her a large sum to stop Mary from going abroad, "Wherever she goes, whatever she does, and no matter what happens to her, Maria is going to succeed. She has a torrential force within her, and no one can restrain that torrent in its course."[26]

The preparations for her departure and the almost daily performances of *Der Bettelstudent* doubtless distracted Mary's attention from the events taking place in the outside world. On 8 September General MacArthur entered Tokyo; in Oslo two days later Vidkun Quisling, the former collaborationist prime minister of Norway, was condemned to death; and in Nuremberg preparations were under way for the trial of German war criminals. In Greece, passions were inflamed by the question of the postwar constitution. Most of the countryside was being terrorized by vengeful bands of armed right-wing extremists, and violent clashes were not infrequent in Athens too. While the Greek Communist party demanded the withdrawal of British forces from Greece, the monarchists and other right-wingers were insisting on a plebiscite, which they hoped would bring back King George II to act as a bulwark against the communist menace. "However, no monarchy can exist with the support of only one faction of its subjects," the moderate centrist newspaper *To Vima* editorialized on the very day that Mary left Greece.

On Wednesday 12 September, the day of Mary's last appearance in *Der Bettelstudent*, Achilleas Mamakis reported in *To Ethnos*: "Miss Mary Kaloyeropoulou, a principal in the G.N.O., is leaving Greece on Friday morning. . . . Her place will be taken by her understudy Madame Zacharatou, a member of the chorus." And two days later, on 14 September, he informed that, "The stage director Mr. Dino Yannopoulos and Miss Mary Kaloyeropoulou of the National Opera sailed for America at nine o'clock this morning." Dino Yannopoulos did leave that day, but on a freighter from Volos in central Greece, bound for America via Turkey and Algeria. Such was the demand for tickets to New York that his father, an admiral, had not been able to secure a passage for Dino on the boat on which he himself was traveling with his wife. At any rate Mary had their company on board, and it is very likely that the admiral's American wife, who had often entertained Mary with tea and cookies during the occupation, invited her to join them in the first-class dining salon during the long voyage. The day before the *Stockholm* arrived in New York the captain asked Mary to sing at the traditional last-night party, just as she had sung on board the *Saturnia* eight and a half years previously. On that occasion the untrained thirteen-year-old had agreed to sing and had charmed the captain and the rest of her audience. This time, however, as a well-established soloist with the G.N.O., she refused, insisting that one could not sing opera in such surroundings.[27]

The strength of Mary's resolve when she left Greece is illustrated by the answer she is said to have given Elvira Mataranga when asked what she was going to do in America: "*I'm going to rejoin my father, and I will also go to the Met—to sing!*" Her listeners thought she was crazy, and Mataranga asked, "What if they don't give you an audition?" "*Oh, then I'll go there every day and sit on the doorstep. One day they will get fed up with me and give me an audition,*" Mary answered, as if that was a perfectly natural solution to her problem. In the event, though she did not actually sit on the doorstep of the Metropolitan Opera, she was so persistent with her telephone calls and so importunate in her solicitations that within two months of her arrival, by her own unaided efforts, she was accepted for an audition by Edward Johnson, its general manager. Before leaving Greece she had obtained some letters of introduction from Ulysses Lappas, who still had contacts in America, but these do not appear to have helped her. Also to no avail, she pestered Nicola Moscona to arrange an interview for her with Toscanini, and succeeded only in alienating him.* In fact she had even brought with her a letter of introduction to Moscona from the G.N.O. baritone Takis Tsoubris, a friend of his, although the famous bass already knew of her through having auditioned her in 1938.[28] So it is clear that Mary had prepared the ground very thoroughly to meet the challenges that would confront her in her early days in New York. Most important of all, however, she had left Greece armed with courage and determination.

The fact is that Mary did not sail off into the blue with nothing to sustain her but hope, or without knowing whither she would turn on arrival in America, as so

---

*When Mary asked Moscona to arrange an audition with Toscanini for her, Moscona (who was then at the peak of his career, having just sung in the famous Met production of *Il Trovatore* with Milanov and Warren) did nothing about it, and from that time on probably started avoiding her. Mary made cutting remarks to her mother about him, which she repeated to the much older bass himself just four years later, in Mexico City (May 1950), when she sang Aida and Leonora with Moscona as Ramfis and Ferrando. Now that her reputation had overtaken his, she "paid him back for his neglect," as her mother puts it. "'Poor, poor Niky,' Maria allegedly purred at him. 'So famous—but why don't they let you sing Mephistopheles?'" (LITSA 88, 107.) Mephistopheles was in fact one of his favorite roles, which Moscona had sung at the Pallas Theater in Athens for his farewell appearance in 1936.

many writers have romantically suggested. That would have been totally out of keeping with her character and her habit of planning all her really important moves down to the last detail. In taking the momentous step of giving up the steady (if limited) career on which she was already firmly launched, it would have been surprising if she had not worked out beforehand whose help she could count on in the early stages, where she would live, and how she could obtain an entrée into the American musical world. In the first place, her father had returned from San Francisco to New York and was living on West 157th Street: she would go and live there with him; then her beloved godfather Leonidas Lanzounis, who was to turn out to be the only absolutely firm rock in her troubled life, would also be near her; and it must have been quite encouraging for her to know that in New York she would find Dino Yannopoulos, a good friend of hers whom she really liked and who had set his sights on a goal similar to her own. As for the various letters of introduction to musicians, these too might indeed have opened some doors to her for crucial auditions, as she probably hoped, but in fact their main importance lay in the moral support they gave her.

It is widely believed that Mary left for America "with no certainty about her future and with half a sandwich in her pocket," and one author has written that she had few clothes and only a hundred dollars with her.[29] However, the fact that the ticket bought for her by Takis Sigaras included all meals on board proves that this is yet another Callas myth, the myth of the young heroine taking off on a hazardous venture without a penny to her name. It was cultivated by Maria herself, who once said, "*I took three or four dresses with me and didn't have a cent in my pocket. . . . A few minutes before embarkation I was fervently advised: 'Be careful and don't lose your money. Where have you put it?' 'There's no danger,' I replied, 'I don't have any.' They couldn't believe me. They took my pocketbook, turned it inside out, and didn't find anything. The Stockholm was to leave Piraeus at three, and at that hour the banks were closed. None of them could help me, but I waved at them happily. I was going to meet the unknown; nevertheless, at that moment I felt with extraordinary clarity that I need not be afraid.*"[30]

"Her departure from Greece was quite sudden. She was helped by God, who made Synadinos treat her in such a way that she left rather earlier than she would otherwise have done," says Andreas Paridis with bitter irony.[31] In Greece Mary had had a hard time, living through events and situations that would leave a deep impression on anybody, and most of all on a young girl growing to adulthood. In the end the G.N.O., and Synadinos in particular, had betrayed and disappointed her, and several of her fellow singers had threatened and deeply wounded her. Poverty and hardship had tested her courage and, above all, the events and circumstances of her private life had turned her irrevocably against her mother. What with Litsa's conduct during the occupation, added to her attitude to her husband, Mary's father, it is easy to understand her subsequent implacable and "heartless" rejection by her daughter. It is also easy to see how the absent father had come to occupy such an important place in Mary's thoughts—chiefly in her imagination, alas—by the time the *Stockholm* sailed from Piraeus.

Mary left Greece on 14 September 1945, two and a half months before her twenty-second birthday. She had arrived on 6 March 1937, aged thirteen and a quarter, and had lived there continuously for eight and a half years, studying and laying firm foundations for her brilliant career. During that time she had acquired a varied repertoire unusual for her time, most of it—apart from the works imposed on her by the G.N.O.—chosen by Elvira de Hidalgo. She had sung seven leading roles in fifty-six performances, she had given five and possibly seven solo recitals, and she had sung in fourteen concerts. In 1954, only nine years after she had left Greece, Maria Callas would remark casually, "*[In Greece] I sang thirty or forty performances, in 'Tosca,' 'Fidelio,' Tiefland,' 'Cavalleria Rusticana,' 'Boccaccio,'*" seemingly without attaching much importance to the fact. But in the memoirs which she dictated late in 1956 she would say that, comforted by the evidence that fame and the public's favor had arisen around her name in Greece, she had decided to win a place for herself in New York: "*In the final analysis, I told myself, I was a singer who had seven years of an intense career behind her.*"[32]

—⁂—

I had a big career in Greece—eight years' hard work.
To Derek Prouse, London (*The Sunday Times*, 2 April 1961)

PART SIX

Epilogue, Postscripts, and Appendix

EPILOGUE

Reappraisals and Conclusions

I know that God has given me a voice that will amaze the world; so I feel a
responsibility to do my best in order that I shall not disappoint Him.

To Carlos Díaz Du-Pond, Mexico City, c. 1950
(*Opera*, April 1973)

One has only to read an account of Maria Callas's life up to the age of about
twenty-two, including a description and analysis of her relations with her
family and the people she worked with, to be led to conclusions that conflict
starkly with the accepted picture of Maria Callas, the woman and the singer. Her
"mythology" is based on this picture, which contains distortions of the truth cultivated in many cases by Maria herself. The main reason for this was her desire to
emphasize the magnitude of her achievements in the face of professional antagonism and other difficulties. Eventually there came a time when her fabrications
were accepted by both the pro-Callas and the anti-Callas sections of the press, and
from then on she did nothing but feed them appropriately whenever she was
pressed, or it suited her. Despite her denunciations of the untruths published over
the years, her own distortions and frequent self-contradictions have been a minefield for her biographers, most of whom have fallen into some of the traps laid by
Maria herself. This biography does not pretend to be totally exempt from such
mistakes, but it has aimed at correcting as many as possible, often in light of new
evidence.

To start, with regard to family relations and psychological traumas during
her childhood in New York, Mary did not suffer particularly, either from an overeating disorder, or a weight problem, or from parental pressure to excel in the arts.
In general, her mother's influence on her at that time was not destructive, apart
from the deep trauma of Litsa's constant display of aggression and open rancor
toward her unambitious, lackluster, unfaithful husband. Conversely, it has to be
acknowledged that Litsa—perhaps with ulterior motives of her own, but that is
beside the point—was responsible for guiding Mary in the direction of vocal
music.

Nevertheless, the wound that Litsa inflicted on Mary's filial love for George
disposed her daughter negatively toward her already in New York; and one serious

511

outcome of Mary's negative feelings toward her mother, which grew steadily into hatred, was that she unconsciously assumed the role of her father's champion. Overlooking the part George had played in the break-up of the marriage, she reacted aggressively to her hysterical and frustrated mother, thus suffering and aggravating her own feelings of stress. Litsa's behavior deteriorated seriously in Athens during the enemy occupation, due to her financial predicament and other causes of insecurity but also to her slack moral standards. She then openly lived a parasitical life of ease, taking advantage of her daughters and passing on to them her unscrupulous, materialistic, and fundamentally amoral principles. Her already negatively charged relations with Mary became even more difficult as a result of the atrocious conditions of life, but even more so by Litsa's encouragement of her younger daughter to exploit the appeal of at least her musical talent in circles of the occupation authorities, mainly Italian. When Mary slowly but steadily distanced herself from her mother after her success in the 1942 *Tosca*, Litsa reacted with hasty and ill-considered counterpressures, which led eventually to their irrevocable breach in 1951.

As for the problems of Mary's excessive weight, acne, and generally unattractive appearance, they were periodical and stemmed mainly from psychological stress. Especially between 1938 and 1940, these problems were due to the separation from her father and the disruption of a family existence, no matter how distressing it had been. The stress factor probably exacerbated some hormone disorders, which led to periodic fluctuations in her weight. Overeating was to remain a matter of serious concern to her for the rest of her life, but the only lasting complex she suffered from with regard to her appearance was self-consciousness about her fat legs and ankles, which she had difficulty in disguising even after she had lost a great amount of weight, in 1954.

Maria Callas is a supreme example of a person whose extraordinary creativity blossoms *despite* and *because of* psychic conflict. Even if one allows for the role of hereditary predisposition to hypersensitivity and mood swings in her personality, the fact remains that her childhood life experiences must have vastly contributed to the narcissistic vulnerability and the contradictions she exhibited throughout her adult life. Indeed, not only did she often say the exact opposite of what she had said earlier, but she tended to try out different names, calling herself Mary, Mary Ann, Mary Anna, Maria, Marianna, Marie-Anna, and perhaps occasionally Marika. Then again, in her effort to consolidate a sense of identity, she was hardly ever satisfied with herself, always fretting that she had fallen short of perfection—by her own unfailingly utopian standards, that is. She also showed neurotic traits in pre- and early adolescence, such as nail-biting and food-craving (especially for sweets). Furthermore, frequent changes of mood; sudden violent outbursts; a tendency toward self-examination; the constant need for reaffirmation of one's worth; feelings of emptiness and melancholy; self-doubts; and repeated questioning of life's meaning—all symptoms which Mary/Maria displayed in abundance throughout her life—can be seen as presumptive evidence of narcissistic imbalance. One side of her was weak, introverted, solitary, and riddled with anxiety and stress, but at times she was capable of carrying all before her like a steamroller, exercising an iron will and tremendous self-control, often subordinating her emotions to the most rigid self-discipline.[1]

In later life Maria made a number of statements about herself which tend to confirm these characteristics. "*I am not as brash and bold as I seem,*" she remarked in 1964. "*This has been a front to hide all the natural human fears that have been within me as they are inside any other human being. . . . We are all vulnerable. I am extremely so and naturally have tried not to show it for my own self-preservation. My shyness and insecurity have often made me seem arrogant—it's a form of self-protection of timid people. . . . I have to be praised and boosted up all the time because I am a born pessimist.*" In 1968, in a series of conversations with John Ardoin (who described her words as "claustrophobic"), Maria voiced her feelings of insecurity and anxiety in a manner that sounded almost hysterical: "*The more famous you become, the more difficult things are, the more you are disliked, especially if you are not a cry-baby. . . . Nothing has come to me the easy way. But so long as the result was good, I didn't care what the sacrifice was. . . . Glory terrifies me. You are quite uncomfortable up there. . . . So I am always on the defensive. I get aggressive. Since my childhood I've been aggressive. Do you blame me?*" she asked in an outburst. A year later, in 1969, she stated explicitly in public, "*It's as if I had a dual personality: the woman (or the person) who guides and the one who criticizes.*" In 1970, when her morale was very low, she admitted that she suffered from terrible stress when she had to make a decision; and in another interview the same year she said: "*Happiness lasts three, five minutes. . . . What does it mean, to be happy? . . . In general, to be happy, one depends on others. And that is the beginning of the end.*"[2]

Several friends of hers and close observers of her behavior have also gone on record with remarks that bear out many of these statements. Dorle J. Soria, the wife of the head of Cetra Records in New York, and Walter Legge, managing director of EMI, both wrote about Maria after her death. According to Soria, "She was capricious, unpredictable, often irritating, suspicious even of her most loyal friends . . . a contradictory person, simple but complex, frank but secretive, wise but childish, always fascinating." Legge believed that Maria suffered from "a superhuman inferiority complex" that was the driving force behind her basic characteristics, namely "her relentless, ruthless ambition, her fierce will, her monomaniacal egocentricity, and insatiable appetite for celebrity"; and he emphasized her "obsession with self-improvement in every facet of her life and work." John Ardoin, who knew her well and was a perceptive analyst of her character, suggested that her "temperament" was due to stubbornness rather than willfulness. Her general intolerance, her irascibility, her unwillingness to compromise, and her choleric impatience with musicians lacking in artistic integrity he identified as manifestations of an oversized ego, which caused her to interpret everything in terms of herself. Such ego, according to Ardoin, is a means of insulation, and in her case it was as outsized as her talent, her insecurities, and her feelings. "She tends to overreact, often to see things in an exaggerated manner. These things served her well in the theater but have often been her enemy in life," he commented shrewdly, and—to his credit—while Maria was still alive.[3]

Despite her serious psychological problems, Maria never sought professional advice, a sure sign of her inability to depend or to trust. "*Psychoanalysis? I don't believe in it. I do my own psychoanalysis all the time,*" she said in 1970, adding that she had never confessed her faults to anyone: "*I prefer to make my confession to myself. . . . I never ask for anything because, if I ask for something, I don't like being refused.*" And on another occasion she said, "*I'm proud. I don't like to show my feelings. I want people to show their interest, but I never ask for anything for fear of being disillusioned. I don't like to lose.*" She usually knew what she wanted and was never satisfied until she had got it. But even when she was suffering agonies in secret, she found it hard to "open up," knowing that her tendency to bottle things up—giving an appearance of self-sufficiency that was only a façade—was a grave handicap. "*Communication is the most important thing in life. It is what makes the human predicament bearable,*" she asserted in 1970. Yet she found it difficult to communicate verbally, except on a superficial level, and so she tried (unsuccessfully) to convince herself that art is "*the most profound way in which one person can communicate with another*" and music "*the highest way of saying things.*"[4]

To her dying day, Maria had a basically conservative and puritanical outlook on life, but her conservatism and puritanism were neither extreme nor pathological. She liked the feeling of "moral order" and often used words like "respect" and "integrity." But this was no more than a front, a protective mask which she wore in public and dropped when she relaxed in the company of the few people she felt she could trust. Then she did open up, revealing herself as a very accessible person, well adapted to the times she lived in. True, she was always a law unto herself and was obsessed by certain fixed ideas, but she could often be surprisingly refreshing, cheerful, even provocative. It should nevertheless not be forgotten that Mary was born into a petit-bourgeois family in the Greek ghetto of Astoria in New York, and that she grew up in a similar environment in Greece, where her musical accomplishments made it possible for her to break out of the class to which she belonged. Although she later rose on her own merits to the very peak of the musical establishment and moved in the highest society, although she became at home in surroundings of affluence and luxury, she retained the petit-bourgeois outlook all her life, with all the narrow-mindedness, the prejudices, and the tastes of her class. She always liked the social conventions to be observed; she needed to have order around her, with everything and everybody in their proper places; good manners were important to her; it was her belief that everybody has an inescapable destiny; as she herself did not mind admitting, she liked light music such as rumbas, jazz, and gypsy music; she loved films and television (especially westerns), admired Walt Disney cartoons, Greta Garbo, and Laurence Olivier; red was her favorite color and the gardenia her favorite flower. All these—as well as her perfectionism, which was so useful to her in her career—absolutely admirable though they may be, are also typical of a conservative middle-class background. And Maria admitted as much in 1969: *"People have often criticized me for being too bourgeois, or rather what I would call 'a good girl.' That's nothing to be ashamed of,"* she protested. *"But they say it's very bourgeois to be like that nowadays."*[5]

Giuseppe di Stefano, the Sicilian tenor who had shared some of her past triumphs and had been her lover when she was well on the way downhill, summed her up after her death: "Maria was a simple, elemental, spontaneous person with incredibly petit-bourgeois dreams. . . . She was possessive, domineering, a real ballbreaker."[6] However, those who, like di Stefano, thought her possessive and domineering were usually people who made no distinction between her professional and her private life and were annoyed by her extreme perfectionism and somewhat strict moral standards. "Maria has an extraordinary character," said Luchino Visconti in her presence in 1969. "She is a perfectionist, and people who are not perfectionists themselves think she is a difficult person. But that's not true: it's just that *they* don't like working or perfecting their work." Similarly, Walter Legge, always a stern critic, wrote in 1977, "I had found a fellow-perfectionist as avid to prove and improve herself as any great artist I have ever worked with."[7] As early as November 1948, when Maria was not yet twenty-five, she had written to Meneghini a remarkably perceptive analysis of the canker that was gnawing at her: *"Everything I do, I am convinced I am doing it badly, and then I start feeling nervous and discouraged. Sometimes I get to the point of wanting death to release me from the torments and the anguish that constantly afflict me. You see, I would like to give so much more to everything I do, both to art and to my love for you. When singing, I would like my voice to do what I want at all times. But it seems I am asking too much. The voice is a thankless instrument and doesn't produce what I want it to. In fact I would say it is rebellious and does not want to be ordered about, or perhaps I should say dominated. It always wants to break free, and I suffer for it. If I go on like this you will have a neurotic on your hands. And it's the same with my love for you. I suffer because I can't give you more. I would like to be able to go on offering you more and more."*[8]

As these confessions amply show, it was in her private existence that Maria was more human and straightforward: there was a curious shyness or reserve about her which caused her to suppress her more romantic, tender-hearted, sensitive side. *"There is a very poetic side to me, which, I need hardly say, I keep hidden,"* she confided to Micheline Banzet in 1965. *"I think everyone has some little corner like that, where everything is beautiful, everything is honest, everything is wonderful."* This natural introversion evidently annoyed her and made her feel stifled: *"We shouldn't be afraid to give of ourselves, and we shouldn't be afraid to be ourselves,"* she stressed. *"It is fair to say that if you're afraid you'll never be able to rise to great heights."* However, being Greek through and through, Maria was endowed with more than her fair share of *philotimo,* a word usually translated as "self-esteem" or "amour-propre," though neither conveys the full meaning of this peculiarly Greek characteristic, with its readiness to take offense at real or imagined slights. *"You have to wait for the right moment to speak the truth, even though that truth is often something we are well aware of,"* she told Banzet. *"If I am given advice brusquely, I really see red. With kindness, people can get me to do anything—absolutely anything, to the point of stupidity!"*[9]

—⁜—

Quite a number of the conclusions reached in this book about Mary during the occupation in Greece, demolish the views that have hitherto been accepted as fact. To begin with, she did not suffer particularly badly from hunger or other deprivations during the war, nor indeed from a weight problem. Although corpulent by the standards of those days, she was less fat and unattractive than she was made out to have been; and as for food, she ate more and had a better diet than most people did then. However, Mary was well aware of the conditions endured by most of her fellow Athenians in those awful years, and we should not overlook the psychological implications of this indisputable fact. In the words of Margarita Dalmati, "Kaloyeropoulou was one of those who did not suffer in the occupation. But do you feel happy when you visit a hospital, yourself hale and hearty, and see the wards full of sick people? That's more or less how that girl must have felt then."[10]

With regard to the antagonism of her professional rivals, it was neither particularly unusual nor inexplicable. It was the natural consequence of her obviously superior talents and of the threat that she represented to some of the older singers. Unpleasant as these early experiences must have been for Mary, and badly as she may have been scarred by some of them, we should not underestimate the value of the lessons they taught her for her future career in the great opera houses of the world. Though still a novice, she showed rare determination in standing up to the older and much more experienced singers in the company. Their hostility strengthened her tenacity and hardened her resolve to make her mark in the field which she believed destiny had marked out for her. However, the antagonism of her fellow singers had little to do with her decision to leave Greece in the autumn of 1945.

The question of Mary's attitude toward the forces of occupation has been much debated—the subject seems to never lose its attraction—and the truth has been much distorted in the process. It has come to be generally accepted that she was quite unscrupulous in using the occupation authorities to further her own interests on every possible occasion. Although relations and support on the part of Italians and Germans undeniably existed, such generalized judgments lead to an unfair oversimplification of the truth. It must be remembered that musicians in Greece, with very few exceptions, continued to practice their profession even when they were "requested" (in other words ordered, to all intents and purposes) to entertain the occupation forces. On the one hand the Germans and Italians respected musicians and loved classical music, while the musicians for their part—most of them impoverished and underfed—were in no position to refuse to comply with their overlords' wishes. In addition, musicians loved their work and naturally wanted to further or at least keep up their careers, and they had no alternative but to go on working for the few available employers, most of whom were inevitably controlled by the occupation authorities. Actors could always join one of the many independent theater companies, while performers of light music could play or sing at independent theaters or nightclubs; but the same was not true of classical musicians, and opera singers were worst placed of all. For if they wanted to remain opera singers, they were confronted with Hobson's choice: either they sang at the only opera house—the state-run G.N.O., which of course was controlled—or else they gave up their careers, in which case some of them would probably have died of starvation.

Mary believed herself to be—and indeed she was—an outstandingly talented musician. She had hardly started her career, and she aspired to reach the top. Believing implicitly in her own worth, she underestimated or was blind to the discreditable nature of some of her friendships and some of the means she used to achieve her ends. Furthermore, besides craving admiration and recognition of her talent, she had a natural need for love and affection, which she had never had at home. As if all this were not enough, she had a mother who, instead of helping and supporting her, encouraged her to enjoy the perquisites of consorting with members of the occupation forces and set her a bad example in this respect. Indeed, Mary's reputation suffered increasingly from the fact that Litsa openly entertained German and Italian officers at the house she shared with her daughters. What is more, Mary suffered from bouts of another sort of craving, which made the "offer" of foodstuffs from the enemy an irresistible temptation. In any case she was not cut out to be a heroine of the resistance, and no one has the right to criticize her for that. Consider the circumstances: she was an up-and-coming singer, not yet twenty years old, and whether she did what she did because she was encouraged by her mother, or because she was hungry, or because she liked or had fallen in love with one of "the enemy," or because she found it gratifying that the Italians and Germans admired her singing, or simply because she wanted not to give up her career but to promote it, it would be an exaggeration to accuse her of collaboration with the enemy. On the contrary, she used her contacts to help her fellow musicians whenever she had a chance: we saw her procuring a barrowload of food for the G.N.O. staff, helping to push it all the way up from Piraeus to Athens with torn and bleeding feet.

Nevertheless, these considerations do not acquit Mary of all guilt. They simply lessen her responsibility and explain some admittedly very hard choices and decisions that she had to make. The fundamental driving force that influenced her behavior and guided her actions in those difficult years was undoubtedly her unwavering determination to become a great opera star, an ambition she regarded not only as a worthwhile goal in her life but as the main counterbalance to her practical and family problems and all the complexes that stemmed from them. Elisabeth Schwarzkopf made a relevant point in an interview in 1986, referring to her own troubles during the war: the bombing raids (for she had spent a good deal of time in an air raid shelter in Berlin, as Mary had done in Athens), the misery, fear, and pain, the consciousness of death lurking round every corner. "And you still have to concentrate on your singing," she pointed out. "I think every big singer has to have built-in this desire of shoving everything aside, not noticing what's going on around him or her and concentrating on getting on with this voice and working with it and learning all there is to learn."[11] However, the risk inherent in this sort of mentality—without which it is impossible to rise to the heights of a Schwarzkopf or a Callas—is that one will be accused of being ruthlessly self-interested, and in time of war perhaps even traitorous. This is true in any country, and especially in Greece, where it has been a commonplace occurrence since the war for people with an ax to grind to charge others with collaboration or to falsely claim a fine resistance record for themselves. One who fell a victim to this kind of mudslinging was young Mary Kaloyeropoulou, extra-multitalented and therefore expendable. Certainly she did fraternize with the enemy, and certainly she was rewarded for it with gifts of food, or with a few recitals and roles at the National Opera; but never did she act unpatriotically or for motives that were in any way political. She never joined any political party or organization and offered her help whenever possible, without any political discrimination. All in all, in those extremely hard times she behaved no differently from most of her fellow musicians, none of whom were pilloried as she was.

This very delicate area of Mary's conduct is important not only for what it tells us about her ethical principles but also because it seems to have hardened her negative attitude toward her mother, making the ultimate breach between them inevitable. Her G.N.O. colleagues' reactions, the appalling civil war that followed the German retreat, and the gradual emergence of the truth about Nazi and Fascist atrocities all over Europe, not least in Greece, must have made her realize before long that some of her actions and some aspects of her private life reflected badly on her. She therefore tried to sweep them under the rug as far as possible, sometimes by getting friends to testify on her behalf, but more often simply by never referring to them and pretending to have forgotten all about that period of her life. At the same time she conveniently laid all the blame for her own actions on Litsa, who had admittedly encouraged her to make use of people and situations and, by consorting with enemy officers herself, had set an example and provided Mary with a useful plea in mitigation of her own fraternization.

Mary's realization that some of her conduct had been seriously reprehensible set the seal on the rejection of her mother, the primary cause of which, however, was Litsa's treatment of her husband. Maria's decision to break off all relations with her mother from the early 1950s—a decision she upheld impenitently for the rest of her life, with extremely damaging consequences to herself—can only be explained in terms of this twofold grievance. Yet, although this uncompromising attitude made her appear odiously hard-hearted and had a disastrous effect on her public image, Maria persisted in condemning her mother, without ever being able to explain her reasons publicly. *"I've never said anything, not really, while she kept blabbing to all the newspapers,"* she is alleged to have said in 1972. *"If I'd said anything, anything that was the real truth, who would have believed me? . . . She'd still be the poor suffering mother of La Diva. Well, it wasn't like that in the war. That lousy war and the rest of it."*[12]

Another subject that is illuminated by new evidence is Mary's relations with men. After 1942–43 she emerges as a vivacious young woman, much more attractive to the opposite sex than the moody, complex-ridden creature she is generally supposed to have been. Most of the people who knew Mary during the occupation—apart from those who talk carelessly about her "affairs" with Italians and Germans—state airily that she had never had a real love affair in her life. The evidence for this view, such as it is, varies from "She wasn't interested in anything except her singing" to "She never said anything about having a date or being in love." Even her sister, for reasons of her own, makes her out to have been congenitally unattractive to men. Yet the truth, as we have clearly seen, was different. In the early years in Greece (from 1937 until the success of the 1942 *Tosca*), when Mary was overweight and suffering from skin problems, it is true that she spent her time practicing, to the exclusion of all else. At the very time when she was beginning to feel the first stirrings of her own sexuality and the need to assert her femininity, she deliberately chose to try to win recognition by means of musical studies and her voice: "To Maria, music was a substitute for a lot of other things," as Elli Nikolaidi asserted.[13]

From 1943, however, the situation changed rapidly. Mary's newfound self-confidence made her more attractive as a woman and easier to get on with as a person, and her relationships with her admirers followed the natural course of any young person's first close relationships. Even her mother, who makes no mention of these relationships and maintains that Maria was a virgin when she met Meneghini, admits that her daughter "never lacked the quality known as sex appeal, and some men were more attracted to her than to her sister."[14] As an adolescent she had developed a very strong desire to be loved and to have a family, for which she would probably have been willing to give up her career. From now on, however, her career was her first concern, and her private affairs and love life were relegated to a normal but lower level of importance. Yet considering what a fiery personality she was at all times, and perhaps most of all on stage, then surely she must have been the same in affairs of the heart too; and it would be naïve to imagine that with such a temperament she had never given way to physical passion.

Even in her youth and adolescence, nearly all the men she found attractive were considerably older than she. Besides being older, most of the men in her early life were also useful to her by virtue of their social, financial, or simply artistic standing, consequently offering her the feeling of security she so much needed. Already at the conservatory Mary was friendly with much older male fellow students such as Vyron Simiriotis, Evangelos Lakadzis, and Spyros Salingaros, respectively nine, fifteen, and ten years her senior when she herself was only fifteen. There followed her crush on her dentist and then her attachment to seventeen-years-older Dr. Ilias Papatestas, most probably a formative experience for her. At the age of eighteen to nineteen she was in love with Attilio De Stasio, the highly placed Italian who was probably twice her age. Then came her romance with the industrialist Takis Sigaras, twelve years her senior. Finally, her great love during this period, the principal baritone at the G.N.O. Evangelos Mangliveras, was a year older than Sigaras. We know of only two amours with men of about her own age. One was her brief but passionate fling with the Italian paratrooper Angiolo Dondoli, who was about seven years older than she. The other, just after the liberation, was her romance with the British officer Ray Morgan, only three years her senior. The first lasted only a week (although it left a lasting impression), the second died a natural death after about a month and a half. After leaving Greece Mary had some kind of emotional and perhaps sexual involvement with the impresario and lawyer Eddie Bagarozy, a considerably older married man. Immediately afterward, when still only twenty-four, she fell in love with—and two years later married—the industrialist Giovanni Battista Meneghini, twenty-eight years older than she and thus about the same age as her mother. And the most shattering love of her life came to her when she was thirty-six, in the person of Aristotle Onassis, who was about twenty-three years her senior.

Mary always felt she needed a protective presence in her life. In her childhood in New York she had been deprived of the companionship of her father, who left home every day not only to go to work but also to escape from the unbearable Litsa. When Mary was taken to Greece in 1937, leaving her father behind in New York, her sense of insecurity deepened. Being thirteen and just entering adolescence, she then looked for love and affection in older men who could offer her both emotional support and practical security. By the end of 1942, however, when her career prospects were looking promising, she was less troubled by feelings of insecurity and her longing for marriage and a family was overtaken by dedication to her professional future. This explains why, about five years later, when she was in Italy and striving to make a career there and a name internationally, she married a man who not only offered her love and financial security but had decided to devote himself to the furtherance of her career. "*I am very proud of having made a success of my marriage. It's the main thing in the life of a woman, I feel, especially for an artist*," she said in 1958, just a year before she fell in love with Onassis and simply walked out on the officiously possessive Meneghini.[15]

Three years later, in 1961, Maria described her walk-out as a very important step in her life, adding, "*Apart from my natural instinct to regard marriage as a per-*

manent contract, the memory of my own parents' incompatibility had instilled in me an especial caution." In 1970—by which time she was alone, having been tossed aside by the man she truly loved, she reverted to the subject of family life once again: *"Yes, I would have preferred to have had a happy family and have children. . . . But destiny brought me into this career, I couldn't get out. . . . I would have given it up with pleasure. This will probably amaze people, but I would have!"* Nevertheless, so bitterly was she disappointed at the way life had treated her that, in 1974, she declared that she did not believe in marriage. Having by that time given up all hope of ever marrying Onassis (who was now seriously ill), and having recently lost some of her closest friends as well as her father, she was suffering again from feelings of insecurity just as badly as she had been thirty years earlier in Athens. The wheel had come full circle: *"The most important thing for a woman,"* she reiterated, *"is to have a man of her own, to make him happy. I don't think that singing is a woman's job."*[16]

—⁂—

Some of the other major errors which this book sets out to correct are concerned either with the reasons for Mary's leaving Greece or with the level of vocal and operatic accomplishment she had attained in Greece.

Mary did not leave Greece as a result of the hostility of jealous rivals, as so many journalists and biographers have alleged. Although that hostility undoubtedly helped to create an atmosphere that she found unbearable, she left primarily because she saw it as the best way of achieving her musical ambitions, and secondly because she longed to see her father again. Other factors of lesser importance behind her decision to leave were her bad relations with her mother, the difficult and dangerous conditions of life in Greece, and the antagonism toward her in the Greek National Opera. Maria herself was largely responsible for disseminating the alternative, much more simplistic version of the story. As the main reasons for her departure from Greece she usually cited the hostile environment in which she had to work and the attitude of her mother. Quite possibly she ended by believing this, as she ended by believing some other perversions of the truth. *"I left Greece feeling embittered because those in charge had refused to give my talent the recognition it really deserved. I used to spend half my nights practicing, but I was always sidelined,"* she once told a Greek confidante. *"I bear no malice toward anybody,"* she would say condescendingly on another occasion in Greece, at the height of her fame. *"Like all other opera singers in Greece, I went through a lot in the war. We suffered, we went hungry, we shared the hardships of the ordinary people with a song on our lips. We had put everything we had into creating an opera company worthy of our country's long artistic history. And we did achieve something. I have met Germans who even now cannot forget the 'Fidelio' they heard in those bleak days."*[17]

When she left Greece Mary was almost fully developed as a singer and as an actress: besides her innate genius, she already possessed an extensive armory of acquired skills and experience. The suggestion that Maria Callas owed everything to Tullio Serafin and to Italy—as has been widely accepted—is disproved by the facts and numerous critical opinions. While no one, least of all Maria herself, would question the importance of Tullio Serafin's role in her development from August 1947, the testimony of people qualified to judge the standard she had reached by the end of her studies and early career in Greece overwhelmingly supports the view that she had already reached a very high level of artistic achievement. Maria herself frequently stressed the importance of what she called her first career, referring to the period from 1947 onward as her "second," "main," or "great" career: *"My first career . . . I call the one in Athens, in other words during the war,"* she said in 1968. *"That is what gave me my experience, I am sure, because I had my training there, I had my stage experiences, I had my ups and downs. By the time I came to Italy—for the big career, shall I say—I had already learned so many roles. I had been singing for eight years. . . . So, you see, there was no surprise for me. That is why I say that this first career was most necessary to me."*[18]

With regard to the voice problems that had troubled her from her earliest years in Athens: the "change of gear" in the transition from one register to another and, more particularly, the excessive vibrato on her high notes, they can be traced back to her childhood in New York, when Mary, encouraged by her ignorant and ambitious mother, pushed her voice too hard without professional guidance. Unfortunately she continued to strain her voice after moving to Greece, partly owing to the inexperience and lack of firmness of her first teacher, Maria Trivella, and partly through her own youthful impatience and her mother's pressure to start an early lucrative career. Elvira de Hidalgo later succeeded in eliminating the wobble with fairly lasting results, but the problem—whether inherent or acquired —was to reappear in 1954, with consequences that proved fatal to her career.

Another factor that may have contributed to the relative brevity of Maria Callas's career is the fact that she was taken on at the Greek National Opera at a very early age and given leading roles almost at once. To all intents and purposes, Mary was a prima donna from the very outset, obliged to sing roles that were unsuitable for and probably damaging to her voice, such as Tosca, Marta, Santuzza, Smaragda, and Leonore. Her own view of the matter, expressed in 1955, was: *"Either you've got the voice or you haven't, and if you've got it, you begin singing the lead parts right away."* However, she was to revise that opinion when she had acquired greater maturity. Indeed, if Mary had started more slowly, not necessarily in the chorus but at least in well-chosen small parts, it is quite possible that the faults which eventually ruined her voice would have been eradicated once and for all. That was probably why, in later life, she herself was always so insistent that young singers should not be in too much of a hurry.[19]

The best way to assess what Maria's voice was like in the autumn of 1945 is by examining the testimony of those who heard her sing in Greece and those who heard her soon afterward, either in America or during and immediately after her first appearance at Verona in the summer of 1947.

The prevailing view among Greeks was stated by Polyvios Marchand as long ago as 1983. When Maria appeared at the Arena in Verona, less than two years after leaving Athens, "She was not an inexperienced and artistically undeveloped novice, a Galatea who had suddenly met her Pygmalion in Italy." Maria Callas, Marchand maintains, evolved in a process of unbroken continuity from Mary Kaloyeropoulou. He fully accepts that a man like Serafin would have brought out, perfected, and made the most of the gifts that nature had lavished on her. Indeed, when Serafin took her on he found those qualities somewhat raw and unpolished, as Mary had not fully mastered the technical or intellectual demands of interpreting a role. "Her art," Marchand concludes, "was dominated by an effortless spontaneity, sometimes not quite under control but so very characteristic of youth. . . . [However,] the outstanding artist was already there, and indeed with eight years' stage experience behind her."[20] His view has been reaffirmed by numerous Greek musicians who knew Mary in the 1940s. Pianist Tonis Yeoryiou, for example, a fine musician who had heard many great singers when he was living in Vienna, has given it as his considered opinion, on the basis of what he heard her sing in 1945, that "Maria had already reached a very high standard here in Greece." Andonis Delendas, the tenor who had partnered Mary in five of her seven leading roles on the Athenian stage, said in 1957, "She was already great in Greece, but if she had not gone abroad she would have remained obscure and unknown to the international public."[21]

Others, however, while agreeing that Mary had reached a high level of attainment in Athens, lay more emphasis on the influence of Serafin's subsequent guidance. Among them are tenor Andonis Kalaidzakis and director Dino Yannopoulos. In Kalaidzakis's opinion it was not until Mary went to Italy that her potential was fully appreciated and exploited. The systematic extension of her range, downward into the contralto register and upward to F above the stave, and the disciplines of supporting the voice firmly with the diaphragm and breathing correctly (which, as we have seen, de Hidalgo had learned instinctively and taught empirically), these accomplishments so vital for a *soprano sfogato* or a *soprano assoluto*, "resulted from the advice of Serafin and others in Italy, and also, of course, from her own hard work." Yannopoulos agrees that Mary was already a full-fledged musician when she left Athens, but he too considers Serafin's later work on her to have been of capital importance: "Yes, her voice was very good in Greece, but she often used it badly. The standard of music in Athens was also good, but we should not forget that the 1941 *Entführung,* for which Mary spent some time in rehearsal, was the first complete Mozart opera ever performed by a wholly Greek cast in Greece."[22]

As an indication of the high standard Maria had reached, however, Yannopoulos himself cites the fact that Edward Johnson offered her a contract at the Metropolitan Opera as soon as she arrived in New York. "Just before Christmas 1945, when I went to sign my first contract with the Met," he recalls, "the general

Mary in New York, spring 1946, a few months after her December 1945 auditions at the Metropolitan.

manager asked me, 'By the way, do you happen to know a certain Callas?' When I said I did, Johnson asked me, 'Is she mad?' I asked him what he meant, and he told me that they had liked Maria very much and had offered her a three-year contract. But since she hadn't as yet sung anything in their repertoire except *Tosca* and *Cavalleria*, they told her she would have to start with small roles and work her way up in the second year. In the third year they would be able to give her a pre-mière in a leading role. 'She refused and, turning to me,' Johnson went on, 'she said, *"Mr. Johnson, I am the greatest singer in the world, and one day you will come to me on bended knee and beg me to sing! And then I shall say no!"'* To be offered that contract was quite something, never mind the fact that she thought it wasn't good enough for her and refused it!" Yannopoulos concludes.*

Maria's incredible nerve, which at the time was regarded with good reason as sheer effrontery, amazed her biographer George Jellinek: "Anybody who knows

---

*YANNOPOULOS. Mary auditioned twice at the Met, on 3 and 21 December 1945, on the roof stage and on the proper stage, respectively. On the first occasion she sang "Vissi d'arte" and "Casta diva" privately to Paul Breisach, who commented, "Exceptional voice—ought to be heard very soon on stage"; on the second she sang the same two arias plus an aria from *Trova-tore*, Frank St. Leger commenting, "Good material—needs work on her voice." (Information provided to Frank Hamilton by Robert Tuggle, director of the Metropolitan Opera archives.) Maria herself told Edward Downes twenty-two years later that she had sung *Trovatore* first and then *Norma*, and Johnson had thought that this was "a funny way to warm up," suggest-ing that she ought to have started with *Norma* and then gone on to *Trovatore*. (DOWNES.) There seems to be no formal proof that an offer was actually made to Callas by the Met. How-ever, in her brief memoirs and in her interview with Downes (1956 and 1968 respectively), Maria said she had refused an offer of *Fidelio* because she would have had to sing it in English. She also said she was offered a part in *Butterfly* and turned that down as well, because she was too fat to play a petite Japanese girl: "*I refused without hesitation.*" (MARIA 26–27.) In an inter-view published in *The New York Post* in 1958, Edward Johnson said, "She was quite over-weight, but that didn't come into our thinking at all—the young ones are usually too fat. . . . We offered her a contract but she didn't like it—because of the contract, not because of the roles. She was right in turning it down—it was frankly a beginner's contract. But she was with-out experience, without repertory." (Quoted in JELLINEK 31 and LITSA 88.) Litsa adds that Mary claimed to have asked Johnson to let her sing *Tosca* or *Aida* without pay, but he refused, whereupon Mary retorted, "*Some day the Metropolitan will go down on its knees to me, begging me to sing. When that time comes, I shall not do it for nothing.*" Stamatis Tsoutis, in his unreliable 1963 biography (a rambling confection, full of imaginative descriptions and conversations, which does contain some believable material but never names the sources), maintains that Mary was willing to sign a contract at the Met unconditionally. According to him, Johnson offered her parts in *Fidelio* and *Butterfly* for the 1946–47 season and the overjoyed Mary could not wait to sign the contracts, which she did the next day after merely glancing through them. When rehearsals started, however, "It turned out that Mary was fatter than they had thought, was too inexperienced and would not have enough time to learn the parts. In addition, her repertoire was considered too limited for the Met. Eventually, after much vacillation by the management and despite Mary's desperate entreaties, the contracts were annulled by Johnson himself, who had put his signature to them when Mary originally signed them in his office." Mary was shattered, according to Tsoutis, who asserts that that was the moment when her character changed and she became tough and determined to "fight by fair means or foul, with-out scruple or sentiment, in order to succeed." (TSOUTIS.)

what a Met contract means to an aspiring opera singer must throw up his hands in disbelief at the very thought of this gesture! . . . Anyone else in her shoes certainly would have seized the opportunity. But this was Maria Callas, aware of what she wanted. And, apparently, she did not want to get ahead at *any* price."[23] Maria mentioned this episode in 1956, adding: "*[In 1946, in America] I went from one movie house to another, not to see the films, but so as not to go out of my mind from torturous thoughts about my uncertain future.*" In 1965 she elaborated: "*People said I was quite mad and I told myself I was mad, too, because I thought I would never have a chance like that again. My secret was to be able to say no, to be able to pick and choose. And also, of course, to wait—to wait in an agony of torment, but [at least] to be able to wait. To say no, not just as the whim took me but after thinking things over and taking everything into consideration. It is a matter of instinct.*" And in 1971 she had this to say about her own character: "*I am a Sagittarius, a hunter with a bow pulled ready to draw. When I believe, I can stand like a monument waiting for the right moment. Timing is very important in life.*"[24]

On Mary's voice then, the views of Eddie Bagarozy and of his wife, Louise Caselotti, a mezzo-soprano with whom Mary had lessons in 1946–47, should certainly be considered. Bagarozy commented later that her voice was "unusual in range, a little tight on top, a little rough in the bottom register, with noticeable breaks in between, but it was an unusually expressive instrument, nevertheless. Reminiscent of Emmy Destinn."[25] As for Caselotti's opinion, she thought that when Mary arrived in New York her voice had suffered as a result of her recent operetta singing. She felt that the young singer she probably first heard at the Louise Taylor Voice Studio on East Ninth Street, Manhattan, was basically a dramatic soprano and that de Hidalgo had harmed her pupil's voice by trying to "lighten" it so that she could sing coloratura and lyrical roles. Mary, of course, would never agree with Caselotti on this point, and it need hardly be added that de Hidalgo would have none of it. Indeed, when listening to the radio in Ankara, in March 1949, the Spaniard heard the broadcast of Mary's triumph as Kundry in *Parsifal* at the Rome opera house, and she wrote to her saying jubilantly that her method had been vindicated: whereas "others" had considered Mary to be a dramatic soprano, she had made her sing as a *leggera*.[26]

Caselotti taught Mary the part of Turandot for a production in Chicago, scheduled for the end of January 1947, which eventually came to nothing. She went to Italy with her in June 1947, and later said that Callas's performance in the Venice production of *Turandot*, early in 1948, fell far short of the standard of the rehearsals in New York at the end of 1946: "The soaring high notes I admired when we were preparing the part for Chicago had lost their freedom, and wavered badly. Her low register was also weak. I knew that she was on the wrong track and told her so." But this criticism—coming as it did from Caselotti, who seems to have taken the view that the only time Mary had no problems was when she was having lessons with her—may well have been prompted by personal rivalry. Some years later, on the famous occasion at La Scala when Maria, unable to see clearly without her glasses, picked up a bunch of radishes from the stage and brandished them in front of the audience, it was thought that Caselotti had thrown them. In fact Maria is reported to have said of Caselotti, *"I don't want to set eyes on her. If I hadn't stopped having lessons with her before it was too late, she would have ruined my voice—forever!"*[27]

Mary's engagement by Giovanni Zenatello to sing at Verona was largely due to the advocacy of Serafin's future son-in-law, the Russian-Italian bass Nicola Rossi-Lemeni, who later recalled: "I met her in America in 1947, when nobody thought anything of her even though she already displayed all the gifts that were later to make her famous." According to Zenatello's daughter Nina, her father offered to give lessons to Mary, who had "some obvious defects in a voice that was a surging torrent of sound, not always under control." In the ensuing two months or so, Zenatello tried—not entirely successfully, according to his daughter—to correct a minor flaw in the middle register of the "black pearl" of a voice which he had discovered.[28] As soon as Mary arrived in Verona—just twenty-one months after her departure from Greece—Serafin heard her sing two or three arias so that he could judge the ability of the unknown prima donna Zenatello had sprung on him. Experienced conductor that he was, he saw her potential immediately, and, although he knew that Mary was too nearsighted to see his baton, he felt no unease when he conducted her in that historic *Gioconda* a few days later. When the production was over he advised her to have lessons with Emma Moglioli, to whom he wrote a letter of recommendation: "Signorina Kallas . . . has a truly exceptional voice that can cope with the sternest challenges. Strong, powerful sounds, but also effortless, sweet *pianissimi*, natural agility." Later Serafin would qualify Maria's musicality as "extraordinary, almost frightening."[29] When she went to Italy Mary started her *"really great career,"* as she herself told Lord Harewood in 1968. And she explained: *"Then you learn to really become a musician. After becoming a singer you have to put your instrument to the service of music, not only to the bel canto. . . . This I learned with Maestro Serafin. . . . I drank all I could from this man. He was the first maestro for me, and I am afraid he is the last man of his kind. . . . Today they don't take the trouble, they don't have that much experience, they start too young and don't have enough humility toward music. . . . What I learned from Serafin is that you must serve music . . . it is our first and main duty."*[30]

Others who heard Maria's voice at that time were her fellow singers in that Verona production of *La Gioconda.* Among them, besides Rossi-Lemeni, was the Bulgarian mezzo-soprano Elena Nicolai, who evidently never had any great affection for Maria but commented forty years after the event, "Her voice, at any rate to start with, was ugly, uneven, unsteady. . . . But all of us in the profession realized that Callas was capable of greatness."[31] The fullest description of Mary's voice, however, as it had been in the Verona *Gioconda* was given by Lord Harewood in conversation with Maria herself in 1968: "At that time, while a very individual

"Drinking music" from Tullio Serafin, 1953.

voice, it was a very bright one, a very strong dramatic voice; but it also had tremendous bright overtones. There was tremendous—not only power—but brilliance then. There always has been brilliance in your voice," he told her, "but not quite as bright brilliance. Can one talk about a darker brilliance now? The brilliance is always there, but it was brightness then, more flashing. Not flashy, but flashing." And in 1972 Harewood described the Callas of 1947 as a *soprano sfogato* like Giuditta Pasta, meaning that she was strong in the mezzo-soprano range with an extension into the high soprano range. More specifically, he pointed out that Mary's voice and style already possessed some of the characteristics that were to become famous as her personal hallmarks, such as "an exemplary attack and a power that was almost steely when she sang at full throttle," as well as "considerable flexibility" and "a smooth and expressive legato."[32]

What clearly seems to be the generally accepted view—though there are some, mainly Italians, who still have reservations about it—was well summed up by the Italian theatrical director and musicologist Leonardo Bragaglia: "The Italian début of the twenty-four-year-old Maria Callas was a point of arrival: the result of ten years of assiduous, intensive, enlightened study. . . . Callas's technique was already formed, complete. So no one—apart from Serafin and then Francesco Siciliani, both of whom gave her the opportunity to show what she already was—can boast of having helped Callas. Vocally, technically, even dramatically, Callas was already fully developed thanks to her innate sense of tragedy and her visceral knowledge of Greek tragedy. All she needed was to put the final touch to her outward appearance; but that was to be taken care of six years later by Luchino Visconti." Nor can we ignore Elvira de Hidalgo's emphatic statement to the Italians, made while she was actually living and working in Milan: "It is often said today that when she landed in Italy Maria was still nothing, and that it was only in Italy, after her marriage to Meneghini, that she managed to complete her [musical] education. These are absurd things to say, and no one is in a better position to know than I am."[33]

—⚭—

I am a passionate artist and a passionate human being. I am impatient when I am asked to conform to standards of work and behavior which I know are inferior. . . . To live in a way you can tolerate for yourself, you must work. Work very hard. I do not believe with Descartes: "I think, therefore I am." With me it is "I work, therefore I am."

To Kenneth Harris
(*The Observer Review*, 8 and 15 February 1970)

The Final Breach
with Her Mother

"*Finally I've come to my beloved America and I'm really very happy,*" Mary wrote to Vangelis Mangliveras three months after her arrival in New York. Most of all she was thrilled to be reunited with her father, who was also very happy to see his younger daughter after more than eight years. For some time George spoiled Mary in an unprecedented way: "*My father literally adores me and I lack nothing,*" she went on. "*I have shopped for everything, I have plenty of pocket money of my own. I have also acquired two fur coats! He refuses me nothing! Let me tell you, dearest Evangelos, God took pity on me and rewarded me for what I went through. You know what my life was—how I worked like a dog in order to support my family, and surely you will acknowledge some good points in my character!*"[1]

Soon, however, Mary's feelings underwent profound changes. In the first place, she was able at last to demythologize her father. "*I was so looking forward to seeing my father and returning to America,*" she told the wife of her godfather Leonidas Lanzounis, "*but it isn't at all the way I expected. I've had quite a shock. . . . I'm certainly not ready to share his affections with that Papajohn woman.*" George made no secret of his relationship with Alexandra Papajohn, and Mary was deeply hurt by it. As Lanzounis and Jackie remarked to Nadia Stancioff later, she would never forgive Alexandra for "robbing" her of George's affection.[2] She felt betrayed by her father, and never got over that feeling of disillusionment completely. What is more, George would always remain the uneducated son of a Peloponnesian farmer, the immigrant pharmacist working with his nose to the grindstone, in a country whose language he never learned properly.

Yet, in spite of the various barriers between them and even though he took practically no interest in her career, Mary never ceased to love him, not necessarily for anything he had actually done for her but simply because he was her father and had never persecuted her or harmed her in any way. And unlike Litsa, George acknowledged Mary's achievement as purely her own: "Thanks only to your own efforts, your dreams [are] realized and your endeavors and desires fulfilled," he wrote her in 1949. "I take pride in being one of the happiest fathers in the world, and I often remember you telling me, '*Father, if only I were offered the opportunity*

Mary in New York,
spring 1947, happy
with both her
parents.

to prove who I am in my art, you will see!' Indeed, I boast because you have proven
that you were and are deserving from every point of view."[3] Mary distanced herself from him in the last eight years of his life, only because in 1964 he finally reg-
ularized his long-standing relationship with Alexandra by marrying her.*

Once across the ocean, distance and time softened Mary's traumatic memories of the occupation. She also found release from the tyranny of her mother, and
even started missing Litsa and the good times they had occasionally had together.
Most probably she began to feel remorse about some of her past outbursts and
cruel words, and there is no doubt that she was secretly hoping that Litsa and
George would get together again. In her early letters to Vangelis Mangliveras Mary
described her life in New York and referred to Litsa and Jackie in terms of endear-
ment that surprise: "*The musical season hasn't started here yet, so all I'm doing is buying clothes and going to see people. As you see I am staying at the Hotel Times Square,
a very good place, and so I have no household duties to keep me busy. I eat out with my
father, and to put it briefly I am having a wonderful, lovely time. I only miss my dear
mother, whom I love so much, and Jackaki. Do go and see them some day, they'll be so
pleased. They love you! That's all for now. I hope you will write me a long, newsy letter very soon. It will give me so much pleasure—oh, so much! With my love always,
Maria.*"[4] About a year after her arrival, she wrote suggesting that Litsa should
come to New York, enclosing a ticket for the purchase of which she had borrowed
seven hundred fifty dollars from her godfather.

However, these feelings of affection died away soon after Mary reencoun-
tered her mother's despotic ways in New York. By the time Mary left for Italy, on
17 June 1947, the friction between her parents had revived unpleasant memories
of her childhood, and these memories had reactivated her hostility toward her
mother. Yet, even then—according to Litsa—Mary was so touched by the advice
her mother gave her before she sailed, that she cried.[5] Maria later shocked the
conservative Catholic Meneghini by telling him all about her confused feelings. "If
I referred to her mother, she would say, '*I don't want to hear you mention that
woman's name.*' On certain occasions . . . she would say that her mother had
robbed her of her childhood. Even when she was only three, her mother forced her
to practice the piano hour upon hour, forbidding her to play. She had her perform
in public, like a trained dog." Nevertheless, at Meneghini's urging, Maria made
fresh overtures to her mother. And when Litsa sent her flowers for her name day,
in August 1948, Maria—again according to her mother's memoirs—wept with
emotion and wrote to thank her "golden mother." Maria's feelings were obviously

---

*When Maria was informed of the marriage, which took place just before George was to undergo
a critical operation in New York, she wired Leonidas Lanzounis: "*Was shocked at his marriage.
. . . Most disgusted and unhappy.*" Later in the same year she wrote to him, "*So, dear Leo, make
it quite plain to him. He chose others. He can keep them. I'm out for good.*" (STASSINOPOULOS 225;
see 224–225 and 274 for more about Maria's refusal to countenance her father's second marriage and the remorse she felt when he died, in 1972, without her ever having seen him again.)

split in two; her favorite photograph, for example, which she dedicated to Mene-ghini at the time of their wedding in 1949, was one that she had evidently intended to send to Litsa as well, with the affectionate dedication: "*To my darling mother with all my love and respect, Maria.*" But in the end she never sent it; it was found among the personal effects she had left at Sirmione in 1959, when she abandoned Meneghini for Onassis.[6]

Maria just before her marriage, Verona 1949.

On 18 September 1949 Litsa wrote to Mary the following letter, in Greek, full of hysterical crescendos, obsessive accusations, and scurrilous arguments that could only exasperate her now fully independent, married daughter. As for the occasionally sound advice and otherwise fair moralizing, it usually went against Litsa's own practices. That is why, when Mary read this long missive, she must have either laughed bitterly or simply taken little, if any, notice:

My beloved Maria,

Following two months of silence, I received your brief letter today. . . . As you know well, anything that you may write to me unrelated to your career is indifferent to me, and for this you should love me all the more, because I am such a glory-seeker and want to know everything that happens in your career. You don't inform me where you have sang and when, to make me happy; I feel ashamed as news reaches me now and then from strangers.

As you now touch upon the question of my not appearing to rejoice over your wedding, you provoke me into speaking to you as a mother to her child; and do not fly into your usual selfish defense and fits of anger, my daughter.

It is not that I don't like your husband, about whom [nevertheless] I haven't the slightest idea—what sort of person he is, what his eyes are like or his face. Sending a photo to your parents you consider absolutely superfluous. . . . Believe me, Maria, I do not recognize you. How you have changed . . . Who should I blame? Your fame or your surroundings? I knew you to be selfish over your career, but not over your personal life.

It is you who oblige me to complain to you as a mother. Up until you left my care you seemed to be a conscientious and sensible girl, aware of your duties and of my demands. As an unfortunate mother, I thought you would always remain as I educated you, with the rare foundations you yourself claim I offered you. But instead of more love or trust towards me, I see things that surprise and disappoint me.

I brought you up from a tender age not just to have a head full of knowledge and operas, but to be a person with a soul and goodness. Now you may well be saying that I am crazy and self-interested. Not at all. Everything you do and all your letters show a lack of gratitude rather than trust in your mother, whom you know to have a sensible and rare soul and sensitivity.

You decided to marry so soon, too soon. . . . You should at least have opened your heart before deciding, asked my opinion even through our correspondence, out of courtesy and as a duty to the mother who bore you, if only as a point of form. But you went and married without further thought and without showing the superiority of your character even to your husband himself. . . .

You did not need to marry anybody, or become rich in three years— you would become much richer than Battista—nor cut yourself off in Italy. . . . To feel such joy for fame and fortune is sinful. You are so young and strong that you could have overcome any obstacle and fatigue. If you couldn't have eight furs, two would do. We don't just live for ourselves, nor for great wealth. There are so many other things that unfortunately are watched and discussed in society, and these are the ones that a young artist like you, with moral and family principles, ought to heed. . . .

You even allow Battista to feel that you don't care about your relatives, which is a hair-raising thing to come from my child, Mary. How I wish—Maria, it is my soul that speaks to you now—that you were still the Mary of 1945! I would have wanted you to be kinder, more generous, more tender. . . . I would have liked you to be Maria the good and caring, and your fame to give me joy. You rose to fame very young, you made your own money, you don't need a man any longer. If you become sweeter and more human, you will live better and God will protect you doubly. My soul is sad and my heart aches for you when I think that you have cast me aside despite your promises, you have broken the family bond. But marriage ought to bring people together rather than divide them.

You write to me that I ought not to worry about you and lead my own life. Why, my daughter, are you being silly? To lead what life? You, of course, do not care if I mop floors and I live in a cemetery. Shame on you! Don't you know that, until her death, a mother will only care for the life and the happiness of her children and nothing else? If you think differently, my Maria, never become a mother. . . .

How you have changed, little Mary. Think back a bit what I went through for you, the beautiful youth I sacrificed. And never write bitter words to me. . . . You write twice that you are not rich but only well-off; then you ought not to have thought of marriage. And next time don't write that your house is so small that it has no space for your mother. How dare you? Did it not hurt your hand to write such a thing? Mary, think what you write, for God's sake. . . . I forgive you because other reasons probably pushed you into writing so thoughtlessly. There is always room for Mother. Anyway, I did not ask to come [to Verona] during the honeymoon, but as a mother I have the right to see my child again and to meet my son-in-law; and you must show the world and your new relatives that you have parents. You know what cinema artists of humble origins do [as soon as they become rich]. In the first month they spend their first money to make a home for their parents and spoil them with luxuries; and they send their mothers for six months to a school to learn manners, how to appear and behave, in order to present them in their homes. You have nothing like that to fear. At least I can't imagine you do. What have you got to say, Maria?

I hope that you read this letter quietly and without anger. I have a duty to remind you of some things, and your youth induces me to be a little harsh. I do hope that you will revert a little to your past. . . . I kiss you and do not tarry replying for it saddens me.

Mama [7]

In June 1950, again probably at Meneghini's instigation, Maria made one last attempt to mend fences with Litsa by inviting her to join her in Mexico City, where she would be singing. Shortly before that though, she had written a letter to her husband saying: "*She does not get along with my father. He also is not well. He still has diabetes and now a heart condition. My mother wants to leave him, but I said to her, 'How can you abandon him now, when he's old and sick?' Battista, she wants to come and live with us. May God forgive me, Battista, but right now I want to be alone with you in our home. Under no circumstances am I willing to compromise my happiness and my right to be alone with you a little. We deserve that, don't we? But how can I explain all this to my mother? . . . I will give her money so she can go somewhere to rest, in the mountains or the country, but I do not believe it is fair that she leave my father now."* Obviously Maria confused her feelings for her father, who was about to be abandoned again, with her legitimate fear of the overbearing Litsa settling in Verona and poisoning her newly found marital bliss. And a few days later Maria informed Meneghini about a nasty letter in which Litsa accused her of thinking only of herself and leaving her mother to die in poverty. *"I'm so disgusted I'm considering severing all relations with her,"* Maria concluded ominously.[8]

In Mexico relations between mother and daughter went from bad to worse. "You'll be pleased to have her with you," her colleague Giulietta Simionato remarked to Maria. *"Pleased?"* she answered. *"I would rather kill her! You don't know, but one day I'll tell you . . ."* And she asked Simionato to have meals with them, *"otherwise we'd tear each other's hair out!"*[9] In her memoirs Litsa does her best, as always, to paint a picture of an idyllic atmosphere between them, but even she has to admit that Maria "seemed as cold as ice" and that "the old mother-daughter relationship was gone." Needless to say, nowhere does Litsa consider the possibility that she herself might have been to blame for Maria's coldness, not only because of her usual overbearance but also by her amorous behavior with a member of the Mexico Opera chorus.[10] In the quieter moments of their stay in Mexico, Maria and her mother sometimes touched on the thorny subject of Litsa's relationship with George. The account that Litsa gave later is typical of the unscrupulous way in which she was later prepared to distort facts or even invent them. It is hard to believe, for example, that Maria actually asked her straight out why she had not divorced George, as Litsa alleges: *"'Jackie and I used to talk about it,'* she said. *'We thought you were stupid not to divorce him.'"* To which Litsa gave the classic answer: "I didn't divorce him because of you two." And when she asked her daughter, "How would *you* act if your Battista behaved to you as your father does to me?" *"I'd take a hammer and break everything he owns with it,"* Maria supposedly said, and her next remark, again as reported by Litsa, even vindicated Litsa against Maria's own contrary beliefs and repressed emotions: *"You are very stupid, Mother, not to get a divorce. You have plenty of cause."*[11] When one considers all the facts set out in the pages of this book, and Maria's own admissions of the pain she suffered when her mother finally broke with her father for good, it seems safe to assume that Litsa's accounts of conversations like this one must have been fabricated with mischievous intent.

One crucial moment in Mexico City came when Maria, lying one day on her mother's bed, checked under the mattress and discovered a bank statement showing that, while constantly asking for more, Litsa had put aside a not negligible sum. Maria wrote of this *"nest egg of 1,500 or two thousand dollars"* in late 1956 with indignation. Another significant tête-à-tête occurred when Litsa urged Maria to give Jackie one of two diamond rings that Meneghini had offered her. Giulietta Simionato, who witnessed the scene, described it afterward and still remembers it vividly: "Maria reacted very badly to this request. Pushing her mother out of the dressing room, she said to her, *'When my sister is working as I am and has found a husband like my husband,* then *she can claim something from me!'* She slammed the door in Litsa's face and flung herself into an armchair, exhausted. . . . *'I can't stand that woman: she has ruined my life!'"* Whereupon she started crying "like a little girl" and Simionato perceived that "hidden behind that hard shell was a fragile, sensitive woman."[12]

By this time Maria decided that the only way out of the fatally destructive relationship with her mother was to break with her completely. Having come to this conclusion, she treated Litsa politely but coldly, bought her a fur coat, gave her enough money to keep her for a year, and paid for her return air ticket. Maria left Mexico a few days before her mother, without having said anything about her hardening resolve to have nothing more to do with her. When they said goodbye at the airport, it was to be the last time they ever saw each other. Maria's coldness and unapproachability over the next few months gradually made it clear to Litsa that things were serious. When Maria went back to Mexico for another season, in 1951, she invited her father to go with her instead of her mother. Litsa was livid and informed her daughter—almost vindictively, one might say—of her decision to leave George for good and go back to Athens. Maria felt that Litsa's move to desert her husband, now a sick man approaching seventy, simply added insult to injury: to her it was the last straw which aggravated unbearably her own deepest trauma.

Back in Athens and penniless, Litsa was once again reduced to sponging on Jackie and Jackie's lover of thirteen years' standing, Miltiadis Embirikos. After trying unsuccessfully to obtain an allowance from George, she redoubled her pressure on Maria in a stream of letters which Jackie describes as "intemperate" and "badly expressed." To Meneghini Litsa wrote asking, "Who is Maria? . . . Her duty is to write her mother every week, no matter how hard up for cash she is." She went on to say she intended to go to Verona to see her daughter that winter: "I will not ask her if she likes it or not," she added. "I never ask my children what I am going to do or not do." Maria then confided to her godfather that her mother *"wrote a letter cursing, etc., as is her usual way (she thinks) of obtaining things, saying also that she didn't bring me into this world for nothing—she said she gave birth to me, so I should maintain her. That phrase—I'm sorry, but it is hard to digest."* And Jackie comments: "If we hadn't long ago realized that Evangelia had been as much concerned about getting away from George as she had been about helping either of her daughters, these pleas might have received a more sympathetic hearing. As it was, both Maria and I knew that Mother was utterly selfish." Gradually Maria stopped even bothering to reply, and Litsa decided to sue George for maintenance in the New York courts. She won her case and was awarded twenty-five dollars a week (which was never paid), but by taking this course she only hastened the final breach with Maria: "Her mother refused to heed her advice, and left George Callas," Meneghini notes in his memoirs. "Maria became incensed once again and told me that under no circumstances was I ever to mention her mother again."[13]

Litsa, whose letters at this time Jackie describes as "bordering on the unhinged," now asked Maria to send her a regular monthly allowance of a hundred dollars. Was it not her due? After all she had sacrificed etc. etc. etc., she wrote. This letter was probably written by Jackie herself, who says: "When Mother finally left my father, she landed on me. So I wrote and told Maria that I wasn't asking for anything for myself, but that she ought to send Mother something, say a hundred dollars a month. That was nothing to her, whereas I felt bad about being a constant burden on Milton. Very stingy, however, my sister was! So she thought that if she suddenly broke off relations with her mother, her mother would never ask her for money again. Some pretty nasty letters were exchanged, and that was that." Litsa's version of the story of those notorious letters is that, having temporarily broken off her engagement to Miltiadis, Jackie asked Maria to help her start a musical career in Italy, and that the first of Maria's insulting letters was her reply to this request from her sister. According to Litsa, it was in a second letter, this time to herself, who had written asking for an allowance of a hundred dollars a month, that Maria poured irreverent abuse upon her.[14]

Whether there was one begging letter or two, Jackie states that Maria's answer was vicious in the extreme: "Not only was there to be no money and no further correspondence, but she went on to tell Mother that as she, Maria, had to 'bark' for a living, why didn't Mother also get a job? But it was the ending that shocked us both: *'Now that it is summer, go to the shore and get some fresh air. If, as you say, you still have no money, you had better jump in the river and drown yourself.'*" In Litsa's version the equally obnoxious rebuff was worded slightly differently: "*I can give you nothing. Money is not like flowers, growing in gardens. . . . I bark for my living. You are a young woman, and you can work. If you can't earn enough to live on, throw yourself out of the window.*" Apparently Litsa wrote once more, asking her daughter why she was being so hard-hearted, to which Maria is supposed to have answered tersely, "*Don't waste time and ink.*"[15] These retorts have been widely quoted and have come to be accepted without question. However, no one has ever seen them in black and white and it is reasonable to wonder, if not whether the letters actually existed, at least exactly how they were worded. While Litsa states that at the time of writing her memoirs (1959–60) she still had that letter (from Maria to Jackie), Jackie wrote that she tore up the offending letter (from Maria to Litsa) after reading it aloud to her mother. In conversation, however, she said it was torn up by Litsa "in a fury," together with all her other letters from Maria. In conclusion, the content of that letter (or letters) remains unverified:

clearly the tone must have been very unpleasant, but Maria always denied—even in private conversation with John Ardoin—that she had used the words and phrases attributed to her.[16]

Although Jackie was to write later that she was "not unsympathetic to Maria's anger," it would seem that she never really appreciated its depth and intensity. Consequently she tried to convince her that "despite all the exaggerations, [Maria] owed a great deal to Mother's obsessive promotion of her talents, whatever her underlying motives may have been." Needless to say, the only result was to provoke her sister to still greater fury. "I didn't speak to her again for nine years—not until 1960, when father came to Greece and we made it up," Jackie says now. To her mother, on the contrary, Maria never spoke another word nor did she have any contact with her, except occasionally to give her money, and this always through an intermediary. Whatever she sent, however, seems never to have been enough. Twenty-four years later, in August 1975, she wrote in exasperation to her godfather Lanzounis: "*As for my mother and sister—how my sister can buy and furnish a lovely home on her own and beg for a part-time maid to me, I cannot understand. I also give my sister some money every month and I know she does not need [it]. She's had Embiricos's inheritance. Then why beg for $200? . . . It's the cheapness of their souls I cannot stand! They never say, Maria, how are you? Do you need anything? Are you sick? Everybody cares about me but [in reality] they never gave a damn about me. It's not new but I still cannot get used to it. Only when they need money do they write. Never mind—forgive my complaining but it's a pity we are not a united family. We all would have been less lonely.*"[17]

—⚬⚬⚬—

Among Meneghini's papers were three letters that Maria had kept in a blue envelope. On it he had written in red ink: "Lettera [sic] Maria della sua Mama." These hitherto unpublished letters, written in Greek, are of great interest for what they tell us not only about the feud between mother and daughter but also about Litsa's character and—to a lesser extent—Maria's character as well.[18]

Athens, 14 Aug. '51

Dear Maria,

I simply can't bear not to wish you many happy returns on your name day. You seem to have grown tired of me, but I, as a mother, do not grow tired of the children I brought into the world, especially you, whom I have worshipped as a god, and more. Maria, I should like you to know that all my life I have taken no risks with my children or my own good name. Now, however, if my own children are in a position to judge me harshly—well, there's nothing to stop you, nothing I can do about it. Thank you for the money you offered to send, but I would rather you paid off your debt to your father, which he thinks is 2,000 dollars [plus]

25 dollars to the St. Moritz Hotel where you stayed with Simionato and
3.50 for the telegram he sent to Mexico for you. You remember I was ill
in hospital. I heard about it afterward, to my sorrow, as he spends his
time dallying in *caffeteries* [?]. But I, the "crazy old woman," prevented
him from writing to your husband to ask him for that money. I am a
straightforward person, unhypocritical, and I lose out; your good father
is notoriously two-faced and a hypocrite, and he comes out on top. I may
never see you again before I die, but I shall write and tell you about a
great secret of your father's, which I have been keeping to myself all these
years. I hope your triumphs continue, and I hope you stay well.

> Best wishes from your sister. I kiss you.
> Mother

The inference to be drawn from this letter is that by this time Maria had
already rebelled openly against her mother and had called her a "crazy old woman,"
either orally or in writing. She had, nevertheless, offered to send a certain sum of
money to her. Litsa, an extremely angry woman with vitriol in her pen, turns
treacherously against her husband with calumnious insinuations and the vague
hint that she knows a "great secret" about him. Asked today what this could be,
Jackie can only suggest the situation that, according to Litsa, had made George im-
migrate to America: leaving the mayor of Meligalas's young daughter with child.
But she thinks it more likely that the "great secret" was no more than evil slander,
at which "mother was always first!"[19]

In the same blue envelope Maria had also kept a letter from Meneghini to
Litsa, translated ungrammatically into Greek, in Litsa's handwriting and without
date, and subsequently sent by Litsa to her husband in New York, with additional
comments and a covering letter, also in Greek.

> Most honored and beloved Mother,
>
> I have felt for some time that the letters Maria has received from home
> have been upsetting her and making her angry. To prevent this from
> happening any more, with consequences that could be disastrous, I have
> decided to write to you myself. I took your last letter to a Greek [here
> Litsa adds, "A whopping lie," insinuating that Maria herself had read
> them to him], who translated it for me. To my great displeasure I saw that
> the letter was malicious, vindictive, and offensive, and those things can-
> not be written by a good mother. You are full of vindictiveness which my
> wife does not deserve, and I return your insults to you. I also have to
> think of my wife's health and her dignity, seeing that she can't expect
> that from you. I warn you, if you write another letter I will have it trans-
> lated and I will not give it to Maria. But I hope that does not happen.
> Think carefully, signora, about every sentence you write. Remember, sig-

nora, I have obligations to the family that I have made with her and to any children we may have. And I will not allow our life to be spoiled by anybody. And I shall send your letters back with the same effrontery as you show in writing them. You are a woman who has lived her life, and I do not think Maria will forget her responsibilities and her family. And I have taken on all the responsibilities, signora, but it is Maria who comes next after me. Maria has done more than she needed to, especially in Mexico, and she has given you a large sum of money to keep you for a whole year, and next year <u>we shall see</u>. And I will not allow you to indulge in the insulting and degrading language you have heaped on her, otherwise we shall reach the point of breaking off our friendly relations. Be very careful not to behave in a vulgar way, and <u>do not utter any threats</u>. You would do better to consider your station—Maria is up to her ears in her work—and not to say whatever comes into your head.

We are glad you are having a good time with Jackie. Last year we had her to stay with us in Italy, but she [soon] decided to heed the pressing call of Athens.

[Here Litsa adds to George: "He means Milton, swine that he is, but what a letter for Jackie to have written to him! As we were told by that Greek-Italian lady who read us his letter, he is shockingly common in his language."]

And Litsa continues in her covering letter:

George, I forgot to mention that your son-in-law said in his letter that it is too soon for Jackie to ask for her sister's hospitality. "We have had her to stay with us before, some years ago," [he added]. "And if you happen to be passing through Italy, signora, we may invite you to stay, too." So now, if he happens to write to you too (for as you see he is a real swine), you must send us his letter and we will send you a letter in Italian to put him in his place. I have told them that to me Maria is dead, and as for him, I consider him a stranger and shall simply ignore him. Never in my life did I imagine she would so degrade her family in the eyes of those Italians. Write to her at once and tell her that it was wicked of her to get her family involved and worse still to get that Italian to insult her mother, and tell her to pay you back the money you spent for her, and never again say that you have a daughter. She once said that we were exploiters. Write and tell her to rejoice in her money, wallow in it, and enjoy her life with the Italians. It is appalling, absolutely unheard-of anywhere in the world that anyone should make four people unhappy for no reason. And it was all because I said to her, "Maria, your father is sick and, as you know, sometimes he works and sometimes he doesn't, so please, if you possibly can, give me a small sum of money every month so that I don't have to be a burden on Milton any more, because it reflects badly on us, and I'll never bother you again once the matter of your sister is settled." Write to her at once and mention that terrific present she gave you, that wallet. [Here a line is crossed out in black ink.] And it would be a good thing if you put it in an envelope and sent it to her by registered post with a letter saying, "As you have done so much for your family, have your wallet back, you may need to sell it." If you don't do that, you're a fool. She told me in Mexico that you should consider it a fine present and you oughtn't to complain because it cost 20 dollars, what more can you ask. "Look here, my girl," I said to her, "when you've been away for three years, bathed in glory, is that all he's worth, an old man like him—a wallet?" And she answered, "It's more than he's worth." I didn't want to tell you that as I was afraid it would upset you. If you get a letter from her, put her in her place. And send it to us.

Litsa

The most striking thing about these nauseating letters is the strong language used by both Litsa and Meneghini, who was almost the same age as his mother-in-law. Litsa talks disparagingly about the Italians, having seemingly forgotten about her own dealings with them in the occupation and her love affair with Mario Bonalti. Even more significant, however, is her ill-concealed duplicity and her attempts to play father and daughter off against each other. She even urges George to demand repayment of Maria's "debt" to him (not forgetting three dollars and fifty cents for a telegram) and to disown her forever! Altogether her letters typify the sort of person Litsa was; and that is why Maria had kept them meticulously.

Maria made brief allusion to this subject in 1956, saying that when she received her mother's letter she was so upset that she had to take to her bed. Meneghini then had it read and, unable to control himself, had replied on his own that *"he would not allow my mother to do anything that would distress me. Another painful exchange of letters followed, and we ended up, unfortunately, breaking off relations."*[20] Seventeen years later, Maria denied in a television interview that she had ever written to her mother in the forthright terms quoted above and repeatedly referred to in books and articles: *"No, I have never said that. That was 'Time' magazine, a certain de Carvalho, who wanted to be very smart, so he had to create a very sensationalist story. As a matter of fact, I have never spoken against my mother, though I could have, frequently. . . . [Yes, I did cut her off completely] because at a certain moment she used blackmail, unfortunately. . . . I mean, she said: 'Either you give me this and that or otherwise I'll* [inaudible] *you against all the newspapers.' And that she did. But I cannot give in to her."*[21]

Also found among Meneghini's papers was a sheaf of handwritten notes by Maria refuting statements made by George de Carvalho in his article "The Prima Donna" (*Time*, 29 October 1956). On the subject of her quarrel with Litsa over

Excerpts from Litsa's letter to George Kaloyeropoulos.

money, she has this to say: "*It is true that my mother asked me for money at that time and I refused, because two months earlier I had paid (she was with me in Mexico, at my expense, of course) about two thousand dollars to the state for my return journey from Greece and for money lent to me by the state, which I naturally passed on to my mother for household expenses, and then I had bought her a three-quarter-length mink coat (the furrier, X? of Mexico, can testify to that) and I had also given her a thousand dollars for her personal expenses, which she promised me should last her a year, as she did not need money as she was living with my father and had set aside a nest egg of 1,500 or two thousand dollars!! I left Mexico without a penny. Also because I had repaid 750 dollars to my godfather for her journey from Greece to America. And I was not rich then—far from it! Nor did I want to be a great burden on my husband—for anyone who has the sensibility to understand that—because in the first year of one's married life it is embarrassing to be continually asking for money. And then she wanted to get a divorce from my father, and that was what made me angry.* [Here she has crossed out the words: "*I couldn't bear the idea of divorce.*"] *At that age people do not get divorced. And on top of all that [my mother] had written offensive letters to Battista.*"[22]

Maria admits in this revealing text that what gave her the greatest pain of all was the fact that her mother had walked out on her father. This admission touches

Excerpt from "Smentite di articolo 'Time,'" Mary's notes refuting George de Carvalho's "calumnies" in *Time* magazine, 29 October 1956.

on the very heart of the matter and lays bare the underlying cause of Maria's estrangement from Litsa. The process of her disaffection had started when little Mary heard her mother continually heap abuse on her father. It was completed in 1951, when Litsa "officially" left George and sued him for maintenance. Maria, of course, would never have dreamed of breathing a word about the other reasons for the ultimate rejection of her mother—Litsa's amorality and self-degradation, especially during the occupation in Athens—even though it was so painful to her, or rather for that very reason. To what has already been said on the subject one need only add the shocking revelation Maria made to John Ardoin in 1968: *"One evening when I was working late in a classroom at the conservatory, one of the teachers assaulted me and tried to rape me. I broke free and ran home in tears to tell my mother. Do you know what she said to me? 'A pity he didn't manage it—then we would have made him marry you and that would have been that!'"*[23]

Litsa later defended herself histrionically, as one might expect. In an interview with a Greek journalist she said, "We all know what's being said about me, but there isn't a grain of truth in any of it. I have always tried to do the best I could with my children. Being human, I may have done some things wrong, but not at my children's expense. I'm not about to be judged by human beings but only by God, when He sees fit to call me, because only God knows how much I went through to bring up those children." She was presumably alluding to her dealings with the occupying forces, but also to her daughter's accusations concerning the break-up of her marriage with George Kaloyeropoulos. In 1957, in Athens, Maria thundered, *"And who told her to leave him and come and live over here? Let her go back to my father!"*[24] And this, of course, was the most deep-rooted trauma, the one from which she suffered all her life. Maria Moundouri, the distant cousin from Thessaloniki with whom she always was on the best of terms (in 1957 she even took her on as her secretary and companion), says now, "That was the root of the trouble: it was a great blow to her when her parents separated. Divorce wasn't as common then as it is now, and I know she felt very bitter about it." Maria's feelings on the subject are also illuminated by the testimony of her first cousin Katie Dimitriadou, the daughter of Litsa's brother Filon, who had got to know her uncle George well when he was back in Greece, living with his second wife, Alexandra Papajohn: "Maria once asked me to look after her father and told me straight out, *'I adore my father because he has always treated me right; and I also have a soft spot for him because we weren't living together for long.'"* But when Katie attempted to talk about Litsa, Maria interrupted her abruptly: *"Please drop that subject! I don't want to talk about it. For me the matter is closed!"*[25]

Litsa was a frustrated, cantankerous, stubborn, obdurate person, and in the final analysis a complete failure as a mother according to the testimony of her own children. Being endowed with strength of character and sublime egocentricity, she approached her personal relationships, especially those with her husband and children, in an uncompromising spirit and without the least trace of discretion or flexibility. At the same time, seemingly out of stubbornness, she was always being gratuitously aggressive, as in that 1951 letter to Mary in which she called George a two-faced hypocrite. Needless to say, this kind of attitude was bound to widen the breach with her daughter. In her memoirs Litsa reveals that she discussed the problem with a number of psychiatrists. She thought that she had alienated her daughter by "excessive devotion," and that the "ugly duckling" and "friendless" childhood stories were tales Mary "may have told herself as a child" and which she still believed. Mary really was an insecure little girl who needed someone strong to cling to, Litsa believed, and "who must convince herself that she needs to depend upon no one but herself." The voice of Maria when under stress, which Litsa heard on the radio or television, reminded her of little Mary's voice after her road accident in 1929 or when she wept inconsolably on seeing her canaries dead in 1944. She summed up categorically that her daughter accepted "kindness and friendships and love" from those whom she later ignored, because she was afraid to admit to herself that she was "like anyone else who needs help and security."[26]

Admittedly there may be a measure of truth in some of Litsa's opinions, but they completely ignore all the factors that had been instrumental in turning Mary against her. Of her own treatment of her husband in New York, of her blatant affairs with other men in Athens, of the way she showed off Mary's talents on the radio in America and to her Italian and German admirers in Greece, of the pressure she put on her daughter to go out and start making money in a third-rate job, of the fundamentally amoral approach to life she instilled in her children, of the example she set and the encouragement she gave to the formation of liaisons with officers of the occupying forces, of her constant interventions in Mary's private life, of her never-ending financial demands: of all this Litsa does not say a word. In 1962 she would go so far as to claim unblushingly in public that her husband had abandoned her and that she had never had a fight in her life: "In fact we were so happy in Greece that Greek people were jealous of us. We were three beloved in nest, so close . . ." she would claim in imperfect English, concluding disingenuously: "I don't know what happened to her . . ."[27]

"Litsa was a terror—spiteful and ungrateful. If we don't understand what sort of person her mother was, we will fail to understand many traits of Maria's character." So says a family friend who still remembers how in the mid-1950s Litsa, to spite Maria (who by then had broken off relations with her), thought up the idea of putting Jackie forward as a second and greater Callas. "She humiliated poor Jackie with this thoroughly evil and ill-conceived scheme of hers, just so that she could use her as a tool in her own feud with Maria." Evidently the unscrupulous mother resorted to every kind of psychological pressure, including table-turning and consultations with a medium, to secure the collaboration of her compliant elder daughter against the "ungrateful" Maria. Weak-willed Jackie agreed to give it a try, for she did have a good voice. When it turned out that she could not cope with the unrelenting demands of a professional career ("I had a voice, but not the

Litsa Dimitriadou-
Kaloyeropoulou.

other necessary attributes," she admits today), Litsa's feelings toward the one who had "failed her" underwent a profound and lasting change. "Indeed, Litsa was the shame of the whole family!" her cousin Titina Koukouli reflects today.[28]

Needless to say, at the very least there would have been less acrimony between them if Litsa—and to a lesser extent Maria—had been by nature less aggressive; and much else would probably have turned out differently, too. It may be true that Maria's behavior toward her mother was occasionally harsh, but on the whole it was justified and even inevitable. Nevertheless, her predilection for her father was to a considerable extent prejudiced, since George, by his attitude and conduct in general, had certainly contributed to the breakdown of the marriage. Showing unmistakably what a little person he really was, in June 1949 he wrote his newly married daughter with nauseating disregard for the truth: "Be sure that I am the best of husbands, that I've loved, I love, and will love my wife. May your husband love you as much as I love my wife."[29] Furthermore, George had never actually done anything to encourage or support his daughter in her musical career; and toward the end of his life he too had pestered her for a regular allowance. But Maria tended to overlook these failings of his, whereas she sustained her implacable hostility to the pitiful Litsa, whom she blamed for nearly everything. In the final analysis it was Jackie who really suffered most at the hands of their mother. Maria, whom Litsa always considered to be indebted to her for the discovery of her "golden voice," fortunately had the strength of character to leave home and manage her own life, without being weighed down by an exaggerated sense of obligation to her parents. Meanwhile, whether she liked it or not, she had learned some lessons—a good many, some would say—from the terrible Litsa. Looking back on it now, from this distance in time, having overcome numerous difficulties in her life, Jackie may perhaps be able to derive some satisfaction from the thought that some of her sacrifices indirectly helped her sister to develop into the miracle known as Maria Callas.

—⚬—

God, how many mothers would have adored to have a child like me?

To John Ardoin, Dallas, September 1968

Maria Callas: An Assessment

The historical importance of Maria Callas is twofold: she renewed the operatic repertoire and she upgraded the importance of its dramatic element. With regard to the first, she rescued from oblivion works which, though of not inconsiderable merit, had been long forgotten because for decades there had been no singers with the vocal and histrionic talents to perform them. As Rodolfo Celletti remarked in 1996 on the occasion of the revival of *L'Ultimo Giorno di Pompei*, a forgotten opera by Giovanni Pacini (1796–1867), "Fifty years ago no one would have thought of rediscovering Pacini. Today, everything is being discovered anew. Thus musical theater is still alive. And that is partly due to one singer: Maria Callas."[1] Naturally, there is a backlash among some people who think there was no reason to disinter works which, in their opinion, had rightly been forgotten: works like *La Vestale* or *Poliuto*, for example, add nothing to the known masterpieces of the operatic repertoire, nor do today most "new" operas performed worldwide. However, quite apart from the fact that such opinions are subjective and liable to change from one decade to the next, those people forget that such operas as *Medea*, *Anna Bolena*, *Armida*, and even the rather uninspired *Il Pirata*, as performed by Maria Callas in the 1950s, had a thoroughly revitalizing effect: they paved the way for the rehabilitation and meaningful revival of truly great composers such as Bellini, Donizetti, and Rossini, all of whose works—apart from a doctored *Norma*, a mangled *Lucia*, and the hackneyed *Barbiere*—had been completely neglected.

The second and more important side of Callas's historical contribution to opera was her more theatrical approach, in other words the reinstatement and enhancement of drama vis-à-vis music. Leaving aside the relative merits of the resuscitated operas and composers, the expansion of the repertoire that she initiated created new openings for the singers who came after Callas, encouraging a more professional attitude to their work and above all a more theatrical comportment on stage. Callas was totally convincing in her performance of these forgotten operas and, by her brilliant dramatic approach to their purely musical and vocal material, she gave meaning and stature to the operas themselves. Her achievement is complex: having mastered the techniques of sheer virtuosity, the unerring runs and vocal fireworks—all superficially dazzling but in themselves meaningless—she applied them in such a way as to bring her various roles to life convincingly, using the musical element of opera in order to emphasize equally its dramatic dimension. In other words, Callas made use of her purely technical accomplishments to discipline her singing and exercise absolute control over her vocal resources; this made it possible for her to give the characters of her heroines the dramatic individuality and consistency that was characteristic of her performances. Thanks to this historic contribution of hers, singers since her time, even if they lack her qualities, have followed her example by adopting a more theatrical and therefore more convincing approach to a form of art that had previously been moribund.[2]

In 1960, during the preparation of *Norma* in Epidavros, Tullio Serafin described Maria Callas as "the greatest prima donna the world has ever seen." While this statement, which appeared only in the Greek press, has hitherto remained unknown, one piece of testimony that Callas's detractors have seized upon with glee is a statement made by none other than the same Serafin: "Let's have no illusions about it, the real vocal phenomena of our century have been Rosa Ponselle, Titta Ruffo, and Caruso. All the others have been merely good singers."[3] When, in 1995, Lord Harewood, who had followed Maria's career ever since 1947, was asked why Serafin had not included Callas among his "miracles," he answered shrewdly: "As an Italian, he ultimately came down to voice. I think he thought that Callas hadn't got as good a voice as Ponselle, Ruffo, and Caruso, and he might well have been right. But he taught her to do more on the whole than most of what even they achieved." In 1958, shortly after Maria had provoked a furor by dropping out halfway through a gala performance of *Norma* attended by the president of Italy in Rome, Serafin had already said, "Of course I can't feel any affection for Callas, considering how much gratitude she has shown me and how she has behaved toward me, but when people start making comparisons and talk about replacing her, I really can't understand it. Or rather, it seems to me that *they* don't understand that Callas is an actress, a great actress, while the others, even the best of them, are merely singers."[4]

Then in 1965, three years before Serafin died, Stelios Galatopoulos asked him if he thought that Callas's voice was ugly or beautiful. "Which voice?" Serafin asked in return. "Norma's, Violetta's, Amina's? I have known many of Callas's voices; I could go on; there was Isolde . . . Do you know, I have never really considered whether her voice was ugly or beautiful. I only know that it was always the right one, and this is more than beautiful!" The eighty-seven-year-old maestro explained what he meant: "Those singers were endowed by nature with a truly miraculous beauty and intensity of voice. Technically, too, their voices were highly accomplished. Of course they perfected their vocal technique, but they had started with exceptional and perhaps unprecedented vocal resources. Yet they did not have the genius of Callas, nor did they shed any real new light on their art. Callas was not a miracle. She was very gifted by nature, but all the gifts of God had been given to her as raw material only. In order to succeed she always needed a great deal of hard work, determination, and absolute dedication. Perhaps that is why she left her art richer than she had found it."[5]

Alas, the extraordinary vocal range of a *soprano drammatico d'agilità*—in Callas's case from the A below middle C to F above the stave—can only be acquired and maintained at a price. With very few exceptions, the cost includes unevenness of sound, inequality of registers, tone problems, loss of control in some parts of the range, reduced volume, and harshness in some notes (the high ones, in Callas's case). Vocal fluency—that is to say the coloratura—of the *soprano drammatico* tends to be somewhat restricted, and usually runs and *fioriture* cannot be sung as rapidly as by a *soprano leggero*. On the other hand, the slightly slower speed makes for more meaningful and expressive interpretation, with the result that singing is not merely a matter of vocal acrobatics devoid of substance and significance, as it used to be before Callas's time. This leads us naturally on to the way in which Callas actually made good use of the defects of her voice, whether those defects were intrinsic or accidental, natural or acquired. For the fact is that one of her greatest qualities was, indeed, her ability to acknowledge her vocal problems, and, when she could (which was usually the case, except for her wobble), to put them to constructive use in her interpretation of the part. During the famous "Callas Debate" in November 1969, the Italian musicologist Fedele D'Amico made some perceptive remarks about the importance of "faults" in the history of music. The failure of musical instruments to achieve their original aim of imitating the human voice, he pointed out, had led to a continuous process of invention, giving rise to the idea of music as an autonomous art that relies solely on instruments, without reference to words or dramatic action. "*Mutatis mutandis* Maria Callas has done precisely the same thing," he continued. "If she had been born with an immaculate, velvety, perfect voice, . . . no doubt she would have succeeded as a singer, perhaps even been quite spectacular, but only as many (or perhaps few) others have been. She was in fact forced to become what she is precisely because of those natural imperfections of her 'instrument.'"[6]

Since Callas did not mind and, in fact, deliberately sacrificed a certain amount of what is traditionally called beauty of voice in order to perfect the interpretation of the part she was playing, the occasions when the "defect" was unintentional were indistinguishable from those when it was due to her own artistic choice. For example, when she was playing Lady Macbeth, she deliberately made her voice hard (or, in the opinion of many purists, harsh and ugly) so as to convey the blackness of heart of that particular heroine. And when talking about the way she sang Medea, Callas would use a rhetorical question, "*Could one say 'Serpenti, venite a me'. . . with a velvety voice?*"[7] But when she could not avoid straining her voice or making the transition from one register to another with a noticeable change of timbre, as was often the case, she took care to use the vocal flaw as an integral part of her interpretation and thus to make it, if not beautiful, at least unnoticeable or "inevitable." The final outcome was that Callas always succeeded (as long as her wobble was under control) in making the listener feel that there could not possibly be any better way of interpreting whatever it was she was singing, even if she was singing in a voice with rough edges or technical defects. "She makes you feel each time that her way is not just the best, but the only way," as Stelios Galatopoulos summed it up. And that in a repertoire spanning a hundred sixty years, from *Alceste* (1767) to *Turandot* (1926)![8]

Maria Callas's career, then, was a turning point in the history of opera, which she revitalized dramatically when it most needed it. To put it simply, perhaps over-simply, it was thanks to Callas that opera came back to life and became, more than ever before, not only music but theater as well. Theatrical interpretation, unlike musical interpretation, is able to renew itself and keep up with the times: stage directing, scenery and costume design, lighting, color schemes, and indeed the whole approach to performance are constantly being updated. Opera, too, from the time of its resuscitation through the art of Maria Callas, acquired a capacity for self-renewal which it still has and will probably have for a long time to come. This immortality, if we may call it that, is largely due to the kiss of life given to it by the gifted Greek diva. As for other great sopranos who came after her—again stating the argument in its simplest terms—Joan Sutherland, for example, was undeniably a great singer; but Sutherland would never have been Sutherland *if Callas had not gone before*. In other words, even if one accepts the opinion that there are and have been since Callas's time other sopranos with equally good or even better voices, dramatic talent, or stage presence, the fact remains that no other has possessed the magic *combination of all these talents* that made Callas unique.

Nevertheless, there are some who insist on denying Maria Callas's historical importance in the revival of bel canto and in the development of opera since the mid twentieth century. According to them, whereas Adelina Patti sang to please the frivolous musical taste of the Victorians with her displays of vocal acrobatics, in the 1920s and '30s Claudia Muzio, Rosa Ponselle, and some other less well-known singers made an almost conscious effort to apply Verdi's famous dictum, "Ritorniamo all'antico e sarà un progresso." This point of view has been stated in writing by Rupert Christiansen, who asserts that the bel canto revival started long before Callas, between the wars, when many dramatic sopranos—whose principal mentor was Serafin—resuscitated forgotten operas by some of Verdi's precursors such as Rossini, Bellini, and Donizetti, emphasizing their dramatic rather than their purely technical vocal potentialities. This revival, Christiansen maintains, was interrupted by World War II, but even without Callas it would have regained its momentum in the 1950s.[9] History, however, cannot be written on the basis of unsubstantiated hypotheses, and in the early postwar years no trace can be found of the continuation of a revival whose previous existence is, in any case, itself largely hypothetical.

Indeed, in the few years after the war, it was Maria Callas, and she alone, who suddenly rose to her full stature and placed her tremendous gifts at the disposal of the astonished and excited Serafin. Undoubtedly, for decades past, Serafin had worked with all the great sopranos of the day, but none had raised true bel canto out of the oblivion into which it had sunk. That is why, when Maria sang for Serafin and for Francesco Siciliani "Qui la voce" for the first time, in October 1948, Siciliani was overwhelmed and Serafin had tears streaming down his face. When Callas heard recordings of Luisa Tetrazzini and Amelita Galli-Curci, she scorned their way of singing. Having studied with Elvira de Hidalgo, who was cast in the same mold as them, she appreciated their genuine vocal accomplishments; but she did not consider those accomplishments sufficient. For Callas, as Bruce Burroughs wrote in 1989, "purely vocal ease and excellence . . . had to be mated to and, when necessary, sacrificed for a perfect musical and dramatic truth." So, when she made her appearance in Italy, most living prima donnas lamented, among other things, the unevenness of her voice, which they found appalling; in contrast, they held up Tebaldi, and her "angelic" voice, as a paragon. *After my début in Italy I was not loved that much,*" Maria recalled twenty years later. *"I was something new to listen to and they disliked anything that took them away from tradition."*[10]

This sort of reaction was perhaps not altogether unconnected with the renowned preference of the Italians for their own singers. Be that as it may, the fact remains that Maria's obvious superiority was overlooked resolutely for a full four years, while those responsible at La Scala gave the limelight to second-rate (now mostly forgotten) Italian sopranos, even in operas in which Maria was already creating a sensation in smaller Italian theaters.[11] Even then, of course, there existed some "illuminated" exceptions, to begin with Tullio Serafin and Francesco Siciliani, who supported and promoted the young Callas as much as they could. Naturally, by the time she first sang Lucia at La Scala—under Karajan in 1954—things had changed and Callas's genius had been widely ackowledged. Toscanini's celebrated Lucia, Toti dal Monte, who was in the audience, went to Maria's dressing room after the performance and confessed to her, with tears in her eyes, that her interpretation had made her realize that she had never understood the role at all. Yet, not only had dal Monte heard all the most famous interpreters of Lucia and similar roles in her day, but she herself had been singing at the time of the supposed bel canto revival, and not just under Toscanini but under Serafin as well.[12]

—∞—

Maria Callas was not a well-read person and her general knowledge outside the field of music was very limited, sometimes shockingly so. Yannis Tsarouchis remembered showing her photographs of the Pompeii frescoes, which she was very taken with: *"What beautiful colors, what beautiful painting!"* she exclaimed. *"What a great artist this Pompeii was! When did she live?"* However, we should not forget that Maria grew up in an uncultured petit-bourgeois environment and left school at the age of thirteen. *"I am not an intellectual,"* she admitted once. *"Far from it. I deplore intellectualism,"* she went on, in a weak attempt to vindicate her own lack of it, *"which is the ruin of so many people. There is too much culture nowadays, and not enough instinct!"*[13] But where music was concerned, it was a very different matter. Walter Legge relates that Victor de Sabata once said to him, "If the public could understand, as we do, how deeply and utterly musical Callas is, they would be stunned." And Carlo Maria Giulini, who had the good fortune to conduct one of the greatest of Callas's performances, *La Traviata* at La Scala in 1955, frankly admitted that she knew the score of that opera better than he did.[14]

It is well known that Maria Callas hardly ever sang songs, and the few occasions when she did were all in Greece up to 1945, when she was required to sing them for examinations or recitals. Her detractors point to this as an indication that she did not possess the special vocal and cultural qualities needed for lieder singing, arguing that the various forms of art song are more difficult and demanding than opera. The widow of German-trained conductor Filoktitis Ikonomidis—with whom we saw Maria clashing on several occasions—was probably expressing her husband's view when she said, "The great singers of the past who sang all kinds of music, such as Lotte Lehmann, had the necessary education and rightly positioned voices. To sing anything other than Italian opera, one needs more culture."[15] Maria would flatly reject this point of view and argue passionately in defense of the paramount importance of instinct in art, as opposed to the purely cerebral exercise of the intellect. Then she would doubtless have gone on to explain that this was a myth cultivated by those who had not made the grade in opera, and that considering that she had studied under Elvira de Hidalgo and had had a natural leaning toward bel canto since her childhood, she had no time to take on lieder as well, with the seriousness that she always put into everything that she undertook.

Callas's astonishing success in Italian opera—and not only Italian, as her successes also included *Die Entführung aus dem Serail, Tiefland, Fidelio, Tristan und Isolde, Die Walküre, Parsifal,* and a fine recording of *Carmen*—had crowned her as the greatest prima donna of this century. In all probability she thought that singing lieder, *mélodies,* or *romanze* was something she might not do so well, and in any case it was a field she could explore in depth later in her career. Indeed, when her voice problems became more serious, she started singing songs which she believed were less taxing to her diminished vocal resources. Apart from *mélodies* of Fauré and those of Duparc—which, according to Michel Glotz, "she knew by heart"—she is said to have studied lieder by Liszt and *canzonette* by Bellini, and the last private recordings that were made of her voice in March 1976, with Jeffrey Tate at the piano, were the scene and concert aria "Ah, perfido!" by Beethoven (which was perhaps the first piece she had been given to learn by de Hidalgo in 1938), and shortly afterward, with Vasso Devetzi at the piano, "Im wunderschönen Monat Mai" from Schumann's *Dichterliebe.*[16] Maria did not live long enough to really concentrate on lieder, but that does not mean that she was incapable of distinguishing herself in that field as well. "It was entirely her own choice," insists her first concert accompanist, conductor Andreas Paridis. "If she had lived longer, she would most probably have done so. Many great singers turn to songs only when their voices start deteriorating, mainly because it is difficult to make one's name and an international career as a singer of lieder and *mélodies*."[17] And anyway, as George Jellinek wrote perceptively in 1960, "To understand her true significance we must also define her limitations. Maria Callas is *not* a universal singer in the sense Lilli Lehmann was or Victoria de los Angeles is today. The realm of the lied, the art song repertoire, oratorios, and the music of the baroque period do not engage her interest. Even in opera . . . as an absolute soprano, she has the means at her disposal that would assure technical mastery of practically all operatic roles. But . . . the Callas repertoire is composed of impersonations which have captured her sense of drama, human characters in which she can believe and whose feelings, emotions, reactions she can communicate through her interpretive art."[18]

—⁓—

The endless possibilities for "reliving" Maria Callas's voice and her art by means of the latest electronic sound reproduction systems could deal a body-blow to her legend. Continuous exposure will diminish and may eventually efface a great deal of the "mythical" quality of Maria Callas. The fact that we can never hear the recorded voices of Malibran, Pasta, Lind, or other great names of the distant past has undoubtedly helped to perpetuate their mythical dimension, a dimension that is much less noticeable in the reputations of singers of the more recent past. Although there is no reason to believe that Patti or Ponselle was in any way inferior to the legends of the first half of the nineteenth century, the existence of recordings of their voices, no matter how poor those recordings may be, has diminished their mythical stature. Imagination has turned into reality, exposed to cavil and faultfinding criticism, and reality usually erodes and eventually destroys the legend. While we have never heard the voices of the great prima donnas of the nineteenth century—even the pictures we have of them are the work of painters and engravers—the divas of the early twentieth century can be heard singing (or even talking) on remastered CDs, while their appearance is known to us from contemporary films, photographs, programs, magazines, and newspapers. The fact that Maria lived even more recently, combined with the intrusive attention she received from the sensation-seeking media of her time, puts her in a still more disadvantageous position.

Nevertheless, despite having to contend with this demythologizing process, Maria Callas today—more than twenty years after her death—is more of a legend and, at the same time, more alive than any other diva in the history of opera. Why is this? Could it be because the events of her life—especially her involvement with Aristotle Onassis—made her name known to a wide public that had probably never seen or heard an opera? Or because her unhappy last years and relatively early death provided ample scope for myth-making, which compensated for the negative effect of wide publicity and the frequent airing of her voice? One cannot help wondering how much would be left of the Callas myth today had she written her memoirs or autobiography, probably with much less success in "putting the truth straight" than she herself said she wanted. And how long would the myth have lasted, in spite of her significance as a historic phenomenon and the magic of her interpretative genius, if she were still alive, a white-haired old lady of seventy-something doing what so many other prima donnas have done and still do: teaching privately or in a conservatory, occasionally sitting as one of the judges at an international competition, giving the odd interview to the newspapers or on television? She might have dispensed valuable advice to singers of the younger generations, giving them the help of her immense experience. Indeed, she would probably be worshipped in operatic circles. But the Callas myth would probably not have been born, and would certainly not be growing still—as it does.

Above all, however, the Callas myth came into being—and will continue to exist—because of her greatness *as an interpreter*, not just as a great singer, nor as an incomparable actress (of which, alas, practically no visual testimony survives), but as an interpreter of such caliber that when we hear recordings of her voice we feel we can almost see her. Callas will always convey an almost visual impression of her art using aural means alone. When we hear Maria sing we see Medea, Lady Macbeth, Amina, or Anne Boleyn, whose personalities she assumed: "*It becomes a stage of identification, at times so complete that I feel I am her!*" she said in 1961.[19] When we listen to Callas singing now, more than fifty years after her incomparable performances, we actually see Norma, Lucia, Violetta, or Floria Tosca reincarnated in her form, the form of Maria. "Callas creates real people," said Fedele D'Amico in 1969. "She belongs to that rare species of actors—rare even in the straight theater —who manage to appear physically different according to the character they are playing."[20] Not only do we feel what someone once called her *sospiroso entrare*, but we feel the eyes of the audience riveted on her as if mesmerized. And then, listening only to the sound of her voice, we can feel all her changes of mood: now weeping, suffering, in torment, now cheerful, happy, exuberant, now loving and caressing, now full of hatred and imprecations.

Of course we lament the fact that there is so very little film footage of Maria Callas the actress, who too "fused in her person the grandeur of Sarah Bernhardt and the human modesty of Eleonora Duse."[21] Ultimately, however, this may help to sustain the Callas myth, her legendary dimension. More than twenty-three years after her death and almost forty years after the virtual death of her voice, the discovery of an unknown recording of one of her performances is still hailed as a major artistic and commercial event, however bad the quality of the sound may be or late in her career the recording made. For a new generation of listeners—the overwhelming majority of whom are too young to have heard or seen her in the flesh—Callas has been until recently the best-selling opera singer in the world, male or female, alive or dead. Only the antics of "the three tenors" temporarily eclipsed her commercial supremacy, and that is without counting the innumerable pirated recordings on the market, for which no statistics are available. In 1997 it was estimated that more than 30,000,000 of her records, cassettes, or CDs had been sold worldwide, with sales continuing to run at over 750,000 a year. Twenty years after the three tenors have taken their show off the road and certainly twenty years after their death—which may well be sixty or seventy years after the death of Maria—the public will probably still be buying recordings of Callas's historic performances, whereas it is doubtful whether they will be much interested in those of today's stars, who largely owe their fame to marketing and the media.

—m—

It is not enough to have a beautiful voice. When you have to interpret a role you have to have thousands of colors during the performance to portray the words you [sing], happiness, joy, unhappiness, sorrow, fear . . . even if you have to sing harshly at times—which I have done frequently. It is a necessity of expression, it is written there, you have to do it, even if people will not understand. But in the long run they will, because you have to persuade people of what you are doing.

To John Ardoin, Dallas, September 1968

POSTSCRIPT III

The Mirror Cracked

Remember always that only a happy bird sings, while an unhappy one creeps into its nest and dies.

To Peter Dragadze (*Life*, 30 October 1964)

As we have seen, Mary enjoyed the opportunity that *Der Bettelstudent* gave her to prove herself to hostile elements in the Athenian musical world. For many years afterward she continued to be motivated by the desire to demonstrate to all her antagonists in Greece that she had been right all the time and had come through with flying colors. At first the incessant demands of her international career and her relationship with Meneghini left her no time even to think of Greece. However, she did receive news through her correspondence with Vangelis Mangliveras, Elvira de Hidalgo (who was living in Turkey but kept in touch with her friends in Athens), her mother and sister (until 1951), and perhaps others too. De Hidalgo once wrote that Maria's letters at that time were full of nostalgia for Greece, that she was dreaming of the time when she would sing for the Greeks and show them what she had become. In two letters to Maria, de Hidalgo looked back at their time together in Athens and the feeling of "unfinished business" that she had when she thought about it. "I wish I could give you a big hug for your success in *Aida*," she wrote in October 1948. "Well done, dear Maria! I expect you are calm and contented now, you have won, as you said, so you see it wasn't too long a struggle. Think of the others—so many humiliations and tears before they achieved one-third of what you have done." And five months later: "I spent twenty days in Athens. I read all the newspapers you sent me. The friends were delighted about your triumphs, of course, and the enemies turned green with envy." A few years later, during an intermission at La Scala, a Greek visitor told Maria that her records were selling like hotcakes in Greece, and "her eyes lit up with satisfaction."[1]

"*Everything I achieved, I achieved by hard work,*" Maria said in the mid-1960s. "*I had to make my name abroad, and at La Scala in particular, before the mandarins in Greece appreciated my worth. I wanted to get what they had owed me for years: recognition.*"[2] This secret longing of hers was only partially satisfied by her successful appearance in Greece in 1957, because of the unpleasant politicking behind the scenes. On that occasion she also received a lot of obscene, offensive, and un-

558

believably venomous anonymous messages that brought back memories of the worst moments of her past life in Greece.[3] Full satisfaction was not to come until 1960 and 1961, when she triumphed as Norma and Medea in the ancient theater of Epidavros. "At last, Greece viewed with a vengeful eye from the Shipowner's yacht," wrote Vassilis Vassilikos—a reference to the fact that Maria was now the official mistress of Aristotle Onassis, on whose yacht *Christina* she usually stayed when visiting Greece.[4] Her revenge, now, was twofold: she was unassailably and indisputably at the top, not only of the musical ladder but also of the moneyed social hierarchy.

Onassis was originally attracted to Maria for a variety of reasons: he was quite cynical in his pursuit of publicity, he wanted an entrée into the artistic world (which had always snubbed him, with good reason), and the challenge of possessing a woman who seemed so unapproachable also appealed to him. Maria, for her part, fell for the dazzle and personal charm of the fabulously wealthy tycoon, the determined courtship and rugged virility of the wily Levantine lover. And she soon realized that until then her experience of the joys of sex had been pale and unexciting. "*With Meneghini I believed that I was in love,*" she confided to Giulietta Simionato in 1969, "*but that was not love, it was gratitude! I had not really known what love is until I met Onassis!*"[5] Most of all, however, their relationship was based on the fact that they both spoke the same language and had the same mentality, derived from the ethnic and social roots they had in common. "Under the grandiose surface, the couple's petit-bourgeois interests prevailed," remarks Nadia Stancioff: "Aside from their physical attraction for each other, it seems clear to me that their middle-class Greekness was their strongest bond."[6]

Stancioff quotes in her book some perceptive comments made by Hélène Rochas and Prince Michael of Greece, two of Maria's friends in Paris who saw her regularly. According to Rochas, Maria had a nineteenth-century sense of respectability: "She suffered from a 'backstreet complex'—of being the mistress. She needed the conventional status symbol of being a wife. Another thing that bothered her was social acceptance. She would like to have been, how shall I say, better born. She was uneasy in some social situations and, being anxious, her behavior was often impulsive, awkward." And Stancioff confirms that, "Despite the strict moral views she had professed when any of her friends were going through a divorce or being unfaithful to their partners, Maria considered her adulterous relationship with Onassis irreproachable." As for Prince Michael's opinion, Maria and Aristo were linked together by "that sense of destiny, that Greekness" that they had in common. Maria too was "profoundly" Greek: "When she spoke French or other foreign languages, she put on an air of sophistication, but in Greek, she was herself, totally natural . . . . When the conversation was on her art, she was the epitome of the self-assured professional. When it was general, she turned into a hesitant, middle-class Greek discussing curtains, carpeting, and little dogs like all those Athenian ladies."[7]

The fundamental problem in Maria's relationship with Onassis was that while she belonged heart and soul to the world of nineteenth-century opera he was a combined personification of Hermes—the god of wealth and cunning—and the resourceful Odysseus. While Maria was dying as Violetta or singing "Casta diva" like an ethereal angel, Aristo was the very embodiment of the cosmopolitan self-made man, the ruthless wheeler-dealer whose only aim is success in business. The two worlds they represented are, indeed, poles apart and nothing can alter that fact, even if practical considerations, personal needs, and mere coincidences do happen to bring them together for a time. The truth of the matter is that artists generally look down on those whose goal in life is mere money, while the latter nearly always suffer from an insuperable inferiority complex toward those who live for the arts. And so it was with Maria and Aristo: they were separated by an abyss—unacknowledged but unbridgeable—that was bound to bring their relationship crashing down sooner or later, unless one of them sacrificed his or her world for the other. "She treated Onassis with condescension from the high throne she occupied as the Queen of Song. Two incompatible worlds, too far apart," commented Giuseppe di Stefano. Onassis, for his part, often treated Callas with the vulgarity of the world to which he really belonged. There are plenty of people who still remember him insulting and humiliating Maria in public (he once lifted her skirt to expose her "weak point," her legs!), even using physical force on her. "Remember that here [on the *Christina*] you are a guest, not the mistress of the house," he was in the habit of warning her.[8]

In the final analysis, although there were advantages for her in the relationship, it was Maria who sacrificed herself for Onassis; but she sacrificed herself in vain. And perhaps the most tragic thing of all is that Onassis probably did not even realize this "immolation." There is not the slightest doubt that Maria was utterly enthralled with Onassis, that she loved him passionately and with amazing generosity. One of the big secrets of her life was that within a year of first meeting him she had borne him a son, who died only two hours after birth.[9] When she reportedly became pregnant again in 1966, Onassis is said to have insisted on her having an abortion.[10] Even if these instances existed only in her imagination, owing to her longing for motherhood, Callas must surely have realized that Onassis was the most unsuitable sort of partner for her—not only the wrong man to be the father of her children, but the wrong person to have with her for the remainder of her artistic career, such as it might be. Nevertheless she accepted the risk, and for about ten years she battled to get a divorce from Meneghini. When she eventually found a solution, it was too late: by that time Onassis had acquired his next status symbol, the former First Lady of the United States.

It seems clear that in giving herself unreservedly to the crafty Greek charmer, Maria was acting out a role that epitomized all her great stage roles, from Medea, who sacrificed herself on the altar of love by killing her own children, to the immeasurably passionate Isolde, to Marta, gazing up from the lowlands to the high mountains, to Norma, Violetta, Floria Tosca, and so many other heroines who expiate their mortal frailties by dying for the loved one. "*In operas so many times I've played heroines who die for love,*" she said in 1961, "*I would surely have done the same in their place.*"[11] After she achieved the success and glory for which she had worked with such dogged determination, Onassis entered her life and she was cast in the role that was to lead to her own Liebestod. Self-sacrificially, like another Isolde, Maria would then renounce all else in order to offer herself up and gain redemption through love, which, when the storm of passion has subsided, is transcendentalized in death.

To Onassis, whose attitude to Maria is the key to their whole relationship and her sacrifice, her appeal undoubtedly lay in the artistic renown and international fame of the great diva. She attracted him as a bright light attracts a moth, but Onassis would never allow himself to be burned up by the white heat of her brilliance. At the same time, her artistic glory and fame remained a persistent irritant to him, as they made him feel that in one respect he was hopelessly inferior to her. "Maria, what a lucky woman you are to be loved by such an important man, such a great tycoon!" gushed a guest aboard the *Christina* one day, when both of them were present. "In this particular case I should say Aristo was the lucky one," a relative and colleague of Onassis was brave enough to remark. "In fifty years' time no one will remember Onassis, but Maria's name will live forever."[12] And Onassis was well aware of that. He may possibly have been in love with her, but he was a true Levantine at heart ("*My pasha,*" the dutiful and devoted Maria often called him). A Levantine who would never allow anything to threaten or even touch his out-sized ego or his business interests. So when Maria was no longer useful to him, when the glitter of her fame had faded, he took on the president's widow in her place in order to attract worldwide publicity to himself once again.

Whether Onassis met his match in Jackie Kennedy—an even more calculating person than he—is irrelevant to the subject at hand, except inasmuch as it must have given Maria some secret satisfaction. Scant consolation that would have been, however, for her abandonment, a bitter blow from which she never recovered. When Onassis died in the spring of 1975, after years of separation during which he had still turned to her whenever he needed love and solace, Maria, who by then had virtually no voice at all, was again afflicted with a terrible sense of insecurity. The loss of her financial adviser (for Onassis had managed her assets for her by setting up a system of interlocking holding companies too complicated for her to understand) brought flooding back to her all the anguished uncertainty about herself and her life that had its origins in 1938, when she and her mother and sister were about to be thrown out into the street from the unfurnished Athenian apartment on Harilaou Trikoupi Street. As early as 1964 she had expressed this anxiety openly: "*My fear has always been to live my old age or die in poverty,*" she said then, aged only forty and by no means poor or sick. And it was this fear, together with loneliness ("*In my life I had some great successes, some great moments,*" she told Giulietta Simionato in 1969, "*but I was admired, not loved.*"[13]) and the inglorious end of her career, that led to her decline. Fortunately for her, death came mercifully out of the blue, taking her quickly and painlessly.

—⁓—

The last years of Maria's life were hardly more than one long void, which she spent mainly in trying to hold on to the memory of anything precious to her from the past. The present was depressing and unworthy of comparison, while the future was dark and uncertain. The vocal problems that marred her last, tired operatic performances, from 1963 to 1965, had stifled her desire ever to sing again. When Yannis Tsarouchis visited her in her dressing room at La Scala on 29 May 1963, just before she trod those famous boards for the last time, she had already said to him, "*I have 'flu. The doctor tells me it's psychological 'flu [grippe morale]. I don't want to sing. Why should I sing? Maria Malibran died long before she reached my age, and she is forever Malibran. There's a statue of her in the Scala Museum.*" And when Tsarouchis visited her in her dressing room again, a year or so later, this time at the Opéra in Paris, she had said to him with a touch of anger, but in a very depressed tone, "*This is the only place I can sing, where they know nothing about music and only look at my figure. And in Greece too, of course: that's my home coun-try, they adore me, it's a different thing. But in Italy they're all ready to boo me if I'm a quarter-tone out. They don't count the number of right notes, but only the wrong ones.*"[14]

When Andreas Paridis visited Maria in Paris in March 1969, she chatted with him about the "good old days" in Athens, which she would never forget, and asked him to send her any photographs or other mementos of those times that he could find. She had not yet managed to lay hands on her old letters and photographs, as these had been left behind at Sirmione in 1959, together with many other personal possessions of hers, when she made her hurried departure to join the man who had so utterly turned her head. Casting about for something to do with her life, she told him, she had hit on the idea of writing her memoirs.* Paridis remembered that Maria had then taken him by the arm and led him over to a big window over-looking the garden. "She showed me a tall tree whose topmost branches were level with the second floor, exactly opposite her bedroom window. *'You see that tree?'* she said. *'It's all I have for company, it's the thing I love! It's the first tree to come out in spring and the last to shed its leaves in the autumn. But when night falls I feel so alone.'*"[15]

By then Maria's existence had sunk to a nadir of unhappiness: an aching void with no prospects, no man, no likelihood of relief for her pain, and, worst of all, no voice. Andreas Paridis, appearing like a fairy godfather, stirred old memories in her—memories which she generally had made out to be very painful but which now, filtered through time, she had begun to long for, at least as far as some of her nicer colleagues and good friends were concerned. Maria kept up with Kiki Xa-kousti, who often visited Paris and still called her friend Mary. They often went to the movies together: "*Not to the theater, Kiki, because you can't slip out into the dark without being seen,*" Maria would say. Kiki, more than anyone else, was her secret link with her Greek past, someone who shared many of her private memories but was not connected with singing or the G.N.O. It was at about the same time, between 1968 and 1970, that Maria was visited by Maria Alkeou, another person who brought back good memories, this time of the Athens Conservatory and her early days in the opera. "She had recently been thrown over by Onassis, that Greek rotter whom she had fallen in love with because he could order her about," Alkeou reflects. "I went and knocked on her door without warning. Someone opened, and from inside the apartment came a smell like a chemist's dispensary. She was still asleep and I left a note with my telephone number. When she rang me, it was

---

*Maria refused to "pay" the twenty percent of her eventual royalties demanded by those who offered to "ghost" for her. (A. Savvakis, *Ioannis Tsarouchis*, Athens 1993, 309.) The result was that, apart from what she dictated for *Oggi* late in 1956, and her extensive autobiographical arti-cle, "I Am Not Guilty of All Those Callas Scandals," published in *Life* magazine on 25 May 1959, she never did leave any proper memoirs.

as if we had spoken to each other just the other day. I mentioned the medicinal smell, and she said, '*Oh, Maria, I'm finished, done for. I'll never even sing again!*' 'What *are* you talking about?' I retorted. '*Believe me, Maria, I'm finished! Finished!*' she insisted." That her morale had broken down also became obvious to Andy Embirikos, a close friend of her last years, when he remarked one day that she "wasn't herself." Maria then turned to him and said simply, "*But the real me doesn't exist any more.*"[16]

She did make some despairing attempts to keep her life going, it is true. Little is known about her love life after Onassis, but it would seem that her celebrity status made it difficult for her to have close friendships with men. When, in an interview after the break-up of her relationship with Onassis, she described him as "charming, very sincere, spontaneous" and "the finest of friends," she was then asked how she defined a good friend: "*Somebody you can count on at any moment of your life,*" she answered. But by that time she had lost all confidence in her ability to handle any personal relationships. "*Celebrities don't know who their real friends are,*" she told her interviewer.[17] This, of course, had its roots in wartime Athens, in the atmosphere and the infighting among singers at the G.N.O., in a period of her life when betrayal could be a matter of life and death. But her mistrust of everybody around her had intensified after she became a famous diva and even more after she met Onassis, who was equally mistrustful of anyone who came near him. This made it harder for her to enter into relationships, even with men she may have liked. Any man who tried to be friends with her was likely to be suspected of ulterior motives and brushed off, even if he had managed to pass the acid test of her initial scrutiny.

In the summer of 1969 she agreed to act in a film for Pier Paolo Pasolini, her new mentor, with whom she had a curious sentimental involvement.[18] But it was not a film of an opera. To us, today, it seems a tragic loss that we have not a properly made record of her work on film, except perhaps the second act of her 1964 Tosca at Covent Garden. The main reason for it, apart from her own diffidence and perfectionism, was that Luchino Visconti did not believe in making films of operas and had made no secret of his views to Maria, who had her own reservations on the subject in any case.[19] By the time she met Pasolini her voice was long and well past its best, of course. The part she eventually agreed to play in the film was one of her favorite heroines, Medea, but not in Cherubini's singing version. This was Pasolini's Medea, and as Giulietta Simionato commented, "[Medea] without Cherubini was not *her* Medea."[20] If Maria had still been her uncompromising self and acted upon the principles she herself advocated in several interviews at about that time, she might perhaps have avoided becoming involved in that nonmusical version of *Medea*. But by this time she had reached the point where she could no longer afford not to make compromises, and one can only admire the unflinching honesty which made it possible for her to say, in 1970, "*The minute you make concessions or compromise, you've sold yourself to the Devil. It is the beginning of the end,*

Maria Callas dedicates her photo to her friend Kiki Xakousti and signs it "Mary" in Greek, Athens 1957.

Resting during the shooting of Pasolini's *Medea*, summer 1969, photographed by her secretary Nadia Stancioff.

because you then start making the one concession, then the other, and then you are finished!"[21]

Maria gave two courses of master classes at the Juilliard School of Music in New York, in October 1971 and February 1972. In April 1973 she co-directed *I Vespri Siciliani* with Giuseppe di Stefano at Turin's Teatro Regio, which was not a success. Then, in 1973 and 1974, came her pitiful concert tours around the world with di Stefano, a veteran of her great triumphs in the 1950s, himself now long past his best. It was he who egged her on when she had given up all thoughts of ever making another appearance. To be fair to di Stefano, he must have hoped that together they might recapture some of the glories of their past; but even so he cannot escape the charge of acting out of self-interest in the belief that only some-one of Callas's stature could raise him out of the slough into which he, too, had sunk. However, di Stefano failed to take into account (and perhaps did not even realize) that he was no more than a very good tenor, whereas Maria, whose repu-tation was bound to be compromised by his eagerness to stage a joint comeback, was a legend in her own lifetime with a whole chapter in the history of music all to herself. At all events he led her blindly into a minefield, selfishly taking advantage not only of her desire to sing again but also of the emotional attachment to him that she had formed in her panic for human support and love. Di Stefano returned her love, but his personal and family commitments made it impossible for him to offer her what she really needed just then. And so his unhappy involvement in

Maria's life remained bound up with that desperate attempt to reverse a downward slide, which would better have been left to follow its natural, inevitable course.[22]

—∿∿—

Maria still visited Greece regularly, mostly for summer holidays by the sea, even after her relationship with Onassis ended. She always loved the sea and enjoyed swimming in the Aegean. Whereas she normally lived on a diet of steak, or steak tartare, in Greece she could never have enough fish and seafood. One of the last treats she gave herself was a visit to Halkidiki in the summer of 1976. She hoped to remain incognito—all she wanted to do was to stay at her hotel, happily swimming in the nearby sea with her mask and snorkel, sometimes giving her two poodles a ride on her back—but the paparazzi eventually caught up with her. Vasso Devetzi later revealed that it was on this visit that Maria first heard attentively the bouzouki music of Vassilis Tsitsanis, which reawakened her memories of Athens during the occupation. After their return to Paris, Devetzi went regularly to her apartment in the Avenue Georges Mandel, where she often found her "utterly absorbed in listening to *rebetika* songs with the volume turned down low." Shortly before her death Maria was planning another trip to Greece, this time to stay with a friend in Tsangarada, on the slopes of Mount Pilion, overlooking the Aegean.[23]

Despite the unpleasantnesses that Maria had endured in her Greek years (and her harping on about them, exaggerating their awfulness and veiling the truth in vague generalizations about hardships and deprivations); despite the stress and disenchantment that often marred her visits to Greece; despite the fact that she was born American, married an Italian, and made France her adopted home; despite the confusion about her identity that she confessed late in her life—despite all this, Maria felt Greek more than anything else. "*The blood in my veins, my character, my thoughts, all are Greek,*" she told a Greek journalist in 1957.[24] In the years following that first return to Greece she made statements in the same vein more and more frequently, and when she was excited and in a Greek environment she was always coming out with typically Greek expressions. In 1958, in her dressing room in Dallas after the triumphant production of *Medea* with a Greek director and Greek stage and costume designer, she shouted out in Greek, "*Long live Greece! We are the greatest!*"[25] And in 1964 she confided to Corinna Spanidou, the physiotherapist on board the *Christina*, "*Even if Aristo and I end up going our separate ways, we will always have respect for one another. We have the same roots, we are both true Greeks.*"[26]

Although she did not believe in life after death, Maria was not afraid of death. When she was told by her doctor in 1974 that her glaucoma might possibly deprive her of her sight, she implored Vasso Devetzi, "*If I ever go blind and haven't the courage to die, don't leave me blind!*" She didn't want to die, Devetzi told Vassilis Vassilikos, but she didn't want to live to be eighty either: "she wanted to be always *en pleine possession de forme.*"[27] The question of whether Maria died naturally or committed suicide has been much debated, chiefly in the tabloid press but

Sailing with her poodle Toy on the Aegean, mid-1970s.

also by several of her biographers. That she was cremated four days after her death (and immediately after the funeral service instead of the customary following day) and that her ashes were later scattered over the Aegean Sea—both these actions having been taken on the initiative of Devetzi, who insisted that they were in accordance with Maria's express (but oral, hence unproven) wishes—led many to conclude that she committed suicide. Those who still believe this feel sure that the reason for the hasty cremation and subsequent scattering of the ashes was to make it impossible for the cause of her death ever to be determined by scientific analysis. "It appears that cremation was the easiest way to achieve a possible cover up," is also Galatopoulos's conclusion. And, naturally, the prime suspect in the *faits accomplis* arranged by Devetzi is Devetzi herself who, according to Meneghini, supplied Maria with potent pills such as Mandrax, "in order to oblige and perhaps make her feel in some way dependent on her."[28]

With regard to the suicide version of Maria's death, an interesting question was raised by Renzo Allegri's reference to a note dated "Summer 1977" found in a prayer book that Maria had in the bedroom of her Paris apartment, where she died. On headed notepaper from the Savoy Hotel in London, where she had stayed a few weeks before her death, Maria had written out the words of La Gioconda's famous aria: *Suicidio! In questi fieri momenti, tu sol mi resti. E il cor mi tenti. L'ultima voce del mio destino, ultima croce del mio cammin.*[29] Yet Maria did not commit suicide: she simply let herself die. "She didn't want to go on living, she was waiting for death," di Stefano said later. "When I met her in 1972 she said to me, '*Caro Pippo, ogni giorno, per fortuna, un giorno di meno.*'"[30] What was there left in her life? From time to time she took a vacation to relieve her boredom (but always with the fear of being tracked down by the paparazzi), she watched television and occasionally went to a movie (but always with the fear of being recognized), she went out to dinner now and then (but was always worried about putting on weight), she still kept up with her singing practice (but all that really did for her was to deepen her sense of loss), she had the company of the few people who attached themselves to her and whose presence she tolerated to take the edge off her loneliness (which was how Devetzi came to be numbered among her "friends"[31]). But toward the end of her life she was an automaton, living because she could not do otherwise. She no longer saw any real reason for staying alive, because in the things that mattered to her—singing and having a loving relationship—she had reached the top and was now on a long and irreversible descent. As Meneghini acknowledged in the end, "Certainly in her last years she was full of despair, especially after the death of Onassis, when she had lost everything, even hope. . . . Suicide? Maybe. But it is also possible that she killed herself unwittingly. What I mean is that she was killed by that continuous abuse of pills and various drugs. She was definitely a woman who no longer wanted to live."[32]

With her excessive reliance on drugs, mainly those that helped her to sleep and —who knows?—to dream of past glories and moments of happiness, Maria wore down her health by overstraining her heart and tampering with her already deficient blood circulation. "She would take three pills, and then forget and take three more," di Stefano recalled, and in one of her moments of despair she herself wrote, *"Never in my life have I been dependent on anybody. Now I am a slave to a box of pills."*[33] Many of those who knew her in the last five years of her life believe that her reliance on drugs had turned her into an addict. According to Devetzi, "She didn't take drugs, only multivitamin pills," but Devetzi was clearly alone in this view. Perhaps she glossed over the truth because she felt responsible for Maria's addiction, which she either could not or did not try to prevent. In a truly heartrending, misspelled note written sixteen months before she died, in a trembling hand betraying the effects of one of her drugs, Maria set down on paper her confused feelings about her tragic fate: *"Je pens pour moi sort esultante la fine de ma vie pas de felicité, d'amis, de la drogue! Maria 5/9/76."*[34]

Just three days before her death Maria was practicing Verdi's *Requiem* at home with Devetzi at the piano. This was a work she had never sung, not even in the days when her voice was up to it: it was almost as if she had been waiting to sing it for herself when she reached the end she longed for. Finally, on Friday, 16 September 1977, the God she believed in, the God to whom she prayed for strength to endure whatever it was His will to send her, delivered her from an existence that had become so pointless and wearing for her. With hardly any forewarning and a minimum of suffering, she passed from life to death in the space of a few minutes, dying—probably of a pulmonary thromboembolism[35]—in the arms of her beloved Bruna, her faithful housekeeper. *"Giulia, remember my words,"* she had told Giulietta Simionato eight years earlier, *"I started dying when I met this man and when I gave up music."*[36] Those who saw her on her deathbed have said how moved they were by her astonishing beauty as she lay there, with her hair lying in a plait on her pillow and her long-fingered hands crossed for the last time on her lifeless body. The only sign of death was a slight purplish tinge coloring her now peaceful face.

—⁓—

In his book *The Eviction*, Greek novelist Vassilis Vassilikos included a 130-page-long novella entitled "Record of a Personal Memoir that Was Never Written: About the Diva."[37] On 1 September 1985 Vasso Devetzi invited Vassilikos to her apartment in Passy and asked him to ghostwrite her memoirs, which she considered "the only authentic testimony" relating to Maria Callas. Every morning for about three weeks Vassilikos went to Devetzi's home to study the much-vaunted "archives" and listen to her reminiscing about Maria. Unfortunately Devetzi refused to allow a tape recorder to be used, even by the man she herself had chosen to set her memoirs down on paper. In the end the book was never written, and so Vassilikos's memoir is of considerable historical importance, not just as it records her views on some events that followed Maria's death, but also as a proof that

Maria's precious private papers and related documents, tapes, and so forth were in Devetzi's illegal possession until at least the end of 1985.[38] Jackie's revealing comments in her published memoirs, together with documents and her more recent oral statements (as well as those of her husband, Dr. Andreas Stathopoulos), provide the necessary counterweight to Devetzi's one-sided testimony as reported by Vassilikos after her death.

"With Callas dead, Devetzi immediately took control of everything," according to Stelios Galatopoulos: "Using her assumed authority as Maria's confidante, she forced her way into the apartment and within minutes Callas's personal papers had disappeared from the study." Galatopoulos, who asserts that Maria had told him that she had written a will taking good care of her family and her servants, as well as leaving money to the Callas Scholarship Fund and Milan's Institute for Cancer Research, even contemplates the possibility that "Devetzi might have removed it from Callas's study."[39] Be that as it may, from the very outset Devetzi cleverly managed to make herself indispensable not only as the administrator of the affairs pertaining to Maria's estate but also as the guardian of Maria's memory as a musician. Taking advantage of Litsa's and Jackie's lack of experience and naïveté, she was given a free hand in settling the complex problems of inheritance "as Maria would have wanted." Having failed to persuade Maria to leave everything to her, Devetzi felt wronged: in her own words, according to Vassilikos, the Diva had left her with her position unsecured because she had "not had time to make the necessary legal provisions."[40] All she had in her favor was the dubious moral argument that Maria's feelings toward her mother and sister made it very unlikely that she would have wanted them to inherit her estate—certainly not *all* her tangible assets and her royalty rights, which were valued at the time at an estimated twelve million dollars.

Two main factors worked then in Devetzi's favor. One was the rapacity of Meneghini, who now reappeared on the scene after being out of Maria's life for eighteen years. Having been reminded by a friend that in 1954 Maria had made a private will appointing him her residuary legatee, he quickly proceeded to find the precious paper and, as Italian law did not yet recognize divorce, rushed to Paris claiming his "lawful share" of the inheritance. The other factor in Devetzi's favor was the complicated state of Maria's affairs. Indeed, with many of her assets, including the apartment in the Avenue Georges Mandel, registered in the name of companies with bearer shares (presumably for the purpose of tax avoidance), the French authorities had been on to Maria for some time, poisoning her last years with threats of eviction and retrospective tax bills.[41] Jackie was clearly incapable of dealing with all these problems on her own, while Litsa did not even attend her daughter's funeral. So Devetzi offered to help out, and she started by cultivating an arrangement that Maria would have found doubly objectionable: the assets and royalty rights were to be shared out between her mother and Meneghini, that usurper from the past, whose name Maria would not allow even to be mentioned in her house. Rather than get involved in costly and highly publicized litigation, the two women accepted the compromise.

There followed the macabre business of sharing out the spoils, of which Vassilikos gives a vivid description based on Devetzi's account. The first item on the block was Maria's half share in a ship: "In a gray room of a gray bank in gray Switzerland the lambs were led to the slaughter. . . . On one side was the shipping company's representative. Facing him, a shipowner who was in cahoots with him. . . . Value of ship: at least eight million dollars. Tender received from the only bidder [for a fifty-one percent share]: half a million. . . . Honor among thieves. If they don't like it this way they'll have to pay taxes. At four o'clock the heirs' resistance breaks down and they say yes. They take a quarter million each and away they go." Next on the list was the jewelry, again to be shared in the gray Swiss Discount Bank. "The Manufacturer [as Vassilikos calls Meneghini] arrived with sheets and towels to wrap it up in, the sister with polyethylene bags. . . . The Italian spent the whole time being rude about the Shipowner's [Onassis's] presents to the Diva. His own were better, he said, because he had taste. The Shipowner only had money. . . . The last item, an old Venetian necklace, went to the sister, but as it looked old and in bad condition, and as the ex-husband seemed to want it, she sold it to him in cold blood for twelve thousand dollars, cash down."[42]

Devetzi's only involvement in all this was as a provider of moral support for Jackie, but what followed was a different matter, starting with the distribution of Maria's personal and household effects from the Paris apartment at the beginning of 1978. "Eventually the legal formalities were completed and one day the Manufacturer and the sister entered the apartment. The division of the spoils was a truly heartrending affair. Druna [as Vassilikos renames Maria's housekeeper Bruna Lupoli] didn't come down from her den. She couldn't bear to see the vultures descending on the Diva's possessions. . . . 'And the sister?' I asked her. 'Didn't she take anything?' 'She did . . . but she was on her own. What chance did she have? That man was there with his fat housekeeper and five or six thugs. They filled the crates, they cleared the lot. The sister didn't get a look-in.'"[43] Jackie's memoirs fill in some of the gaps that Devetzi left in the version she gave to Vassilikos. According to Devetzi, "The Manufacturer came with his lorries and the sister with a van," the implication being that each took away his or her share then and there. But Jackie discloses that Maria's clothes and personal effects were packed into a hundred ninety-four crates, half of which went to her mother and herself, and these Devetzi offered to store temporarily at her own house. Of those ninety-seven crates, Jackie eventually received precisely seven! When pressed, Devetzi accused Meneghini of having stolen the other ninety.[44]

The next step in the pathetic proceedings was the much-publicized auction of the furniture and sundry other items from the apartment, a sorry affair which took place at the Hôtel Georges V on 14 June 1978. Many of the lots were bought by Meneghini but most were knocked down to complete outsiders, often at give-away prices. The story goes that while that poignant sale was in progress a huge mirror in the main lounge of the hotel suddenly cracked from top to bottom with a deafening report, for no apparent reason.[45]

Jackie, anxious and unable to speak French, was a pawn in the hands of Devetzi, who used her position and influence to good effect. Not the least of her achievements was to persuade Jackie to surrender to her the *droit moral*, that is to say the guardianship of Maria Callas's artistic reputation. This she followed up with a proposal to create a foundation to help young musicians, in accordance with a wish that Maria had expressed in Greece in 1960. Naturally enough she herself would be its president, with carte blanche to manage its affairs and the right to use its funds as she thought fit. To cover her until such time as the foundation came into existence, Devetzi even persuaded Jackie to draw up a will in her favor: "If I left it all to her, [she explained], she would see that it would one day go to the right places," says Jackie pathetically in her memoirs. Utterly overpowered, she drew up the will (in Geneva, on 18 December 1979) and continued sending Devetzi personal remittances for the needs of the foundation. Between 1978 and 1980 she sent her $792,000 (as confirmed by the copies of the vouchers still in Jackie's possession). And as Jackie wrote and reaffirms today, she also gave Devetzi cash on several occasions, bringing the total closer to $1,250,000—no mean sum by any standards. Of course, none of this money was used to perpetuate the artistic reputation of Maria Callas.[46]

Next came the sale of the large Paris apartment, a subject that Devetzi did not even mention to Vassilikos. Telling Jackie that she had found a rich Arab buyer willing to pay one million dollars or more, she first persuaded her to buy out Meneghini for $420,000. Once all the anonymous shares were in the hands of the guileless Jackie ("again in the gray Swiss bank," as Jackie remembers), Devetzi reached over, took them from her, put them into a plastic bag, and announced that she would "look after them" until all the formalities relating to the property sale were completed. Jackie immediately realized her mistake but was too astonished to protest. As soon as she was alone she crossed herself, as she later wrote. Shortly after, Devetzi announced that the Arab buyer had disappeared, and nearly two years later she informed Jackie that the French Inland Revenue had levied heavy taxes which had eaten up almost the entire value of the property. Finally, in 1982, just a few months before Litsa died and only after intense pressure had been brought on her, Devetzi sent Jackie the princely sum of eighty thousand dollars as her share of the sale proceeds![47]

In November 1984, now advised and guided by Andreas Stathopoulos whom she had married in December 1983, Jackie revoked from Devetzi the power of attorney concerning the *droit moral* of Maria. Although Devetzi fought back—even presenting a fake typed letter of Maria's naming her as her sole heir only three days before she died—the court rejected her attempt. Earlier in 1984, Devetzi had received a further sum of £102,000 from Callas royalties, which was also never credited to the foundation, as subsequently confirmed in writing by Christos Lambrakis, her successor as its president. In 1985 Jackie and her husband went to visit the foundation's offices in Fribourg, but soon realized that it existed only on paper. Unable to see even the notary in charge, a certain Herr Burgknecht, they wrote to him repeatedly requesting information on the finances of the foundation. They never received any, but, in answer to a similar enquiry, Devetzi's German lawyer, Herr Wunderlich of Munich, confirmed that sums totaling $792,000 had never been registered in the accounts of the famous Callas Foundation.

Jackie and her husband further discovered that Devetzi had established a commercial company named Callas International S.A., with her Paris home address as its seat, through which she collected royalties from the sale of video tapes of Callas's two concerts in Hamburg (1959 and 1962). Devetzi never accounted for these sums with regard to the foundation of her "friend," whose "memory" she so devoutly championed. But now, already in bad health, she found herself being threatened with legal action for having "with incredible audacity," according to Stelios Galatopoulos, "swindled Callas's sister out of a fortune."[48] By 1987, with conclusive evidence against her, Stathopoulos was poised to start legal proceedings against the one who was president, vice-president, treasurer, and sole member of the board of the foundation, all in one, and who had refused to account for its affairs when asked by Jackie to do so. Devetzi must have lived out the last months of her life in dread that her actions would be publicly exposed. Death, on 1 November 1987, saved her from being engulfed in a humiliating scandal.

A matter of even more consequence in the long term is the fate of Maria's personal papers which, according to Vassilikos, comprised letters, interviews, and all sorts of other documents that had never been—and, today, still have not been —touched by her various biographers. Presumably they would also have included recordings of her practice sessions and private conversations, as Maria had taught herself to use a tape recorder and had meticulously kept a living record of all that still mattered to her. Devetzi never left Vassilikos alone to search through the suitcases and trunks where the materials were kept. She and a niece of hers stood guard over them like Cerberus: "They hovered around me like birds of prey, to watch me and make sure I did not spirit any of the precious documents away."[49] We can only hope that one day these important papers will be found, although the question of their rightful ownership is beset by complex legal problems. If they have disappeared forever, it will be an enormous loss to music history and historians.

One of the saddest chapters in the posthumous history of Maria Callas's personal effects is the story of what happened to the half share taken by Meneghini, who lived to enjoy his spoils for only three years. During that time he was dictating his memoirs and making plans to set up a Meneghini-Callas foundation to which he would donate his Callas memorabilia. But the man whose reputation as a great miser yet survives never showed himself capable of rising to the heights to which circumstances had thrust him. When he died, in January 1981, he had at his

Sirmione villa not only everything he had "inherited" or bought since 1977 but also various other personal possessions of Maria's, notably her private papers, which included all her correspondence up to 1959. Most of this collection has now been dispersed, having been sold off by his residuary legatee, his former housekeeper Emma Roverselli-Brutti, who also turned the villa into a paying proposition by dividing it up into fourteen apartments. The result is that many of Maria's personal effects and documents are unfortunately being hoarded by Callas buffs and are therefore unavailable for study by her biographers and music historians.[50]

Lastly, let us reflect on the fate of the sheets of paper on which Maria jotted down her innermost thoughts in the last years of her life: about a hundred fifty loose pages of emotional outpourings, so personal that she did not dare put them in a diary. Devetzi removed these sheets from Maria's belongings and gave them to the lawyer administering Callas's estate on Devetzi's behalf. These strictly personal and very moving documents the lawyer transferred to a safe deposit box in a bank, with instructions that in the event of his death they were to be entrusted to Dr. Ivano Signorini. When they came into the latter's possession, in 1994, Signorini fortunately realized that their contents required scrupulously careful and conscientious treatment. And so, to this day, the priceless heirloom lies hidden away from impious eyes and pens, in the care of one who admittedly respects it but has no proper right to it. Sole responsibility for this shameful smothering of Maria's most revealing private thoughts must be borne by the self-appointed guardian of her memory, Vasso Devetzi.[51]

Some further idea of Devetzi's duplicity can be gained from her behavior with regard to the cremation of Maria's body and the scattering of the ashes that followed. The hurried decision in favor of cremation—based solely on Devetzi's verbal assurance that that had been Maria's declared wish—has since been questioned by a number of people, including close friends of hers who think that the idea of cremation did not accord with her moral or religious beliefs. The climax of the proceedings came with the stage-managed scattering of the ashes on the waters of the Aegean, a ceremony conceived by Devetzi, who had naturally reserved the leading role for herself. There would be nothing odd about this story if the casket had not been stolen in January 1978 and then found thrown somewhere in the Père Lachaise cemetery, as a result of which Devetzi herself declared that it no longer contained Maria's ashes.[52] Yet, even so, she blithely pressed on with her plans, and on 3 June 1979 the mediocre pianist assumed the guise of a bad actress, pretending to believe that the casket—which she herself had ceremoniously brought from Paris as if it contained a holy relic—really did contain the ashes of Maria Callas. And when the Greek minister of culture, Dimitris Nianias, was devoutly emptying the casket over the waves, a spiteful gust of wind blew the ashes into the faces—even into the mouths—of some of the participants in a rite at which it seems most probable that Maria Callas was not actually present.

Vasso Devetzi's sad performance, 3 June 1979, standing by as Minister Nianias prepares to scatter the ashes.

—⁓—

Wouldn't it be lovely to be a sun-basking Mediterranean sea gull?
I'm not sure I like that idea. Sea gulls have such ugly voices.
Make a special request. Ask to be a sea gull with the voice of a nightingale.
In that case, I accept. Think how wonderful it will be not to have to answer the phone, not to have to give interviews to journalists who change everything you say.

To Nadia Stancioff, c. 1970
(*Maria: Callas Remembered*, London 1987)

APPENDIX

Appearances and Repertoire (1938–1945)

Mary's performances up to September 1945 can be divided into two categories: (1) *those of which there is some kind of printed record*, mainly press announcements of forthcoming events, press reviews of her public appearances, programs of those events, a few other relevant documents, and the Athens Conservatory examination records for the four years from 1939–40 to 1942–43 (in which the program was written in by hand by Mary's teacher, Elvira de Hidalgo); and (2) *those for which the only evidence comes from personal recollections, either oral or published*, these being mostly private performances or else public concerts that were not advertised or reviewed in the newspapers of those troubled times. Although there is more certainty about the ones in the first category, even they are not absolutely indisputable because the newspapers rarely gave notice of a cancellation. Absolute certainty would be possible only if the stage book had survived or if the archives of the National Theater and National Opera were complete.

It is quite likely that a few of Mary's performances are missing from the list because nothing is known about them. They would have been private functions or semi-formal events organized by private individuals or societies, or even by officers of the occupation authorities acting privately or in their official capacities. One such event, organized by the Society of Pyrgians in Athens, took place in about 1939 at the Hotel Acropole, where Mary, standing on a makeshift stage, sang some solo pieces with piano accompaniment to a large audience.[1] Then there is the occasion mentioned by her mother, who says that Mary sang "the *Stabat Mater*" at a memorial service for a German officer; this must have taken place either at the German Evangelical Church on Sina Street or at the Catholic cathedral on Panepistimiou Street, perhaps at the German Cultural Institute on Rigillis Street or even at one of the cinemas or theaters requisitioned by the Wehrmacht for the entertainment of German soldiers, such as the theater in Victorias Square, the Rialto on Kypselis Street, or the Kentrikon on Kolokotroni Street. Other unconfirmed appearances include a concert attended by numerous Germans, perhaps at the Olympia Theater under the baton of Dimitris Michailidis, though he has no recollection of it; a performance of a *Stabat Mater*, perhaps Rossini's, at Thessaloniki in the summer of 1943; and an appearance "for the Germans" in 1944, including excerpts from *Fidelio*, perhaps at the Odeon of Herodes Atticus.[2]

—ɯ—

Even before she had her first singing lessons, Mary had sung at school. The only stage works in which she is known to have performed are *The Mikado* and *H.M.S. Pinafore* by Gilbert and Sullivan and *Countess Maritza* by Kálmán. On her own, with hardly any tuition, she sang a number of light songs such as "A Heart That's Free" and the well-known "La Paloma." Other pieces that have been mentioned are the Bach/Gounod Ave Maria and the Habanera from Bizet's *Carmen*. In those days Mary used to imitate singers she heard on the radio or phonograph in pieces from the *leggero* or *drammatico* repertoire (such as "Je suis Titania" from *Mignon* by Ambroise Thomas, "Ombra leggera" from *Dinorah* by Giacomo Meyerbeer, excerpts from *Aida*, and supposedly the entire role of Carmen), which may have done serious and possibly irreparable damage to her voice.

In Greece, besides the pieces and whole operas or arias listed below, we know that in 1939–40 Mary also studied Beethoven's scene and concert aria "Ah, perfido!" and that in the operatic repertoire she also learned Rossini's *La Cenerentola*, which de Hidalgo set her to lighten her voice. In November 1941 she learned the role of Konstanze in Mozart's *Die Entführung aus dem Serail* to be ready to understudy Frangiska Nikita. During the academic years 1940–41, 1941–42, and 1942–43 she also studied *La Traviata*, *La Gioconda*, and *Dido and Aeneas*, "various" Handel arias (as she told Lord Harewood in 1968), and perhaps the aria "Qui la voce" from Bellini's *I Puritani*. She is also mentioned as having sung several Greek songs, unspecified lieder by Schubert and Brahms, Pizzetti's *I Tre Canti Greci*, and Delibes's "Les Filles de Cadix." The pieces she learned in those two years also included *"many arie antiche"* (as she herself told John Ardoin in 1968) and arias from Bach's *Saint Matthew Passion*, Handel's *Messiah*, and Mozart's *Requiem*. And, of course, there is absolutely no doubt that Mary also studied many other pieces, of all kinds, which she never performed and which were never mentioned, either in written or in spoken word.

—⁓—

Particulars given in square brackets are uncertain. Chapter indications in parentheses refer to the description of each entry in the text.

1. **Early September 1937.** Audition for Maria Trivella (Chapter 10), Trivella's home, 5 Hoffmann St., Athens.
    "L'amour est un oiseau rebel" (Georges Bizet, *Carmen*)
    "La Paloma" (Sebastián Yradier)

2. **11 April 1938.** Exhibition concert, Maria Trivella's 1937–38 classes, National Conservatory (Chapter 12), Parnassos Hall, Karytsi Square, Athens. Piano accompanist: Stefanos Valtetsiotis.
    "Leise, leise, fromme Weise" (Carl Maria von Weber, *Der Freischütz*)
    ["Plus grand dans son obscurité"] (Charles Gounod, *La Reine de Saba*)
    "Two Nights" (Ioannis Psaroudas)
    "O dolci mani" (Giacomo Puccini, *Tosca*), duet with Zannis Kambanis
      (Mario)

3. **8 June 1938.** Proficiency test, National Conservatory (Chapter 12), Parnassos Hall, Karytsi Square, Athens. [Piano accompanist: Elli Nikolaidi.] Program not known.

4. **4 July 1938.** Celebration of American Independence (Chapter 12), Rex Theater, 48 Panepistimiou (now El. Venizelou) St., Athens. Piano accompanist not known.
    Unspecified "American and Greek songs"
    [Encore: "Casta diva"] (Vincenzo Bellini, *Norma*)
With Vangelis Mangliveras, baritone, and Nota Kamberou, soprano.

5. **September 1938.** Audition for Nicola Moscona (Chapter 12). Modern dance school in Akadimias St., Athens. Piano accompanist: Lysimachos Androutsopoulos. Program not known.

6. **September 1938.** Audition for Elvira de Hidalgo (Chapter 12), De Hidalgo's home, 8 Codringtonos St., Athens.
    "O patria mia" (Giuseppe Verdi, *Aida*)

7. **2 April 1939.** Exhibition concert given by National Conservatory students (Chapter 13), Olympia Theater, 59 Akadimias St., Athens.

Pietro Mascagni, *Cavalleria Rusticana*. Role: Santuzza.

With Vyron Simiriotis (Turiddu), Pepi Efthymiadou (Lola), Afroditi Kopanou (Mamma Lucia), Christoforos Athineos (Alfio). Ad hoc orchestra conducted by Michalis Vourtsis.

8. **22 May 1939.** Exhibition concert, Maria Trivella's 1938–39 classes, National Conservatory (Chapter 13), Parnassos Hall, Karytsi Square, Athens. Piano accompanist: Stefanos Valtetsiotis.

> "Belle nuit, ô nuit d'amour" (Jacques Offenbach, *The Tales of Hoffmann*), duet with Anita Bourdakou (Nicklausse)
> "Ocean! thou mighty monster" (Carl Maria von Weber, *Oberon*)
> "Ritorna vincitor" (Giuseppe Verdi, *Aida*)
> "I Shan't Forget" (Ioannis Psaroudas)
> "O terra addio" (Giuseppe Verdi, *Aida*), duet with Zannis Kambanis (Radamès)

9. **23 May 1939.** Concert given by graduating and top-grade National Conservatory students (Chapter 13), Parnassos Hall, Karytsi Square, Athens. Piano accompanist: Stefanos Valtetsiotis.

> "Ocean! thou mighty monster" (Carl Maria von Weber, *Oberon*)
> "Dis-moi que je suis belle" (Jules Massenet, *Thaïs*)

10. **25 June 1939.** Exhibition concert given by the opera school classes of the National Conservatory (Chapter 13), Olympia Theater, 59 Akadimias St., Athens. Piano accompanists: Elli Nikolaidi (*Un Ballo in Maschera*) and Stefanos Valtetsiotis (*Cavalleria Rusticana*).

> "Ve' se di notte" (Giuseppe Verdi, *Un Ballo in Maschera*), with Christoforos Athineos (Renato), Petros Hoidas (Sam), Nikos Aliprandis (Tom)
> "Morrò, ma prima in grazia" (Giuseppe Verdi, *Un Ballo in Maschera*)
> "Voi lo sapete" (Pietro Mascagni, *Cavalleria Rusticana*)
> "Tu qui, Santuzza?" (Pietro Mascagni, *Cavalleria Rusticana*), duet with Michalis Koronis (Turiddu)

11. **16 or 25 September or 5 October 1939.** Entrance examination, Athens Conservatory (Chapter 15), Great Hall, Athens Conservatory, 35 Pireos St., Athens. [Piano accompanist: Yerasimos Koundouris.]

> ["Ocean! thou mighty monster"] (Carl Maria von Weber, *Oberon*)

12. **23 February 1940.** Charity concert in aid of scholarship fund for needy students, Athens Conservatory (Chapter 16), Great Hall, Athens Conservatory, 35 Pireos St., Athens. Piano accompanist: Yerasimos Koundouris.

"Mira, o Norma" (Vincenzo Bellini, *Norma*), duet with Arda Mandikian (Adalgisa)

13. **3 April 1940.** Opera soirée, Athens Radio, live broadcast (Chapter 16), Athens Radio studio, Zappion Hall, Athens. [Piano accompanist: Yerasimos Koundouris.]

"Mira, o Norma" (Vincenzo Bellini, *Norma*), duet with Arda Mandikian (Adalgisa)

14. **28 May 1940.** End-of-year examinations, Elvira de Hidalgo's classes, Athens Conservatory (Chapter 16), Athens Conservatory, 35 Pireos St., Athens. [Piano accompanist: Yerasimos Koundouris.]

"Care selve" (George Frederic Handel, *Atalanta*)

"Casta diva" (Vincenzo Bellini, *Norma*)

["D'amor sull'ali rosee"/"Tacea la notte placida"] (Giuseppe Verdi, *Il Trovatore*)

"Élégie" (Henri Duparc)

15. **16 June 1940.** Exhibition concert, Elvira de Hidalgo's opera class, Athens Conservatory (Chapter 16), Great Hall, Athens Conservatory, 35 Pireos St., Athens. Piano accompanist: Yerasimos Koundouris.

Giacomo Puccini, *Suor Angelica*. Role: Suor Angelica.

With Popi Efstratiadou [Arda Mandikian?] (La zia principessa), Iris Streulein (La badessa), Maryitsa Konstantinou (La suora zelatrice), Arda Mandikian [Popi Efstratiadou?] (La maestra delle novizie), Aliki Zografou (Suor Genovefa), Anna Spavera (La suora infirmiera).

16. **21, 22, 23, 24, and 27 October 1940.** Sings from the wings in the incidental music of the Greek National Theater's production of *The Merchant of Venice* (Chapter 17), Greek National Theater, 48 Ayiou Konstantinou and Koumoundourou Sts., Athens. Orchestra under Yorgos Lykoudis and singers both on the stage and in the wings.

Excerpts arranged from Engelbert Humperdinck's *Hänsel und Gretel*

17. **Between 15 February and 9 March 1941.** Between two and ten but probably five or six (of seventy-one) performances (Chapter 18), National Opera, Pallas Cinema, 1 Voukourestiou St., Athens. National Opera orchestra and chorus. Conductor: Walter Pfeffer/[Leonidas Zoras].

Franz von Suppé, *Boccaccio*. Role: Beatrice.

With Michalis Koronis/Nikos Glynos (Boccaccio), Zoe Vlachopoulou/Zozo Remoundou (Fiametta), Kitsa Damasioti/Mitsa Kourahani (Isabella), Nafsika Galanou/Mary Kaloyeropoulou (Beatrice), Spyros Kaloyeras/Titos Xirellis (Lotteringhi), Marika Papadopoulou (Marianna), and the actors Thodoros Androulis, Dimitris Horn, Michalis Kaloyannis, Evangelos Mamias, Athanasia Moustaka, Yannis Stylianopoulos.

18. **19 June 1941.** End-of-year examinations, Elvira de Hidalgo's classes, Athens Conservatory (Chapter 19), Athens Conservatory, 35 Pireos St., Athens. Piano accompanist: Yerasimos Koundouris.

> Unspecified aria (François Boieldieu, *Béniowski, ou Les Éxilés de Kamtchatka*)
> ["Abscheulicher!"] (Ludwig van Beethoven, *Fidelio*)
> "Von ewiger Liebe" (Johannes Brahms)
> ["Pace, pace mio Dio"] (Giuseppe Verdi, *La Forza del Destino*)

19. **3–15 July 1941.** Probably five or six but possibly ten (of fifteen) performances (Chapter 20), National Opera, Park Theater, Mavrommateon St., Athens. National Opera orchestra and chorus. Conductor: Leonidas Zoras.

> Franz von Suppé, *Boccaccio*. Role: Beatrice.

With same cast as for No. 17.

20. **29 May 1942.** End-of-year examinations, Elvira de Hidalgo's classes, Athens Conservatory (Chapter 21), Athens Conservatory, 35 Pireos St., Athens. Piano accompanist: Yerasimos Koundouris.

> "Et incarnatus est" (Wolfgang Amadeus Mozart, Great Mass in C minor, K. 427)
> "La mamma morta" (Umberto Giordano, *Andrea Chénier*)
> "Bel raggio lusinghier" (Gioacchino Rossini, *Semiramide*)
> "Il Ballo" (Ildebrando Pizzetti)

21. **7 June 1942.** Concert in celebration of 150th anniversary of Rossini's birth (Chapter 22), Pallas Cinema, Nikis Ave., Thessaloniki. Piano accompanist: Andreas Paridis.

> "Bel raggio lusinghier" (Gioacchino Rossini, *Semiramide*)
> ["Selva opaca"] (Gioacchino Rossini, *Guglielmo Tell*)
> ["Una voce poco fa"] (Gioacchino Rossini, *Il Barbiere di Siviglia*)
> [Unspecified duet, trio, and/or quartet from Rossini operas]

With Mireille Fléri and Fanny Papanastasiou, sopranos, Petros Epitropakis, tenor, Spyros Kaloyeras, bass.

22. **Summer 1942.** Singing in nightclub (Chapter 22), name and exact location not known but near Omonia Square, Athens. Piano accompanist not known.

"Il Bacio" (Luigi Arditi)
"Mattinata" (Ruggiero Leoncavallo)
Unspecified Greek and Italian songs

23. **27, 28, and 30 August, 2, 4, 6, 8, 10, 12, 13, 16, 18, 20, 22, 24, 26, 27, and 30 September 1942.** Eighteen performances (Chapter 23), National Opera, Klafthmonos Square open-air theater, Athens. National Opera orchestra and chorus. Conductor: Sotos Vassiliadis.

Giacomo Puccini, *Tosca*. Role: Floria Tosca.
With Andonis Delendas/Ludo Kouroussopoulos (8 September and two performances thereafter sung in Italian) (Cavaradossi), Titos Xirellis (Scarpia), Totis Stefanidis/Thanos Tzeneralis (Angelotti), Nikos Doufexiadis (Spoletta), Petros Hoidas (Scarone), Mitsa Kourahani (Pastore), Thodoros Androulis (Il sagrestano).

24. **Winter 1942–43.** Concert with Andonis Delendas and Mitsa Kourahani (Chapter 24), Casa d'Italia, 47 Patission St., Athens. Piano accompanist not known.

Unspecified oratorio
"Vogliatemi bene" (Giacomo Puccini, *Madama Butterfly*)

25. **9 January 1943.** Concert in celebration of 150th anniversary of Rossini's birth (Chapter 24), Casa d'Italia, 47 Patission St., Athens. Piano accompanists: Stefanos Valtetsiotis and Andreas Paridis.

"Quis est homo" (*Stabat Mater*), duet with Mitsa Kourahani, mezzo-
soprano
"Sancta Mater" (*Stabat Mater*), quartet with Mitsa Kourahani, Michalis
Kazandzis, tenor, and Yorgos Moulas, bass
"Nacqui all'affanno" (*La Cenerentola*)
"Bel raggio lusinghier" (*Semiramide*)
With Mary Tambassi, soprano.

26. **19 February–20 March 1943.** Probably nine (but perhaps twelve) performances, unspecified dates (Chapter 25), National Opera, National Theater, 48 Ayiou Konstantinou and Koumoundourou Sts., Athens. National Opera orchestra and chorus. Conductor: Leonidas Zoras.

Manolis Kalomiris, *O Protomastoras* (*The Master Builder*). Role: One of
seven soloists (the others were Kitsa Damasioti, Eleni Kokkori, Irma
Kolassi, Mitsa Kourahani, Frangiska Nikita, Aliki Zografou) reinforcing the chorus for the Intermezzo.

With Andonis Delendas (Master Builder), Zozo Remoundou (Smaragda), Nafsika Galanou (Singer), Anita Bourdakou (Mother), Christoforos Athineos (Archon), Petros Hoidas/Manolis Doumanis/Nikos Papachristos (Old Man).

27. **28 February 1943.** Charity concert in aid of the Hestia of Nea Smyrni (Chapter 25), Sporting Cinema, Nea Smyrni. Piano accompanist: Yerasimos Koundouris.

["Ritorna vincitor"/"O patria mia"] (Giuseppe Verdi, *Aida*)
"Vissi d'arte" (Giacomo Puccini, *Tosca*)
With Petros Epitropakis, tenor, Kitsa Damasioti, mezzo-soprano, Xeni Evangelatou, harp, Raimondi Spyraki, violin, and male chorus under Takis Glykofrydis.

28. **21 April 1943.** Concert for the Fascist celebration of the anniversary of the foundation of Rome (Chapter 24), Casa d'Italia, 47 Patission St., Athens. Piano accompanist not known

"Ritorna vincitor" (Giuseppe Verdi, *Aida*)
"Il Ballo" (Ildebrando Pizzetti)
Encore: unspecified *romanza da camera*
With Andonis Delendas, Petros Epitropakis, and Lambros Mavrakis, tenors, Lysimachi Anastasiadou, mezzo-soprano, and Mary Tambassi, soprano.

29. **22 April 1943.** Easter concert (Chapter 25), Istituto di Cultura Italiana per la Grecia, 3 Zalokosta St., Athens. Small string orchestra conducted by Yorgos Lykoudis.

Stabat Mater (Giovanni Battista Pergolesi)
With Arda Mandikian, mezzo-soprano.

30. **16 May 1943.** Concert for "Italians Around the World Day" (Chapter 24), Casa d'Italia, 47 Patission St., Athens. Piano accompanist: Stefanos Valtetsiotis.

Unspecified arias and duets from Italian operas
With Andonis Delendas, tenor, Lysimachi Anastasiadou, mezzo-soprano, and small string orchestra conducted by Giovanni Battista Dantone.

31. **27 May 1943.** End-of-year examinations, Elvira de Hidalgo's classes, Athens Conservatory (Chapter 21), Athens Conservatory, 35 Pireos St., Athens. Piano accompanist: Yerasimos Koundouris.

["Che farò senza Euridice?"] (Christof Willibald Gluck, *Orfeo ed Euridice*)
"Et incarnatus est" (Wolfgang Amadeus Mozart, Great Mass in C minor, K. 427)
"Suicidio!" (Amilcare Ponchielli, *La Gioconda*)
"Il Ballo" (Ildebrando Pizzetti)

32. **17, 21, and 31 July 1943.** Three performances (Chapter 25), National Opera, Klafthmonos Square open-air theater, Athens. National Opera orchestra and chorus. Conductor: Sotos Vassiliadis.

Giacomo Puccini, *Tosca.* Role: Floria Tosca.

With Andonis Delendas (Cavaradossi), Titos Xirellis (Scarpia), Totis Stefanidis/ Thanos Tzeneralis (Angelloti), Nikos Doufexiadis (Spoletta), Petros Hoidas (Scarone), Petros Efthymiou (Pastore), Thodoros Androulis (Il sagrestano).

33. **21 July 1943.** Recital (Chapter 25), Second Musical Afternoon of Greek Artists, first part (second part, Nikos Dikeos, violin), Moussouri Theater, Mavrommateon St., Athens. Piano accompanist: Andreas Paridis

"Care selve" (George Frederic Handel, *Atalanta*)

"Nacqui all'affanno" (Gioacchino Rossini, *La Cenerentola*)

["D'amor sull'ali rosee"/"Tacea la notte placida"] (Giuseppe Verdi, *Il Trovatore*)

"Io son l'umile ancella" (Francesco Cilèa, *Adriana Lecouvreur*)

"My True Love's Getting Married" (Nikos Lavdas)

34. **31 August or 1 September 1943.** Recital (Chapter 26), White Tower Theater, Thessaloniki. Piano accompanist not known.

Unspecified Schubert lieder

Unspecified Brahms lieder

"Inflammatus" (Gioacchino Rossini, *Stabat Mater*)

["Ah! si, per voi già sento"] (Gioacchino Rossini, *Otello*)

["Assisa a piè d'un salice"] (Gioacchino Rossini, *Otello*)

35. **[Late August/early September 1943.]** Recital (Chapter 26), White Tower Theater, Thessaloniki. Piano accompanist not known. Program not known.

36. **26 September 1943.** Charity concert in aid of Greek students from Egypt (Chapter 26), Olympia Theater, 59 Akadimias St., Athens. Piano accompanist: Kostas Kydoniatis.

"Abscheulicher!" (Ludwig van Beethoven, *Fidelio*)

"Et incarnatus est" (Wolfgang Amadeus Mozart, Great Mass in C minor, K. 427)

"Dis-moi que je suis belle" (Jules Massenet, *Thaïs*)

"Ritorna vincitor" (Giuseppe Verdi, *Aida*)

"Canciòn Española" (Joaquin Turina)

"My True Love's Getting Married" (Nikos Lavdas)

With Poupa Kokkinaki, Dimitris Myrat, Eleni Papadaki, Yorgos Pappas, Angelos Sikelianos, and Emilios Veakis (all reciting); dancers Linda Alma, Angelos Grimanis, Yannis Fléri, and students' ballet; Marios Laskaris, piano; and Kostas Persis, bass.

37. **12 December 1943.** Charity concert in aid of insurance workers suffering from tuberculosis (Chapter 26), Rex Theater, 48 Panepistimiou (now El. Venizelou) St., Athens. Piano accompanist: Lysimachos Androutsopoulos.

"Abscheulicher!" (Ludwig van Beethoven, *Fidelio*)

"Bel raggio lusinghier" (Gioacchino Rossini, *Semiramide*)

["D'amor sull'ali rosee"/"Tacea la notte placida"] (Giuseppe Verdi, *Il Trovatore*)

"Canciòn Española" (Joaquin Turina)

With Maria Cheroyorgou, piano, Dimitris Efstratiou, bass, Loukia Heva, mezzosoprano, Michalis Kazandzis, tenor, Frangiska Nikita, soprano, and Kostas Persis, bass.

38. **22, 23, 25, 27, and 29 April, 4, 7, and 10 May 1944.** Eight performances (Chapter 28), Greek National Opera, Olympia Theater, 59 Akadimias St., Athens. G.N.O. orchestra and chorus. Conductor: Leonidas Zoras.

Eugen d'Albert, *Tiefland.* Role: Marta.

With Andonis Delendas (Pedro), Vangelis Mangliveras (Sebastiano), Zoe Vlachopoulou/Galatea Amaxopoulou (4, 7, and 10 May) (Nuri), Yorgos Moulas (Tommaso), Christoforos Athineos (Moruccio), Lambros Mavrakis (Nando), Zozo Remoundou (Pepa), Mitsa Kourahani (Antonia), Anita Bourdakou (Rosalia).

39. **6 May 1944 and one more performance before 16 June 1944.** Two (of between nine or ten and possibly twelve) performances (Chapter 30), Greek National Opera, Olympia Theater, 59 Akadimias St., Athens. G.N.O. orchestra and chorus. Conductor: Totis Karalivanos.

Pietro Mascagni, *Cavalleria Rusticana.* Role: Santuzza.

With Andonis Delendas (Turiddu), Mitsa Kourahani (Lola), Anita Bourdakou (Mamma Lucia), Takis Tsoubris (Alfio).

40. **21 May 1944.** Charity concert in aid of needy actors and musicians (Chapter 30), Olympia Theater, 59 Akadimias St., Athens. G.N.O. orchestra. Conductor: Leonidas Zoras.

"Casta diva" (Vincenzo Bellini, *Norma*)

With Kitsa Damasioti, mezzo-soprano, Andonis Delendas, tenor, Nafsika Galanou, soprano, and Vangelis Mangliveras, baritone; the actors Manos Filippidis, Maria Kalouta, Vassilis Logothetidis, Kostas Moussouris, Eleni Papadaki, Yorgos Glynos, Iro Hanta, Dimitris Horn, Anna Kalouta, Kostas Maniatakis, Vasso Manolidou, and Rena Vlachopoulou; pianist and jazz composer Yannis Spartakos; and the dancers Loukia Kotsopoulou, Nina Pavlowska, Bella Smaro, Tatiana Varouti, Yannis Fléri, Angelos Grimanis, and Stavros Spyropoulos. The orchestra was also conducted by Hans Hörner, Petros Petridis, Yorgos Vitalis, and Alekos Ainian.

41. **30 July and [5] August 1944.** Two (of six) performances (Chapter 30), Greek National Opera, Odeon of Herodes Atticus, Athens. G.N.O. orchestra and chorus. Conductor: Manolis Kalomiris (possibly Lysimachos Androutsopoulos on 5 August).

Manolis Kalomiris, *O Protomastoras*. Role: Smaragda.
With Michalis Koronis/Andonis Delendas (5 August) (Master Builder), Vangelis Mangliveras/Christoforos Athineos (5 August) (Archon), Nafsika Galanou (Singer), Anita Bourdakou (Mother), Petros Hoidas (Old Man).

42. **14, 15, 17, 20, 22, and 31 August, 1, 3, 6, 9, and 10 September 1944.** Eleven (of fourteen) performances (Chapter 32), Greek National Opera, Odeon of Herodes Atticus, Athens. G.N.O. orchestra and chorus. Conductor: Hans Hörner.

Ludwig van Beethoven, *Fidelio*. Role: Leonore.
With Andonis Delendas/Michalis Koronis (three times) (Florestan), Vangelis Mangliveras/Dimitris Efstratiou (once) (Pizarro), Zoe Vlachopoulou (Marzelline), Yorgos Moulas/Kostas Persis (once) (Rocco). Three performances (19 August, 2 and 7 September) were given with a second cast: Zozo Remoundou, Galatea Amaxopoulou, Michalis Koronis, Dimitris Efstratiou, and Kostas Persis, conducted by Leonidas Zoras.

43. **14, 15, and 24 March 1945.** Three performances (Chapter 34), Greek National Opera, Olympia Theater, 59 Akadimias St., Athens.
Eugen d'Albert, *Tiefland.* Role: Marta.
With same cast and conductor as for No. 38.

44. **20 March 1945.** English Musical Afternoon (Chapter 34), Greek National Opera, Olympia Theater, 59 Akadimias St., Athens. Accompanied by ad hoc quintet under Totis Karalivanos.
"Willow, Willow" (traditional)
"Love, I Have Won You" (Landon Ronald)
"On Wenlock Edge" (Ralph Vaughan Williams)
With Kitsa Damasioti, mezzo-soprano, Spyros Kaloyeras, baritone, and Zoe Vlachopoulou, soprano, accompanied by Yerasimos Koundouris, and the G.N.O. ballet in a suite based on Henry Purcell's dances; in the second half (apart from Mary Kaloyeropoulou), Andonis Delendas, tenor, and Mireille Fléri, soprano (again accompanied by Koundouris), the G.N.O. chorus, the dancer Loukia Kotsopoulou, and the corps de ballet.

45. **30 March 1945.** "A Nite of Stars" (Chapter 34), for the European division of air transport command, 1418th American Air Force Base, Ellinikon, near Athens airport. Members of the G.N.O. orchestra. Conductor: Leonidas Zoras.

"Vissi d'arte" (Giacomo Puccini, *Tosca*)
"Casta diva" (Vincenzo Bellini, *Norma*)

With Mireille Fléri, soprano, Michalis Koronis, tenor, and Zoe Vlachopoulou, soprano.

46. **9 May 1945 [and possibly again on the following day].** Recital (Chapter 35), Third Army Corps Club auditorium, d'Espérey St., Thessaloniki. Piano accompanist: Tonis Yeoryiou. Same program as for No. 47.

47. **17 May 1945.** Recital (Chapter 35), White Tower Theater, Thessaloniki. Piano accompanist: Tonis Yeoryiou. According to Tonis Yeoryiou and Kyriakos Patras, the arias that Mary probably sang in this and the previous (No. 46) recitals were as follows:

"Ocean! thou mighty monster" (Carl Maria von Weber, *Oberon*)
"Leise, leise, fromme Weise" (Carl Maria von Weber, *Der Freischütz*)
"Or sai chi l'onore" (Wolfgang Amadeus Mozart, *Don Giovanni*)
"Una voce poco fa" (Gioacchino Rossini, *Il Barbiere di Siviglia*)
"O mio Fernando" (Gaetano Donizetti, *La Favorita*)
"Casta diva" (Vincenzo Bellini, *Norma*)
"Abscheulicher!" (Ludwig van Beethoven, *Fidelio*)
"Ah! je ris de me voir si belle" (Charles Gounod, *Faust*)
"Ritorna vincitor" (Giuseppe Verdi, *Aida*)
"E strano . . . Ah! fors' è lui . . . Follie, follie" (Giuseppe Verdi, *La Traviata*)
"Où va la jeune Indoue?" (Leo Delibes, *Lakmé*)
"O mio babbino caro" (Giacomo Puccini, *Gianni Schicchi*)
"Mild und leise" (Richard Wagner, *Tristan und Isolde*)

48. **20 May 1945.** Second subscription concert of Thessaloniki Symphony Orchestra (Chapter 35), National Theater, Thessaloniki. Conductor: Evripidis Kotsanidis.

"Ritorna vincitor" (Giuseppe Verdi, *Aida*)
"Casta diva" (Vincenzo Bellini, *Norma*)
Encore: "O mio Fernando" (Gaetano Donizetti, *La Favorita*)

49. **3 August 1945.** Farewell concert (Chapter 36), Rex Theater, 48 Panepistimiou (now El. Venizelou) St., Athens. Piano accompanist: Aliki Lykoudi.

"Batti, batti, o bel Masetto" (Wolfgang Amadeus Mozart, *Don Giovanni*)
"Bel raggio lusinghier" (Gioacchino Rossini, *Semiramide*)
["Ritorna vincitor"/"O patria mia"] (Giuseppe Verdi, *Aida*)

["D'amor sull'ali rosee"/"Tacea la notte placida"] (Giuseppe Verdi, *Il
  Trovatore*)
"Ocean! thou mighty monster" (Carl Maria von Weber, *Oberon*)
Unspecified Spanish songs ["Canciòn Española" (Joaquin Turina)]
Unspecified Greek songs by Thodoros Karyotakis ["Anastasia," "The
  Dream," "Caravel from Chios"] and Yorgos Poniridis ["Our Lady of
  Sparta," "The Anadyomene"]
Encore: two unspecified English songs ["Willow, Willow'
  (traditional)/"Love, I Have Won You" (Landon Ronald)/"On
  Wenlock Edge" (Ralph Vaughan Williams)]

50. **5, 6, 7, 8, 9, 11, and 12 September 1945.** Seven performances (Chapter 37),
Greek National Opera, Alexandras Avenue Theater (now the Metropolitan), 14
Alexandras Ave., Athens. G.N.O. orchestra and chorus. Conductor: Antiochos
Evangelatos.
    Karl Millöcker, *Der Bettelstudent.* Role: Laura.
With Michalis Koronis (Simon), Petros Epitropakis (Ollendorf), Kitsa Damasioti
(Palmatica), Marika Papadopoulou (Bronislava), Michalis Kazandzis (Casimir),
Mitsa Kourahani (Richthofen), Petros Hoidas (Wangenheim), Nikos Papachris-
tos (Schweinitz).

—⁓—

By the time she left Greece, Mary had sung **seven leading roles** in **fifty-six performances** on stage (Santuzza 3, Suor Angelica 1, Tosca 21, Marta 11, Smaragda
2, Leonore 11, Laura 7), besides taking one minor role (Beatrice in *Boccaccio*)
probably a dozen times and singing in the chorus of nine performances of *O Protomastoras*. She had given **at least five and perhaps seven solo recitals** and had
sung in **fourteen concerts**, including one orchestral concert in which she was the
only soloist. In addition, she had sung in at least **ten student concerts and examinations** and in **one live radio broadcast.**
    Not counting the private venues at which she had sung, she had appeared in
twenty theaters, concert halls, and other auditoriums (in Athens: National Conservatory, Athens Conservatory, Olympia Theater, Odeon of Herodes Atticus,
Parnassos Hall, National Theater, the Rex, Pallas, and Sporting indoor theaters,
the Klafthmonos Square, Park, Moussouri, and Alexandras Avenue open-air theaters, Casa d'Italia, Italian Cultural Institute, and the American base at Ellinikon;
in Thessaloniki: National Theater, White Tower Theater, Third Army Corps
Club, Pallas Cinema). This is equivalent to **about one-seventh of the total number of auditoriums in her whole career,** as she was to sing in another 123 theaters
and concert halls after leaving Greece.[3]
    One last point worth stressing is the major part played by Andonis Delendas,
who was undoubtedly Maria Callas's first regular tenor. He played opposite her in

five of her seven lead roles and forty of her fifty-six appearances (*Tosca* 18, *Tiefland* 11, *Fidelio* 8, *Cavalleria Rusticana* 2, and *O Protomastoras* 1), which means that he was by her side at the most important moments of her career in Greece.

FIRST APPEARANCES

1. **At a public student exhibition concert:** Aged 14 and 4 months, **11 April 1938**. Parnassos Hall, class of Maria Trivella.

2. **At a public performance, not all musical:** Aged 14 and 7 months, **4 July 1938**, Rex Theater, American Independence Day celebrations.

3. **At a public student opera performance:** Aged 15 and 4 months, **2 April 1939**, Olympia Theater, *Cavalleria Rusticana*, as Santuzza, conducted by Michalis Vourtsis.

4. **At a public professional opera performance:** Aged 16 and 2 months, **February 1941**, Pallas Cinema, National Opera, *Boccaccio*, as Beatrice, conducted by Walter Pfeffer.

5. **In a leading role:** Aged 18 and 9 months, **27 August 1942**, Klafthmonos Square open-air theater, National Opera, *Tosca*, as Floria Tosca, conducted by Sotos Vassiliadis.

6. **At a public recital with piano accompaniment:** (i) *Participation in mixed program*: Aged 18 and 6 months, **7 June 1942**, Thessaloniki, Pallas Cinema, with Andreas Paridis. (ii) *Solo for one half of program*: Aged 19 and 8 months, **21 July 1943**, Moussouri Theater, with Andreas Paridis. (iii) *Full solo recital*: Aged 19 and 9 months, **31 August** or **1 September 1943**, Thessaloniki, White Tower Theater, accompanist not known.

7. **At a public concert with orchestra:** Aged 21 and 5 months, **20 May 1945**, Thessaloniki, National Theater, second subscription concert of the Thessaloniki Symphony Orchestra, conducted by Evripidis Kotsanidis.

—⚭—

I like to think that [Callas and Maria] both go together, because Callas has been Maria, and in my singing and in my work my own self has been there every second. I've done nothing falsely, I've worked with all honesty, so Maria has [done]. If one really tries to listen to me seriously, one will find all of myself in there. So, probably you can't detach. Only that Callas is sort of a celebrity...

To David Frost, New York, December 1970

Sources, Bibliography,
and Abbreviations

PERSONAL INTERVIEWS

In the course of my research to gather material for this book I spoke to many people who, each in his or her own way, gave me valuable assistance. All of them, from viewpoints representing a wide range of occupations and positions, had something important to say about Mary and her relatives or about other persons, events, and the general climate of the period. Without their testimony, no account of Maria Callas's years in Greece could have been written, or at any rate it would certainly not have been as full as I hope this one is. I should like to thank them all once again for their cooperation and support. With one exception (Anthi Zacharatou, who would not allow it), our conversations are recorded on tape.

The list below gives the occupation or status of each person at the time to which their recollections refer and the date of my first interview with each of them. Small capitals denote the abbreviations by which their names are referred to in the Notes. G.N.O. stands for Greek National Opera. And a note on Greek names: The masculine and feminine of surnames usually have different endings. Names ending in *os*, *is*, and *as* in the masculine become *ou*, *i* or *ou*, and *a*, respectively, in the feminine; the masculine ending *ou* remains unchanged.

ADALI	Penelope Adali, niece of Maria Trivella, 18 Jan. 1994
ALKEOU	Maria Alkeou, actress, pupil of de Hidalgo, 30 Apr. 1993
AMAXOPOULOU	Galatea Amaxopoulou, soprano, pupil of de Hidalgo, 7 Oct. 1994
ANEMOYANNIS	Yorgos Anemoyannis, stage director at G.N.O., 9 Nov. 1993
CHEROYORGOU	Maria Cheroyorgou, pianist, student at National Conservatory, 28 Apr. 1993
CHIOTAKIS	Stefanos Chiotakis, tenor, chorus member and comprimario at G.N.O., 20 Nov. 1993

591

DALMATI	Margarita Dalmati, occasional pupil of de Hidalgo, 31 May 1993
DAMASIOTI	Kitsa Damasioti, student at Athens Conservatory, mezzo-soprano at G.N.O., 2 May 1993
DIORIDOU	Elli Dioridou, soprano, pupil of de Hidalgo, 31 May 1993
DOUFEXIADIS	Nikos Doufexiadis, tenor, comprimario at G.N.O., 30 Apr. 1993
DOUNIAS	Kostas Dounias, tenor, chorus member at G.N.O., 2 Dec. 1993
EFFIE	Effie Dimitriadou-Hadzimitakou, first cousin of M.C., 23 Nov. 1993
EMBIRIKOS	Hariton Embirikos, brother of Jackie's "fiancé" Miltiadis E., 11 Nov. 1994
EXAKOUSTOU	Eleni Exakoustou, wife of pianist Tonis Yeoryiou, 10 May 1994
FLÉRI	Mireille Fléri, soprano at G.N.O., 20 Apr. 1993
GOUDELIS	Yorgos Goudelis, lawyer, family friend, 27 May 1994
HADZIS	Manolis Hadzis, a member of de Hidalgo's circle, 25 Sept. 1993
IKONOMIDI	Kalliopi Ikonomidi, wife of conductor and principal of the Athens Conservatory Filoktitis I., 9 Apr. 1994
KALAIDZAKIS	Andonis Kalaidzakis, tenor, chorus member at G.N.O., 7 Nov. 1993
KALOYEROPOULOU	Jackie (Yakinthi) Kaloyeropoulou-Stathopoulou, M.C.'s sister, 8 Apr. 1993
KAMARA	Lalaki Kamara, friend and patient of Dr. Papatestas, 6 Sept. 1996
KAMBANIS	Yannis (Zannis) Kambanis, tenor, pupil of Trivella, 30 May 1991
KAMBOURI	Anna Kambouri, second cousin of M.C., 13 Dec. 1993
KAMBOURIS	Nikos Kambouris, second cousin of M.C., 13 Dec. 1993
KATIE	Katie Dimitriadou-Zerva, first cousin of M.C., 18 Dec. 1993
KOLASSI	Irma Kolassi, mezzo-soprano, répétiteur at G.N.O., 22 Mar. 1995
KOPANOU	Afroditi Kopanou, soprano, fellow pupil at National Conservatory, 31 May 1997
KOUKOULI	Christina (Titina) Koukouli, first cousin of M.C.'s mother, 30 Apr. 1994

KOURAHANI	Mitsa Kourahani-Kounelli, mezzo-soprano at G.N.O., pupil of de Hidalgo, 22 Apr. 1993
KOUROUSSOPOULOU	Xenia Kouroussopoulou, wife of tenor Loudovikos K., 18 Nov. 1993
KRASSA	Marina Krassa, third wife of conductor Leonidas Zoras, 26 May 1993
KYDONIATIS	Kostas Kydoniatis, professor at Athens Conservatory, accompanist, 15 May 1993
LOUVI	Ypatia Louvi-Maratou, soprano, pupil of de Hidalgo, 13 May 1993
MAKRIYANNI	Katie Makriyanni, piano student at Athens Conservatory, 7 Feb. 1995
MANDIKIAN	Arda Mandikian, mezzo-soprano, pupil of de Hidalgo, 12 May 1993
MANGLIVERAS	Christos Mangliveras, brother of the baritone Vangelis M., 13 May 1993
MATARANGA	Elvira Mataranga, student at National Conservatory, chorus member at G.N.O., 6 Oct. 1993
MATSOUKI	Klada Matsouki, pianist, de Hidalgo's class accompanist, 27 Sept. 1993
MICHAILIDIS	Dimitris Michailidis, piano student at Athens Conservatory, accompanist, 18 Jan. 1994
MIRKA	Mirka Dimitriadou-Dendrinou, first cousin of M.C., 19 May 1993
MORGAN	Raymond George Morgan, British officer, romance with M.C. in Oct.–Nov. 1944, 30 Nov. 1993
MOUNDOURI	Maria Moundouri, distant cousin of M.C. in Thessaloniki, 8 Oct. 1993
NIKOLAIDI	Elli Nikolaidi, chorus mistress at National Conservatory and G.N.O., 28 Mar. 1992
NINON	Ninon Dimitriadou-Kambouri, first cousin of M.C., 19 Jan. 1994
PAPACHRISTOS	Nikos Papachristos, bass, chorus member and comprimario at G.N.O., 2 Nov. 1994
PAPADOPOULOU	Marika Papadopoulou, pupil of de Hidalgo, soprano at G.N.O., 2 May 1993
PARIDIS	Andreas Paridis, pianist, accompanist, 20 Sept. 1993
PATRAS	Kyriakos Patras, violist, Thessaloniki Symphony Orchestra, 11 May 1994
PATRIARCHEAS	Yorgos Patriarcheas, assistant stage designer at G.N.O., 17 Dec. 1994

POLITOU	Ekaterini Politou, soprano, pupil of de Hidalgo, 31 May 1993
RITSOU	Lola Ritsou-Zolota, soprano, pupil of de Hidalgo, 25 Sept. 1994
SALINGAROS	Spyros Salingaros, baritone, chorus member and comprimario at G.N.O., pupil of de Hidalgo, 4 Apr. 1993
SALTA	Antigone Salta, mezzo-soprano, chorus member at G.N.O., 18 May 1994
SIGARAS	Takis Sigaras, industrialist, intimate friend of M.C., 25 May 1993
SIMIONATO	Giulietta Simionato, mezzo-soprano, later colleague and friend of M.C., 22 May 1998
SIMIRIOTIS	Vyron Simiriotis, tenor, student at National Conservatory, 2 Dec. 1993
SKORDOULI	Lela Skordouli, soprano, pupil of de Hidalgo, chorus member at G.N.O., 2 Dec. 1993
THIVEOU	Ismini Thiveou, sister of a neighbor of M.C., 15 Oct. 1993
TZAKA	Nada Tzaka, niece of a neighbor of M.C., 16 Nov. 1993
VAROUTI	Tatiana Varouti, G.N.O. dancer, wife of conductor Leonidas Zoras, 19 May 1993
VASSILIADOU	Haris Vassiliadou, wife of conductor Sotos V., 18 May 1994
VLACHOPOULOU	Zoe Vlachopoulou, soprano at G.N.O., pupil of de Hidalgo, 28 Nov. 1992
XAKOUSTI	Kiki Xakousti, close personal friend of M.C., 15 Dec. 1993
YANNOPOULOS	Dino Yannopoulos, stage director at G.N.O., 2 June 1993
YENNAROPOULOU	Ioanna Yennaropoulou, wife of tenor Dionysis Thanos, 23 Sept. 1994
YEORYIOU	Tonis Yeoryiou, pianist, accompanist, 13 Nov. 1993
ZACHARIOU	Nikos Zachariou (Nicola Zaccaria), bass, chorus member and comprimario at G.N.O., 26 May 1993
ZACHAROPOULOU	Niki Zacharopoulou, piano student at Athens Conservatory, 2 Nov. 1993

Besides these, many others also helped me, often no less materially but perhaps at shorter length or in different ways, for example in telephone conversations. The names of those are to be found only in the text and in the relevant notes. I am grateful to them all for the information they gave me as well as for their cooperativeness and good will.

UNPUBLISHED SOURCES

Capitals denote the abbreviation by which the following are referred to in the Notes.

ELIA	Hellenic Literary and Historical Archives Society (Theodoros Synadinos papers)
M.B.G./G.N.O.	Minutes of the board of governors, Greek National Opera
M.B.G./N.T.G.	Minutes of the board of governors, National Theater of Greece

Callas, Maria, "Smentite di articolo 'Time'" (MS, in Italian, 1956). The MS was preserved in Meneghini's papers; he passed it on to Renzo Allegri when the latter was ghostwriting his memoirs. Allegri also used it in *La vera storia di Maria Callas* (Milan 1991), and he kindly allowed me to use it freely.

Examination records, archives of the Athens Conservatory.

Linardos, Petros, *Musikleben in Athen, 1941–1944: Der Einfluss der deutschen und italienischen Besatzung*, unpublished masters thesis, Institut für Musikgeschichte, Vienna 1987.

Register book of the National Theater, 13 Nov. 1943–23 Mar. 1945, archives of the National Theater of Greece.

"Works and Sundry Festivals, Receptions, Concerts, etc., of the Royal Theater of Greece, 19 Mar. 1932–27 May 1956," manuscript book, archives of the National Theater of Greece.

PUBLISHED WORKS

Small capitals denote the abbreviation by which the following are referred to in the Notes.

ALLEGRI	Renzo Allegri, *La vera storia di Maria Callas*, Milan (Mondadori) 1991.
ARDOIN	John Ardoin and Gerald Fitzgerald, *Callas*, London (Thames and Hudson) 1974.
DE CARVALHO	George de Carvalho, "The Prima Donna," *Time*, 29 Oct. 1956.
GARA	Eugenio Gara, *Maria Callas*, Milan (Ricordi) 1957.
GENTE	Renzo Allegri, "La Callas: Diva per vendetta, parla la maestra del celebre soprano greco," *Gente*, June 1968.

HARRIS   Kenneth Harris, "Callas," *The Observer Review*, 8 and 15 Feb. 1970.

DE HIDALGO   Interview of Elvira de Hidalgo to *Oggi*, published in full in Bruno Tosi's *Giovane Callas*, Padua 1997, 159–167.

JACKIE   Jackie Callas, *Sisters*, London (Macmillan) 1989.

JELLINEK   George Jellinek, *Callas: Portrait of a Prima Donna*, London (Dover) 1986; first published New York (Ziff-Davis) 1960.

LEGGE   Walter Legge, "La Divina: Callas Remembered," *Opera News* 42, no. 5, Nov. 1977. (Reprinted in Elisabeth Schwarzkopf, *On and Off the Record: A Memoir of Walter Legge*, London 1982, 192–203).

LITSA   Evangelia Callas, *My Daughter, Maria Callas*, London (Leslie Frewin) 1967; first published New York (Fleet) 1960.

MARCHAND   Polyvios Marchand, *Maria Callas: Her Greek Career*, Athens (Gnossi) 1983.

MARGRIET   "Maria Callas," anonymous article-interview, *Margriet* (Amsterdam), no. 12, 1959.

MARIA   English translation of Callas's memoirs in David A. Lowe, ed., *Callas As They Saw Her*, London (Ungar) 1987, 15–51. Dictated in late 1956 and first published in five installments by Anita Pensotti in *Oggi*, 10, 17, 24, and 31 Jan., and 7 Feb. 1957. The first part was titled "I miei anni terribili in Grecia."

MENEGHINI   Giovanni Battista Meneghini, *My Wife Maria Callas*, New York (Farrar, Straus & Giroux) 1982; first published as "La mia vita con Maria Callas," *Gente*, 31 Oct. 1980–24 Apr. 1981.

PROUSE   Derek Prouse, "Maria Callas Speaks," interview in *The Sunday Times*, 19 Mar., 26 Mar., and 2 Apr. 1961.

SCOTT   Michael Scott, *Maria Meneghini Callas*, London (Simon & Schuster) 1991.

STANCIOFF   Nadia Stancioff, *Maria: Callas Remembered*, London (Dutton) 1987.

STASSINOPOULOS   Arianna Stassinopoulos, *Maria: Beyond the Callas Legend*, London (Weidenfeld and Nicolson) 1980.

SUTHERLAND   Robert Sutherland, "Diary of a Tour with the Superstar," *Sunday Telegraph*, 31 Aug. and 7 Sept. 1980.

TSOUTIS   Stamatis Tsoutis, "Maria Callas: The First Authentic Biography of the Great Greek Soprano," *Niki*, 20 July–

	30 Aug. 1963 (part 1, 35 installments) and 31 Aug.– 18 Sept. 1963 (part 2, 15 installments).
VASSILIKOS	Vassilis Vassilikos, *The Eviction*, 2nd ed., Athens (Gnossi) 1989.
VASSILIOU	Vassilis Vassiliou, "Maria Callas," *Ekloyi*, no. 187, 14 Aug. 1960, reprinted in *Kathimerini*, 18–23 Sept. 1977.

The following selection of books and articles does not include reviews of performances.

A. B., "Konzrertbericht aus Saloniki," newspaper clipping dated 2–3 Sept. 1943, reprinted with commentary by Kurt Wenzel, "Maria Callas und Rossini," *Orpheus* (Berlin), no. 6, June 1983, where the source of the original article is given as the *Deutsche Nachrichten in Griechenland.*

Allegri, Renzo, and Roberto Allegri, *Callas by Callas*, Milan (Mondadori) 1997; English-language edition (Universe Publishing) 1998.

Amis, John, "Callas via Legge," *Uw Maria Callas Brief* (Holsbeek), no. 18, Dec. 1989.

Ardoin, John, "Callas Today," *Musical America*, Dec. 1964.

———, "Maria Callas: The Early Years," *Opera Quarterly* 3, no. 2, summer 1985.

———, *The Callas Legacy*, London (Duckworth) 1988.

———, *Callas at Juilliard: The Master Classes*, London (Robson Books) 1988; first published New York (Alfred A. Knopf) 1987; corrected reprint published Portland (Amadeus Press) 1998.

"At La Scala, the Triumph of U.S.–Born Maria Callas," *Newsweek*, 10 Jan. 1955.

Barnes, Clive, "Callas, the Unique," *Music and Musicians*, Jan. 1964.

Barry, Naomi, "Maria Callas: 'The Singer Is Nothing But the Servant of Genius,'" *International Herald Tribune*, 30 June 1971.

Beer, Manfred, "Mit Lili Marleens Lied . . . ," *Die Welt*, 6/7 May 1970.

Bottero, Irene, *Maria Callas, croce e delizia*, Mondovì (Nuova Editrice Italiana) 1997.

Bragaglia, Leonardo, *L'arte dello stupore*, Rome (Bulzoni) 1977.

Bronte, André, "Les quatre grands combats de la Callas," *France-Dimanche*, 3, 10, 17, and 24 Oct. 1977.

Burroughs, Bruce, "Maria Callas, 'Yes, But . . . ,'" *Opera Quarterly* 6, no. 4, summer 1989.

Callas, Maria, "I Am Not Guilty of All Those Callas Scandals," *Life*, 25 May 1959.

———, unsigned interview with, *Elle*, 9 Feb. 1970.

"Callas the Woman," unsigned obituary, *The Sunday Times*, 18 Sept. 1977.

Cartier, Jacqueline, "Callas immortelle," five-part article, *France-Soir*, 1981–82.

———, "La vie passionnée de la Callas," *France-Soir*, 18–19 Sept. 1977.

Cassidy, Claudia, "Splendor in the Night," *Opera News* 42, no. 5, Nov. 1977.

Caviglia, Pier Luigi, "Il fenomeno vocale storico umano di Maria Callas," *Discoteca*, June 1967.

Celletti, Rodolfo, "La voix," *Opéra International, Spécial Maria Callas*, supplement to no. 5, Feb. 1978.

————, "Una voce per la storia," *Musica Viva*, Jan. 1988.

————, "Maria Callas," *Musica*, June 1984.

————, "Maria Callas—Sopranistin, Kultfigur, Musik-wissenschafterin," *Neue Zürcher Zeitung*, 25 June 1996.

Celli, Teodoro, "Una voce venuta da un altro secolo," *Oggi*, 20 Mar. 1958.

————, "Perchè la sua strana voce è bella," *Oggi*, 27 Mar. 1958.

————, "La sua voce commuove perchè contiene un drama," *Oggi*, 3 Apr. 1958.

Celli, Teodoro, and Giuseppe Pugliese, *Tullio Serafin, il patriarca del Melodramma*, Venice 1985.

Christiansen, Rupert, *Prima Donna*, London (Penguin Books) 1984.

————, "Callas: A Polemic," *Opera*, June 1987.

Cristallo, Michela, "Fragile dea," *Elle* (Italian edition), June 1990.

Crutchfield, Will, "The Story of a Voice," *The New Yorker*, 13 Nov. 1995.

Dalmati, Margarita, "Maria Callas," *Nea Skepsi*, nos. 176–177, Nov.–Dec. 1977.

————, review of Polyvios Marchand's book, *Nea Estia*, no. 1365, 15 May 1984.

"Der einsame Tod der Maria Callas," *Neue Revue Illustrierte*, no. 40, 26 Sept. 1977.

Díaz Du-Pond, Carlos, "Callas in Mexico," *Opera*, Apr. 1973.

"Die Primadonna," *Der Spiegel*, no. 7, 13 Feb. 1957.

di Stefano, Maria, *Callas, nemica mia*, Milan (Rusconi) 1992.

Dragadze, Peter, "My Lonely World: A Woman Looking for Her Voice," *Life*, 30 Oct. 1964.

————, "Ma che vita inutile, una vita senza figli," *Gente*, 1 Oct. 1977.

————, "Parla la madre di Maria Callas," *Gente*, 15 Oct. 1977.

Drakos, Th., "The Callas-Onassis Romance," 42 installments, *Thisavros*, nos. 531–572, 4 Oct. 1976–18 July 1977.

Dufresne, Claude, *La Callas*, Paris (Perrin) 1990.

Eggington, Joyce, "My Famous Daughter Will Never Be Happy," *Sunday Dispatch*, 2 Dec. 1959.

"Faüle Tomaten für Grösste Sängerin," *Kasseler Zeitung*, 1 Dec. 1956.

Filippas, Filippos, "Maria Callas's Mother Reveals . . . ," *Thisavros*, no. 22, 24 Nov. 1977.

————, "Maria Callas Forever," *Reportage*, no. 2, June–July 1979.

Fotinos, A., "Maria Callas, a Living Legend," *Evropaia*, 3 Feb. 1983.

Galatopoulos, Stelios, *Callas: Prima Donna Assoluta*, London (W. H. Allen) 1976.

————, "The Art of Callas," *Mousiki*, no. 22, Sept. 1979.

————, *Maria Callas: Sacred Monster*, London (Fourth Estate) 1998; subsequently published New York (Simon & Schuster) 1999.

Gastel-Chiarelli, Cristina, *Maria Callas*, Venice (Marsilio Editori) 1981.

"Geliebt und Gehasst: die Callas," *Radio Revue* (Berlin), no. 51, 20 Dec. 1959.

Gregor, Ella, "Die Callas," 21 installments, *Abend*, 4–25 May 1959.

Gregory, John M., "Maria Callas: 'I Am Not Stubborn, I Am Right,'" *The Star Weekly Magazine*, 5 Sept. 1959.

Gruen, John, "Maria Callas: 'I Am a Very Normal Human Being,'" *The New York Times*, 31 Oct. 1971.

Guandalini, Gina, *Callas, l'ultima diva*, Turin (Eda) 1987.

Hannine Vallaut, J.-J., *Giulietta Simionato*, Parma (Azzali) 1987.

Haralambopoulos, H. D., "The Autobiography of Colonel Konstantinos Petrou Dimitriadis, Secretary to General Yannis Rangos in the War of 1821," *Bulletin of the Historical and Ethnological Society of Greece* 22, 1979.

Harewood, Earl of, "The Art of Maria Callas," based on the Adrian Boult Lecture, Queen Elizabeth Hall, 10 Apr. 1978, *Recorded Sound*, no. 10, 1979.

————, chapter 15 in *The Tongs and the Bones*, London (Weidenfeld and Nicolson) 1981.

Herzfeld, Friedrich, *La Callas*, Berlin (Rembrandt Verlag) 1959.

Herzog, Friedrich W., "Callas Athene, mit Hilfe der PK 1943 bei ihren Landsleuten durchgesetzt," *Die Wildente* (Hamburg), no. 21, Oct. 1959.

————, "Die Primadonna des Jahrhunderts, als Maria Callas noch Maria Kalojeropoulou war," 1959 press clipping, with no indication of source.

Hume, Paul, "Maria Callas, Fiery Opera Star of Dramatic Power," *The Washington Post*, 17 Sept. 1977.

Jackson, Paul, *Saturday Afternoons at the Old Met: The Metropolitan Opera Broadcasts 1931–1950*, Portland (Amadeus Press) 1992.

Jellinek, George, "The Background to a Callas Biography," *The Maria Callas International Club Magazine*, no. 10, Oct. 1993.

Jessup, Laura, "Maria Callas Versus Everybody," *Opera News*, Sept. 1958.

Karakandas, Yorgos, *All About Opera*, Athens 1978.

Kesting, Jürgen, *Maria Callas* (Eng. trans.), London (Quartet Books) 1992.

Krineos, Petros, "A Heavenly Voice, a Frosty Eye," interview given by Maria Trivella to an Athens newspaper, c. 10 Mar. 1957 (in Trivella's papers).

Lalas, Thanassis, "The Callas I Remember," *To Vima tis Kyriakis*, 14 Mar. 1993.

Lazaridis, Odysseas, "Maria Callas the Great," *Tachydromos*, 22 Sept. 1977.

Leibowitz, René, "Le secret de la Callas," *Les Temps Modernes*, July 1959.

Leontaritis, Yorgos, "From the Old Phonograph to the Triumph at Carnegie Hall," 13 installments, *Acropolis*, 18 Sept.–2 Oct. 1977.

Leotsakos, Yorgos, "Elvira de Hidalgo: Her Life and Work," *Proini*, 31 Jan. 1980.

————, *Greek Opera: 100 Years, 1888–1988*, Athens 1988.

Linakis, Steven, *Diva: The Life and Death of Maria Callas*, London (Peter Owen) 1981.

Lorcey, Jacques, *Maria Callas*, Paris (PAC) 1977.

Lowe, David A., ed., *Callas As They Saw Her*, London (Ungar) 1987.

Mamakis, Achilleas, "What's Up with Maria Callas?" *To Ethnos*, 26 Feb. 1957.

Mancini, Roland, "Biographie," *Opéra International, Spécial Maria Callas*, supplement to no. 5, Feb. 1978.

Marcilly, Jean, "La Callas jette son masque, 'Je voudrais mourir muette,'" *Noir et Blanc*, 22 July 1964.

Mathers, Steven, "Callas the Savoyard," *The Callas Circle*, no. 2, Feb. 1995.

Matz, Mary Jane, "We Introduce Maria Meneghini Callas," *Opera News*, 3 Dec. 1956.

Meneghini, Pia, "Sette anni con Maria," in Bruno Tosi, *Giovane Callas*, Padua 1997.

Merlin, Virginie, "Dans l'intimité de la Callas," *Le Match de Paris*, Sept. 1987.

Neville, Robert, "Voice of an Angel," *Life*, 31 Oct. 1955.

Orfanos, Yorgos, "Maria Callas: Anatomy of a Genius," *Odos Panos*, no. 32, Sept.–Oct. 1987.

Palesti, Marika, *Why Voices Are Destroyed Prematurely, Like That of Callas*, Athens 1962.

Pensotti, Anita, "Maria, ti chiedo perdono," *Oggi*, 1 Oct. 1977.

Pettitt, John, "Maria Callas: The Early Struggle," *The Maria Callas International Club Magazine*, no. 17, Feb. 1996, and no. 18, June 1996.

Pilichos, Yorgos, "Beautiful, Tragically Human, and Lonely," *Ta Nea*, 29 Mar. 1969.

———, "The Human Face of Maria Callas," *To Vima tis Kyriakis*, 13 Sept. 1992.

Pilloli, Carla, "Sì, lo sapevo: Maria Callas si è lasciata morire," *Gente*, 9 Dec. 1978.

Pisani, Chiara, "La Callas fugge la sua madre," *Oggi*, 5 Mar. 1958.

"Processo alla Callas," panel discussion, *Radiocorriere TV*, no. 48, 30 Nov. 1969. English translation ("The Callas Debate") by Madeleine Fagandini first published in *Opera*, Sept.–Oct. 1970, and reprinted in D. Lowe, ed., *Callas As They Saw Her*, London (Ungar) 1987.

Rasponi, Lanfranco, *The Last Prima Donnas*, London (Gollancz) 1984.

Ravazzin, R., "Intervista con la 'Gioconda' giunta da oltre oceano," *Il Gazzettino*, 22 July 1947.

Rémy, Pierre Jean, *Callas, une vie*, Paris (Ramsay) 1982.

Restrepo, José Félix Patino, "Maria Callas' Health and Illnesses," *The Maria Callas International Club Magazine*, no. 15, June 1995.

Riemens, Leo, *Maria Callas*, Utrecht (Bruna & Zoon) 1960.

Roussos, Yorgos, "I'm Not Like the Others: The Case of Callas," *Tachydromos*, 10 Aug. 1957.

Santini, Aldo, four articles, *Oggi*, nos. 39–42, 24 Sept.–15 Oct. 1986.

Savvakis, Alexios, *Ioannis Tsarouchis*, Athens (Kastaniotis) 1993.

Schickel, Richard, "Callas," *Look*, 17 Feb. 1959.

Schifano, L., chapter 16 in *Luchino Visconti: The Flames of Passion*, London (Collins) 1990.

Schroeter, Werner, "Der Herztot der Primadonna," *Der Spiegel*, no. 40, 26 Sept. 1977.

Segalini, Sergio, *Callas, les images d'une voix*, Paris (Francis van de Velde) 1987.

———, "Singing Rediscovered," in D. Lowe, ed., *Callas As They Saw Her*, London (Ungar) 1987.

Serafin, Tullio, "A Triptych of Singers," *Opera Annual*, no. 8, 1962, first published in *Discoteca*, Sept. 1961.

Sievewright, Alan, "Callas Remembered," *Opera* 28, no. 11, Nov. 1977.

Signorini, Alfonso, "Ecco le lettere, i documenti e le foto che conservo della mia amica Callas," *Gente*, 2 and 9 Nov. 1992.

Soria, Dorle J., "Greek Sorceress," *Opera News* 42, no. 5, Nov. 1977.

Spanidou, Corinna, *Onassis As I Knew Him*, Athens (Estia) 1996.

Tosi, Bruno, *Casta diva, l'incomparabile Callas*, Rome 1993.

———, *Giovane Callas*, Padua 1997.

Tripeleff, *Un amore di Maria Callas*, Pavia (Liber) 1994.

Vannozzi, Eraldo, and Teresa Bryk Ovi, *Storia del paracadutismo in Maremma, 1946–1987*, Novara (Banca Popolare) 1987.

Vokos, Yorgos, "Maria Callas Arrived the Day Before Yesterday, Full of Emotion But Saying Nothing," *Acropolis*, 30 July 1957.

———, interview with Maria Callas in *Acropolis* and *Apoyevmatini*, 17 Sept. 1977.

Wisneski, Henry, *Maria Callas: The Art Behind the Legend*, New York (Doubleday) 1975.

Zoras, Leonidas, "First Steps at the Conservatory, the National Opera, and the Escape Toward Glory," *To Theatro*, nos. 59–60, Sept.–Dec. 1977.

CALLAS INTERVIEWS AND CONVERSATIONS

Small capitals denote the abbreviation by which the following are referred to in the Notes.

BANZET	Radio interview, "Trois jours avec Maria Callas," with Micheline Banzet, RTF, Paris, 8 Feb. 1965.
CALONI	Radio interview, "Hommage à Maria Callas," with Philippe Caloni, Radio-France Musique, Paris, 1976.
DOWNES	Radio interview with Edward Downes for the Metropolitan Opera broadcast intermissions, New York, 30 Dec. 1967 and 13 Jan. 1968.
FLEETWOOD	Radio interview with Harry Fleetwood, New York, 13 and 27 Mar. 1958.
FROST	Television interview with David Frost, *The David Frost Show*, New York, 10 Dec. 1970.

HAREWOOD   Television interview with Lord Harewood for the BBC,
                "Maria Callas Talks to Lord Harewood," Paris, 23–26 Apr.
                1968.
L'INVITÉ   Television program, *L'invité du dimanche*, Paris, 20 Apr.
                1969.
MURROW   Television interview, *Person to Person*, with Edward R.
                Murrow, New York, 24 Jan. 1958.

Radio interview with Achilleas Mamakis, Athens, 4 Aug. 1957.
Radio interview with Mr. Rodrini, Milan, Sept. 1957.
Television interview with Norman Ross, Chicago, 17 Nov. 1957.
Television interview (together with her father, George Callas) with Hy Gardner,
    New York, 26 Feb. 1958.
Radio interview with David Holmes, London, 23 Sept. 1958.
Radio interview with Charles Trenet, Paris, 1959.
Radio interview with Michel Glotz, Paris, 25 May 1963.
Radio interview with William Weaver, Paris, 10 Apr. 1965.
Private conversation with John Ardoin, Dallas, 13 Sept. 1968.
Television interview with Mike Wallace, New York, 3 Feb. 1974.
Television interview with Barbara Walters, New York, 15 Apr. 1974.

Notes

PREFACE

1. The number of pages devoted to the period from 1923 to 1945 by the writers who give the most coverage to those years is as follows: Maria Callas herself, in her memoirs (dictated in late 1956) in *Oggi*, Jan.–Feb. 1957, 11 of a total of 36 pages (28 percent); her mother Evangelia (Litsa) Callas and her sister Jackie Kaloyeropoulou, who cover the whole of Maria's life (up to 1977), 85 of 175 (48 percent) and 85 of 250 (34 percent), respectively, but the latter figure includes a good many pages exclusively concerned with Jackie herself; Eugenio Gara (1957) 3 substantial pages on her childhood and her Greek period out of a total of 22 (13.6 percent); Leo Riemens (1960) 6 of 156 (3.9 percent); and George Jellinek (1960) 26 of 355 (7.3 percent). The corresponding figures for Callas's biographers who cover her whole life are as follows (in order of publication): John Ardoin (1974) 3 informative pages of 21 in the biographical chapter of a 282-page book (3 percent); Henry Wisneski (1975) 20 of 422 (4.8 percent); Stelios Galatopoulos (1976) 20 of 353 (5.6 percent); Jacques Lorcey (1977) 23 of 432 (5.3 percent); Roland Mancini (1978) 8 of 108 (7.5 percent); Arianna Stassinopoulos (1980) 35 of 329 (10.6 percent); Cristina Gastel-Chiarelli (1981) 14 of 213 (6.1 percent); Steven Linakis (1981) 25 of 170 (14.8 percent); Mario Pasi (1981) 10 of 320 (3.1 percent); Pierre Jean Rémy (1982) 23 of about 315 (7.3 percent); Giovanni Battista Meneghini (1982) about 10 scattered pages of 350 (3 percent); Martin Monestier (1985) 23 of 270 (8.5 percent); Nadia Stancioff (1987) 32 of about 280 (11 percent); Gina Guandalini (1987) 20 of 320 (6.2 percent); Claude Dufresne (1990) 40 of 283 (14.1 percent); Michael Scott (1991) 27 of 312 (8.7 percent); Alberto Petrolli (1991) 30 of 461 (6.5 percent); Renzo Allegri (1991) 33 (useful) of 271 (12.2 percent); Jürgen Kesting (1992) 9 of 416 (2.2 percent); Eleni Kanthou (1995) 10 of 168 (6 percent); Carla Verga (1995) 4 of 132 (3 percent); Renzo Allegri and Roberto Allegri (1997) 18 of 170 (10.6 percent); Irene Bottero (1997) 15 of 240 (6.3 percent); Bruno Tosi (1997) 48 of 230 (20.8 percent); David Bret (1997) 26 of 380 (6.8 percent); Galatopoulos (1998) 38 of 564 (6.7 percent). The figures show that less than ten percent of about nine thousand pages cover the first twenty-two of Maria Callas's fifty-four years, that is to say, about forty percent of her lifespan.
2. FROST.
3. STANCIOFF 35.
4. Her relatives and most of her oldest and closest Greek friends went on calling her Mary throughout her life; and she herself, the world-famous Maria Callas, often continued to use the name Mary when she was writing or dedicating photographs to those close friends from "the old days."
5. MURROW: "*Not only was I born in New York . . . but I was brought up in America, in New York, and I am rather proud of that too.*" FLEETWOOD: "*I was born in New York City, right on Manhattan!*" On the other hand, she was reported as saying that she had spent so much time out of the United States that she felt "*more European than American*" (M. J. Matz, "We Introduce Maria Meneghini Callas," *Opera News*, 3 Dec. 1956).

6. V. Vassiliou, *Acropolis*, 7 Aug. 1957; radio interview with Achilleas Mamakis, Athens, 4 Aug. 1957; interview for National Greek Radio, Athens, 9 Aug. 1960, broadcast and reported in the papers the next day: "*We are Greek. . . . Don't forget that during the war we were together, we suffered together, went hungry together, worked together.*" PROUSE (1961): "*My blood, may I say, is pure Greek.*" BANZET (1965): "*I was born in America and I have pure Greek blood.*"

7. Y. Pilichos, "The Human Face of Maria Callas," *To Vima tis Kyriakis*, 13 Sept. 1992.

8. D. Lowe, ed., *Callas As They Saw Her*, London 1987, 2–3.

9. STANCIOFF 3–4: "*They haven't an inkling who Maria is. I just want to make sure someone tells them. Maybe I should write my autobiography . . . set the record straight. . . . Oh, wait till that book comes out. A lot of people will wish me dead then.*" To Alan Sievewright, July 1977, quoted in "Callas Remembered," *Opera* 28, no. 11, Nov. 1977.

CHAPTER 1

1. STASSINOPOULOS (274) says that George was eighty-six when he died, almost blind, in early December 1972, which would mean that he was born in 1886 or possibly at the end of 1885. LITSA (10, 12) maintains that she herself was born on 1 January 1898 and that George was "in his thirties" when she married him in 1916. Leonidas Lanzounis, a childhood friend of George and godfather to Mary, told Nadia Stancioff that George was thirteen years older than Litsa (STANCIOFF 51–52), but according to the particulars on Mary's birth certificate, in 1923 George was thirty-five and Litsa twenty-five. As Litsa was actually born in 1894 or 1895, George must have been born not before 1881 and not after 1885.

2. E. Nikolopoulou, "Maria Callas's House Many Years On, Altered Beyond Recognition," *Ta Nea tis Kyriakis*, 10 Mar. 1985; letter from Panayotis Kaloyeropoulos (son of George's brother Mitsos and owner of the family home), ibid., 31 Mar. 1985; letter from Dimitris Gouliamos, ibid., 12 May 1985.

3. When asked in 1959, Maria said she did not know whether her father had ever served in the Greek army. (MARGRIET.)

4. LITSA 10.

5. H. D. Haralambopoulos, "The Autobiography of Colonel Konstantinos Petrou Dimitriadis, Secretary to General Yannis Rangos in the War of 1821," *Bulletin of the Historical and Ethnological Society of Greece* 22, 1979, 479–530.

6. LITSA 139.

7. Not only has the family estate been broken up, but the land is bisected by the Athens–Thessaloniki highway, which passes only 10 meters away from the chapel and the memorial to Colonel Dimitriadis. The exterior of the chapel is in good repair but the features of the bust are blurred, because the marble has been eroded by the salty sea air and exhaust fumes from the main road. The house still stands, half a kilometer away and about 50 meters back from the main road, in relatively good condition.

8. The eldest son, Petros, and the second, Dimitris, followed in their father's footsteps and joined the army. Dimitris married but died childless, and all his life he envied his brother Petros for having a large family. But Petros died younger, having "only" reached the rank of colonel, whereas Dimitris rose to be a general, lived in the fashionable Kolonaki district of Athens, and, according to Litsa, was "close to King Constantine." The third son, Doukas (1859–1898), was a pediatrician. He studied abroad, in Munich or Paris, and may have remained abroad for a time after qualifying. He married a foreign girl against his family's wishes but died young; part of his estate went to his nephew, also called Doukas, the third son of his brother Petros. The two daughters of Konstantinos and Marigo, Xenia and Eleni, married local notables and spent most of their lives in the Stylis area. Eleni Dimitriadou's husband, Nikolaos Kambouris, came from Konitsa near the Albanian border but settled in Stylis. One of their five children, Iraklis Kambouris, bought the house and land at Stylis from Petros Dimitriadis. The grandchildren of another, Konstantinos, were the cousins whom Mary met occasionally when she was living in Athens. (KAMBOURIS; KAMBOURI.) See also Chapter 17.

9. S. Terra, "Un'altra Callas mira alla Scala," *Epoca*, Feb. 1958; LITSA 11. A similar anecdote that is easier to believe is that one day in Patras, singing as he shaved by an open window, he was heard by an Italian impresario who offered to promote him as a singer. Not surprisingly, he decided not to give up his career as a regular officer, but the incident must have gratified his long-suppressed hankering to be a musician. (KOUKOULI.)

10. Frosso's father, Efthymios, was a brother of Nikolaos Louros, also an army officer, whose son Konstantinos (1864–1957) was an obstetrician and gynecologist and Frosso's first cousin. His son Nikolaos (1898–1986), also an ob/gyn and a member of the Academy of Athens, was a second cousin of Maria's mother Litsa Dimitriadou. The Louros family, originally from Souli in northwestern Greece, fled to Nafpaktos on the Gulf of Corinth in 1819, when the British sold the area to the (in)famous Ali Pasha.

11. EFFIE; KOUKOULI.

12. LITSA 28–29; EFFIE.

13. MIRKA.

14. LITSA 29; KALOYEROPOULOU; MIRKA.

15. LITSA 10–11; EFFIE.

16. EFFIE; KOUKOULI.

17. LITSA 11–12; STANCIOFF 52.

18. Terra, op. cit. JACKIE (33) says that her parents were married "within six weeks of the funeral," and that it was only after Petros's death that Frosso "encouraged" Litsa to marry George. But her version of the story is probably a touched-up narrative of events at which she herself, of course, was not present.

CHAPTER 2

1. LITSA 12, 139; JACKIE 28, 33.

2. LITSA 12.

3. JACKIE 28, 33; KALOYEROPOULOU.

4. MARGRIET. Maria said that Vassilis died in the summer of 1923, but that is impossible, as she herself was born only three or four months later and Litsa was not pregnant when Vassilis died. So, if he died in the summer, it must have been the summer of 1922.

5. LITSA 13; JACKIE 29, 31.

6. JACKIE 29.

7. But see note 1 in Chapter 3.

8. KALOYEROPOULOU; JACKIE 32.

9. KALOYEROPOULOU; JACKIE 33; MIRKA.

10. MARGRIET; also JACKIE 33–34; KALOYEROPOULOU. Michael Scott hypothesizes that George had decided to go to America in order to escape the problems caused by his involvement in an affair with the wife of a prominent citizen of Meligalas (SCOTT 5).

11. MARGRIET.

12. Jürgen Kesting (*Maria Callas*, London 1992) is the only biographer who gives a different departure date (21 August), also stating that the family left from Athens. Elsewhere he says that Litsa's decision to return to Greece was made at the *end* of 1937, although he then goes on to describe events that took place in Athens in *September* of that year (p. 84). It is easy to imagine what howlers are to be found in less serious publications, both Greek and foreign. For example, in an article by E. Thomopoulos ("Maria Callas Is To Give a Performance," *Athinaiki*, 3 Aug. 1957) Jackie is described as Maria's *younger* sister by her mother's *first marriage* and it is said that the family emigrated to America *toward the end of World War I*, that Maria *was taken to Athens when she was six months old*, that *her parents separated in 1938*, and that *her father then went back to America*. Chiara Pisani ("La Callas fugge la sua madre," *Oggi*, 5 Mar. 1958) emulates this effort by stating that Litsa had found George—an American of Greek origins who ran a drugstore—in New York, married him in Brooklyn, and decided to leave him *and* the children before they had finished school! These are extreme cases, of course, but serious errors and numerous inaccuracies are to be found even in books that have sold widely around the world.

CHAPTER 3

1. It was exactly twenty-four years later, on 2 August 1947, that Maria Callas made her début in Verona, in *La Gioconda*, under the baton of Tullio Serafin. However, the date of the family's arrival in New York and the mournful atmosphere of that day could well be the result of Litsa's inventiveness, as on Mary's passport application of 15 February 1937 it is stated that her father emigrated to America "on or about 4 June 1923." (Photocopy of application to the State Department kindly provided by Jackie Kaloyeropoulou.) In this case the family's departure from Greece should also be placed two months back, to mid May 1923.

2. LITSA 13; JACKIE 34. For the period covered by Chapters 3–8 (up to March 1937) the only primary sources—apart from statements made by Maria herself (scattered about in books, newspapers, magazines, and recordings of oral interviews) and Jackie's oral reminiscences—are the memoirs of Litsa and Jackie (published in 1960 and 1989, respectively). A few of Maria's biographers, namely Jellinek (1960), Ardoin (1974), Stancioff (1981), and Scott (1991), have each added a certain amount of original evidence concerning this period. Linakis (1981) also gives some new information but cites no other source but himself, and his credibility has been badly dented by Jackie (see note 2 in Chapter 4). All the others, without exception, have simply reworked the old material and perpetuated past errors and inaccuracies.

3. JACKIE 34; KALOYEROPOULOU. Cf. LITSA 9: "We had Greek friends near us in Astoria." Their first address is given as the home address of Mr. and Mrs. Kalos on Mary's birth certificate (SCOTT 5).

4. LITSA 9; JACKIE 34; STANCIOFF 49. "By the time he obtained a license it was too late. In five years he spent all the money he had brought from Greece." (KALOYEROPOULOU.)

5. SUTHERLAND (conversation recorded in Seoul, 10 Oct. 1974).

6. KALOYEROPOULOU.

7. Litsa entitled the relevant chapter of her book "Child of the Storm" (LITSA 9–25). For no known reason, she says that on the day of Mary's birth there was a terrible snowstorm, although the records show that the weather in New York City was fine that day. Most of Callas's biographers assert that Leonidas was the doctor who actually delivered Mary. Litsa is to blame for this, for she refers to Lanzounis as "my obstetrician" (LITSA 60). STANCIOFF 48; LITSA 10; cf. J. Lorcey, *Maria Callas*, Paris 1977, 40; C. Dufresne, *La Callas*, Paris 1990, 23; ALLEGRI 23–24. Litsa admits that there may be some truth in the suggestion that her initial reaction may have scarred Mary: "This may be true. I did want a son, but I loved Mary and I still do." (LITSA 148.)

8. STANCIOFF 44. SCOTT (6 and n. 6), writing four years later, gives the following additional particulars: "Certificate and Record of Birth: State of New York, No. 49149, dated 10 Dec. 1923." The certificate, filed in the record bureau of New York City's health department, was first published in *Uw Maria Callas Brief*, no. 30, 2 Dec. 1993.

9. MARIA 16. She said much the same to GARA (9) and in her interview for the Dutch magazine *Margriet* (MARGRIET).

10. LITSA 14; JACKIE 35; KALOYEROPOULOU.

11. STANCIOFF 48. The name Anna was given to her by Lanzounis, Maria by Karouzos, who then seems to disappear from her life. (KALOYEROPOULOU.)

12. SCOTT 6.

13. JACKIE 35–37.

14. MARIA 17; LITSA 147.

15. JACKIE 35–36.

16. JACKIE 36–37.

17. MARIA 17; GARA 10.

18. LITSA 15; E. Gregor, "Die Callas," *Abend,* 4 May 1959; J. M. Gregory, "Maria Callas: 'I Am Not Stubborn, I Am Right,'" *The Star Weekly Magazine,* 5 Sept. 1959; JACKIE 36.

19. LITSA 18; JACKIE 39; VASSILIOU.

20. F. Filippas, "Maria Callas's Mother Reveals . . . ," *Thisavros,* no. 22, 24 Nov. 1977; VASSILIOU; unsigned article, *Acropolis,* 18 Sept. 1977; LITSA 15; MARIA 17.

21. SUTHERLAND (conversation recorded in Paris, 20 Dec. 1973); television interview with Norman Ross, Chicago, 17 Nov. 1957; J. Cartier, "Callas immortelle," five-part article, *France-Soir*, 1981–82. However, there was one occasion when Maria expressed no regrets for her lost childhood: "*It was no trouble for me, because I didn't really enjoy myself playing around as children [do] then.*" (HAREWOOD.) And two years later, when asked by David Frost whether she had enjoyed her childhood, she replied, "*Ah, yes. The little I did have I really did enjoy.*" (FROST.)

CHAPTER 4

1. STANCIOFF 51.
2. JACKIE 38; S. Linakis, *Diva: The Life and Death of Maria Callas*, London 1981, 13–14. However, it must be said that when asked about Linakis Jackie said: "We didn't know him. He is from the same part of the world as my father, but not related to us. He came to see my father once, but my father didn't know him from Adam. Mother met him on her second trip to America, in 1946–47. Everything he has written is untrue and I can prove it. I doubt if he ever met Maria." (KALOYEROPOULOU.) It is therefore difficult to assess the value of Linakis's book as a source. He claims, among other things, that his mother was a Kaloyero-poulou, that he was seven months older than Mary and remembers playing with her under the dining room table in her family's apartment where he lived from the early 1930s until Litsa left for Greece. (Linakis, op. cit., 13.) As for his chapters dealing with the Greek period, they are a hodgepodge of "faction" and information culled from Litsa's book, retold with transparent distortions and generously larded with cheap humor. Linakis betrays his unreliability as a source when he states that Mary wrote a letter soon after arriving in Athens describing the family's move to the apartment at 61 Patission Street, a move that did not take place until two years later.
3. MARGRIET.
4. STANCIOFF 51; JACKIE 38. Cf. KALOYEROPOULOU: "She made us hate our father."
5. KALOYEROPOULOU; JACKIE 39.
6. LITSA 148. In what looks like a willful misrepresentation of Mary's feelings for her father, Litsa goes on to remark disingenuously, "It is possible that Maria's announced love for her father is the result of a childhood desire for an affection denied her [by George]."
7. DOWNES; A. Pensotti, "Maria, ti chiedo perdono," *Oggi*, 1 Oct. 1977. Di Stefano continued, "That was Maria all over: she wanted other people to understand what she meant, while she hid within her shell."
8. LITSA 15–16, 147; MARIA 24.
9. LITSA 15–16, 146–147; GARA 10; MARIA 24. Cf. JACKIE 39–40; SCOTT 6–7. Scott says (without reference to his source) that Mary was sent home the same evening, suffering from nothing worse than scrapes and shock. Jackie said in conversation, "I can hardly remember anything about it. She didn't stay long in the hospital, and I don't think it did her any lasting harm." (KALOYEROPOULOU.) It has been suggested that the accident may have resulted in a hormone imbalance that caused Mary to suffer from pathologically insatiable hunger (A. Bronte, "Les quatre grands combats de la Callas," *France-Dimanche*, 3–24 Oct. 1977), but this argument is far-fetched, considering that her overeating did not start until much later and had other, psychological, causes (see Chapters 9 and 21).
10. JACKIE 41–42. Yorgos Kritikos was a sponge merchant and, according to Jackie "something in shipping." His daughter Eleni, a childhood friend of the Kaloyeropoulou girls, now lives in New York, the widow of Yorgos Arfaras. (KALOYEROPOULOU.)
11. STANCIOFF 49–50. George never repaid this loan nor even mentioned it, except that he once said jokingly to Lanzounis, "I'll see you after we die." (STANCIOFF 51.)
12. JACKIE 35–36; KALOYEROPOULOU.
13. MARIA 17; MARGRIET.

CHAPTER 5

1. STANCIOFF 52; JACKIE 42–43; KALOYEROPOULOU.
2. SCOTT 7. Scott, who did a good deal of research on the subject, says that between 1929 and 1937 Mary attended six different public schools in New York: P.S. 228, P.S. 9, P.S. 43, P.S. 192, P.S. 164, and P.S. 189. He gives no dates, but we know from other sources that P.S. 189 was the last and that she spent her last three or four years there, from fifth to seventh or eighth grade. Therefore the other five schools must all have been in her first three or four years, from first or second through fourth grade.
3. JACKIE 41, 46.
4. LITSA 20–21; JACKIE 51.
5. LITSA 20; JACKIE 40.
6. LITSA 145, 148.
7. JACKIE 40; KALOYEROPOULOU.
8. GARA 10.
9. R. Neville, "Voice of an Angel," *Life*, 31 Oct. 1955, reprinted in *The New York Times*, 30 Oct. 1956. LITSA (138) comments that she has no recollection of any such fan club, that Mary did not have an autograph album until she was eleven or twelve, that she took it with her to Greece, and that the remark about "the girl with the golden voice" was probably written in it after she had left school. Mary's autograph album must have held very special memories for her. She kept it all her life, and it was included at the posthumous exhibition "L'opéra secret de Maria Callas," Musée Carnavalet, Paris, 10 Apr.–20 May 1979 (exhibition catalog, p. 6). Its whereabouts are now unknown (but see Chapter 37).
10. This statement first appeared in print in George de Carvalho's article "The Prima Donna," *Time*, 29 Oct. 1956.
11. Radio interview with Johnny Carson, New York, 1962; LITSA 17–18; Jackie agrees that the incident "occurred," though she does not remember it herself. (KALOYEROPOULOU.)
12. JACKIE 44.
13. In 1991 Jackie recalled that, "Mother bought us everything to hear and took us to the library." (Discussion with members of the Maria Callas International Club, London, 8 Oct. 1991.)
14. The particulars of these historic broadcasts, which must surely have formed the basis of Mary's early musical education, come from P. Jackson, *Saturday Afternoons at the Old Met*, Portland (Amadeus Press) 1992: see the detailed list on pp. 507–522.
15. LEGGE; DOWNES. A self-taught singer, Rosa Ponselle (1897–1981) began her career singing in vaudeville and cabaret, often with her elder sister Carmella. In 1918 she was heard by a former valet of Jean de Reszke, a music-lover who arranged an audition for her with Caruso. After hearing her sing two arias (from *Aida* and *Il Trovatore*), Caruso calmly informed her that she would be singing with him at the Met. Sure enough, she appeared with him in *La Forza del Destino* at the age of twenty-one, at which time she had heard only two operas in her life! Altogether she sang twenty-two roles in 360 performances with the Met. She retired at forty but continued singing privately, giving lessons to a few hand-picked pupils and taking an active part in the musical life of Baltimore, where she spent the rest of her life. See J. A. Drake, *Rosa Ponselle: A Centenary Biography*, Portland (Amadeus Press) 1997.
16. To Rudolf Bing, introducing the cast of *Lucia* on the Met broadcast, New York, 8 Dec. 1956. Quoted in "La Callas Speaks," *The Callas Circle*, no. 1, Nov. 1994.
17. "*I think it was, if I'm not mistaken, 'Aida.*'" (Radio interview with William Weaver, Paris, 10 Apr. 1965.) P. Jackson, *Saturday Afternoons at the Old Met*, Portland (Amadeus Press) 1992, 507–522.
18. GARA 12.
19. C. Díaz Du-Pond, "Callas in Mexico," *Opera*, Apr. 1973. Jackie recalled that when once, before the end of 1936, they heard a recording of Rosa Ponselle at a friend's house, "Mary said, '*I am going to be more famous than her!*' And everybody laughed." (Discussion with members of the Maria Callas International Club, London, 8 Oct. 1991.) When I ques-

tioned her, however, Jackie appeared uncertain about whether the singer was Ponselle or someone else. (KALOYEROPOULOU.)

20. JELLINEK 8. JACKIE (48), however, states explicitly that "her [Mary's] favorite was Lily Pons" and that she used to sing along with her on the radio. This is corroborated by PATRI-ARCHEAS, who, as an assistant stage designer at the G.N.O. in 1943–44, heard Mary expressing the greatest admiration for Pons. Lily Pons (1898–1976), after several undistinguished years in provincial French opera, was "discovered" by Giovanni Zenatello and his wife, María Gay, who arranged for her March 1930 Metropolitan Opera audition. With her small but sweet coloratura voice, she was a great success as Lucia, Amina, and Lakmé. She was a diva at the Met from her début in 1931 until 1960, when she retired at the age of sixty-two.

21. LITSA 18; KALOYEROPOULOU; R. Mancini, "Biographie," *Opéra International, Spécial Maria Callas*, supplement to no. 5, Feb. 1978.

CHAPTER 6

1. O. Lazaridis, "Maria Callas the Great," *Tachydromos*, 22 Sept. 1977.

2. Roland Mancini ("Biographie," *Opéra International, Spécial Maria Callas*, supplement to no. 5, Feb. 1978) is one of the few writers who have expressly acknowledged that the Callas phenomenon was due to Litsa. Also P. J. Rémy, *Callas, une vie*, Paris 1982, 22: "If there really was anything remarkable about Maria's childhood, it is actually the astonishing presentiment of her mother, who saw below the surface and divined the talents of her younger daughter."

3. Radio interview with Johnny Carson, New York, 1962. Cf. J. M. Gregory, "Maria Callas: 'I Am Not Stubborn, I Am Right,'" *The Star Weekly Magazine*, 5 Sept. 1959; F. Filippas, "Maria Callas's Mother Reveals . . . ," *Thisavros*, no. 22, 24 Nov. 1977.

4. Y. Orfanos, "Maria Callas: Anatomy of a Genius," *Odos Panos*, no. 32, Sept.–Oct. 1987.

5. DE CARVALHO; "Der einsame Tod der Maria Callas," *Neue Revue Illustrierte*, no. 40, 26 Sept. 1977.

6. JACKIE 47; KALOYEROPOULOU.

7. S. Terra, "Un'altra Callas mira alla Scala," *Epoca*, Feb. 1958.

8. ARDOIN 26.

9. J. Cartier, "Callas immortelle," five-part article, *France-Soir*, 1981–82. In the same article, the imaginative Cartier explains that Mary decided at one stage that she wanted to be a dentist, not a surgeon like her beloved godfather Leonidas, because a dentist is "a torturer who, armed with his drill, holds his patient in a position where he cannot resist. A surgeon operates on someone who feels nothing, but a dentist on someone who feels terrified"—in other words, persecuted, as she herself was.

10. LITSA 21, 144.

11. MARGRIET.

12. Maria wrote these autobiographical notes ("Smentite di articolo 'Time,'" MS, in Italian, 1956) in refutation of the malicious charges made against her in de Carvalho's article ("The Prima Donna," *Time*, 29 Oct. 1956). They remained unpublished until 1991, when lengthy excerpts were published in ALLEGRI (139–143). Cf. MARGRIET: "*I don't know how the story got about that my mother used to make me eat 250 grams of cheese for breakfast every day to keep my vocal cords in good condition.*" Also MENEGHINI 105: "Some people even ascribed a psychological interpretation to her 'ravenous' appetite, postulating that she ate in compensation for a lack of affection. These suppositions are fantasy. . . . She was still slim when she left the United States in 1937."

13. STANCIOFF 53; LITSA 137; JACKIE 46. The lowest weight that Maria was to reach after slimming dramatically in 1953–54, according to her own statement, was 53.5 kilos (118 pounds), a bit less than she weighed when she was eleven years old and measured 13 centimeters less than her final height of 5 feet 8 inches (1.73 meters).

14. Lazaridis, op. cit.

15. SUTHERLAND.

16. STANCIOFF 52; KALOYEROPOULOU.

17. Cf. STASSINOPOULOS 14, 15: "In Evangelia's mind love, happiness, fame, and money were convertible currencies," and "All the love and approval Maria was given during this time was strictly conditional." Likewise P. J. Rémy (op. cit., 24–25), after reminding us that, when she was twelve, the great Malibran used to practice vocalises and roulades encouraged by kicks and blows from her father, says equally speciously, "*Autres temps, autres moeurs,* but nothing has really changed. All they do is stuff Maria with tidbits . . . and drag her off to awful competitions, to teach her not to be afraid of the public: even genius can be learned, and for that one pays a higher price still."

CHAPTER 7

1. MURROW; DE CARVALHO; M. Callas, "Smentite di articolo 'Time'" (MS, in Italian, 1956), para. 3.

2. LITSA 19; JELLINEK 10.

3. MURROW; "At La Scala, the Triumph of U.S.–Born Maria Callas," *Newsweek*, 10 Jan. 1955; MARGRIET.

4. MARIA 18. Cf. ARDOIN 26: "To this day, she often masks her insecurities with the cover of aloofness."

5. "She only had to hear a song once or twice on the phonograph and she would immediately pick it up and sing it in the same key" (Y. Leontaritis, "From the Old Phonograph to the Triumph at Carnegie Hall," *Acropolis,* 18 Sept. 1977); MARGRIET; GARA 10.

6. KALOYEROPOULOU; JACKIE 47. Jackie calls the Swede a "singing coach" rather than a teacher. She adds: "Mary had a sweet voice, a child's voice; [with hindsight] it began to be recognizable only when she started having lessons in Greece." (KALOYEROPOULOU.)

7. FLEETWOOD.

8. KALOYEROPOULOU (but cf. JACKIE 47); MARIA 18; *Alexandrian Literature,* booklet published for a festival held on 12 Sept. 1943 in aid of Greek students from Egypt, ed. Marios Vaianos, Athens 1943. The next sentence in this last source states that in both competitions "she won from a field of four hundred students and graduates."

9. The main sources of information on the first of these competitions, besides Maria's own recollections of the event in later years, are JACKIE 47 and LITSA 18. ARDOIN 26. When Norman Ross interviewed her (Chicago, 17 Nov. 1957), he said, "You sang here on the radio before you went to Athens," and Maria concurred. This was subsequently interpreted as indicating that she had sung in Chicago, whereas Maria had simply taken "here" to mean "in America," not "in Chicago." The only other competition about which Maria mentioned anything specific was one on radio station WUSR, where she met well-known contralto Gladys Swarthout. (FROST.)

10. J. Ardoin, *The Callas Legacy,* London 1988, 1–3. Although Ardoin first presented the case as no more than a hypothesis, which gradually came to be accepted as fact, it seems that he later came around to believing in his discovery. On seeing in MARCHAND (16) that the handwriting on Foresti's entry form was not Mary's, he wrote, "This earliest example of Callas's handwriting is certainly not the same as that of her application letter for the *Major Bowes Amateur Hour,* two years earlier. It is obvious that this letter . . . was, as I long suspected, written by either her mother or a friend." (J. Ardoin, "Maria Callas: The Early Years," *Opera Quarterly* 3, no. 2, summer 1985.) A transcript of Foresti's dialogue with Major Bowes is given in "La Callas Speaks," *The Callas Circle,* no. 1, Nov. 1994.

11. STANCIOFF 41–43; KALOYEROPOULOU. The judges gave Foresti a D and noted: "Faint possibility for future." Most writers who mention the "Foresti affair" question its truth (cf. SCOTT 281, n. 4). Jackie was equally emphatic in public: "It's a trick! It's not her voice. It's not true! It's not Maria!" (Discussion with members of the Maria Callas International Club, London, 8 Oct. 1991.) Nevertheless, a 1997 EMI release of live Callas material included this Pandora's box of a piece.

12. LITSA 18, 20; radio interview with Johnny Carson, New York, 1962; JACKIE 49; STANCIOFF 42; KALOYEROPOULOU. Jackie believes her mother could not bear the thought of

either of her daughters going into a profession even vaguely connected with medicine, because anything of that kind "had been rendered repugnant by her life with Father."

13. M. J. Matz, "We Introduce Maria Meneghini Callas," *Opera News*, 3 Dec. 1956; *The New York Times*, 30 Oct. 1956, quoted in LITSA 136–137; STANCIOFF 54–55.

14. KOUKOULI; MURROW. Maria said exactly the same thing to David Frost almost thirteen years later (FROST). Mary made more boasts about her future stardom to relatives of hers soon after arriving in Athens in 1937, which shows that Litsa passed on her artistic ambitions to her daughter at a very early age.

15. S. Mathers, "Callas the Savoyard," *The Callas Circle*, no. 2, Feb. 1995; STANCIOFF 55. LITSA (20) says that Mary had been wearing glasses since she was five, but the school nurse's report, where she is described as "a quiet, reserved, quick-witted child," records that she first wore them when she was in fifth grade, in the school year 1934–35 (STANCIOFF 53).

16. FROST. An account of the graduation ceremony (pp. 1–2) and the photograph (between pp. 50–51) were first published in 1960 by JELLINEK.

17. Radio interview with Johnny Carson, New York, 1962.

18. MARIA 17. Similarly, speaking to David Frost in 1970, Maria said: "*I remember the first time. I never was terrified, I thought, but I went on stage and I got such a dry throat that I couldn't open my mouth—nothing came out!*" (FROST.)

19. ARDOIN 26. Linakis (*Diva: The Life and Death of Maria Callas*, London 1981, 3) tells how once, when Mary was accompanying herself on the piano with almost fanatical intensity, he asked her, "Who do you think you are? Grace Moore?" "*Better, much better!*" she answered.

CHAPTER 8

1. JACKIE 45, 51.
2. S. Linakis, *Diva: The Life and Death of Maria Callas*, London 1981, 14; LITSA 147.
3. JACKIE 43, 51.
4. JACKIE 52–53.
5. JACKIE 53–54; LITSA 22.
6. JACKIE 55.
7. MARIA 18.
8. JACKIE 54; KALOYEROPOULOU.
9. The Christmas Day performance of Humperdinck's *Hänsel und Gretel* at the Met was broadcast live, as it was every year. It was followed next day by Saint-Saëns's *Samson et Dalila*. Productions in the New Year included *Tristan und Isolde* with Melchior and Flagstad on 2 January, *Carmen* with Ponselle on 9 January, and performances of *The Tales of Hoffmann*, *Aida*, *Manon*, *Die Walküre*, and *Siegfried*. The last opera broadcast from the Met that Mary is likely to have heard was *Lucia* with Lily Pons on 27 February 1937. Cf. P. Jackson, *Saturday Afternoons at the Old Met*, Portland (Amadeus Press) 1992, 507–522.
10. LITSA 22–23. When Litsa went back to New York in 1946 she found that the piano and all the furniture and curtains had been sold for twenty-five dollars to defray the unpaid storage charges.
11. MARGRIET.
12. Photocopied documents kindly provided by Jackie Kaloyeropoulou. JELLINEK 7. Jellinek obtained his information about the New York years from George Kaloyeropoulos himself as early as 1959 or 1960. "I learned a great deal about Maria's New York years, the family's early struggles, and also about the deep hostility that existed between her parents." ("The Background to a Callas Biography," *The Maria Callas International Club Magazine*, no. 10, Oct. 1993.)
13. LITSA 136; M. J. Matz, "We Introduce Maria Meneghini Callas," *Opera News*, 3 Dec. 1956.
14. LITSA 24. In 1959 and 1960, when Maria was in the process of separating from her husband, Meneghini, in order to rebuild her own life, she was just six or seven years younger than Litsa had been at the time of her return to Greece in 1937.
15. JACKIE 60.

CHAPTER 9

1. LITSA 24–26. The precise date of their arrival in Patras, 6 March 1937, is first stated on Mary's application for registration as an American citizen in Athens, on 15 March 1938. (Photocopied document kindly provided by Jackie Kaloyeropoulou.)

2. LITSA 21–22, 24; JACKIE 48. The canaries had been given to them by George. The oldest, already approaching the evening of his days, was Stefanakos; the second, less well endowed vocally, was Elmina, who officially belonged to Jackie; and the youngest, the best singer of them all, was David, who belonged to Mary.

3. LITSA 24.

4. LITSA 25; J. Cartier, "Callas immortelle," five-part article, *France-Soir*, 1981–82. The only record we have of Maria really playing, having fun, is given by Frédéric Simogli, one of her hairdressers during her last years in Paris, who said: "When she was happy, she played like a child with her two poodles. She would pretend to bite them, laughing and rolling around with them on the carpet." (V. Merlin, "Dans l'intimité de la Callas," *Le Match de Paris*, Sept. 1987.)

5. LITSA 27–28; JACKIE 59.

6. EFFIE.

7. LITSA 30; JACKIE 60.

8. LITSA 30; MIRKA; EFFIE; GOUDELIS.

9. JACKIE 59; KALOYEROPOULOU. Another account of Mary's first arrival in Greece is given by LITSA (28–30), who says that the first house they lived in was "beyond the Acropolis" (and by implication near it). She describes it in some detail, but the house she had in mind is unlikely to have been the one in Sepolia, even though that too did have a view—a rather distant view—of the Acropolis. "I can't remember ever living in a house near the Acropolis," Jackie says. (KALOYEROPOULOU.)

10. EFFIE; LITSA 30; JACKIE 59; KALOYEROPOULOU; NINON.

11. EFFIE.

12. JACKIE 59–60. "She spoke only broken Greek when we reached Athens; today she speaks it perfectly." (LITSA 33.)

13. BANZET.

14. EFFIE; NINON.

15. NINON.

16. JELLINEK 12; LITSA 31; JACKIE 61; KOUKOULI.

17. KOUKOULI.

18. JACKIE 60. Although Jackie acknowledges freely that their mother was "terribly domineering," she says, displaying a more forgiving spirit than perhaps Litsa deserves, "All right, so maybe she pressed Mary to sing sometimes, but Mary would have wanted it herself." (KALOYEROPOULOU.) STASSINOPOULOS (22) describes Mary as being little more than an "auditioning machine" during those years, and in an interesting projection she suggests that Maria's refusal to sing for Winston Churchill on board Onassis's yacht may have been a reaction to the pressure that had been put on her to sing for relatives, friends, and "useful" acquaintances. A more plausible interpretation, however, would be that her refusal was simply due to the uncultured atmosphere generally prevailing on the yacht *Christina*, where, despite the existence of a piano, Maria rarely sang or studied.

19. KOUKOULI; MARIA 18.

20. KOUKOULI.

21. FROST. David Frost expressed surprise that someone like Maria, "known as a very independent and strong person," had allowed herself to be manipulated in this way by her mother and husband. To which Maria replied, *"I would be inhuman if I wasn't run every now and then. . . . Has it occurred to you that life is a fight on who commands the other? Mother commands the child. Then, at school, everybody is trying to believe in doing what they want, and if you don't do what they want they get very angry and they accuse you and you are in fights all the time. I think that life is a struggle for independence. I have struggled lately to gain independence. I have always strived for independence of thinking, without bothering anybody else, because I lead my own life; but my life is not a normal life."*

22. MARIA 18. Maria later repeated the same argument in several interviews. In 1976 she insisted she would only study music if she won scholarships, otherwise she would give it up: "*I was sure that I would not win the scholarship—absolutely sure, sure four times over! But I kept winning scholarships and so I had no choice, I had to go on.*" (CALONI.)

23. O. Lazaridis, "Maria Callas the Great," *Tachydromos,* 22 Sept. 1977.

24. MARIA 18.

25. LOUVI.

26. LOUVI.

27. LOUVI.

CHAPTER 10

1. JACKIE 60–61 (but cf. KALOYEROPOULOU: "I don't remember anything much about it, not even whether Mary sang or Kambanis either."); KAMBANIS. Kambanis (1908–1991) had several strokes shortly before his death, and both his memory and his mind were almost gone. With his splendid *lirico-spinto* tenor voice, he was engaged to sing Enzo (*La Gioconda*) and Turiddu (*Cavalleria Rusticana*) at La Scala in 1940, but his contract was annulled on the outbreak of war between Greece and Italy. Returning to Athens, he made his first appearance at the National Opera as Turiddu, but in 1943 he went back to Italy and enrolled at the Accademia di Santa Cecilia in Rome. While there from 1943 to 1945 he was given several principal roles at Teatro Reale: Radamès (*Aida*), Alvaro (*La Forza del Destino*), Manrico (*Il Trovatore*), and Turiddu at the express wish of Mascagni himself, who considered his voice ideal for the part. After the war he had a highly successful career all over the world (São Paulo, Buenos Aires, Tokyo, Boston, Montreal, Sydney, Munich, Barcelona, Lisbon, Monte Carlo, Vienna), which was concluded at the G.N.O. in Athens, where he sang until 1959. Many Greeks, however, never forgave Kambanis for "having it easy" in Italy while Greece was at war with that country.

2. LITSA 32–33; JACKIE 64. According to Jackie, "She must have heard her sing 'La Paloma' or 'A Heart That's Free.'" (KALOYEROPOULOU.) Yorgos Leontaritis ("From the Old Phonograph to the Triumph at Carnegie Hall," *Acropolis,* 18 Sept. 1977) asserts that Mary sang the Habanera and Ave Maria.

3. Y. Vokos, "Maria Callas Arrived the Day Before Yesterday, Full of Emotion But Saying Nothing," *Acropolis,* 30 July 1957.

4. P. Krineos, "A Heavenly Voice, a Frosty Eye," interview given by Trivella to an Athens newspaper, c. 10 Mar. 1957 (clipping in Trivella's papers).

5. Vokos, op. cit.; GARA 12; HAREWOOD.

6. LITSA 33.

7. Television interview with Barbara Walters, New York, 15 Apr. 1974. Maria said more in the same vein in 1958: "*My mother and my sister brought me over [to Greece] on a trip, and they brought me to the conservatory and they had to fake my age, because of course I was then thirteen years old and no conservatory would accept you. And I was very tall and well built, so I easily passed for seventeen.*" (FLEETWOOD.)

8. It has often been falsely asserted (for example, JELLINEK 14) that Trivella was Italian, or at least of Italian descent. The only germ of truth in that allegation is that her mother's family were distantly descended from Venetian colonists.

9. Compiled from statements made by Trivella to Vokos (op. cit.) and Krineos (op. cit.).

10. ADALI.

11. Y. Karakandas, *All About Opera,* Athens 1978, 633, and letter in *Embros,* 18 Nov. 1977.

12. Undated typewritten note by Kalomiris (Kalomiris papers, archives of the National Conservatory); L. Zoras, "First Steps at the Conservatory . . . ," *To Theatro,* nos. 59–60, Sept.–Dec. 1977. Litsa even managed to involve their influential relative, Konstantinos Louros: "I don't forget when, as a young girl, I took you to Kalomiris, to get you a place, and you told me, '*I have, dear uncle, great confidence in myself.*' (Letter from Louros to his "beloved Mary," Athens, 9 Jan. 1951, now the property of Ilario Tamassia.)

13. In the academic years 1937–38 and 1938–39, respectively, the conservatory had 1,427 and 1,775 students, of whom 942 and 947 were at the central campus in Athens. Of those,

418 and 419 were in the school of pianoforte and 204 and 209 in the school of singing. (Bulletins for the Academic Years 1937–38 and 1938–39, archives of the National Conservatory.)

14. Bulletin for the Academic Year 1938–39; conversation with Filippos Tsalahouris, keeper of the Kalomiris papers, 16 Oct. 1993; mark sheet for Trivella's class for the year 1937–38 (archives of the National Conservatory).

15. MARIA 18; LITSA 33–34.

16. LITSA 34.

17. Y. Karakandas, *All About Opera*, 633–634, letter in *Ta Simerina*, 21 July 1977, and letter in *Embros*, 18 Nov. 1977; ADALI. Cf. S. Galatopoulos, *Maria Callas: Sacred Monster*, London 1998, 27 ("Maria, kneeling, tearfully begged for forgiveness pledging never to be impertinent again.")

18. FROST.

19. Yorgos Karakandas, letter in *Ta Simerina*, 21 July 1977; HAREWOOD; LITSA 34. Speaking about *Lucia* in 1956, Maria admitted that she had not bothered to read Sir Walter Scott's novel *The Bride of Lammermoor*. "*It's not important, for it is the music that matters. The Mad Scene is a result of Donizetti's genius and not of the novel. The literary works are the springboard, but what really matters is what the composer does with them. There is nothing Scottish about the way Donizetti interprets Lucia.*" (L. Rasponi, *The Last Prima Donnas*, London 1984, 579.)

20. ADALI; HAREWOOD.

21. Yorgos Vokos, *Acropolis* and *Apoyevmatini*, 17 Sept. 1977.

22. Y. Leontaritis, "From the Old Phonograph to the Triumph at Carnegie Hall," *Acropolis*, 2 Oct. 1977.

23. Yorgos Vokos, *Acropolis*, 2 Oct. 1977.

24. KAMBANIS; SIMIRIOTIS. Vyron Simiriotis (b. Athens 1915) studied music with no intention of making a musical career, as he was by profession an architect and interior designer. His singing teacher at the National Conservatory was Smaragda Yennadi. He was a *tenore lirico-drammatico* and apparently showed considerable promise. (SIMIRIOTIS.)

CHAPTER 11

1. LITSA 31.

2. KOPANOU.

3. JACKIE 64; EFFIE. The root cause of the final breach was the feeling of Litsa's siblings that because of her they had had a raw deal financially.

4. JACKIE 64.

5. JACKIE 61–62; EMBIRIKOS.

6. In 1937 Maria Drakatou was still a student in Smaragda Yennadi's advanced class at the National Conservatory. She is mentioned by A. Hadziapostolou (*History of Greek Opera*, Athens 1949, 105, 124) as a soprano who "played second leads and minor parts and went with the Hellenic Melodrama on some of its tours." Nothing more is heard of her. Cristina Gastel-Chiarelli (*Maria Callas*, Venice 1981, 17) suggests that Mary had heard de Hidalgo as Violetta in Athens and that was why she wanted to be taught by her, but this is not true. De Hidalgo made her last stage appearances as Violetta and Gilda on 20 and 22 May 1937 (see Chapter 14): this was only two months after Mary's arrival in Athens and before Jackie had even met Miltiadis Embirikos.

7. JACKIE 68–69. Although Jackie adds that, from that moment on, Mary went to see "whatever she could," there is no evidence of her having been to other performances; and if there were any, they would most probably have been few and far between. Even later on, according to VLACHOPOULOU, she very rarely went to see whatever was on at the Greek National Opera. SALINGAROS corroborates this: "The management had reserved a box for us at the theater. Mary, however, very seldom came."

8. The new address, Harilaou Trikoupi 70, is stated on Mary's application for registration as an American citizen in Athens, 15 March 1938. (Photocopied document kindly provided by Jackie Kaloyeropoulou.)

9. JACKIE 64.
10. JACKIE 65–67.
11. Ismini Thiveou says: "Most of what I know I heard from my sister Christina, which means that it comes straight from Litsa. I also heard some things from my other sisters, Daisy Thiveou, who worked in the same bank as Marina Papayeorgopoulou (the tenant of the Kaloyeropouloses at 61 Patission Street), and Pepi Garofalidou, another of Litsa's close friends for many years." (THIVEOU.) Nada Tzaka, who was then only seven, often came to stay with her aunt Christina Katifori on Harilaou Trikoupi Street. Her accounts of incidents that she did not see or hear herself are derived from her subsequent conversations with her mother and aunts. (TZAKA.)
12. Conversation with Dinos Petroyannis, 3 Jan. 1997.
13. TZAKA.
14. Letter from Litsa to Maria, Athens, 18 Sept. 1949 (now the property of Ilario Tamassia).
15. JACKIE 67.
16. THIVEOU; TZAKA; conversation with Dinos Petroyannis, 3 Jan. 1997.
17. ZACHAROPOULOU; statement by Nadia Stancioff in Alan Palmer's film *Maria Callas*, 1987.
18. THIVEOU; KALAIDZAKIS.
19. TZAKA; CHIOTAKIS; SALINGAROS; JACKIE 67.
20. JACKIE 67–68; KALOYEROPOULOU; TZAKA.
21. JACKIE 69.
22. Conversation with Dinos Petroyannis, 3 Jan. 1997.
23. TZAKA. Mary appears to have been on surprisingly good terms with Menis Fotopoulos, to judge by the dedication she wrote on the back of a photograph of her father and herself, which she sent him from New York in 1947: "*To my dear Menaki, so that you won't forget me.*" (From Maria's private photograph album, now owned by Renzo Allegri.)
24. TZAKA; THIVEOU.
25. THIVEOU.
26. TZAKA; SIMIRIOTIS; THIVEOU.

CHAPTER 12

1. The *G* (between her surname and the initial *M* for Mary) stands for her father's name, George. JACKIE 68; letter from Trivella, *Ta Nea*, 30 Aug. 1960. With regard to Mary's late enrollment, the wording of the relevant sentence in the first biographical note on Mary Kaloyeropoulou (see note 6 in Chapter 26) is also interesting: "In March 1937 she came with her family to settle in Greece, and six months later [that is to say, in September] she started having singing lessons *in order to be admitted* to the conservatory" (my italics).
2. LITSA 35 (letter from Trivella); program, first published in MARCHAND (19). Stefanos Valtetsiotis (1876–1975) studied composition and piano in Milan. He held the positions of director of the Hellenic Melodrama (1912–29) and professor of opera both at the Athens (1917–26) and the National Conservatory (1926–44). An opera composer and considered by many to be the best Greek opera conductor ever, he was one of the most highly respected musicians in Athens in the late 1930s.
3. "Falcon" for the vocal attributes of French soprano Cornélie Falcon, who won great fame in Paris between 1832 and 1836, aged eighteen to twenty-two, on account of the tremendous vocal demands of the parts given or created for her, such as Valentine in Meyerbeer's *Les Huguenots*.
4. Ioannis Psaroudas (1871–1952) studied music in Athens and from 1890 in Paris. He composed mainly songs, some of them very fine, in the spirit and form of French *mélodies*, particularly those of his teacher Jules Massenet.
5. JACKIE 69. Jackie described Kambanis as an "imposing figure" on the stage beside the "diminutive" Mary, whereas ironically enough the truth of the matter, visually at least, was exactly the reverse: Kambanis was about five inches shorter than Mary, who had reached her final height of 5 feet 8 inches (1.73 meters). Psaroudas, who regularly reviewed the class exhibition concerts of the various conservatories, failed to give the concert a notice because

at the same time on the same day there was a concert of the Athens Conservatory Orchestra conducted by Filoktitis Ikonomidis, with Alfred Cortot playing the Schumann Piano Concerto. And a small footnote for history: the day after Mary's first public appearance in Athens, the great Chaliapin died in Paris.

6. KAMBANIS.

7. KAMBANIS.

8. KAMBANIS. Although none of these incidents can be precisely dated, they must all have taken place between the spring of 1938 and the spring of 1939.

9. Clipping from an unidentified Athens newspaper (in Trivella's papers).

10. *Acropolis*, 17 Sept. and 2 Oct. 1977; L. Zoras, "First Steps at the Conservatory . . . ," *To Theatro*, nos. 59–60, Sept.–Dec. 1977; NIKOLAIDI; VLACHOPOULOU; DOUNIAS. Tenor Kostas Dounias (1904–1998) was one of the first group of fourteen men taken on by the G.N.O. for its chorus in 1940.

11. PROUSE; VLACHOPOULOU; *Epikaira*, 22 Sept. 1977.

12. Nikos Moschonas, known as Nicola Moscona (Athens 1907–Philadelphia 1975), was a self-taught singer. He developed his outstanding vocal talent in Athens around 1930, with the support and guidance of Stefanos Valtetsiotis. After several appearances in Greece and in Egypt, in 1936 he won a City of Athens scholarship and went to Italy, where he was immediately engaged to sing at the major opera houses. At La Scala he was heard by Edward Johnson (the same person who was to hear Mary in New York eight or nine years later), who invited him to sing at the Metropolitan. He made his début at the Met in December 1937, as Ramfis in *Aida*. A *basso cantante* with a very wide repertoire, Moscona was highly regarded by Toscanini and sang with every one of the top names in opera until 1961.

13. HADZIS.

14. LITSA 53; also VASSILIOU. Without citing his source or specifying the date, JELLINEK (13) says: "Moscona . . . commented on the girl's excellent potential, and he urged the most serious and concentrated study." Moscona left Athens on 30 September 1938.

15. HADZIS.

16. *Kathimerini*, 17 Sept. 1977; *Acropolis*, 18 Sept. 1977. Totis Karalivanos (1901–1987) was one of the pillars of the Hellenic Melodrama from 1926 and subsequently of the G.N.O., conducting almost a thousand performances in all. He was extremely knowledgeable about opera and was highly complimented by Tullio Serafin on his preparation of the 1960 Epidavros production of *Norma* with Maria Callas.

17. SIMIRIOTIS; DALMATI. The tenor Michalis Koronis, himself a pupil of Kalfopoulou, also mentioned that Mary "went to Kalfopoulou" (information provided by journalist Yorgos Pilichos).

18. VLACHOPOULOU.

19. A student who did well in the licentiate (*ptychio*) examination had the choice of either taking the proficiency test or going straight on to the diploma examination. But if a student wanted to skip the licentiate and proceed straight to the diploma, he had to take the proficiency test first.

20. NIKOLAIDI; PAPADOPOULOU; Bulletin for the Academic Year 1937–38 (archives of the National Conservatory).

21. MURROW. Although Maria did not mention the date or any other particulars, this statement of hers is important because her recollection, now corroborated by the discovery of the original program, establishes the fact that she made no public appearance before 4 July 1938.

22. Mary's registration was renewed by the American consular service on 4 June 1940 and 28 March 1945. (Photocopied documents kindly provided by Jackie Kaloyeropoulou.)

23. MANGLIVERAS; *Eleftheron Vima*, 3 and 4 July 1938; program of the Independence Day celebrations found among Vangelis Mangliveras's papers (in the author's collection).

24. P. Krineos, "A Heavenly Voice, a Frosty Eye," interview given by Trivella to an Athens newspaper, c. 10 Mar. 1957 (clipping in Trivella's papers).

25. THIVEOU. Among the well-established singers who performed on Athens Radio during this period were Angelopoulos, Xirellis, Fléri, Moulas, Efstratiou, Galanou, Kalfopoulou,

Mangliveras, and Moscona (when he was in Athens). The younger singers included Glynos, Kambanis, Mavrakis, Koronis, Athineos, Nikita, Anastasiadou, Mavridou, Efstratiadou, Salingaros, and Vlachopoulou, all of whom appear in this book.

26. ALLEGRI 37; VLACHOPOULOU.

27. DE HIDALGO; S. Galatopoulos, *Maria Callas: Sacred Monster*, London 1998, 30.

28. See Chapter 15. John Ardoin says—and this interesting piece of information must have been given to him by Maria herself—that she sang Rezia's aria for de Hidalgo when auditioning "later in 1939." (J. Ardoin, "Maria Callas: The Early Years," *Opera Quarterly* 3, no. 2, summer 1985.)

29. DE HIDALGO.

30. De Hidalgo herself was responsible for the error that has been perpetuated in every book and article in which she appears, namely that she came to Greece just before the war and stayed on teaching in Athens because she was caught there by the outbreak of hostilities. The facts are quite different: see Chapter 14.

31. ALLEGRI 38; GENTE.

32. The most likely hypothesis is that, after being approached by Litsa, de Hidalgo had heard about Mary from Lakis Vassilakis or someone else who had described Mary as a "phenomenon," and that from then on she claimed to have discovered Mary herself. It has sometimes been mistakenly reported in the Greek press (in *Niki*, 25 Aug. 1963, for example) that Mary's audition with de Hidalgo was arranged by de Hidalgo herself, who had heard Mary singing at the National Conservatory. But in the opinion of most of de Hidalgo's pupils and others who knew her, that could never have happened.

33. SALINGAROS; TSOUTIS.

CHAPTER 13

1. Mark sheet for the year 1938–39 (archives of the National Conservatory). Michalis Vourtsis (1908–1983), composer, conductor, and chorus master, was a product of the National Conservatory. As director of the G.N.O. chorus from 1943 he worked with many great conductors, and he was the chorus master for the 1961 Epidavros production of *Medea* starring Maria Callas.

2. VLACHOPOULOU; *Apoyevmatini*, 17 Sept. 1977.

3. DE HIDALGO 161.

4. CALONI.

5. CHIOTAKIS.

6. Notice advertising the performance, *Proia*, 27 May 1939; S. Galatopoulos, *Maria Callas: Sacred Monster*, London 1998, 28; untitled typescript by Kalomiris (Kalomiris papers, archives of the National Conservatory). JACKIE (70) confirms that it was Karakandas who fought for her sister to be given the role of Santuzza.

7. JACKIE 70; Th. Drakos, "The Callas-Onassis Romance," 42 installments, *Thisavros*, nos. 531–572, 4 Oct. 1976–18 July 1977.

8. NIKOLAIDI. "I would compare Callas with Chaliapin," the Russian-born Nikolaidi remarked. "He didn't have a beautiful voice either, but he did have great talent and acting ability. He too had the same passion for practicing. And he too was not one to stand at the front of the stage and sing to the audience: he acted the part. So did Maria: it wasn't her voice but her wonderful expressiveness that sent you into ecstasies."

9. DOUNIAS; SIMIRIOTIS.

10. Y. Karakandas, *All About Opera*, Athens 1978, 633; S. Galatopoulos, *Maria Callas: Sacred Monster*, London 1998, 28.

11. SIMIRIOTIS; KOPANOU.

12. Y. Orfanos, "Maria Callas: Anatomy of a Genius," *Odos Panos*, no. 32, Sept.–Oct. 1987. Orfanos probably had this information from Trivella.

13. Program, first published in MARCHAND (20). *Proia* and *Eleftheron Vima*, 2 Apr. 1939. This celebrated photo was probably taken especially for this occasion; the copy of it which Mary inscribed to Trivella appears later in this chapter.

14. MARIA 19 (cf. J. Cartier, "La vie passionnée de la Callas," *France-Soir*, 18–19 Sept. 1977: "*I was very, very ill. There was something wrong with my teeth, I was swollen up and felt very miserable*"); MARGRIET.

15. Only a month and a half later Kodzias was to deprive Athens of the fifty-year-old Municipal Theater on Athinas Street, an opera house with a capacity of only fifteen hundred, but built well up to western European standards and a very attractive building. Ironically, the square bears the name of Kodzias to this day, while Athens is still without a proper opera house.

16. KOPANOU; ADALI.

17. SIMIRIOTIS; S. Galatopoulos, *Maria Callas: Sacred Monster*, London 1998, 28; untitled typescript by Kalomiris (Kalomiris papers, archives of the National Conservatory); NIKOLAIDI; MARIA 19; *Eleftheron Vima*, 20 Apr. 1939. LITSA (39, 141) wrote that *Cavalleria* was "no thundering triumph," adding that, although both she and Trivella were very proud, it never occurred to either of them that this was Mary's operatic début. Although JACKIE (70) says that Mary was in a different class from the other young singers, she evidently had no clear memory of the performance, for she describes it as being without scenery or costumes. In general, Litsa's and Jackie's comments on Mary's stage and concert performances are of little or no account, apart from some purely descriptive details. Mention must be made here of a curious statement attributed to de Hidalgo by Renzo Allegri (GENTE): "The others [Ikonomidis and other teachers at the Athens Conservatory] had reservations [about admitting Mary to the Athens Conservatory and giving her a scholarship: see Chapter 15], chiefly because they knew that she had already studied at another conservatory, where she had been made to discontinue the part of Santuzza in *Cavalleria Rusticana*." No evidence has come to light to explain this statement of de Hidalgo's, which suggests that Mary had had a failure in the part.

18. ADALI; Karakandas, op. cit., 634–635; SIMIRIOTIS.

19. Bulletin for the Academic Year 1939–40 (archives of the National Conservatory); LITSA 35 (letter from Trivella to Litsa); ADALI.

20. Program, first published in MARCHAND (22–23); Ioannis Psaroudas in *Eleftheron Vima*, 31 May 1939.

21. Program, first published in MARCHAND (24–25); Ioannis Psaroudas in *Eleftheron Vima*, 27 May 1939.

22. Program, first published in MARCHAND (26–27).

23. The dramatic tenor Michalis Koronis (1914–1979) had passed the proficiency test at the same time as Mary, had just got his diploma, and was now on the threshold of a long career. He was to be one of the pillars of the G.N.O. from the time of its very first production (*Die Fledermaus*) in March 1940, making a name for himself both in purely dramatic roles and in operetta. "A great voice, but not a very sensitive musician," was Zoe Vlachopoulou's verdict on him. (VLACHOPOULOU.)

24. Dimitrios Hamoudopoulos in *Proia*, 28 June 1939; Bulletin for the Academic Year 1939–40; mark sheet for Trivella's class for the year 1938–39 (archives of the National Conservatory).

25. MARIA 18–19; J. Ardoin, "Callas Today," *Musical America*, Dec. 1964; HARRIS.

26. This photo, taken by a Patission Street photographer in the early spring of 1939, as well as the accompanying earliest surviving sample of Maria Callas's writing, is now in the author's collection and was exhibited for the first time at the Callas exhibitions in Athens (Gennadeios Library, Jan. 1998) and in Paris (Hotel de Ville, Mar.–June 1998).

27. LITSA 34–35.

28. MAKRIYANNI.

29. JACKIE 48; P. Jackson, *Saturday Afternoons at the Old Met*, Portland (Amadeus Press) 1992, 507–522.

30. SKORDOULI. As to another possible cause of Mary's wobble, Litsa makes this interesting suggestion in her book: "In addition to Trivella and Hidalgo, Maria had another teacher, . . . her canary David. . . . Now she began to sing with David, trying to find out how he did it, putting her fingers on her own throat and watching his, trying to control her voice as he

did his song. This hurt her and tired her; sometimes she was forced to stop singing and rest while he sang on." (Litsa 37–38.) It is quite possible that Mary, in her inexperience, aggravated the harm she had done to her voice as a child in America in the way that Litsa describes.

31. Adali. A similar opinion was expressed in the late 1940s by Louise Caselotti (see the Epilogue).

32. Louvi; Kopanou.

33. Skordouli; Adali.

34. Adali; P. Krineos, "A Heavenly Voice, a Frosty Eye," interview given by Trivella to an Athens newspaper, c. 10 Mar. 1957 (clipping in Trivella's papers).

35. Letter from Maria Trivella, *Ta Nea*, 30 Aug. 1960.

CHAPTER 14

1. Dimitri Mitropoulos was born in Athens in 1896. After graduating from the Athens Conservatory in 1919 he spent four years in Brussels and Berlin before returning to Athens, where he enjoyed a highly successful career until 1937. He moved to Minneapolis in January 1938 and conducted the Minneapolis Symphony until 1949, establishing his reputation as one of the great conductors of his time. He then became the director of the New York Philharmonic, which he took on tour to Athens in 1955 and was lionized on his first appearance there in seventeen years. He conducted Maria Callas for the first and only time at the Metropolitan Opera in 1956, in *Tosca* (see the first footnote in Chapter 24). He died in Milan on 2 November 1960, struck down by a heart attack while rehearsing Mahler's Third Symphony at La Scala. See W. R. Trotter, *Priest of Music: The Life of Dimitri Mitropoulos*, Portland (Amadeus Press) 1995.

2. As told by de Hidalgo to her pupil Ileana Konstantinou. (Conversation with Ileana Konstantinou, 6 May 1993.)

3. Harewood. In another interview, in 1968, Maria said that de Hidalgo had made her stage début at the age of thirteen. (Downes.)

4. Leo Riemens in his book *Maria Callas* (Utrecht 1960, 18–19) mentions a conversation he once had with the Italian tenor Attilio Salvaneschi (1873–1938), who had played Count Almaviva to de Hidalgo's Rosina in Prague in 1908. Salvaneschi, who had heard and sung with the greatest coloratura sopranos of his day (including Galli-Curci and dal Monte), told him that de Hidalgo was second to none vocally—for she had a much fuller, darker voice than her rivals—and even more outstanding dramatically: her performance of the Mad Scene in *Lucia*, for example, made an unforgettable impression on all who saw it.

5. Nikolaidi.

6. The great baritone Yannis Angelopoulos (1881–1943) studied in Athens and started his career there. His voice was so big and had such an enormous range—from a low F to a high A or even B-flat—that in his early years he was sometimes cast as a bass and sometimes as a tenor! As early as 1913 he sang Rigoletto, the role at which he excelled, in Bucharest, and the story goes that his astonishing vocal and dramatic prowess so discouraged Giuseppe de Luca that the latter made his excuses and went back to Milan. Titta Ruffo later voiced his admiration for Angelopoulos, and it is said that on one occasion, when Angelopoulos was on tour with the Neapolitan Teatro San Carlo in Egypt and vying for supremacy with Riccardo Stracciari, "everyone acknowledged the Greek singer's superiority." Between 1920 and 1924 he made highly successful appearances at opera houses all over Italy. His Rigoletto was seen by King Vittorio Emanuele III (who is reported to have remarked, "What a shame! Rigoletto was born in Italy, but it turns out he's Greek . . .") and Benito Mussolini; and then there was a historic run of the same opera at Palermo's Teatro Massimo, in April 1922, with Toti dal Monte as Gilda. Apparently Toscanini wanted to engage him to sing at La Scala, but his plan was frustrated by the jealousy of leading Italian baritones, especially Carlo Galeffi. Angelopoulos returned to Greece in August 1924, probably out of ideological opposition to Fascism, and continued his brilliant career until 1940. The foundation of the Greek National Opera brought his career to a premature end, as he was not engaged to

sing with it although still in fairly good form vocally. Despite his poverty, he refused to sing for the Italians and Germans, and hunger and illness resulted in his untimely death in utter destitution on 5 December 1943. Fortunately the voice of "the Greek Chaliapin," as Angelopoulos was called by German musicologist Sigrid Neef, has been preserved for posterity on some forty records. It is fair to suggest that if he had been born Italian he would now be spoken of in the same breath as the legendary Italian operatic idols of his time. See Y. Leotsakos, *Greek Opera: 100 Years, 1888–1988*, Athens 1988, 100–113.

7. Ioannis Psaroudas, "Piraikos Syndesmos, Second Symphony Concert, Elvira de Hidalgo," *Eleftheron Vima*, 23 Mar. 1938.

8. VLACHOPOULOU. "When I went to the Athens Conservatory in 1937, de Hidalgo and Vassilakis saw a lot of Fléri and her second husband, the tenor Nikos Glynos. They used to play cards together, which was one of de Hidalgo's favorite pastimes. From being close friends all together, Vassilakis and Fléri became lovers. Their affair knocked Glynos flat and ruined his career, while de Hidalgo suffered a blow from which she never recovered." (VLACHOPOULOU.) In 1947, when de Hidalgo left Greece to teach in Ankara and later in Istanbul, it seems that the real reason for her going was to get over the trauma of her abandonment by Vassilakis. "With Karandinos, who had been so shattered when she left him that he almost died of a broken heart, she always remained good friends, but she never forgave Vassilakis, especially because he later married Fléri." (Conversation with Ileana Konstantinou, 6 May 1993.) De Hidalgo helped Vassilakis a good deal in the early stages of his career, both with the Hellenic Melodrama and with the Greek National Opera, and she also provided him with capital to open a shop in central Athens selling radios and radio equipment.

9. The biographical material on Elvira de Hidalgo comes partly from statements she made to some of her pupils and partly from various written sources. The two best are both by Yorgos Leotsakos: *Greek Opera: 100 Years . . .* , 122–127; and "Elvira de Hidalgo: Her Life and Work," *Proini*, 31 Jan. 1980. See also SCOTT 12–13.

10. Filoktitis Ikonomidis (1889–1957) studied in Athens and started teaching advanced theory at the Athens Conservatory in 1910. In 1921 he founded the Athens Choir, with which he gave the first Greek performances of great choral works of the classical and modern repertoire. He started conducting the Athens Conservatory Orchestra in 1927 and was principal of the conservatory from 1935 to 1939. He was one of the prime movers behind the transformation of the Athens Conservatory Orchestra into the Athens State Orchestra in 1942, and he conducted it from then until his death. In 1954 he was managing director of the G.N.O. In the course of his career he made guest appearances with the Berlin Philharmonic, the Vienna Symphonic Orchestra, and the New Philharmonia, among other orchestras. But it is true that he was prejudiced against Italian opera: "Not that he thought it inferior, but it was his belief that it takes more 'culture' to sing other kinds of music such as oratorios, masses, or lieder," commented his widow, Kalliopi, no doubt echoing his own views. (IKONOMIDI.)

11. The old Athens Conservatory building, including the historic little auditorium, is now used by the drama school of the National Theater. Classroom 25, where de Hidalgo taught Mary Kaloyeropoulou, has been turned into a boiler room.

12. L'INVITÉ. De Hidalgo added, "[Singers nowadays] do little work, and sometimes they do it badly. They think of nothing but having a big voice, and they think that's enough. For example, they come to me to be auditioned and I ask them, 'What kind of voice have you got? Dramatic, lyric, mezzo-soprano?' The first thing they say is 'Dramatic.' Not one has ever said lyric. Oh, no! Dramatic! And they have small voices which they have overstrained, their natural voice being much lighter."

13. CALONI.

14. Edward Downes, "Bel Canto in 1956," *Opera Annual*, no. 3, 1956.

15. R. Celletti, "Maria Callas," *Musica*, June 1984. This generally accepted view of bel canto is rejected by Rupert Christiansen ("Callas: A Polemic," *Opera*, June 1987). Briefly, Christiansen's argument is that the term "bel canto" was never used until near the end of the nineteenth century and, when it did make its appearance, "It meant nothing deeper than a

bright, clear and flexible vocal style. . . . To suppose that there was a specific set of Masonic rules of bel canto, on the basis of which that well-matched trio of Rossini, Donizetti, and Bellini wrote all their operas, and with which the Italian singing masters hypnotized their pupils, is utter nonsense." He goes on to deny that Callas resurrected bel canto and concludes, "The art of bel canto had never been lost, simply because it had never existed." But see Postscript II.

16. PROUSE.
17. HAREWOOD.

CHAPTER 15

1. GENTE.
2. GENTE; ALLEGRI 38.
3. SKORDOULI.
4. DE HIDALGO 159; JELLINEK 15.
5. The annual tuition fees in 1939–40 were Drs. 1,150 for singing and Drs. 750 for opera.
6. Data from the class registers in what remains of the Athens Conservatory archives. Polyxeni Mattei (1902–1999) started out as a pianist. She studied in Athens and Leipzig, staying on in Germany for a few years after she graduated: among other things, in 1930 she performed some pieces by her friend Nikos Skalkottas under the baton of Wilhelm Mengelberg. She then went to study with Carl Orff, whose educational principles she applied in the field of dance on her return to Greece.
7. What follows does not set out to be an in-depth analysis of Maria's voice and vocal problems. For a fuller discussion of the subject, see "Processo alla Callas" (*Radiocorriere TV*, no. 48, 30 Nov. 1969, English translation by M. Fagandini, *Opera*, Sept.–Oct. 1970, and in D. Lowe, ed., *Callas As They Saw Her*, London 1987, 81–104); R. Celletti, "Maria Callas," *Musica*, June 1984, and "La voix," *Opéra International, Spécial Maria Callas*, supplement to no. 5, Feb. 1978; T. Celli, "Una voce venuta da un altro secolo," "Perchè la sua strana voce è bella," and "La sua voce commuove perchè contiene un dramma," *Oggi*, 20 and 27 Mar. and 3 Apr. 1958, "A Song from Another Century," *The Saturday Review*, 31 Jan. 1959, and "La donna che diventò voce," *Il Messagero*, 8 Apr. 1973; unsigned article, "Die Primadonna," *Der Spiegel*, no. 7, 13 Feb. 1957; R. Leibowitz, "Le secret de la Callas," *Les Temps Modernes*, July 1959; W. Crutchfield, "The Story of a Voice," *The New Yorker*, 13 Nov. 1995.
8. LEGGE. Walter Legge was an influential figure in the postwar musical world who, as artistic director of EMI, produced a number of recordings encapsulating the art of Maria Callas. In a filmed interview about his wife, Elisabeth Schwarzkopf, he said, "She and Callas were the two best [singers] I have ever worked with" (*Elisabeth Schwarzkopf, A Self-Portrait*, EMI Classics, video, 1995). De Hidalgo, who believed voices should be classified according to their timbre rather than their range, expressed this opinion: "Callas sang what she sang because she worked hard, but also because the timbre of her voice remained as it was." In other words, she never tampered with or forced her natural timbre, which was so rich and so inimitable. (L'INVITÉ.) Rupert Christiansen, on the other hand, believes that de Hidalgo "brightened and colored" Callas's timbre and remarks, "By normal pedagogic standards, de Hidalgo was absolutely the wrong teacher for a potential Turandot or Gioconda" ("Callas: A Polemic," *Opera*, June 1987). However, he seems to overlook the much more important point that de Hidalgo also taught a potential Norma or Lucia. Referring to the roles of Lucia, Gilda, and Rosina, he says, "She thus left her pupil in the odd position of having a great dramatic voice trained to sing little-girl roles like de Hidalgo's own favorites." (*Prima Donna*, London 1984, 305–306.)
9. MATARANGA; POLITOU; SKORDOULI. Others of Mary's classmates have similar recollections, and Klada Matsouki, de Hidalgo's assistant pianist, who quite often accompanied Mary at her practice sessions in her early days at the conservatory, agreed that her voice was "lovely but fraught with problems, because it wasn't at all well placed." (MATSOUKI.)
10. HAREWOOD.

11. NIKOLAIDI; Giuseppe di Stefano, *L'arte del canto*, Milan 1989, 38; L'INVITÉ.

12. VLACHOPOULOU; conversation with Maryitsa Konstantinou, 6 May 1993.

13. PROUSE; FLEETWOOD; DOWNES.

14. J. Ardoin, "Callas Today," *Musical America*, Dec. 1964.

15. L'INVITÉ.

16. M. Fleuret, "Les dons de la maîtrise technique," *Nouvel Observateur*, no. 672, 26 Sept. 1977.

17. Letter from Verdi to Count Arrivabene, 27 Dec. 1877; Stendhal, *Vie de Rossini*, 1824 (both cited in JELLINEK 320). In "Processo alla Callas" (op. cit.), Eugenio Gara quoted the words used by Wagner of Wilhelmine Schroeder-Devrient, the first Leonore/Fidelio: "No, she had no voice; but she knew so well how to handle her breathing and thereby to create, with so marvelous a musicianship, the true soul of a woman, that one thought no longer of singing nor of voice."

18. PROUSE.

19. MATSOUKI. Matsouki's comment on de Hidalgo is reminiscent of what Mary said about opera to Ypatia Louvi at about this time. See Chapter 13.

20. SALINGAROS.

21. HARRIS.

22. DE HIDALGO 161; GENTE.

23. Interview with Mr. Rodrini for Philadelphia Radio, Milan, Sept. 1957; PROUSE.

24. GARA 25. In her interview with Mary Jane Matz ("We Introduce Maria Meneghini Callas," *Opera News*, 3 Dec. 1956) Maria said that she spent hours working on Concone and Panofka to perfect her coloratura. And in her master classes at the Juilliard School of Music in New York (1971–72) she reverted to the subject once again, calling the exercises of Concone and Panofka *"a singer's bible"*: *"To be a proficient vocal instrumentalist, you need Concone and Panofka. They are your homework as long as you are a singer. These studies will place your voice, will exercise it, will answer any questions about trills, gruppetti, accaciature. They are not just for display—it is impossible to become a valid singer without them. It would be like a pianist attempting to perform without having worked on Czerny."* (J. Ardoin, *Callas at Juilliard: The Master Classes*, London 1988, 61–62.)

25. Conversation with Ileana Konstantinou, 6 May 1993.

26. PARIDIS.

27. ALKEOU; VLACHOPOULOU.

28. PAPADOPOULOU; STANCIOFF 61.

29. NIKOLAIDI; conversation with Ileana Konstantinou, 6 May 1993; VLACHOPOULOU. Whereas Vlachopoulou does not remember ever doing any trill exercises with de Hidalgo, Ileana Konstantinou relates that when her former teacher heard Joan Sutherland performing superb trills in about 1960, she commented: "She walks like a horse, like the Statue of Liberty. She has nothing except her trills!"

30. AMAXOPOULOU; SALINGAROS; POLITOU.

31. HARRIS; MARIA 19.

32. Letter from de Hidalgo to Maria, Ankara, 15–18 Mar. 1949 (now the property of Ilario Tamassia), in B. Tosi, *Casta diva, l'incomparabile Callas*, Rome 1993, 103–105, and *Giovane Callas*, Padua 1997, 174.

33. Cf. L. Rasponi, *The Last Prima Donnas*, London 1984, 584; SCOTT 13.

34. S. Galatopoulos, *Maria Callas: Sacred Monster*, London 1998, 32.

CHAPTER 16

1. VLACHOPOULOU.

2. SALINGAROS.

3. DIORIDOU; ALKEOU; MANDIKIAN.

4. E. Gregor, "Die Callas," *Abend*, 5 May 1959 (source not cited).

5. ZACHAROPOULOU. Yorgos Tsirigotis, the principal horn player in the G.N.O. orchestra, recalled once standing behind Mary in the line at the cashier's office waiting to be paid, and

seeing lice in her hair. That was quite unremarkable in those days, but nevertheless he did remember it later. (Telephone conversation with Vasso Rizioti, daughter of Yorgos Tsirigotis, 17 July 1996.)

6. VLACHOPOULOU; SALINGAROS.

7. DE HIDALGO 163.

8. MARIA 19–20.

9. The *Eleni* began life as one of Tsar Nicholas II's private yachts, the *Cherno More* (*Black Sea*).

10. EMBIRIKOS; JACKIE 71; conversation with Sophia Destouni-Xanthakou, 6 Mar. 1996; LITSA 38. See Chapter 33.

11. KALOYEROPOULOU; MIRKA; STASSINOPOULOS 26; JACKIE 71; HARRIS.

12. SALINGAROS; VLACHOPOULOU; POLITOU. Those of de Hidalgo's pupils known to have gone on these outings with Mary include Spyros Salingaros, Apostolos Hadziioannou, Christos Dalamangas, Thanos Tzeneralis, Vangelis Lakadzis, Zoe Vlachopoulou, Elli Dioridou, Ekaterini Politou, Arda Mandikian, Pepi Andreadou, and Iris Streulein.

13. VLACHOPOULOU; *Niki*, 19 Aug. 1963.

14. PROUSE.

15. JACKIE 72; PROUSE. Maria said much the same in 1970: "*We began work at ten o'clock in the morning. We would have a short break for lunch, or maybe eat sandwiches in the school, and then we would begin again. We would work until eight o'clock at night. . . . I did not want to go home. I wouldn't have known what to do if I had gone home or gone out.*" (HARRIS.)

16. L'INVITÉ; Gregor, op. cit. (source not cited); DE HIDALGO 163; GENTE; PROUSE.

17. MANDIKIAN; VLACHOPOULOU; S. Galatopoulos, *Maria Callas: Sacred Monster*, London 1998, 31.

18. GENTE; MARIA 21; television interview with Norman Ross, Chicago, 17 Nov. 1957.

19. When interviewed by singer Charles Trenet for the French radio station Europe 2, in 1959, Maria was asked what piece de Hidalgo had first given her to study, and she answered, "*I think it may have been 'Ah, perfido!' from 'Fidelio' [sic].*" This was something that de Hidalgo regularly assigned her pupils; Zoe Vlachopoulou sang it the same year and included it in the program for her diploma examinations. "It suited Maria's voice better than mine," she now says. (VLACHOPOULOU.)

20. MANDIKIAN; telephone conversation with Lakadzis's widow, 17 May 1996. Mary also helped Lakadzis to transliterate the Italian words into the Greek alphabet.

21. HAREWOOD; DOWNES. In her memoirs, too, Maria had said, "*I remember that at that period my only preoccupation was my hands. I never knew where to put them: they seemed useless and cumbersome.*" (MARIA 19.)

22. GENTE; ALLEGRI 40.

23. LOUVI.

24. MANDIKIAN; TSOUTIS.

25. *Alexandrian Literature*, booklet published for a festival held on 12 Sept. 1943 in aid of Greek students from Egypt, ed. Marios Vaianos, Athens 1943, 19.

26. Y. Roussos, "I'm Not Like the Others: The Case of Callas," *Tachydromos*, 10 Aug. 1957. According to an unsigned article ("The Diva of the Century," *Tachydromos*, 5 Aug. 1961), "[Lykoudis] had to hustle her out of the radio station. '*One day you will beg me to sing and I shan't come!*' yelled the aspiring prima donna, before slamming the door in Lykoudis's face." Yorgos Lykoudis, who in April 1943 conducted Mary in Pergolesi's *Stabat Mater* (see Chapter 25), seems to have been one of those people who never liked Mary, perhaps as a result of that inauspicious first meeting.

27. KYDONIATIS; J. Gruen, "Maria Callas: 'I Am a Very Normal Human Being,'" *The New York Times*, 31 Oct. 1971.

28. Examination records, school of singing, advanced class of de Hidalgo, 28 May 1940 (archives of the Athens Conservatory); GENTE. The other candidates sang arias from *Tannhäuser* (Wagner), *Hamlet* (Thomas), *Le Cid* (Massenet), and *Il Guarany* (Gomes), and lieder by Borodin, Rimsky-Korsakov, Duparc, Saint-Saëns, Benedict, Delibes, Brahms, and Strauss.

29. Program, first published in MARCHAND (39); Alexandra Lalaouni, "At the Opera Examinations," *Vradyni*, 19 June 1940.
30. SALINGAROS; HADZIS.
31. LOUVI; GENTE. On another occasion de Hidalgo said much the same in different words (as recorded in B. Tosi, *Casta diva, l'incomparabile Callas*, Rome 1993, 99): "She astonished everybody and scored a personal triumph. I realized on that occasion that Maria genuinely had the potential to become a great actress, she had the sort of single-minded obsession that few artists in the world possess; and I perceived that she had a wonderful future ahead of her."
32. Lalaouni, op. cit.; PROUSE.

CHAPTER 17

1. An excerpt from the contract is published in MARCHAND (43). Marchand kindly provided a copy of the full text. The original was in the G.N.O. archives at least until 1982 (see the Preface).
2. Kostis Bastias (1901–1972) studied law at Athens University and started a successful career in journalism in 1923. He launched the literary review *Ellinika Grammata* in 1927 and the daily newspaper *Icho tis Ellados* in 1935, and he wrote a number of books. His great love, however, was the theater, and he had several plays performed on the Athenian stage, the first when he was only twenty-two. He was appointed general manager of the National Theater when it was reopened in 1930.
3. Ioannis Sideris, "What the Director of State Theaters Said," *Paraskinia*, no. 120, 31 Aug. 1940. The idea of combining an opera house with a theater aroused a good deal of adverse criticism and gave rise to numerous jokes: one journalist suggested that this arrangement had perhaps been made "to give Oedipus Rex a way of spending a few Nights in Venice with a Merry Widow"!
4. Walter Pfeffer (Vienna 1897–Athens 1970) studied under Felix Weingartner and probably also under George Szell, and was acquainted with Franz Lehár. He began his career in about 1925, conducting *Die Fledermaus* at the Vienna Volksoper. Thereafter he went on several tours with tenor Richard Tauber and held appointments in Munich, Zurich, Berlin, and Vienna. In 1935 he visited Athens with a ballet ensemble from the Vienna Staatsoper. When Hitler annexed Austria in 1938 Pfeffer fled to Brussels, and it was from there that Bastias brought him to Athens for the National Opera. To avoid arrest after the Germans occupied Greece, he made a hair-raising escape to Palestine in 1941 and stayed there until 1946. He then returned to Greece and resumed his post as chief conductor of the Greek National Opera (1946–58), where he conducted more than twenty operettas and some operas.
5. Renato Mordo came from a family of Sephardic Jews settled in Corfu. He was born c. 1895 in Vienna, where he was educated. He very quickly made a name for himself as a stage director after World War I, mostly in Germany, though he also worked in Vienna and occasionally in the Netherlands, Italy, Britain, and France. In 1931 he was appointed director of the Prague Opera, where he was regarded as an innovator, his productions of *Carmen* and operas by Wagner and Mozart being described as "reformist." He was especially fond of classical operetta, and Lehár himself engaged him to direct some of his works in Italy. The rise of Nazism led him to contact Manolis Kalomiris when the latter happened to be in Prague in 1938, and Kalomiris put him in touch with Bastias. As he had a Greek passport, he was ready to leave for Athens as soon as the Germans entered Prague. Some of the trials and tribulations he endured during the German occupation of Greece will be described in the following chapters. After the war he stayed on in Greece for a while before leaving to work first in Ankara and then in Germany, where he died c. 1955. ("In a Year We Shall Have Opera: R. Mordo Speaks," *Paraskinia*, no. 67, 26 Aug. 1939; NIKOLAIDI.)
6. Sasha Machov, born in Prague c. 1900, studied in Paris and won an international reputation by his performances in many European cities and in New York. Settling in Prague, he founded an avant-garde theater company, organized ballet ensembles, and worked with

the Prague Opera as the leading male dancer and as a choreographer until the city fell to the Germans in March 1939. Presumably his contacts with the fledgling National Opera in Athens were effected through Kalomiris, as in the case of Renato Mordo. In Athens Machov built up a very good dance ensemble to work with both the opera and drama divisions of the National Theater, creating a style based partly on Greek folk dances, which he had studied as soon as he arrived in Greece. A naturally gentle and sensitive man, Machov suffered great physical and mental torment during the German occupation, and the Nazi atrocities eventually drove him to suicide. ("Mr. Machov Speaks," *Paraskinia*, no. 80, 25 Nov. 1939; NIKOLAIDI.)

7. *Eleftheron Vima*, 11 Nov. 1939; M.B.G./N.T.G. no. 183, 27 Dec. 1939, "Engagement of artistic personnel for the National Opera"; NIKOLAIDI. The first soloists to be engaged were Nafsika Galanou, Elli Katsirelli, Marika Papadopoulou, Zoe Vlachopoulou, Michalis Koronis, and Spyros Kaloyeras.

8. Real old-timers such as Michalis Vlachopoulos, Ilias Ikonomidis, Artemis Kyparissi, and a few others could not expect to be given a place in a new opera company, and no one was suggesting that they should; but several well-established younger singers omitted by Bastias at this time—notably Petros Epitropakis, Andonis Delendas, Vangelis Mangliveras, and Mireille Fléri—were to figure prominently in the history of the National Opera over the next two decades. The omission for which Bastias came under the heaviest fire was that of Yannis Angelopoulos, the baritone who for thirty years had rendered services of the highest order to the Hellenic Melodrama. However, it should not be forgotten that Angelopoulos was then fifty-eight, with not much of a future ahead of him: in fact he had given a "farewell recital" of light and popular songs at the Kotopouli Theater on 28 April 1938. Admittedly, to have found a place for him in the opera company would have given him public recognition in well-deserved recompense for a truly outstanding musical career, but it would have run counter to the sensible policy that Mordo had strongly advocated and Bastias wanted to follow scrupulously. Bastias was also accused of passing over Angelopoulos for political reasons, as the latter was a left-winger. However, this charge does not really stand up, considering that Bastias personally foiled a move by the extreme right-wing Metaxas dictatorship to arrest the actor Emilios Veakis, another left-winger. (NIKOLAIDI, herself a left-winger.) Despite this, Veakis was bitterly hostile to Bastias: he accused him in his diary (26 Oct. 1940) of "acts of charlatanry which he passes off as great feats" and maintained that "the National Opera, by which I mean not serious opera but operetta" was the assassin's knife with which Bastias had dealt a mortal blow to the theater. Indeed there was a general feeling of fierce antagonism—which lasted throughout the occupation—between the opera company and the exponents of legitimate drama, with the latter regarding the former as interlopers in their territory.

9. TSOUTIS.

10. DE HIDALGO 163–165.

11. TSOUTIS; SKORDOULI. At the same meeting (M.B.G./N.T.G. no. 198, 20 June 1940) the board approved the employment of seventeen male choristers at a monthly salary of Drs. 2,500 as well as the soloists Nikos Glynos (10,000) and Frangiska Nikita (8,000). Nine other soloists—Michalis Koronis (10,000); Zoe Vlachopoulou (8,000); Spyros Kaloyeras (8,000); Nafsika Galanou (7,000); Aliki Zografou (5,000); Anna (Zozo) Remoundou, Kitsa Damasioti, and Irma Kolassi (4,500 each); and Manolis Doumanis (4,000)—had been engaged a month and a half earlier. Maria confirmed in 1968 that she never sang in the chorus, and she glossed over the fact that she had once had a contract of employment as a chorus member: "*After six months of training [sic] with de Hidalgo I was immediately taken—engaged, shall we say?—by the then six-months-old opera in Greece.... They needed a dramatic soprano and they had engaged me for one year on an agreement that I would not sing anywhere else. And de Hidalgo had seen to that contract so that I would have a sum of money that would give me the possibility of studying patiently, without having the necessity of going around to work.*" (HAREWOOD.)

12. Interview for National Greek Radio, Athens, 9 Aug. 1960. Maria was in Greece to sing *Norma* at Epidavros, and it happened that Bastias was again general manager of the G.N.O.

"I am grateful to Kostis. I remember the bad times, but I remember the good moments as well," she added in an aside to journalists standing near her, to remind them that she had not forgotten the infighting of which she had been a victim. She then announced that she would donate her fee to endow scholarships in her name: *"Just as I was in need then, and I was helped, so now I would like to do the same for a youngster who needs help in the early stages."*

13. LITSA 32; KALOYEROPOULOU. The family had never had a telephone in any of their homes in Athens. Apropos of Litsa's blue color scheme, it is interesting to note that twenty-five years later Maria was to choose that color for a study in her apartment on Avenue Georges Mandel, Paris, which she called "the blue room."

14. Letter from Dimitris Gouliamos, *Ta Nea tis Kyriakis*, 12 May 1985; MIRKA.

15. KAMBOURI; KAMBOURIS.

16. F. Filippas, "Maria Callas's Mother Reveals . . . ," *Thisavros*, no. 22, 24 Nov. 1977; SALINGAROS.

17. TSOUTIS.

18. SKORDOULI; SALINGAROS.

19. ZACHAROPOULOU; SALINGAROS; conversation with Nikolaou's pupil Anastasia Parisi, 15 Nov. 1995.

20. MARGRIET; SALINGAROS.

21. JACKIE 75–76.

22. The only surviving records from the year 1940–41 are the examination records of June 1941 and, of course, the Bulletin for the Academic Year 1940–41, which was the last to be issued until after the war (archives of the Athens Conservatory).

23. JACKIE 72–73.

24. VASSILIOU; Achilleas Mamakis, interview with Alexis Minotis, *Ikones*, no. 287, 21 Apr. 1961; Alexis Minotis, *Distant Friendships*, Athens 1981, 117; letter from Michalis Papadakis, *Ikones*, 12 May 1961; Maria Karavia, "Notebook," *Kathimerini*, 23 Sept. 1977.

25. ALKEOU.

26. Emmanuele Grazzi, *I Archi tou Telous* (*Il principio della fine*), Athens 1980, 268–269.

CHAPTER 18

1. MARIA 19; HAREWOOD.

2. TSOUTIS.

3. PAPACHRISTOS.

4. Conversation with Dimitris Horn, 29 Aug. 1993. Horn did not have anything to do with Mary during that production, apart from sometimes exchanging a few words with her during the intermissions. When Maria met him again in 1960 she pretended not to remember him at first, but then, laughing, she asked him to do his imitation of Galanou yelling for help.

5. VLACHOPOULOU; KALAIDZAKIS; HAREWOOD.

6. Ioannis Psaroudas (*Eleftheron Vima*, 31 Jan. 1941) said that the company deserved to be congratulated and that "all the soloists were good." In the role of Boccaccio, usually sung by a woman, he felt that Michalis Koronis had not been a success, "though without being bad," and he found Zoe Vlachopoulou's voice "rather cold" while acknowledging her charm and technical accomplishment. His greatest plaudits he reserved for the conductor, Walter Pfeffer. This was the only time Pfeffer ever conducted Mary. The stage director was Renato Mordo, the sets were designed by Kleovoulos Klonis, the choreography was by Sasha Machov, and the costumes were designed by Andonis Fokas. The chorus included many singers whose names reappear in these pages: Galatea Amaxopoulou, Anthi Zacharatou, Mitsa Kourahani, Antigone Salta, and Lela Skordouli among the women, and Kostas Dounias, Andonis Kalaidzakis, Nikos Papachristos, and Nikos Doufexiadis among the men.

7. JACKIE 77; LITSA 39–40.

8. DOWNES.

9. Undated postcard from Maria Kaloyeropoulou to Vangelis Lakadzis (now the property of his son Yannis). When Vangelis came back from the front he dropped out of the Athens

Conservatory. In 1960 he met Maria again, and she told him that circumstances had been "unkind to his voice." He died in 1992.

10. Michalis Payidas, interview with Nafsika Galanou, *Acropolis*, 1 July 1979.

11. Ibid.

12. NIKOLAIDI. Nafsika Galanou (1905/08?–1982) was the daughter of writer Demosthenes Voutyras. She studied at the National Conservatory and then in Vienna, where she met Walter Pfeffer. She was temperamentally best suited to German music and Viennese operetta and was excellent in roles such as Hanna Glawari in *The Merry Widow*. Although her voice was not of the highest quality, she always looked wonderful, her articulation was very good, and she had a distinctive and stylish stage presence. However, she was quite unscrupulous in promoting her own interests and invariably sided with whoever happened to be in the ascendant at any given moment.

13. AMAXOPOULOU; TSOUTIS.

14. ALKEOU.

15. S. Galatopoulos, *Maria Callas: Sacred Monster*, London 1998, 35.

16. MARIA 44; BANZET.

17. FROST.

18. Discussion between Jackie Kaloyeropoulou and members of the Maria Callas International Club, London, 8 Oct. 1991.

19. Conversation with Alkis Papayeorgopoulos, 19 July 1996.

20. JACKIE 71; discussion between Jackie Kaloyeropoulou and members of the Maria Callas International Club, London, 8 Oct. 1991.

21. JACKIE 73–74; recollections of Despina Karydi (a neighbor living at 5 Marni Street), May 1997.

22. JACKIE 75.

23. Maria Malibran was to be one of Maria's lifelong idols and favorites, so much so that although Callas was never a great collector she acquired several Malibran memorabilia. Among the items included in the exhibition "L'opéra secret de Maria Callas" at the Musée Carnavalet, Paris, 10 Apr.–20 May 1979, were a portrait of Malibran (as well as one of Giulia Grisi); two programs of performances of hers at Covent Garden; a manuscript of Donizetti's "Lamento per la morte di Bellini" dedicated to her; the silver spade used in laying the foundation stone of her house in Belgium; and an oval portrait medallion of her (exhibition catalog, pp. 4–6). All these are now said to be "lost" (see Postscript III).

24. TSOUTIS.

25. LITSA 42–43.

26. JACKIE 75–76; FLEETWOOD.

27. TSOUTIS. According to Tsoutis, Papatestas remarked that Mary had once said to him, "*I'm not at all frightened by these air raid alerts. If I come down to the shelter, I do so as an elementary precaution for my own safety, because I think it's stupid to expose yourself to unnecessary risks.*"

28. STANCIOFF 60.

29. TSOUTIS; JACKIE 76.

CHAPTER 19

1. LITSA 44. "*I don't like this kind of hypocrisy.*" (FROST.)

2. RITSOU. Lola Ritsou, now married to former Prime Minister Xenophon Zolotas, never took up music professionally.

3. GENTE; ALLEGRI 39.

4. L'INVITÉ.

5. TSOUTIS.

6. C. Gastel-Chiarelli, *Maria Callas*, Venice 1981, 15, 17; JACKIE 76–77; LITSA 49.

7. The other candidates from the advanced class (Aliki Zografou, Maryitsa Konstantinou, Lela Skordouli, Galatea Amaxopoulou, and Arda Mandikian) sang arias from *Dido and Aeneas* (Purcell); *Fidelio* (Beethoven); *Mignon* (Thomas); *Il Re Pastore, Die Zauberflöte*, and

Le Nozze di Figaro (Mozart); and *Le Cid*, *Thaïs*, and *Werther* (Massenet); and songs by Brahms, Tchaikovsky, Félicien David, Rimsky-Korsakov, and the Greek composers Lavdas and Pallandios. (Examination records, 1940–41, archives of the Athens Conservatory.)

8. S. Galatopoulos, *Maria Callas: Sacred Monster*, London 1998, 32; RITSOU; telephone conversations with Thomas and Regina Apostolou, spring 1995.

9. LITSA 44; KOURAHANI; JACKIE 80.

10. LITSA 139; STANCIOFF 59; E. Thomopoulos, "Maria Callas Is To Give a Performance," *Athinaiki*, 3 Aug. 1957; *Embros*, 2 Sept. 1961 (cf. L. Jessup, "Maria Callas Versus Everybody," *Opera News*, Sept. 1958: "For the next four years Maria fed the family by singing for Italian and German soldiers, who paid her with food"); MARGRIET.

11. Gastel-Chiarelli, op. cit., 18.

12. STANCIOFF 59–60. Cf. JACKIE 78–79.

13. S. Terra, "Un'altra Callas mira alla Scala," *Epoca*, Feb. 1958.

14. Letter from Litsa to Maria, Athens, 18 Sept. 1949 (now the property of Ilario Tamassia).

15. The only time his name is mentioned is in STASSINOPOULOS 35, but as usual the author does not name her source.

16. LITSA (46–48) and JACKIE (77–78) are the only original sources for this episode.

17. LITSA 48–49; JACKIE 78–79.

18. For historical background on the occupation of Greece, see Hagen Fleischer, *Im Kreuzschatten der Mächte: Griechenland 1941–1944*, Frankfurt/Bern/New York 1986, and Mark Mazower, *Inside Hitler's Greece*, New Haven/London 1993.

19. TSOUTIS.

20. JELLINEK 20.

21. STASSINOPOULOS 34.

22. R. Allegri and R. Allegri, *Callas by Callas*, Milan 1997, 27–28.

23. GENTE; DE HIDALGO 163.

24. Letter from Renzo Allegri to the author, Milan, 9 Feb. 1994.

25. Conversation with Yorgos Pilichos, 5 Aug. 1995. Mary also became friendly with a violinist, Giovanni Battista Dantone, himself a friend of Sylvano Guerri, a sergeant-major who lived in a requisitioned room in the house of music critic Sophia Spanoudi, whose daughter Athina he would later marry.

26. ALLEGRI 42; letter from Renzo Allegri to the author, Milan, 9 Feb. 1994.

27. LITSA 149.

28. SUTHERLAND (conversation recorded in Portland, Oregon, 29 Sept. 1974).

29. ALLEGRI 42. Mary's confession to her classmate Mitsa Kourahani, that her mother made her sing for Italians and Germans *"so that they would bring us food,"* and that she *"had often rebelled"* (KOURAHANI), confirms Meneghini's statement.

30. SIMIONATO. Maria made this confession in Rome, in 1969, on her way to Turkey for the filming of Pasolini's *Medea*.

31. LITSA 139–140; KOPANOU. Litsa met Kopanou in the early 1960s, when Maria was angry with her for wanting to extract a lump sum from Onassis instead of regular monthly payments. She accused her daughter of taking this line only out of a desire to get even with her. "She's getting her revenge on me," she said. When Kopanou asked her why, she told her the story.

32. H. A., "Kameradeschaftsabend der Lufthansa," *Deutsche Nachrichten in Griechenland*, 23 June 1942. On Saturday, 20 June 1942, Sophia Vembo sang at the musical soirée of the Lufthansa Frontreparaturwerstätten at a villa in Kifissia which had been requisitioned and converted for use as a German club (*Kameradschaftsheim*) with a small movie theater, facilities for cards and other games, and a Viennese-style Weinstube in the garden. On that particular evening, typical of many at that time, the tables were set out under the trees, there was plenty to eat and drink, and the party lasted well beyond midnight. The organizer had arranged for musicians from the German radio station (Sender Athen der Wehrmachtsendergruppe Südost), which broadcast the musical portion of the proceedings. After the obligatory opening address, a Luftwaffe band conducted by maestro Neumann played a selection of "spirited, lilting melodies." Then Ingeborg Friedemann sang some arias from

operettas, Corporal Fesselmayer performed on the accordion, two NCOs played accordion duets, and Heinz Kohlhaas entertained the guests with humorous stories. "Something of a climax was reached with the appearance of the famous Greek singer Sophia Vembo, giving her first performance for the [German] radio station in Athens. She sang Greek songs—including 'S'agapo'['I love you'], which she rendered with controlled passion—and received a tremendous ovation."

33. PARIDIS.
34. S. Galatopoulos, *Maria Callas: Sacred Monster*, London 1998, 45.
35. YENNAROPOULOU.
36. DE HIDALGO 163.
37. ALLEGRI 41–42.
38. MARIA 20.

CHAPTER 20

1. Nikos Yokarinis had met Mussolini and probably become personally acquainted with him in the 1920s, when he was the *Proia* correspondent in Rome. From 8 December 1942 he was senior press officer in the prime minister's office, working for the Italian propaganda machine, while still retaining his post at the National Theater. He was dismissed on 12 May 1943, a victim of a political crisis and the diminution of Italian influence in Greece. He left the country at the time of the German withdrawal in 1944, going first to Rome and then to Berlin before settling briefly in Paris; he returned to Greece in October 1950, gave himself up, and was immediately imprisoned.
2. *Athinaika Nea*, 6 and 10 May 1941; M.B.G./N.T.G. no. 1, 15 May 1941.
3. M.B.G./N.T.G. no. 10, 26 June 1941; no. 11, 14 July 1941. The soloists' contracts were renewed at this time, at salaries ranging from Drs. 4,000 to 10,000.
4. L. Zoras, "First Steps at the Conservatory . . . ," *To Theatro*, nos. 59–60, Sept.–Dec. 1977; S. Galatopoulos, *Maria Callas: Sacred Monster*, London 1998, 35.
5. From the summer of 1941 to August 1942 the National Opera staged *The Land of Smiles*, *The Gypsy Baron*, and *Giuditta* (three operettas which de Hidalgo presumably considered at best unnecessary and at worst quite unsuitable for Mary), *Die Entführung* (in which Mary did take part unofficially), *Carmen*, *Barbiere*, and *Traviata* (for which she was not yet ready), and *Cavalleria Rusticana* and *Gianni Schicchi* (which were outside de Hidalgo's repertoire).
6. MARCHAND 65–66; TSOUTIS; NIKOLAIDI.
7. Only four of the twenty-one were men, one being the baritone Konstantinos (Dinos) Engolfopoulos, a first-year student in the lower class, who was to sing Ernesto opposite Maria's Imogene in Bellini's *Il Pirata* in New York eighteen years later. The eight girls in the advanced singing class were G. Amaxopoulou, M. Vassiliou, E. Dioridou, A. Zografou, M. Kaloyeropoulou, M. Konstantinou, A. Mandikian, and E. Skordouli.
8. TSOUTIS. Theodoros Vavayannis (1905–1988) studied at the Athens Conservatory, played percussion in the conservatory orchestra, and was its conductor from 1942. From 1931 to 1939 he was the faithful assistant of Dimitri Mitropoulos, from whom he learned a lot, and in 1938–39 he was in Berlin for further studies at the Hochschule für Musik. From 1950 onward he conducted various orchestras in the United States and Europe, including the Orchestre de la Suisse Romande and the Berlin Philharmonic.
9. MAKRIYANNI.
10. MAKRIYANNI; KALOYEROPOULOU.
11. MAKRIYANNI; LOUVI; DALMATI.
12. Y. Lazaridis, *Flashback*, previewed in *Adesmeftos Typos*, 18 Oct. 1997; DAMASIOTI; MAKRIYANNI; M. Dalmati, "Maria Callas," *Nea Skepsi*, nos. 176–177, Nov.–Dec. 1977.
13. KOURAHANI.
14. MARIA 19; conversation with John Ardoin, Dallas, 13 Sept. 1968.
15. RITSOU.
16. KOURAHANI; MARGRIET; RITSOU.
17. HAREWOOD; conversation with John Ardoin, Dallas, 13 Sept. 1968.

18. Letter from de Hidalgo to Maria, Ankara, 3 Jan. 1949 (now the property of Ilario Tamassia), in B. Tosi, *Casta diva, l'incomparabile Callas*, Rome 1993, 103, and *Giovane Callas*, Padua 1997, 173.
19. HAREWOOD.
20. R. Neville, "Voice of an Angel," *Life*, 31 Oct. 1955, reprinted in *The New York Times*, 30 Oct. 1956; HAREWOOD.
21. Conversation with John Ardoin, Dallas, 13 Sept. 1968.
22. ARDOIN 32; NIKOLAIDI; RITSOU.
23. PROUSE.
24. Radio interview with David Holmes, London, 23 Sept. 1958.
25. HAREWOOD.

CHAPTER 21

1. M. J. Matz, "We Introduce Maria Meneghini Callas," *Opera News*, 3 Dec. 1956; MARIA 20. Similarly, *"In Greece, yes—and it wasn't anybody's fault but the war—then I really suffered hunger."* (Television interview with Norman Ross, Chicago, 17 Nov. 1957.) Another time, in a different mood, she said of the occupation: *"That was hard. I confess that that was a bit hard, but it doesn't hurt anybody. Hardship does one good."* (FROST.)
2. DE HIDALGO 163; ALLEGRI 42; GENTE.
3. MARIA 20–21. See also the views expressed by Giuseppe di Stefano to Anita Pensotti (presumably Maria's views) in "Maria, ti chiedo perdono," *Oggi*, 1 Oct. 1977.
4. E. Thomopoulos, "Maria Callas Is To Give a Performance," *Athinaiki*, 3 Aug. 1957; unsigned article, "La madre della Callas scrive un libro esplosivo," *Gente*, 18 Oct. 1958; LITSA 51–52, 139.
5. KALOYEROPOULOU; JACKIE 78.
6. STANCIOFF 60.
7. KAMBOURIS.
8. Television interview with Norman Ross, Chicago, 17 Nov. 1957; MARIA 20. LITSA (139) confirms that "many others" also helped them.
9. GOUDELIS.
10. MARIA 21.
11. PAPADOPOULOU.
12. LITSA 140; JACKIE 79.
13. M. Callas, "Smentite di articolo 'Time'" (MS, in Italian, 1956), para. 1. See also ALLEGRI 35.
14. JACKIE 79; LITSA 52; conversation with Dr. Panayotis Papapanayotou, 20 Nov. 1997. Arda Mandikian told Nadia Stancioff that Litsa "made Maria go through all kinds of home beauty treatments to improve her complexion." (STANCIOFF 66.)
15. Yorgos Vokos, *Acropolis*, 17 Sept. 1977.
16. Article in *Vradyni*, 22 Sept. 1977.
17. M. Dalmati, review of Polyvios Marchand's book, *Nea Estia*, no. 1365, 15 May 1984.
18. C. Cassidy, "Splendor in the Night," *Opera News* 42, no. 5, Nov. 1977; Callas, op. cit., para. 8. Cf. MARIA 27: *"I was in fact convinced that I was a 'fatty.' In reality I weighed 176 pounds and 176 pounds is a lot, but not excessive for a tall woman like me, five feet eight inches."* When Litsa went to New York at the end of 1946 she found Maria changed: "I asked her why she had let herself gain so much weight, and she laughed and said, 'So what?' I . . . took her in hand. She had been eating enormous breakfasts of eggs, bacon, ham, and butter; I began to cook breakfasts for her consisting of two poached eggs, no ham, no bacon, no cream. In forty days Maria was no longer the fat daughter who had kissed me at the *Queen Elizabeth*." (LITSA 86–87.)
19. Letter from Mary to Vangelis Mangliveras, New York, 12 Jan. 1947 (in the author's collection).
20. Callas, op. cit., para. 8.
21. JELLINEK 108; FROST. See also J. F. P. Restrepo, "Maria Callas' Health and Illnesses," *The Maria Callas International Club Magazine*, no. 15, June 1995.

22. M.B.G./N.T.G. no. 7, 3 Oct. 1941; no. 9, 10 Oct. 1941; no. 20, 25 Nov. 1941; no. 24, 16 Dec. 1941.

23. YANNOPOULOS. The principal female roles were taken by Frangiska Nikita (Konstanze) and Zoe Vlachopoulou (Blonde), with Andonis Delendas as Belmonte and Nikos Papachristos as Osmin.

24. M.B.G./N.T.G. no. 35, 7 Mar. 1942; no. 36, 13 May 1942.

25. JACKIE 80–81; LITSA 46.

26. JACKIE 85–87.

27. LITSA 67, 68–69, 101–102.

28. According to her statement, sworn at the U.S. consulate in Venice, 19 January 1950, Maria arrived in Naples on 28 June 1947 (affidavit by native American to explain protracted foreign residence; photocopy kindly provided by Jackie Kaloyeropoulou). She arrived in Verona next day, 29 June 1947, by train. (MARIA 28; MENEGHINI 12.)

29. G. B. Meneghini, *My Wife Maria Callas*, New York 1982, 20; ALLEGRI 70; JACKIE 121.

30. SKORDOULI.

31. The items sung by Mary's classmates that year were arias from *Barbiere, Lucia, Don Pasquale, Mefistofele,* and *Carmen* and songs by Benedict, Hahn, Liszt, Johann Strauss, and Gordigianni. (Mark sheet and examination record, archives of the Athens Conservatory.)

CHAPTER 22

1. PARIDIS. Andreas Paridis (1916–2000) started his career as a pianist and impressed the critics with his virtuosity and interpretative skills. After the war he studied conducting under Bernardino Molinari at the Accademia di Santa Cecilia in Rome, and while there he followed Maria's early progress in Italy. It was Maria who recommended him to Tullio Serafin, who took him as a pianist to the Maggio Musicale in Florence. In 1951 Paridis was appointed permanent director of the Athens State Orchestra, but he shone as an opera conductor as well. He conducted in many European countries and in America, and it is generally agreed that he was the most talented Greek conductor after Dimitri Mitropoulos.

2. LITSA 60–61.

3. FLÉRI; PARIDIS. Mezzo-soprano Popi Efstratiadou, whose name appears on the permit, was to have been an additional member of the party. A point of interest, because of its psychological implications for Mary, is that Litsa was already using her maiden name, Dimitriadou, although she was not yet divorced.

4. FLÉRI; LITSA 62. PARIDIS remembers them all suffering from severe intestinal disorders, the result of their overeating.

5. *Apoyevmatini*, 6 June 1942; "Celebrazione Rossiniana a Salonico," *Il Giornale di Roma*, undated clipping (probably 9 or 10 June 1942), Petros Epitropakis papers (now the property of Stathis Arfanis).

6. LITSA 62; PARIDIS; FLÉRI; *Il Giornale di Roma*, loc. cit.; *Nea Evropi*, unsigned articles entitled "Theater News" (10 June 1942) and "Rossini" (11 June 1942). SCOTT (18) states that Mary also sang Matilda's aria "Selva opaca" from *Guglielmo Tell*, but mentions no source.

7. JACKIE 88.

8. FLÉRI.

9. LITSA 49–50; M. Callas, "Smentite di articolo 'Time'" (MS, in Italian, 1956), para. 6.

10. DE CARVALHO. Remoundou is named by SCOTT (17) as the offending soloist, and Fléri by Claude Dufresne (*La Callas*, Paris 1990, 44–45), who adds (without substantiating his allegation), "On another occasion a backstage worker was rewarded for his pains by being hit over the head with a stool, in consequence of a rude remark." Galatopoulos (*Callas: Prima Donna Assoluta*, London 1976, 16–17) relates that the young director Nikos Zografos made some hasty alterations to a shapeless black velvet dress that he found in the wardrobe, to disguise Mary's corpulence, but Zografos himself remembered no such incident and there is no reference to him as having been involved in the 1942 production. The story of the alleged assault on Mary in 1941 has been retold with many variations by all Maria's biographers. It has even been blithely repeated by persons who claim to have witnessed the

episode, such as Nikos Zachariou, who was not working at the National Opera until December 1942 but is reported saying that Mary "seized the impertinent spectator [not the soloist's husband] by the scruff of the neck and hit him so hard that she broke his nose" (Y. Leontaritis, "From the Old Phonograph to the Triumph at Carnegie Hall," *Acropolis*, 21 Sept. 1977). Interestingly enough, even Litsa mentions a fracas connected with *Tosca*, which she says took place "in the courtyard of the Royal Theater before a small but fascinated audience." According to her, "[The absent soloist] sent her husband to stop Maria from entering the theater, but when he tried to bar her way to the stage entrance she flew at him and scratched his face. Again I was proud of my daughter for her courage. She came home with a black eye." (LITSA 56–57.) Callas, op. cit., para. 6. JELLINEK (21) places the incident in July 1942 but comments that Maria "roundly denies that there was a fight."

11. Telephone conversation with Louisa Terzaki, 10 Feb. 1995; M.B.G./N.T.G. no. 3, 10 July 1942.

12. The figures are taken from the payroll records and daybook of the National Theater. At that time there were twenty-two men and eighteen women on regular contracts with the opera, with salaries ranging from Drs. 5,800 to 16,000 per month (or Drs. 87,000 to 240,000 per annum, including the Easter, summer, and Christmas bonuses).

13. Michalis Raptis, *A Brief History of Greek Opera and the Greek National Opera, 1888–1988*, Athens 1989, 257.

14. O. Lazaridis, "Maria Callas the Great," *Tachydromos*, 22 Sept. 1977. On another occasion Maria is alleged to have said of her mother: *"When I was fourteen she sent me out to sing just to make money."* (Unsigned article, *Embros*, 5 Aug. 1961.)

15. SIMIONATO.

16. The occupation authorities had taken over several nightclubs on Dorou Street and its environs for the exclusive use of Italians and Germans. They had done the same with brothels: their soldiers were not allowed to go wherever they wanted, for reasons of security.

CHAPTER 23

1. Radio interview given by Ludo Kouroussopoulos to Maria Karavia, National Greek Radio/Television, Sept. 1977. Tenor Loudovikos (Ludo) Kouroussopoulos (1910–1985), born into a naval family, attended the Naval Academy and graduated as a midshipman in 1930. On leaving the service in 1936 he had a year's singing lessons with de Hidalgo and then went to Naples on a four-year scholarship for further studies with Massimo Periti. A soloist with the G.N.O. until 1965, he sang at Buenos Aires in 1950 (Cavaradossi) and at Leipzig and Dortmund in 1957–58. On his retirement he stayed with the G.N.O. as head of protocol and chief librarian.

2. NIKOLAIDI; KALAIDZAKIS; letter from Ulysses Lappas to Maria, 6 Feb. 1949 (now the property of Ilario Tamassia); *Ethnikos Kiryx*, 11 Aug. 1960. Dramatic tenor Ulysses Lappas (1890–1971) was by this time already a towering figure in Greek operatic circles, having won worldwide renown. He had an impressively long career (as Enzo Grimaldo in *La Gioconda*, Milan and Rome, 1915; as Canio in *Pagliacci*, Monte Carlo, 1950 and 1951; as Loris in *Fedora*, Athens, 1952) and sang under some of the most famous operatic conductors of his time. One of the truly great tenors of the 1920s and '30s, he made his mark on opera in Greece, where he sang fairly regularly. From the mid-1930s, when he lived in Athens and was singing less abroad, he was involved in the campaign to start a state opera company in Greece. See Y. Leotsakos, *Greek Opera: 100 Years, 1888–1988*, Athens 1988, 86–97; V. Sambas, *Ulysses Lappas: Forty Years of Singing*, Athens 1957.

3. Lyric baritone Titos Xirellis (1898–1985) studied at the Athens Conservatory with Nina Foka as his singing teacher and Filoktitis Ikonomidis for theory. He made his first public appearance as a singer in 1918, accompanied at the piano by Dimitri Mitropoulos, who had been in the army with him. Between 1925 and 1930 he lived and worked in Milan and Berlin and sang at concerts in various other parts of Germany as well. After spending another five years in Athens (1930–34) and at least three in the United States (1935–38), mostly in New York and Chicago, he settled permanently in Athens. His best roles were

Amonasro, Rigoletto, Scarpia, and old Germont: of his performance as Germont in 1933, Manolis Kalomiris wrote that it was the best ever heard in Athens. See Leotsakos, op. cit., 66–73.

4. KALAIDZAKIS.

5. Sotos Vassiliadis (1905–1990) studied the violin and theory of music at the Thessaloniki State Conservatory, and orchestration and composition with Manolis Kalomiris. Besides the now famous 1942 *Tosca*, he conducted Ulysses Lappas's last concerts in 1951.

6. Sotos Vassiliadis, letter in *Ta Nea*, 21 May 1983, and article in *Mousiki*, no. 22, Sept. 1979, published in MARCHAND (82).

7. HAREWOOD.

8. VASSILIADOU.

9. VASSILIADOU.

10. VASSILIADOU.

11. TSOUTIS.

12. KALOYEROPOULOU; LITSA 83; KALAIDZAKIS.

13. KOUROUSSOPOULOU.

14. YANNOPOULOS. Dino Yannopoulos was born in Athens in 1919, the son of a Greek admiral who served for a time as military attaché in Vienna. There Dino studied history and philosophy at the university while simultaneously taking a drama course at the Reinhardt Seminar, which he had been attending since 1933. As the assistant to Herbert Graf, who was then directing for Toscanini, Yannopoulos spent two summers (1936, 1937) working at the Salzburg Festival. He returned to Greece in the spring of 1940 and joined the National Opera in 1941 on the recommendation of Pfeffer and Mordo, whom he had known in Vienna. He left Athens in September 1945 for America, where he had a highly successful career (his first engagement with the Met was as early as 1946), making periodic trips to direct in Greece. In 1958 he had a short spell as general manager of the Greek National Opera.

15. Interview for National Greek Radio, Athens, 9 Aug. 1960. She then went on to say, speaking as an established prima donna: *"Personally, if there's any question of not doing my work well, I would rather make less money and sing better. So in summer I rest. . . . The only thing I have agreed to do this time is Epidavros, for the National Opera and for Greece."*

16. FLEETWOOD. She later admitted: *"When I was young and trying to establish my career, I had to take whatever was given to me."* (VLACHOPOULOU; KALAIDZAKIS; M. Callas, "I Am Not Guilty of All Those Callas Scandals," *Life*, 25 May 1959.) Cf. Richard Schickel, "Callas," *Look*, 17 Feb. 1959: *"When you're young you have to take chances."*

17. HAREWOOD.

18. *To Vima tis Kyriakis*, 16 Nov. 1980; MARCHAND 3.

19. A. Fotinos, "Reminiscences of the Theater," *I Theatriki*, no. 30, Nov. 1980.

20. T. Lalas, "The Callas I Remember," *To Vima tis Kyriakis*, 14 Mar. 1993.

21. KALAIDZAKIS.

22. CHIOTAKIS.

23. KALAIDZAKIS; YANNOPOULOS. The incident has also been described by Ella Gregor ("Die Callas," *Abend*, 6 May 1959): "Exerting her animal strength, the well-built Maria grabbed the poor little baritone, lifted him up as if he were a feather and hurled him on to the boards with all her might. The whole stage shook. Painfully the singer picked himself up and limped off. The whole of Athens enjoyed the story."

24. SALINGAROS; KOUROUSSOPOULOU; statement by Visconti to the architect Panayis Psomopoulos, who related it to me in a telephone conversation, 17 July 1996.

25. DOUNIAS; L. Bragaglia, *L'arte dello stupore*, Rome 1977, 20; KOURAHANI. "When we sang together at the conservatory, Mary's voice had a sob in it which was eliminated, or at any rate reduced, after she went to Italy." (KOURAHANI.)

26. FROST.

27. Andonis Delendas (1906–1960), who studied the violin and singing at the Athens Conservatory, started his musical career as a violinist in the Athens Conservatory Orchestra. His first public appearance as a tenor was in 1928, as Turiddu with the Hellenic Melodrama.

From 1938 until war was declared on Greece he worked in Germany, making successful appearances in Berlin, Hamburg, Kiel, and Leipzig. His repertoire was extensive, ranging from oratorio to Wagner to operetta. For twenty years he was one of the pillars of the National Opera, singing thirty-seven different roles (see Yorgos Kousouris, *Greek Opera Soloists*, Frankfurt 1978, 58–59).

28. KALAIDZAKIS; DOUFEXIADIS.

29. SALINGAROS; Fotinos, op. cit.; KALAIDZAKIS.

30. KOUROUSSOPOULOU. Haris Vassiliadou tells how one day, when she went to Mary's dressing room, she found her applying her makeup with the help of her mother. Pausing for a moment, Mary looked at Haris, told her straight out that her lipstick did not match the red scarf on her head and advised her what kind of rouge to use. (VASSILIADOU.) Maria's own everyday makeup of a few years later has been described by Pia Meneghini, with the comment: "I must say it was always a pleasure to see her making up. . . . She did it all herself, quickly and without fuss." (Pia Meneghini, "Sette anni con Maria," in B. Tosi, *Giovane Callas*, Padua 1997, 111.)

31. KOUROUSSOPOULOU.

32. KOUROUSSOPOULOU; PAPACHRISTOS; YANNOPOULOS; LITSA 56, 124–125, 142. According to Litsa, Xirellis's voice "was not up to his looks," while Delendas, though a magnificent singer and actor, was "the fattest Mario since Caruso"—so huge that "when he and Maria sang impassioned duets, I sometimes had to close my eyes." It is true that Delendas was a compulsive eater. Litsa tells us he was reputed to eat two pounds of pasta at a sitting, and Spyros Salingaros remembers that during the occupation his fellow singers used to tease him by describing dishes so mouthwatering that the very thought of them made him weep.

33. BANZET.

34. Radio interview with William Weaver, Paris, 10 Apr. 1965; L. Schifano, *Luchino Visconti: The Flames of Passion*, London 1990, 295; L'INVITÉ ("I think that even if you had not sung in opera you would still have been tremendous [as an actress]," Visconti added turning to Maria); P. Dragadze, "Parla la madre di Maria Callas," *Gente*, 15 Oct. 1977. Tsarouchis also spoke to her about Euripides's *Ion*, prompting her to exclaim, *"What wonderful things there are, what masterpieces, and I don't know them!"* (A. Savvakis, *Ioannis Tsarouchis*, Athens 1993, 305.)

35. Sotos Vassiliadis, article in *Mousiki*, no. 22, Sept. 1979, published in MARCHAND (82).

36. M. Callas, "Smentite di articolo 'Time'" (MS, in Italian, 1956), para. 6.

37. Alexandra Lalaouni, "*Tosca*," *Vradyni*, 28 Aug. 1942. See also Ead., "La Tosca al Teatro Nazionale," *Il Giornale di Roma*, 28 Aug. 1942. In her review of the Italian version (*Vradyni*, 9 Sept. 1942) Lalaouni called Mary "a real marvel" and concluded prophetically, "This is a singer the theater needs, and one who obviously has a great future."

38. Sophia Spanoudi, "The Première of *Tosca*," *Athinaika Nea*, 28 Aug. 1942; Petros Koulmassis, "*Tosca* im Nationaltheater," *Deutsche Nachrichten in Griechenland*, 29 Aug. 1942; Dimitrios Hamoudopoulos, "*Tosca*," *Proia*, 29 Aug. 1942.

39. *Proinos Typos*, 29 Aug. 1942. This critic's opinion was subsequently backed by Marika Palesti, a dramatic soprano who made her name in the Moscow Opera in Tsar Nicholas II's reign. In August 1961, apropos of Maria's appearance as Medea at Epidavros, Palesti wrote to her "to save you from the ruin that awaits you if you go on singing things like *Medea*, *Norma*, and *Aida*," as she put it. In her letter she said, "You, my dear Maria, have a dramatic temperament, but your voice is a lyric-coloratura soprano, and instead of suiting your repertoire to your voice you have followed the dictates of your dramatic temperament, starting in Athens with *Cavalleria*, *Tosca*, *Tiefland*, *O Protomastoras*, etc. Do you remember, when you sang *Tosca* with Kouroussopoulos during the occupation and invited me to your house to hear what I thought of it, I said, 'My dear Maria, you are a lyric-coloratura soprano,' and that was proved in *Der Bettelstudent*. When you did not have to make yourself sing harshly you were outstanding, because your voice is cut out for operas like *Traviata*, *Lucia*, *Faust*, and *Madama Butterfly*." (M. Palesti, *Why Voices Are Destroyed Prematurely, Like That of Callas*, Athens 1962, 16–17.)

40. Ioannis Psaroudas, "*Tosca,*" *Eleftheron Vima,* 29 Aug. 1942. However, it should be noted that Psaroudas found the Italian production "altogether much better than the first run, and it gained greatly by being performed in Italian." (*Eleftheron Vima,* 24 Sept. 1942.) Sophia Spanoudi was also more complimentary about Mary in the Italian version: "She is settling into the role of the heroine, a role she is made for," she wrote. (*Athinaika Nea,* 9 Sept. 1942; see also Ead., "Tosca in Sonderbesetzung," *Deutsche Nachrichten in Griechenland,* 17 Sept. 1942.)

41. MARCHAND 81; KOUROUSSOPOULOU. The dates of the *Tosca* performances were 27, 28, and 30 Aug. and 2, 4, 6, 8, 10, 12, 13, 16, 18, 20, 22, 24, 26, 27, and 30 Sept. The first performance in Italian (with Ludo Kouroussopoulos as Mario and Lakis Vassilakis as Scarpia) was the one on 8 September, but I have been unable to establish the dates of the other two.

42. NIKOLAIDI; PAPACHRISTOS.

CHAPTER 24

1. SKORDOULI; KOUROUSSOPOULOU.

2. JACKIE 83. Besides several fellow students and colleagues, Hariton Embirikos, the brother of Miltiadis, also described Jackie as having been jealous of Mary. He remembered her singing to him "some time later" in an attempt to convince him that she had a better voice than her sister. This became much more of an issue in the mid-1950s, when Litsa, in the throes of her bitter feud with Maria, had no hesitation in using the elder daughter to annoy the younger. She then managed to cajole the compliant Jackie into taking singing lessons, no doubt making the most of Jackie's "inferiority" to her famous, rich, and now married sister. Andonis Kalaidzakis, who taught Jackie, comments that she had "an excellent voice, perhaps of better quality and with greater clarity of tone than Maria's," but that she did not have the other qualities needed to make a career as a singer. (KALAIDZAKIS.) See also Postscript I.

3. JACKIE 82; LITSA 58–59, 108.

4. PAPADOPOULOU. Papadopoulou then reminded Mary of the risk of exposing her voice to the damp night air, to which she retorted, "*I don't mind about* that*!*" In 1957, when Papadopoulou asked her what had caused the breach between her and her mother, Maria answered: "*You're the one person who shouldn't have to ask! You know very well how my mother treated me and what she did to me!*"

5. VASSILIADOU.

6. MAKRIYANNI.

7. KAMARA.

8. XAKOUSTI.

9. XAKOUSTI; PAPADOPOULOU.

10. THIVEOU; KALOYEROPOULOU.

11. KAMARA.

12. KAMARA.

13. KAMARA; *To Ethnos,* 2 Aug. 1957; *Vradyni,* 5 Aug. 1957.

14. TSOUTIS. Jackie heatedly insists that the views attributed to Papatestas were in fact those of Maria herself: "I tore up the newspaper, I practically had a fit. Really, she ought to be ashamed of herself! If your family's like that, it reflects on you too. How can you be any different?" (KALOYEROPOULOU.)

15. TSOUTIS.

16. T. Lalas, "The Callas I Remember," *To Vima tis Kyriakis,* 14 Mar. 1993.

17. Conversation between Andonis Kalaidzakis and Nikos Loundzis, Dec. 1996.

18. PROUSE; Y. Roussos, "I'm Not Like the Others: The Case of Callas," *Tachydromos,* 10 Aug. 1957.

19. *The New York Post,* 2 Mar. 1958; C. Spanidou, *Onassis As I Knew Him,* Athens 1996, 160.

20. MATARANGA; KOURAHANI.

21. NIKOLAIDI; DOWNES; DE CARVALHO. Cf. Litsa 129: "Maria never backs down in the face of the enemy. She is at her best when under fire." In 1974, talking about the petty

spite of artists in general, Maria would say, "*Singers are the worst!*" (SUTHERLAND, conversation recorded in New York, 15 Mar. 1974).

22. LITSA 55; PAPADOPOULOU, payroll records of the National Theater. The bass Nikos Zachariou, who made his début as a comprimario in *The Merry Widow* in December 1942, recalls that his early salaries were actually equal to the salary of a naval officer. (ZACHARIOU.) Payroll records of the National Theater show that Mary did not receive a loan or an advance on her salary after the 1940–41 season, as many of the other singers did during the war years.

23. LITSA 36.

24. SALINGAROS.

25. KOURAHANI.

26. Mario Alberici da Barbiano, "Vivo successo alla Casa d'Italia del concerto rossiniano," *Il Giornale di Roma*, 10 Jan. 1943.

27. "Il Natale di Roma rievocato alla Casa d'Italia fra l'entusiasmo dei camerati," *Il Giornale di Roma*, 22 Apr. 1943.

28. "'Tag des Auslandsitalieners' in Athen, Festliche Feier und Konzert in der Casa d'Italia," *Deutsche Nachrichten in Griechenland*, 18 May 1943.

29. KALOYEROPOULOU; JACKIE 88–89.

30. Conversation with General Kyriakos Papayeorgopoulos, 29 Nov. 1993.

31. For example, "Il saluto dei Fascisti recato alle CC.NN. in armi delle Gerarchie atenensi" and "Il decennale del Nazionalsocialismo solennemente celebrato al Vittoria," *Il Giornale di Roma*, 2 Feb. 1942; "Die deutsche Maifeier in Athen," *Deutsche Nachrichten in Griechenland*, 2/3 May 1942.

32. LITSA 62–63.

33. JACKIE 89–90.

34. KALOYEROPOULOU; JACKIE 91.

CHAPTER 25

1. Legends of innocent victims being immured alive to ensure that a building will stand are common to many European and Asian cultures. The beautiful bridge spanning the River Arachthos in western Greece was built in the seventeenth century to replace another which had collapsed and been rebuilt several times since the third century. Ludo Kouroussopoulos, the Cavaradossi of the 1942 "Italian" production of *Tosca*, belonged to a resistance group, through which he heard that the Italians were intending to blow the bridge up; he went to plead for it with a senior Italian officer mentioning that the history had even been made into an opera. (KOUROUSSOPOULOU.) And so the bridge of Arta was saved and remains intact.

2. F. W. Herzog, "'Der Baumeister,' Manolis Kalomiris' musikalische Tragödie im Athener Nationaltheater," *Deutsche Nachrichten in Griechenland*, 21 Feb. 1943. MARCHAND (89) lists twelve performances of *O Protomastoras* (19, 21, 23, 26, 27 Feb. and 2, 5, 6, 11, 13, 16, 20 Mar.), but the manuscript book in the archives of the National Theater entitled "Works and Sundry Festivals, Receptions, Concerts, etc., of the Royal Theater of Greece, 19 Mar. 1932–27 May 1956" mentions only nine performances without giving dates. The principal roles in this production were sung by Andonis Delendas (Master Builder) and Zozo Remoundou (Smaragda).

3. Copy of the program in Petros Epitropakis's papers (now the property of Stathis Arfanis), published in *The Maria Callas International Club Magazine*, no. 10, Oct. 1993. Cf. MARCHAND 90 and *Estia Neas Smyrnis*, vols. 14–15, 1978, 59.

4. "L'Istituto di Cultura Italiana e la sua attività in Grecia," *Il Giornale di Roma*, 22 Dec. 1942; JACKIE 89; MANDIKIAN. The program of this concert was first published in MARCHAND (91).

5. MANDIKIAN; *Eleftheron Vima*, 24 Apr. 1943; JACKIE; MAKRIYANNI. In the early 1950s Hadzidakis started composing an opera entitled *Rinaldo and Armida* especially for Maria Callas, but he never finished it. According to Stamatis Tsoutis, Mary was on her way home from the Holy Thursday concert when the curfew came into force, and she was stopped by

an Italian patrol shortly before she reached 61 Patission Street. She answered their questions in Italian, telling them that she sang at the opera, and soon had the patrol commander eating out of her hand. (TSOUTIS.)

6. JACKIE 88; KALOYEROPOULOU.

7. P. Dragadze, "Ma che vita inutile, una vita senza figli," *Gente*, 1 Oct. 1977.

8. Jackie Kaloyeropoulou, discussion with members of the Maria Callas International Club, London, 8 Oct. 1991.

9. KALOYEROPOULOU; Stelios Galatopoulos to Nikos Charalambopoulos, in conversation, spring 1996; MENEGHINI 5–6, 131. See also Postscript III.

10. M.B.G./N.T.G. no. 9, 28 Jan. 1943; PAPACHRISTOS.

11. L. Rasponi, *The Last Prima Donnas*, London 1984, 350. Cf. SCOTT 19.

12. TSOUTIS. In the spring of 1944, Andreas Paridis was offered a scholarship to go to Berlin to study the piano further, on the recommendation of the German chargé d'affaires, von Grävenitz, who was a music-lover and a pianist himself. Paridis got out of it by saying he wanted to be a conductor. (PARIDIS.)

13. SKORDOULI.

14. End-of-year 1942–43 examination records (archives of the Athens Conservatory); A. Mamakis, "What's Up with Maria Callas?", *To Ethnos*, 26 Feb. 1957.

15. Conversation with Frangiski Psacharopoulou-Karrori, 13 July 1996; PATRIARCHEAS.

16. JACKIE 84–85; letter from D. Gouliamos, *Ta Nea tis Kyriakis*, 12 May 1985.

17. M.B.G./N.T.G. no. 1, 12 June 1943; no. 2, 17 June 1943; no. 4, 28 June 1943; program, first published in MARCHAND (94–95); Alexandra Lalaouni, *Vradyni*, 19 July 1943.

18. *Kathimerini*, 24 July 1943; F. W. Herzog, "Maria Kalojeropoulou als Tosca," *Deutsche Nachrichten in Griechenland*, 20 July 1943.

19. PARIDIS; VLACHOPOULOU.

20. Program, first published in MARCHAND (100).

21. F. W. Herzog, "Konzertabend im Kosta Moussouri," *Deutsche Nachrichten in Griechenland*, 23 July 1943; Alexandra Lalaouni, *Vradyni*, 24 July 1943.

22. F. W. Herzog, "Callas Athene . . . ," *Die Wildente*, no. 21, Oct. 1959.

23. Ibid. Herzog touched on the subject of the support given to Mary by the Germans in another article, also written in 1959: "The opinions of the German newspapers in Athens carried so much weight that her Greek 'colleagues' dropped their guarded attitude toward her," he wrote. ("Die Primadonna des Jahrhunderts . . . ," 1959 press clipping, with no indication of source, kindly provided by Polyvios Marchand.)

24. "Mit Lili Marleens Lied . . . ," *Die Welt*, 6 May 1970. Cf. P. J. Rémy, *Callas, une vie*, Paris 1982, 37: "So it seems that someone called Friedrich Herzog was the person who did the little pushing that was necessary to set her career firmly on course."

25. Clipping from German magazine, without title or date, but probably 1959 (in the author's collection).

CHAPTER 26

1. LITSA 64. Dimitris Moundouris was an ex-officer working for the city of Thessaloniki as a municipal engineer.

2. MOUNDOURI.

3. LITSA 64.

4. A.B., "Konzertbericht aus Saloniki," newspaper clipping, 2/3 Sept. 1943, reprinted with commentary by Kurt Wenzel, "Maria Callas und Rossini," *Orpheus*, no. 6, June 1983, where the source of the original article is given as the *Deutsche Nachrichten in Griechenland*. Wenzel had found the clippings in the personal papers of the tenor Anton Dermota in Vienna, with the words "*Deutsche Nachrichten in Griechenland*" written on them. Despite a thorough search, however, I was unable to find this article, and Wenzel admitted it was possible that the clipping (which was somewhat tattered) might have come from another newspaper. (Telephone conversation with Kurt Wenzel, 25 Sept. 1996.)

5. Telephone conversation with Andonis Kosmatopoulos, 11 May 1994; LITSA 64.

6. The full text reads: "Born in New York, America, in December 1924 [sic]. Her vocal talent became apparent in her childhood and she therefore started having piano lessons, making such good progress that at the age of ten she was playing Chopin waltzes with the greatest of ease. She had to give up piano lessons soon afterward, however, and only resumed them two years ago. But she kept up her singing on her own, and whenever an opportunity presented itself she sang [in public] and impressed her listeners. At the age of eleven she took part in two competitions organized by the biggest radio networks in America, which she won from a field of four hundred students and graduates. In March 1937 she came with her family to settle in Greece, and six months later she started having singing lessons in order to be admitted to the conservatory. In 1939, at the age of fifteen [sic], she sang in Mascagni's *Cavalleria Rusticana*. Her success in that work and the discovery of her rich seam of talent caused her to have second thoughts, and she went to Mme. Elvira de Hidalgo for further studies. The year before last she was taken on by the National Theater (National Opera) and appeared as Beatrice in *Boccaccio*. She then continued with her studies and last year she appeared again in the difficult role of Tosca, where she scored a great success. She has sung in concerts, radio broadcasts, etc." Some clarification is called for with regard to the sentence concerning Mary's work in *Cavalleria Rusticana*: it hardly seems logical that her success—if it was a success—should have made her decide to move from Trivella to another teacher.

7. KYDONIATIS.
8. *Kathimerini*, 2 Oct. 1943.
9. TSOUTIS.
10. YANNOPOULOS; TSOUTIS.
11. VASSILIADOU; conversation with Eleni Mangou, 18 May 1994; ZACHARIOU; T. Lalas, "The Callas I Remember," *To Vima tis Kyriakis*, 14 Mar. 1993.
12. Michalis Raptis, *A Brief History of Greek Opera and the Greek National Opera, 1888–1988*, Athens 1989, 256.
13. DOUNIAS; VASSILIADOU; conversations with Eleni Mangou, 18 May 1994, and Lela Stamos, 20 Jan. 1996.
14. CHIOTAKIS.
15. "The Unknown Callas of EAM," *Eleftherotypia*, 19 May 1983; ALKEOU; DALMATI; Aspasia Papathanassiou, *Pages of Memory*, Athens 1996, 63.
16. CHIOTAKIS.
17. M.B.G./N.T.G. no. 6, 7 July 1943; no. 8, 14 July 1943.
18. Handwritten summaries of the statements made to the board by Lakis Vassilakis (22 Oct. 1943), Lysimachi Anastasiadou (22 Oct. 1943), and Mary Kaloyeropoulou (23 Oct. 1943) from the latter's personal dossier, which has disappeared from the G.N.O. archives. Photocopies of these statements were given to Polyvios Marchand in 1982 at the request of Elli Nikolaidi (see Preface).
19. Ibid.
20. KRASSA.
21. M.B.G./N.T.G. no. 6, 7 July 1943; no. 18, 13 Sept. 1943; no. 19, 20 Sept 1943; no. 20, 24 Sept. 1943; no. 37, 24 Jan. 1944; and data from payroll records (archives of the National Theater).
22. Payroll record of "Kaloyeropoulou M., opera actress" for the year 1943–44 (archives of the National Theater).
23. On 3 October 1943 Terzakis had signed a contract leasing the Olympia Theater from the Karandinos brothers, and the necessary conversion work was begun straightaway. Until it was ready, orchestral rehearsals were held in the National Archaeological Museum, in the room that was also used for rehearsals of the Athens State Orchestra (as the Athens Conservatory Orchestra had been renamed when it was reorganized in the autumn of 1942).
24. M.B.G./N.T.G. no. 10, 26 July 1943; no. 16, 30 Aug. 1943; no. 24, 18 Oct. 1943; no. 25, 25 Oct. 1943.
25. LITSA 65; JACKIE 91.
26. STANCIOFF 66.

27. SUTHERLAND (conversation recorded in Paris, 20 Dec. 1973). Yet in an earlier interview she declared, "*When I was performing in Athens during the war, the Germans did not bother me in any way even though I held an American passport.*" (Joachim Schilling, "Man hat mich seelisch gelyncht," *Der Spiegel*, no. 4, 2 Feb. 1958.)

28. *Eleftheron Vima*, 16 Dec. 1943.

29. VASSILIOU.

CHAPTER 27

1. VLACHOPOULOU.

2. Maria Cheroyorgou-Sigara remembers Takis telling her he had once said to Mary, "Maria, I love you too much to marry you, because I'll ruin your career." She herself has her own views on Mary's relationship with Takis: "Not having a boyfriend or lover, Maria wanted to show that she could at least have a well-off male friend, which gave her a certain standing."

3. Y. Roussos, "I'm Not Like the Others: The Case of Callas," *Tachydromos*, 10 Aug. 1957; unsigned article, "The Diva of the Century," *Tachydromos*, 5 Aug. 1961; TSOUTIS.

CHAPTER 28

1. SALINGAROS; KALAIDZAKIS.

2. *Athinaika Nea*, 12 Jan. 1933; *Neos Kosmos*, 15 June 1935.

3. MANGLIVERAS. In politics, Mangliveras started out as a socialist in reaction to the Fascism then sweeping Europe. As time went by, the problems posed by his way of life and personal circumstances caused him to water down his ideals, but he always remained true to democratic principles.

4. MATARANGA.

5. MANGLIVERAS. "Mangliveras wielded a lot of power in those days, as he was collaborating fairly openly with the Italians. However, he was a democrat at heart, a good singer, and generally well liked, and that was why he was never accused of having been a collaborator." (SALINGAROS.)

6. Letter from Mangliveras to Angelos Terzakis, 29 June 1943 (G.N.O. archives).

7. Letter from Mangliveras to the board of the National Theater, 27 Apr. 1944 (G.N.O. archives).

8. ALKEOU; KOLASSI; KALAIDZAKIS; KOUROUSSOPOULOU; MATARANGA. No recordings of Mangliveras's voice were known until, after his brother's death in 1999, a tape with "De la splendeur immortelle" from *Benvenuto* by Eugène Diaz and a 78 rpm record with "Largo al factotum" from Rossini's *Il Barbiere* were found. They both attest to a singer and interpreter of the very highest caliber, by any standard.

9. VLACHOPOULOU; TSOUTIS; KALAIDZAKIS.

10. KOURAHANI; VLACHOPOULOU.

11. DOWNES.

12. Conversation with Eleni Mangou, 18 May 1994.

13. HAREWOOD.

14. KOURAHANI.

15. M.B.G./N.T.G. no. 42, 27 Feb. 1944; no. 43, 13 Mar. 1944; no. 44, 20 Mar. 1944; no. 45, 27 Mar. 1944; Manolis Kalomiris, "Report on the Activities of the Greek National Opera during the Past Winter Season," 7 July 1944 (ELIA). Although the National Opera had in practice been independent of the National Theater for some time, its official existence as an autonomous entity dates from 9 May 1944, when a Cabinet resolution declared it to be an independent public corporation and its name was changed to Greek National Opera (*Government Gazette*, no. 160A, 9 May 1944).

16. Undated handwritten lists signed by Kalomiris and initialed by Rallis (ELIA); M.B.G./ N.T.G. no. 50, 24 Apr. 1944; M.B.G./G.N.O. no. 4, 3 June 1944. On 10 April Kalomiris had requested that the salaries of certain National Opera soloists should be equated with

those of the National Theater, but Rallis had refused on the grounds that the theater was financially self-supporting while the opera was not (M.B.G./N.T.G. no. 48, 10 Apr. 1944; no. 50, 24 Apr. 1944).

17. Answering the criticism that Papadaki had won the right not to be replaced in any role for which she had been cast, Rallis, who was a close friend of Papadaki, said that that condition "also applies to Miss Kaloyeropoulou of the National Opera." Lappas and Kalomiris agreed that "outstanding" artists should be allowed to set their own conditions (M.B.G./N.T.G. no. 70, 4 Sept. 1944).

18. Data from contracts in the soloists' personal dossiers in the G.N.O. archives.

19. CALONI.

20. KRASSA; L. Zoras, "First Steps at the Conservatory . . . ," *To Theatro*, nos. 59–60, Sept.–Dec. 1977.

21. Ibid.; MARIA 20.

22. MATARANGA; KRASSA; VAROUTI; Zoras, op. cit. Leonidas Zoras (1905–1987) was a protégé of Kalomiris and had married his daughter Krinó. He had started out as a tenor, so he knew something about singing. As a conductor he was thorough, meticulous about details and strict with the orchestra, but he had quarreled with most of his fellows, especially Ikonomidis, accusing him of never doing anything to promote Greek music. Being "an honest man who stood up for his principles," as he was described by Tatiana Varouti, Zoras had no hesitation in openly challenging the authority of Kalomiris sometime in 1944, probably at a rehearsal for *O Protomastoras*, with the result that his general manager and ex-father-in-law sent him to the disciplinary board. One of the key witnesses of this incident was Mary, who was invited to testify at the hearing of the case. (Statement by the general manager of the G.N.O., 25 June 1944, ELIA; resolution referring Leonidas Zoras to the disciplinary board, M.B.G./G.N.O. no. 7, 26 June 1944.)

23. KOURAHANI.

24. CHEROYORGOU.

25. *Deutsche Nachrichten in Griechenland*, 23 Apr. 1944; information received from Polyvios Marchand, who had been told by Michalis Papadakis, the actress's brother.

26. TSOUTIS; VLACHOPOULOU. Xenia Kouroussopoulou also remembers Mary's cold: "I went to her dressing room before the performance. She was burning hot all over—her temperature must have been 39°C [102°F]—and she was frightfully worried about going on stage. In the event there was one high note that she didn't get very well and she was generally a bit insecure. After the performance she looked very upset with herself, although she had acted her heart out and done fantastically well." (KOUROUSSOPOULOU.)

27. SKORDOULI; NIKOLAIDI; VASSILIOU.

28. VLACHOPOULOU; Zoras, op. cit.; P. L. Caviglia, "Il fenomeno vocale storico umano di Maria Callas," *Discoteca*, June 1967.

29. "Finally, what is a sound if not a means of expressing thought? What is a note without the feeling that it colors and by which it is brought to life?"

30. "It is extreme sensitivity that makes mediocre actors; it is mediocre sensitivity that makes the vast number of bad actors; and it is the absolute lack of sensitivity that leads to sublime actors."

31. GARA 17, 19, 22.

32. VLACHOPOULOU. Zoe Vlachopoulou also talked about Mary's nearsightedness to Stamatis Tsoutis in 1963: "When Maria sits down to study her role she is not content to study her own part only. She has the whole score with her, so first she reads all the other parts and then the whole score until she has learned it all by heart, and only then does she concentrate on learning her own part. . . . In the end she doesn't really need the conductor to bring her in in the right place, because by listening to the other singers she automatically knows when to come in, without anybody to help her." (TSOUTIS.)

33. G. B. Meneghini, *My Wife Maria Callas*, New York 1982, 29; M. J. Matz, "We Introduce Maria Meneghini Callas," *Opera News*, 3 Dec. 1956; L'INVITÉ.

34. NIKOLAIDI; PAPACHRISTOS; KOURAHANI; PAPADOPOULOU.

35. MATARANGA; DOUFEXIADIS; George London, "Prima Donnas I Have Sung Against," *High Fidelity*, Mar. 1987.

36. MANDIKIAN.

37. Zoras, op. cit.

38. Conversation with John Ardoin, in *Callas at Juilliard: The Master Classes*, London 1988, 6; HAREWOOD.

39. *Vradyni*, 23 Apr. 1944; *Kathimerini*, 24 Apr. 1944.

40. *Eleftheron Vima*, 25 Apr. 1944; *Athinaika Nea*, 25 Apr. 1944. Reviews were also written by Dimitrios Hamoudopoulos and Angelos Doxas (in *Proia* and *Acropolis*, respectively, both 25 Apr. 1944). Doxas called Mary "a welcome revelation," while Hamoudopoulos said of her: "With her fine dramatic voice she was brilliant in her interpretation of the thankless and extremely difficult role of Marta. . . . And so this singer passed triumphantly through the golden gate of music to the great roles."

41. F. W. Herzog, "'Tiefland' in der Griechischen Staatsoper," *Deutsche Nachrichten in Griechenland*, 23 Apr. 1944.

42. Konstantinos Ikonomou, "D'Albert: *Tiefland*," *To Radiophonon*, no. 45, 30 Apr.–6 May 1944.

43. Letter from Mangliveras, *To Radiophonon*, no. 46, 7–13 May 1944. See also N. P. Vergotis, "Apropos of a Review," *To Radiophonon*, no. 48, 21–27 May 1944.

44. F. W. Herzog, "Eine Griechische Staatsoper in Athen," *Deutsche Zeitung in den Niederlanden*, 9 May 1944; "'Tiefland' in der Griechischen Oper in Athen," *Wiener Illustrierte*, 21 June 1944 (reprinted in MARCHAND 119–121).

45. Zoras, op. cit.

46. LITSA 66; VASSILIOU.

47. Manolis Kalomiris, "Report on the Activities of the Greek National Opera during the Past Winter Season," 7 July 1944; undated report from M. Molotsos to Kalomiris (ELIA).

CHAPTER 29

1. KOURAHANI; PROUSE.

2. MANGLIVERAS; SALINGAROS; S. Galatopoulos, *Callas: Prima Donna Assoluta*, London 1976, 19 (without reference to his source).

3. Maria was later to state in writing that her tough bargaining with opera houses over pay and conditions was usually dictated to her by Meneghini, a former brick manufacturer who brought the hard capitalist mentality into the world of music. In time she accepted her husband's tactical approach and perhaps adopted it herself. See ALLEGRI 243–244.

4. AMAXOPOULOU; conversations with Louisa Terzaki, 10 Feb. 1995, and Vyron Kolassis, 20 Jan. 1996; SKORDOULI.

5. SALINGAROS; PAPACHRISTOS. However, on the subject of Mary's attitude to sex, it is worth noting Takis Sigaras's unequivocal assertion that with him there had been "no surges of sexual passion" on her part. The exact nature of her relationship with Mangliveras remains unclear, and most people prefer to keep their opinions to themselves on this matter. Mangliveras's brother is evasive, saying cryptically, "Even if it was the case [that they had a sexual relationship], Vangelis was not the first." (MANGLIVERAS.)

6. LITSA 58–59.

7. STANCIOFF 66; MANDIKIAN; S. Galatopoulos, *Maria Callas: Sacred Monster*, London 1998, 47.

8. F. W. Herzog, "Callas Athene . . . ," *Die Wildente*, no. 21, Oct. 1959; S. Galatopoulos, *Callas: La Divina*, London 1963, 20. See also S. Galatopoulos, *Callas: Prima Donna Assoluta*, London 1976, 20. The next writer to mention a proposal of marriage was JELLINEK (22).

9. S. Galatopoulos, *Maria Callas: Sacred Monster*, London 1998, 47.

10. MANGLIVERAS; letter from Mary to Vangelis Mangliveras written in Greek on notepaper headed "Hotel Times Square, Forty Third Street, West of B'way, New York City," 2 Jan. 1946; 1945 Christmas card with the printed sentiment, "It's extra warm and true—this Christmas wish—'Cause it's for You!" (in the author's collection).

11. Letters from Mary to Vangelis Mangliveras, New York, 2 Jan. 1946 ("*Give my love to Artemis and you know who*") and 12 Jan. 1947 (in the author's collection). Kalliopi Vrettou is said

to have once approached Mary, telling her that she was the mother of Mangliveras's children. The story goes that Mary then said, *"I'm glad to meet you, but there is nothing between Vangelis and me. We just have a good working relationship and he encourages me—nothing more than that."* (AMAXOPOULOU.)

12. Letter from Mary to Vangelis Mangliveras, New York, 12 Jan. 1947 (in the author's collection). The entire Chicago project fell through.

13. KALOYEROPOULOU; JACKIE 91–92, 94–95.

14. Letters from Mary to Vangelis Mangliveras, New York, 2 Jan. 1946 and 12 Jan. 1947 (in the author's collection); LITSA 66; S. Galatopoulos, *Maria Callas: Sacred Monster*, London 1998, 47.

CHAPTER 30

1. VAROUTI; TSOUTIS.

2. TSOUTIS.

3. SIGARAS.

4. LITSA 67; JACKIE 92. "You couldn't just throw him out of the house. They were very nice people, both he and the colonel." (KALOYEROPOULOU.)

5. JACKIE 92; LITSA 68–69; ALKEOU. Marina Krassa is another who says that Mary once talked to her "in tears" about her mother's pressure in connection with a German officer. (KRASSA.) The only other German whose name has been linked with Mary's (the allegation being that "she used to go and see him in his apartment") is a man named Burg or something similar. (KALOYEROPOULOU.)

6. KALOYEROPOULOU; LITSA 68; conversation with Alkis Papayeorgopoulos, 19 July 1996; JACKIE 92–93.

7. Spyros Tsiros, *Kathimerini*, 17 Sept. 1977.

8. F. W. Herzog, "Die Primadonna des Jahrhunderts . . . ," 1959 press clipping, with no indication of source.

9. F. W. Herzog, "Callas Athene . . . ," *Die Wildente*, no. 21, Oct. 1959.

10. Conversations with Vyron Kolassis, 20 Jan. 1996, and Anthi Zacharatou (not taped), 8 July 1993; PARIDIS; MATARANGA.

11. MATARANGA; conversation with Filippos Tsalahouris, keeper of the Kalomiris papers, archives of the National Conservatory, 16 Oct. 1993.

12. KOURAHANI.

13. L. Zoras, "First Steps at the Conservatory . . . ," *To Theatro*, nos. 59–60, Sept.–Dec. 1977; ZACHARIOU. Says Nikos Zachariou, "I didn't know Maria at all in the occupation, but I did sing in the chorus in *Tiefland, O Protomastoras*, and *Fidelio*. I really got to know her in 1953 at La Scala."

14. PATRIARCHEAS.

15. VASSILIOU.

16. "Journal of Performances at the National Opera from Monday 1 May to Sunday 7 May 1944" (ELIA).

17. Totis Karalivanos, unpublished paper, "The Chronicle of the Greek National Opera, 1940–1982" (now the property of Yorgos Leotsakos); Spyros Tsiros, *Kathimerini*, 17 Sept. 1977. Karalivanos, a veteran of the Hellenic Melodrama, was generally acknowledged to be more able than most other conductors, who tried to keep him (and Stefanos Valtetsiotis too, for that matter) on the sidelines. On the other hand, he has been described as "bad and lazy" (PARIDIS) and "two-faced and self-interested" (VLACHOPOULOU), and he was nicknamed "the Cobra."

18. Telephone conversation with historian Manos Eleftheriou, 15 Mar. 1998.

19. Telephone conversation with architect Panayis Psomopoulos, 17 July 1997.

20. KOURAHANI; SCOTT 22; MATARANGA.

21. Schedules of performances from the founding of the National Opera to December 1945 (ELIA); PATRIARCHEAS. The performance schedules, which unfortunately do contain some errors and omissions, list only eight performances of *Cavalleria* in 1944, while Kalomiris in

an official report gives the number as ten, and MARCHAND (124) has a total of twelve (6, 19, 14, 16, 19, 23, 25, 27, 28 May and 1, 8, 16 June 1944). Marchand's dates are taken from newspaper announcements, but some performances may have been canceled at the last minute. At all performances Turiddu was played by Delendas, Lola by Kourahani, and Lucia by Bourdakou.

22. *Athinaika Nea,* 7 May 1944.

23. *Proia, Eleftheron Vima,* and *Vradyni,* 10 May 1944.

24. P. Linardos, *Musikleben in Athen, 1941–1944: Der Einfluss der deutschen und italienischen Besatzung,* unpublished masters thesis, Institut für Musikgeschichte, Vienna 1987.

25. The La Scala broadcasts, some of which Mary would surely have heard, included in 1943 *Tosca* (7 and 22 Sept.), *Bohème* (28 Sept. and 2 Dec.), *Don Pasquale* (12 Oct.), *Barbiere* (2 Nov.), *L'Amico Fritz* (6 Nov.), *Trovatore* (9 Nov.), *Favorita* (16 Nov.), *Traviata* (22 Nov.), *Rigoletto* (6 Dec.), and *Butterfly* (28 Dec.), and in 1944 *Cavalleria* (4 Jan.), *Pagliacci* (11 Jan.), *Aida* (18 Jan.), *Lucia* (25 Jan. and 6 Apr.), and *Turandot* (1 Feb.).

26. Most of these particulars are taken from Linardos, op. cit.; *To Radiophonon,* and *Deutsche Nachrichten in Griechenland.*

27. F. W. Herzog, "Callas Athene . . . ," *Die Wildente,* no. 21, Oct. 1959.

28. The program is published in MARCHAND (126). See also *To Theatro,* no. 3, 20 May 1944; *Athinaika Nea* and *Vradyni,* 22 May 1944. The production expenses were borne by the Germans and the entire proceeds—a large sum—were shared among needy actors, musicians, and theater technicians.

29. Y. Roussos, "I'm Not Like the Others: The Case of Callas," *Tachydromos,* 10 Aug. 1957.

30. Unsigned article, "Geliebt und gehasst: die Callas," *Radio Revue,* no. 51, 20 Dec. 1959.

31. Zoras, op. cit.; F. W. Herzog in *Deutsche Nachrichten in Griechenland,* 24 May 1944, and "Callas Athene . . . ," *Die Wildente,* no. 21, Oct. 1959.

32. Cast list for *O Protomastoras,* register book, 13 Nov. 1943–23 Mar. 1945 (archives of the National Theater).

33. M.B.G./N.T.G. no. 2, 22 May 1944; no. 8, 19 June 1944; no. 10, 17 July 1944; no. 11, 24 July 1944; PAPACHRISTOS; MATARANGA.

34. Altogether 6,701 tickets were issued, of which 1,277 and 935 were for the performances of 30 July and 5 August, in which Mary was singing ("Financial Year 1944–45, First Season," G.N.O. archives).

35. "Greek National Opera," a schedule of performances from 1 Apr. to 3 Dec. 1944, signed by stage manager Kostas Pomonis, and "Schedule of G.N.O. productions from 5 March 1940 to 11 July 1945" (both in ELIA); Alexandra Lalaouni, *Vradyni,* 9 Aug. 1944; S. Galatopoulos, *Maria Callas: Sacred Monster,* London 1998, 41.

36. Conversation with Filippos Tsalahouris, keeper of the Kalomiris papers, archives of the National Conservatory, 16 Oct. 1993. He had been told the story by Leonidas Zoras.

37. KALAIDZAKIS; MATARANGA. The unsuitability of Kalomiris's music for Mary's voice and the fact that she had problems with the part of Smaragda are confirmed by Litsa, who describes *O Protomastoras* as "a very difficult modern Greek opera which nearly broke her voice." (LITSA 58.)

38. TSOUTIS; SALINGAROS; MATARANGA.

39. NIKOLAIDI.

40. B. Burroughs, "Maria Callas: 'Yes, But . . . ,'" *Opera Quarterly* 6, no. 4, summer 1989.

41. FLÉRI; KOLASSI; NIKOLAIDI. On the important part played by Ferruccio Cusinati (1872–1954) in the early years of Maria's career in Italy, see the testimony of his daughter in B. Tosi, *Giovane Callas,* Padua 1997, 195–197.

42. A. Signorini, "Ecco le lettere, i documenti e le foto che conservo della mia amica Callas," *Gente,* 2 Nov. 1992. Mary was probably thinking of her singing exhibition on board Embirikos's S.S. *Eleni,* during the trip to Corfu in the summer of 1939.

43. SIMIONATO. Cf. I. Bottero, *Maria Callas, croce e delizia,* Mondovì 1997, 212–213.

44. P. Dragadze, "My Lonely World: A Woman Looking for Her Voice," *Life,* 30 Oct. 1964; interview in Alan Palmer's film *Maria Callas,* 1987; P. Dragadze, "Ma che vita inutile, una vita senza figli," *Gente,* 1 Oct. 1977. Will Crutchfield ("The Story of a Voice," *The New*

Yorker, 13 Nov. 1995) argues cogently that Maria's vocal problems were congenital and had therefore been present long before 1959, when—after a life of total dedication to the art of opera singing—she met Aristotle Onassis and her lifestyle changed completely. However, he does not explain the cause of the problems. Crutchfield, an admirer of Maria Callas who places her on the highest pedestal in the history of opera (and likes to refer to her as an American), ought to have added that, even if the "Onassis period" was not the primary cause of her vocal problems, it surely created conditions conducive to the more rapid aggravation of irreversible symptoms.

CHAPTER 31

1. M.B.G./N.T.G. no. 50, 24 Apr. 1944; unsigned MS dated 26 Apr. 1944 (ELIA); F. W. Herzog, "Callas Athene . . . ," *Die Wildente*, no. 21, Oct. 1959, and "Die Primadonna des Jahrhunderts . . . ," 1959 press clipping, with no indication of source; M.B.G./N.T.G. no. 51, 1 May 1944. Oskar Walleck, described by Herzog as being "in the cultural service of the Reich," had worked at Coburg and Munich and was at that time general manager of the German Theater in Prague. He had directed operas (mostly by Mozart, Wagner, and Verdi) in Paris, at La Scala in Milan, at the Maggio Musicale in Florence, and at Teatro Reale in Rome.
2. SIGARAS.
3. Petition from Fléri to the board of the G.N.O., 3 June 1944 (ELIA); FLÉRI; telephone conversation with Fléri, 9 Feb. 1995.
4. MARIA 21–22; FLEETWOOD.
5. KOLASSI; A. Mamakis, "What's Up with Maria Callas?", *To Ethnos*, 26 Feb. 1957.
6. Cast list for *Fidelio*, 3 June 1944 (ELIA); conversation with Kostas Paschalis, 30 Dec. 1994; AMAXOPOULOU; VLACHOPOULOU; MATARANGA.
7. KOLASSI; PATRIARCHEAS; VAROUTI.
8. KALAIDZAKIS.
9. SALTA.
10. Photocopy of written statement submitted by Mary Kaloyeropoulou to Manolis Kalomiris, undated [20 July 1944], from her now lost personal dossier, given to Polyvios Marchand in 1982.
11. Ibid.
12. Register book, 13 Nov. 1943–23 Mar. 1945 (archives of the National Theater).
13. M.B.G./G.N.O. no. 6, 19 June 1944; "Announcement," no. 205, signed by Kalomiris, 1 July 1944; cast list, 28 Aug. 1944 (ELIA).
14. Cast list, 8 Sept. 1944 (ELIA).
15. PROUSE.
16. VASSILIOU.

CHAPTER 32

1. Fotini Pipili, "Maria Callas," *Pantheon*, no. 631, 4–17 Oct. 1977; NIKOLAIDI. Maria was always very fond of Elli Nikolaidi and had great respect for her. When she came to Athens in 1957 she recognized her immediately at the airport and greeted her as "the Russian," the nickname she had always used for her because of her Russian origins.
2. KOLASSI; HAREWOOD.
3. HAREWOOD.
4. PARIDIS; VLACHOPOULOU; *To Radiophonon*, no. 33, 6–12 Feb. 1944, and no. 39, 13–19 Mar. 1944. Hans Hörner (who was born in Munich in 1903 and worked as a répétiteur in Berlin from 1932 to 1941, when he was appointed director of the Leipzig radio station) loved Greece and fell in love with a Greek violinist in his orchestra, Melita Andreadou. When the Germans withdrew from Greece very soon after *Fidelio*, Hörner deserted and was hidden by Andreadou. After a while they both escaped to Turkey, where he conducted the Ankara Symphony Orchestra for an unknown length of time. (PARIDIS; conversation with Vyron Kolassis, 20 Jan. 1996.) In 1959, when Maria was giving a recital in Germany, the

Münchner Illustrierte (no. 50, Dec. 1959) published an article with an old photograph of Mary and Hörner together. By that time Hörner was back in Germany, getting occasional engagements to conduct the Stuttgart Philharmonic. He never managed to re-establish himself in postwar Germany, probably on account of his "Nazi past." The fact that he had been an officer in the Wehrmacht with no other duties than conducting music was seen as a sign of special favor, although all the Greek musicians who worked with him were sure he was anti-Nazi. He ended his career in Japan, though it is not known when he went there, and he died in Tokyo in May 1968. (Particulars taken from the *Deutsche Bühnenjahrbuch* and kindly provided by Klaus Thiel, head of opera at the Freie Berlin radio station.)

5. KOLASSI. (Irma Kolassi admits she did not like Mary's voice: "I thought highly of Kaloyeropoulou's work, her personality, and her acting, but I did not like her kind of voice.") The prevailing opinion of Greek conductors at that time was expressed by a critic who described them as "thoroughly slapdash, men of meager talent and education whose conducting is nothing more than experimentation at the expense of the music and the very long-suffering public" (N. Rudzin, *To Radiophonon*, no. 33, 6–12 Feb. 1944). Most soloists and choristers in the G.N.O. at that time were and still are broadly in agreement with this opinion.

6. FROST; LITSA 107.

7. HAREWOOD. On Maria's method of preparation see also PROUSE; JELLINEK 323–324.

8. *O Kallitechnis*, no. 1, 8 Aug. 1944; PAPADOPOULOU; VLACHOPOULOU.

9. VLACHOPOULOU; HAREWOOD.

10. M.B.G./G.N.O. no. 6, 19 June 1944; no. 8, 3 July 1944.

11. SIGARAS; IKONOMIDI. It is worth mentioning here that Filoktitis Ikonomidis is held to have been one of the prime movers of the psychological warfare against Dimitri Mitropoulos that caused him to leave Greece. So, ironically enough, it could be said that he indirectly helped to promote the international careers and reputations of two of the greatest musicians of our time, and certainly the two greatest Greeks: Mitropoulos and Callas.

12. A. Mamakis, "What's Up with Maria Callas?", *To Ethnos*, 26 Feb. 1957.

13. JACKIE 93–94.

14. The original of this document is in the author's collection. According to Elvira Mataranga, the decision to ban children under fourteen from the opera had been made a few months earlier, after a performance of *Tiefland* at which Mangliveras's five-year-old daughter had screamed "He's killing Daddy!" when Delendas was "strangling" him. (MATARANGA.)

15. KALOYEROPOULOU; THIVEOU (Garofalidou's sister). A similar anecdote was related many years later by Meneghini: "When she was singing at La Scala, we would dine at Biffi Scala around seven in the evening. Maria would consume a twenty-eight-ounce steak; everyone who saw her must have wondered how she could possibly sing with all that food sitting on her stomach." (G. B. Meneghini, *My Wife Maria Callas*, New York 1982, 105–106.)

16. Conversation with Thodoros Veroulis, 13 Feb. 1994; letter from Mary to Vangelis Mangliveras, New York, 12 Jan. 1947 (in the author's collection).

17. MATARANGA; S. Galatopoulos, *Maria Callas: Sacred Monster*, London 1998, 87–88.

18. MATARANGA; W. Schroeter, "Der Herztot der Primadonna," *Der Spiegel*, no. 40, 26 Sept. 1977.

19. T. Lalas, "The Callas I Remember," *To Vima tis Kyriakis*, 14 Mar. 1993; SALINGAROS. A similar opportunity for venting anti-German feeling had arisen in July 1943 at the end of the second act of *Carmen*, where Carmen (Kitsa Damasioti) says to Don José (Andonis Delendas), "Et surtout la chose enivrante: La liberté! La liberté!" and the chorus repeats "La liberté! La liberté!" The audience erupted, and the Germans insisted on having the "dangerous" word removed. When, at the next performance, Carmen and the chorus sang instead "Dans la montagne! Dans la montagne!" the audience erupted again ("the mountains" being virtually synonymous with the resistance).

20. MANGLIVERAS; KOURAHANI; Y. Roussos, "I'm Not Like the Others: The Case of Callas," *Tachydromos*, 10 Aug. 1957; IKONOMIDI; S. Galatopoulos, *Maria Callas: Sacred Monster*, London 1998, 44.

21. *Eleftheron Vima, Vradyni, Athinaika Nea, Proia*, all 17 Aug. 1944; *Kathimerini*, 18 Aug. 1944.

22. Christos Mangliveras remembered seeing a German broadcasting van outside the Odeon of Herodes Atticus.

23. Several writers (see, for example, JELLINEK 22) have asserted wrongly that *Fidelio* was staged in German, presumably because the conductor and stage director were both German. However, as John Ardoin notes, "With few exceptions the operatic material of these years was sung in Greek. In a number of Callas's scores dating from this period that I have seen— *Aida,* for example (which she used during her classes at the Juilliard School of Music)—you can see where she has written the Greek translation above the original text." (J. Ardoin, "Maria Callas: The Early Years," *Opera Quarterly* 3, no. 2, summer 1985.)

24. The upper (and much larger) section of seating in the Odeon of Herodes Atticus was not then in use, which meant that the total capacity was only about two thousand. ("Financial Year 1944–45, First Season," G.N.O. archives; "Greek National Opera," a schedule of performances from 1 Apr. to 3 Dec. 1944, ELIA.) The first performance with the alternate cast (Remoundou, Amaxopoulou, Koronis, Efstratiou, with Leonidas Zoras conducting) took place on 19 August and was followed by two more on 2 and 7 September 1944.

25. LITSA 57; JACKIE 94.

26. Conversation with Thodoros Veroulis, 13 Feb. 1994.

27. MARIA 26; TSOUTIS.

28. LITSA 58, 60, 131. Although Maria would always remember the Louros family's standoffishness, when she went back to Greece in 1957 she feigned amnesia, mainly because of the prevailing climate of hostility toward her, and in that way she gained the support of some of her "disloyal" relatives, notably that tardy admirer of hers, Nikos Louros.

CHAPTER 33

1. SIGARAS; LITSA 87.

2. M.B.G./N.T.G. no. 73, 18 Sept. 1944; register book, 13 Nov. 1943–23 Mar. 1945 (archives of the National Theater); M.B.G./N.T.G. no. 78, 25 Sept. 1944 to no. 85, 10 Nov. 1944.

3. MATARANGA.

4. Handwritten minutes, 21 Oct. 1944 (ELIA).

5. LITSA 70–71, 112; JACKIE 95.

6. MATARANGA.

7. MATARANGA.

8. MARIA 22.

9. Memorandum to the management of the G.N.O., 28 Oct. 1944, signed by 122 members of the company (ELIA).

10. Petition presented by 114 members of the company to the management of the G.N.O., 18 Nov. 1944; statement by Kalomiris notifying the G.N.O.'s artistic, administrative, and technical personnel of the petition of 18 Nov. 1944 (both in ELIA).

11. MARGRIET.

12. TSOUTIS.

13. Lieutenant Ray Morgan, whom Mary met on or about 20 October, jotted down her office address in his notebook at their first meeting as follows: "Miss Mary Callas, Gen. direct. 1st floor G.H.Q." This means that Mary had started work with the British almost as soon as they moved into the Tameion building.

14. MARIA 22.

15. Ray Morgan wrote a memoir of the period ("Athens: October–December '44," *The Athenian,* Dec. 1987) in about 1960. He taught music to the senior boys of All Saints School, Maidenhead, before becoming its deputy head and then deputy head of Harrow Junior School. In 1965 he became headmaster of Merton Park Primary School, Wimbledon, London. Since 1985 he has been living in Athens with his Greek wife, and I have been able to talk to him at some length. The account of events given on the following pages has been put together from his published memoir and our conversations, filled out with connecting narrative drawn from other sources as well as my own comments.

16. On political affairs, Maria was later to say: *"Politics doesn't interest me. I don't want to get involved. I have my opinions, but I keep them to myself"* (*L'Express*, 19 Jan. 1970); and again, *"I never mix myself in politics. We artists should only be artists"* (J. Gruen, "Maria Callas: 'I Am a Very Normal Human Being,'" *The New York Times*, 31 Oct. 1971).

17. Television interview with Hy Gardner, New York, 26 Feb. 1958; MARIA 24.

18. LITSA 73; JACKIE 95–102; KALOYEROPOULOU. Jackie still gets quite upset when talking about her mother's attitude. "That woman! She was crazy! It wouldn't have been so bad if she had been well-off, but she wouldn't have had two pennies to rub together if it hadn't been for Milton." (KALOYEROPOULOU.)

19. LITSA 76–77, 155; JACKIE 103. Maria was no doubt forcibly reminded of the canaries by an incident that occurred in 1964. Sitting in the main square of Lefkada, she took it into her head to sing Santuzza's aria "Voi lo sapete" accompanied on the piano by Kyriakos Sfetsas, a young musician who happened to be present. When she had finished, "[A barber], carried away by her singing, ran into his shop, picked up the cage containing his beloved canary and gave it to her. Callas was very touched. She adored the canary. One day, as we were drinking our after-lunch coffee in the pool lounge, Onassis told the chief steward to bring him the cage. . . . He opened the door and let the canary out. . . . He maintained that he did not like seeing birds cooped up in cages." (C. Spanidou, *Onassis As I Knew Him*, Athens 1996, 164.)

20. LITSA 74–75.

21. MARIA 25; LITSA 75–76. Although Maria later stated that she had not been able to leave the building for the whole of those three weeks, she may possibly have ventured out to her old neighborhood of Harilaou Trikoupi Street, with her heart in her mouth, to ask Christina Katifori if she could give them any provisions. It is also possible that Christina's brother-in-law, Nikos Katiforis, who had the right connections, may have instructed the communist guerrillas around the Polytechnic to leave Litsa and her daughters alone. (Conversation with Christina Katifori's nephew, Angelos Papadimitriou, 2 June 1996.) Be all this as it may, there is no particular reason to doubt Stamatis Tsoutis's statement that Mary twice tried to go out to get food "but could not, because of the fierce fighting in the area." (TSOUTIS.)

22. JACKIE 103; LITSA 78; MARIA 25.

23. MARIA 25; LITSA 78; JACKIE 103–104.

24. TSOUTIS.

25. LITSA 79; JACKIE 103–104.

CHAPTER 34

1. LITSA (29, 73) misrepresents the truth by stating that Filon was killed by the communists. Their sister Pipitsa was also a communist sympathizer: one day she was arrested and their brother Efthymios, who knew the chief of police, had to plead for her release. (EFFIE; KATIE.)

2. *Megali Ellas*, 7 and 8 Feb. 1945.

3. Inaugural address of Synadinos on taking over as general manager, 16 Feb. 1945, and report to the board of the G.N.O., 25 July 1945 (both in ELIA). Synadinos calculated that in the 1,825 days of its existence the G.N.O. had given a total of 883 performances of twenty-five different works, of which seven were operettas, five were one-act operas, and two were ballets.

4. The numbers of tickets sold and complimentaries given out for each performance were 14 March, 355 and 9; 15 March, 295 and 16; and 24 March, 408 and 18. ("Financial Year 1944–45, First Season," G.N.O. archives.)

5. Only 568 tickets were sold. ("Financial Year 1944–45, First Season," G.N.O. archives.)

6. EMBIRIKOS.

7. K. Amandos to I. Sideris, 10 Mar. 1945; T. Synadinos to I. Sideris, 13 Mar. 1945 (both in ELIA); M.B.G./G.N.O. no. 1, 4 Mar. 1945; no. 2, 8 Mar. 1945.

8. M.B.G./G.N.O. no. 5, 29 Mar. 1945.

9. Letter from seventeen soloists to the board of the G.N.O., 6 Apr. 1945 (ELIA); M.B.G./ G.N.O. no. 6, 4 Apr. 1945; no. 7, 12 Apr. 1945.

10. Letter from Synadinos to the board of the G.N.O., 25 July 1945 (ELIA).

11. Handwritten report of Lysimachos Androutsopoulos to the management of the G.N.O., 4 Apr. 1945; M.B.G./G.N.O. no. 7, 12 Apr. 1945; no. 8, 14 Apr. 1945; handwritten lists of soloists drawn up by Zoras, Evangelatos, Mordo, Triandafyllou, and Synadinos (all in ELIA).

12. L. Zoras to T. Synadinos, 14 Apr. 1945 (ELIA).

13. Handwritten lists of soloists drawn up by Zoras, Evangelatos, Mordo, Triandafyllou, and Synadinos (ELIA).

14. M.B.G./G.N.O. no. 8, 14 Apr. 1945; no. 9, 16 Apr. 1945.

15. It was not long before the new salary rates were readjusted: by the summer of 1945 they had risen from Drs. 40,000 to 53,340 for Grade AA and from Drs. 35,000 to 46,670 for Grade A, and on 1 November 1945 they were raised again to Drs. 72,000 and 63,000, respectively (complete payroll records of G.N.O. personnel, 1945; Totis Karalivanos, unpublished paper, "The Chronicle of the Greek National Opera, 1940–1982," now the property of Yorgos Leotsakos). Thus the "restructuring" remained a dead letter and in spring 1946 Synadinos was replaced, being judged to have failed in his mission.

16. MARIA 22–23; MARGRIET. Cf. Maria's statement in C. Cassidy, "Splendor in the Night," *Opera News* 42, no. 5, Nov. 1977: *"My colleagues went to protest. The director said, 'The whole theater is against you.' I tore up my contract."*

CHAPTER 35

1. Unsigned article, "Geliebt und gehasst: die Callas," *Radio Revue*, no. 51, 20 Dec. 1959 (source not cited); MARGRIET.

2. *Nea Alithia* and *Makedonia*, 26 Apr. 1945. Litsa gives the date of this trip wrongly as 1944 (LITSA, caption of photo between pp. 80 and 81).

3. The photograph is now in the author's collection. It was found in Maria's album, which she left in the house she had shared with Meneghini at Sirmione (together with other personal effects and her correspondence up to 1959), not imagining that she would never set foot there again.

4. MOUNDOURI; YEORYIOU.

5. The announcement appeared again in *Nea Alithia* on 9 May, the day of the first recital, and in *Makedonia* on 2, 5, 8, and 9 May 1945.

6. YEORYIOU.

7. YEORYIOU; EXAKOUSTOU.

8. YEORYIOU; EXAKOUSTOU.

9. YEORYIOU; EXAKOUSTOU.

10. Maria never once mentioned singing the Liebestod in Greece. In fact, describing how Serafin had asked her to sing Isolde in 1948, she admitted that her answer to him—that she knew it—was not true.

11. YEORYIOU; PATRAS.

12. In the first part of the 1942–43 season the Thessaloniki radio orchestra was conducted by Hartmann, an efficient organizer but not a very good musician nor a likable person (unlike his counterpart in Athens, Hans Hörner). Early in 1943 he was replaced by the thirty-year-old Fricke, until then musical director of the Leipzig radio orchestra, who was succeeded for the 1943–44 season by Yung, a former conductor of the Saarbrücken radio orchestra. It seems that Yung was a more accomplished musician than his predecessors and more open-minded, even going so far as to play Tchaikovsky at the very time when Germany was losing the war with Russia.

13. PATRAS.

14. PATRAS; *Makedonia*, 9 May 1945; *Nea Alithia* and *Dimokratia*, 11 May 1945; telephone conversation with Kiki Chrysafi-Marinaki, 13 May 1994.

15. Evripidis Kotsanidis (1890/95?–1968), like his fellow conductors Alexandros Kazandzis and Vassilis Theofanous, taught the violin at the Thessaloniki State Conservatory. Since

1919 he had been conducting the small orchestra that gave regular concerts in the park on the waterfront near the White Tower. For several years past the main musical events in the Macedonian capital had been Kotsanidis's "Musical Thursdays," for which he augmented the orchestra with up to twenty extra players and, instead of playing Strauss waltzes and Suppé overtures, tackled meatier works like Beethoven's First and Schubert's Unfinished Symphony.

16. PATRAS.
17. *Makedonia*, 12 May 1945; *Fos*, 13 May 1945.
18. YEORYIOU.
19. *Nea Alithia*, 16 and 18 May 1945; *Makedonia*, 16, 18, 19, and 20 May 1945; *Fos*, 16 and 18 May 1945; *Laiki Foni*, 20 May 1945.
20. PATRAS; YEORYIOU.
21. PATRAS.
22. LITSA. See also MARCHAND 142.

CHAPTER 36

1. LITSA 71, 81–82; JACKIE 106–107.
2. On the first photograph, a scene from the second act of *Tosca*, she wrote, "*To my dear Father, with love, Maria. P.S. Here you see me with Xirellis.*" (From Maria's private photograph album, now owned by Renzo Allegri.) On the other she wrote rather smugly, "*I am sending you a memento of a 'historic event,' as the newspapers described this production. Your little daughter, Maria.*" (Published in S. Segalini, *Callas, les images d'une voix*, Paris 1987, 17. It was "given" to Segalini by Vasso Devetzi; see Chapter 37.)
3. TSOUTIS; T. Lalas, "The Callas I Remember," *To Vima tis Kyriakis*, 14 Mar. 1993.
4. ARDOIN 44.
5. S. Linakis, *Diva: The Life and Death of Maria Callas*, London 1981, 8. It is interesting to note that Maria is said once to have used almost exactly the same words to describe the way she was exploited by her husband, Meneghini: "*He never gave me credit either for my talent or for the terrible struggle I had to reach the top. I was just a machine for making money.*" (C. Spanidou, *Onassis As I Knew Him*, Athens 1996, 151.)
6. KALOYEROPOULOU; JACKIE 121.
7. YEORYIOU. Tonis did meet her once more when he went to *Tosca* at Covent Garden in 1965 (sitting next to Noël Coward, who roared, "Mariaaaaa! Divaaaaaa!"). After the performance he went backstage, where he found her in her dressing room. "As soon as she saw me, after twenty years, she cried '*Tony, darling!*' and threw her arms round me."
8. LITSA 82.
9. G. B. Meneghini, *My Wife Maria Callas*, New York 1982, 18–19.
10. A. Mamakis, "What's Up with Maria Callas?", *To Ethnos*, 26 Feb. 1957; report of Synadinos to the board of the G.N.O., 25 July 1945 (ELIA).
11. M.B.G./G.N.O. no. 15, 24 May 1945; no. 17, 7 June 1945.
12. D. K. Evangelidis, "The National Opera," *To Ethnos*, 28 June 1945, and "The National Opera Needs Restructuring," *To Ethnos*, 30 June 1945.
13. *Vradyni*, 2 July 1945; *To Ethnos*, 7 July 1945.
14. MARIA 23. GARA (13) takes the view that the "parenthesis" of operetta—which even the great Wagnerian Kirsten Flagstad had not been able to escape in her youth—was a useful counterweight to the dramatic roles that Mary had had to sing until then.
15. *To Ethnos*, 7, 9, and 10 July 1945; data from soloists' personal dossiers (G.N.O. archives).
16. *To Ethnos*, 18 July 1945; M.B.G./G.N.O. no. 24, 9 Aug. 1945.
17. Application for registration, affidavit by native American to explain protracted foreign residence, Athens, American Consular Service, 28 March 1945, and other related documents. (Photocopies kindly provided by Jackie Kaloyeropoulou.) See also JELLINEK 25.
18. Oath of allegiance and application for the renewal of her passport in the name of Sophie Cecelia Kalos, Athens, American Consular Service, 23 July 1945; passport No. 358 (FS122034), issued 4 Aug. 1945 in the name of Sophie Cecelia Kalos. (Photocopies kindly

provided by Jackie Kaloyeropoulou.) See also *The Maria Callas International Club Magazine*, no. 15, June 1995.

19. Maria 23; Fleetwood.

20. Alkeou; conversation with Polyvios Marchand, 28 Feb. 1992.

21. Kouroussopoulou.

22. Skordouli.

23. Letter from de Hidalgo to Maria, Ankara, 3 Jan. 1949 (now the property of Ilario Tamassia), in B. Tosi, *Casta diva, l'incomparabile Callas*, Rome 1993, 103, and *Giovane Callas*, Padua 1997, 173; letter from de Hidalgo, *To Ethnos*, 5 Aug. 1957.

24. Litsa 82; Tsoutis; *To Ethnos, Vradyni, Eleftherotypia, Kathimerini, Ta Nea*, 2 and 3 Aug. 1945.

25. No program was published for this recital and the pieces referred to are only those mentioned in Spanoudi's and Psaroudas's reviews. The best known of the early songs by Thodoros Karyotakis (1903–1978) are "Anastasia" (words by Sotiris Skipis), "The Dream" (words by Miltiadis Malakassis), and the folk song "Caravel from Chios." The best-known songs written by Yorgos Poniridis (1887–1982) before August 1945 are "Our Lady of Sparta" and "The Anadyomene," both dating from 1942, which are settings of poems by Angelos Sikelianos.

26. Litsa 82; Artemis Matsas, "Maria Left in a Huff," *To Ethnos*, 15 Sept. 1990.

27. *Ta Nea*, 8 Aug. 1945.

28. *To Vima*, 12 Aug. 1945.

CHAPTER 37

1. Tsoutis.

2. Litsa 84; Jackie 106–107; M. Callas, "Smentite di articolo 'Time'" (MS, in Italian, 1956), para. 17.

3. Department of State, refusal of passport extension, 9 June 1947; U.S. government office memorandum on the subject of the passport case of Sophie C. Kalos), 24 September 1947. (Photocopies kindly provided by Jackie Kaloyeropoulou.) Maria herself eventually repaid the debt, on 4 October 1948, in order to have her passport renewed until 3 August 1949.

4. Sigaras.

5. Waiver signed by sixty-three members of the artistic and technical staff, 20 Aug. 1945; M.B.G./G.N.O. no. 26, 27 Aug. 1945. The dispute had gathered enough momentum for the remaining orchestral players, choral singers, and ballet dancers to keep up their protests until, on 20 October (by which time Mary was in New York), they declared a general strike and the G.N.O. closed down for a time. This campaign signaled the beginning of the end for Synadinos, who was deposed in the spring of 1946.

6. *To Ethnos*, 25 Aug. 1945.

7. *Estia*, 1 Sept. 1945; *To Ethnos*, 30 Aug. 1945.

8. *To Ethnos*, 30 Aug. 1945.

9. *To Ethnos*, 30 Aug. 1945 and 26 Feb. 1957.

10. Tsoutis; Salingaros; Chiotakis.

11. Salingaros; Amaxopoulou; Mataranga.

12. Salingaros; Kourahani; Papachristos.

13. Conversation with Anthi Zacharatou (not taped), 8 July 1993; manuscript in Synadinos's handwriting (ELIA).

14. The villain of *Der Bettelstudent*, Colonel Ollendorf, decides to settle a score with the impoverished Countess Palmatica by marrying off her daughter Laura to Simon, a convict whom he passes off as a wealthy aristocrat. Simon agrees to play Ollendorf's game, but he falls in love with Laura and tries unsuccessfully to tell her the truth just before the wedding. Once Simon and Laura are safely married, Ollendorf reveals the secret with malicious glee. Simon reacts threateningly, whereupon Ollendorf flees in terror. The countess urges her daughter to leave her "impostor" of a husband, but Laura is by now in love with Simon and refuses.

The Polish revolution breaks out, the "beggar student" becomes a national hero, and the story ends—as always in operettas—with laughter and rejoicing.

15. *To Vima*, 19 Aug. 1945; conversation with Yorgos Anemoyannis, 29 Nov. 1993. When Anemoyannis happened to meet Maria "with a retinue of porters carrying her luggage" at Milan railway station in 1954, she recognized him and said, *Do you still remember that 'Bettelstudent'?*"

16. PAPADOPOULOU; MATARANGA; CHIOTAKIS.

17. *To Ethnos*, 6 Sept. 1945; *Ta Nea* and *To Vima*, 7 Sept. 1945; "Financial Year 1944–45, First Season" (G.N.O. archives). Reviews were also published by "Red," *Acropolis*, 6 Sept. 1945; by Dimitrios Hamoudopoulos, *Eleftheria*, 9 Sept. 1945; by E.A., *Embros*, 11 Sept. 1945; by Vassilis Rotas, *Elefiheri Ellada*, 8 Sept. 1945; by Alexandra Lalaouni ("The Greek National Opera Production"), *Vradyni*, 9 Oct. 1945; and by Fivos Anoyianakis ("The National Opera and *Der Bettelstudent*"), *Filologika Chronika*, 15 Oct. 1945. Several hundred more people, besides those 4,916, must have attended with complimentary tickets. One performance was broadcast on Athens Radio, though it is not known whether it was with Mary or Zacharatou in the lead. Having failed to overcome the G.N.O.'s financial and other problems, in which Mary would have become bogged down had she stayed, the management took the easy way out as usual and ran *Der Bettelstudent* for sixty-two more performances until 2 December 1945 (from 20 October at the Olympia), with Anthi Zacharatou as Laura for all except two, in which she was replaced by Lela Zografou.

18. SALTA; PAPADOPOULOU; conversation with Michalis Kazandzis, 28 Mar. 1994.

19. SALINGAROS; TSOUTIS; FLEETWOOD.

20. SIGARAS.

21. STASSINOPOULOS 41; JACKIE 107–111; LITSA 84; MARIA 23.

22. LITSA 84–85; JACKIE 112; MARIA 23.

23. DE HIDALGO 165; JELLINEK 25.

24. SKORDOULI.

25. MARIA 27 (Romani skillfully parried Mary's request for lessons); ALLEGRI 37.

26. DE HIDALGO 165; JELLINEK 26. The identity of the person who offered to pay to keep Mary in Greece remains a mystery.

27. *To Ethnos*, 12 and 14 Sept. 1945; YANNOPOULOS; TSOUTIS.

28. MATARANGA; YENNAROPOULOU; MATARANGA.

29. Unsigned article, "The Diva of the Century," *Tachydromos*, 5 Aug. 1961; Alberto Petrolli, *La divina Callas, vita e arte*, Rovereto 1991, 42 (without reference to his source).

30. MARIA 23.

31. PARIDIS.

32. Claudia Cassidy, *Chicago Tribune*, 21 Nov. 1954 (quoted in H. Wisneski, *Maria Callas: The Art Behind the Legend*, New York 1975); MARIA 26. Maria made statements in the same vein to Harry Fleetwood in 1958 ("*In Greece I made an eight years' career, from thirteen and a half or fourteen to twenty-one years old. . . . You can imagine the wonderful time I had during the war! But I was singing there and I was the first soprano, as they called it. We were engaged by the year.*" FLEETWOOD.), to Micheline Banzet in 1965 ("*We should not forget that I had a short career of eight years in Greece. I was very young, but . . . . that was a great piece of good luck for me.*" BANZET.), to Lord Harewood (HAREWOOD) in 1968, and to John Ardoin (*Callas at Juilliard: The Master Classes*, London 1988, 5): "*My performances in Greece were a sort of early, preparatory period; the completion, so to speak, of my school days. There I learned how far I could go and what my possibilities were.*"

EPILOGUE

1. Conversation with Dr. Nicholas Kouretas, 28 Mar. 1997.

2. P. Dragadze, "My Lonely World: A Woman Looking for Her Voice," *Life*, 30 Oct. 1964; ARDOIN 45; L'INVITÉ; interviews in *Elle*, 9 Feb. 1970, and *L'Express*, 19 Jan. 1970.

3. D. J. Soria, "Greek Sorceress," *Opera News* 42, no. 5, Nov. 1977; LEGGE; ARDOIN 33.

4. Unsigned interview, *Elle*, 9 Feb. 1970; to John Ardoin, 1968 (ARDOIN 45); HARRIS.

5. BANZET; FROST; radio interview with Charles Trenet, Paris, 1959; L'INVITÉ.

6. A. Pensotti, "Maria, ti chiedo perdono," *Oggi*, 1 Oct. 1977.

7. L'INVITÉ (cf. ARDOIN 32); LEGGE.

8. Letter from Maria to Meneghini, 18 Nov. 1948, published in R. Allegri and R. Allegri, *Callas by Callas*, Milan 1997, 58.

9. BANZET.

10. M. Dalmati, review of Polyvios Marchand's book, *Nea Estia*, no. 1365, 15 May 1984.

11. Television interview with Melvin Bragg, London, 1986.

12. S. Linakis, *Diva: The Life and Death of Maria Callas*, London 1981, 8.

13. NIKOLAIDI.

14. LITSA 83.

15. MURROW.

16. PROUSE; FROST; television interview with Barbara Walters, New York, 15 Apr. 1974.

17. C. Spanidou, *Onassis As I Knew Him*, Athens 1996, 153; V. Vassiliou, *Acropolis*, 7 Aug. 1957.

18. DOWNES. Maria made statements in a similar vein to Micheline Banzet in 1965 and to Lord Harewood in 1968.

19. R. Neville, "Voice of an Angel," *Life*, 31 Oct. 1955, reprinted in *The New York Times*, 30 Oct. 1956.

20. MARCHAND 8.

21. YEORYIOU; "Musicians Speak about the Nonappearance of Callas," *Vradyni*, 3 Aug. 1957.

22. KALAIDZAKIS; YANNOPOULOS.

23. JELLINEK 31–32. Jellinek considers it quite likely that Nicola Moscona put in a good word to Johnson on Maria's behalf. Stamatis Tsoutis also wrote that Moscona accompanied Maria to the Met and introduced her to Johnson. (TSOUTIS.)

24. MARIA 27; BANZET; N. Barry, "Maria Callas: 'The Singer Is Nothing But the Servant of Genius,'" *International Herald Tribune*, 30 June 1971.

25. JELLINEK 29. Soprano Emmy Destinn (1878–1930) had a superlative voice with an extraordinary range, which allowed her to sing over eighty operatic roles. She was born in Prague and started her career as Santuzza (a first coincidence) at Dresden in 1897. In 1901 she sang Senta at Bayreuth. She premièred the roles of Madama Butterfly in London (1905) and Salome in Berlin (1906). She made her first appearance at the Metropolitan Opera in 1908 as Aida (with Caruso as Radamès and under the baton of Toscanini, who was also making his house début), and soon afterward as Marta (a second coincidence) in the first New York production of *Tiefland*. In 1910 she created the role of Minnie in *La Fanciulla del West*, opposite Caruso and Amato. Her brilliant career ended in 1926, and she lived out the rest of her life in Bohemia, honored as a national heroine.

26. JELLINEK 30; letter from de Hidalgo to Maria, Ankara, 15–18 Mar. 1949 (now the property of Ilario Tamassia), in B. Tosi, *Casta diva, l'incomparabile Callas*, Rome 1993, 103–105, and *Giovane Callas*, Padua 1997, 174.

27. JELLINEK 44–45; Anita Pensotti, "Maria Callas," in B. Tosi, *Giovane Callas*, Padua 1997, 35. It is certainly quite possible that Caselotti's strictures were motivated partly by jealousy of the rising young star, as she herself had never been given a part in Italy. She may also have been aware of her husband's liking for Mary, with whom Bagarozy evidently had some kind of involvement (see Mary's letters to Bagarozy, in Allegri and Allegri, op. cit., 44–51). Be that as it may, the consequence of her outspoken criticism was that Mary and Meneghini would have nothing more to do with her and she eventually returned to New York. Nevertheless, it is quite possible that Caselotti exercised a considerable influence on Mary, first in New York and later in Italy. Litsa wrote Meneghini about her daughter's "former friend Louise" in one of her frantic letters in the summer of 1951: "I will tell you the truth, Mr. Meneghini, before she met that woman, my daughter Maria was perfect, a lovely girl. After her friendship with Louise she has changed entirely." (Letter from Litsa to Meneghini, Athens, 31 Aug. [1951], now the property of Ilario Tamassia.) It is rumored that while Maria was studying with Caselotti in New York several 78 rpm records of her singing were made; these Bagarozy is said to have given to a lawyer when he instituted legal proceedings against her in 1955, and they have not been heard of since.

28. Statements by Nicola Rossi-Lemeni in *Per Maria Callas*, San Lazzaro (Bologna) 1977, 31, and Nina Zenatello in B. Tosi, *Giovane Callas*, Padua 1997, 187.

29. Letter from Tullio Serafin to Emma Moglioli, 20 Aug. 1947, in Allegri and Allegri, op. cit., 46; T. Serafin, "A Triptych of Singers," *Opera Annual*, no. 8, 1962 (translation of an article first published in *Discoteca*, Sept. 1961).

30. HAREWOOD.

31. Aldo Santini, *Oggi*, 1 Oct. 1986.

32. HAREWOOD; Lord Harewood, "The Art of Maria Callas," *Recorded Sound*, no. 10, 1979. As Maria was quick to point out to Lord Harewood, her voice was "younger" then.

33. L. Bragaglia, *L'arte dello stupore*, Rome 1977, 21–22; DE HIDALGO 165.

POSTSCRIPT I

1. Letter from Mary to Vangelis Mangliveras, New York, 2 Jan. 1946 (in the author's collection).

2. STANCIOFF 69. Mary—who, a few days earlier at the port of New York, had hugged her father "as though he had been raised from the dead" and had cried on his shoulder with joy—left the West 157th Street apartment (until her father had agreed not to share it with Alexandra Papajohn) and went to stay at the central Hotel Times Square on West Forty-third Street. *"In that year and half that I lived with him, he treated me like a queen, making up for everything that I had suffered,"* she later mentioned cryptically, without any reference to Alexandra. (MARIA 25–26.) Jackie maintains that it was not with Alexandra that Mary found her father living in 1945 but with his housekeeper, "whom Mary soon drove out of the house." (KALOYEROPOULOU.)

3. Letter from George to Maria, New York, 10 Nov. 1949 (now the property of Ilario Tamassia).

4. Letter from Mary to Vangelis Mangliveras, New York, 2 Jan. 1946 (in the author's collection).

5. LITSA 94–95. Litsa had committed her words of wisdom to paper and referred to them as her "thirteen points." Among others she urged Mary to believe in God and be grateful to Him for her golden throat; always to be strong despite setbacks and disappointments; never to betray a friend or be unkind to a relative; when she married, to tolerate her husband's faults; and never to forget to help the poor. Although Litsa herself had failed to practice most of what she preached, twelve years later she still remembered her "thirteen points" well enough to take a sly dig at her daughter: "Looking back at this counsel today, I would say that Maria has certainly not forgotten my advice to be strong."

6. MENEGHINI 121; LITSA 100. Meneghini subsequently gave the photograph to Renzo Allegri together with a quantity of other material to assist him in setting up a Meneghini-Callas foundation, a project which came to nothing.

7. Letter from Litsa to Maria, Athens, 18 Sept. 1949 (now the property of Ilario Tamassia).

8. MENEGHINI 125, 129.

9. SIMIONATO.

10. LITSA 103–111; PARIDIS.

11. LITSA 108.

12. KOUKOULI; M. Callas, "Smentite di articolo 'Time'" (MS, in Italian, 1956), para. 17; SIMIONATO; A. Signorini, "Ecco le lettere, i documenti e le foto che conservo della mia amica Callas," *Gente*, 2 Nov. 1992. See also J.-J. Hannine Vallaut, *Giulietta Simionato*, Parma 1987, 89.

13. STASSINOPOULOS 77; letter from Litsa to Meneghini, Athens, 31 Aug. [1951] (now the property of Ilario Tamassia); JACKIE 130; MENEGHINI 132–133.

14. JACKIE 130; KALOYEROPOULOU; LITSA 118–119.

15. JACKIE 131; LITSA 118–119; "Die Primadonna," *Der Spiegel*, no. 7, 13 Feb. 1957.

16. JACKIE 131; KALOYEROPOULOU; ARDOIN 33. Meneghini relates that Maria's offensive words about her mother were spoken as a retort to a journalist who had exasperated her with his personal questions. (MENEGHINI 120.)

17. JACKIE 131; KALOYEROPOULOU; autograph letter from Maria to Leonidas Lanzounis, Aug. 1975, reproduced in facsimile in STASSINOPOULOS 275–276.

18. They were given by Meneghini to Renzo Allegri, who has kindly provided them.

19. KALOYEROPOULOU.

20. MARIA 40.

21. Television interview with Mike Wallace, New York, 3 Feb. 1974.

22. M. Callas, "Smentite di articolo 'Time'" (MS, in Italian, 1956), para. 17.

23. As told to the author by John Ardoin at the First International Congress Dedicated to Maria Callas, Athens, Zappeion Megaron, 11–14 Sept. 1997.

24. F. Filippas, "Maria Callas's Mother Reveals . . . ," *Thisavros,* no. 22, 24 Nov. 1977; KAMBOURIS.

25. MOUNDOURI; KATIE.

26. LITSA 113, 134, 137, 148, 150–151, 155–156.

27. Radio interview with Johnny Carson, New York, 1962.

28. Telephone conversation with the family friend, who wishes to remain anonymous, Apr. 1995; KALOYEROPOULOU; KOUKOULI.

29. Letter from George to Maria, New York, 18 June 1949 (now the property of Ilario Tamassia).

POSTSCRIPT II

1. R. Celletti, "Maria Callas—Sopranistin, Kultfigur, Musik-wissenschafterin," *Neue Zürcher Zeitung,* 25 June 1996.

2. See also P. L. Caviglia, "Il fenomeno vocale storico umano di Maria Callas," *Discoteca,* June 1967.

3. *Kathimerini* and *Eleftherotypia,* 11 Aug. 1960; quoted in Italian in G. Guandalini, *Callas, l'ultima diva,* Turin 1987, 16. See also T. Serafin, "A Triptych of Singers," *Opera Annual,* no. 8, 1962.

4. John Pettitt, "David Mellor with Lord Harewood on BBC Radio 3, Dec. 31, 1994," *The Maria Callas International Club Magazine,* no. 14, Feb. 1995; Tullio Serafin to Giuseppe Pugliese, 4 May 1958 (excerpt from diary), in Teodoro Celli and Giuseppe Pugliese, *Tullio Serafin, il patriarca del Melodramma,* Venice 1985, 231. This is an allusion to the fact that in 1956, when Maria's contract with Cetra prohibited her from making another recording of *La Traviata* before 1957, Serafin had agreed to record that opera for EMI with Antonietta Stella. Maria had been wild with fury and had sworn never to make any more recordings with Serafin. "It was a decision that soon became part of the folklore of ingratitude and ruthlessness that was to surround Maria." (STASSINOPOULOS 133.)

5. Dictated personally by Stelios Galatopoulos, Athens, Sept. 1997, and included in his article "The Art of Callas," *Mousiki,* no. 22, Sept. 1979. Cf. S. Galatopoulos, *Maria Callas: Sacred Monster,* London 1998, 81–82, where Serafin is reported saying: "I remember [all the great artists I worked with]—their faces, their mannerisms, their names but not their voices, except Callas's voice."

6. "Processo alla Callas," *Radiocorriere TV,* no. 48, 30 Nov. 1969 (English translation by M. Fagandini, *Opera,* Sept.–Oct. 1970, and in D. Lowe, ed., *Callas As They Saw Her,* London 1987, 81–104). Taking part in the panel discussion were Fedele D'Amico, Rodolfo Celletti, Eugenio Gara, Giorgio Gualerzi, Luchino Visconti, and Gianandrea Gavazzeni.

7. S. Segalini, "Singing Rediscovered" in D. Lowe, ed., *Callas As They Saw Her,* London 1987, 120.

8. S. Galatopoulos, "The Art of Callas," *Mousiki,* no. 22, Sept. 1979.

9. R. Christiansen, *Prima Donna,* London 1984, 306.

10. B. Burroughs, "Maria Callas: 'Yes, But . . . ,'" *Opera Quarterly* 6, no. 4, summer 1989; DOWNES. With regard to Tebaldi's voice, Maria once remarked cuttingly, "*I am built by an unknown artisan, but my instrument is played by Paganini. She, instead, is a Stradivarius played by an amateur.*" (Related by Anita Cerquetti to Lanfranco Rasponi and quoted by him in *The Last Prima Donnas,* London 1984, 571.)

11. See J. Pettitt, "Maria Callas: The Early Struggle," *The Maria Callas International Club Magazine*, no. 17, Feb. 1996, and no. 18, June 1996.

12. Segalini, op. cit., 118–119.

13. Conversation with Yannis Tsarouchis, 6 June 1990; A. Savvakis, *Ioannis Tsarouchis*, Athens 1993, 305; CALONI.

14. LEGGE; D. Lowe, ed., *Callas As They Saw Her*, London 1987, 10.

15. IKONOMIDI.

16. The Schumann song (duration 1:00) and an excerpt from Leonora's aria "Madre pietosa Vergine" from *La Forza del Destino* (duration 1:35, and the last known recording of Maria's voice, made in August 1977, about a month before her death) were selected by Vasso Devetzi from the practice tapes that Maria recorded regularly on a Revox tape recorder with a special microphone (now in the author's collection) for inclusion in the background music for the exhibition "L'opéra secret de Maria Callas" at the Musée Carnavalet, Paris, 10 Apr.–20 May 1979. On "Ah, perfido!" and the circumstances of her practice sessions with Jeffrey Tate, see M. Vandenbergh, "Maria at the Théatre des Champs Élysées," *The Callas Circle*, no. 7, May 1996.

17. PARIDIS.

18. JELLINEK 322–323.

19. PROUSE. Maria always went to her dressing room several hours before a performance to prepare herself both physically and mentally, but especially mentally. Michel Glotz, one of her last intimate friends in Paris, commented perceptively: "What made her a great actress was that she tried to keep the balance between one half of her brain, absolutely crystal-clear, and the other half of her brain, absolutely gone." (Statement by Michel Glotz in Alan Palmer's film *Maria Callas*, 1987.)

20. "Processo alla Callas," *Radiocorriere TV*, no. 48, 30 Nov. 1969 (English translation by M. Fagandini, *Opera*, Sept.–Oct. 1970, and in D. Lowe, ed., *Callas As They Saw Her*, London 1987, 81–104).

21. Words used by theatrical director Alexis Solomos to describe the great Greek actress Eleni Papadaki.

POSTSCRIPT III

1. Elvira de Hidalgo, letter in *To Ethnos*, 5 Aug. 1957; letters from de Hidalgo to Maria, Ankara, 6 Oct. 1948 and 15–18 Mar. 1949, in B. Tosi, *Casta diva, l'incomparabile Callas*, Rome 1993, 101, 103–105, and *Giovane Callas*, Padua 1997, 174; VASSILIOU.

2. C. Spanidou, *Onassis As I Knew Him*, Athens 1996, 153. Cf. ZACHARIOU: "The people in authority in those days could not hear the difference between Maria and someone like Remoundou. They still hadn't realized what she was capable of doing with her vocal cords and her whole stage presence. Callas on stage was a different person from the Maria you met in the street. On stage she was a lioness!"

3. For samples of the offensive messages, see ALLEGRI 196–197. According to Tatiana Varouti, Maria was hesitant even about accepting the invitation to sing in Athens in 1957. Achilleas Mamakis, then director of the festival, only managed to change her mind thanks to the parting shot he delivered at the end of his fruitless negotiations: "All right, then, don't come, but it's a pity they won't be able to see you as you are now, Maria," he said, alluding to her slim figure. What persuaded her to sign the contract was her feminine vanity and, even more, her secret desire "to show them." (VAROUTI.)

4. VASSILIKOS 256.

5. SIMIONATO.

6. STANCIOFF 145.

7. STANCIOFF 142–143.

8. A. Pensotti, "Maria, ti chiedo perdono," *Oggi*, 1 Oct. 1977; Spanidou, op. cit., 59.

9. "An attempt to have a child in the first year of their relationship, but without success, as the infant dies two hours after being born. On the spur of the moment she christens him Angelos." (VASSILIKOS 254–255.)

10. Maria's friend and biographer John Ardoin (in Alan Palmer's film *Maria Callas*, 1987) and her secretary Nadia Stancioff (STANCIOFF 161), both of whom were in a position to discuss the matter with Maria, believed that the second pregnancy was not imaginary. But see Chapter 25 for Meneghini's different opinion and about Maria's early menopausal problems. Nicholas Gage (*Greek Fire: The Story of Maria Callas and Aristotle Onassis*, New York [Alfred A. Knopf] 2000, ch. 14) also offers new evidence against this second pregnancy, arguing that Callas—aiming to avenge her abandonment by exposing Onassis's cruelty—spoke about his having forced her to have an abortion only after he had married Jackie Kennedy. As to the first pregnancy, Gage quotes, twice, Meneghini's statement to Galatopoulos that Maria's gynecologist Carlo Palmieri had diagnosed symptoms of early menopause in 1957 and "prescribed a series of injections which delayed [menopause] for about a year." Gage concludes that these injections possibly rendered a "superfertile" Maria who could well have conceived a child by Onassis on the *Christina*, in August 1959. Whether this background is correct or not, the evidence—including documents that Gage indirectly attributes to the archival material taken by Vasso Devetzi after Callas's death (see Chapter 37)—seems quite convincing that on Wednesday morning, 30 March 1960, Maria bore Onassis a son named Omero Lengrini, who died within hours. What remains inexplicable is her decision to hasten the birth by about a month, just four days before Onassis's expected arrival in Milan, and the doctor's willingness to perform an unnecessary cesarean in an ill-equipped private clinic.

11. PROUSE.

12. Spanidou, op. cit., 157–158.

13. P. Dragadze, "My Lonely World: A Woman Looking for Her Voice," *Life*, 30 Oct. 1964; SIMIONATO.

14. A. Savvakis, *Ioannis Tsarouchis*, Athens 1993, 307–309.

15. Yorgos Pilichos, *Ta Nea*, 29 Mar. 1969.

16. XAKOUSTI; ALKEOU; statement by Andy Embirikos to Tassos Kriekoukis, then secretary of the Greek embassy in Paris, who was involved in making arrangements for Maria's funeral in September 1977 (conversation with Tassos Kriekoukis, 6 June 1997).

17. FROST.

18. Tripeleff's book *Un amore di Maria Callas* (Pavia 1994), a fictional re-creation of Maria's relationship with Pasolini, is both interesting and well-written.

19. Visconti would tell Maria his negative opinion on the subject even in public. (L'INVITÉ.)

20. SIMIONATO; "Interview by Our Readers," *The Callas Circle*, no. 7, May 1996.

21. FROST. Not long before she died Maria would admit ruefully, "*Yes, I have made some [concessions], but I have paid very dearly for them. When I was younger I made fewer concessions. Later, as people were saying I had such a reputation for being 'difficult,' I started making concessions, and that made me annoyed with myself. An artist should never make concessions!*" (CALONI.)

22. For interesting insights into the relationship between Maria and di Stefano, see Maria di Stefano, *Callas, nemica mia*, Milan 1992, the memoirs of his embittered wife (which must be treated with caution); also SUTHERLAND.

23. Savvakis, op. cit.; VASSILIKOS 301; conversation with Yorgos Pilichos, 5 Aug. 1995.

24. V. Vassiliou, *Acropolis*, 7 Aug. 1957.

25. Letter from Yannis Tsarouchis to fellow painter Yannis Moralis, 7 Oct. 1957, in *My Dear Yannis . . .* , Athens 1997, 51. Tsarouchis continues: "She always spoke Greek to Greeks, French to Frenchmen, English to Americans, and Italian to Italians. If we ever said anything to her in a foreign language, she would reply in Greek."

26. Spanidou, op. cit., 167.

27. VASSILIKOS 305.

28. S. Galatopoulos, *Maria Callas: Sacred Monster*, London 1998, 455, 458.

29. ALLEGRI 258. ["Suicide! In these proud moments, you are all that is left me. And my heart tempts me. The last voice of my destiny, the last cross on my way."] Galatopoulos believes that although the writing is Maria's, the date and address "a T" ("to Titta") was forged by Meneghini in order to "show the world that Maria's last message was for him." (*Maria Callas: Sacred Monster*, London 1998, 458–459.)

30. *"Pippo dear, every day means one day less, thank goodness."* (Statement by di Stefano in Alan Palmer's film *Maria Callas*, 1987.)

31. Vasso Devetzi (1925–1987) studied with Teo Kaufmann, a Belgian piano teacher at the Thessaloniki Conservatory. Still very young during the occupation, she aroused strong feelings in local musical circles—much more than did Mary in Athens—by consorting with members of the German authorities and frequently playing under German conductors. An ambitious woman who learned early to maintain good contacts in the right places, she had a long-standing affair with Oberfeldwebel Wolfram Zeller, an excellent pianist and conductor then posted at Thessaloniki and reputedly a personal friend of Goebbels. After the liberation Devetzi suffered the cost of her fraternization, but she managed to rehabilitate herself in Paris, mainly with the backing of the French composer Henri Sauguet (1901–1989), whose Piano Concerto she played regularly. There followed a period in which she enjoyed the support of the Russian musical establishment, thanks to her carefully cultivated friendship with the famous trio of Richter, Oistrakh, and Rostropovich. Finally, being a person who ever enjoyed basking in reflected glory, she insinuated herself into the good graces of the unhappy but still world-famous Maria Callas. On Devetzi as a pianist the well-known Alexandrian Greek pianist Tassos Yannopoulos (who often played with Thibaud and Casals) once remaked, "There are three kinds of pianists: the good ones, the bad ones, and Devetzi." (Conversation with Vyron Kolassis, 20 Jan. 1996.)

32. G. B. Meneghini, "Sì, lo sapevo: Maria Callas si è lasciata morire," *Gente*, 9 Dec. 1978.

33. Statement by di Stefano in Alan Palmer's film *Maria Callas*, 1987; in R. Allegri and R. Allegri, *Callas by Callas*, Milan 1997, 158.

34. *"I think about myself, my 'brilliant' fate, having to spend the end of my life without happiness, [without] friends, [but only] with drugs!"* VASSILIKOS 302. A photocopy of this note, written on notepaper headed "36 Avenue Georges Mandel, Paris 16e," was kindly provided by Renzo Allegri. Vasso Devetzi admitted to Vassilis Vassilikos that a lot of people considered Maria to have been addicted to drugs toward the end of her life. (VASSILIKOS 305.)

35. Most writers have supported this version, that Callas died as a result of heart failure. According to Dr. Andreas Stathopoulos, however, the statement of Bruna to Nadia Stancioff shortly after the event ("The night before her death she complained of a sharp pain in her lower and middle back. She asked me to massage her back. She said it helped and told me to call a masseuse for her the following day." STANCIOFF 246.) contains information that—together with Maria's chronically deficient circulation and low blood pressure, the problems of her middle-age and depression, and her abuse of various pills—rather indicate a pulmonary thromboembolism. These symptoms and problems exacerbate a generally slow circulation, which leads to the formation of blood clots—in Maria's case in her legs, which swelled so often. The fatal thrombus must have blocked a branch of the pulmonary artery on the night of 15 September, causing the "sharp pain in her lower and middle back" and prompting Maria's request for a masseuse. (Conversation with Dr. Andreas Stathopoulos, 30 Nov. 1997.)

36. SIMIONATO.

37. VASSILIKOS 231–309.

38. These most precious papers and other documents, together with all the personal effects, are reputedly in the possession of her successors; however, a well-established rumor has it that at least part of the "loot" has recently been transferred to a well-known Athenian musical establishment.

39. S. Galatopoulos, *Maria Callas: Sacred Monster*, London 1998, 457, 459. Nadia Stancioff also recalled Maria telling her she had written a will. (STANCIOFF 247.)

40. VASSILIKOS 241.

41. VASSILIKOS 269–271. These threats explain the title of Vassilikos's book.

42. VASSILIKOS 279, 281.

43. VASSILIKOS 295.

44. JACKIE 233, 240; KALOYEROPOULOU; S. Galatopoulos, *Maria Callas: Sacred Monster*, London 1998, 460.

45. See auction catalog, *Succession Maria Callas*, Etude Claude Boisgirard—A. de Heeckeren, Paris, Hôtel Georges V, 14 June 1978; VASSILIKOS 295; JACKIE 234.

46. This and the following three paragraphs are based chiefly on Jackie's written memoirs (JACKIE, chapter 8) and oral reminiscences (KALOYEROPOULOU); on Vassilis Vassilikos, *The Eviction*, 2nd ed., Athens 1989, 231–309; on documents provided by Dr. Andreas Stathopoulos; and on the latter's written memoir on "the Devetzi case," addressed to the author on 25 November 1997.

47. This actually represented daylight robbery, since the apartment at 36 Avenue Georges Mandel belonged to Onassis's company Trenton, and its owner (initially Maria Callas) carried anonymous Trenton shares of a value equal to that of the property. Naturally, the eventual tax liabilities would have fallen on Trenton, while Devetzi would have quietly sold or cashed in the shares she had grabbed from Jackie. The price never became known, but, according to Dr. Andreas Stathopoulos, it should not be less than eight hundred thousand dollars. JACKIE 248–258. Many people still vividly remember Devetzi's forays into Parisian high society in the years following Maria's death. Among others she threw lavish receptions at Maxim's, which she hired specially for the occasions.

48. S. Galatopoulos, *Maria Callas: Sacred Monster*, London 1998, 460.

49. VASSILIKOS 242. According to Hervé Guibert ("La voix hors du feu," *Le Monde*, 11 Apr. 1979), Maria had equipped one room of her apartment as a recording studio: "She never uttered a squeak without recording it. . . . Until the day of her death she was always working on her voice, listening to herself, criticizing, starting all over again. Sheer perfectionism."

50. Fortunately photocopies exist of much of her correspondence, and it is to be hoped that one day these letters will be edited by a serious historian and published. Many original documents were auctioned off in Paris on 2 and 3 December 2000.

51. Information received from Renzo Allegri, to whom the "diary" was to have been given. See also Allegri and Allegri, op. cit., 7, 158.

52. VASSILIKOS 264.

APPENDIX

1. Conversation with Odysseas Dimitrakopoulos, 28 Mar. 1996, whose parents were present on that occasion.

2. LITSA; ZACHAROPOULOU.

3. See Karl van Zoggel, "De theaters van Maria Callas, een compleet overzicht," *Uw Maria Callas Brief*, no. 20, 16 Sept. 1990.

Index

Numbers in bold refer to illustrations. Operas and major musical works are indexed under the name of their composer.

659